C.A.Chandraprema

Gōta's War

The Crushing of
Tamil Tiger Terrorism
in Sri Lanka

C.A.Chandraprema

Gōta's War

The Crushing of
Tamil Tiger Terrorism
in Sri Lanka

Published by the
Ranjan Wijeratne Foundation

Published in 2012

ISBN 978-955-54087-0-7

Cover Photo (top)
*Colonel Vijaya Wimalaratne and
Major Gōtabhaya Rajapaksa
during the Vadamarachchi Operation 1987*

Cover & page design by
Ranjith Liyanage

Printed by
Piyasiri Printing Systems

To

Ranjan Wijeratne,
Vijaya Wimalaratne,
Lalith Athulathmudali,
Gamini Dissanayake,
Lakshman Algama,
and Janaka Perera
all of whom the present writer knew and held
in high regard, and all the others
who fell in the war against terror.

Contents

Introduction

The conflict between the majority Sinhala and minority Tamil political parties in Sri Lanka began in 1956. What first began as a political power game later gave rise to terrorism and finally a full blown civil war. Sri Lanka provides a text book example of confrontational politics escalating into terrorism and war in the absence of restraint and good judgement on the part of politicians. The story of Sri Lanka is in that sense, a cautionary tale for all multi-ethnic, multi-religious states.

In any power struggle, the character of the conflict is decided not so much by the establishment as by the party challenging the status quo. As such the character of the Sri Lankan conflict was determined first by the Tamil political party the *Ilangei Tamil Arasu Kachchi* (ITAK) and in later times by the Liberation Tigers of Tamil Eelam.

There was always an international dimension to the conflict in Sri Lanka. In the 1950s, the initial inspiration for the political conflict that sparked off the war in Sri Lanka, came from Dravidian/Tamil separatist politics in South India. The shift from politics to terrorism was a local development, but without the help of the Indian central government, it would not have escalated to the level where it posed a threat to the Sri Lankan state. After India lost control of things in 1990 and stepped aside, the Western powers began playing a role in the Sri Lankan conflict.

Usually, foreign intervention would mean that a foreign country would be able to influence, guide or control events in the country subject to the intervention. Yet in Sri Lanka, no foreign power ever held the reins in their hands. No foreign power could switch things on or off in Sri Lanka as they pleased. The epicentre of the conflict always remained firmly in Sri Lanka. All foreign powers who thought they could manipulate or even influence things in Sri Lanka were to realise that they were only handmaidens and not mistresses. A recent Norwegian government commissioned report on their peace mediation efforts in Sri Lanka candidly admitted as much.

The Sri Lankan war is one of the most written about conflicts in the world, but almost everything that has been written has been based on half truths and misunderstandings. It is because policy making on the Sri Lankan issue was based on wrong information and assumptions that so many who tried to intervene or mediate in the Sri Lankan conflict failed to achieve any tangible result. Why for instance, did India make such a tragic mess of their policy with regard to Sri Lanka in the 1980s? All the assumptions they had worked on with regard to this country were proved entirely wrong. This despite the close geographical proximity and cultural affinity between the two countries. If India operated on wrong assumptions, it was hardly surprising that the West which is far removed from Sri Lanka would end up doing the same. Two decades after the Indians, the Norwegians, the USA, and the EU which functioned as the overseers of the Sri Lankan peace process were to find that the plans they had for Sri Lanka were not working out either.

All these failures and embarrassments were due to the fact that nobody really took the trouble to study the history of the Sri Lankan conflict carefully and understand the nature of the political project that lay at the root of the problem. Both the Indians and the Western powers naively expected a compromise in Sri Lanka when a compromise was never on the agenda even in the 1950s when the conflict first began.

From the 1990s onwards, both the Indians and the Western powers did come to the realization that the main stumbling block in working out a compromise was the LTTE, and not the government of Sri Lanka. In contrast to the LTTE, they found the alternating Chandrika Kumaratunga and Ranil Wickremesinghe governments between 1994 and 2005 to be quite flexible and accommodating. In that respect perhaps the regime that went furthest to find an accommodation with the LTTE was the Premadasa government of 1989-1993.

President R.Premadasa's accommodating attitude toward the LTTE was widely recognised. After his assassination by an LTTE suicide bomber on 1 May 1993, *The Economist* declared in its 8 May 1993 issue *"Mr Premadasa was the closest thing the Tigers had to a political friend."* Hamish MacDonanld writing in the *Far Eastern Economic Review* of 13 May 1993, was to express surprise that the LTTE would want to assassinate President Premadasa. He wrote, *"If the LTTE link is true – it has been denied by the Tigers – this is even more alarming than Premadasa's death on its own. It would indicate that the LTTE is far more resistant to a negotiated settlement than anyone had suspected."*

But this was enlightenment coming in dribs and drabs. Both the Western powers and India never came to a full theoretical understanding of what the Sri Lankan conflict is about. Every time their plans failed to work, they would naively wonder what went wrong, but since one cannot simply give up, they would shake off their doubts and perplexities and start all over again only to end up at square one yet again. Things had been going round in circles in this manner for years and decades until the Rajapaksa regime managed to put an end to the unending cycle of violence.

The resistance of certain Western powers to the ending of the conflict showed that even as late as 2009, after everything they had seen for the past two decades and more, the West was still befuddled and not clear in their minds about the Sri Lankan issue. Due to the outrages committed by the LTTE, almost all Western countries had banned it as a terrorist organization, but they were still opposed to the destruction of the LTTE due to the impression that despite the intransigence and brutality of the LTTE, their political project had some justification. The West had first become aware of the Sri Lankan problem through propaganda carried out by the Tamil separatist lobby where the Sri Lankan government was cast in the role of the oppressor and first impressions continued to hold sway despite anything that may be seen to the contrary. Indeed even in Sri Lanka, the conventional wisdom applicable to this problem has been largely shaped by years of Tamil separatist propaganda.

It would be impossible to understand why things had to end the way they did on the banks of the Nandikadal lagoon, without going back to the years 1956, 1957 and 1958, when communal politics came to the fore in Sri Lanka. The resolutions passed at conventions of the ITAK during these years are especially relevant in this regard. These resolutions were published in full in the newspapers of the time. Journalists attended these events and did spot interviews with ITAK leaders about the decisions arrived at, which also got prominence on the front pages of the newspapers. Such documents provide the missing link in the evolutionary tale of the Sri Lankan conflict. Just reading the Bandaranaike-Chelvanayagam pact or the Dudley-Chelvanayagam pact as many people tend to do today, will not reveal the true nature of the political project at the root of the Sri Lankan problem.

In a sense, one cannot blame foreigners for having the wrong impression of the conflict, because they are finally dependent on material coming out of Sri Lanka to form their opinions. As such this book is aimed first and foremost at correcting some of the half truths and misrepresentations that pass off as facts about the Sri Lankan conflict.

The story of the war that followed bad politics is an epic tale in itself that needs to be told. In piecing together the story of the four decade long war against Tamil terrorism, we have relied on the memories of retired and serving armed services personnel, as well as that of pioneers and leaders of the Tamil militant movements. We have perused the operation completion reports of most of the major operations conducted by the Sri Lanka army starting from the Vadamarachchi operation of 1987 and concluding with the reports of the divisions that participated in the final Vanni battles in 2007-2009. Interviews were conducted with soldiers who had been involved in these battles. Dates were matched with the news reports of the time and army operation completion reports and other such documents and a picture of what happened has been built up in that manner. Former Tamil militants filled in the rest of the picture with a narrative of the parallel developments on their side. This book spans the entire period from 1956 to 2009 and seeks to provide a comprehensive account of the Sri Lankan conflict.

This is a war that would not have ended if not for the drive, vision, experience and commitment of one man, Gōtabhaya Rajapaksa who orchestrated the war against the LTTE on behalf of his brother President Mahinda Rajapaksa's government. Gōtabhaya served in the Sri Lanka army through the period that politics graduated into terrorism and finally into a fully fledged war. Gōtabhaya himself and many of the field commanders who led the final onslaught against the LTTE were either students or subordinates of the late Vijaya Wimalaratne arguably the single individual most responsible for turning the Sri Lanka army into a professional fighting force. One may say that it was Gōtabhaya who took Wimalaratne's legacy and applied it across the board not just to the army, but the entire security apparatus of the state.

12

Sri Lanka is the only country in the world that has triumphed against terrorism in recent times and has become an inspiration for many countries beset by intractable political violence. Why Gōtabhaya succeeded while everybody else failed, is because unlike all the others, he had the fullest backing of his brother President Mahinda Rajapaksa. No other president would have taken the decision to go for a head on confrontation with the LTTE which was considered by many Western powers to be undefeatable. No other president would have taken the political risk of prosecuting a war considered to be un-winnable even by dominant sections of the local political establishment. No other president would have stayed the course so resolutely despite setbacks on the military front and tremendous pressure coming from overseas. Without Mahinda there would have been no decision to wage war. Without Gōtabhaya, no victory.

Chapter 1

Into the Eye of the Storm

Gōtabhaya Rajapaksa joined the Ceylon Army as an officer cadet on 26 April 1971 at the height of the insurgency launched by the Marxist *Janatha Vimukthi Peramuna* (JVP). Prime Minister Sirima Bandaranaike was later to report to parliament that a total of 74 police stations all over the country had been attacked by terrorists. In the entire administrative district of Kegalle, only one police station was still in government hands. Less than a year earlier in May 1970, a new government had been voted into power with a two thirds majority in parliament in the sixth peaceful election in the 22 years since the British had granted independence to Ceylon.

Gōtabhaya's elder sibling Mahinda Rajapaksa had been elected to parliament for the first time in 1970 as the youngest member of the supreme legislature through a coalition made up of the Sri Lanka Freedom Party, The Lanka Sama Samaja Party (Trotskyite) and the pro-Moscow Communist Party of Ceylon. Ceylon was shaken to its foundations by the JVP's attempt to overthrow the democratically elected government through the force of arms. A small island of 65,610 square kilometres with a population of 12.3 million in 1971, Ceylon was then a model democracy. Indeed the British colonial masters used this country as a testing ground to see whether representative government would work in the colonies. Ceylon was granted universal adult suffrage in 1931, and between 1931 and 1948, there was a system of partial self-government with seven members of the elected legislature wielding ministerial power over certain subjects.

In the years after independence, a two party democratic system evolved, with a breakaway group from the conservative United National Party – the party that ushered in independence – becoming its social democratic rival as the Sri Lanka Freedom Party. Gōtabhaya's father D.A.Rajapaksa played a pivotal role in the formation of the two party democratic system as he crossed the floor of parliament with S.W.R.D.Bandaranaike in 1951 to form the Sri Lanka Freedom Party. Gōta, as he was called by everybody, hailed from a very political family, his paternal uncle D.M. Rajapaksa, his father D.A.Rajapaksa, his first cousins Lakshman and George Rajapaksa and now his brother Mahinda were all elected members of the supreme legislature of the country at various times in the decades before and after independence. Even in the parliament elected the previous year in 1970, there were two members of the family, his cousin George Rajapaksa and his brother Mahinda.

Elections, representative government and the political party system were what many members of the Rajapaksa clan had made careers out of. They owed their prominence in Ceylonese society to this system which was now being assailed by the JVP. The ruling coalition had been shaken to the core by the sudden uprising. Many ruling party parliamentarians including Mahinda found that among the revolutionaries who tried to overthrow their democratically elected government, were young men and women who had worked indefatigably for them at the parliamentary elections of 1970 and were at least partly responsible for obtaining for them the unexpected two thirds majority.

In Mahinda's case, one of his main election campaign workers, Mahinda Wijesekera, a tall gangling youth from Matara in the deep south, was among those who had led the insurgency. Mahinda came into politics straight from his job as a library assistant at the Sri Jayewardenepura University. Wijesekera had been a JVP student leader in that university at the time the election of 1970 came around. Wijesekera had gone to see Mrs Sirima Bandaranaike the leader of the Sri Lanka Freedom Party and urged her to nominate Mahinda Rajapaksa and had assured her that he together with other student activists would go to the Beliatte electorate and ensure that he wins.

True to his word, Wijesekera had taken up residence at the Rajapaksa home in Medamulana and worked hard to ensure Mahinda's victory. Gōta's association with Wijesekera had been minimal as it had been mainly his younger sibling Basil who had handled the political campaign for Mahinda. Though he came from

15

a political family, politics had never really interested Gōta. However, it was through Mahinda that Gōta had got the opportunity to join the Ceylon army.

Mahinda and his close friend Anura Bandaranaike the son of the prime minister were in the habit of calling on Lt General Sepala Attygalle, the amiable commander of the army and enjoying his hospitality. During one of these convivial meetings, Attygalle had suggested that Mahinda should encourage one of his brothers to enlist in the army. A natural suggestion perhaps, because Mahinda's elder sibling Chamal was already a serving police officer. When Mahinda took the suggestion to Gōta who had just finished his schooling at the leading Buddhist boy's school in Colombo, Ananda College , the young man was overjoyed. Gōta had been the quietest and most reserved of the Rajapaksa siblings and Chamal who knew the set up in the police, had doubts whether he would fit into a military environment.

With his experience as a police officer, Chamal had told Gōta that it was not going to be easy for him in the army and had tried to discourage him from joining. When Gōta made up his mind however, Chamal had relented and even signed his service bond as surety. Those days getting into the army, navy, air force and the police force, was not as easy as it became later. At that time joining the armed services was joining the social elite of the country. A few years before Gōta joined the army, all officer cadets were trained at the Sandhurst Military Academy in England. This was at a time when going abroad was a rare privilege. The final interview panel to select officer cadets for the armed forces comprised of some of the highest officials of the land. When Gōta went for his final interview, he faced a panel comprising the then deputy minister of defence, Lakshman Jayakody, Mr Mackie Ratwatte a brother of Prime Minister Sirimavo Bandaranaike as the representative of the Prime Minister's Office, defence secretary Walter Ratnavale and the army commander Lt General Sepala Attygalle.

At army headquarters in Colombo, Gōta joined 20 other officer cadet recruits who were to be taken to the army training school in Diyatalawa in the hill country, where the world's finest tea is grown. Usually, the raw recruits would be taken to the Maradana railway station in Colombo and put on a train to Diyatalawa. Once they reached Diyatalawa, their baptism of fire would begin right at the station. They were expected to carry their bag and baggage and trudge all the way to the army training school a distance of a few kilometres.

Gōta's intake however, did not have to go through this because of the JVP insurgency. Taking the recruits to Diyatalawa by train was not considered safe, so they were taken by bus.

This was the largest officer cadet intake into the Ceylon army ever. In the previous intake which had 15 officer cadets, were Sarath Fonseka, Shantha Kottegoda and Sarath Munasinghe among others. When Gōta started his cadetship, Sarath Fonseka's intake had completed their training and were waiting for their graduation parade. Once the gates of the Diyatalawa army training school slammed shut behind them, the raw officer cadets entered a different world. As in any military, the training was gruelling. The first two weeks were particularly tough. On the day that the recruits arrived in Diyatalawa, they were issued with their kit called an 'ali-kakula', (elephant's leg) because of the shape of the tall round duffel bag which was used for the purpose. They had to carry the heavy bag with them while they were taken to be shown around the army training centre.

During the first three months, the officer cadets were considered ordinary recruits. They were put up in billets to start with and given a taste of what the ordinary soldier's life was like. These billets were referred to as the 'beast billets' by the senior cadets to indicate that was how the raw recruits were going to be treated. The food served to the officer cadets was the same as that served to ordinary soldiers and in much the same manner. In the first three months of the course, the recruits were not supposed to walk. If they were on their way from one place to another, they had to jog.

In addition to the usual regimen of early morning physical training, parades and drill, there was the ragging by the seniors to put up with. Having got up at the crack of dawn for physical training, the exhausted rookies would fall asleep only to be woken up at various odd hours of the night for an 'inspection' of their gear by the seniors. During the first two weeks, the rookies hardly got any sleep. The seniors were allowed to drink alcohol in the cadet's mess and they would come to the junior cadets' billets after drinking and inspect their kit and get the juniors to entertain them by singing songs. If you didn't sing, they meted out punishments such as sit-ups and push-ups. Sometimes the seniors would make sure the recruits got no sleep at all and they had to go through the training programme the next day without having slept at all the previous night. Among the senior cadets, the three terrors the juniors did not like to see coming into their billets were Sarath Fonseka, Saliya Udugama and Abdul Zahir.

Chapter 2

Gōta Meets 'Jungle Wimale'

In the second term, the cadets were given a room and moved up to the cadets' mess. The recruits had to work their way up, from the billets into individual rooms. Mess nights had to be attended by the cadets in full dress uniform where the highest standards of social etiquette were maintained. With the JVP insurgency raging in the outstations, Gōta's intake was to undergo training for six months after which they were to be deployed in quelling the insurgency and brought back to Diyatalawa later to follow the remainder of the course. Everything was fast tracked for Gōta's intake by squeezing in more activities into a day.

Earlier, officer cadets would train only from 6.00 am to around 2.00 pm. But Gōta's intake would train from 6.00 am to 6.00 pm and then they had to play a role in defending the army training centre from possible JVP attacks in the night. Because of the insurgency, the officer cadets began their weapons training the day after their arrival in Diyatalawa. However the insurgency fizzled out after several weeks and they were able to complete the full course. Because they had covered so much ground during their first three months, their course was actually shorter by three months.

The Diyatalawa army training school is located in an area populated mostly by Indian Tamil estate workers who took no part in the insurgency. Hence, the new recruits hardly felt there was an insurgency raging outside except for the fact that they had to do more guard duty in the nights than the previous intakes.

The JVP was led by Rohana Wijeweera, a young man who had been radicalized in the heady atmosphere of the Patrice Lumumba University in Soviet Russia. He hoped to seize political power in a simultaneous and countrywide surprise attack on the security organs of the state. It was a bold and daring scheme and in the context of Sri Lanka at that time, not as half as daft as it may seem. As Felix Dias Bandaranaike, a powerful minister in that government was to admit later, the JVP insurgency caught them completely off guard and during the first two weeks the situation was so precarious that nobody knew who would run out of ammunition first, the insurgents or the government.

Given the state of the armed forces at that time, Wijeweera's hope of overwhelming the government with a surprise attack, was not too far-fetched. Where Sri Lanka was in military terms at that time can be gauged from an anecdote being passed down from generation to generation in the air force. The first offensive operation of the air force was during the 1971 insurgency and the tiny Bell G-47 helicopters, a bubble with a skeleton frame, had been used to drop grenades on gatherings of JVP insurgents in the jungles. When the pin is removed from a grenade, the spring pops out and it explodes in a matter of seconds. The air force had improvised a method to use grenades for aerial bombing by putting the grenade into a glass container and then pulling the pin so that the glass prevents the spring from popping out. When the glass is dropped, it shatters on impact releasing the spring for the grenade to explode. That was how the air force bombed the enemy at that time.

It was only the premature and isolated attack on the Wellawaya police station at 5.00 am on 5 April 1971 instead of 5.00 pm on the same day that threw the entire plan awry. If not for this blunder which was due to a miscommunication of the time to the Wellawaya cadres, the entire government would have been caught unawares, and the state apparatus may not have been able to bring the situation under control. A few days into the insurgency, with a shortage of ammunition looming, prime minister Sirima Bandaranaike had to appeal to prime minister Indira Gandhi of India for emergency supplies of ammunition for the ageing World War II .303 rifles, Self Loading Rifles (SLRs) and other weapons used by the armed forces at that time.

The use of terrorism for political purposes that started in 1971 would take nearly four decades to run its course in this country. The JVP insurgents had killed 35 policemen, 15 soldiers, 6 naval ratings and 4 airmen and injured a total of 312 security forces personnel, the majority of them being policemen. The JVP insurgency was crushed ruthlessly by the government and everything was over by July 1971. According to the government, 1,560 insurgents had been killed and 14,000 imprisoned. This was to be a dress rehearsal for what was to come later. This was the first time that Sri Lanka had graduated from riots and civil commotion to full blown insurgency and terrorism.

Speaking later about the causes of the JVP insurgency, Minister Felix Dias Bandaranaike would say that when his government took over in 1970, there were 12,000 unemployed graduates whereas during Mrs Sirima Bandaranaike's first term of office in the first half of the 1960s, there was not a single unemployed graduate in the country. Felix Dias stressed that "young people when they go to school, must feel that there is a life ahead of them, a future to look forward to". He also spoke of the impatience that young people have with the slow processes of democracy. Unemployment became a permanent feature in Sri Lanka during the decade of the 1960s and the radicalization of young people to the extent of resorting to violence took place among the Tamils and the Sinhalese at around the same time, as we will see in the coming chapters.

It was at the army training school that Gōta first met Captain Vijaya Wimalaratne, who would be his mentor and role model for the next twenty years. Captain Wimalaratne, a product of the elite Colombo public school Royal College, and the Dehra Dun military school in India where he was trained in 1961, was a dark, soft spoken man of middling height, a man who with the rise of separatist terrorism, would emerge as one of Sri Lanka's most formidable military commanders. Captain Wimalaratne was a course instructor in Diyatalawa and he specialized in war strategy. Usually, only the best officers were assigned to the training establishments. Diyatalawa was a different world to the officer cadets, with polished mahogany furniture, and the old colonial ambiance of the officer's mess which took pride in maintaining the highest standards.

The values of integrity and discipline were dinned into the young recruits during their training. At the training school, Gōta's forte was 'military appreciation' a subject taught by Capt. Wimalaratne. What is meant by military appreciation is really a skill in sizing up things, a kind of military SWOT (strengths, weaknesses, opportunities and threats) analysis. This is a skill that can be applied to any sphere of life. As the rank of the officer goes up, the factors taken into account in military appreciations would become wider in scope and at the very highest level of a military appreciation, even political factors will be taken into account. But the officer cadets were looking at military appreciation at the level of a platoon commander. At this level, sizing up the situation the platoon commander finds himself in, consists of an assessment of the terrain, whether it has open spaces, whether it is forested, whether it is a mountainous region etcetera. An assessment also takes into account the positioning of self and the enemy in this terrain and the relative manpower, supplies and ammunition positions of the two parties. Even at the platoon commander's level, a military assessment takes into account the motivation of the enemy and the question of why he was there.

As a platoon commander the task given was to attack and capture a position. This involves thinking about the options available. This necessitates an assessment of the flanks and assessing whether a day attack or night attack would be more advantageous. To the young cadet officers, Wimalaratne was a strict disciplinarian but a man who inspired lifelong loyalty. One change that occurred in the training schedule of new recruits as a result of the JVP insurgency was the introduction of a one month jungle warfare course in the Lahugala jungles conducted by Wimalaratne towards the end of their cadetship. Wimalaratne, who had undergone a jungle warfare training course in Malaysia was known among the cadets as 'Jungle Wimale'.

Gōta graduated from army training school and was commissioned as a Second Lieutenant in the regular force of the Sri Lanka army on 26 May 1972. Ceylon had become Sri Lanka with the promulgation of the republican constitution of 1972 a few days before Gōta was commissioned. He was in the fourth intake of officer cadets to be trained entirely in Sri Lanka. The 19 graduates of Gōta's intake were assigned to various units. Gōta joined the Signals Corps. The most sought after regiments those days were the Armoured Corps, Artillery, Engineers and Signals. The infantry units were not necessarily favoured because they were non-technical. Among his contemporaries who will figure in this narrative, H.R.Stephen joined the Sinha Regiment, Nanda Mallawarachchi the Sri Lanka Light Infantry, Gamini Gunasekera the Service Corps and Palitha Fernando the Sri Lanka Electrical and Mechanical Engineers.

The army at that time had only three infantry units, the Sri Lanka Light Infantry, the Gemunu Watch and the Sinha Regiment. After his commissioning as a Second Lieutenant and joining the Signals Corps, Gōta was sent on a Signals Young Officers' course to Rawalpindi in Pakistan. Young officers' courses at that time were invariably held overseas, mainly in India and Pakistan.

Chapter 3

The Creation of Conflict

In a multi-ethnic, multi-religious society, differences always exist. All it takes is for some people to articulate and exacerbate these differences for a conflict to emerge. In Sri Lanka, conflict between the Sinhalese and the Tamils is as old as history itself. However, in centuries past, the conflict was always couched in terms of Tamil invaders from the Indian mainland and not in terms of conflict between the Sinhalese and indigenous Tamil communities living in the country. Tamils served even in the army of the 2nd century BC Sinhala hero Dutugemunu, who vanquished the Tamil King Elara, and unified the whole country as a Buddhist state.

The last Sinhala Kingdom of Kandy was ruled from 1739 to 1815 until it finally capitulated to the British, by a Tamil dynasty which had legally been acceded the throne by the Kandyan aristocracy upon the death of the last Sinhala King. The founder of the Tamil dynasty Sri Vijaya Rajasinha was the Tamil brother-in-law of the last Sinhala King who died without a legitimate heir. So even though there was conflict between the Tamils and the Sinhalese, it is not as if these two communities have been at war throughout history. In the early decades of the 20th century under British colonial rule, Sinhala-Tamil relations started off on a good footing with the creation of the Ceylon National Congress in December 1919, to agitate for self rule.

A Tamil, Sir Ponnambalam Arunachalam was its first president and his leadership was acknowledged by both the Sinhalese and Tamil elites. But soon afterwards the Ceylon National Congress split over the question of the allocation of a seat in the then Legislative Council for Tamils in the Western Province. A separate body called the *Tamil Mahajana Sabha* was born in 1921 and the Ceylon Tamil League led by Ponnambalam Arunachalam was formed in 1923. It is a supreme irony that the Tamil-Sinhala conflict in the modern era began not with a cry for separatism but a cry for greater integration, with the Tamil elites demanding guaranteed representation in the Western Province, where they live in sizable numbers.

Even though Sinhala-Tamil skirmishing began long before independence, the issue was at that early stage restricted to jostling for more representation for Tamils. When a commission headed by Lord Soulbury was appointed by the British government in the mid-1940s to go into the question of granting independence to Ceylon, the then leader of the Tamil Congress G.G.Ponnambalam asked for parity of representation for the Sinhalese on the one hand and the Tamil, Muslim and other minority communities on the other. The Soulbury Commissioners rejected this suggestion as preposterous. What they had in mind was a system of representative government akin to that which existed in Britain. After independence however, the Tamil Congress gave up their demand for parity of representation and joined the first independence government and became a conservative Tamil party in alliance with the conservative UNP. This was a partnership that was to last many years.

The two party system evolved in the Tamil areas before it manifested itself at the national level. In 1949, a group broke away from the conservative Tamil Congress to form the more radical *Ilangei Tamil Arasu Kachchi* (ITAK) or the Ceylon Tamil State Party. The immediate reason for the split in the Tamil Congress was the decision of its leader G.G. Ponnambalam to support a bill in parliament which would deny citizenship rights in the newly independent Ceylon to the Indian Tamil labourers living in the plantation areas in the hill country. The Tamil Congress supported the bill on the grounds that the Indian Tamils were a transient population that had come to this country as plantation workers and still maintained their links with India and looked to India as their native land.

Of the seven Tamil Congress MPs in the first parliament, five voted for the legislation and two including the future leader of the ITAK, S.J.V.Chelvanayagam voted against it. Thus the beginnings of Ceylon Tamil radicalization can be traced back to an issue pertaining only to the Indian Tamil population. The supreme irony being that in the sixty years between 1949 and the bloody end of Tamil terrorism on the banks of the Nandikadal lagoon in 2009, the Indian Tamil population remained conservative and never sought to join their northern and eastern brethren in the struggle for an independent state.

The other great irony was that while Chelvanayagam walked away from the Tamil Congress because the Indian Tamil workers had not been given citizenship rights, India herself was to later accept that these people were indeed Indian, and agree to accord the majority of them Indian citizenship. Prime Minister Lal Bahadur Shastri of India came to an understanding in 1964 with Sirima Bandaranaike to take back 525,000 Indian Tamil workers over a period of 15 years along with their natural increase provided Ceylon gave citizenship to another 300,000 and their natural increase. The fate of the remaining 150,000 was to be decided later. In 1974 another agreement was concluded between Indira Gandhi of India and Mrs Bandaranaike for India and Sri Lanka to split the remaining 150,000 and their natural increase equally between the two countries.

What all that indicated was that these workers were indeed Indian, and many of them did opt to take Indian citizenship. In the 1980s, the J.R.Jayewardene government gave citizenship to all remaining Indian Tamil workers and the problem was finally laid to rest. Ironically, the Indian Tamil issue was the beginning of a conflict that raged everywhere else other than in the areas inhabited by the Indian Tamil workers. In fact even at the height of the LTTE's campaign of terror, the up-country areas inhabited by the Indian Tamils were always far safer than Colombo. When the ITAK was formed by Chelvanayagam on 18 December 1949, issues relating to the Indian Tamils had no relevance for the Tamils of the north and east whom the ITAK sought to represent. In order to make the new political entity relevant to the Ceylon Tamils, a new grievance was added to the list – Sinhalese colonization of land irrigated under schemes such as the Galoya project in the eastern province.

Even this was a non-issue. In his classic 1957 book, *Pioneer Peasant Colonisation in Ceylon*, B.H.Farmer has described the standard procedure adopted at that time to select colonists for schemes like Galoya. It was landless peasants from the area in which the scheme was located who were given first preference. It was only if there weren't enough applicants from the locality that outsiders were brought in. In acknowledgement of this fact four Tamil academics of the well known organization, University Teachers for Human Rights (Jaffna) were to write as follows in their 1990 book *The Broken Palmyra*. *"… It is probably wrong to say that Mr. D. S. Senanayake was involved in a deep anti-Tamil conspiracy to bring about Sinhalese domination. Nor is it possible to make a case that Mr. Senanayake was hatching a diabolical master plan to colonise Tamil areas with Sinhalese. When work for the Gal Oya settlement scheme in the Eastern province had been completed, first preference was given to people from the province. It was only after about six months, when faced with the paucity of local applicants, that the doors were opened to applicants from other provinces."*

Four decades after the formation of the ITAK, the authors of *The Broken Palmyra* who were living through what Chelvanayagam had created would observe ruefully that the Tamil leadership from the 1940s preferred to do what *'appeared clever rather than what was principled'* and that there was a *'predominance of manipulation over morality'* in their actions. With the formation of the ITAK, a two party system came into being in the north and east with the Tamil Congress and the ITAK vying for the votes of the Tamils. Two years later in 1951, a two party system came into being at the centre as well, through the formation of the Sri Lanka Freedom Party by S.W.R.D.Bandaranaike and Gōta's father D.A.Rajapaksa among others.

From this time onwards, things tended to be driven by the needs of these contending forces in the political arena to either win or retain power. The emergence of a two party system at the national level can be considered a positive development because all working democratic systems in the world are two party systems. However, the emergence of two parties vying for the north-eastern Tamil vote was to have fateful consequences. After its formation in 1949, the ITAK unsurprisingly hit the doldrums because their reasons for opposing the dominant Tamil Congress had no resonance among northern Tamil voters. At the next parliamentary election held in 1952, S.J.V.Chelvanayagm himself lost his Kankesanthurei seat to the UNP candidate S.Natesan. The ITAK won only two seats, Kopay in the Jaffna peninsula and Trincomalee in the east.

What gave the defeated ITAK a new lease of life was the language controversy of 1955/6. The language issue was under discussion in this country even before independence. It was J.R.Jayewardene, then an up and coming young legislator who first brought a resolution in the State Council on 4 May 1944, suggesting that Sinhala should replace English as the language of the state. Jayewardene, a member of the Ceylon National Congress and a well known Indophile, drew inspiration from the Indian National Congress which had declared that Hindi should be the language of the state in India. While agreeing that Tamil should be the language state business is transacted in Tamil speaking areas, he expressed apprehensions about giving Tamil parity of status with Sinhala because there were over 40 million Tamil speakers in neighbouring South India and his fear was that giving parity of status to the two languages would lead to the swamping of Sinhala by the more widely used Tamil. Despite these reservations, Jayewardene declared that he will not stand in the way of the Tamils if they wanted parity of status with Sinhala.

In the debate that followed, S.W.R.D.Bandaranaike who was also a member of the State Council made a speech on 25 May 1944, agreeing with Jayewardene's proposal and saying that both Sinhala and Tamil should be made the state languages of Ceylon. A decade later, Bandaranaike was to change his stance. The partnership between the elitist and conservative UNP and the equally elitist and conservative Tamil Congress had worked well into the 1950s. In 1955, the then UNP prime minister Sir John Kotelawala made a passing comment at a meeting in Jaffna about making both Sinhala and Tamil state languages, and this set off agitation in the Sinhala dominated south against granting parity of status to Tamil.

On 19 October 1955, the leader of the socialist (Trotskyite) Lanka Sama Samaja Party Dr N.M.Perera brought a resolution in parliament suggesting that both Sinhala and Tamil should be made the state languages. Dr Perera argued that in order to eliminate any suspicions the communities may have of each other, and to generate inter-communal harmony, it was necessary to make both Sinhala and Tamil official languages. By this time, Bandaranaike was a member of the opposition in parliament, as the leader of the recently formed SLFP. Drawing attention to the previous debate on this matter in the state council back in 1944, Bandaranaike said that at that time, everybody was thinking only of replacing English with indigenous languages and that none of them had thought of the real implications of making a language a state language.

He admitted that his thinking had changed somewhat since then and that his party the SLFP has decided that Sinhala should be the state language while provision will be made for the reasonable use of Tamil in public administration, education and the courts. He argued that two languages can be state languages only in a federal state. Taking Switzerland as an example, he pointed out that in Geneva the state language was French while in Bern, the state language was German and that worked because Switzerland was a federal state. If in a unitary state, two languages were to be state languages, confusion could result if a Sinhala speaking defendant is brought before a Tamil speaking judge. Because both Sinhala and Tamil will be official languages, the judge will be able to order the records of the case to be kept in Tamil which the defendant will not understand.

Moreover, he argued that Tamil is spoken by about 40 million people in South India, in the northern and eastern provinces in Sri Lanka, in the hill country by Indian Tamil workers as well as by the one million or so Tamils living among the Sinhalese in all parts of t he island, and that if Tamil was made a state language the use of Sinhala would become more and more restricted. The UNP suffered because they were identified with the 'parity of status' policy and Bandaranaike was able to capitalize on the mood of the day by adopting the policy of Sinhala as the state language with provision for the reasonable use of Tamil. He won a landslide victory and became prime minister in 1956.

Like Bandaranaike in the south, another politician who benefited from the language controversy of 1955 was S.J.V.Chelvanayagam and his ITAK which won a parallel landslide victory in the Tamil majority constituencies in the northern and eastern provinces. In 1956, Chelvanayagam's ITAK was able to replace the Tamil Congress as the main Tamil political party. At the 1947 parliamentary elections, the Tamil Congress won 7 seats. The party split in 1949 with Chelvanayagam founding the ITAK. At the 1952 elections, the TC won four seats and the ITAK two seats. But at the 1956 elections, the ITAK got 10 seats and the TC only one. Chelvanayagam was now not only back in parliament, but also the principal political leader of the Tamils, eclipsing his erstwhile political boss G.G.Ponnambalam.

The inspiration for Tamil separatism in Sri Lanka came from South India. Dravidian/Tamil separatism had been flourishing in South India even during the era of British colonial rule in the early decades of the 20th century. It started off as an anti-Brahmin movement but the agenda soon came to include a separate sovereign state for Tamils. Even as early as 1921, the Justice Party a Dravidian nationalist, separatist party became the dominant political force in the Madras Presidency which encompassed most of South India. By 1925, E.V.Ramasamy Naikar (Periyar) had started his Self Respect movement against the 'Aryan domination' of the Dravidian south. In 1935, Periyar joined the Justice Party and Dravidian revivalists in South India thus closed ranks.

Dravidian/Tamil nationalism and separatism held sway in South India from 1921 to 1937. In 1937 with the independence struggle sweeping across India, the Indian National Congress managed to wrest control of the Madras Presidency from the separatist Justice Party. After the Congress party captured power in the Madras Presidency, an attempt was made to introduce the Hindi language as a subject in schools. This was opposed by the Justice Party. Despite this setback, the Indian National Congress managed to retain power in the Madras Presidency due to anti-colonial fervour and the heat of the independence struggle.

As the 1930s rolled into the 40s, the call for a separate Dravidian state became more strident with the Justice Party even demanding that the Dravidian areas be governed directly from London by the British Colonial Office as a separate entity from the rest of India. In 1944 the Justice Party was renamed the Dravida Kazagam which continued to advocate the same line of Dravidian separatism. On 1 July 1947, weeks before India gained independence from the British, the Dravida Kazagam held a series of public meetings calling for an independent Dravida Nadu. In 1949, the Dravida Kazagam split with a prominent leader C.N.Annadurai breaking away to form the Dravida Munnethra Kazagam (DMK) which would dominate separatist Tamil politics in India thereafter. Thus the Tamil separatist movement in India was already decades old before S.J.V.Chelvanayagam established the ITAK in Ceylon.

It was clearly the success of Tamil separatism and nationalism in South India that would have shown Chelvanayagam that identity politics was his ticket to power. Chelvanayagam split from the Tamil Congress in the same year that C.N.Annadurai split from the Dravida Kazagam to form the *Dravida Munnethra Kazagam* (DMK). After this, the vicissitudes of separatism in Tamil Nadu would be mirrored in Sri Lanka almost on a one to one basis. For example, the official language became an issue in India before it became an issue in Ceylon. In 1950 with the promulgation of the Indian constitution, Hindi became the official language of India and the Dravida Kazagam and the newly formed DMK spearheaded opposition to Hindi.

The Congress Party government at the centre was alive to the dangers of pan-Dravidian separatism and they set about taking countermeasures. The first step was to isolate the epicentre of Dravidian separatism. The Indian central government set about dismembering the Madras Presidency after independence. The Telegu-speaking northern areas of the Madras Presidency became Andra Pradesh in 1953. A few years later in 1956, with the Indian States Reorganisation Act of 1956, the Malayalam speaking areas of the Madras Presidency became Kerala. What was left now in the Madras State were only the Tamil speaking areas and it was here that separatism continued to flourish. Dravidian separatism died a natural death in the other three states of Kerala, Andhra Pradesh and Karnataka that were carved out in South India.

Chapter 4

The Abyss Opens

The year 1956 marked the defeat of sober conservative politics and the rise of emotional populism. This was as true of the Sinhalese as the Tamils. Caution and reflective introspection was in seriously short supply. The day before the official language bill was presented to parliament on 4 June 1956, Chelvanayagam wrote to prime minister S.W.R.D. Bandaranaike informing him that the ten ITAK parliamentarians and about 200 of their party supporters would stage a sit-in protest on the flight of stairs leading to the main entrance to parliament and he wanted the prime minister to ensure that his men were not prevented from having their protest.

Bandaranaike consulted his advisors and decided that this would not only disrupt the proceedings of parliament but could also lead to a wider breach of the peace, and he wrote back to Chelvanayagam that he could not permit any such protest to take place on the steps of parliament house. Bandaranaike's letter was hand delivered to Chelvanayagam that same evening. The ITAK thereupon shifted their protest to the Galle Face green in close proximity to parliament. Later, ITAK parliamentarian from Kopay C.Vanniasingham was to describe the events that took place on that day 5 June 1956. They had assembled at Galle Face green at around 8.30 in the morning and seen a large concentration of persons 'numbering in the thousands rather than hundreds' and a number of police trucks, vans and police personnel near the precincts of the parliament.

The Tamil protestors were sitting on the grass when the Sinhala mob holding aloft a national flag, had marched past them jeering, shouting slogans and obscenities. But the Tamil protestors had kept silent. Up to this point, only words were exchanged. Then, C.Sundaralingam the independent MP for Vavuniya and G.G.Ponnambalam had arrived on the scene to more jeers and catcalls from the crowd. Vanniasingham says that at this point, Sundaralingam had 'turned and bowed' to the jeering mob. However Sundaralingam was well known to be a maverick politician much given to histrionics and it is unlikely that he just bowed. Gōta's cousin Lakshman Rajapaksa was later that day in parliament, to accuse Sundaralingam of having 'challenged the crowd' at Galle Face green. An unrepentant Sundaralingam responded immediately to the accusation saying "*I confess quite frankly that I have always on the floor of this house, in the press and on public platforms, I have given expression namely to the view that according to the declaration of human rights accepted by the United Nations Organisation, we are entitled as a last resort to rebellion.*"

Be that as it may, it was after Sundaralingam did his thing, his 'bow' as Vanniasingham put it, or his 'challenge' according to Lakshman Rajapaksa, that things graduated from mere verbal abuse to blows and fisticuffs that morning. After Sundaralingam made his appearance and left, The Sinhala mob had grabbed the placards held by the Tamil protestors and thrown them up in the air, and they had come among the protestors, planted the lion flag in the middle and danced around it. Vanniasingham himself and two other parliamentarians were assaulted by the Sinhala mob. One protestor had his ear bitten. After one hour, the police had intervened and formed a cordon around the protestors.

While this was going on, more Tamil protestors who had arrived from Trincomalee came walking in a body from the Fort railway station to the Galle Face green. At this point, the Sinhala mob began throwing stones at the protestors over the police cordon. These were the missiles that had famously injured A.Amirthalingam and a few others. The protest was called off by about 1.00 in the afternoon and the ITAK parliamentarians went back to parliament. The events at Galle Face green were not taking place in isolation. A *hartal* – a complete shutdown of shops, public transport, offices and schools - was being observed that morning in the Tamil areas of the north and east, to protest against the Official Language Act.

With rumours of the events at Galle Face Green spreading, sporadic acts of violence spread to other areas of Colombo with Sinhala mobs looting Tamil shops and throwing stones. The police fired into looting mobs and things cooled off after that. By 7 June, even the taverns were open again. The total damage from the riot was estimated at Rs 300,000 according to a *Ceylon Daily News* headline story. A *hartal* was held in Jaffna to protest against the attack on the *Satyagrahis* on Galle Face green. However Jaffna community leaders led by the Jaffna Mayor S.S.Navaratnam saw to it that the Sinhalese living in Jaffna were protected and no major incidents were reported from the peninsula. In Batticaloa town however, a Sinhalese owned eatery was set on fire and employees of the eatery fired into the Tamil mob killing two. The hotel employees were arrested by the police. About 25 Sinhalese had been injured in Batticaloa in sporadic acts of violence which had included the burning of two Sinhala schools and a house.

Independent Ceylon had experienced its first communal riot as a result of the ITAK's ill conceived plan to agitate against the official language bill outside parliament. This was also the first time that the *Satyagraha* had been used in a major way in Sri Lankan politics. The *Satyagraha* was a mode of protest introduced to the world by Mahatma Gandhi and the term would loosely mean 'capturing the truth'. In actual application however this had nothing to do with any quest for truth but was an instrument of protest, opposition and stubborn defiance while eschewing violence. Speaking of this ITAK *Satyagraha* in parliament, Bandaranaike said that these *Satyagrahas* look peaceful, but they are meant to spread ill-feeling and tension all around, and what is expected is anything but peace. In this Bandaranaike was right. The *Satyagraha* as an instrument of protest was never meant to be peaceful.

It was non-violent only to the extent that actual physical violence was not used by the *Satyagrahis*. In every other respect, the *Satyagraha* was an instrument of confrontation. The fact that this form of protest makes a moralistic pretence of being peaceful and non-violent may irk those at the receiving end of a *Satyagraha* even more than an honest and straight forward riot. As Bandaranaike said, the sight of hundreds of people sitting in sullen silence and exuding hate and resentment in all directions, is not conducive to maintaining the public peace.

Decades later, at the Thimpu talks in 1985, A.Amirthalingam would recount what happened on that day in 1956 when the ITAK tried to stage a protest on Galle face green. *"Government set up hoodlums to attack us. We were beaten up with sticks, pelted with stones, stripped and trampled. I still carry two scars on my head caused by the non-violent stones which the Sinhala patriots threw at the Tamil*

Satyagrahis. When I walked into parliament with my clothes drenched in blood and a handkerchief tied around the gaping wound on my forehead, the then prime minister Bandaranaike remarked, 'honourable wounds of war'. To him, it was a joke... But the Satyagrahis were not the only victims of violence on that occasion. Tamils on the roads of Colombo were pulled out of their cars and buses and beaten up. Mr Sivasittamparam reminds me that one of those beaten up on the roads of Colombo on the occasion was no less a person than the present chief justice Mr Sharvananda. He was not one of the Satyagrahis, then why was he beaten up? Because he was Tamil. This is the reply that the Tamil people get for the first attempt at non-violent Satyagraha against an inequity perpetrated on them."

Yet, anybody with commonsense would have seen that a confrontation was inevitable given the fact that the ITAK disregarded Bandaranaike's warning not to assemble near parliament as it could lead to a wider breach of the peace. On seeing the Sinhala mob already assembled near parliament that morning, Vanniasingham expressed surprise as to how and why these people had been allowed to collect there. Somehow, it did not seem to occur to Vanniasingham that the Sinhala mob had assembled there the same way that the Tamils had assembled at the same place. Tension had been building up over a period of time, and a responsible political party would not have assembled outside parliament if they wanted to avoid a disturbance of the peace.

On the morning of 5 June, the *Ceylon Daily News* headline screamed *"Special police cordon round house, Satyagrahis expected."* The news story stated that the 'strictest security arrangements' would be observed at parliament. Another front page story in the same newspaper said that contingents of *Satyagrahis* from various parts of the north and east led by ITAK parliamentarians C.Vanniasingham from Kopay, and N.R.Rajavarothiam from Trincomalee had started arriving in Colombo the previous day and that another contingent led by C.Rajadurai was on its way from Batticaloa. Then there were special reports of *Satyagrahis* setting off from various other places to converge on Colombo. With such reports in the newspapers, it was inevitable that a Sinhala mob too would be present at Galle Face.

By stubbornly going ahead with their plan to hold the protest, the ITAK was deliberately provoking a backlash. In fact, during the debate on the Official Language Act, in June 1956, Bandaranaike sarcastically asked the ITAK parliamentarians, *"These incidents that occurred are just what you wanted, is that not so?"* Politically motivated mobs do not behave in an enlightened fashion. A good example of this is the way an ITAK mob set upon a fellow Tamil nationalist C.Sundaralingam in Batticaloa town on 28 July 1957. While the ITAK was holding its annual convention in Batticaloa, the independent Vavuniya MP C.Sundaralingam was addressing a meeting close to the Batticaloa town hall when he was set upon and pelted with stones by a crowd of about 400 ITAK members. The police had to baton charge the attackers to rescue Sundaralingam who had been injured and had to be hospitalized.

The moral of the story is that when two different political groups assemble in proximity to one another, conflict is inevitable even if there are shared values between the two groups. What happened between the ITAK and the Sinhala mob in June 1956 is no different to what happened between Sundaralingam and the ITAK in July 1957. Cautious and far thinking politicians will always try to avoid situations that would lead to a breach of the peace and that is where the ITAK erred in 1956. This then raises the question whether a political party has to forego its right to protest simply because there is a risk of a reaction from the other side. The answer to that would depend on how substantial the issue, and how justifiable the protest is. In that respect the ITAK campaign is found wanting.

Firstly, the ITAK's *Satyagraha* was touted as a protest against the 'Sinhala only policy' but, there was never a Sinhala only policy – Sinhala was to be the official language with reasonable provision for the use of Tamil. This was the position that Bandaranaike took in introducing the official language bill in parliament on 5 June 1956. This formula of primacy being given to the language of the majority community with provision for the reasonable use of the language of the minority, was a policy that Chelvanayagam himself wholeheartedly agreed with. He too adopted this formula in the Bandaranaike-Chelvanagayagm pact of 1957. In the proposed Tamil controlled regional councils in the north and east, there was a Sinhala speaking minority and the formula agreed on by Chelvanayagam was that Tamil would be the language of administration in the Tamil majority regional councils with 'reasonable provision' made for Sinhala – a mirror image of the policy that the SLFP had adopted with regard to the whole country.

Twenty years later, in 1976 when Chelvanayagam made the famous Vadukkodai proclamation calling for an independent sovereign Tamil state in the northern and eastern provinces of Sri Lanka, it had a note on the language policy of Tamil Eelam. Once again, the state language of Tamil Eelam was to be Tamil with provision for the reasonable use of Sinhala for the Sinhala minority. Thus Chelvanayagam endorsed Bandaranaike's language policy twice, once in 1957 and again in 1976. There was no need therefore, to have that protest at Galle Face Green in June 1956.

There was the fact that when the Official Language Act of 1956 was passed by parliament, it had no reference to the reasonable use of the Tamil language. However, on 6 June, 1956, speaking at the debate on the official language bill, Bandaranaike explained that even though the Official Language Act would be passed in June 1956, its implementation would be delayed for four and a half years until 1 January 1961, for two reasons – one was to enable the switch over from English to Sinhala in the government service and the courts and secondly, to provide for the reasonable use of Tamil. So provision for the reasonable use of Tamil was very much on the agenda and the ITAK had absolutely no reason to spark off a riot over the language issue.

Chapter 5

A Little Now, More Later

A rational, sober and cautious approach however was not the way to make headway in politics at that time. About two months after the official language legislation was passed, the ITAK held a party convention in Trincomalee on 18 and 19 August 1956. This took the form of a circus with thousands of party activists marching to Trincomalee from various parts of the north and east on foot. Welcoming ceremonies were held for the marchers at towns *en route*. Many activists collapsed from exhaustion as they neared the end of the march thus adding to the drama.

At this convention, it was resolved that the unitary form of government had failed to ensure the rights of the Tamil minority. They cited the passing of the Official Language Act, the disenfranchisement of the Indian Tamils, and the colonization of 'Tamil areas' by state aided Sinhalese settlers. Having stated these grievances, the ITAK issued an ultimatum to the government which went as follows. *"This convention further declares that unless the Prime Minister and Parliament take the necessary steps to constitute a Federal Union of Ceylon by August 20 1957, the Federal Party (ITAK) will launch direct action based on non-violent means for the achievement of this objective."*

Thus the government had a one year deadline to grant the ITAK demands or face a civil-disobedience campaign. The following year, as the deadline set by the ITAK for instituting a federal system of government came dangerously close, a series of frantic discussions took place between the Bandaranaike government and the ITAK and on 26 July 1957, the Bandaranaike-Chelavanayagam pact was announced. The compromise achieved without instituting a federal form of government or repealing the Official Language Act, was to set up a system of regional councils, with the northern province being one regional council and the eastern province being divided into one or more regional councils. The regional councils could amalgamate to form one council by mutual consent, and councillors to the regional legislatures would be directly elected by the people. Subjects like agriculture, cooperatives, land, land development, colonization, education, health, industries, fisheries, housing, social services, electricity, water schemes and roads were to be handled by the regional councils. They were also to have the power to select land allotees within their area except in the areas coming under the Galoya settlement scheme. On language, as we saw earlier, Tamil was to be the language of administration and the courts with reasonable provision for the use of Sinhala.

There is the simplistic belief among many people that had the Bandaranaike-Chelvanayagam pact of 1957 been implemented, that Sri Lanka's ethnic problem would have been solved back then and a brutal war averted. Indeed the problem would have been solved if in the view of both parties, this was a once and for all, permanent solution to whatever problem there was. The meaning of a compromise is that the two parties to a conflict come half way and give up some of their demands in order to come to a settlement. But this was not how the ITAK viewed the Bandaranaike-Chelvanayagam pact. Just two days after Chelvanayagam signed the pact, a special convention of the ITAK was held in Batticaloa.

At this convention, a proposal made by A. Amirthalingam and seconded by S.M.Rasamanickam declared *"The national convention of the Federal Party having considered the agreement reached between its representatives and Premier Bandaranaike and having reviewed the report of the negotiations submitted to it by its representatives, reiterates its unalterable determination to achieve (1) an autonomous Tamil linguistic State or states within the framework of the Federal Union of Ceylon (2) parity of status between the Tamil and Sinhalese languages throughout the island (3) revision and re-orientation of the present unilateral and undemocratic citizenship laws to ensure recognition of the right of every Tamil-speaking individual who has made Ceylon his permanent home to full citizenship."*

The Amirthalaingam-Rasamanickam resolution said further - *"The convention having regard to... (The provisions of the Banda-Chelva pact)...resolves to accept the agreement as an **interim adjustment** and thereby ratifies the decision to withdraw the proposed Satyagraha campaign*

36

scheduled for August 20." The day after the ITAK held their Batticaloa convention, the *Ceylon Daily News* of 28 July 1957 reported on the event in a headline story with the telling strap-line *"Not final but an interim adjustment".* Another front page news item in the same issue reported C.Vanniasingham as saying during his speech at the convention *"This is only the stepping stone to our achievement of our objective – a federal state."* The leaders of the ITAK were very open about their intentions. On 19 August 1957, Chelvanayagam himself told the *Ceylon Daily News "... While we obtain the benefits accruing from the pact, we must continue our struggle to achieve our demands and the gains got will give strength to the future struggle."*

So in the eyes of the ITAK, this was never a permanent solution to the Tamil problem and only a stepping stone to higher things. Implementing the Bandaranaike-Chelvanayagam pact would in fact have solved nothing and would only have exacerbated the problem. None of this was going to make the other side happy about the pact. The opposition UNP held a rally at Victoria Park in Colombo calling on the government to repudiate the Banda-Chelva pact on 18 August 1957 and J.R.Jayewardene sardonically observed *"One party to the pact, the prime minister looks upon it as a permanent solution to the language difficulties he has created. The other party, the federalists and a large body of Tamils consider it a first step towards the creation of an independent Tamil state or states."*

The contents of the Bandaranaike-Chelvanayagam pact and the resolutions adopted at the ITAK convention came in for a great deal of public scrutiny and the Sinhalese in particular were apprehensive about the objectives of the ITAK. Even as the ITAK held its 1957 convention in Batticaloa, Prime Minister Bandaranaike was reassuring anxious bhikkus in Colombo that his pact with the ITAK would not lead to a division of the country. But given the 'a little now more later' policy enunciated at the ITAK convention, the prime minister's words of reassurance sounded hollow. Bandaranaike was trying to argue with anxious Sinhala protestors that had he not agreed to the regional councils system, the results would have been 'catastrophic'. But given the agenda announced at the ITAK Batticaloa convention, many Sinhalese had begun regarding the pact with the ITAK itself as a catastrophe. Pressure mounted on the prime minister from all quarters in the days that followed.

The opposition UNP was issuing statement after statement against the Bandaranaike-Chelvanayagam pact from the very day it was signed. J.R.Jayewardene even organized a 'long march' to Kandy against it in the first week of October 1957. In hindsight, perhaps it was just as well that the Banda-Chelva pact was never implemented. If it was simply an 'interim adjustment', with more having to be conceded later, implementing this pact would have led not to a solution but to exacerbating the problem with the ITAK being emboldened to make further demands. Bandaranaike was bullied into appending his signature to the regional councils proposal with nothing more than the threat of a civil disobedience campaign and that too by a party that never had a clear majority of the votes cast in the north and east.

Bandaranaike's lack of a backbone and his ill-advised intellectual meanderings had much to do with creating many intractable problems in Sri Lanka. When he was a young Colombo Municipal Councillor in 1926, Bandaranaike had at a lecture delivered in Jaffna to the Jaffna Youth Congress, said that a federal system of government would be suitable for Ceylon. This event in Jaffna in July 1926, was just a discussion where various ideas were mooted. Bandaranaike was only 27 years old at the time. One member of the audience was in fact wondering aloud whether the best form of government wouldn't be to remain under British rule. Yet this even this speech of 1926 is being made use of by the Tamil separatist lobby to justify their claim to an independent state. It goes without saying that one offhand comment made by a young and obviously intellectually confused politician in his twenties, cannot possibly be construed as a considered statement of policy that should guide the affairs of state.

Be that as it may, because Bandaranaike appended his signature to the regional councils proposal, it appears as if the government in Colombo has accepted in principle that the Tamils should govern themselves in the north and east. And from that time onwards this idea of a self governing Tamil unit has been the main focus of even the moderate Tamils. This is a text book example of how poor leadership and decision making can create problems that countries are unable to unravel long after those leaders have left the stage of history. The regional councils proposal had been agreed to not because it was deemed the best way to govern and administer this country, but in a headlong rush to avoid agitation by the ITAK.

This was a complete contrast to the manner adopted by the Donoughmore Commission in 1931 and the Soulbury Commission in 1947 which presided over constitution making during British times. The colonial masters simply said NO to any suggestion that seemed unfair or unworkable. The ill conceived Bandaranaike-Chelvanayagam pact was the clearest sign that after independence, Ceylon had fallen into the hands of lesser men.

Chapter 6

Guided by Unreason

In this volatile situation, another issue came up which set the spark to the tinderbox. In mid-March 1958, the first state owned buses with the new vehicle numbering system featuring the letter *Sri* in the Sinhala script arrived in Jaffna. The enterprising Chelvanayagm saw this as another opportunity for agitation and he promptly set about organizing opposition to the Sinhala letter *Sri* on the new buses coming to Jaffna. Chelvanayagam and his party secretary E.M.V.Naganathan met the minister of transport Maithripala Senanayake and told him not to send the *Sri* numbered buses to Jaffna. Minister Senanayake had thought over the matter and decided to send the buses anyway, as they were needed in Jaffna. The ITAK held a rally in Jaffna on 28 March 1958 and instructed their activists to replace the Sinhala '*Sri*' on bus number plates with the same letter in Tamil. On 30 March 1958, Amirthalingam personally led ITAK activists in defacing the number plates on buses in Jaffna.

This naturally set off a reaction in other parts of the country. Sinhala mobs in Colombo 'bare bodied goons with their sarongs held shoulder high and shamelessly displaying their genitals', as Tarzie Vittachchi put it in his classic book *Emergency '58*, had reacted by defacing Tamil lettering on business premises, signboards, buses and wherever else they found Tamil lettering. As the situation careered out of control, an eminent Tamil member of the upper house of parliament S.Nadesan made a forceful speech in the Senate, accusing the government of 'supineness' and declaring that they should either 'govern or get out'. During his speech, Nadesan said that ITAK activists had first replaced the Sinhala letter *Sri* with the Tamil *Sri* on their own vehicles in Jaffna, and the government took no action at that stage. Now the ITAK had been emboldened to change the lettering on state owned buses as well. Because no action was taken with regard to the painters in the north, people in the south also thought they could take the law into their own hands with no consequences. Nadesan asserted that the leaders of the ITAK "had done the greatest disservice to the entire country on this matter". He warned that unless the government took immediate steps, things might lead to bloodshed and the creation of great bitterness between the two communities'.

The disturbances soon spread to other parts of the country as well. Two Tamil shops were broken into in Anuradhapura and in Bogawantalawa in the hill country, an Indian Tamil mob had pursued a bus with the *Sri* lettering and when the driver drove into a police station for safety, the mob threw stones at the police station. Two Tamil rioters died in the subsequent police shooting. Chelvanayagam even made use of this tragedy, organizing a hartal on 5 April 1958 to protest against the Bogawantalawa shootings. Disturbances were reported from Jaffna, Mannar, Batticaloa and Anurahapura. As things spiralled out of control, Prime Minister S.W.R.D.Bandaranaike announced that the Bandaranaike-Chelvanayagam pact could not be implemented because of the actions of the ITAK. Indeed given the situation that had arisen in the country, it would have been suicidal for the government even to attempt to implement such an agreement.

The abrogation of the Bandaranaike-Chelvanayagam pact led to the ITAK stepping up their anti-*Sri* campaign. The ITAK issued a statement on 10 April 1958 saying that Bandaranaike had abrogated the accord and that the Tamils and the Sinhalese were now at the parting of ways and that the Tamil people had the choice of 'either fighting back or for ever being a subject race'. They called upon all Tamils to join in a campaign of civil disobedience. Justifying his anti-*Sri* campaign Chelvanayagam said that the tarring of the letter *Sri* on buses was in support of the political campaign of the Tamil people against the language policy of the government and charged that hooliganism and thuggery was being used to prevent the Tamil people from engaging in non-violent civil disobedience to win their rights.

On 11 April 1958, Chelvanayagam himself announced that in addition to continuing tarring the *Sri* on number plates, ITAK members will refrain from paying taxes and would travel ticketless on public transport to court arrest. Over the next few days, ITAK leaders including Amirthalingam, Vanniasingham and Chelvanayagam himself were arrested while defacing buses. Chelvanayagam's arrest took place in Batticaloa on 13 April 1958. They were all released later on bail. Over 130 ITAK activists had been arrested by 15 April 1958.

The agony of 1958 did not end with that. Senator Nadesan's prophetic warning was to come horribly true in a matter of weeks. The disturbances following the ITAK's anti-*Sri* campaign was to set the stage for much worse things. The battle lines in the country had been drawn and there was a gradual build up of tensions which were soon to explode in a conflagration which would have implications far into the future. On 18 April 1958, in the backdrop of escalating communal tensions, Sinhala settlers in Padaviya held a meeting against the government's plan to settle among them, 400 Tamil families displaced by the closing down of the Royal Navy dockyard in Trincomalee. This set the stage for unrest in the Polonnaruwa and Batticaloa districts. Violence was in the air. In Colombo, even trade union protests turned violent resulting in damage to property. The mood in the country was turning ugly.

C. Sundaralingam the maverick Tamil politician did not help matters by calling for the creation of an independent Tamil State of Eelam in a pamphlet he released on 16 May 1958. It was in the middle of all these tensions that the ITAK's Vavuniya convention was held amidst great hostility to it especially in the Polonnaruwa district. The Polonnaruwa, Anuradhapura and Batticaloa districts had been in a state of tension for several weeks because of the possibility of 400 Tamil families being settled among them. On 23 July, the Colombo-Batticaloa train was stopped near the Polonnaruwa station by a crowd of about 500 and hooligans boarded the train smashed windows and assaulted Tamil passengers who they thought were on their way to the ITAK convention. The unrest was mostly between Polonnaruwa and Batticaloa. The night train was derailed in Polonnaruwa the same night killing one and injuring 13. On 24 July, telecommunications with Batticaloa had been cut and train services to the north and east reduced to the minimum for security reasons. Train services to Jaffna, Batticaloa, Trincomalee and Talaimannar were affected.

In the middle of all this, the ITAK went ahead with their convention and announced on 25 May that the civil disobedience campaign demanding a federal form of government which had been first announced in August 1956 and called off in July 1957, will be held from 20 August 1958. Following this announcement, Polonnaruwa erupted in violence again with mobs stopping vehicles and assaulting Tamil passengers. Armed mobs stormed police stations in Polonnaruwa and Hingurakgoda and four died in police shootings. Security arrangements were beefed up in Trincomalee, Batticaloa, Eravur, Galoya, and Amparai. The army and navy were deployed on the streets of Colombo and all taverns were closed. The government ordered the acquisition of all privately owned firearms in the country. Despite all this, looting was reported even from Colombo Fort. Speaking at a UNP rally in Kurunegala, J.R.Jayewardene said that the government had ceased to govern.

On 27 May, the government declared an emergency and imposed dusk to dawn curfew countrywide. A press censorship was also announced, all schools were closed and all public meetings and processions banned. The ITAK and the Jathika Vimukthi Peramuna, a Sinhala extremist organization led by K.M.P.Rajaratne were proscribed. (This should not be confused with the Janatha Vimukthi Peramuna of later years led by Rohana Wijeweera). ITAK leaders like Chelvanayagam who had houses in Colombo were kept under house arrest while those who did not, were detained at the Galle Face Hotel.

The Sinhala residents of Jaffna took refuge in police stations while the government scotched rumours to the effect that the Nagadipa temple in Jaffna had been attacked and one monk killed. In fact the Nagadipa Temple had been completely destroyed by Tamil mobs and the incumbent monk beaten within an inch of his life. The government rebuilt the temple while the press censorship was still on, and prevailed upon the incumbent monk not to reveal the truth to the public. Royal College in Colombo was turned into a refugee centre for Tamils displaced by the riots. The extent of the displacement can be gauged from the fact that by 3 June 1958, 4,400 Tamils had been transported by ship to Jaffna and 2,100 Sinhalese had been brought from Jaffna to Trincomalee for their safety.

The riot of 1958 was not a one sided affair. Both the Sinhalese and the Tamils turned on one another in the districts where they were in the majority. Outrages were committed on both sides. Decades later, Lt Gen Sarath Fonseka whose parents were school teachers serving in the Ampara district in the east, reminisced how he and his parents had to hide in the jungles in the night to avoid marauding Tamil mobs during this period. Cyril Ranatunga, then a young officer in the army was involved in quelling the riots in the Galoya settlement which had been provoked by the killing in Eravur, of D.A.Seneviratne a Sinhalese and a former Mayor of Sri Lanka's hill capital Nuwara

Eliya. Infuriated Sinhalese mobs had thereupon commandeered bulldozers and other vehicles and gone in search of Tamil homes. Ranatunga's platoon had dispersed one particular mob they had come face to face with, but that hadn't stopped the rioting. There were several massacres of Sinhalese in Batticaloa the one in Karativu where Sinhala fishermen were set upon by a Tamil mob, being the most serious. Tarzie Vittachchi estimates the death toll from that single incident to be more than 11.

The communal riots of 1958 was a cataclysmic event for Sri Lanka. No real casualty figures are available as in the case of all communal riots that took place in Sri Lanka, but it is generally estimated that over a hundred would have been killed, the majority being Tamils and several thousand displaced from both communities as a result of the riots. About two weeks into the emergency, things cooled off. On 17 July, with the ITAK leaders still in custody, Bandaranaike presented the Tamil Language (Special Provisions) bill of 1958 in parliament.

Making hasty arrangements to legislate for the use of the Tamil language in the north and east made it look as if this was an impromptu measure to pacify the Tamils. However this had always been a part of the language policy of the Bandaranaike government. In introducing the Tamil Language (Special Provisions) bill of 1958, Prime Minister Bandaranaike said that this legislation would have come at least one and a half years earlier if not for the insistence of the ITAK, that the language provisions should be introduced together with the regional councils provided for in the Bandaranaike-Chelvanayagam pact. He explained that the setting up of the regional councils needed intricate legislation and could not be done overnight. The Tamil Language (Special Provisions) Act of 1958 provided for the use of the Tamil language in education up to university level and in public service exams, and the use of Tamil in corresponding with government institutions.

The stories he heard of the riots of 1958 would leave an indelible impression on the young Prabhakaran. On 11 March 1984, in an interview with Anita Pratap for the Indian weekly, *Sunday*, Prabhakaran explained why he took to arms *"The shocking events of the 1958 racial riots had a profound impact on me when I was a schoolboy. I heard of horrifying incidents of how our people had been mercilessly and brutally put to death by Sinhala racists. Once I met a widowed mother - a friend of my family who related to me her agonizing personal experience of the racial holocaust. During the riots a Sinhala mob attacked her house in*

43

Colombo. *The rioters set fire to the house and murdered her husband. She and her children escaped with severe burn injuries. I was deeply shocked when I saw the scars on her body. I also heard stories of how young babies were roasted alive in boiling tar. When I heard such stories of cruelty, I felt a deep sense of sympathy and love for my people. A great passion overwhelmed me to redeem my people from this racist system. I strongly felt that armed struggle was the only way to confront a system which employs armed might against unarmed, innocent people."*

The interesting thing is that according to Tarzie Vittachchi's account of the riots of 1958, in the original version of the story it was a Sinhalese baby that had been boiled in tar by a Tamil mob in Batticaloa. With the passing of years, the ethnicity of the baby and the place had got switched around. Another incident during the communal riots of 1958 that motivated the young Prabhakaran to take to arms was the story of the burning to death of the Hindu priest of the Panadura kovil. This incident was however true. In Vittatachi's account, the mobs in Panadura had been driven by blind hate because of a rumour that a female teacher from Panadura who had been serving in Batticaloa had been murdered after her breasts had been cut off and that the mutilated body was being brought back to Panadura.

Mobs killed the Hindu priest in revenge. Later it turned out that there was no teacher from Panadura serving in Batticaloa. It was the story about the killing of the Panadura priest that ignited Jaffna and caused the destruction of the Nagadipa temple. Similarly, the riots in the Polonnaruwa, Anuradhapura and Batticaloa districts and in Padaviya were driven by the story of the killing of D.A.Seneviratne, the former Mayor of Nuwara Eliya - which was also true. Such are the dynamics of a riot. Stories both real and imaginary feed the flames of violence.

Chapter 7

The Ultimate Objectives

With all these histrionics between 1956 and 1958, the ITAK went from strength to strength. At the March 1960 parliamentary election, they won no less than 16 seats. The March 1960 election resulted in a hung parliament and the ITAK with 16 MPs could have tipped the balance either way. In these circumstances, the ITAK leader Chelvanayagam addressed a letter to both the UNP and the SLFP laying down certain conditions if either of the two parties wanted his support to form a government. In the first part of this letter, Chelvanayagam outlined the basic objectives of his party - a federal constitution with autonomy for the Tamil areas, parity of status for the Tamil language throughout the country, the granting of citizenship rights to Indian Tamils settled in Ceylon and stopping the colonization of 'Tamil areas' with Sinhala people. Then he suggests certain compromise measures as follows.

1. *The creation of regional councils in the northern and eastern provinces and the allocation of the functions envisaged in the Bandaranaike-Chelvanayagam pact including the right of one or more regional councils to amalgamate. All colonization to be halted until the establishment of these regional councils.*

2. *Tamil to be the language of administration and courts of the northern and eastern provinces with reasonable provision made for the non-Tamil speakers in these areas (The Bandaranaike formula once again.) Tamil people throughout Ceylon should have the right to be educated in Tamil and to sit competitive exams for recruitment*

to the public service in Tamil. And every Tamil person should have the right to transact business with the government in Tamil.

3. The citizenship act which disenfranchised the Indian Tamil population to be amended.

4. Until such time as the franchise issue of the Indian Tamils is settled, 4 out of the 6 appointed MP's in parliament be selected from among the Indian Tamil community.

These compromise measures came with an important caveat. Chelvanayagam wrote:

"However, since we have asked for an indication of the minimum points on which agreement can be effected between ourselves with a view to my parliamentary group supporting your party to form the government, we are setting down briefly four points which I think should be acceptable, but by making these suggestions we should not be understood to be surrendering or abandoning any of our fundamental objectives."

Chelvanayagam was much more forthright in this letter than he was in the Bandaranaike-Chelvanayagam pact three years earlier. In the earlier instance, the compromise was stated in the pact and the caveat to the compromise only two days later at the ITAK convention in Batticaloa. But here in one letter was everything - the fundamental ITAK objectives, the compromise, and the caveat. The ITAK was offering a compromise which was not a compromise at all but a stepping stone to the final goal. To them a compromise did not entail the giving up of any part of their final objectives. The UNP, which had the best chance to form a government decided to reject Chelvanaygam's invitation to commit political suicide and this led to parliament being dissolved for fresh elections to be held.

When the Official Language Act was passed in 1956, the date for the switch over from English to Sinhala was set as 1 January 1961. The ITAK which never missed an opportunity to agitate against the state, began a *Satyagraha* campaign on 20 February 1961 against Sinhala being the language of the state. This *Satyagraha* campaign consisted of sit in protests in front of *Kachcheris* (government offices) in the northern and eastern provinces, disrupting the work of the offices and bringing public administration and essential services to a halt. After ten days of the ITAK's protests, the military was sent into Jaffna to bring the situation under control. The navy was assigned to guard the Jaffna *Kachcheri* (the provincial centre of administration) but ITAK activists broke through the cordon and continued their *Satyagraha*.

46

There were calls by minority community politicians from other parts of the country for the government to withdraw the troops and initiate talks with the *Satyagrahis*. On 4 March, two weeks into the ITAK campaign, Mrs Bandaranaike appealed to the ITAK to give up their campaign and said that any consequences of the Official Language Act can be discussed, but no discussions will be held so long as the *Satyagraha* campaign was on. She had pointed out the provisions already made (in the 1958 act) for the extensive use of the Tamil language and that it was unfair to say that the government was trying to destroy Tamil culture and identity. As we pointed out in a previous chapter, developments in India tended to be mirrored in Ceylon. The anti-Hindi agitation of 1960 in the Madras State would undoubtedly have influenced the ITAK's *Satyagraha* campaign in Jaffna in 1961.

Buoyed by the success of their *Satyagraha*, the ITAK intensified their campaign on 14 April 1961, by taking their civil disobedience campaign to a higher level. The ITAK started their own postal service and produced postage stamps of their own with Chelvanayagam himself selling the first postage stamps. ITAK post offices were opened in places like Kankesanthurei and Uduvil. They also announced a plan to hold 'land *kachcheris*' to distribute land. This was closely followed by an announcement that they would start a police force of their own as well. This was a seditious announcement that could not possibly be ignored. The government declared an emergency on 17 April 1961. A 48-hour curfew was imposed on the north and east and army officers appointed to coordinate security arrangements in Jaffna, Batticaloa, Trincomalee, Mannar and Vavuniya districts. The government also arrested the leaders of the ITAK.

Mobs in the Jaffna peninsula attacked army patrols with stones and bottles in several places including Velvettiturei, Point Pedro and Kaithady. In Chavakachcheri an army patrol was shot at, injuring two soldiers. Mobs that tried to obstruct the troops were fired upon resulting in at least one fatality in Velvettiturei. To bring the situation under control, the government had to impose draconian emergency regulations imposing the death penalty or life imprisonment for offences such as arson, looting, obstructing transport, or intimidating persons.

The leader of the opposition Dudley Senanayake shared Prime Minister Sirima Bandaranaike's view that the ITAK was up to no good. The day after the declaration of emergency, on 18 April 1961, Dudley spoke in parliament, welcoming the imposition of a state of emergency. Speaking further, he said *"We know what the Satyagragha stands for. We know that any measure asked for now is only a stepping stone to the achievement of the ultimate objectives. Let us be clear about these ultimate objectives. Although Mr Bandaranaike signed that pact (with Chelvanayagam) thinking that it was the conclusion to all differences, we know that the Federal Party (ITAK) only took that as one step forward to fight for their further objectives..."*

A significant thing about the agitation of 1961 was that the upcountry Tamils of Indian origin also made common cause with the northern Tamils, by declaring a strike in the plantation areas in sympathy with the ITAK civil-disobedience campaign. Within the next few years however, events were to occur in India which forced the ITAK to soften its stand. In 1963, the Indian parliament unanimously passed the Sixteenth Amendment to the constitution of India to stem the rising tide of Tamil separatism in that country. This legislation required all politicians to swear an oath to uphold the sovereignty and integrity of India before standing for election to parliament or to a state legislature. The oath was administered once again before assuming duties after being elected to parliament or to a state legislature. This was an ingenious piece of legislation which forced politicians to refrain from campaigning for election on a separatist agenda as a single pro-separatist statement made on the public platform could result in an election petition and a court order declaring his election null and void.

Thus any political party that sought to contest elections, dared not utter a word about separatism lest it disqualified all its elected representatives. This effectively put an end to separatism in the Madras State. After this, the DMK and its offshoots became crypto-separatists. One of the reasons why Chelvanayagam went in for an accommodation with the Dudley Senanayake led UNP in 1965 was probably the banning of separatism in India and the capitulation of the DMK. When the DMK threw in the towel, Chelvanayagam basically followed suit.

As the 1965 parliamentary election approached, Dudley Senanayake and Chelvanayagam arrived at an agreement which became known as the Dudley-Chelvanayagam pact. One aspect of this agreement related to making Tamil the language of administration and the language of the courts in the northern and eastern provinces. In addition to provisions for the use of the Tamil language in the north and east, the Dudley Chelvanayagam pact also had provision for the setting up of district councils. There was also a formula agreed

48

on for the distribution of land in the northern and eastern provinces. In the first instance land allotments were to be made to landless persons within the district concerned. Then to Tamil speaking persons within the northern and eastern provinces and in the last round to people living in other parts of the country with preference once again being given to Tamils.

Dudley Senanayake in agreeing to such a land distribution policy in 1965 was as short-sighted as Bandaranaike had been in agreeing to regional councils in 1957. Chelvanayagam was using various political horse deals to carve out an exclusive, Tamil homeland in the north and east of Sri Lanka. Agreeing to such conditions militated against the very concept of a single multi-ethnic nation. A UNP-led government was elected to power in 1965, and the language demands of the ITAK were met in the Tamil Language (Special Provisions) Act passed in early 1966. This legislation provided for the use of Tamil in the business of government and as the language of record in the northern and eastern provinces. The difference between the two Tamil language special provisions acts of 1958 and 1966 was that the former applied to the use of the Tamil language on a countrywide basis for certain purposes and the latter made provision for the use of the Tamil language in the north and east where Tamil speaking people were the majority.

In fact the CWC, the political party of the up-country Tamils, opposed the Tamil Language (Special Provisions) Act of 1966 because it provided only for the use of the Tamil language in the north and east and the Tamil people who lived in the hill country got no tangible benefit from it. On 8 January 1966 when J.R.Jayewardene presented the Tamil Language (Special Provisions) Bill in parliament, a politically motivated riot ensued. A massive crowd assembled at Viharamahadevi Park and came to the Kollupitiya Junction via Dharmapala Mawatha and all traffic on the Galle Road stopped. The police asked the protestors to disperse which they refused to do. Bottles and stones were thrown at shops and business premises in the vicinity. Missiles were also thrown at the police. Even the Kollupitiya railway station in the vicinity was attacked. Unable to control the situation, the police opened fire killing a monk by the name of Dambarawe Rathanasara. A state of emergency was declared soon afterwards and it took over a week for the situation to be brought under control.

The problem in the 1950s and 60s was that the people themselves had not undergone any enlightening suffering and there was no shortage of Tamil and Sinhala mobs to support the unreasonable and irrational stands taken by their leaders. Never have so many suffered in a game started for the benefit of so few. Be that as it may, the Tamil Language (Special Provisions) Act was passed in January 1966 and this began a period of relative calm in Sinhala-Tamil relations. Prime Minister Dudley Senanayake attended the ITAK annual convention held in Kalmunai and was given a tumultuous welcome by the Tamils. The ITAK was now a constituent of the ruling coalition. This uneasy detente in Sinhala-Tamil relations would continue until 1970 when the SLFP won a landslide victory and romped back to power.

Chapter 8

The First Terrorist Attack

Ironically, it was this very *detente* that had taken place between the ITAK and the UNP after 1965 that gave rise to terrorism among the Tamils. The ITAK was born in 1949 against the Tamil Congress policy of cooperating with the government and Tamil terrorist groups in turn were born because the ITAK itself started 'collaborating' with the government after fifteen years of rabble rousing. The rabble that had been roused, refused to calm down on call. The poisonous contagion spread among the Tamil public was such that anybody having anything to do with the government in Colombo was seen as a traitor. This has been one of the abiding legacies of the ITAK. Even in 1965, the reason why G.G.Ponnambalam who had been a long time ally of the UNP and a loyalist of the Senanayake family, refused to accept a cabinet portfolio was because he did not want to be seen as a 'traitor'.

He wanted the ITAK to accept a cabinet portfolio and be labelled as traitors instead. But the ITAK did not fall for that. They appointed an outsider M.Tiruchelvam, a retired Solicitor General as a minister to the slot allocated to the ITAK without appointing an elected representative of the party. Tiruchelvam, was appointed to the upper house of parliament the Senate, and made a minister in the Dudley Senanayake government on behalf of the ITAK. When such an attitude takes root among both the people and the leaders of an ethnic minority, there is only one way things can go. Politics in Tamil Nadu was also exerting an influence on events in Sri Lanka.

Cyril Ranatunga says his memoirs that one of the first to sound a warning about the influence of Tamil nationalism coming from across the Palk Straits was the then Police Superintendent of Jaffna R.Sundaralingam who had warned that with the victory of the DMK in Tamil Nadu in 1967, publications promoting Tamil nationalism were being brought to the north by the smugglers of Velvettiturei. Up to that time, the Indian National Congress had dominated the politics of the Madras state. Even the change of name from Madras State to Tamil Nadu took place only in 1968 in the wake of the DMK victory. Thus this was a period of rising Tamil nationalism even in India. The issue of DMK publications coming into the country was serious enough for the new Sirima Bandaranaike government to address themselves to the question of banning some of these publications and in July 1970, the minister of information and broadcasting C.Kumarasuriyar was given the task of compiling a list of South Indian publications to be banned. Nothing ultimately came of this as no publications were banned. Unsurprisingly, Velvettiturei was a hotbed of Tamil radicalism by the early 1970s. Their main means of livelihood which was smuggling, also meant that they were constantly clashing with the security forces.

Varatharajah Perumal, the former chief minister of the short lived North-Eastern Provincial Council, recounts what happened in the late sixties as follows. *"In 1965, both the ITAK and the Tamil Congress joined the UNP-led government. Till then the ITAK was known for non-violent but militant politics. They posed as being very aggressive in demanding the rights of the Tamils. The 1956 Satyagraha before parliament, the attacks by the mobs and Amirthalingam going to parliament with a head wound dripping blood made them legends among the people. Amirthalingam was also a fiery orator, so was C.Rajadurai of Batticaloa. Rajadurai was more a Dravidian movement inspired speaker and roused Tamil emotions in the same manner. When even these radicals joined the government in 1965, there was dissatisfaction among the youth. In 1968, V.Navaratnam MP for Kayts left the ITAK saying they had betrayed the cause. He started a party called Tamil Sawahachchi Kazagam (Tamil Autonomy Party). The FP was Federal Party only in English. In Tamil it was Ilangai Tamil Arasu Katchchi (Tamil State Party). So the general understanding among the people was that they were struggling for a Tamil state. The ITAK's campaign meshed with the Tamil Nadu Dravidian movement with its anti-Hindi, anti-Indian anti-establishment campaign. M.Karunanidhi's speeches, M.G.Ramachandran's films all supported the ITAK platform."*

In 1968/69 some militant Tamil youth formed an organisation called the Eelam Tamil Youth Federation. Ponnuthurei Sivakumaran who would later earn notoriety as the first Tamil terrorist in Sri Lanka was a leading light of this movement. It was Sivakumaran who is the real father of terrorism in Sri Lanka, not Rohana Wijeweera. Sivakumaran launched his first attack about ten months before the JVP insurgency broke out and in that respect, the Tamil terrorists had a head start over the Sinhala terrorists. In July 1970, several weeks after the new United Front government came into power, Somaweera Chandrasiri the deputy minister of cultural affairs in the new government went to Jaffna to attend ceremonies at the Jaffna Naga Viharaya and the famous Nagadipa Viharaya at the invitation of the chief monks of those temples.

Deputy Minister Chandrasiri made his visit a cultural tour of Jaffna taking along with him a group of about 30 people which included dancers and drummers. One D.D.Perera a town councillor from Panadura accompanied Chandrasiri as a translator. Even the traditional 'gokkola' (palm frond decorations) were taken to Jaffna from Colombo. The group attended ceremonies at the two temples and on the final day of the visit, a meeting was held near the Nallur kovil in Jaffna where Sinhala and Tamil cultural performances were staged alternately in between speeches. After the meeting was over, Chandrasiri was walking towards his Opel Rekord car when some Harijan (untouchable) protestors who had been sitting on the road, approached him to hand over a petition complaining about the discrimination they were being subject to in Jaffna.

It was these Harijan petitioners who had saved Chandrasiri's life that day. The deputy minister's official car exploded in a ball of fire as he stood a little distance away talking to the Harijan delegation. The car was wrecked. Minister Chandrasiri was flown to Colombo in a helicopter. The government prevailed upon the press to keep the whole affair under wraps for fear that it would set off a communal riot in the country. Thus even though this was the first ever terrorist attack in Sri Lanka, it got no publicity at all at the time. The government had strictly instructed Chandrasiri not to tell even his constituents in Colombo about what had happened in Jaffna. The Sinhala daily *Dinamina*, had a report on 28 July 1970 about Chandrasiri returning to Colombo by helicopter, but said nothing at all about the bombing.

If in the beginning, opportunistic Tamil leaders had to crank up things and create issues artificially, now issues were beginning to come up of their own accord. Education was an important source of social mobility for Tamils in the Jaffna district. Until the early 1970s admission to the universities was through open competition and the Tamils were able to gain admission to universities far out of proportion to their numbers in the population. In the prestigious medical and engineering faculties, the number of Tamils gaining entry was virtually equal to that of the Sinhalese. In the veterinary science course there were over twice as many Tamils as Sinhalese and in the agriculture faculty, there were more Tamils than Sinhalese. It was only in the physical science, biological sciences and architecture courses that the Sinhalese were more than twice the number of Tamils.

It was also around this time that the switch over from English to Sinhala and Tamil was effected in the senior classes in schools. In the liberal arts stream the switch over had been completed by the early 1960s but in the important science stream, the changeover was completed only by the late sixties. As senior Peradeniya University academic C.R.de Silva pointed out in an essay on this issue, so long as public examinations for university admission were carried out in English there was no problem but when examinations began to be conducted in Sinhala and Tamil, a mighty caterwaul was raised that Tamil examiners were favouring Tamil students and therefore they were gaining entry to universities in large numbers.

In fact in August 1970, the marks of 155 Tamil students who had qualified to enter the engineering faculty were sent for rescrutiny because of suspicions that there was favouritism. In October that year, university admissions were held up for the same reason. However, a committee appointed to look into these allegations headed by Prof. B.A.Abeywickrema said that the allegations of discrimination were 'unfounded'. The controversy did not end there. A communal group called the Sinhala Youth Organisation, wanted the findings of that committee reviewed. The president of the Ceylon National Teachers' Union D.Peter Silva chipped in by saying that the candidates from Jaffna excelled because their teachers worked hard to uplift the standards of their students.

The new government elected in 1970 started experimenting with various schemes to address the imbalance in university admissions, and the first scheme they tried out was to introduce language wise standardisation where a student who sat for the examination in Tamil had to get higher marks than a student who sat for the examination in Sinhala. The argument put forward by the government in favour of such a scheme was that Jaffna had some of the best schools in the country and Tamil examiners tended to favour Tamil candidates, leading to serious imbalances in university admission.

According to Dr C.R.De Silva, after this language based standardization scheme was introduced in university admissions in 1971, a Tamil student had to get an aggregate of 250 to get into the medical or dental science faculty while a Sinhalese would get into the same faculty with 229 marks. For the engineering faculty too, it was 227 for a Sinhalese and 250 for a Tamil. In the physical sciences, it was 183 for a Sinhalese and 204 for a Tamil. In the humanities and liberal arts it was the other way about with Tamils gaining entry with 170 marks while a Sinhalese had to get 187. This however meant nothing to the Tamils who more often than not aimed for the science based courses. Because of this language based standardization there was widespread and justifiable resentment among the Jaffna Tamil population who looked to education as a means of social mobility.

There was nothing intrinsically wrong with the principle of standardization where the threshold for university admissions was lowered in the case of less privileged candidates who would not have the same access to a quality education as others. Over the next few years the government experimented with various schemes of standardisation ultimately settling for a district wise scheme whereby 30% of admissions were to be on merit and 70% on district-wise quotas. The government got off to a very bad start with an intrinsically good principle by initially making it a language based standardization instead of a territory based standardization. Veteran Tamil journalist T.Sabaratnam has pointed out that the first student to enter university from the Kilinochchi district got in only because of the standardization scheme and that even though district-wise standardization placed restrictions on Jaffna students, it benefited other Tamil majority districts like Batticaloa, Vavuniya and Mannar. Be that as it may, the end result of this experimentation with university admissions was that Tamils who once had as many places as the Sinhalese in the medical and engineering faculties, had by 1974, gone down to one fifth in the engineering faculty and around one third in the medical faculty.

Now there were over twice as many Sinhala students in dental surgery and veterinary science than Tamils. Needless to say this created a great deal of resentment within the Jaffna district, where everybody wanted to be a doctor, engineer or lawyer. What Felix Dias Bandaranaike said in the wake of the 1971 JVP insurgency about Sinhala school students not having a future to look forward to, and their having taken to arms as a result was becoming true of the Jaffna peninsula as well. It was very easy for enterprising political agitators to tell young school children in Jaffna that they had no future because the 'Sinhala government' in Colombo was shifting the goal posts.

Because of the new UF government's plan to introduce standardization, the Tamil Youth Federation called a protest meeting in Jaffna on 24 November 1970. Thousands of students answered the call by hitherto unknown youth leaders. Students with placards denouncing the minister of education at the time Badiuddin Mahmud were arrested and released on bail after the police recorded their statements. The police also removed an effigy of the minister of education which had been hoisted at Kokuvil junction. This protest had the support of the parent-teacher associations of the schools as well. The success of this protest gave the fledgling militant youth movement the confidence that they had a future outside the ITAK and that they did not need the traditional leaders.

Education was important to the Jaffna Tamils and every family had the feeling that they were directly affected by the standardization issue. The issues articulated by the ITAK earlier such as citizenship for Indian Tamils, and colonization were largely theoretical issues for the northern Tamils. But this question of university admissions was a major issue for every school student and his parents. The Tamil Student League was formed after this mammoth student demonstration in late 1970. The Eelam Tamil Youth Federation disappeared. The new organisation had the leaders of the earlier organization and some new faces as well like P.Satyaseelan a graduate of Peradeniya University. The organization had also now expanded out of Jaffna and demonstrations were held all over the north and east. This new generation of youth leaders did not believe in non-violence.

The first access of the incipient terrorist movement to arms and explosives was through the radicalized smuggling village of Velvettiturei. There were many chemistry students in the Student League who knew how to make bombs from chemicals and all these items could be accessed through Velvettiturei. Around April/May 1971, there was an accidental blast at a hideout in Velvettiturei when some activists of the Tamil Student League were trying to make a bomb. One of those injured in the blast was the teen aged Prabhakaran who had a permanent scar as a result. He was an acolyte of the fledgling terrorist movement at that time.

Chapter 9

Prabhakaran Enters History

With the JVP insurgency of 1971, the army, navy and police were strengthened, recruitment increased, new arms and ammunition were purchased. Even though there was a lull in anti-state activity in the north following the 1971 insurgency, the secession of Bangladesh from Pakistan in December 1971 provided new inspiration to the ITAK and people started believing that with India's help, they would be able to do the same in Sri Lanka.

The ITAK held a rally in Kankesanthurei on 12 January 1972 and the inspiration gained from the independence of Bangladesh was very palpable in the crowd. Varatharajah Perumal who had joined the ITAK that year was a participant at this rally. When Chelvanayagam arrived the people cheered him as the 'future president' and Amirthalingam as the 'future prime minister'. And others were cheered as future ministers. The Vavuniya MP X.M. Sellatambu was cheered as the 'border minister'. At that time there was no separatist agenda and the meeting was actually held as a protest against the new draft constitution of May 1972, but the success of the Bangladeshi liberation struggle had given the ITAK the confidence that they will prevail in the end.

This ITAK meeting did not go unnoticed by the government in Colombo. A few days-later, Minister Felix Dias Bandaranaike came to Jaffna and said at the Jaffna headquarters of the SLFP that there will be no 'Jaffna-desh' in this country. The ITAK was heavily influenced by the Tamil nationalism coming from neighbouring Tamil Nadu. When they formed the Tamil United Liberation Front in May 1976, the symbol they adopted - the rising sun - was the same symbol used by the DMK in Tamil Nadu. This adoption of the DMK symbol by the new Tamil political entity came in for much discussion in parliament later that year.

The Tamil Congress however, led by the elitist and aloof G.G.Ponnambalam, was never influenced by the Dravidian Movement and that made for the difference between the ITAK and the Tamil Congress. ITAK leaders like Amirthalingam had met Ramasamy Naikar, Mutuvel Karunanidhi, M.G.Ramachandran and other leaders of the Dravidian Movement. But according to veteran TC member V.Anandasangaree, Ponnambalam had met the leaders of the Dravidian movement for the first time, only when he attended the Second International Tamil Conference in Madras in 1968. Later when M.G.Ramachandran came to Sri Lanka, he had visited Ponnambalam. The latter however did not seek out a close relationship with the Tamil Nadu leaders, whereas the ITAK leaders did. Ponnambalam preferred to have a close relationship with the leaders of the Congress Party in the Indian central government instead. Their level of education and their social milieu suited Ponnambalam more than the tinsel town figures in Tamil Nadu politics.

Gōta was in the final stages of his cadetship at the army training school in Diyatalawa in May 1972 when the new republican constitution was promulgated by the United Front government. The promulgation of this new constitution was to have a fateful impact on Tamil politics. The two Tamil parties in the north, the ITAK and the Tamil Congress which had always been arch rivals, came together over their opposition to the proposed 1972 constitution and formed the Tamil United Front on May 14 1972. Thus the conservative and sane Tamil Congress which had for one and a half decades fiercely maintained their independent stand, finally capitulated to the adventurist ITAK. G.G.Ponnambalm was by this time a disappointed man. He had gone off to Malaysia soon after his defeat at the 1970 parliamentary election and it was M.Sivasittamparam who had been acting on his behalf as leader of the TC.

The main ITAK grievance was that constitutional status had not been granted to the Tamil language in the fields of education, public administration and in the courts. It was Chelvanayagam who broke the ice between the two parties by going personally to his rival Ponnambalam's house to get his consent to form one united political

58

entity. Initially, Saumyamoorthy Thondaman, the leader of the up-country Indian Tamils also joined the TUF. The Tamil Congress had three MPs in parliament, V.Anandasangaree from Kilinochchi, C.Arulampalam from Nallur, and A.Thiyagarajah from Kayts. G.G.Ponnambalam the party leader had lost his Jaffna constituency at the 1970 general elections. When the UF government set up a constituent assembly to draft a new constitution, the ITAK boycotted it. Two Tamil Congress parliamentarians Arulampalam and Tiyagarajah left the TC and joined the ruling coalition.

At this time, links were formed between the ITAK leaders and the leaders of the radical Tamil Student League. The ITAK leaders would provide the Tamil Student League leaders with legal help if needed. They were at this stage, experimenting with improvised bombs made with chemicals stolen from school labs. Leaders of the Tamil Student League like Satyaseelan also became members of the TUF. Tamil youth joined the anti-constitution movement in large numbers. On 22 May 1972, the day the constitution was passed by parliament, Tamil youth hoisted black flags and wrote anti-constitution slogans on the walls, damaged electricity transformers, and threw bicycle chains on electricity lines to create blackouts. They also cut down trees and blocked the roads.

On 8 June 1972, just two weeks after the promulgation of the new constitution, Sathyaseelan the Tamil Student League leader tried to assassinate Vadukkodai MP A. Tiyagarajah at his house in Bambalapitiya Colombo because he had left the Tamil Congress and joined the government and voted for the new constitution. They had come to his house claiming to be journalists working for a Jaffna newspaper. But the hit-men were inexperienced and even though they fired at point blank range, one bullet whizzed past Tiyagarajah's ear and hit the wall behind him. Then Tiyagarajah had dived under the bed he was sitting on and shouted for help. The would-be assassins had fired another shot at him and fled, leaving him unharmed.

The TUF called for a hartal on 2 October 1972 to protest against the new republican constitution. S.J.V.Chelvanagayagm resigned his seat in parliament so that a by-election could be held by the government to test the popularity of the new constitution among the Tamils. In the middle of all this, on 17 September 1972, some hand bombs were found near the Duriappah stadium in Jaffna, where a carnival was being held. The 17 year old Prabhakaran was widely believed to be behind this attempt to bomb the carnival. The bombs were never thrown. The previous night, there had been a caste clash between Karaiyars and Harijans in the Kariyoor area of Jaffna which had raged for about three hours with the houses of the fishing caste Karaiyars being bombed and burnt and roughnecks fighting with iron rods and bottles on the streets. The police intensified security checks after that and the discovery of the bombs hidden near the Duriappah stadium was a result of the extra vigilance of the police. Ten days later however, there was a bomb throwing incident in Navanthurei in Jaffna which injured seventeen youths.

On one occasion, reminisces Varatharajah Perumal, some members of the TSL were making bombs in a Hindu kovil and the public thought it suspicious that youth were frequenting a temple and tipped off the police thinking there was something immoral going on inside. When the police raided the temple, the young men ran away leaving their bomb making equipment behind. It should be understood that at this early stage, these sporadic acts of violence that the incipient Tamil terrorist movements were engaging in, were not very different to the other acts of violence that were taking place in Jaffna. For example, if some youths were discovered making bombs, they were as likely to be terrorists as warriors belonging to the rival castes.

During this period, there was more violence over the issue whether Harijans should be allowed to enter the Mavaddipuram temple than over any political issue. There was no shortage of people willing to throw bombs at one another over caste rivalries. On 8 July 1970, about 200 members of the outcast Harijan community had entered the Mavaddipuram Kandasamy kovil for the first time, and shops were closed and the police were patrolling the area. Throughout the early seventies there was much tension in Jaffna over this issue. As the police were seen to be facilitating the entry of Harijans into Hindu temples, some anti-state feeling had built up even over this.

In fact in December 1972, V.N.Navaratnam the MP for Chavakachcheri was challenging the government to prove that there was politically motivated violence in Kankesanthurei and the surrounding areas, to which Lakshman Jayakody said that there were five bomb throwing incidents which were politically motivated. This was hotly contested by Navaratnam who contended that one of the incidents referred to was not even a caste clash but a private dispute between two parties. Perhaps the first real indication that politically motivated violence was coming to the fore in Jaffna would have been the attempt to murder A.Tiyagarajah.

Among the 70 or so youths arrested during the anti-constitution protests after May 1972, was Varatharajah Perumal who had been caught painting anti-constitution slogans on the wall of Jaffna Hindu College. The prisons became an incubator of Tamil militancy. When Varatharajah Perumal was in jail, JVP leader Rohana Wijeweera was also in the Jaffna prison but in a separate cell. They were able to see and talk to one another. The young Tamils who found themselves in jail did not have much faith in the TUF which had just been formed. They thought the TUF would confine themselves to parliamentary politics and do nothing more. In fact, soon after the new constitution was promulgated, a meeting of the TUF at the headquarters of the Tamil Congress at Main Street Jaffna was disrupted by Tamil youth demanding that the TUF parliamentarians resign from the legislature *en masse*. Those who tried to explain why the TUF should not do so, were jeered at and shouted down.

By the latter half of 1972, the Tamil Student League became defunct because their leaders were either in jail or in hiding. After about six months, those who were not involved in violent activities were released. After they came out, R.Padmanabha, Varatharajah Perumal and some others began regrouping outside and contacting the young men they had befriended in jail. Their intention was to pressurize the TUF to take a more radical stand. In 1973 January, they formed the Tamil Youth League. Within two weeks however, Satyaseelan, the Tamil Student League leader was arrested and under interrogation, he revealed all the names of those in the underground Tamil youth movements. By this time the ex-members of the Tamil Student League were now in the Tamil Youth League and they had to go into hiding and only a few who had not been involved in the TSL remained out in the open.

The Tamil Youth League got the cooperation of the TUF. They would hold joint public meetings with the TUF and use the TUF office and even the bus and train passes of the TUF parliamentarians to travel within the north and east. Symbolising the spirit of cooperation between the early militants and the established Tamil leadership, in December 1972 Uduvil MP V.Dharmalingam raised issue in parliament about the 'third degree' methods used on Sivakumaran while in police custody. Lakshman Jayakody the then deputy defence minister said that Sivakumaran had been arrested while trying to make bombs and for having a revolver in his possession. Dharmalingam however insisted that Sivakumaran had not been arrested but had voluntarily surrendered to the Nallur police through a lawyer named A.Jegatheesan. He averred that the police were trying to get Sivakumaran to implicate ITAK parliamentarians

61

Amirthalingam and Alalasundaram in militant activities. In 1973, the Tamil Youth League and the TUF jointly organized a programme which consisted of 50 days of fasting in 50 different places in the north and east. The TUF leaders made speeches at these gatherings. As Gōta found his feet in the Sri Lanka army in the early 1970s, Tamil politicians were closing ranks from above and Tamil youth were being radicalized from below. This was to be a mutually reinforcing process that led to the emergence of a separatist movement.

As the 1970s dragged on, separatist sentiments were gaining ground. In September 1973, The ITAK at its annual convention resolved that the Tamils are in every way equipped to be regarded as a separate nation and that the only path for them to follow is the establishment of their right to self rule in their traditional homelands based on the internationally recognized right to self determination. By this time, no Tamil party had actually called for a separate state in Sri Lanka but they were coming perilously close to it. As a wave of Tamil nationalism rose in the north and east, Felix Dias Bandaranaike tried to douse the flames with an impassioned appeal to the Tamils in parliament in July 1974. He said;

"Show me any other country in the world where a communal majority supposed to be oppressing the minority according to you, had created by its very policies conditions which have made the Tamils the richest community in the country in agriculture,...when your city becomes the cleanest in the island, when there is a rush of building activity in every main road,...Is there one single Sinhalese person who has expressed a sense of jealousy? In fact they are lost in admiration of what your people in Jaffna are doing by sheer hard work."

Technically, Felix Dias Bandaranaike was right. Tamil politicians may be upset at the 1972 constitution and students may be upset at the university admissions policy, but the farmers of Jaffna were enjoying a period of unprecedented prosperity under the UF government. The import substitution policy of that government banned the import of certain essential food items like dried red chillies, onions and potatoes and the farmers of Jaffna made huge profits from agriculture. Numerically, there were many more people engaged in farming than those who aspired to get into medical college. But it is never the majority that moves things in politics. It's the inspired and organized few who move the majority. And during the UF government of 1970, that essential nucleus of an organized minority was formed due to issues like the standardization of university admissions and the rabble rousing of Chelvanayagam over the 1972 constitution.

When Dudley Senanayake relinquished power in 1970, anybody advocating separatism in the north would have been regarded as a member of the lunatic fringe but just a few years into the Sirima Bandaranaike government, the idea of a separate state was moving into the centre stage of Tamil politics. So Felix Dias Bandaranaike's appeal to reason fell on deaf ears. By this time every little thing had begun to be misinterpreted as happens in such situations. As the minister of public administration, local government and home affairs, Bandaranaike had issued a circular to all local government authorities to fly a Buddhist flag on Vesak Day. Tamil politicians in Jaffna took exception to that circular and Bandaranaike had to explain in parliament that all he had said was that the ministry had no objection to the Buddhist flag being flown on Vesak day and that there was no compulsion for anybody to do so. The constitution of 1972 had accorded Buddhism the foremost place among religions (another main cause of complaint by the ITAK) and Bandaranaike's Vesak circular was being interpreted as a case of trying to foist Buddhism on the Tamils.

Chapter 10

A Deceptive Calm

When Gōta returned from the young officers course in
Rawalpindi, Pakistan, his first posting was to Palaly in Jaffna as the
signals officer. Even though this was the first time in his life that
Gōta was setting foot in Jaffna, Tamil culture was not unfamiliar to
him because Jaffna had come to his village in the Hambantota district
many years ago in the form of Kamalan Rockwood, a Jaffna Tamil
lady who was married to his much older cousin Lakshman Rajapaksa.
George and Lakshman the sons of D.M.Rajapaksa were Gōta's first
cousins but were more than twenty years older than him. When his
father D.A.Rajapaksa was alive, both of them would turn up in
Medamulana to see DA quite often. When the latter became an invalid,
it was Lakshman Rajapaksa who helped attend to him and when
DA died, Lakshman, as the eldest in the clan, was the master of
ceremonies at the funeral. Kamalan, Lakshman's Tamil wife also
treated D.A.Rajapaksa's bereaved brood with much sympathy.

Kamalan Rockwood was a gregarious lady who would play a
leading role in Lakshman Rajapaksa's election campaigns. She could
speak a little Sinhala and fitted in easily with the Rajapaksa ethos of
providing tea and meals to all those who came to her home. The
village folk were for their part quite fascinated by her sing song Tamil
accent with which she spoke Sinhala. Kamalan had been quite fond
of D.A.Rajapaksa and when Chamal the eldest in that branch of the
family visited them at Weeraketiya for the holidays, they would get
him to stay there for a couple of days and there were times when he

was taken to Colombo and introduced to their family friends in Colombo. Chamal remembers a visit to the home of the Tambiah family, who were family friends of the Rockwoods.

After 1967, Mahinda also used to visit the Weeraketiya residence of Lakshman Rajapaksa quite often. In Later years, George Rajapaksa's daughter Nirupama Rajapaksa would also marry a Jaffna Tamil - Tirukumar Nadesan. George Rajapaksa's maternal uncle George Weeratunga was also married to a Tamil lady, one Amelia Getrude Dawson - a musical celebrity of the time - who went by the stage name of Kokila Devi. Gōta's eldest sister Kamala Wickremasuriya's daughter Anoma would marry a Muslim army officer Fazly Lafir. The latter was like Gōta, a Gajaba Regiment officer and a pioneer of the Special Forces. Lafir was killed in action during the operation to relieve the besieged Mulleitivu camp in 1996. In any event the Rajapaksas were a very cosmopolitan family with Hindu Tamils, Muslims and Christians accepted as part of the extended family. The lady that Mahinda married, Shiranthi Rajapaksa comes from a mixed Buddhist - Roman Catholic background. Unsurprisingly, Gōta's presidential sibling Mahinda is the only Tamil speaking and trilingual head of state or head of government that Sri Lanka has had.

At the time that Gōta started his army career, the army had six commands, the Task Force on Illegal Immigration (TaFII), being one of them. It was TaFII that covered the entire northern province and the coastal belt from Mannar to Trincomalee, with its headquarters in Palaly. Colonel Tissa Weeratunga better known as 'Bull' Weeratunga was the Commander of TaFII at the time Gōta was assigned to his first posting. This was a special unit set up to curb illegal immigration and smuggling along the northern coast of Ceylon. Cyril Ranatunga who also served in TaFII as a mid-career army officer, explains that most of the illegal immigrants who came to Sri Lanka's shores were Indian Tamil workers who had been repatriated to India. The smugglers were enterprising Tamils of the north who brought in goods that were in short supply in Sri Lanka due to import restrictions. In fact in 1973, during Gōta's first tour of active duty, the army earned a record amount of over 1.8 million Rupees in anti-smuggling operations.

Gōta took over the duties of signals officer from Lieutenant Chula Seneviratne. One privilege that a signals officer had was that even very young officers got to join the headquarters staff. Gōta occupied an office next to that of the commanding officer Bull Weeratunga. A thriving smuggling trade between India and Sri Lanka was in operation between point Pedro and Velvettiturei. Even though there was a coral reef in the Velvettiturei area, the smugglers had cut canals into the hinterland so that if seen and chased on sea, they could take the boats through the canals into their villages and the boats would disappear. The soldiers assigned to TaFII would go out to sea in small dinghies with outboard motors and lie in wait for smugglers and illegal immigrants. There were some soldiers who had acquired considerable expertise in this line of work. Those who caught smugglers got cash rewards. Gōta remembers one particular officer, Shantha Silva from the 3rd Gemunu Battalion, who held the record at that time for catching smugglers.

At that time, Sri Lanka had no coast guard and the navy was miniscule. Wasantha Karannagoda, another individual who will figure prominently in this narrative also joined the navy in 1971 when its total strength was around 2000 men and 80 officers. In the decade of the 1960s, the vessels they had owned had been sold off and no officers had been recruited. Two batches of 300 naval ratings each had been recruited in 1966 and 1969. There was no recruitment on a yearly basis. After the 1971 insurgency however, recruitment began taking place on a yearly basis. The navy had a base in Karainagar but their role even in anti-smuggling operations was negligible.

When Gōta was the signals officer in Jaffna, one of his duties was to organize the Roman Catholic Kachchativu festival. The navy took Gōta to Kachchativu Island and he put up a tent and overlooked the control of the crowds that flocked to Kachchativu for the festival. Indians and Sri Lankans would converge on the rocky outcrop for the festival. While this was mainly a religious festival, a lively barter trade took place between Sri Lankans and Indians, with the Indians bringing items like saris and the Sri Lankans taking soap and coconut oil. At the time Gōta did his first tour of duty in the north, a lot of Sinhala people lived in Jaffna. The bakery industry was a Sinhala monopoly. Motor garages were run by Sinhalese. There were fishermen who would come to the coast for seasonal fishing and then there were the Sinhalese officials and government servants such as *Kachcheri* clerks and employees of the private sector. Edgar Gunatunga who later became Chairman of the Samptah Bank, was the branch manager of the Jaffna Hatton National Bank and was a good friend of the TaFII commander Colonel Bull Weeratunga. Gunatunga was often seen in the Palaly camp. The examiner at the Registrar of Motor Vehicles office in Jaffna was a Sinhalese, and at that time, even the Jaffna government agent was a Sinhalese.

Army units under TaFII were deployed from Mollikulam point on the west coast (to the South of Silavathurai), to Kokilai on the east coast. There were army camps in Silavathurei, Tallady, Talaimannar, Pooneryn, Velvettiturei, Madagal, Thondamannar, Mulleitivu, and Kokilai. Then there were many small detachments along the coast of around 10 soldiers each. Sometimes there were no more than four or five personnel in each detachment. But even the smallest detachment, had a radio operator from the Signals Corps. As the TaFII Signals Officer, Gōta had to attend to the pay and allowances of the Signals men in these various detachments. Once every month, he had to do the rounds in all these scattered detachments to pay those under him. The payment had to be handed over to them in cash and Gōta had to look into their other problems as well. Every month he went to all the TaFII detachments from the west coast to the east, a round trip that would take about two weeks.

Gōta had an old Mahindra jeep to do the rounds and he would move around in the north in uniform, with only a driver and no weapons. He would start from Palaly and pay his soldiers in the detachments close by in Madagal, Velvettiturei, Point Pedro, Thondamannar and Elephant Pass. Then he would cut across to Mulleitivu from Pooneryn. From Puthukudiirippu onwards, the road passed through dense jungle. From Mulleitivu he would move through Vavuniya to Mannar, and the Tallady camp from where he would go to Silavathurei and after visiting Talaimannar he would come to Pooneryn, cross over to the Peninsula on the Senguppidy ferry and return to Palaly. At times a technician would accompany Gōta and his driver to attend to the repairs and maintenance of the radio equipment in the detachments.

The significant thing was that Gōta could make this entire round in the north without any weapons in 1972/3 despite all that had been happening in terms of Tamil radicalization as recounted earlier. He and his driver would stop at wayside boutiques to drink tea and have their meals and there was no hostility towards them. Looking back at that period, Gōta says that even though radicalization may have been taking place in the north in the years before he was posted to Jaffna, he never felt any tension at all, when he was serving as the signals officer in Palaly in 1972/73.

Many military officers serving in Jaffna had friends among the Tamil civilian officials in their areas. When Gōta visited other camps such as Pooneryn, he would be invited to a meal at the house of a Tamil friend of his fellow officers. The postmaster of Talaimannar was a good friend of the officers of the Tallady camp. At that time Palaly was mainly a civilian airport and the Tamil officer who was the head of the civilian airport was a very frequent visitor to the officer's mess of the Palaly army camp. Military officers did not mix much with civilians in any case, and the level of interaction with Tamil civilians in the north was to the same extent as interaction with Sinhalese civilians. There was no difference at that time, in the way they interacted with either community.

The reason why Gōta was able to move around the north unarmed and without encountering any hostility until well into the 1970s was because there were two parallel undercurrents in Tamil politics even at that stage. One was the increasingly popular separatist tendency and the other was a strong undercurrent of conservatism. We can gauge the strength of this conservative tendency in the north by the results of elections. In 1956, the ITAK won 10 seats in parliament and became the main Tamil political party in the north and east elbowing out the Tamil Congress.

From that time onwards, it was always the ITAK that would negotiate with the government in Colombo on Tamil issues. The ITAK negotiated the Bandaranaike-Chelvanayagam pact and later the Dudley-Chelvanayagam pact with the respective prime ministers. With these developments, the Tamil Congress was reduced to insignificance. The TC went down from 7 seats in the parliament of 1947, to 4 at the parliamentary election of 1952. They were reduced to just one seat in 1956 and had only one MP in parliament until 1965 when they managed to regain some of the lost ground by winning three seats. They retained three seats in parliament in 1970, even though the TC leader G.G.Ponnambalam lost his seat at that election.

Even though the Tamil Congress had long been a cipher in terms of representation in parliament, an examination of the election results of 1970 will indicate that even though the TC had been in decline for the past one and a half decades and even its leader G.G.Ponnamabalam lost his seat in 1970, still in terms of the absolute number of votes, they were not far behind the ITAK. At the 1970 parliamentary election, in the crucial Jaffna electorate, the ITAK candidate C.X.Martyn barely scraped through with 8,848 votes while Alfred Duriappah (Later the SLFP Mayor of Jaffna) contesting as an independent candidate came a very close second with 8,792 votes. A difference of just 56 votes. In the Point Pedro electorate, the ITAK candidate won with 9,217 votes while the TC came a close second with 8,902 votes, a difference of 315 votes.

In the Kankesanthurei electorate which was represented by S.J.V.Chelvanayagam himself, the ITAK won comfortably with a majority of 5,356 votes over the closest rival V.Ponnambalam who was a member of the pro-Moscow Communist Party. Yet even in Chelvanayagam's own electorate only a minority of Tamil people actually voted for him with V.Ponanambalam and independent candidate C.Sundaralingam together actually getting more votes than Chelvanayagam. In Uduppidy, the ITAK candidate got 12,918 while the TC candidate got 11,662 and the Communist Party candidate got 1,149 votes. Once again the TC and CP candidates got more votes than the ITAK candidate. In Kayts the ITAK candidate won comfortably getting over 8,000 votes but here too the vote was split between two independent candidates and the TC candidate, who together polled 11,438 votes – much more than the ITAK candidate.

In the then Uduvil (Later known as Manipay) electorate, the ITAK candidate won with 14,120 as against the 11,656 of the TC with an independent candidate getting 1,352 and the LSSP candidate getting 1,254. The point being that the ITAK was not getting a clear majority in such electorates and was winning only because the vote opposed to them was divided. In the Vavuniya electorate, the ITAK candidate got 10,947 while the TC candidate got 10,674, and the CP candidate got 3,120 votes. Once again the TC and CP together had more votes than the ITAK. Kopay was one electorate that the ITAK won very comfortably and actually commanded a good majority with a margin of about 3,000 votes. The same can be said of the Chavakachcheri electorate which was won by the ITAK with an absolute majority of the votes cast defeating the TC by over 2,400 votes. The electorates of Vadukkodai, Nallur and Kilinochchi were not won by the ITAK at all and went to the TC.

In the east, especially in the Tamil majority Batticaloa district, this lack of an ITAK monopoly was even more visible. The Kalkudah electorate was won by the UNP as was the Paddirippu electorate. The Batticaloa multi-member electorate was won by the ITAK and another independent Tamil MP. Thus we see that the apparent preponderance of the ITAK in the politics of the north was largely a product of the first past the post electoral system of the time which enabled anybody who gets the biggest block of votes to represent the electorate even though his ascendency may only be the result of splits in the vote and he does not represent the majority in that electorate. Hence, when Gōta was doing the rounds in all these districts in the mid 1970s he could go around unarmed despite the tensions that the ITAK had been trying to fan in those areas since the mid-1950s.

The Tamil people were of many minds at that time. What has to be noted is the strength of the conservative Tamil Congress despite the years in the wilderness. Prof A. Jeyaratnam Wilson says that the Tamil Congress managed to retain significant support among the Tamil middle classes who did not endorse the separatist agenda of the ITAK. It would be interesting to speculate what would have happened if a proportional representation system had been in place at that time – perhaps the slide into extremism precipitated by the ITAK may never have taken place.

When Gōta was serving as the Signals officer in Palaly, Anura Bandaranaike and his brother Mahinda came to Jaffna for an SLFP event that had been organized by Alfred Duriappah the SLFP organizer for Jaffna. Anura and Mahinda stayed at the Kankesanthurei Cement Factory circuit bungalow. Duriappah hosted the guests to dinner at Subash Hotel Jaffna and to lunch at his house. Gōta had also been invited to Duriappah's house to lunch. Duriappah was a popular figure in Jaffna and he paraded Anura and Mahinda throughout Jaffna with blue flags flying. Even though parliamentarians C.Arulampalam and A.Tiyagarajah had joined the SLFP by that time, it was always Duriappah who was the live wire of the SLFP in Jaffna.

Chapter 11

The Whisper of Death

By the time Gōta completed his first tour of duty in Jaffna in the mid-1970s, things were changing for the worse. The conservatives in northern society had capitulated to the radicals with the coming together of the ITAK and the Tamil Congress. In the 1950s, the ITAK needed to artificially create issues. But as their enterprise matured, the issues began rolling in of their own accord. In the early 1970s grievances about the new republican constitution, language-wise standardization of university admissions, the rise of militant youth and student movements due to disenchantment with the older Tamil political parties, the rising tide of Tamil nationalism in Tamil Nadu since 1967, were all beginning to darken the sky over the north.

The very elements seemed to be conspiring to send Sri Lanka down the path it went with even unforeseen and fortuitous incidents contributing to the descent into the abyss. In the first week of January 1974, the International Tamil Research Conference was held in Jaffna. The mood generated among Tamils by the ITAK at that time was such that the Tamil Conference itself turned into an expression of opposition to the state. This was an event organized by Tamil intellectuals worldwide once every three or four years. The first three conferences had been held in Paris, Kuala Lumpur and Tamil Nadu in that order. The fourth conference was held in Jaffna.

The government wanted the conference held in Colombo but the organizers wanted to hold it in Jaffna because that was the heartland of the Tamils. The Tamil people came out in their numbers to support the conference and decorations were put up all over the

71

peninsula for the event. The state too supported it. The Jaffna Municipality building was illuminated and was described as being 'ablaze with lights' in press reports. The then Government Agent Jaffna, Wimal Amarasekera (a Sinhalese) opened the exhibition that was held during the conference at Chundukuli Girl's school. On the last day of the conference, 10 January 1974, a meeting was held at the Jaffna esplanade. A narrow street that led to the meeting hall had been packed with people.

Two policemen on motorcycles who tried to pass through the crowd were assaulted and chased away by the crowd. They were injured and had to be hospitalized. Hearing of the incident the police had then arrived in force with tear gas and riot gear and baton charged the crowd. The public reacted and a street battle ensued. Then the police fired into the air, inadvertently snapping electrical cables overhead. The live wires fell on the crowd and seven people died as a result of electrocution. This was obviously an accident, but the ITAK/TUF leaders, given the mood of the day sought to make political capital of it and described this incident as the "Jalianwala Bagh of Jaffna".

This was a reference to the massacre carried out by Brigadier-General Reginald Dyer in Amritsar in 1919, where unarmed people were killed by the dozens in indiscriminate machine gun fire. That incident was one of the sparks that ignited the Indian independence struggle. P.Sivakumaran, who had been involved in organizing the International Tamil Conference vowed to kill Duriappah and Assistant Superintendent of Police Chandrasekera. The police were put on high alert to capture Sivakumaran. The latter believed in small conspiratorial organizations and was not necessarily a mass organization man. He was a former student of Jaffna Hindu College studying to be a book keeper at the Jaffna Technical College. Varatharajah Perumal and Sivakumaran had been studying for their book keeping exams together.

Due to his widely publicized pledge to kill both Duriappah and ASP Chandrasekera, Sivakumaran became a popular hero overnight with spontaneous support coming from the people. At that time, Amirthalingam had wanted Sivakumaran to be a part of the Tamil United Front but Sivakumaran had always wanted to be independent. However, when the police were closing in on him, Sivakumaran sent emissaries to Amrithalingam asking for help to go to India. Amirthalingam however, did not help the fugitive. Out of desperation Sivakumaran tried to raise money to flee to India by robbing the Kopay branch of the People's Bank on 5 June 1974 but the police got wind of the plan and surrounded the place.

Sivakumaran was cornered with seven of his accomplices. To avoid capture, he swallowed cyanide from a small bottle he was carrying with him. He was arrested at around 3.00 pm and was pronounced dead at 6.00 pm. He had in his possession a loaded revolver and a knife at the time of his arrest. Sivakumaran was the first Tamil terrorist, and the first to take cyanide. The previous experience with Satyaseelan was that if arrested, the police would extract everything they needed to know. So Sivakumaran started the practice of carrying cyanide to take in case of capture. Sivakumaran had told his group to implicate only him if caught, but no one else and that the police will never take him alive. His funeral organized by the Tamil Youth League became a huge event in Jaffna. Even without prompting from the organizers, Jaffna school students came in procession to the funeral. Priests of the Hindu and Christian faiths accorded him both Christian and Hindu religious services.

So the year 1974 from the deaths at the International Tamil Research Conference in January up to the funeral of Sivakumaran in June was a roller coaster ride of emotion directed against the government. When Mrs Bandaranaike visited Jaffna on 6 October 1974, the ITAK and the Tamil Youth League organized a *hartal* in Jaffna, but the formidable Duriappah, managed to muster some crowds for her meetings. In addition to declaring open the Jaffna University, Mrs Bandaranaike also visited the Naga viharaya, the Kandasamy kovil in Nallur, and met the farmers of Jaffna who had benefitted immensely from the policies of her government. She also unveiled a statue of Ponnambalam Ramanathan in the premises of the Jaffna Municipality. The *Ceylon Daily Mirror* described the prime minister's visit editorially as a 'triumph for sanity' and said that this has exploded the myth that no leader from the south could go to the north without the approval of the TUF. The success of this meeting would have been one of the reasons that hastened Duriappah's ultimate end.

In April 1974, Gōta was promoted to the rank of Lieutenant. In October 1974, he decided to join the Sinha Regiment and became an infantryman. Six months after his transfer to the Sinha Regiment in April 1975, Gōta went to Quetta in Pakistan on an Infantry Young Officers Course and returned to Sri Lanka in June 1975. For the next two years, until the change of government in 1977, he was the battalion intelligence officer at the Echelon Square headquarters of the Sinha Regiment in Colombo. At that time, Sarath Fonseka was also stationed at the regimental headquarters.

73

Those were rather uneventful times but one incident stands out during this period. There were regular military exercises held before promotions were granted to officers as well as other rankers and one such exercise was held in late 1976, to promote lance corporals to corporals. During the jungle march, one soldier died. It later transpired that he had died of a heart attack, but within the Sinha Regiment, there was a situation bordering on a mutiny over the death of this soldier. The commanding officer of the Sinha Regiment Colonel Prasanna Dahanayake and three young officers were removed and this helped defuse the situation that was building up.

One of the rising terrorist leaders of the time was Selliah Tanabalasingham better known to history as 'Chetty' who had once been an inmate of the Maggona correctional facility for juvenile delinquents. At Maggona, he had learnt boxing and driving and had a good physique. On 13 June 1972, he escaped from the Anuradhapura jail and walked along the railway track all the way to Jaffna along with three other escapees. It was Dharmalingam Siddharthan the son of ITAK parliamentarian V.Dharmalingam who had found the prison escapee places to stay. After returning to Jaffna, Chetty sent a message to Sivakumaran saying he wanted to join his group. But Sivakumaran turned down Chetty saying that he does not want to take a 'thief' into his group.

All this while Prabhakaran who was wanted for the 1972 discovery of bombs near the Duriappah stadium, was in hiding in India, and he never knew Sivakumaran personally. After being turned down by Sivakumaran, Chetty together with some professional criminals, carried out a robbery. The due share was given to the thieves and Chetty left for India with his share of the money. In India he bought a couple of revolvers and met Thangaturei in Tamil Nadu seeking an invitation to join his group. But once again Chetty was turned down. After the talks failed, Tangathurei and Periya Sothy sent Prabhakaran to see Chetty off in a bus. Prabhakaran went with Chetty and he did not come back.

Prabhakaran and his new found leader Chetty returned to Jaffna several weeks after the death of Sivakumaran in mid-1974. Among the Tamil militant youths Chetty had approached was Varatharajah Perumal. He had shown Perumal a new revolver to impress him, but Perumal had told him that his way forward was different and that he believed in mass action, but that they could always cooperate with one another. Perumal drew his inspiration from the vast mass organizations of the Indian Congress and the DMK in Tamil Nadu.

When he met Perumal, Chetty told him that he had formed an organization called the Tamil New Tigers. After returning to Jaffna with Prabhakaran, Chetty carried out another robbery and bought more arms to strengthen their fledgling organization the Tamil New Tigers.

However, in early 1975, Chetty who was an escaped prisoner was arrested and Prabhakaran ended up becoming the leader of the Tamil New Tigers. When Chetty was arrested, Dharmalingam Siddharthan too was implicated as a person who helped him to hide in Jaffna. His father was tipped off by top officers in the police and Siddharthan was packed off to London. While all this was going on, A.Amirthlingam, the emerging leader of the Tamil United Front was trying to establish some kind of control over these fledgling militant youth movements. He wanted the Tamil Youth League to be under the Tamil United Front, but the TYL did not want to be under the TUF. After the Kankesanthurei by-election in June 1975, a split took place in the TYL and Varatharajah Perumal, C.Phusparajah, R.Padmanabha and others formed the Tamil Eelam Liberation Organisation. (Not to be confused with the organization that would later be founded by Kuttimani and Thangathurei)

The view held by Tamil youth at the time was that the traditional Tamil leaders in the ITAK/TUF were more interested in their parliamentary salaries than in the Tamil people. It was during this time that the Tamil New Tigers was catapulted to fame after Prabhakaran killed Alfred Duraiappah on 27 July 1975. Duriappah was a popular figure in Jaffna. The SLFP-led government he represented had benefitted farmers in Jaffna enormously so he was a formidable force to be reckoned with even for the ITAK which had managed to absorb the Tamil Congress but were powerless against Duriappah. After the capitulation of the Tamil Congress to the radicals, Duriappah became the sheet anchor of the conservatives in Jaffna society.

All radicals in Jaffna were pleased with the news that Duriappah had been murdered. After the Duriappah killing, the government re-arrested all those who had been in prison earlier for anti-state activities. Many Tamil Student League leaders and those who were involved in the agitation of 1972, including Varatharajah Perumal were rearrested. Those who were not arrested went underground or fled to India. For nearly a year after that, there was a lull in terrorist activity. The only significant event during this period being the Putur People's Bank robbery on 5 March 1976 by Prabhakaran which netted the Tamil New Tigers Rs 700,000. This was one of the biggest ever bank heists at the time. It was carried out like in the movies. Prabhakaran and four others dressed in the bell-bottom trousers and long hair that was in vogue at the time, had hired a taxi - an Austin A 40 car – and later overpowered, gagged and trussed up the driver and put him into the boot. They had then driven to the bank and at gunpoint demanded the keys to the safe. They fled with the cash after having fired four shots in the air. The getaway car was found later with the driver still in the boot.

After May 1976, the Tamil Eelam Liberation Organisation started by Varatharajah Perumal, Padmanabha and others became defunct after most of its key activists were arrested in the wake of the robbery of the Rural Bank of the Puloly Multi-Purpose Cooperative Society on 10 May 1976. This was a copycat robbery which followed the script of the previous Puttur robbery. Once again four youths wearing bell bottom trousers hired a taxi, gagged and trussed up the driver, put him in the boot of the Austin A40, robbed Rs 300,000, made their getaway and abandoned the car in Velvettiturei with the driver still in the boot. Clearly, this was a bad time to be a taxi driver driving an Austin A40 car in Jaffna.

On May 15 1976, the ITAK/TC combine took the situation that had been developing to a new level by forming the Tamil United Liberation Front and issuing the fateful Vadukkodai resolution calling for a separate, sovereign Tamil state. The resolution cited a long list of grievances, such as the disenfranchisement of the Indian Tamils, state aided colonization in the 'Tamil homeland', the making of Sinhala the only official language, giving Buddhism foremost place in the constitution of 1972, denying Tamils equality of opportunity in employment, education, and communal violence directed at Tamils in 1956 and 1958, the Army 'reign of terror' in the north in 1961, police violence at the International Tamil Research Conference in 1974, etcetera. The resolution ended with the following words - *"... This Convention calls upon the Tamil nation in general and the Tamil youth in particular to come forward to throw themselves fully in the sacred fight for freedom and to flinch not till the goal of a sovereign state of TAMIL EELAM is reached."*

By the mid-1970s, Chelvanayagam's health was deteriorating. He was able to speak only in whispers. When addressing public meetings, he would stand by the microphone and whisper what he wanted to say to Amrithalingam who would say it out aloud into the microphone. Even in this condition Chelvanayagam remained the rabble-rouser. The desire to take a more cautious and sober approach to politics would never have occurred to him because since 1956, he had succeeded only through reckless intransigence and brinksmanship. The leaders of the country were like putty in his hands and he really had no reason to be careful when the rewards for recklessness were so readily forthcoming.

The TULF followed up the call for a separate state with a *hartal*, ordering the closure of shops, government offices, businesses, factories, and the stoppage of public transport throughout the northern and eastern provinces. In May 1976, Prabhakaran's Tamil New Tigers changed its name to the Liberation Tigers of Tamil Eelam. After the Vadukkodai proclamation demanding a separate state for the Tamils, things would never be the same again in the north and east. The mood of the people underwent a change. The killings began in earnest.

A police constable by the name of A.Karunanithy of the Kankesanthurei police station was shot by the LTTE on 14 February 1977. He died before admission to hospital. This was the first time Tamil terrorists had killed a member of the police force. Soon afterwards the terrorists followed this up by killing two constables both bearing the name of Shanmugathasan when they were waiting for a bus at Inuvil Jaffna on 18 May 1977. They were attached to the CID units in the Kankesanthurei and Velvettiturei police stations. In the meantime, S.J.V.Chelvanayagam, who had made it his life's work to fan the flames of communal hatred in Sri Lanka, died in April 1977 and was succeeded as the TULF leader by A.Amirthalingam. The conservative Tamil leader G.G.Ponnambalam had also died on 9 February 1977. When the TULF contested the July 1977 parliamentary elections, they asked the people for a mandate for a separate, sovereign Tamil state of Eelam. Their main slogan was *"If you vote for the TULF on the 21st, you will get Tamil Eelam on the 22nd!"* The election was won by the UNP in a landslide, giving the party a five sixth majority in parliament. The SLFP was decimated, being reduced to just eight seats in parliament. Gōta's brother Mahinda also lost his seat in Beliatta. The TULF won 18 seats, and Amirthalingam became the leader of the opposition in parliament. In April 1977, a few months before the general election, Gōta was promoted to the rank of Captain.

Chapter 12

The 1977 Carnival Riot

In the short space of about five years there was a palpable change in the atmosphere of the north. On 12 August 1977, just weeks after the UNP's landslide victory in the general election, four off duty policemen tried to enter a carnival held at St Patrick's College grounds in Jaffna without paying the entrance fee. Policemen are accustomed to using public transport and entering places of entertainment without paying the entrance fee. Many members of the force regard this as a harmless privilege they enjoy. The organizers resisted and a scuffle ensued with the uniformed police on duty coming to the aid of their off duty colleagues. The police would later claim that the four policemen had entered the carnival grounds to arrest a suspect. Over the next few days the clashes snowballed with more policemen in civvies going to the carnival and behaving in an unruly manner. There was a shooting incident as well where the police claimed they clashed with terrorists. By this time, three Tamil policemen had been killed by terrorists in Jaffna and tensions were running high within the police force.

The TULF alleged that the next day the police launched reprisals by smashing shops and assaulting any Tamil they came across. Amirthalingam, now the leader of the opposition in the country was to complain that he too was assaulted by policemen when he went to inquire into the violence. Troubles spread to other towns as wildly exaggerated reports of the goings on in Jaffna were circulated by word of mouth throughout the country. The rumour was that Tamil mobs were attacking Sinhalese owned business establishments and government buildings in Jaffna town. Why such a story would gain credence among Sinhalese mobs is easy to see. The TULF had been elected on a platform of forming a separate state in the north and east and the Sinhalese were apprehensive that with the mandate the TULF had clearly got, the Tamils may be trying to chase the Sinhalese out of the north.

With the rumours spreading, there were outbreaks of violence in the Sinhala areas as well. The government declared curfew in the Anuradhapura and Kurunegala districts on 17 August 1977. What led to the riots spreading island-wide however was an act of indiscretion by Amirthalingam. After returning from Jaffna, on 18 August 1977, he responded to the statement of government policy made by the new prime minister J.R.Jayewardene by drawing attention to the mandate given to the TULF by the Tamil people for the 'restoration' of the separate state of Tamil Eelam and asserted that the Tamils had by all internationally accepted standards, the distinct characteristics of nationhood.

The exaggerated stories coming out of Jaffna and Amirthaligam's unnecessarily provocative statements in parliament led to attacks on Tamil homes and shops in Colombo, Kandy, Matale Anuradhapura and many other areas. This again underscores the fact that once a wedge has been driven in and mistrust created between communities, more cause for mistrust just keeps rolling in automatically. Ultimately, a matter of a few carnival entrance tickets ended up with about 115 people killed and a trail of burnt shops and homes throughout the country. Unlike the riots of 1958 however, there were no parallel attacks on Sinhalese living in Tamil areas such as Jaffna. Over three thousand displaced Tamils were transported to Jaffna in ships, and over 4000 were arrested for creating public disturbances and looting. Normalcy was not restored until the end of August 1977.

Amirthalingam for his part, insisted that the TULF had been demanding a separate state from 1976, but that there had been no ethnic riots earlier and the gist of his argument was that it was not his aforementioned statement in parliament that had set off the riots. In fact he was reported in a headline story in the *Ceylon Daily Mirror* as having said that the incidents in Jaffna were not communal in nature at all. Indeed they were not, as it all started out as a matter of a few carnival entrance tickets.

For the fledgling terrorist movements in the north, the riots of 1977 proved to be a great boon. The Sri Lankan Tamil question gained a great deal of publicity in Tamil Nadu as a result of these riots and the sympathy generated would stand them in good stead in the years to come. The Tamil Nadu state legislature passed a resolution on 24 August 1977 expressing shock at the goings on in Sri Lanka and asking the Indian central government to pressurize the Sri Lankan authorities to put a stop to the 'violence and atrocities' that the Tamils in Sri Lanka were being subject to.

In the years and decades to come, both the government and the opposition in Tamil Nadu would fall over one another to show sympathy for the Sri Lankan Tamils as a way of bolstering their political fortunes within Tamil Nadu. In August 1977 both the Tamil Nadu chief minister M.G.Ramachandran and his arch rival and opposition leader M.Karunanidhi wrote to the then Janatha Party prime minister of India, Moraji Desai urging him to send a senior cabinet minister to Sri Lanka to bring pressure on the Sri Lankan government. Desai however had a good rapport with prime minister J.R.Jayewardene and did not do so. But he assured the Tamil Nadu politicians that the Indian high commissioner in Colombo was looking into things on behalf of the Indian government.

A significant thing about the ethnic riots of August 1977 was that even though Amirthalingam himself claimed to have been assaulted by the police, he did not blame Prime Minister J.R.Jayewardene or the ruling UNP. He appears to have been much taken up by Jayewardene and was keen to continue the dialogue he had going with the government. Before the 1977 parliamentary elections, Saumyamoorthy Thondaman, the undisputed leader of the Indian Tamils had arranged a meeting between J.R.Jayewardene and A.Amirthalingam. Following this meeting, the UNP had included a chapter in their election manifesto on the problems of the Tamil speaking people.

The UNP pledged to look into their grievances in the fields of language, education, colonization and employment and they pledged to summon an all party conference to discuss these matters after they are elected to power. The UNP had won a landslide victory just weeks before the 1977 August riots broke out, and Amirthalingam may not have wanted to rock the boat by blaming the new government for what was obviously a case of police indiscipline. Even though Amrithalingam downplayed the issue, for the leader of the opposition to be assaulted by policemen of all people, was a scandalous state of affairs. In the coming years, this was not the only act of indiscipline on the part of either the police or the armed services that we were going to hear of. Clearly what was taking place was a process where rising tempers, frayed nerves and a gung ho attitude on both sides were feeding upon one another in the run up to all out war.

After the Vadukkodai declaration, and separatism became the mainstream of Tamil politics, members of the TULF youth front also started joining the various clandestine terrorist movements. Uma Maheswaran was among those who joined the LTTE from the TULF youth front. Prabhakaran made him the Chairman of the LTTE while retaining real power in his hands. In the meantime, Tangathurei and Kuttimani started functioning again as TELO – not to be confused with the organization by the same name that had been started by Varatharajah Perumal and the others earlier. By this time, the Eelam Revolutionary Organisation of Students had been formed in London. Suresh Premachandran was a member of EROS in 1975/76. Rathnasabathy its leader formed links with the PLO and sent 13 of its members to Lebanon for training in 1977. E.Rathnasabapathy, R.Padmanabha, Suresh Premachandran and Shankar Raji were among those who received military training. They offered the LTTE two of the PLO training opportunities and Uma Maheswaran and another member of the LTTE were sent to Palestine.

After Suresh Premachandran returned to Sri Lanka having completed his military training in Lebanon, he began recruiting Tamil youth into his organisation. When Tamil people from Colombo were sent by ship to Jaffna, after the 1977 riots, Premachandran had been among those waiting to receive and recruit them to his cause. EROS was working at that time with the Tamil Refugee Rehabilitation Organisation founded by a former Colombo based trade unionist, and Tamil people who had been chased away from the south were resettled in Vavuniya. By this time, Padmanabha had returned to Sri Lanka and he came into contact with Varatharajah Perumal. In the aftermath of the cyclone in the east in 1978, Padmanabha, Premachandran and others managed to establish a foothold in the Batticaloa district by engaging in relief work. Thus, by 1978 there were three Tamil terrorist groups - the LTTE, TELO and EROS.

Soon after the change of government in August 1977, Gōta, now holding the rank of Captain was sent to the army training centre in Diyatalawa as an officer instructor, a position he held only for a few months until January 1978 when he was appointed a staff officer in charge of administration at garrison headquarters Diyatalawa. While serving at the garrison headquarters, he also got an opportunity to attend the senior staff and tactics course held at the officers study centre at the army cantonment in Panagoda.

Amirthalingam was in a way right to have been accommodating towards the UNP government of 1977. When the new constitution of 1978 was promulgated, provisions for the use of the Tamil language in the north and east were written into the new constitution and Tamil was made along with Sinhala, one of the two national languages of Sri Lanka, while Sinhala remained the official language. Thus, one of the main grievances the Tamil parties had about the 1972 constitution was redressed. But things were careering out of control. On 27 January 1978, M.Canagaratnam the second MP for Potuvil who had been elected on the TULF ticket but had defected to the ruling UNP was shot by Prabhakaran and Uma Maheswaran outside his home in Kollupitiya, Colombo. He had a deep wound in his chest, his spleen was removed, his liver had been damaged and his intestines ruptured in ten places. He would succumb to these horrific injuries later.

The year 1978 was the year in which the incipient terrorist movements made everyone stand up and take notice. In April came the killing of Inspector T.B.Bastiampillai, Sub-Inspector A.E.Perambalam, Sergeant Balasingham, and police driver Siriwardene. Their bodies were discovered on 10 April 1978. Bastiampillai had gunshot injuries and several slash marks. Siriwardene too had both gunshot injuries and signs of having been hacked at with a sharp instrument. That ended the career of one of the most colourful officers in the police force at the time. Stocky, bald and tough-looking, Bastiampillai was a swashbuckling figure who always packed two revolvers which he would twirl cowboy-fashion while talking to his colleagues. He was the country's foremost expert on the incipient Tamil militant movements and was very secretive about his work.

He was the cop the early Tamil militants feared the most and was well known for being able to squeeze out every bit of information he wanted from a suspect. One may even surmise that he was the reason the cyanide option was introduced to the Tamil terrorist movement by Sivakumaran. Only he and his chosen team in the CID knew what he was doing at any given time. He would be dashing off to the north ever so often in his white Peugeot car and nobody knew where he was bound. When he suddenly disappeared with three others, his colleagues in the CID had to break open his desk and filing cabinets to look for clues as to where he may have gone. Less than a month after the Bastianpillai killing, on 6 May 1978 Inspector K.Padmanathan of the Jaffna police was shot and killed as he was alighting from his vehicle after returning home. Five rounds were fired at him by four gunmen who had been waiting for him. On 9 June 1978 retired police officer Kuttipillai Kumar, was shot and killed outside a Hindu kovil in Jaffna.

On 7 September 1978, an Air Ceylon Avro 748 which had just returned from Jaffna was blown up by a time bomb on the tarmac of the Ratmalana airport after the passengers had alighted. The blast broke the plane in two. Its captain and three others were carrying out a routine inspection of the aircraft when it exploded but miraculously, they were unhurt. On 5 December 1978, the Peoples' Bank branch in Nallur was robbed. Two policemen on guard duty were killed and their submachine gun and two shot guns taken, along with Rs 1.8 million in cash. Killing the policemen was as important a part of the operation for the terrorists as taking the money. When an injured policeman ran away and locked himself in the toilet, a terrorist followed him, blew open the door of the toilet and shot him dead. The autopsy revealed 18 bullet holes in the dead policeman. The clarion call of the Vadukkodai resolution of the TULF, inviting Tamil youth to come forward to fight for Tamil Eelam was working like a dream.

Chapter 13

The International Quest for Eelam

From the moment the separatist call was made in Vadukkodai in 1976, control over what they had begun, began to slip out of the hands of the TULF. By 1979 president Jayewardene made preparations to set up district development councils originally mooted in the Dudley-Chelvanayagam pact of 1965. He had also agreed with the TULF that the existing demographic pattern in the districts of the northern and eastern provinces should not be changed except in the case of lands coming under the major development schemes (mainly the Mahaveli development scheme). In view of these positive developments, Amirthalingam wanted some kind of accommodation with the government in Colombo. The problem however was that Amirthalingam was not able to lead the Tamils in his own right for very long. In just a couple of years after assuming the leadership of the TULF, Amirthalingam himself was being led by nameless Tamil youth with guns.

In the year 1979, the acts of violence in Jaffna continued. On 1 February 1979, constable Gnanasambandan was shot dead in Kokuvil and the terrorists had ridden off on the slain policeman's own bicycle. On 22 March, constable Sivanesan of the Velvettiturei police station was killed. On 1 July 1979, Inspector Gurusamy was shot dead in his home located a few kilometres away from the Jaffna police station. He had received death threats earlier, and the police department had given him a transfer to Kandy, but he had taken no notice of the threats. While this was going on at the ground level, there was a parallel offensive going on at the international level, and that was at a time when the term 'Tamil Diaspora' had not even been heard of. From the very inception, the Tamil separatist project in Sri Lanka combined international relations with terrorism.

Even as early as 1979, an Eelamist expatriate body called the Tamil Coordinating Committee based in London was in contact with Indira Gandhi. Her Indian Congress Party was out of power at that time, and Prime Minister Moraji Desai had a good relationship with the J.R.Jayewardene government in Sri Lanka, which was not to the liking of Indira. It was in this context that the expatriate Tamil lobby began cultivating Mrs Gandhi. The UNP for its part, identified the Gandhi family with their local enemies the Bandaranaikes. Mrs Gandhi was going to harbour a lifelong grudge against J.R.Jayewardene for being thick with her political enemies.

In 1979 Mrs Gandhi wrote to The Tamil Coordinating Committee in London that the Janatha Party government of Moraji Desai was going out of their way to be friendly (with J.R.Jayewardene) and that his government will not take up the suffering of the Tamils of Sri Lanka. A few months after that, in 1980, power was once again in the hands of Mrs Gandhi following the fall of the Janatha Party government. The Tamil Coordinating committee which had befriended Mrs Gandhi when she was out of power, wrote to her requesting among other things, that the Indian High Commissioner in Colombo should always be a Tamil. Mrs Gandhi may not have been able to accede to that request due to the way the Indian civil service functioned. But over the coming years, she would show much greater sympathy to the Eelamist lobby than the Sri Lankan government.

The Tamil expatriate lobby scored some significant successes very early on. The link they established with India was one. The other was cultivating influential sections of the establishment in the USA. On 16 May 1979 they managed to get the Governor of the State of Massachusetts Edward J.King to declare 22 May 1979 as Eelam Tamil's Day. The Governor's proclamation declared that from ancient times, Sri Lanka has had two nations, the Sinhalese and the Tamils with distinct languages, cultures, religions and clearly demarcated geographic territories and that after independence, the two nations were left under a unitary governmental structure resulting in the Tamils living as an oppressed minority in Sri Lanka.

On 8 May 1980, the Tamil lobby managed to persuade Congressman Mario Biaggi of New York to move a resolution in the

85

house of representatives calling upon the president of the United States to get the government of Sri Lanka to withdraw troops from the Tamil areas and to promote self determination for the Tamils. The following year, on June 19 1981, the Massachusetts state legislature adopted a resolution calling upon the president and Congress of the United States to support the struggle for a separate sovereign state of Tamil Eelam.

Thus at the height of the cold war, the Tamil lobby managed to win over a part of the capitalist bloc and a part of the socialist bloc to their cause, cleverly exploiting the naivety of the Americans and the pettiness and self interest of the Indian leaders. India at that time was solidly with the Soviet bloc. A good part of the Indian disenchantment with J.R.Jayewardene was because he tilted to the West in his foreign policy and towards capitalism in his domestic policy. Yet the Tamil lobby was able to deprive the Jayewardene government of support from his own side which shows how sophisticated their operation was.

Many changes were taking place within the terrorist movements in the late 1970s. Chetty Tanabalasingham the founder and leader of the Tamil New Tigers who had been arrested in early 1975, was released from jail in 1977. But by that time Prabhakaran had consolidated his grip over the organization and Chetty was a nobody. In fact while Chetty was in prison, even the name of the Tamil New Tigers had been changed to the Liberation Tigers of Tamil Eelam. He had been warned by his former protégé Prabhakaran not to engage in any political activities. Chetty took the warning seriously and was not involved in any political activity after 1977.

EROS was in possession of some shot guns by the late 1970s, and had commenced rudimentary military training. In 1979, the organisation split and Varatharajah Perumal, R.Padmanabha, Suresh Premachandran and Douglas Devanada among others, formed the Eelam Peoples' Revolutionary Liberation Front. Asked why he left EROS to form a new organization, Devananda says simply, that the EROS leader (E.Rathnasabathy) was an alcoholic and was living in London. The EPRLF had a strong base in the east because of the work they had done there and they would remain the dominant group in Batticaloa until around the mid 1980s when they were elbowed out by the LTTE. In 1979, a split took place within the LTTE too.

Its president Uma Maheswaran had a love affair with an LTTE female cadre called Urmila. Prabhakaran was against members of the organization having love affairs as that would distract them from the cause and in his eyes, Maheswaran was not setting the right example. At the height of this controversy, Urmila died suddenly and Maheswaran thought Prabhakaran had killed her. But Varatharajah Perumal says that Urmila had come to his house a few days before her death and she had a high fever. Perumal's mother in law had looked after her. The fever had been due to complications arising from an abortion. Both Prabhakaran and Maheswaran were in India at the time. Urmila's death exacerbated the enmity between them. The LTTE suffered two splits in 1979. The first was with Uma Maheswaran over his love affair. Then Prabhakaran had a dispute with other members of the LTTE and he too left the organization and went back to his former mentors Kuttimani and Thangathurei and joined their organization TELO.

As the law and order situation in the north deteriorated, on 18 March 1979, Brigadier Bull Weeratunga was sent to Jaffna with a mandate to eradicate terrorism. By this time, the entire Sri Lanka army did not have more than 9,000 men. Gōta was then serving as a staff officer in Diyatalawa. In order to deal with the increasing threat of terrorism, the government promulgated a special law - the Prevention of Terrorism (Special Provisions) Act No: 48 of 1979. Under this law, police could arrest any person, and search any premises, individual, vehicle, vessel, train or aircraft; and seize any document or thing. They could detain suspects for a period of three months initially, and up to 18 months if necessary and no court could call into question such an order. If a statement is made by a person in custody, the burden of proving that such statement is not be admissible as evidence shall be on the person asserting it to be irrelevant.

Soon after Bull Weeratunga was sent off to Jaffna, stories of arrests, torture and the 'bumping off' of suspected terrorists began to circulate. All these were usual characteristics of a crackdown at that time. Bull Weeratunga's principal staff officer was Major Denzil Kobbekaduwa. Among the others on his staff were Majors Cecil Waidyaratne, and Saliya Kulatunga. The leaders of the terrorist groups fled to India as they were unable to face the repression. It was while they were hiding in India during the latter half of 1979 that differences between Prabhakaran and Uma Maheswaran came out into the open.

While he was in Jaffna with a mandate to wipe out terrorism, Bull Weeratunga studied how terrorist sympathisers had infiltrated government offices and the banks. Another study that he did was on the encroachment of government land by the front organizations of separatist terrorist movements such as the deceptively named

'Gandhiyam Movement' with the aid of international non-governmental organizations like CARE, NOVIB and REDD BARNA. The TULF and the terrorist movements encouraged movements such as Gandhiyam to settle people along the so called 'Eelam border'. At that time it was all thick jungle. Settlements had taken place in this manner on state land in the districts of Mannar, Vavuniya, and Batticaloa.

Bull Weeratunga appointed Major V.K.Nanayakkara to study these land encroachments. Nanayakkara was at that time serving in Diyatalawa as an instructor and when he was appointed for this task, he asked Gōta whether he would like to join him. In the team that worked on land encroachments, there was Major Nanayakkara, Gōta, an officer from the Land Commissioner's Department and also a police officer to provide the team with police powers. The team travelled from one district to another in the north and east studying the encroachments that had taken place. If there were army camps they stayed in the camps. If there were no army detachments in the vicinity, they stayed at houses. A report was compiled on the encroachment of state land and handed over to the defence ministry.

After completing this study into land encroachments in the north and east, Gōta returned to Diyatalawa. It was around this time that the government decided to raise a new infantry regiment called the Rajarata Rifles. Lt Gen Denis Perera the army commander entrusted the raising of the new regiment to Lt Col V.K.Nanayakkara and the new unit was inaugurated in January 1980. It was on Lt Col Nanayakkara's invitation that Gōta decided to leave the Sinha Regiment and join the new infantry unit. The purpose of starting this new regiment as stated by Lt Gen Perera, was to meet the emerging threat of terrorism. The plan was to locate the regimental headquarters in Anuradhapura with two volunteer battalions in Batticaloa and Trincomalee. He had planned to set up yet another unit called the Vijayaba Regiment headquartered in Vavuniya with volunteer battalions headquartered in Jaffna and Mannar.

Even as early as 1980, the north was becoming a no-go zone. Even though the army had not by then been called upon to combat the terrorist movements, the violence against the police in the Jaffna peninsula had received wide publicity in the south, and potential recruits were reluctant to join the security forces. Hence the Vijayabahu Regiment was never able to raise the required number of troops. Colonel Tissa Jayatunga was the first commanding officer of the Vijayabahu Regiment. Due to the thinking that this difficulty could be due to the location, the headquarters was shifted from Vavuniya to Minneriya. Later Lt Colonel Viyaya Wimalaratne took over the struggling regiment.

The Rajarata Rifles under V.K.Nanayakkara however got off to a better start and it was able to become operational. It was Gōta as the adjutant to Lt Col Nanayakkara, who selected the 100 acre block of state land in Saliyapura located 7 km from Anuradhapura along the A-12 route from Anuradhapura to Jaffna, where the headquarters of the new regiment was to be located. It was then a patch of jungle. Later this camp would become the headquarters of the Gajaba Regiment that rose on the ashes of the Rajarata Rifles. The land was selected, surveyed, and nine families that had encroached on state land had been evicted and the camp was designed and the construction was carried out with Gōta playing a major role as V.K.Nanayakkara's principal staff officer.

Chapter 14

Tamil Leadership in Chains

It did not take long for the incipient terrorist movements in the north to browbeat the Tamil politicians into submission. For some time, the terrorist movements had been sending unmistakable signals to the democratically elected Tamil leaders, that whoever stepped out of line would lose his life. With this reign of terror, Amirthalingam and the TULF leaders were virtually prisoners of the various terrorist groups by 1980. Anuruddha Ratwatte has recounted in his memoirs that when Mrs Sirima Bandaranaike visited Jaffna in October 1980 at the invitation of Amirthlingam, the visit was literally hijacked by terrorists. It was the terrorists who had greeted Mrs B at the Palaly airport and Amrithalingam had approached his guest only after the terrorists had had their say.

Mrs Bandaranaike's private security detail that had been sent to Jaffna by road with instructions to be at the airport to receive her, had been detained by the terrorists elsewhere and they had arrogated to themselves the role of providing Amirthalingam's guest with security. The terrorists had even tried to persuade Mrs Bandaranaike to travel in one of their vehicles, but it had been explained to them that the SLFP leader would be more comfortable in her own vehicle. During her entire visit, Mrs Bandaranaike was being taken around in Jaffna by terrorists and Amirthalingam, the supposed host was just tagging along - and this was in a year when none of the terrorist movements were really active in Jaffna.

The leaders of the terrorist groups fled to India in the wake of Bull Weeratunga's repression of 1979 and the year 1980 remained for the most part peaceful. The terrorist movements began to get active again in 1981. By this time Prabhakaran was with Kuttimani and Thangathurei in TELO. One of his first acts after returning to Sri Lanka was to kill his erstwhile leader Chetty Tanabalasingham on 16 March 1981. The hit job was carried out by Prabhakaran and Kuttimani in Kalyankadu. It was a sad end for the real founder of the Tamil tiger movement - in addition to the ignominy of being shot by his own acolyte, the *Ceylon Daily Mirror* described him as a 'key police informant' in the front page news item that reported the killing.

A few days later, on 25 March 1981, Prabhakaran and the TELO group he was now working with, robbed the vehicle transporting money belonging to the Peoples' Bank branch in Neerveli, taking 8 million rupees. During this robbery, Prabhakaran was supposed to stop the police jeep in front and shoot the driver. But his gun jammed as he tried to open fire. Sri Sabaratnam had then jumped forward and shot the policemen before they could shoot Prabhakaran. A little more than a week later, Kuttimani, Thangathurei and another cadre were waiting on the beach in Manalkadu for a boat to go to India, when they were arrested by a naval patrol. Many Tamils believe that it was Prabhakaran who had betrayed Kuttimani and Thangathurei.

During his trial in Colombo, Thangathurei had given an interview to *Daily News* journalist T.Sabaratnam where he had hinted that they had been betrayed by Prabhakaran and this story gained currency among the Tamil community. But this may be a misunderstanding. On the day that Kuttimani and Thangathurei were apprehended, Lt Jayantha Perera was the duty officer in the operations room in the Karainagar naval base. A Cheverton inshore patrol craft had detected a high speed terrorist boat off Velvettiturei. This was at around 11.00 am. The terrorist boat was too fast for the Cheverton which could do only 10 to 15 knots. Then the crew on the Cheverton patrol boat informed the Karainagar naval base that the terrorist boat was speeding towards Velvettiturei. A team of 8 naval personnel were rushed to Velvettiturei under the command of Lt S.R.Samaratunga to apprehend the boat. Fishermen in Velvettiturei told the naval personnel that they had seen a boat moving towards Pt Pedro.

With this information, the navy squad went towards Manalkadu and they came across three men walking on the road. By their attire, Samaratunga realised that they were not fishermen. When the three men saw the navy jeep, they started running, but could not run very far in the vast, open sandy area and they soon slowed down to a

91

walk. As the navy jeep came near them, they raised their hands in surrender. Samaratunga was now convinced that they had captured some terrorists. Fishermen did not run on seeing the security forces or raise their hands in surrender. One of them had a parcel in his raised hands. Suddenly a shot rang out. The man with the parcel had tried to kill himself with a pistol he had in the parcel, but he only injured himself slightly. The three captives were taken to the Point Pedro police station where the police recognized the injured man as Kuttimani. It was only later that the other two were identified as Tangathurei and Devan.

The parcel that Kuttimani had been carrying contained jewellery in addition to the pistol. There was no betrayal involved, the navy had simply chanced upon them while pursuing a boat. After the arrest of Tangathurei and Kuttimani, Sri Sabaratnam became the leader of TELO. This led to Prabhakaran leaving TELO and rejoining Mahattaya, Charles Anthony and others in the LTTE. Around this time, the bereaved, embittered and motivated Uma Maheswaran stormed into Jaffna. He had just formed a new organization called the People's Liberation Organisation of Tamil Eelam (PLOTE). Some of the best in the old LTTE had sided with Maheswaran during the split in 1979. In the year 1981, Uma Maheswaran became arguably the most important terrorist leader in the north. The newly formed PLOTE dominated the scene during the District Development Council (DDC) elections of 1981.

It was from the DDC elections of 1981 that the terrorist groups came to dominate the democratically elected politicians and call the shots openly. The setting up of the DDCs was in pursuance of one of the points agreed to in the Dudley-Chelvanayagam pact of 1965, hence the TULF accepted the DDCs and prepared to contest the elections. Writing about these DDC elections, K.M. de Silva in his monumental biography of J.R.Jayewardene, says that it was a mistake for the UNP to contest the DDC elections in Jaffna – the heartland of the Tamils. Silva ascribes this decision to a visit made by the then prime minister R.Premadasa and a team of UNP ministers to Jaffna where they were given a tumultuous welcome. This welcome had given the UNP the impression that they would be able to gain a foothold in Jaffna if they contested. In fact at that time, Saumyamoorthy Thondaman, the leader of the up-country Tamils, had also gone to president Jayewardene and told him not to put forward UNP candidates in Jaffna. But Jayewardene's reply was that the UNP was a national party and he saw no reason as to why he should not field candidates in Jaffna.

Both Thondaman and Silva were speaking of expediency and in favour of allowing the TULF a walkover in the north. But could a national political party that had a five sixths majority in parliament, not field candidates in Jaffna without losing face? Besides, the Jayewardene government had enshrined provisions for the use of the Tamil language in the constitution, and was gradually implementing the Dudley-Chelvanayagam pact with the introduction of the DDCs. Very early on, the UNP government had solved the standardization of university admissions problem to the satisfaction of all parties concerned, so the UNP may have had good reason to think they had earned some political capital among the Tamils.

Be that as it may, what happened was that the UNP contested, and the terrorists reacted violently. The terrorists had good reason to fear the UNP. As we pointed out earlier on, there was a very strong conservative tendency among Tamils which kept the Tamil Congress alive for a very long time after they had lost their position of pre-eminence in Tamil politics. Since the conservative TC had merged with the ITAK to form the TULF, the terrorists may have feared that the conservative Tamil vote would go to the UNP, especially in a context where the UNP was addressing many of the issues raised earlier by the Tamil leadership.

Another cause of worry was that the DDC elections were being held under the proportional representation system. We pointed out earlier that had there been a proportional representation system in the 1950s, the ITAK would never have become the only mouthpiece of the Tamils after 1956. As the conservative tendency in Tamil politics was very strong, the Tamil Congress would also have got a number of seats very close to that of the ITAK and the whole history of Tamil politics would have been very different. If this Tamil conservative vote went to the UNP at the DDC elections and they won a substantial number of seats, that basically would have been the end of the Tamil separatist cause. So from the point of view of the terrorists, making it impossible for the UNP to make a mark at the Jaffna DDC elections, was imperative. One of the problems was that a former Tamil Congress conservative, and ex-parliamentarian for Vadukkodai A.Tiyagarajah who had consistently opposed the ITAK/TULF agenda was leading the UNP campaign in Jaffna.

PLOTE killed Tiyagarajah on 24 May 1981. He had just finished speaking at a UNP propaganda rally in Vadukkodai and was about to get into his vehicle when gunmen shot him. This led to several UNP candidates withdrawing their candidatures due to fear. The terrorists then moved to scuttle the whole election. On 31 May 1981, one policeman was killed and two others injured when they were shot by PLOTE gunmen while on duty at a TULF rally in Kovilady, Jaffna. Enraged policemen went on the rampage that same night and the following night as well. In the two days of reprisals, shops in Jaffna town, the office of the *Elanadu* newspaper, and the house of ITAK parliamentarian V.Yogeswaran, The TULF headquarters, and the Jaffna library were set on fire. The DDC election was held on 4 June.

The Rajarata Rifles regiment was deployed in Jaffna for the elections and Gōta's company was stationed at the Madagal army camp. One of Gōta's platoon commanders at the time, Jayavi Fernando reminisces that at the eleventh hour the Jaffna GA had informed the government that he was unable to hold the election. The government decided to hold the election anyway and made arrangements to bring election staff from Colombo to Jaffna. But the election staff that had arrived by train from Colombo saw Jaffna burning in the two days of police reprisals, and went back to Colombo in the same train.

The government in their desperation had then brought minor employees of the government departments, peons, drivers and labourers and the like to conduct the election. None of them had ever conducted an election before. One ballot box had been brought to the Madagal army camp at around 10.30 in the night by a confused government peon who had innocently wanted to know where he was supposed to take it – he did not know that ballot boxes had to be taken to the counting centre after polling closed. Thanks to incidents like the burning of the Jaffna library and the brief arrest of Amirthalingam in the early hours of polling day, the TULF won all seats in the Jaffna District Development Council.

The terrorists learned through this how malleable the democratic system was. A few people with weapons could manipulate things at will. An action would be taken and a reaction would be provoked. It is not the action but the reaction that delivers what the terrorists want. From this point onwards, it would be the bullet that ruled Tamil politics.

As in the case of the disturbances of 1977, the events surrounding the DDC elections of 1981 were also discussed extensively in the Indian parliament. But at that time, the Indira Gandhi government does not seem to have had a firm plan in mind as to what it was going to do in Sri Lanka. The terrorist movements too were still in an

94

incipient stage and the Indian government dealt mainly with the TULF which had agreed to the DDC scheme. Due to these reasons, P.V.Narasimha Rao the external affairs minister of the Congress Party government struck a conciliatory note. While reporting to parliament that there was an outbreak of violence in Jaffna with spill-overs in Colombo and the hill country, he informed the Indian parliament that these disturbances had been brought under control by the armed forces. He added that the Indian government had been in touch with the Sri Lankan government over these developments. He also stressed that these events were an internal matter for Sri Lanka and that it should not affect bilateral relations between the two nations.

Chapter 15

Gunfire in Madras

Terrorist activity escalated after mid 1981. A landmark achievement was notched up when a PLOTE hit team led by Uma Maheswaran and Sundaram attacked the Annaicoddai police station on 27 July 1981, killing one policemen and taking seventeen .303 rifles, one sub machine gun, five shot guns and about 1500 rounds of ammunition. This was the first time that terrorists in the north had graduated from carrying out attacks on individual policemen to storming police stations. The operation itself was quite simple, the hit team had arrived in a hired van at around 19.30 in the night and knocked on the door of the police station. At that early stage the police stations did not have sentries and were not the fortresses that they became later. Constable Nazeer who was on duty, opened a window to investigate and he was promptly shot. The party broke into the police station and took the arms and ammunition, shooting three other policemen in the process.

The Rajarata Rifles regiment was deployed in Jaffna again following this attack. When the body of the dead policeman was taken for burial to Ratnapura, that triggered off the communal riots of 1981. The burning and looting of Tamil owned shops and houses spread from Ratnapura, to Balangoda and Kahawatte, and to the Batticaloa and Ampara districts. As in 1977, the uninvolved up-country Tamil population bore the brunt of the rioting. During this period, the rivalry between the LTTE and PLOTE began to intensify. With the scuttling of the DDC elections and the Annaicoddai police station attack, it was PLOTE that had the upper hand. In an attempt to regain lost ground, the LTTE now with Prabhakaran back in the fold, shot dead two soldiers who were making purchases from a hardware store in Jaffna town and took one .303 rifle on 15 October 1981.

This was the first time that the terrorists had taken on the army. Up to that time, it was only the police that the terrorists had attacked. Hence Prabhakaran's attack also became a landmark. However even with this, the LTTE could not eclipse PLOTE which just a few days later, carried out another spectacular operation. On 29 October 1981, the Kilinochchi branch of the People's Bank was robbed and cash and gold worth 27 million Rupees stolen. One soldier was killed during the robbery. If things had continued in this vein, the LTTE would have been completely eclipsed by PLOTE. Prabhakaran prevailed over all other Tamil terrorist groups because he was not an idealist, but a ruthless pragmatist. Principles meant nothing to him.

In order to stop the seemingly unstoppable rise of PLOTE, he got Charles Anthony to kill Sundaram (Sathasivam Sivashanmugamoorthy) the second in command of PLOTE and the man largely responsible for the military success of the organization, on 2 January 1982. With that PLOTE's meteoric rise came to a grinding halt. Despite this debilitating setback, PLOTE managed to stay the course and on 13 February 1982, they shot dead one soldier of the Armoured Corps at the Kurikattuwan jetty in Kayts. Two other soldiers narrowly escaped death by jumping into the water and swimming to safety. PLOTE also killed two members of the LTTE in retaliation for Sundaram's killing. Needless to say that tension between PLOTE and the LTTE was now at fever pitch. It was these tensions that led to the shootout between Prabhakaran and Uma Maheswaran when they accidentally came face to face at Pondy Bazaar in Madras on 19 May 1982.

Both Prabhakaran and Maheswaran ended up in a Madras jail after the shootout. Prabhakaran was chased through the streets of Madras by Tamil youths, who caught and roughed him up and handed him over to the police. In Gōta's view, the biggest mistake the UNP government of the time made was to treat the capture of Prabhakaran and Maheswaran in India as a police and intelligence services matter, instead of taking action at the very highest levels with president Jayewardene talking to Mrs Gandhi to get them extradited. At that early stage, the Sri Lankan Tamil terrorists had not come into the consciousness of the Tamil Nadu public either, so the extradition could have been done without much of a problem. But there was an underestimation of the terrorist problem in the north and nobody thought such measures were warranted at the time.

Even the imprisonment in India worked to the advantage of the terrorists. Varatharajah Perumal says that this was the time that Indian intelligence officials first began having contacts with the LTTE and PLOTE. Earlier there had been no real collusion as such and India was being used as a rear base by the Sri Lankan terrorist groups only on the sly. At that time it was not easy for any member of a Sri Lankan Tamil group to travel to India and back. Until Uma and Prabhakaran were arrested, the normal law was applied to anyone arrested smuggling goods or caught crossing the border illegally. After their arrest, things changed and a kind of official tolerance of the Sri Lankan Tamil groups by both the Indian central government and Tamil Nadu, began.

During the first presidential election of 1982, the Rajarata Rifles regiment was deployed in Jaffna and Gōta was in charge of the security arrangements in Jaffna town. The detachment that he commanded was housed in the Sinhala Maha Vidyalaya. On election day, while on his rounds, Gōta got into a conversation with a Catholic priest at a polling booth set up at St John's College who told him that Hector Kobbekaduwa, the SLFP presidential candidate would win in the Jaffna district because the farmers in the peninsula had benefited greatly from the import substitution policies of the SLFP whereas they had been ruined economically by the open economic policy of the UNP. The priest told Gōta about the chilli, potato, onion and tobacco farmers of Jaffna who had benefited from the SLFP policy of import substitution.

Towards the latter half of 1982, tensions were rising in Jaffna, with isolated killings, bank robberies and the like. Gōta was commanding the Elephant Pass detachment in the north when one day a Dutch Catholic priest attached to the small missionary run Church in Iranamadu, had come to see him. In the course of their conversation he told Gōta about the discrimination that Tamil people had to face. He had said that he worked very closely with the fishing community and that the poor Tamil fishermen were not getting boats and nets. Gōta told the priest that this is not discrimination and that these problems were common to both Tamil and Sinhala fishermen and that this was due to underdevelopment, not discrimination. Politicians in the north however were telling the people of the area that they were not getting boats, nets and fishing gear because they were Tamil. Gōta told the priest not to believe these stories and asked him whether he has gone to the south and seen the condition of Sinhala fishermen. He had stressed that these were all common problems but agitators were misinterpreting these issues to their advantage.

Despite the rising tensions in the early 1980s it was still possible for military personnel to move about freely. Harsha Abeywickrema reminisced that when they were air force officer cadets at China Bay, Trincomalee in 1980, a Tamil warrant officer had died (of natural causes). His home had been in Kayts and they had all gone to Jaffna in a truck to accord him a military funeral. When they were in Jaffna, they had walked about freely in the market and the streets. Even after passing out as a pilot, Abeywickrema used to go as a co-pilot on the scheduled flights to Jaffna and they would walk about in the Chunnakkam market and buy items like nelli crush and crabs etcetera to take back home on the return flight.

By 1982, there were five main terrorist groups, the LTTE, PLOTE, TELO, EROS and EPRLF, and all were operational in Jaffna. But these were miniscule groups which did not have large numbers of cadres. Even though separatist ideology was clearly gaining ground in Jaffna, the terrorist groups did not have a ready supply of recruits, and this limited their operational capability. After the arrest of Kuttimani and Thangathurei in 1981, the activities of TELO came to a halt as their successor Sri Sabaratnam was in India. Incidents were occurring sporadically from time to time, but military vehicles moved about freely in the north.

Groups of terrorists were training in the jungles of Tamil Nadu. While there was some tension because of sporadic attacks on police and army personnel, life continued as usual in Jaffna. If there was an army camp on one side of the road, the houses of civilians would be located right in front of it on the other side of the road. There were no 'high security zones' at that time. When Gōta was the officer commanding the Velvettiturei army detachment, he used to get plates of freshly prepared *vadai* from houses in the vicinity. But things were slowly and surely changing. Gone were the days when military men could move around in uniform and unarmed. Now nobody went out unarmed. Gradually, the concept of travelling with back-up vehicles also came into being.

During this period, the army had increased interaction with other branches of the services. Gōta first got to know air force officers Roshan Goonetilleke, Lasantha Waidyaratne, Gagan Bulathsinhala, and navy officers like Prasanna Rajaratne during this period.

99

Wasantha Karannagoda, the second in command of the Karainagar naval base at the time, had been to the same school as Gōta- Ananda College Colombo - and he had been a classmate of Dudley, his younger brother. Among the more noteworthy incidents during Gōta's stint in the north in 1982 were; the ambush of a police jeep at Nelliady junction killing one policemen and injuring three others including the Point Pedro police OIC on 2 July 1982 and the blasting of the Poonlai causeway in an unsuccessful attempt to attack a navy convoy on 29 September 1982. Ten rudimentary landmines made of gelignite and shrapnel were exploded on the causeway as a convoy of navy bowsers moved out to fetch water for the Karainagar naval base. No one was injured, but the road surface was damaged. This was an amateurish operation by the LTTE which was embarrassingly botched.

The LTTE managed to salvage their self respect about four weeks later, when a 12 man team stormed the Chavakachcheri police station at dawn on 27 October 1982. A mini-bus had come up to the gate of the police station and two men clad in *vertis* had approached the police station as if to lodge a complaint. In the ensuing attack three policemen were killed and two others injured. A bullet hit the police station clock and it stopped at 5.27 am, the exact time of the attack. Two sub-machine guns, one revolver, nine .303 rifles and 19 repeater shotguns were stolen. The terrorists escaped in the mini-bus, firing at approaching vehicles as they went. The LTTE had seized the initiative again. Prabhakaran who had been in prison in Madras following the Pondy Bazaar shootout, had come back to Jaffna after his release and commenced work. Charles Anthony was shot in the leg during the Chavakachcheri attack.

That was the situation when Gōta went to Staff College in Wellington, India in January 1983. Officers were selected for the staff college course through a competitive exam. Gōta came first and went to staff college much earlier than some of those senior to him in service like Sarath Fonseka. In the meantime, sporadic terrorist attacks continued in Jaffna. On 18 February 1983, the officer in charge of the Point Pedro police station E.K.R.Wijewardene was shot dead along with his driver while his vehicle was parked near Siri's café in Pt Pedro. On 4 March, terrorists had shot and injured two soldiers in Paranthan when they tried to investigate a suspicious looking vehicle parked on the road.

It was with such sporadic acts of violence in the background that the country went to the local government elections of May 1983.

100

The terrorist groups wanted all parties including the TULF to boycott the election. On 29 April, three UNP local government candidates were shot dead in Pt Pedro, Chavakachcheri and Velvettiturei and this led to a spate of resignations of candidates in the Jaffna MC and Point Pedro UC. Even the TULF candidates were intimidated. On 8 May 1983, the LTTE disrupted a meeting of the TULF in Ottumadam while Amirthalingam was addressing the gathering. As terrorists invaded the venue firing in the air, people had fled in all directions leaving Amirthalingam alone on the stage. The terrorists had then driven away in Amirthalingam's car which was found later with the windscreen smashed and tyres slashed. *The Island* reported the incident in a headline story titled *"Guns boom at TULF meeting, Amir's car hijacked."*

The Rajarata Rifles regiment was asked to send a company of soldiers to Jaffna for election duty. At the time however, one company of the Rajarata Rifles was deployed in Vavuniya and another in Batticaloa and the other was in Colombo for an army tattoo and there were no troops to send. Army headquarters refused to release the company that had gone for the army tattoo and they were told to send whatever troops were available. Hence, three platoons were formed of the medical orderlies, the cooks the drivers at the regimental headquarters. One of the platoon sergeants was a professional cook with no combat experience, another was the pot-bellied ration sergeant. Then there was the stores sergeant who according to one officer, had not conducted a patrol in his life. There were no officers available either, so Captain G.A.Chandrasiri an Armoured Corps officer was sent to be in charge of this company. Then there was a young officer who had just passed out of the army training school and was undergoing an infantry training course in Amparai. He was pulled out of the course and placed in charge of a platoon.

Chapter 16

The Rajarata Rifles Mutiny

On election day, 18 May 1983, the Kandaramadam polling booth which was guarded by three soldiers of this rag tag Rajarata Rifles Company was attacked and one soldier J.S.S.Jayawardene killed. Another soldier fled the scene, but the lone soldier left in the polling booth, a raw recruit, kept the terrorists at bay until reinforcements arrived. The terrorists could not take the ballot box. At the time the attack took place, it was almost time for the polling to close. The reinforcements from two different army units that arrived at the scene set fire to several shops, houses and vehicles in the vicinity. The blame however fell on the Rajarata Rifles. On their way back to the Jaffna Kachcheri with the ballot box, the soldiers had fired at random along the roads as they went.

The Rajarata Rifles company was stationed at the Sinhala Maha Vidyalaya in Jaffna with troops of the 1st Sinha Battalion which was commanded by Lt Jayantha Kotelawala. That night the soldiers vented their fury by setting fire to the Jaffna market. Captain Chandrasiri had no control over the troops because he was from another unit and didn't know the men he was commanding. The Gajaba 25th Anniversary publication says euphemistically that upon private Jayawardene's death, soldiers of the Rajarata Rifles had behaved in an 'unruly manner' – which means in effect that the soldiers went on the rampage against Tamil civilians.

The soldier who was killed happened to be from Anuradhapura and on the day of his funeral, there were hand written posters all over Anuradhapura with emotionally charged slogans designed to arouse communal feelings. The funeral was attended by massive crowds, and buses had been used to transport mourners. Col Cecil Waidyaratne was sent to the Rajarata Rifles regimental headquarters to handle the situation. A board of inquiry was appointed about a week later and four sergeants who were in charge of the platoons that went to Jaffna were discharged from the army. The board of inquiry set up comprised of Col Harsha Gunaratne Chairman, Col Vijaya Wimalaratne, and Lt Col K.M.S.Perera the commanding officer of the Rajarata Rifles. But Lt Col Perera disagreed with the findings of the board of inquiry. Things were supposed to end with that. The army obviously did not want to take the action any further.

But what happened next was that about 60 troops walked out with the four dismissed sergeants and deserted the army *en masse*. The troops who walked out had gone to the Anuradhapura railway station and were waiting for the 4.00 pm train to Colombo. The OIC of the Anuradhapura police station feared that there would be trouble in the town because all the deserters were together and spoke to Col. Waidyaratne about it. Waidyaratne asked Lieutenant Vikum Siriwardene to go and speak to the deserters. Lt Siriwardene had gone to the railway station and tried to talk the troops into coming back but he failed. In a situation where the strength of a battalion at that time was less than 400, for 60 to 70 soldiers to desert *en masse* was a serious matter. At this point, Col Waidyaratne summoned a meeting of those who stayed behind at the regimental headquarters and announced that he had been appointed the commander of the unit and that Lt Col K.M.S.Perera had been sent on compulsory leave. Col V.K.Nanayakkara who had been out of the Rajarata Rifles for more than a year by that time and was area commander Diyatalawa, had also been sent on compulsory leave.

Five officers who remained were placed under 'open arrest' which meant that they could not leave the camp. At this, one Lieutenant and three Second Lieutenants refused to serve under Waidyaratne and gave in their resignations. Not to be outdone, Waidyaratne said that he will not allow them to resign, but will see to it that their commissions were withdrawn. Later Waidyaratne called the five officers and told them that they were young and should not get carried away by emotions but he was not able to change their resolve to leave the army.

It was only those soldiers attached to the Saliyapura camp that were involved in the mutiny. Other companies of the battalion were in Minneriya, Vavuniya and Batticaloa and these detachments were not affected. After the mass desertion, the entire unit was brought to the Diyatalawa army training school. During the mutiny the next most senior officer in the unit was Gōta, then holding the rank of Major, but he was away at staff college in India.

As the retraining programme of the Rajarata Rifles drew to a close, the July 1983 communal riots broke out and one company of the regiment was sent to Colombo to help quell the riots. After the riots were over, the company in Colombo was brought back to Diyatalawa where they were told that the regiment was to be disbanded and amalgamated with the struggling Vijayaba Regiment which had never really got off the ground. On 13 October 1983, all personnel of the Rajarata Rifles and the Vijayaba Regiment removed their badges. They got to know that the new regiment was going to be called the Gajaba Regiment, but even by February 1984, only a crude outline of an insignia for the Gajaba Regiment had been designed.

With the amalgamation of the Rajarata Rifles and the Vijayaba Regiment, Lt Col Vijaya Wimalaratne became the commander of the new unit that was formed. The then army commander Tissa Weeratunga explained the rationale for the decision to amalgamate the two regiments in the following words. *"We urgently need manpower to fight terrorism. Both the Rajarata Rifles and the Vijayabahu Regiment lacked the manpower to take up active duties and it would take time to supply the manpower and equipment, so the battalions were amalgamated"*. The army commander explained further that trying to find NCOs and officers to build up two units would have been a drain on other units. This was October 1983, a time when the battle against terrorism was intensifying.

Had the Commander of the Gajaba Regiment been anyone other than Lt Col Wimalaratne, it would have been just another infantry unit with nothing to distinguish it from the other infantry units of the army. But from day one, the Gajaba Regiment became a special entity in the army. It was born with the war against terrorism and officers trained and inspired by Wimalaratne would play a major role in ending it decades later. For years after the new regiment was formed, Wimalaratne displayed the badges and symbols of both the Vijayaba and Rajarata Rifles regiments in his office, to build the *espirit de corps* of the new unit. In forming the Gajaba Regiment, Wimalaratne as the founding commander, penned the following words in his message delivered on the occasion: *"A Regiment is not a group of men living in sprawling buildings with modern weapons, kit and equipment. It is a living organization with a soul and character of its own. The Regiment's personality is the collective personality, achievements and aspirations of all its officers and men."* In his inaugural message to the regiment, Wimalaratne stressed the principles of good discipline, high standards of training, efficiency, high morale and *esprit de corps.* Throughout all these events Gōta was away in India at staff college. He went to staff college as a Rajarata Rifles officer and came back to Sri Lanka in November 1983 as an officer of the Gajaba Regiment.

In the meantime, Col Waidyaratne had dealt with the Rajarata Rifles deserters harshly. He had them arrested by the military police, shaved half their heads, bundled them into a truck and dropped them off at various points in the Vavuniya jungles to find their own way back. The army always dealt harshly with any kind of indiscipline, contrary to a view that has been propagated by some quarters. A soldier was expected to do exactly what he was told and nothing more, nothing less. The last thing the officer cadre wanted were soldiers who did as they pleased or took the law into their own hands. Hence the sacking of the four sergeants who had gone to Jaffna, for not being able to control their men even though cooks and ration clerks can hardly be expected to control anybody. It was really the army itself that was at fault for not releasing an operational company and sending off a motley crew of non-combat personnel to Jaffna for election duty.

Despite the propaganda that the Sri Lankan armed forces engaged in ethnically motivated violence, the army always punished anything that was outside the orders given to their men. In May/June 1981 during the DDC elections the Rajarata Rifles had been deployed in Jaffna for election duty and even on that occasion, 32 men were punished for disorderly behaviour. It was not that they participated in the burning of the Jaffna Public Library and other incidents that were blamed on the police. Their offence was of a different nature. When shops in Jaffna town were set on fire, the army was sent to do the fire fighting with water bowsers. While putting out the fires, some of the soldiers had helped themselves to things in the shops. One of the soldiers in the fire fighting party had dropped his beret in a jewellery shop that had been on fire. Lt Col Lyle Balthazar who had gone to the town later had found the beret in the jewellery store and wanted to know who had come back last evening without his beret. And an army cook was arrested by the military police. On information elicited from him, a string of arrests took place and all of them were given various punishments. Nobody was discharged, but some were given detention and some had their seniority lowered. Colonel Hamilton Wanasinghe headed the inquiry.

While the army punished anything even slightly smacking of indiscipline, the question arises as to what motivated the rank and file policeman or the soldier who committed these infringements? Terrorism and sustained anti-state activity was at that time a new phenomenon to Sri Lanka. The armed forces and the police were not used to being attacked and had not at that time, evolved the practices and procedures or even the attitude of mind to cope with such situations. On 1 June 1983, when two airmen were killed in the vegetable market in Vavuniya town, air force men in civvies had gone berserk burning down the market complex in retaliation. Besides, this was more than a quarter of a century ago and the world was different at that time.

It is only after the end of the cold war that these new fangled notions of politically correct wars came to the fore. The problem with the Sri Lankan issue is that this is a four decade long affair straddling both eras and people tend to look at the past by the standards of the present. That there were reprisals by the armed forces and the police against civilians in the 1980s in not in doubt - the most prominent instance being the events in the run up to the DDC elections of 1981. Reprisals against civilians were not state or military policy but given the mood of the times, such incidents tended to happen. What is most important to note is that none of this was really ethnically motivated. If policemen had been shot at and killed while on duty even in a Sinhala dominated area, the police in 1981 would have reacted in exactly the same way that they did in Jaffna during the DDC elections. Such behaviour was normal at that time and if the army or police was attacked, reprisals were considered their right.

On 20 January 1981, a clash had taken place between policemen of the Colombo Fort police station which was then located where the Colombo Hilton Hotel now stands, and soldiers of the Sinha Regimental headquarters. The soldiers smashed up the police station and destroyed all its communication equipment. Following this clash, soldiers of the Sinha Regiment were sent on leave and the buildings sealed with the Armoured Corps taking over guard duties. The police were not Tamil but the army reacted to them in the same way that they would have at that time reacted to anyone seen to be challenging them. In March 1981, Lt Col Cecil Waidyaratne was appointed the commanding officer of the Sinha Regiment. Here too, Waidyaratne's iron fist was applied to impose discipline. Disciplinary measures were taken even though it was not possible to identify the culprits behind the attack. So the expedient adopted was to dismiss all the soldiers who had been occupying the billets closest to the police station while reinstating everyone else. A soldier was expected to attack only on command and wherever any attack of any kind took place without express orders, the army came down hard on the perpetrators. This is what enabled the army to survive long enough to finish the war. If unauthorized arbitrary actions had been allowed to go unpunished, the army would not have survived as an institution beyond the mid-1980s and the whole fabric of Sri Lankan society would have unravelled.

Even though many people think these various acts of indiscipline went unpunished, that was not true. Even the policemen involved in the reprisals during the DDC elections in May/June 1981 were charged. The Chunnakkam police filed charges in the Mallakam magistrate's court against one sub-inspector and 12 constables who had been attached to the same police station during the incidents of May/June 1981. They were charged with unlawful assembly and causing damage totalling Rs 230,000 to Kanapathipillai Stores and Ranjana Café in Chunnakkam.

* * * * *

The various branches of the Sri Lankan armed forces got involved in the war in stages. From the beginning to the end of the 1970s, it was the police that was at the forefront. From then until the mid-1980s, it was the army and to a lesser extent the navy as well. The air force was the last to join the fray. Before the July 1983 riots, the air force had a fixed wing transport aircraft squadron and a helicopter squadron. The helicopter squadron had about six Bell Jet Ranger helicopters and two French Dauphin helicopters which were used by the president and the prime minister. In 1982, only two pilots passed out of the flight training school, in China Bay - Harsha Abeywardene and Kolitha Gunatilleke, both of whom would serve as directors of operations in the air force during the final war in 2006-09. The previous year there had been only three pilots qualifying, all of whom had joined the helicopter squadron. When Harsha Abeywickrema and Kolitha Gunatilleke joined the fixed wing squadron, it had only six other pilots.

At that time, for the air force to do combat flying was unheard of. The air force in fact did not possess combat aircraft at all, even in the early eighties. Training took place first on Chipmunks, a two seater single engine plane and then on Cessna 150s which also were two-seater single-engine planes. The air force at that time had mainly civil aviation duties. After graduation Kolitha Gunatilleke was assigned to the fixed wing squadron in Katunayake which flew the Cessna 337 - an odd looking aircraft capable of carrying four passengers with two engines, one in front and the other behind, the De Havilland Herron, a four engined aircraft much bigger than the previously mentioned ones, and the Riley-Herron which was a Herron modified with new engines by Sri Lankan air force engineers. There was one Avro which the Air Force had inherited from Air Ceylon. It could carry 44 passengers. There were very few Avro flights at that time because there were seldom that many passengers. At that time there was no need to transport goods by air so it was basically a passenger service.

Every week there would be a flying schedule mainly for air force personnel or those of the army and navy as well, to commute between Colombo and the outstations. On Mondays it was to China Bay and back. The flight leaves Katunayake at 8.00 am, stays at China Bay till 2.00 pm and comes back. On Tuesdays it was to Palaly with touchdowns at Anuradhapura and Vavuniya and a return trip on the same day. On Wednesday it was to Koggala and Weerawila. Thursday was to Ampara and Batticaloa. On Friday it was again to China Bay and back. There was more movement between Colombo and China Bay because of the flight training school located there. The plane to Palaly was the Cessna 337 which could carry only four passengers and sometimes even that was not full. If there was a bigger crowd, a Herron would be used which could carry up to 14 passengers.

At that time most of the air fields belonged to the Civil Aviation Authority and there was not much staff. Sometimes when the plane flew to Ampara, there would be no response from the control tower. Then the plane would fly to Ampara town and circle over the house of the air traffic controller who would then be seen rushing to his vehicle for a quick dash to the airport to give them clearance to land. Those were laid back days for members of the security forces. If the pilots went to Weerawila they would be airborne by 8.00 am and when they got to Weerawila there was nothing to do. They would watch a movie, read the papers or have a nap until it was time to return after having lunch. Rear Admiral Jayantha Perera reminisced that in 1978, the year that he joined the navy, officers had a few drinks after lunch and did hardly any work in the afternoon. Some would have a nap. Others would have a leisurely lunch, drinking till 4.00 o'clock and then go home.

Before 1983, offensive operations carried out by the air force took the form of an airman firing a T-56 assault rifle out of the open door of a single engine Cessna 150. In an operation in Trincomalee, Kolitha Gunatilleke, then fresh out of flight training school, had been instructed to fire on a patch of jungle with a T-56 before the ground troops went in. At that time even the helicopters were not equipped with guns. Only hand held weapons from the choppers were used. If one looks back at the Sri Lanka air force before 1983 and the LTTE's own incipient air force in 2007/8, it can be seen that the LTTE was far more advanced in their use of light air craft for combat operations.

Chapter 17

The July 1983 Riots

By mid 1983, president J.R.Jayewardene was frustrated and angry. The goalposts kept shifting in his dealings with the TULF. The president was well aware that a new element, the terrorists had taken over Tamil politics. In an interview with the *Daily Telegraph* of London, on July 9 1983, president Jayewardene expressed his frustration saying *"The TULF is useless. They are in fear of their lives. They say one thing to me and something else to somebody else. I am sorry for them."* Throughout this interview, president Jayewardene kept stressing the need to eliminate terrorism without which even the TULF would not be allowed to function. He was also stressing the fact that he had gone as far as the District Development Councils and could go no further. President Jayewardene expressed his resolve to deal with the terrorist issue 'without quarter'.

It was soon after this declaration by president Jayewardene that the security forces scored another major victory akin to the capture of Kuttimani and Tangathurei. This was the killing of Prabhakaran's chief hit man Charles Anthony alias Seelan in a chance encounter with the army on 15 July 1983. But this success was to have unforeseen consequences. The attack launched by Prabhakaran to avenge Charles Anthony would soon change the trajectory of Sri Lankan history. Before July 1983, there were sporadic attacks in the north but only one or two individuals were killed in such attacks. The first major attack was the ambush of an army patrol near the Jaffna University at Tinneveli on the night of 23 July 1983. This was an attack personally led by Prabhakaran.

As a patrol of the Sri Lanka Light Infantry commanded by a Second Lieutenant, went past the Tinneveli junction, a landmine was exploded under the jeep in front and the LTTE terrorists fired on and threw grenades at the soldiers in the truck that followed as they scrambled for cover. Thirteen of the 15 soldiers died in the ambush. When Gōta who was then at Staff College in Wellington Tamil Nadu, read of the ambush in the Indian press, he was shocked. He couldn't believe that 13 soldiers had been killed in just one incident. His feeling of disbelief was shared by most Sinhalese. This was the first time in Sri Lankan history that such an event had taken place. Even though the JVP insurrection of 1971 also saw members of the police and armed forces coming under attack, there was never anything as deadly as this single incident.

This was followed by a communal riot which Indian author M.R.Narayanan Sawmy described as the biggest conflagration that South Asia had seen since the partitioning of India in 1947 - and he was probably right. The 50th anniversary publication of the army says quite candidly that soldiers in Jaffna had gone 'berserk' following the Tinnaveli ambush but the situation had been brought under control on the arrival of the army commander in Jaffna. As the bodies were brought to Colombo for burial, riots broke out in Colombo and soon spread to the provinces. Sinhala mobs went on the rampage against Tamils all over the country. Many of those who have written about these incidents opine that had the bodies of the 13 soldiers been sent to their respective villages instead of being brought to Colombo for a mass funeral the riots may never have broken out, but this is only a matter of conjecture.

In 1981, the body of a policeman who died in the Chavakachcheri police station attack was sent back to Ratnapura and that too sparked off a riot that spread to many areas. In July 1983, Tamil owned shops, industries and homes were burnt and many ordinary Tamils killed. The government stood paralysed as the attacks on Tamils spread throughout the country. Nobody has compiled accurate figures of the number of Tamils killed in the July 1983 riots. Even the University Teachers' for Human Rights (Jaffna) are unable to provide even an approximate figure. The claim made by the leader of the opposition Amirthalaingam was that nearly 2000 Tamils had been killed.

Whatever the death toll, what was certainly true was that Tamil-owned property was systematically destroyed all over the Sinhala majority areas of the country. In August 1983, the number of displaced as reported to the *Lok Sabha* by the Indian external affairs minister was 50,000. Douglas Liyanage, then the secretary to the ministry of state in Sri Lanka in a press briefing on 5 August 1983, confirmed that the number of displaced people in Colombo was 52,000 with 12,000 more in the outstations. H.W.Jayewardene, the brother of president Jayewardene when he went to India as the special representative of the president, had mentioned a figure of 80,000 displaced, at the initial stages which had however rapidly gone down to 30,000. Amirthalingam had given the Indians the figure of 135,000. Whatever the figures, this was a cataclysm of the kind that Sri Lanka had never before experienced.

On 18 August 1983, the Indian external affairs minister Narasimha Rao announced in the *Lok Sabha* that of the thousands of Tamils who ended up in IDP camps, around 25,000, had gone to Jaffna, another 5000 to Batticaloa and Trincomalee and yet another 25,000 had either gone back to their own homes or gone to live with friends or relatives in Colombo or other parts of Sri Lanka. The Indian government had provided three ships to take the displaced people to Jaffna. The damage to property during the riots had been estimated at Rs 4 billion by the Sri Lankan government.

Even Tamil terrorist suspects detained in the jails in Colombo were done to death by the Sinhala prisoners. The attacks on prisoners took place in the Welikada jail while Varatharajah Perumal was detained next door in the Magazine prison. He had been arrested in April 1983 in Batticaloa while holding a meeting to commemorate the Karl Marx centenary. Fortunately for him, nothing happened at the Magazine prison. From inside prison, Perumal was able to see the smoke rising as Colombo burned and pieces of ash and burning paper and cloth carried along by the wind fell into the jail. When the riots took place in Welikada, Perumal heard that Kuttimani and others had been killed the first day.

Perumal had been lucky because the officers at the Magazine prison had taken special care that nothing should happen to the inmates of their prison. A little known fact is that the Sinhala prisoners targeted only the Tamil terrorist suspects. The other Tamil remandees and convicts of whom there were a good number, were completely unharmed. This was revealed by J.P.Delgoda the Commissioner of Prisons in the inquiry held subsequently. What this means is that the Sinhala criminals in the prisons were more 'disciplined' than the armed forces of the time, who vented their fury on ordinary Tamils following terrorist attacks whereas the Sinhala prisoners carefully separated the ordinary Tamil criminals and killed only the terrorist suspects!

After the riots, Perumal and the other Tamil prisoners were transferred to the Batticaloa prison. It was the air force that transported the prisoners between Colombo and Batticaloa. A Douglas DC Dakota, a twin engined aircraft which could carry 28 passengers and the Riley-Herron which could carry 14, were used for the task. Donald Perera and Kolitha Gunatilleke flew the Riley Herron. There was some concern about unarmed pilots flying with 14 prisoners and just one jail guard. The Herron had a single row of seats and the convicts were seated with one hand handcuffed to the hand of the prisoner behind him with his other hand handcuffed to the one in the seat in front. One of the prisoners, who had got his first plane ride in this manner had told Flight Lieutenant Gunatilleke, "Now I don't mind even if I die, because I have finally travelled by air!"

In the wake of the July 1983 riots, many Western nations opened their doors to Tamil refugees thus giving rise to the phenomena of overseas Tamil groups that have remained staunchly supportive of the separatist cause. The riots of 1983 may also be seen as a main reason for the sympathy that the Western nations in general have shown the Tamil cause over the years. As we saw earlier, the reaction to the events of 1981 in Jaffna was muted even in India. But the events of July 1983 captured the attention of the entire world.

The J.R.Jayewardene government of 1977 was arguably the most pro-Western government this country has ever had. Yet the Eelamist lobby was so active and so successful in portraying the Sri Lankan government as an oppressor of an ethnic minority that from the mid-1980s onwards, the West baulked at providing Sri Lanka with weapons. Cyril Ranatunga has stated in his memoirs that the Americans approved a tender for armoured cars placed by Sri Lanka but without the guns. The British refused to supply ammunition for the Saladin armoured cars they had sold to Sri Lanka earlier. So from the beginning of the war to the very end it was countries like China, Israel, Russia, Pakistan and later Ukraine and Brazil that provided Sri Lanka with her needs. Even India despite various internal political limitations, provided some equipment.

Needless to say, the July 1983 riots in Sri Lanka was extensively discussed in the Indian parliament as well. N.Gopalswamy a radical Tamil MP from Tamil Nadu fulminated "...*The Jayewardene government speaks about Dharmista Society. Is it the formula of the Dharmista society to kill loot and rape? Is it not the duty of our government to give an ultimatum? Tamil Nadu is also part and parcel of this country. That is why we have come here to raise this matter. We are also part and parcel of this country. That is why we have come here crying and begging. Is it not your duty to protect our people?"*

When Anita Pratap asked Prabhakaran in her 11 March 1984 interview in the Indian weekly *Sunday*, whether it was not the LTTE's killing of 13 soldiers that led to the riots, Prabhakaran refused to accept that his attack could have been the cause of the riots. He told Pratap that to say so, was an oversimplification, and that there were ethnic riots even before the emergence of the LTTE. He said that anti-Tamil violence cannot be traced to a single event and that there had been guerrilla attacks previously where police and armed forces personnel had been killed and that the July ambush was only a part of the protracted guerrilla campaign they were engaged in. Thus, Prabhakaran denied that it was his attack which killed 13 soldiers that provoked the ethnic riots.

In 2006, following the Israeli military action in southern Lebanon, Hassan Nasrallah the Lebanese Hezbollah leader in a candid acceptance of responsibility, said that had they known that the capture of Israeli soldiers would have led to Israel declaring war on Lebanon, they would definitely not have done it. A responsible political leader will not provoke attacks on the people he leads. Tamil leaders from Velupillai Chelvanayagam to Velupillai Prabhakaran consistently denied that their actions would have provoked some of the untoward things that happened in this country.

We explained earlier how Chelvanayagam refused to accept that he provoked the 1958 riots by tarring the letter *Sri* on the number plates of state owned buses. And here we have Prabhakaran a quarter of a century later, also refusing to acknowledge that his killing of 13 soldiers could have had anything to do with the riots of July 1983. These provocations were the very lifeblood of the political project started by Chelvanayagam and carried forward by Prabhakaran. It was the ethnic riots of 1958 provoked by Chelvanayagam that gave the young Prabhakaran the stories to feed his antipathy towards the Sinhalese. It was the riots of July 1983 that would give Prabhakaran in turn the mileage that he needed to build his terrorist movement.

The events of July 1983 were subject to embellishment and exaggeration and even misrepresentation as the information was relayed by word of mouth. One Indian legislator said in the *Lok Sabha* that the killing of the 13 soldiers had been in retaliation for the rape of Tamil girls by Sinhala soldiers. However, in his first interview with the Indian journalist Anita Pratap, referred to earlier, Prabhakaran himself would confirm that the Tinneveli ambush was to avenge the death of Charles Anthony. It was after the riots of July 1983 that enlightenment dawned on the Sinhala mobs that their actions only played into the hands of the Tamil terrorists, gaining them sympathy in Tamil Nadu and in the Western capitals as well.

The riots of July 1983 marked the end of the era of Sinhala mob rule. As we saw earlier, the era of Tamil mob rule had ended with the DDC elections of 1981 after the terrorists began asserting open control over the elected leadership of the Tamils. After this, there would be no Sinhala mobs to attack Tamils and no Tamil mobs to attack Sinhalese. Sri Lanka had passed the era of politically motivated mobs and entered the era of organized terrorism.

The Wellington Military Academy where Gōta was doing his Staff College course during these cataclysmic events back home, is located in the Nilgris hills of Tamil Nadu. A lot of Indian Tamil workers from Sri Lanka who had been repatriated under the Sirima-Sastri pact, and engaged in the tea industry in Tamil Nadu would congregate in the small town of Kunoor close to the military academy. Gōta was one of two Sri Lankan military officers at the staff college and special security was provided for him by the college with a military policeman even posted outside his room. The events in Sri Lanka had been discussed at the military academy with many Indian officers expressing shock at the breakdown of law and order in Sri Lanka. When Gōta came back from staff college in November 1983, he went back to his unit which had changed its name from Rajarata Rifles to Gajaba. Usually after staff college, an officer is assigned to a staff vacancy at army headquarters. However the situation was changing and Gōta was assigned straightaway to his unit.

When Gōta resumed duties in the Gajaba Regiment at the end of 1983, a radical change had taken place in the ground situation. The government made a lot of mistakes during the 1983 ethnic riots. The first mistake was to allow things to get out of hand. The second mistake was to send internally displaced people to Jaffna. Gōta had heard while he was still in India that when the ships carrying displaced Tamils started arriving in the Kankesanthurei harbour, the LTTE and other terrorist groups had been waiting on the pier to enlist recruits from among the enraged and embittered riot victims. Unbridled hate was a necessary ingredient in getting a terrorist movement off the ground. Up to 1983, hate was not being manufactured in sufficient

115

quantities to make terrorism the mainstream among the Tamils. What really got things rolling was the riot of July 1983. The terrorists now found a ready supply of new recruits which vastly increased their operational capability.

Karuna Amman was one of the young people who joined the LTTE immediately after the July 1983 riots. He was 19 at the time. Tamil refugees arriving in his village in Batticaloa had told them harrowing stories of Sinhala cruelty towards ordinary Tamils. The LTTE had distributed a leaflet saying *"You see what has happened? We need a separate state to live in!"*. This was what had motivated Karuna to join the LTTE. The Tigers with their characteristic efficiency, had a well oiled mechanism to send the new recruits for training. The recruits from Batticaloa had left their homes at seven in the morning and were taken to the northern coast and put on speed boats. By midnight they had been in India. Dharmalingam Siddharthan of PLOTE says that before 1983, none of the organizations including the LTTE had more than 25 to 30 people. But after 1983, all the groups grew phenomenally.

Before Gōta left for Staff College at the end of 1982, it was still possible for a relatively small number of soldiers to cover a large area in cordon and search operations. It was for example possible to cordon off the whole of Nelliady town with around 100 soldiers. After his return however that was no longer possible and the army had to operate in much bigger formations. Before the 1983 July riots, water for the Karainagar naval base was brought from a location about 15 kilometres away. In those more relaxed days, the navy water bowser used to go out with just one naval rating with a gun sitting astride the tank. But after the Tinneveli ambush, the bowser was sent out with a back up vehicle.

After the riots, most of the 35,000 Sinhalese resident in Jaffna and the Northern Province left, fearing reprisals. A young novice monk then resident at the Nagadipa temple, came in a fishing boat to the naval base in Karainagar and said that he was carrying a message from the chief monk and that the temple had no protection and requested the navy to do something. A platoon of naval guards was assigned to the Nagadipa temple under the command of Lt Jayantha Perera. Lt Perera slept in the single room in the temple with the chief monk. The Tissa Viharaya, another Buddhist temple in Kankesanthurei was closed down in early 1984 due to the lack of patronage as almost all Buddhists had left Jaffna.

Chapter 18

India's Proxy War

After the July 1983 ethnic riots, the Indians began to play a more overt role, mediating between the Tamil groups and the Sri Lankan government. G.Parathasarathy was appointed as India's special envoy to Sri Lanka. There began a bewildering exchange of letters and proposals and counter proposals between the government of Sri Lanka, the TULF, the terrorist groups, and India, which would culminate four years later, in the Indo-Lanka Peace Accord of 1987. At the opening of the new session of parliament, J.R.Jayewardene was to ruefully admit that *"Sri Lanka cannot shut its eyes and ears to the international consequences arising from what happened in July (1983)."*

The government convened an all party conference in January 1984. This all party conference unlike the one convened on 20 July 1983, got off to a better start and was attended by the SLFP, the CP, LSSP, the TULF, and the CWC. The SLFP walked out soon afterwards, but the dialogue continued between the government and the Tamil parties. The TULF had withdrawn from the District Development Councils in late 1983. The solution that the TULF had agreed to accept was thus jettisoned due to pressure from the terrorists. In October 1983, the TULF was no longer able to remain in parliament due to their refusal to take an oath under the Sixth Amendment to the constitution against separatism. From that time onwards, they would reside mainly in India. In fact Amirthalingam was to request S.Thondaman to represent not only the Indian Tamils but the northern Tamils as well in parliament as there was now nobody to represent them. From the time of the July 1983 riots, Sri Lanka-India relations were on a downward spiral. By the end of 1983, exchanges had begun between the Sri Lankan government and the government of India, about Tamil terrorist training camps on Indian soil.

On 23 March 1984, the Sri Lankan parliament discussed an article in *India Today* which revealed the existence of training camps for Tamil terrorist groups in Tamil Nadu. Lalith Athulathmudali the then national security minister read out passages from *India Today* which had provided details of a training camp in Kumbakonan in Tamil Nadu. The figures given in the magazine of the number of terrorists trained by that date had been 2000, with 2000 more in training. Quoting these figures, Athulathmudali said that what these numbers mean is that they were planning for pitched battles with the Sri Lankan armed forces and not just the hit and run tactics the terrorists had used up to that time.

The Indian *Lok Sabha* for its part, discussed how anti-Indian feeling was rising in Sri Lanka. Indian external affairs minister P.V.Narasimha Rao deplored the build up of 'anti-Indian' sentiment in the Sri Lankan media and especially the contribution that the Prime Minister R.Premadasa was making towards that. There were also questions raised in the Indian parliament by Narasimha Rao about sketchy reports of escalating violence in Jaffna. Later Lalith Athulathmudali would explain that this was just a case of the armed forces reacting to the killing of police and armed forces personnel and Tamil civilians by the terrorists.

The Indian central government was under pressure from within their own country over the Sri Lanka issue. One legislator P.Upendra was arguing *"Gone are the days when we can say that what is happening in a neighbouring country is not our concern. Particularly in countries with multi-racial populations which have got bonds with the populations of neighbouring countries, the problem always gets internationalized, and it cannot remain a domestic problem."* In his reply to this Narasimha Rao the external affairs minister seemed to agree. He said *"This is no longer a Tamil Nadu issue. The most encouraging feature is that the whole of the Indian people are behind their Tamil brethren who are being subjected to untold suffering and harassment."* By May 1984, the Indian external affairs minister was expressing the view that the presence of large numbers of troops in Jaffna was aggravating ethnic tensions.

In the middle of all this, Lalith Athulathmudali was trying to fend off criticism. He said in Parliament on 8 May 1984, in response to the accusations coming from India, *"I am getting reports now which show that the way in which the army is carrying out its work is much more acceptable than before. There is a great deal of politeness. Doing cordoning off and searches are inevitable. Particularly in an area where information is not forthcoming readily. What other way is there to find out and separate terrorists from innocent people? But cordoning off and searching anyone is a distasteful thing. Nobody can be happy about it. The person being searched and the person doing the search both find it distasteful. But it has to be done."*

These exchanges between India and Sri Lanka would increase in stridency and Premadasa was soon challenging India to invade Sri Lanka openly without fighting a proxy war. The Indians were later to raise issue over the 'intemperate language' being used by Premadasa. As 1984 progressed these exchanges continued unabated. In August 1984, The Indian government was complaining of large scale arrests in Jaffna and the shelling of the Velvettiturei town by the navy and Indira Gandhi herself was complaining that 40,000 Sri Lankan refugees had arrived in Tamil Nadu from Sri Lanka since July 1983.

Indian support for the terrorist movements would have fateful consequences for the Tamil people of Sri Lanka as well. The reliance of the Tamil terrorist groups on India for a rear base and for training as well as weapons and money, meant that these terrorists were independent of the population they sought to control. After initially relying on the Indians for support, the LTTE later began relying on expatriate Tamils who had migrated overseas in their thousands after the riots of July 1983. What this meant was that the Tamil terrorists were never really dependent on the goodwill of the people of the north and east for their survival. Much of the suffering that the Tamil people had to undergo was a result of their representatives not really being dependent on those whom they claimed to represent. The authors of *The Broken Palmyra* said that to the terrorist movements the people were just 'demonstration fodder' during this period. Later after voluntary recruits dwindled, the LTTE began forced conscription and with that the Tamil people would also become cannon fodder for the LTTE.

Indira Gandhi who began this self defeating process of trying to use terrorists as proxies to wage a war of attrition against an independent minded neighbour, was assassinated on 31 October 1984 and was succeeded by her son Rajiv Gandhi. But the policy of promoting terrorism in Sri Lanka continued. First it was free access to India that was provided followed by weapons training and later still, actual arming of the terrorists. The EPRLF got about 40 to 50 people trained by the Indians during this period. The total number of EPRLF cadres trained up to the Indo-Lanka peace Accord of 1987, was not more than 200. The training of the Sri Lankan terrorist groups had taken place mainly in Tamil Nadu and Uttar Pradesh.

At this stage however the Indian government did not provide arms. They provided only training. It was only after the talks with the Sri Lankan government faltered in 1984 and Mrs Indira Gandhi got frustrated that the Indian government started giving the terrorists just a few weapons. This was just before she was assassinated. That at least is the experience of the EPRLF to whom the Indians gave only around 30 or 40 weapons in total, mostly submachine guns, with a few AK-47s and a few revolvers and pistols. A little more may have been given to the other groups. The terrorist movements however had been given a free run of Tamil Nadu and allowed to maintain their camps and move between Sri Lanka and India at will.

By mid-1983, even before the July riots, Sri Lanka-India relations was on a downward spiral. The then Sri Lankan High Commissioner in India Bernard Tillekeratne had been summoned by the Indian external affairs secretary K.S.Bajpai and told that the measures that the Sri Lankan government was taking to meet the situation in Jaffna would have repercussions in Tamil Nadu, and he had specifically referred to emergency regulation 15A that had been invoked which enabled the disposal of dead bodies by a police officer above the rank of ASP without holding an inquest. This led to the Acting Indian High Commissioner in Colombo being summoned to The Sri Lankan foreign ministry where a strong protest was registered at Indian interference in the internal affairs of Sri Lanka. Atal Behari Vajpaee then a member of the Indian opposition, was to raise a pertinent question in the *Lok Sabha,* wanting to know whether India protested when similar provisions were invoked by the Sri Lankan government in 1958 and 1971, (during the communal riots and the JVP insurgency respectively).

It was not that India was at any time supporting separatism in Sri Lanka. Way back in 1984, the Indian mediator G.Parathasarathy had told Dharmalingam Siddharthan, that India will never allow an Eelam in Sri Lanka. So what they were doing was using the Tamil terrorist groups as proxies to establish some kind of control over Sri Lanka. A separate Tamil state would have posed a danger to India as that would have encouraged separatist tendencies in Tamil Nadu as well. By this time the Indian government had misgivings about the foreign policy trajectory of the right-wing, pro-Western government of J.R.Jayewardene. J.N.Dixit the Indian High Commissioner who served in Sri Lanka during the latter half of the turbulent 1980s says in his memoirs that the setting up of a Voice of America transmitting station in Sri Lanka posed a major problem because the Indian government had got information to the effect that it was also to be used for espionage.

Another sticking point was the awarding of a contract to rehabilitate the old British World War II oil tank farm in Trincomalee to an American conglomerate despite India also having made a bid for the tender. Getting the help of Pakistan and Israel to quell Tamil terrorism also made India wary. There was also the fact that Mrs Gandhi was not willing to forgive J.R.Jayewardene for fomenting close relations with her political foes in India. Another reason that Dixit avers for Indira Gandhi's attitude towards Sri Lanka was the fact that the Jayewardene regime deprived Mrs Sirima Bandaranaike a close friend of the Gandhi family, of her civic rights in 1980 which meant that she would not be restored to power anytime soon and J.R.Jayewardene and his pro-Western policies would be in place for a considerable time to come. Thus a complex congeries of reasons both political and personal made India adopt the highly counterproductive strategy of promoting Tamil terrorism in Sri Lanka.

Chapter 19

The Gajaba Regiment on Duty

After the July 1983 riots, there was a lull in terrorist activity which lasted till the first quarter of 1984. Varatharajah Perumal and some others who had been transferred from prisons in Colombo to the Batticaloa prison, escaped on 23 September 1983 with the connivance of the jail guards. Altogether 271 prisoners escaped. One of the escapees - Panagoda Maheswaran staged the Kattankudy People's Bank robbery on 13 January 1984, taking cash and jewellery worth 35 million Rupees - the biggest bank heist up to that time. In Jaffna, there were nine lamp-post killings in the first quarter of 1984. On 11 January 1984, two guns and two pistols were taken from a customs warehouse by terrorists after tying up the two watchmen on duty. On 13 February 1984, the People's Bank branch in Chavakachcheri was robbed and Rs 5 million taken.

On 24 February 1984, an unsuccessful attempt was made to rob money being transported from the Velani branch of the Bank of Ceylon across the Pannai causeway and one terrorist died in the shootout with the police. As a result of this the Bank of Ceylon and the People's Bank decided to close down all branches in the north except for those located near police stations or army camps. It was not only the banks that were closing down. After the attacks on the Annaicoddai and Chavakachcheri police stations, those stations in areas considered vulnerable were also closed down and when the Gajaba Battalion was posted for its first tour of duty in Jaffna in April 1984, only the Jaffna town, Kankesanthurei, Velvettiturei, Point Pedro, Kayts, Chavakachcheri, Chunnakkam and Kilinochchi police stations were still functioning.

On 1 April 1984, the newly formed Gajaba Regiment was assigned to the north and headquartered in Palaly with detachments in Mankulam, Kokavil, Pooneryn, Elephant Pass, and the Jaffna peninsula. The deployment in the peninsula included detachments in the Duriappah Stadium in Jaffna town, Velvettiturei, Madagal and Pt Pedro. The Mankulam camp covered a large extent of territory on both sides of the A-9 road in the heart of the Vanni extending up to Tunukkai in the west and Oddusudan in the east. In 1984, just one company of about 100 men had no problem in holding the Elephant Pass - Pooneryn area despite the escalation of terrorist activity.

During this period, troops used to come to Jaffna by train and when they disembarked in Jaffna, they were taken in buses under escort to Palaly. On 9 April 1984, just days after the Gajaba Regiment had been posted to Jaffna, this regular convoy was ambushed. A massive car bomb explosion hit one of the trucks in the convoy just as it was passing a Church on Hospital Street Jaffna, and LTTE cadres fired on the rest of the convoy from the church. The troops fired back and the church was pock marked with bullet holes as a result. Ten soldiers died in this attack. The officer in charge of the convoy on that occasion, was Lt Fazly Lafir, who would later marry Gōta's first cousin Anoma. The terrorist groups then orchestrated a massive protest by Tamil civilians over the damage to the church.

Gōta's company was deployed at the Duriappah stadium with the soldiers billeted on the grandstand, and Gōta and his platoon commanders taking up residence in the dressing rooms. Next to the dressing rooms were about four toilets and showers for everybody. The Duriappah stadium detachment was tasked with controlling Jaffna town. The morning after the hospital road incident, Gōta saw smoke rising in the distance and from the general direction he guessed that it was coming from the Naga Viharaya in Jaffna town. (This should not be confused with the *Nagadipa* temple) He got some soldiers together and rushed to the scene. When they reached the spot, they found tyres burning and barricades put up along the approach roads. A crowd had assembled in the vicinity of the Naga Viharaya to protest against the damage to the church the previous day.

Having dispersed the crowd, Gōta saw that a group of terrorists was trying to destroy the Naga Viharaya. The incumbent monks had been packed off in a bus to Colombo by the LTTE. Seeing the army, the LTTE fired a few shots at them and fled. In the two days of anarchy that followed, the Jaffna branch of the Bank of Ceylon was robbed and Rs 1.2 million taken. The Point Pedro police station was burnt to the ground as the policemen fled. The government announced that 50 people had been killed in the three days of unrest. But the Jaffna Citizens Committee held that 214 had been killed. Things were back to normal by 12 April 1984. On 21 April, 15 guns and 10 pistols were stolen from the Jaffna high courts stores. Guns were always in short supply for the various terrorist movements. Even as late as the latter part of 1983, some terrorists had even been using toy pistols in holdups and robberies.

There were also the usual killings of alleged informers and numerous robberies. Among the more notable incidents this year was the LTTE's spiriting away of Nirmala Nityanandan from the Batticaloa prison on 11 June 1984. The LTTE rescue party had come dressed as prison guards and once inside the jail, had overpowered the real guards and taken away Ms Nityanandan who had treated Charles Anthony when he was injured during the raid on the Chavakachcheri police station in 1982. Then there was the 28 June bomb blast in a room of the Oberoi Hotel in Colombo. The Oddusudan police station was attacked on 5 August 1984 by about 60 terrorists and two policemen were killed. On the same day, police superintendent Arthur Herath was killed in Vavuniya inside his office. A time bomb had been placed under his table.

On 5 August 1984, terrorists tried to prevent the army from taking casualties from the Jaffna hospital to Palaly to be transferred to Colombo, by engaging the army from surrounding buildings. This was one of the first face-to-face confrontations between terrorists and the army at the time. Apart from the robberies of the Bank of Ceylon, the People's bank and the National Savings Bank in Jaffna, involving small amounts of money, the major event that gained both local and international attention was the 6 August 1984 bombing of the Meenambakkam airport in Madras. A powerful suitcase bomb made by Panagoda Maheswaran meant to explode in Colombo after being sent from Madras to Colombo in an Airlanka flight, exploded prematurely at the Meenambakkam airport in Madras, killing 35 and wounding scores of others.

There was a landmine blast in Mannar on 12 August which killed six security forces personnel. Another bomb blast in Pt Pedro on 2 September killed 4 police commandos and injured another ten. Another major event was the explosion of bombs in Colombo on 22 October 1984. Colombo was rocked by multiple bomb blasts at the Fort railway station, in Kotahena near the foreshore police station, in Peliyagoda and Torrington square. The only fatalities were three terrorists who died when the bombs they were carrying exploded prematurely. On 19 November 1984, Colonel A.Ariyapperuma the then northern commander was killed in a landmine blast in Telippalai, Jaffna. On 21 November 1984, the Chavakachcheri police station was attacked by TELO. The attackers had come in army uniform and taken everybody by surprise. At the time of the attack, there had been around 75 policemen in the station which included 20 police commandos. No less than 24 policemen and three civilians had been killed, and the building damaged in a massive explosion caused by an explosives laden vehicle. After the attack, *The Island* reported that five Sinhala and 8 Tamil policemen were missing in action. When the army rushed in reinforcements, they were ambushed in Kaithady.

It was in late 1984 when Gōta was serving in the north that the conflict began spilling out of Jaffna into the east as well. On 30 November 1984, the LTTE carried out the first of the many civilian massacres they would carry out in the years and decades to come. Two LTTE parties attacked the open air prison camps known as the Dollar and Kent Farms about ten kilometres to the north of Parakramapura in the Welioya area and killed over eighty prisoners and prison guards. The next night, on 1 December 1984, the LTTE carried out yet another massacre of Sinhalese seasonal fishermen operating out of the Nayaru and Kokilai villages on the coast, and killed another sixty civilians. This massacre too occurred within the Welioya area. By the end of 1984, there were over 15,000 internally displaced Sinhalese mainly in the east, as a result of attacks on civilians by terrorists.

Gōta served in the detachments in Jaffna town, Mankulam and Elephant Pass until his regiment was finally withdrawn to their Saliyapura headquarters in Anuradhapura on 19 January 1985. When the Gajaba Regiment was withdrawn from Jaffna and the Sri Lanka Light Infantry took over, the withdrawing Gajaba troops went on foot from Jaffna to Elephant Pass. They did not travel by vehicle due to the fear of landmines. It was only at Elephant pass that they got into vehicles for the trip back to Anuradhapura. Between Elephant Pass and Vavuniya, whenever the withdrawing soldiers saw a culvert on the road, they would stop, ensure that there were no buried land mines and then resume their journey.

In the mid 1980s, landmines were the principal weapon of the terrorists. In the early days, landmines buried on the road could be easily noticed in the daytime with their tell-tale patches on the road with the hole dug for the explosives and the detonating wire. The

Tinneveli attack carried out by Prabhakaran in July 1983 was not really a landmine attack but a conventional ambush, because the landmine was used only to stop the convoy and the soldiers were killed by gunfire. Soldiers who had been in the doomed patrol had got down and sprayed bullets around them and it had been one of these bullets that had killed Sellakkili. After this, the LTTE and other terrorist groups improved their landmines so that the fatalities would occur with the impact of the land mine without relying on gunfire and grenades to finish the job.

During this period, the armed forces started using armoured personnel carriers to transport troops to minimize the harm from landmines. A special armoured personnel carrier squadron was set up in the Armoured Corps and drivers specially trained to handle the lumbering vehicles. The LTTE would take the lead and ratchet up the use of technology, with the army only reacting to the use of a new weapon. In the early stages the army could detect the mines by the patches on the road. Later the terrorists began tunnelling under the road to bury the mines which made them impossible to detect from a vehicle. Then the army began to sweep the roads for mines on foot before the vehicles moved out. It was during Gōta's tour of duty in the north in 1984, that the landmine became the principal weapon of the terrorists against the army. From the latter half of 1984 into 1985, a spate of land mine attacks took place all over the north and east.

To meet this threat Lt Gen Tissa Weeratunga, the then commander of the army obtained a Mazda truck chassis from a private company in Colombo and this was used to improvise the first armoured personnel carrier for the army in order to minimize casualties from landmine blasts. The idea was to at least have the bodies intact after a blast. When an ordinary vehicle was hit by a landmine, the bodies would be torn to pieces and this was demoralizing the soldiers. It was a known fact that when a blast took place, the pieces of flesh would all be gathered together and divided into the number of soldiers who died and this cocktail of human remains would be what was sent back in the sealed coffin.

The symbol of the Sri Lanka Electrical and Mechanical Engineers (SLEME) of the army which designed and built this armoured personnel carrier was the horse. Therefore, their creation was called the *Unicorn*. Based on pictures in military catalogues of South African *Buffels* and other such armoured personnel carriers, SLEME adopted the V shaped hull to divide the force of the landmine blast and reduce damage: The first batch of 25 vehicles had spaced steel plates with a two inch gap in between. The V hull was made of ½ inch steel plates while the plates on the sides of the personnel carrier were ¼ inch thick. Major Palitha Fernando was one of those involved in turning out the improvised personnel carriers.

The South African *Buffles* were built on Mercedes Unimog truck chassis which were made only in Germany and were very expensive. The Sri Lankan *Unicorns* were built on a purpose made chassis manufactured by TATA in India. These armoured personnel carriers provided at least a psychological sense of protection against the feared landmines. The terrorists had put the security forces into a steep learning curve. New weapons were being acquired which the army did not know how to use.

While the Gajaba regiment was still in the northern province, Gōta was made the commanding officer of the Elephant Pass detachment after his stint at Mankulam. The commanding officer of the Elephant Pass camp Major Malik Deen, took over Mankulam from Gōta. During this period, new equipment was being purchased to meet the threat posed by the LTTE. Among the new items being introduced was a new type of baby grenade. It was first issued to the police. When this stock of new grenades was received, the officer in charge of the Mankulam police station which was right opposite the army camp, had approached Gōta and asked him whether he could train his men in the use of these grenades. He had also brought a box of the new grenades with him.

Gōta had told the police officer that he is moving to the Elephant Pass camp and to speak to the new detachment commander when he comes. Later this police officer had approached Major Deen and made the same request. In the older grenades, when the pin is removed, a striker hits the detonator. Striker tests had to be made to see whether the grenade would work properly. To do the striker test, the grenade is held to the waist and the pin is released so that the striker hits the belt. The new grenades however worked differently. They were already primed and a detonator was not necessary. Major Deen gave the new grenades to a sergeant major who did the striker test. The resulting blast killed the sergeant major, Major Deen and some others. The only survivor in the room was an army pay clerk. The army was learning to use new technology the hard way.

Chapter 20

The Fighting Intensifies

There was an intensification of terrorist activity from the end of 1984 and the beginning of 1985 onwards. This was obviously because of the logistical support given to the terrorists by India to carry out attacks in Sri Lanka. On 19 January 1985, TELO blew up the Colombo-Jaffna train, the *Yal Devi* with a cluster of bombs buried on the tracks near Murukandy killing 48 of whom 28 were army personnel and injuring another 50 people. The scale of the blast was unprecedented. Around 1000 kilos of gelignite had been used in nine improvised explosive devices, eight of which had gone off. One unexploded bomb that was recovered weighed 100 kilos. Eleven carriages were completely destroyed.

Even as late as the mid 1980s Sri Lanka was surprisingly ill-equipped to fight terrorism. In late 1984, president J.R.Jayewardene's son Ravi Jayewardene had come to China Bay in Trincomalee while on his rounds to distribute shotguns to the villagers in the east that had come under terrorist threat. Harsha Abeywickrema then a young flight lieutenant in the air force happened to be a classmate of Ravi Jayewardene's eldest son Pradeep who had accompanied his father. Abeywickrema told Pradeep to tell his grandfather the president, that the air force does not have a single aircraft that had guns fitted onto them and that they were using small arms to fire on the enemy from inside aircraft. In short the air force was still nothing more than an airborne attacking platform for foot soldiers!

The air force was helpless to stop the terrorist boats that crossed the Palk Straits between Sri Lanka and India because small arms fired from inside a fixed wing aircraft or helicopter were not accurate enough to hit a moving target below them. It was after Abeywickrema's appeal that six SIAI Marchettis had been bought for the air force in mid-July 1985. This was an entry-level ground attack aircraft, below what was really needed in Sri Lanka. The SIAI Marchetti is a single engine aircraft which could carry two .50 gun pods with around 150 rounds each, and two rocket pods which could carry seven rockets each, or two small bombs of around 75 kg each. Everything with regard to the war was from the very beginning, pegged at the lowest common denominator because of financial constraints on the one hand, and due to an underestimation of the terrorist problem on the other. The military leaders themselves were not convinced about how much firepower was required to combat the terrorist threat.

The Bell 212 helicopters purchased in January 1984, were also fitted with forward firing guns and rocket pods and used as gunships. The Bell Jet Rangers that the air force already had were single engine helicopters while the new Bell 212s were twin engine choppers. The passenger load was also different with the Bell 212s being able to accommodate 10 passengers as against only 4 in the Jet Rangers. The Bell 212 was a utility helicopter which could be used for many purposes. The Jet Ranger however was mainly a training helicopter. Two rocket pods with 14 rockets and two .50 gun pods with 260 rounds of ammunition were fitted onto the Bell 212s in addition to two .50 general purpose machine guns mounted on either side.

Initially chopper pilots would fly 1500 feet above the ground and give guidance to the ground troops below and do reconnaissance on enemy movements and concentrations and use the side gunners to fire at the enemy. That height was generally sufficient to avoid small arms fire coming from below. After the LTTE acquired .50 calibre weapons which had a range of 4500 feet, the choppers had to fly higher to avoid being hit. The main helicopter base was in Katunayake with choppers stationed in Palaly, Batticaloa, Vavuniya and Anuradhapura. As the hostilities escalated, the air traffic to the north also increased. From the four seater Cessna 337 that was originally used for these weekly flights to Jaffna, it became a 14 seater Herron, then a 28 seater DC Dakota and finally the 44 seater Avro. From one flight a week, it became a daily flight. By 1986 there were three daily flights to Palaly. At times fresh supplies like eggs and meat would also be transported on the planes to Jaffna in addition to taking passengers.

When no longer in use to transport passengers, the Cessna 337 which could stay airborne for about five hours was used to do coastal surveillance to prevent arms smuggling from India. This reconnaissance would be carried out from Palaly for around 8-9 hours a day. This aircraft had a small baggage hatch on the undercarriage and the last two seats could be removed to make room for one person to lie down with a T-56 assault rifle to fire on the high speed terrorist boats. A bigger gun could not be used because it would have been difficult to use inside the small plane. The gunner at the back of the Cessna 337 had to be constantly reminded not to shoot the rear wheel off in his excitement. Some boats were fired at in this manner but no boat was destroyed or even stopped. This plane would also report back to naval headquarters about the location of naval craft so that navy headquarters would be able to keep tabs on whether their patrol craft were where they were supposed to be, and as a result the Cessna 337 was known in the navy as the *kelama* (tale carrier).

It was on 23 January 1985 that the LTTE first mounted a rocket propelled grenade attack on the air force. Indeed that was the first RPG attack to take place anywhere in Sri Lanka. The DC Dakota troop transport plane had just taken off from Palaly, when the LTTE fired at it from the perimeter of the Palaly airport. The RPG hit the plane but did not explode and the plane made an emergency landing. That was the first time the Sri Lankan military saw an RPG and many did not recognize it for what it was. It was described by some airmen as an object that looked like 'the front part of an umbrella'.

The Gajaba Regiment which had returned to Saliyapura in mid-January 1985, was posted to Welioya in early February 1985. Thus this regiment which had just been withdrawn from one theatre of conflict, was assigned to yet another in what was to become a familiar pattern in the coming years. The task of the Gajaba battalion was now to secure the Welioya defences. New detachments were established in Kokkuthuduwai and Kokilai among other places. Lt Col Janaka Perera was the brigade commander of Welioya with his headquarters located in the new town of Janakapura established in the vicinity of the abandoned Dollar and Kent farms.

On 13 February 1985, barely days after it was established, the Kokilai detachment was attacked by the LTTE. This was the first attack ever launched by the terrorists with a view to overrunning an army camp. They had conducted raids on police stations in Annaicoddai and Chavakachcheri in 1981 and 1982 respectively, but this was the first time they had tried to overrun an army detachment. The attack began at around 2.00 am and continued till dawn. It was successfully repulsed and Lt Shantha Wijesinghe who commanded the detachment at the time of the attack, was promoted to Captain in a field promotion – the first ever such promotion in Sri Lankan history. There was only one platoon in the Kokilai camp - about 30 men, but they were able to kill 14 LTTE attackers. The LTTE used rocket propelled grenades (RPGs) to attack the camp. At that time, the army did not have RPGs. The LTTE attacking party had been well equipped with even night vision goggles.

Despite confrontations between the army and the terrorists, the ordinary people were not as antagonistic towards the army as one may expect. Soldiers would distribute the ginger biscuits and toffees they get with their ration packs to children at the checkpoints outside their camps. At that time a checkpoint still did not denote a bunker but just two barrels placed on the side of the road. Patrols would also go along the roads on foot. The people had ways of warning the soldiers of possible terrorist attacks. At times the warning came direct with someone whispering in their ears of a possible landmine or small arms attack.

When foot patrols moved along the roads, the people would often give the soldiers water or king coconut water or whatever drink was available. On days that an attack was imminent, the people would not give the foot patrols water and this was a warning which the soldiers had learnt to recognize. If no water was being offered they can expect to be shot at any moment. Another warning that the soldiers learnt to recognize was if children did not turn up at their checkpoints for sweets or if people were seen to be avoiding certain areas. It was mainly the older and more conservative people or the children who would show friendliness towards the troops. Sometimes people would tell the troops that the dogs were heard barking in the night and that there would have been some kind of LTTE activity in the night like burying a landmine. When such warnings were received, they would search the area and something would often be found.

A very significant development during this period was that the five Tamil terrorist organizations LTTE, PLOTE, TELO, EPRLF and EROS formed an umbrella group styled Eelam National Liberation Front (ENLF) on 10 April 1985. The very next day, the Jaffna police station was attacked leaving four policemen dead. News reports on this attack were censored by the government and the newspapers could not publish the real details. The LTTE would claim that the policemen retreated into the Jaffna Fort and that they destroyed the buildings and took away 35 sub-machine guns, 80 automatic weapons, 175 grenades, 100 tear gas shells, 50 revolvers and a huge quantity of ammunition.

On 5 May 1985, the EPRLF made an abortive attempt to overrun the Karainagar naval base with an improvised armour plated bulldozer to crash through the naval defences. They were forced to withdraw under a withering counterattack which killed 22 of their cadres including a woman cadre by the name of 'Sôba' - the first female terrorist to be killed. Aware of the fear they had instilled in the minds of the Sinhala public with their attack on the Kent and Dollar farms and in Nayaru and Kokilai some months earlier, the LTTE outdid themselves by carrying out yet another atrocity. On 14 May 1985, an LTTE hit team dressed in army uniforms and headed by Victor, their Mannar leader attacked pilgrims in Anuradhapura killing 146 and injuring another 85. These were 'shock and awe' atrocities to cow everybody into submission by the sheer scale and brutality of the massacres. Gōta's company was in Mannar at the time and on the morning of the massacre, he was airborne in a helicopter flying to Anuradhapura for official work when he heard about the incident.

In 1985, Lt Colonel Wimalaratne went to Israel to follow a course in counter-insurgency operations and rehabilitation. After he returned, a counter-terrorism training programme for all the non commissioned officers in the army was held at the Saliyapura camp. Wimalaratne took leave of his responsibilities as commanding officer of the Gajaba Regiment to train 300 volunteers from various units in special operations in July 1985. This was the precursor of what would later become the elite Rapid Deployment Force (RDF) which in turn would become the Special Forces of the army. The training was conducted by the Pakistani Special Forces. The one-armed Brigadier Tariq Mohamed of the Pakistani army - a living legend in his own country - was in charge of training the troops at the Saliyapura camp.

Gōta had the opportunity to work with the Pakistani trainers. There were two teams working in three month rotations. This was another land mark in getting the army transformed into a professional fighting force. It was in fact the police that first began to receive specialized training from overseas instructors. This started with the police Special Task Force - the elite police paramilitary force created in 1983 by Ravi Jayewardene. Originally the idea was to give police officers military training and deploy them for VIP security duties – primarily the protection of president Jayewardene himself. Initially, about 60 serving police officers were given military training by the army. Subsequently retired SAS officers from Britain gave them further training. Apart from VIP security duties, a good part of the STF was traditionally deployed in the Batticaloa and Ampara districts.

In 1985, the Gajaba Regiment raised a third battalion with its headquarters in Vavuniya. In the meantime, terrorist attacks continued unrelentingly in the run up to the Thimpu talks brokered by India. On 12 May, 10 soldiers died in a shootout with terrorists during a cordon and search operation in Karativu in the Batticaloa district. There was another major shootout between the armed forces and the LTTE near the Manampitiya bridge in Polonnaruwa. In Eravur, a landmine attack and ambush left two police commandos dead. A Sinhala village in the Trincomalee district was attacked and five killed and dozens of houses burnt to the ground.

Chapter 21

The Thimpu Fiasco

The Indian brokered ceasefire of 18 June 1985, which preceded the Thimpu talks actually strengthened the terrorist movements rather than bringing about a settlement. In fact even before the ceasefire agreement was signed, the terrorist groups were expressing doubts about the usefulness of the proposed talks but they said in the same breath that they would abide by the ceasefire so as not to embarrass their benefactor India. By that time the terrorists were everywhere in the north and east, but they did not control any territory. It was because of this very ceasefire that the terrorists first began controlling territory. It was this ceasefire that taught Prabhakaran the importance of ceasefires in advancing the interests of the terrorists. From that time onwards, ceasefires became an integral part of LTTE strategy.

The ceasefire agreement of 18 June 1985, was an elaborate affair with four phases. In the first phase, the army was to carry out cordon and search operations only in the presence of a local magistrate or civil officials and in the final phase they were to cease all raids and search operations completely. The army at that time maintained a presence in Jaffna through its headquarters in Palaly and detachments stationed in other towns. The way they controlled terrorist activity was through cordon and search operations and to stop this was effectively to confine the army to barracks and to give the terrorists a free run of Jaffna to do as they pleased. It was from this point onwards that the army came to be restricted to just holding the area of their camp perimeter and nothing more. The terrorists made full use of the ceasefire to mine the roads extensively and to make movement outside virtually impossible. Even the main roads were now no longer secure.

Naval personnel going on leave from the Karainagar base went by boat to Kankesanthurei harbour and then by road to the air strip at Palaly after 1985. Gōta knew how genuine the government of the time was in trying to adhere to the ceasefire. Lalith Athulathmudali the national security minister had personally issued orders to the army that they were not under any circumstances to move out of their camps in the north and east.

When the talks between the Sri Lankan government and the Tamil groups began in Thimpu, the TULF was very keen to talk. The terrorist groups however were euphoric with the unity that had been achieved and were feeling invincible. On 8 July 1985, the very day the Thimpu talks began, the terrorist groups organized *hartals* in Jaffna and Vavuniya in opposition to the peace talks and youths staged demonstrations on the roads, shouting pro-Eelam slogans. The next day, there was a bomb attack in Jaffna near the Duriappah stadium. How determined the terrorist movements were to scuttle the Thimpu talks can be gauged from the fact that on 11 July 1985, an alert cop stumbled upon an attempt to assassinate president J.R.Jayewardene. At around 6.45 am, the policeman had seen some youths in a van parked near St Lucia's cathedral in Kotahena, Colombo. When he approached them thinking their behaviour suspicious, they had taken to their heels. But the policeman had managed to apprehend the driver.

One of the youths who had run away was caught by members of the public and handed over to the police. There was a huge bomb in the van with 120 kilos of gelignite wired and with a timer set to explode at 9.00 am. The captured terrorists had admitted to being members of EROS and the van bomb was to be positioned near the presidential secretariat in the old parliament building at Galle Face to explode when president J.R.Jayewardene's motorcade came in. Needless to say that the first round of the Thimpu talks ended inconclusively and the second round was fixed for 12 August.

The attitude of almost all Tamil delegates except the TULF at the Thimpu talks was that they did not have to settle for anything less than Eelam. India had clearly indicated that they were not for separation and Rajiv Gandhi had ruled out even federalism and had said that what had to be envisaged was devolution up to the point practiced in India. What the delegates thought was that in the course of time, India might eventually agree to a separate state for Tamils if they went on fighting. Hence the format in which the talks took place was that the head of the Sri Lankan delegation H.W.Jayewardene would read out various proposals and the Tamil delegates would find some reason to reject them saying that one thing or the other does not satisfy Tamil aspirations.

The whole episode was a charade meant to give the impression to the Indian government that the Tamil delegates were interested in a political solution but that it was the Sri Lankan government that was refusing to budge from their position. It was Varatharajah Perumal who formulated the famous 'Thimpu principles' to ensure that nothing would result from the talks. The idea was to put forward a set of principles to which the Sri Lankan government could never agree. They told the government to agree to these principles after which they could go on to the next phase. The Thimpu principles included the following:

1. Recognition of the Tamils of Sri Lanka as a distinct nationality.
2. Recognition of an identified Tamil homeland and the guarantee of its territorial integrity.
3. Recognition of the inalienable right of self-determination of the Tamil nation.

From this point onwards, the terrorists would use the 'Thimpu principles' as a stalling tactic whenever they were trying not to come to a settlement with the Sri Lankan government. A ceasefire was supposed to be in place but the violence was continuing with no let up. On 27 July 1985, the LTTE shot dead C.E.Anandarajah the principal of St John's College in Jaffna, a highly respected educationist and community figure in northern Tamil society. Later Prabhakaran would explain to the Indian journalist Anita Pratap why he killed Anandarajah. He accused Anandarajah of organising a cricket match between the armed forces and the boys of his school at a time when the Sri Lankan forces were 'arresting, killing and torturing Tamil youths and raping Tamil women'. The government was going to use the cricket match to portray to the world that the Tamil civilians had cordial relations with the armed forces and that the ethnic problem was something created by a handful of militants.

Terrorists attacked the Welikanda army camp on 6 August 1985. During this period, 200 employees of two state owned farms in the east fled their homes after receiving death threats, as did some Sinhala villagers in the Vavuniya district. On 11 August, five police personnel were killed in a bomb blast in Vavuniya town and in the reprisals that followed, 20 shops were burnt and nine persons killed. The next day, a seven kilo gelignite time bomb was discovered on the night mail train from Jaffna which had arrived at the Colombo Fort railway station. The train came in at 6.33 that morning, and an alert passenger had seen an unattended parcel and reported it. The parcel turned out to be a bomb timed to go off at 7.45 am, at the height of the morning rush hour. During this period, a landmine near the Vavuniya army camp killed 21 civilians and injured another 18. Twenty nine Sinhala villagers were massacred in Namalwatte in the Trincomalee district. Four soldiers were killed in a landmine blast in the east.

By 22 August the second round of the Thimpu talks had also collapsed. After the collapse of the talks, on 2 September 1985, two TULF politicians, C.Alalasundaram former MP for Kopay and V.Dharmalingam former MP for Manipay were abducted and killed. Dharmalingam's son Siddharthan was one of the PLOTE representatives in Thimpu. Siddharthan was in Madras convalescing after coming down with hepatitis when he heard that his father had been killed. Amirthalingam warned Siddharthan not to go to Jaffna for the funeral. Siddharthan had later found that TELO was behind both killings. The idea had apparently been to wipe out the TULF completely, leaving only the terrorist movements as the sole representatives of the Tamils.

At the end of June 1985, *The Hindu* had published an article quoting an ENLF press statement which had stressed that the TULF should now abdicate its assumed role as the legitimate representatives of the Tamil people. Thus the decision to end the political role of the TULF appears to have been taken collectively by all the terrorist groups. Only four of the former TULF parliamentarians V.Dharmalingam, C.Alalasundaram, T.Tureiratnam, and S.Rajendran were still living in Jaffna at the time.

After the Thimpu talks broke down and the Tamil delegates had returned to Madras, Rajiv Gandhi wanted to talk to the leaders of the Tamil terrorist groups again. But he was deliberately kept waiting by Prabhakaran, so much so that even the other terrorist leaders were beginning to feel uncomfortable. Sri Sabaratnam had told Padmanabha that it was very unfair to keep the prime minister of India waiting like this, and that if Prabhakaran was not coming, the other leaders should go and meet Gandhi. Padmanabha however argued that their strength was in unity and they should go together. After Prabhakaran finally agreed to see Gandhi, he along with the other terrorist leaders met M.G.Ramachandran to canvass support for their intransigence and after that, Prabhakaran, Balasingham, Padmanabha, Uma Maheswaran and others went to meet Rajiv Gandhi on 17 September 1985.

During his talks with the Sri Lankan Tamil groups Gandhi had told them that the 'Thimpu principles' were in fact a demand for separation. The Tamil delegates argued that this is not a demand for separation but 'an attempt to forge unity while accepting these principles'. To this Gandhi said if they are not demanding separation, they have to put forward their proposals and that will show whether they are demanding separation or not. The Tamil groups however said that it was the responsibility of the government to put forward a proposal accommodating the four Thimpu principles. Dixit who was present at these talks says that Prabhakaran had said that unless J.R.Jayewardene gives them a guarantee that Eelam will be granted within a given time frame, they were opposed to any half-way-house arrangements!

Thus was the world treated to the unedifying sight of the leader of the world's largest democracy, literally begging a group of stubborn terrorists to come back to the negotiating table. After the meeting with Gandhi failed, Romesh Bandari tried to make a last ditch attempt to salvage the talks. During a heated discussion with the terrorists, on 5 October 1985, N.Satyendra, a TELO delegate had shouted at Romesh Bandari "You buggers are trying to betray us!" Bandari was stunned. Amirthalingam apologized to him on behalf of all the others.

The government of India, thrashing about in an impotent rage, deported the outspoken N.Satyendra, Anton Balasingham and even C.Chandrahasan the son of S.J.V.Chelvanayagam. The weapons of all the groups in Tamil Nadu were confiscated. Dixit says that the Indian government was fed up with the intransigence of the Tamil groups by this time. It was after this that the Indian government started negotiating directly with the Sri Lankan government. They would have felt that there was no point in getting the Tamil groups involved. From this point onwards, Indian ministers P.Chidambaram and K.Natwar Singh became the delegates the Sri Lankan government spoke to.

The urgency of bringing about a settlement to the Tamil problem in Sri Lanka would have been impressed upon the Indian authorities because as the Tamil separatist struggle gathered momentum, LTTE propaganda began hinting at what Dixit referred to as the 'higher political purpose' of re-establishing a Tamil super-state reminiscent of the Cholan empire with the northern and eastern parts of Sri Lanka, the whole of Tamil Nadu, the Mauritius Islands, and parts of Indonesia, Malaysia and Singapore. The fact that hints at such a plan began emerging in LTTE propaganda material would have been a warning to India that Tamil separatism in Sri Lanka had gone far enough and had to be terminated before the contagion infected Tamil Nadu as well.

Chapter 22

A Deadly Ceasefire

It's still unclear as to what advanced the cause of terrorism more in this country - gunfire or ceasefire. Once the army lost their dominance in the Jaffna peninsula by being confined to barracks during the Thimpu peace talks, they never really regained the ground lost. When the Thimpu talks broke down the troops could not simply start again from where they had left off. They were besieged by the terrorist groups who were firing their home made mortars into the camps. In the beginning the improvised mortars had a range of about 500 meters and the perimeters of the military installations in the Jaffna peninsula were expanded to get out of LTTE mortar range. As the LTTE mortars improved, the perimeters also expanded creating the 'forward defence lines' that were to be fact of life in Sri Lanka for a quarter of a century.

Suresh Premachandran says that it was the EPRLF that had first developed improvised mortars in the mid 1980s, which the LTTE was to perfect later. The initial development of the improvised mortar had been done for the EPRLF by an agriculture graduate of the Peradeniya University and two individuals from Tamil Nadu. They had military catalogues and other literature which they had used to build the improvised mortar. All the necessary material was available in India and they had experimented for several months. On several occasions, the shells had exploded prematurely and even killed one person, but thereafter they had been able to turn out a fairly reliable product. Kittu, the LTTE's Jaffna leader had once complimented Premachandran on the EPRLF's technical ingenuity.

After the Thimpu talks, it became necessary to keep the army detachments in the Jaffna peninsula supplied by air. Gagan Bulathsinhala recalls having done 57 landings a day to pick up and drop off supplies or personnel from one point to another as a young flying officer during this period. Supplies and personnel were ferried from one location to another in just two Bell 212 helicopters stationed at Palaly each of which could carry a load of 700 kg. The camps in Elephant Pass, Mannar, Mankulam, Mulleitivu and Kilinochchi were kept supplied with one Bell 212 helicopter operating from Vavuniya.

There was a roster whereby each of the camps was kept supplied with a given number of helicopter loads of food or ammunition per day. Even these supply runs were more like combat missions, with the choppers coming under enemy small arms fire as they landed or took off. They would very often come back with bullet holes. There were even some emergency situations with fuel tanks being hit and choppers landing with fuel streaming out. Even the Palaly air base was not immune to enemy attack. On 23 January 1986, an Avro troop transport plane was shot at while trying to land.

* * * * *

On 27 September, 1985 Gōta was at the Saliyapura camp in Anuradhapura, which had married quarters and his wife was living with him in the camp. A few months earlier, in April 1985, he had been appointed the second in command of the 1st Gajaba Battalion. That night he was in his quarters when there was a knock on his door around midnight and a soldier informed him that the area commander wanted to talk to him as there was an attack in progress on the Mahavilachchiya police station. Gōta was told about the attack and asked to do something. Saliyapura was a rear headquarters, and all troops were deployed elsewhere and there were no soldiers in the camp. His battalion the 1st Gajaba was deployed in Batticaloa. But there were some new recruits who were being trained in the camp. Gōta had rounded up around 50 of those trainees and their instructors. It was about 40 kilometres to Mahavilachchiya from the Saliyapura camp along a badly maintained road.

As they approached the Mahavilachchiya police station, they saw many people who had come out on to the road upon hearing the sounds of the attack from the direction of the police station. By the time Gōta and his motley crew got to the police station the firing had ended and the attackers had withdrawn. Gōta guessed that they would have come from Mannar and would be withdrawing in the same direction though the Wilpattu jungles. Then an army sergeant who was attached to the Salaiyapura camp and was on leave in Mahavilachchiya, turned up at the police station. When Gōta said that he wanted to pursue the attackers, this sergeant said that he knows a route by which they could overtake them.

A stretch of jungle had been cleared to demarcate the border of the Wilpattu forest reserve. The sergeant suggested that they cut across to the Tantirimale temple and take a shortcut from there to the Wilpattu border. The sergeant was absolutely certain that the terrorists would have to pass a certain point to get to Mannar and that they should lay an ambush at that point. The party then went to the Tantirimale temple, parked their vehicles at the temple and walked through the jungle until they came to the cleared stretch of land which marked the border of the forest reserve. When Gōta examined the area, he found foot prints which indicated that the party had gone towards Mahavilachchiya but no marks that indicated that they had gone back to Mannar.

Then Gōta went along the road leading towards Mahavilachchiya looking for a good ambush site. By this time it was daylight. A sergeant-major who happened to be walking ahead of him was the first to spot the returning terrorists. He said to Gōta in a whisper, "Sir the tigers are coming!" There was a bend on the road and Gōta could see the terrorists approaching in the distance. He ordered all his men off the road and into the jungle and they waited for the terrorists to come into view. When the whole group was within range Gōta opened fire. The recruits who knew nothing about controlled fire, fired with reckless abandon and Gōta had to bellow at them to stop. At the end of it, There were seven dead bodies on the road. Some had managed to crawl into the jungle and a few managed to escape into the wilderness. One soldier had been killed in the confrontation. The dead bodies were taken to the Tantirimale temple. This incident hit the headlines of *The Island*.

Days later, two of the escapees had been caught by the villagers. They had got lost in the jungle and spent a day or two on top of trees and ultimately unable to bear the hunger and thirst had come out of the jungle and had been captured by the villagers. The captives had revealed that they had set off from Adampan in Mannar. Usually when terrorists launched attacks on a police or military installation, reinforcements would be rushed in to defend the position, but the attackers would not normally be pursued. The terrorists were therefore completely unprepared for Gōta's ambush. The significant thing was that this ambush had been carried out mainly by raw recruits led by a few experienced people.

Gōta became one of the first recipients of the gallantry awards to be presented by the then President J.R.Jayewardene. His name had been proposed for a medal by the Gajaba regiment but due to a mistake made by army headquarters, what he got was a commendation. Be that as it may Gōta was one of the first 15 soldiers to be given gallantry awards in the first such awards ceremony at the incipient stages of the war. The supreme irony was that at the very moment Gōta was fighting terrorists on behalf of the Sri Lankan state and even being commended for bravery in the line of duty by the president himself, his politician brother Mahinda was languishing behind bars at the Welikada jail having been arrested over an incident at the Mulkirigala by-election in September 1985 at which the eldest in the family Chamal was the candidate of the SLFP. Mahinda was exonerated of all charges later, but he was brought in handcuffs to their mother's funeral in October 1985. Gōta always saw the distinction between the state and the people on the one hand and politics and governments on the other. The fact that the incumbent government had imprisoned his brother and probably hastened the death of his mother did not distract Gōta from his duty to the state.

*　*　*　*　*

By the last quarter of 1985, hostilities between the government and the terrorists had returned to normal and were being conducted without any pretence of adhering to a ceasefire. On 30 October 1985, the Thondamanaru army camp came under attack for over two hours. A week later, two landmine attacks in Trincomalee and Batticaloa left seven policemen and three soldiers dead. By December the government announced that since the ceasefire had come into effect on 18 June 1985, there had been 1191 ceasefire violations with 368 murders and 257 abductions of which only about two dozen had returned and the others were believed to have been killed. The dead included 82 armed forces personnel.

A highlight of the post-Thimpu period was the LTTE's move to establish its hegemony over the Tamil separatist struggle. The relationship between the rival terrorist groups had always been uneasy at best. There were differences among the terrorist groups that had not been eliminated by their coming together to form the ENLF in April 1985. Besides, old wounds continued to fester and it was only a matter of time until it broke out onto the surface. So long as the

142

terrorists were carrying out hit and run attacks in a peninsula dominated by the security forces, no terrorist group could emerge supreme as they were all on the run. But from the time the troops were confined to their camps and the terrorists had a free run of the peninsula after the Thimpu talks, perhaps a war for hegemony over the vacated territory was inevitable.

Around the last quarter of 1985, problems emerged between TELO and the LTTE. Das, the Vadamarachchi leader of TELO had even banned the LTTE from entering the Nelliady town. At that time TELO had the upper hand. Das was a tough and recklessly brave man. TELO controlled the town of Nelliady and on one occasion when Mahattaya the LTTE's deputy leader was cycling along, he had been signalled to stop at a TELO checkpoint but he had ignored the call to stop. Das had stopped Mahattaya himself and said that this was TELO territory and that he could not do as he wanted. Then he had rapped Mahattaya on the head with his knuckles as a teacher would do to an errant schoolboy. When things were getting bad for the LTTE, Prabhakaran had gone to the Madras office of the EPRLF to meet Padmanabha. Varatharajah Perumal who had been there told Prabhakran that Padmanabha had gone out but would be back soon. Prabhakaran had waited for Padmanabha who had arrived after about 15-20 minutes. Prabhakaran had argued with Padmanabha that what TELO was doing was wrong and that this was not good for the Tamil cause and that there should be unity among the militant groups.

Thereupon, Padmanabha and Perumal had gone to Sri Sabaratnam's house – all the terrorist group leaders were living in India at that time – and tried to plead Prabhakaran's case. But Sabaratnam had been furious with Prabhakaran for trying to encourage some members of TELO to kill him. The conspirators had been caught by Sabaratnam's loyalists. Sabaratnam was of the view that the LTTE had to be finished off. Padmanabha had argued for about an hour with Sabaratnam and in the end, the latter had relented and told Padmanabha *"I will tell them to stop only because you want me to."* Even as he agreed to stop the fighting, Sabaratnam added *"But I still don't trust that fellow."* Professor K.Sivathamby and members of the Jaffna Citizens Committee also interceded to stop the fighting between TELO and the LTTE.

Chapter 23

The LTTE Gains Supremacy

Up to the beginning of 1986, the other terrorist groups and the LTTE were more or less on an equal footing. However, in early 1986, the LTTE got a consignment of arms from Lebanon which they had bought on the open market with the money provided by M.G.Ramachandran the chief minister of Tamil Nadu. Among these were assault rifles and sophisticated communication equipment as well as weapons like rocket propelled grenades, and light machine guns which other groups did not have. Even in the procurement of arms from outside, the LTTE was not the trail blazer. Earlier in 1985, PLOTE had brought a container load of weapons from South East Asia to the Madras port. At that time no terrorist group had the capacity to transfer cargo in mid sea to smaller boats, and the shipment was brought to India in the hope that they would be able to get the weapons across to Sri Lanka by boat, but the Indian customs seized the PLOTE arms shipment.

However, Ramachandran helped the LTTE to clear their shipment through the Indian customs. The LTTE now had better weapons and more ammunition than the other terrorist groups. In the meantime, hostilities between the terrorists and the security forces in the first few months of 1986 followed the usual pattern. There was sporadic mortar fire exchanged with the now penned in armed forces, and landmine attacks were carried out to restrict troop movements. The armed forces for their part occasionally sallied out of their camps to launch surprise attacks on terrorist positions. A landmine attack in Kantale killed 39 civilians and four soldiers. Eight irrigation workers were killed by terrorists in Namalwatte in Trincomalee. An improvised gelignite mine was found buried in the airstrip of the Palaly air base. A huge landmine in Kokuvil killed eight soldiers and opened up a large crater on the road. Relief parties that rushed to the scene were shot at.

None of these incidents in the ding dong battle between the terrorists and the armed forces were of a magnitude to change the course of the future. What would shape the future would be the internecine fighting between the terrorist groups themselves. In early March 1986, Das, the TELO leader for the Vadamarachchi area was killed by a rival TELO faction in a shootout in the canteen of the Jaffna hospital. The death of Das and the disunity in TELO gave Prabhakaran the opening he had been waiting for. But Sri Sabaratnam, the TELO leader was blissfully unaware of the gathering storm. Even in the fateful month of April 1986, what absorbed his attention was the fight with the Sri Lankan state. As late as mid-April, with only three more weeks to live, Sri Sabaratnam was quoted by *The Hindu* as saying that foreign shipping should not come into Sri Lankan waters because they had laid sea mines on the shipping lanes.

He was trying to choke Sri Lanka's very lifeline. With just days to D-day, on 24 April, TELO carried out an attack on the Anuradhapura oil storage facility. A petrol bowser that had come in from Jaffna had exploded inside the facility killing nine and causing extensive damage to the facility. It was on 29 April 1986, that the LTTE moved on TELO. Pitched battles erupted between the two organisations in the Nallur area. On 1 May the Kalyankadu headquarters of TELO was completely destroyed and the LTTE put up posters announcing that TELO cadres should surrender if they valued their lives.

The entire LTTE had been mobilized for this operation against TELO. Large numbers of cadres had assembled in Kalyankadu before launching the attack on the TELO headquarters. Since the army was confined to their barracks, and fighting a defensive battle to hold just the camp perimeter, TELO had not fortified their headquarters and had only a few weapons at hand. The LTTE had the advantage of surprise and TELO was completely outgunned. After the attacks commenced, frantic attempts had been made by TELO to get arms from the EPRLF, but by that time, it was too late. TELO leader Sri Sabaratnam was killed on 7 May 1986. The EPRLF held public protests against these killings. Not to be outdone, the LTTE made the case that TELO was an organisation of anti-social types and displayed

145

hundreds of items they claimed had been stolen from the public by TELO. Among the items displayed were cars, television sets and video players etcetera.

The government, trying to take advantage of the situation, made an announcement asking the embattled TELO cadres to seek refuge in the nearest security forces camp. LTTE terrorists took up position outside the Jaffna hospital to ensure that no injured TELO cadres received treatment. The most enduring image of this LTTE operation was of TELO cadres being hunted down, shot, doused with patrol and burnt in public in broad daylight in several places in the Jaffna peninsula. Later, the authors of *The Broken Palmyra* were to say that the LTTE was now practicing on the Tamils the same 'shock and awe' tactics that they practiced on the Sinhalese during the Anuradhapura massacre.

The government was not going to allow this internecine fighting among the terrorist movements in the north to go unexploited. Speaking in parliament in 20 May 1986, two weeks after the killing of Sri Sabaratnam and the destruction of TELO, the minister of national security Lalith Athulathmudali explained that the terrorists were firing mortars and RPGs into the army camps and that this was not a situation that could be allowed to continue. He explained how the Karinagar Naval base had been surrounded by the LTTE and they were laying sea mines off Kayts and the army had to storm into Kayts to secure the island, because it was important for the security of the Karainagar naval base.

At that time, offensive operations to retake territory dominated by the terrorists was new to the army. Back in January that year, the government had mooted the idea of declaring a one kilometre security zone around army camps and they tried to make use of the internecine fighting between terrorist movements to expand the area held by the army. The Indians opposed this move on the grounds that the offensive was causing civilian casualties. Troops broke out of the Jaffna Fort and established a beach-head on Mandaitivu Island, providing a safe means of ferrying troops and supplies into the Jaffna Fort. Up to that time, helicopters landing inside the fort regularly came under fire by terrorists. The army also succeeded in widening the perimeters of its camps in Thondamanaru and Velvettithurai. The destruction of TELO had in fact created a temporary manpower crisis for the terrorist groups which the army fully exploited.

In mid-July 1986, the Gajaba Regiment was once again posted to Jaffna and they would remain there until the end of the Vadamarachchi operation in July 1987. Gōta was in Palaly with

146

Brigadier Wimalaratne. Because of increased terrorist activity, it was now no longer possible for a single battalion to hold the entire northern province. The Jaffna peninsula was now being held by two battalions, the 4th Sinha and the 1st Gajaba. There were Gajaba detachments in Velvettiturei, Point Pedro and Thondamanaru and Sinha detachments in Jaffna Fort and the Telecom Complex, Navatkuli, and the Kankesanthurei harbour. After having left Jaffna in January 1985, the Gajaba regiment had been mostly in Welioya with a short stint in Batticaloa as well. They had been out of Jaffna for eighteen months and they were now returning to a radically changed situation. At the time the Gajaba Regiment took over, the Gemunu Watch was garrisoning Jaffna and they were confined to the camps. Even the food was being airlifted to these camps by helicopter. The limited operations to expand the perimeter of the camps that had been launched in May 1986 had not changed the situation much.

The situation was such that when Gajaba troops were inducted into the Velvettiturei camp, this had to be done by sea and air. They had to literally fight their way in, as the LTTE had surrounded the camp. The soldiers in the Velvettiturei camp had been eating canned food because they were not able to go into the kitchen to cook. There were at that time no high security zones around the camps. There was the camp perimeter and the LTTE was right outside. The camps too were small, extending only a few hundred meters on either side. The troops could not even look out of the camp because any exposure risked a sniper's bullet. After the Gajaba regiment was posted to Jaffna, one of the issues they had to deal with was the state of siege faced by the Karainagar naval base. The Karainagar base at that time covered an area of about 1500 by 1500 meters and was manned by about 300 naval personnel.

Mortar attacks on the camp were commonplace. Those in the detachment did not sleep in the night till after 1.00 am. They'd stay up but without talking. Everybody would play scrabble or chess without talking and all communication was by hand signals. When a mortar is fired it gives off a popping sound and that gives them a few seconds to dive into the bunkers. The commander of the Karainagar naval detachment asked Col. Wimalaratne to help them expand the defence lines so that the LTTE would not be able to come within mortar range. One day, Wimalaratne and Gōta had gone to Karainagar to discuss the operation and Wasantha Karannagoda who was then a middle ranking naval officer, had accompanied them with 30 naval ratings on a reconnaissance mission outside the base.

About 200 meters away from the Karainagar base was a *Gamudawa* housing project. When they approached the housing project, the LTTE had started firing at them from three directions and the reconnaissance party was pinned down. They had to call for a helicopter gunship to fire rockets at the enemy to enable them to withdraw. During this time the Joint Operations Commander was Cyril Ranatunga. On one occasion, he came to Palaly and wanted to visit Jaffna Fort. It was Gōta who escorted him from Palaly to Jaffna Fort. The helicopter they were in landed in Mandativu and they came over the Pannai causeway into the Jaffna Fort. When Ranatunga and Gōta were in the Telecom building, an RPG was fired at one of the army bunkers by the LTTE who knew that some dignitary had arrived from Colombo and they wanted to send the visitor a message.

Lt Col Wimalaratne decided that this situation of being besieged and constantly watched by the enemy cannot be allowed to continue. He ordered limited operations to clear the vicinity of the camps. In one such operation, the detachment that held Velvettiturei sent two platoons to fight their way to the Thondamanaru detachment which lay to the south. Lt Shavendra Silva was one of the two platoon commanders involved in that limited operation.

One would think that with the terrorist movements killing one another, attacks on the state would cease at least for a while. On the contrary, there was an intensification of terrorist attacks. It was almost as if some third party was determined not to let the Sri Lankan government reap the benefit of the infighting among terrorists. It was on 3 May 1986, at the height of the LTTE-TELO clashes in the north that a Tri-Star jet belonging to Airlanka was blown up on the tarmac of the Katunayake international airport. The massive blast broke the plane in two, killing 23 and injuring scores of others. That morning, Lalith Athulathmudali had just commenced a conference with Indian ministers Natwar Singh and P.Chidambaram at the ministry of national security when he got a phone call informing him of the incident. A furious Athulathmudali had told the Indian ministers, that this was the work of RAW to bring pressure on the Sri Lankan government. Four days later, a time bomb went off in the Central Telegraph Office in Colombo Fort killing 11 and injuring over 130.

The main suspect in the Central Telegraph Office bomb case, a member of EROS named Neranjan was captured later by the CID. He revealed that he placed the bomb inside the CTO and watched from a distance as it exploded. When he saw injured people being taken to hospital, his conscience was disturbed and he had even gone to the hospital to donate blood. The police checked whether this story was true and they found from the Blood Bank records that he had indeed donated blood on that day. Later Neranjan was released at the request of the Indian government which proved beyond any doubt that the Indian intelligence agencies had a direct hand in planning and executing the terrorist attacks that took place in Colombo in the mid-1980s.

These were followed by attacks on similar soft targets. The Muslim village of Sinnakinniya in the Trincomalee district was attacked and 78 shops, and a dozen houses were burnt while five Muslims were killed. The Sinhala village of Mahadivulwewa also in the Trincomalee district was attacked leaving 20 villagers dead and 16 injured. A bomb in a lorry that had brought in empty bottles from the north destroyed the Elephant House soft drink bottling plant in Slave Island, Colombo killing eight employees and injuring over 100. The internecine fighting had depleted the number of terrorists available for attacks on the security forces and the kind of operations launched during this period were ones that did not need much manpower. Even though TELO had been decimated, EPRLF and PLOTE would continue to function until the end of 1986.

Bomb blasts and civilian massacres continued. Sixteen civilians were killed in the Trincomalee district. In Gomarankadawela in the Trincomalee district, 645 families out of 739 had left the area and ten villages lay completely depopulated. A bomb went off in the central bus station in Vavuniya killing 4 and injuring 19. The more noteworthy attacks during this period included a bus bomb in Vavuniya which killed 30 civilians, an attack on a Sinhala village in Medirigiriya where 20 persons were killed and an attack in Kattankudy that left 20 Muslims dead.

There were also landmine attacks in Vavuniya, Vakarai, Ampara and other places which left more than two dozen security forces personnel dead. In early November 1986, the LTTE moved against PLOTE. After PLOTE gave up virtually without a fight, the LTTE turned on the EPRLF in December 1986. By mid-December, 28 EPRLF camps along with weapons like mortars had fallen to the LTTE. Kumaran Pathmanathan, the LTTE's chief arms procurer says that there were certain factors that gave the LTTE an advantage over all other groups. The money given by M.G.Ramachandran and the arms shipment they got from Lebanon was one factor. Apart from that, the LTTE was smaller, better disciplined, and each individual member was better armed than members of other groups.

Because it didn't do mass recruitment like the other groups, its financial resources were not overstretched and the whole organization was on a sound and sustainable footing. Prabhakaran had openly expressed his disdain for the recruitment policies of his rivals and always held that numbers should be increased only if sufficient weapons and other logistical back up was available. So the LTTE ended the year 1986 as the sole terrorist group in the north and east. The only low point for the LTTE during the year 1986 was the death of Victor, their Mannar leader and the 'butcher of Anuradhapura' in an army offensive in Adampan on 13 October 1986.

India Led by the Nose

The main reason why the other terrorist groups simply dissolved in the face of the LTTE onslaught was that none of them were led by fighters. Sri Sabaratnam is described by those who knew him, as 'a very nice man'. He was not a fighting type. One of his bodyguards in fact said that he had never seen Sabaratnam carrying a gun. Much the same could be said about V.Balakumar, the leader of EROS, R.Padmanabha the leader of EPRLF and Uma Maheswaran of PLOTE as well. Kumaran Pathmanathan says perhaps with much justification, that of the early Tamil militant leaders, only Prabhakaran had the right frame of mind to lead a terrorist movement. Even as far back as 1984, Prabhakaran had a huge collection of books on guerrilla warfare and terrorism as well as detailed maps of Sri Lanka and he was very serious about what he was doing. If someone coming from overseas asked him what he wanted, he would ask for a book on war, or for issues of *Jane's Defence Weekly*.

In contrast to Prabhakaran says Pathmanathan, Sabaratnam for example would have been happy with a shirt as a gift. When the present writer spoke to Varatharajah Perumal about the fighting qualities of the non-LTTE militant leaders, he explained that in the army, one becomes a commander only after having served in a junior capacity on the field, but that in the militant movements, the commanders were not battle hardened individuals who had risen from the bottom and that they did not have the necessary experience.

In an interview with N.Ram of *The Hindu*, soon after the LTTE became the only Tamil terrorist group operating in the north, Prabhakaran said that the state expected them to be weaker after the other terrorist movements had been destroyed but that on the contrary, the Tamil separatist movement was now stronger than ever. Prabhakaran's claim was that the LTTE successfully resisted the army push against them after May 1986 and that this increased the support that the people had for them. In September 1986, Prabhakaran in another interview with Ram, exulted that the army was now so much under siege in Jaffna that the army camp in Thondamanaru had appealed to the LTTE through the Citizens Committee of the area not to cut off their water supply. In Jaffna too, the army had been communicating directly with LTTE and asking for basic supplies like firewood, which the LTTE had graciously allowed.

The LTTE engaged in a clever manoeuvre at this time, mainly with a view to pacifying the Indian government after the massacre of TELO. The Sri Lankan government had come up with a new set of proposals which was given to the Tamil groups by Natwar Singh and M.G.Ramachandran. The agreement reached between the EPRLF and the LTTE was that the Sri Lanka government's proposals would be rejected. But the LTTE played a more sophisticated game. Instead of opposing the proposals outright, they said that 'if the proposals meet their aspirations' they will be willing to accept it. By this time, the LTTE had learnt the art of making the Indians hang on their every word. Even an offhand indication that they 'may be' willing to consider a proposal was enough to send the Indian mediators into paroxysms of joy.

This had the desired effect and the increasingly desperate Indian government began to talk to Prabhakaran and only him. By this time, the Indians had realized that the TULF was a dead letter and that only Prabhakaran mattered. It was from this point onwards that the LTTE began making the claim that they were the sole representatives of the Tamil people and that this had been recognized by the Indian government as well. By a combination of ratcheting up tensions in Sri Lanka, provoking more confrontations and getting more refugees into India, The LTTE managed to get off scot free after killing off all other Tamil terrorist groups, especially those that were close to India.

Despite the demonstration of Tamil terrorist intransigence in Thimpu, the Indians had not learnt anything from what they had experienced. They thought they could still get the LTTE to agree to a settlement if they could wring more out of the Sri Lankan government. There was also the problem that the Indian government had got used to thinking of the Sri Lankan government as the party that was in the wrong. The most important thing however was that the original reasons that had motivated the Indians to foster terrorism in Sri Lanka, the Westward tilt in Sri Lankan foreign relations and Sri Lanka's friendliness with countries that India was not comfortable with, were still unresolved. Hence the year 1986 saw the ratcheting up of tensions between the two countries.

On 27 February 1986, the Indian external affairs minister B.R.Baghat told the *Lok Sabha* that the number of refugees from Sri Lanka had swelled to 125,000 and that around 7000 to 8000 people had been killed in the north - some of whom had been harvesting their crops. For the first time, he described what was happening in Sri Lanka as 'genocide'. The Sri Lankan government reacted strongly to such statements. In a hard hitting speech in parliament on 4 March 1986, Merrill Kariyawasam, a parliamentarian who was especially close to J.R.Jayewardene, accused both the Indian central government and Tamil Nadu of allowing freedom of movement to terrorists on Indian soil and providing funding, arms, ammunition, military training, and even travel documents for terrorists to travel outside India. Most significantly, he also accused India of providing professional direction for terrorist operations on Sri Lankan soil.

In what can be described as the lowest point in Indo-Lanka relations ever, on 5 March 1986, the Indian government made a formal complaint to the UN Commission on Human Rights in Geneva, about the violation of the rights of the Tamil minority in Sri Lanka.

India was now doing the talking on behalf of the Tamils of Sri Lanka. This approach was typified by the December 19th (1986) proposals which emerged from talks between president J.R.Jayewardene and the two Indian ministers P.Chidambaram and K. Natwar Singh. It was through these proposals that the basic contours of a 'political solution' were worked out - such as a provincial councils system, the merger of the northern and eastern provinces, etcetera. As they lost control over the Tamil terrorist movement in Sri Lanka, the Indians erroneously believed that by working out a package that would meet 'Tamil aspirations', they would be able to counter the rise of the LTTE. Hence we saw the phenomenon where the more the LTTE strengthened itself, the more pressure the Indian government put on the Sri Lankan government to work out a 'political solution'.

* * * * *

By about 1986, the LTTE set up the sea tiger unit. Up to this time, they had been using fast boats and dinghies to ferry men and material between India and Sri Lanka. But after 1986, the scope of these operations would expand enormously, culminating in the setting up of an international arms supply network and an offensive capability on the sea that would place enormous strain on the Sri Lanka navy. When Wasantha Karannagoda joined the Sri Lanka navy in 1971, it had only one ocean going vessel, a frigate called the *Gajabahu* and several patrol craft that had been acquired in the late 1960s. The navy got five fast gun boats from China after the 1971 JVP insurgency.

In 1975, five Cheverton inshore patrol craft were acquired from Britain and Colombo Dockyard Ltd, built six 20 meter coastal patrol craft and two 40 meter offshore patrol vessels to add to the fleet. In 1980, two more 'Shanghai class' fast gun boats were acquired from China. This was the Sri Lanka Navy when the challenge posed by the Tamil terrorist groups came up from the early 1980s onwards. Sri Lanka's navy was ill-equipped to meet the challenge posed by the terrorist boats. In the 1970s the role of the navy had been confined mainly to anti smuggling operations, preventing illegal fishing in Sri Lankan waters, and preventing illegal immigration. The gunboats could not go deep into sea and the maximum range they operated in was 100 km.

In the late 1970s and early 1980s, the terrorists never confronted the navy on the sea, and they always tried to make a get away when accosted. The naval gunboats had high calibre guns and their firepower on the sea was much greater, but the speed of the terrorist boats was a problem faced by the navy. Around April 1984, a naval surveillance zone was established from Mannar in the west, to Chundikulam in the east. All the available boats of the navy were deployed in that area. Soon after this surveillance zone was established, the Sri Lanka navy experienced their first sea battle . On 21 April 1984, Lt Somatilleke Dissanayake was in charge of a Cheverton inshore patrol craft with eight other crew members. That night they were patrolling off Velvettiturei at around 9.00 pm when they noticed a boat on the sea. Fishing had been banned and there was not supposed to be any movement on the seas. The sea was rough at that moment and was to the advantage of the Cheverton rather than the boats used by the terrorists.

At that time, except for the large gun boats, none of the naval craft were equipped with fixed guns. All the guns available on the Cheverton were hand held weapons, which included a 7.62 calibre Bren gun and several .303 rifles. Even the searchlight was manually operated. With this searchlight Dissanayake was able to see that the suspicious craft was a terrorist boat full of men which was moving towards India. Warning shots were not able to stop them. However, because of the rough seas and a full load, the terrorist boat could not travel at full speed and the much slower Cheverton was able to draw close and start firing at it. The terrorists fired back. This was the first naval battle that the Sri Lankan navy had ever engaged in. At one point the two boats were touching one another as they fired small arms at one another at close range in the darkness.

It had taken about one and a half hours to get the terrorist boat to stop and by that time most of its occupants were dead. The boat sank shortly afterward and four survivors were rescued by the navy and handed over to the Talaimannar police. This was a batch of recruits being taken to India for training. They had been accompanied by two senior LTTE cadres who had died in the confrontation and the recruits had been left to fend for themselves. Over the next two and a half decades until the end of the war, the Sri Lanka navy would have well over 200 confrontations with the terrorists.

Mainly to address the issue of speed, two Dvora fast attack craft were bought from Israel in 1985. The Dvoras combined firepower with speed. Over the years, more of these boats were bought and the Dvoras and similar fast attack craft would become the backbone of the navy. Another problem that the navy faced in the early days was that terrorist sea movements took place mostly under cover of darkness and the navy did not have sophisticated radar or night vision equipment. In the mid-1980s the navy's night vision equipment was limited to illuminator flares and searchlights. One reason why so few terrorist boats were apprehended or destroyed was because of their ability to blend into the darkness. It was only towards the late eighties that night vision binoculars were introduced.

After the fast attack craft were brought in, a problem that the navy encountered was that the facilities for the fast attack craft were available only in Trincomalee in the east and the extra distance that had to be travelled to get to the main theatre of surveillance – the Palk Straits – reduced the endurance of the craft at sea, as no refuelling and resupplying was available on the western coast. To make the patrolling of the Palk Straits more efficient, six merchant vessels were converted into 'command and surveillance' ships to be used by the smaller fast attack craft for logistical support and rest and recreation for the crews. These surveillance and command ships were also equipped with radars to detect movement of terrorist boats. The fast attack craft and 22 foot dinghies with 75 horse power out board motors were used with these surveillance and command ships as 'pouncers'. For a while this arrangement proved to be relatively successful even though the navy was never able to halt terrorist movements between India and Sri Lanka.

Chapter 25

Countdown to July 1987

From late 1986 onwards, on another initiative taken by Col Wimalaratne, Israeli instructors were brought in to train troops in close quarter combat in Maduruoya where a close quarter firing range had been constructed for the purpose. Fighting in the heavily built up areas of the Jaffna peninsula entailed that kind of warfare. Gōta was among the officers given this specialized training. In the meantime, the expansion of the area held by military installations continued into 1987. The military had little choice in the matter. On 5 March 1987, a Chinese built Y-12 transport plane coming into Palaly came under small arms fire and landed with bullet holes in the fuselage. Despite all the perimeter expansion that had been going on since May 1986, even the Palaly airstrip was still within small arms range of the LTTE.

On 8 January 1987, troops moved out of the Jaffna Fort and took over the adjoining Telecommunications department complex which was vital to the security of the fort. A massive operation to clean up Kokkadicholai in the Batticaloa district was launched by the STF on 28 January following a landmine attack that killed 12 police commandos. On 10 February, a limited operation was also launched in Adampan and the Madhu church area in the Mannar district against LTTE concentrations by Brigadier Denzil Kobbekaduwa. During these limited military offensives, India kept calling for a halt to the hostilities with Rajiv Gandhi himself writing to J.R.Jayewardene, expressing his concern. President J.R.Jayewardene told the Indians on 1 March 1987 that the military operations will stop if the terrorism stops.

India deliberately overlooked the fact that terrorist attacks were taking place on a daily basis all over Sri Lanka and that the military operations were a reaction to such incidents. During the first few months of 1987, eight soldiers were killed in a confrontation in Kilinochchi and two soldiers were killed and six injured in a landmine attack in Talaimannar. The Oddusudan police station was attacked on 20 April and two policemen killed in a gun battle that raged from midnight till dawn. The first half of 1987 also saw a series of terrorist attacks on civilians and civilian targets. On 15 January 1987, a major disaster in Colombo was averted when two terrorists believed to be members of EROS were caught in the vicinity of the Kolonnawa oil refinery with a bomb containing 20 kilos of C-4 explosives which they were trying to plant in a bowser going into the oil refinery complex. They were detected in the nick of time by two alert policemen.

Three days later, a similar time bomb exploded on a bus in Badulla killing 7 and injuring 57. On 25 January, a time bomb in a briefcase was discovered in an office building on Canal Row, Colombo Fort, in close proximity to President's House. On 4 February, 12 Sinhala civilians were killed and 14 injured in a village in the Ampara district by LTTE death squads. Over 300 families fled the area following this massacre. Four days later, 28 village folk were killed in Arantalawa, also in the Ampara district. On 7 March, a landmine explosion killed 17 civilians in Medawachchiya. This was followed by the killing of 26 civilians in Serunewa in the Anuradhapura district. The worst atrocity during this period was the Aluthoya massacre of 19 April 1987 in the Trincomalee district which left 120 Sinhala civilians dead. The very next day, Jayanthipura, another village in the Trincomalee district was attacked and 18 civilians killed. The day after that, on 21 April 1987 came the car bomb in Pettah, Colombo which claimed the lives of 111 people.

This was an intensification of hostilities the likes of which Sri Lanka had never seen before. In Jaffna, apart from the usual lamp post killings, on 14 February 1987 there was the Navatkuli bowser bomb which went off prematurely killing 14 LTTE terrorists along with about 46 Tamil civilians. The bowser bomb had been meant for the Navatkuli army detachment. Then in early April 1987 were the reprisal killings in Jaffna for the grenade attack on Kittu which claimed the lives of at least 150 members of the EPRLF and PLOTE.

During this period, the LTTE tried to overrun some army detachments in the Jaffna peninsula. By the beginning of 1987, the various detachments in the Jaffna Peninsula were manned by company strength contingents i.e. 80 to 100 men. The Jaffna Fort in the heart of Jaffna town was manned by two companies of the 4th Sinha Regiment. Since the Jaffna Fort was surrounded by the LTTE and there was no supply route by land, the 4th Sinha also dominated Mandativu Island 3 km off the Jaffna coast. Helicopters landed on Mandativu and it was through the Pannai causeway that both personnel and supplies reached the Jaffna Fort. Adjoining the Jaffna Fort was the government owned Jaffna Telecommunications complex which housed the telephone exchange.

This telecommunications facility was also taken over by the army because it provided cover for the vital causeway that functioned as the supply route to the Jaffna Fort. Supplies were brought from the Karainagar naval base along the causeway linking Karainagar, Kayts and Mandativu islands and movement was mostly at night. Even the causeway was not safe. If the army lost the Telecom building, they would lose the fort as well. The total area held including the Jaffna Fort and the Telecom building would have been around 1½ by 2 ½ kilometres. Civilians working in the telecommunications facility would come in the morning for work as usual and return home in the evening.

In the early hours of 23 March 1987, the LTTE launched simultaneous attacks on Jaffna Fort, the Telecom building and the Mandativu and Kayts islands as well. The simultaneous attack on other installations was to deflect attention from the LTTE's real objective which was to secure the Telecom building outside the Jaffna Fort. As the diversionary attacks on other places proceeded, a small group of LTTE infiltrators made their way through an open sewage drain into the Telecom complex. Private Ananda Alwis of the 4th Sinha Battalion was in Mandativu when the attack started. The attackers who had infiltrated the Telecom complex had been wearing army uniforms and they managed to kill five or six soldiers before the army realised that there were attackers inside the defences. After the guard points had been silenced, many more LTTE infiltrators had made their way into the Telecom complex. By morning however, reinforcements from the Jaffna Fort had gone into the Telecom building and secured the area once again. About five soldiers lost their lives in this attack. Five soldiers and three policemen had also been abducted by the LTTE during the confrontation and were reported missing in action.

If the Telecom building had been taken over by the LTTE, it would have had catastrophic consequences for the detachment in the Jaffna Fort. Four years later, in 1990, we were to be given a demonstration of what would happen to the Jaffna Fort detachment without the Telecom complex to provide its supply route with cover. After the 1987 attack on the Telecom building, Tamil civilians stopped coming to work in the facility. Until the arrival of the IPKF, the Sri Lanka army kept the Jaffna telephone exchange working as best as they could, with personnel brought from Colombo.

On 2 April 1987, the LTTE launched an attack on the Velvettiturei army detachment which was then manned by a company of the 1st Gajaba Battalion. The previous day, the LTTE's Jaffna commander Kittu had been seriously injured in a grenade attack and the furious LTTE may have been trying to salvage their self respect by overrunning an army camp. There were about 120 troops under Captain Deepal Subasinghe in the Velvettiturei camp, along with a platoon of police personnel (about 25 men), under a Sub-Inspector. The police post was located inside the camp because by this time, a police station could not function outside and the few police personnel there were supposed to do whatever police work that came their way if arrests were made and investigations were necessary.

On the day of the attack the Assistant Superintendent of Police who was in charge of the police stations in the area visited the Velvettiturei camp and he stayed overnight. This camp was located about half a kilometre to the west of the Velvettiturei town on the coastal highway that linked Kankesanthurei and Velvettiturei. The camp extended about 350 meters from the beach to the interior and straddled both sides of the coastal highway, and the extent of the camp from west to east was about 400 meters. Four young platoon commanders, Chandana Weerakoon, Sahampathi Ekanayake, Mangala Wimalasuriya, and Samanatha Jayasundara, held the perimeter. Wimalasuriya held the western end which was much narrower than the rest of the camp.

The Velvettiturei camp was shaped like a truck with the part controlled by Wimalasuriya resembling the bonnet of a truck. Between 11.00 and 12.00 pm, on 2 April 1987, Second Lt Ekanayake who was manning the eastern end of the detachment, heard the sound of small arms fire. At first he thought it was just a few shots routinely fired by sentries at any suspicious movement. Then the firing increased in intensity, and there were a series of explosions. He realized then that this was a full scale attack. All other attacks on camps had come between 11.00 pm and 1.00 am and everybody in the camp was awake.

The LTTE usually attacked and withdrew before dawn under cover of darkness. That day in fact, the Velvettiturei detachment as well as all other camps along that stretch of the coast had been forewarned that they should expect an attack. The explosions Ekanayake heard was that of the LTTE using Banlglore torpedoes - improvised explosive devices which when exploded on the ground, sets off vibrations that makes the anti-personnel mines along its path go off. The LTTE was clearing a path through the minefields around the camp.

The LTTE rained 60mm mortars on the camp. Their own improvised 'Baba' mortars, came screaming through the darkness to explode sending shrapnel hurtling through the air. The LTTE attempt was to isolate the bonnet shaped western end from the rest of the camp and finish it off before fighting their way into the main part of the camp. The LTTE did manage to open up a breach in the defence line and the struggle then was to close the gap. One of Weerakoon's men was shot clean through the forehead and fell dead next to him during the battle that continued till dawn. At one stage, Wimalasuriya on the other side of the wedge that the LTTE had driven through the defence lines, was frantically asking for more ammunition.

The ammunition was sent into the beleaguered western sector along the beach. Supporting artillery fire came from the Thondamanaru camp located 3-4 kilometres away and the Point Pedro camp located about 8 km away. Despite the LTTE's barrage of mortar fire, they were unable to isolate the western end of the detachment and by 4.00 am, the attackers been beaten off and the breach in the defence line sealed. About four or five LTTE cadres were detected inside the camp and they too were speedily dispatched.

By morning, about 15 dead bodies of LTTE cadres lay strewn about both inside and outside the camp. Some had stepped on anti-personnel mines while retreating and were found lying outside the camp. The dead LTTE cadres were described as being well built men. Some of them had brought heavy machine guns for the attack. Among the captured firearms were RPG launchers and a gun with a double grip that the army had never seen before. Only two soldiers were killed, and four injured.

Less than three weeks later, on 22 April 1987, came a similar attack on the Kankesanthurei detachment which provided security for the harbour area. At that time the Kankesanthurei cement factory was still functioning and the army suspects that there would have been LTTE activists who had been working as labourers in the factory or on the jetty who would have studied the movements of the troops before the attack. There were only two police personnel and just one soldier at the check point on the road that went past the harbour.

160

On the night of the attack, the LTTE had forced civilians living in the vicinity of the harbour to leave quietly. The army failed to notice the absence of people mainly because everybody was behind closed doors in the night. The LTTE attacking party had assembled in an open spot close the road that led to the Kankesanthurei jetty, and engaged the sentries at the checkpoint. While this confrontation was going on, a lorry came up to the jetty and started firing at the sentries. The LTTE had converted the back of the lorry into a kind of mobile bunker with sand bags for the attackers to take cover. Sixteen 4th Sinha soldiers lost their lives in this attack, but the LTTE was beaten back, with reinforcements arriving by sea in dinghies from the main detachment which was located in the Harbour View Hotel. By morning the LTTE attackers had withdrawn. It was after these three consecutive attempts to overrun army camps that the army realized that such attempts would only increase in frequency and they had to push the LTTE out of the Jaffna peninsula or risk being pushed out themselves.

Chapter 26

The Vadamarachchi Operation

By late February 1987, the LTTE had got wind of the fact that the government was planning an all out offensive to clear the entire Jaffna peninsula. They thought the army would break out of Jaffna Fort and the Elephant Pass camp. To meet this anticipated offensive the LTTE adopted tactics that they would perfect a quarter of a century later, cutting anti-tank trenches, and building bunkers outside the Jaffna Fort and the Elephant Pass camp. According to the government's estimate there were around 2200 LTTE terrorists at that time. Col Wimalaratne had originally told his officers that they were going into Jaffna town and to prepare plans for the operation. The purpose was to deliberately allow the news to leak out so that the LTTE would be misled. The government also announced that the Jaffna hospital would be closed down.

The LTTE's deputy commander in Jaffna, Rahim, threatened to blow up the hospital along with the patients inside if the government tried to close it down. To the LTTE, the attempt to close the Jaffna hospital was a sure sign that the troops would break out of the Jaffna Fort. They assumed that the government was trying to minimize the risk of civilian casualties. So the LTTE wanted to see to it that the hospital remained right where it was as a buffer. Earlier on 9 March, retaliatory fire from the Jaffna Fort at LTTE mortar positions had resulted in 48 civilian deaths, and the LTTE knew that the army was wary about offensives in heavily populated areas. Brigadier Kobbekaduwa and Col. Wimalaratne who were to lead the operation kept their plans to themselves. Even Gōta was given the impression that the offensive was to be launched from Jaffna Fort. It was only at the last minute that they were told that they were not going into Jaffna town but into Vadamarachchi, on the other side of the Jaffna peninsula.

Four battalions were to take part in the operation, the two regular Gajaba Battalions and a battalion each from the Gemunu Watch and the SLLI. Gōta then a Major, commanded the 1st Gajaba Battalion during the Vadamarachchi operation because Colonel Wimalaratne assumed command over a brigade. When Gōta took over command of the battalion, he appointed as his adjutant Lt Shavendra Silva, an officer who many years later, would play a crucial role in ending the war. The Vadamarachchi operation was the first time that the Sri Lankan army operated in battle groups. One brigade was commanded by Kobbekaduwa and the other by Wimalaratne. The area that Gōta's battalion had to take over was the coastal stretch from Palaly to Pt Pedro, along the coast.

When the Vadamarachchi operation commenced on 26 May 1987, leaflets were air dropped over the area, giving civilians three hours to gather at designated civilian enters. Rajiv Gandhi issued a strong statement against the operation stating; *"Violence has already claimed thousands of lives in Sri Lanka. The military option is adding to the carnage. The horrific loss of innocent life of this magnitude is totally disproportionate to the avowed aim of exterminating the Tamil militant groups. The calculated, cold blooded slaughter of thousands of Sri Lankan citizens by their own government cannot promote a solution....While India was patiently and painstakingly working towards a political solution, it is apparent now that the Sri Lankan government was buying time for pursuing a military option. The present offensive is part of this plan..."*

The claim of working 'painstakingly' towards a political solution alluded to the talks that had been going on between the Chidambaram-Natwar Singh duo and the Sri Lankan government. Gandhi seemed oblivious to the fact that the Indian efforts at mediation had failed in 1985 because the terrorist groups did not want a solution and given the intensification of hostilities, the Sri Lankan government had no choice but to launch an all out military offensive. When the operation commenced, the 1st Gajaba battalion broke out of Thondamanaru and in the first two hours of the operation, there were heavy casualties due to anti-personnel mines and booby traps.

Each battalion had an armoured personnel carrier as a command vehicle for the operation. Gōta's command vehicle was destroyed about an hour into the operation in a massive land mine blast. The other battalion commanders thought that Gōta himself had been a victim of the blast, but he was on foot at the time and not in the command vehicle. Other than the casualties from booby traps and anti-personnel mines at the starting point in Thondamanaru, there was no real resistance by the LTTE. By the next day, Gōta's battalion had advanced 12 km. Anticipating tough resistance as he approached Velvettiturei, Gōta decided not to approach the town along the coastal road, but to make a detour, and attack from the landside.

As the 1st Gajaba Battalion made the detour and were approaching Velvettiturei, Gōta got a piece of bad news. A nephew of his, Prasanna Wickremasuriya who was a 2nd Lieutenant in his battalion, had been hit. As his battalion executed the detour, they met with some resistance and while trying to clear the area, Wickremesuriya was shot through the chest. The regimental sergeant major who knew Gōta's close relationship to the young officer informed him personally that his nephew was dead because he expected the injury to be fatal. Later Gōta got to know that Wickremasuriya was not dead and that he had been evacuated to Colombo. By the time the 1st Gajaba Battalion stood poised to take Velvettiturei town it was around 3.00 in the afternoon. The town was taken by around 8.30 pm.

At that time, Velvettiturei was the main command centre of the LTTE. After taking Velvettiturei in the night, tragedy struck the Gajaba regiment as Captain Shantha Wijesinghe, the defender of Kokilai, was killed the very next morning. In an inexplicable act of indiscretion, he clambered onto a parapet wall to survey the Pt Pedro side, and was promptly shot by an LTTE sniper. He was evacuated to Colombo, but the next night, Col Wimalaratne himself informed Gōta that Wijesinghe had died in hospital.

Throughout the Vadamarachchi operation there were air force men embedded with the army who would direct the aircraft in giving close air support. Instructions were given with the help of a map with small numbered circles close to one another called a 'bola map'and the same map would be with both the air force man moving with the ground troops, and the pilot. The airman on the ground would only have to give the pilot the number of the circle that needed to be attacked. Even if the LTTE was monitoring army radio communications, they would not know which area the number denoted. The numbering patterns would be changed every few days in case the map leaked to the LTTE. This was a system that the military would use right up to the end of the war a quarter of a century later.

From Velvettiturei, the 1st Gajaba Battalion, fought their way to Pt Pedro. It was to Pt Pedro that all other advancing columns converged and the victory photograph was taken under a tree in Pt Pedro town. By 28 May, the entire Velvettiturei, Uduppidy, and Pt Pedro areas had been cleared. This was as far as the army would get. While the Vadamarachchi operation was on, the Indian envoy J.N.Dixit had met president Jayewardene and bluntly told him that India will not stand by idly and allow Jaffna to fall into the hands of the army, and if the military operation continued, there could be unforeseen consequences. Asked to explain what these 'unforeseen consequences' could be, Dixit had told Jayewardene that military aid may be given by India to the LTTE leading to the possible dismemberment of Sri Lanka.

The Indians were building up a case for direct intervention on the number of refugees coming into India. Even before the Vadamarachchi operation commenced, Natwar Singh speaking in the *Lok Sabha* on 1 May 1987, said that the number of Sri Lankan refugees in India had gone up to 140,000. There were internally displaced people in Jaffna as a result of the Vadamarachchi operation and the Indians worked on the assumption that these displaced people too would end up in India. They at first requested permission from the Sri Lankan government to send food aid to Jaffna for the displaced people. The Sri Lankan Foreign Minister A.C.S.Hameed replied to the Indian government saying that there was no situation in Sri Lanka requiring outside assistance.

On 2 June 1987, Rajiv Gandhi informed J.R.Jayewardene that food aid in 20 fishing boats would arrive the next day in Jaffna. In reply to this Jayewardene said that these items can be accepted only if they are handed to the Sri Lankan government. The next day, the cabinet issued a statement to the effect that any foreign vessel coming into the territorial waters of Sri Lanka would be dealt with according to Sri Lankan law, and that no goods will be permitted to be unloaded except under the direction of Sri Lankan authorities.

The Sri Lankan navy halted the Indian flotilla of food aid boats on 3 June 1987. The command and surveillance ship *Edithara*, four Chinese built fast gun boats and the five Israeli fast attack craft took part in the operation in the sea off Kachchativu Island at the maritime border between the two countries. The next day, the Indians issued a statement saying that since the delivery of food aid by boat was blocked, it would be air dropped over Jaffna. The Sri Lankan government responded describing this proposed air drop as an outrage and an assault upon the sovereignty of Sri Lanka. The Sri Lankan government also issued frantic orders to the armed forces in the peninsula not to fire on the Indian aircraft. The food aid was dropped over Jaffna at around 5.00 pm on the same day, by five transport planes escorted by four Mirage fighter planes. The food parcels containing about 19 tonnes of food had been dropped over Vadamarachchi, Urumpirai and Kankesanturei.

The Sri Lankan government virtually capitulated to Indian pressure after the food drop. More food aid was sent later, this time with the concurrence of the Sri Lankan government and all such 'aid' was unloaded at the Kankesanthurei harbour in the presence of Sri Lankan officials. The Vadamarachchi operation came to a halt on 9 June 1987. By latter day standards, the operation had been carried out with few casualties - just 33 killed and 182 wounded. Around 2,340 terrorist suspects were arrested during the operation and transported to the Boossa internment camp in the deep south of Sri Lanka by ship. After the operation was halted, some apprehended LTTE suspects were brought to Boossa by ship by a young naval officer Lt Jayantha Perera. The national security minister Lalith Athulathmudali came to Galle within 24 hours and ordered Lt Perera to take back all the suspects to Jaffna again the same night because the Indians were keen to see them released.

Chapter 27

An Elusive Peace

The troops were disappointed at the halting of the Vadamarachchi operation. The army however did not abandon Vadamarachchi. They set up detachments and continued to dominate the area. After the military operation had been halted Lt Shavendra Silva, Gōta's adjutant, was injured in an LTTE grenade attack. He was trying to cut his way through a steel fence when terrorists lobbed a grenade at him from a distance using a kind of throwing stick they had devised to enable the grenade to travel further. Silva survived the grenade attack because he had his body armour on.

The authors of *The Broken Palmyra* claim that during a conversation between Kumarappa the LTTE's Batticaloa leader and Col Vijaya Wimalaratne in Palaly after the Indo-Lanka Peace Accord, the former had said that both Prabhakaran and Soosai had indeed been in Velvettiturei but had escaped before Gōta's battalion took the town. While the Vadamarachchi operation was on, the LTTE in their desperation was stepping up attacks elsewhere. On 2 June 1987, they carried out what they hoped would be a strategic killing that would precipitate a communal backlash – the brutal hacking to death of 29 bhikkus and a few Buddhist laymen in Arantalawa. The expected backlash however did not materialize.

Even after the Vadamarachchi operation had been halted, skirmishes continued right up to the signing of the Indo-Lanka Peace Accord. On 12 June, a landmine killed three soldiers and over a dozen Tamil civilians. Another landmine on the same day on the Anuradhapura-Trincomalee road killed another 16 Tamil civilians who happened to be Tamil detainees from Boossa who had been released and were returning to their homes. Again on the same day an LTTE death squad attacked the Godapotta village in the Polonnaruwa district and killed nine civilians. Less than a week later, the Girihanduseya Buddhist temple in Tihariya, Anuradhapura was completely destroyed by the terrorists. Twelve soldiers were killed in a confrontation in Kokilai in the east coast on June 30.

In Jaffna, army detachments in Vasivilan, Kurumbasetty and Kattuwan came under mortar attack on 12 June. A few days later the Jaffna Fort also came under attack. It was during this period that the landmark attack on the Nelliady army camp took place. The Nelliady camp had been established in a school during the Vadamarachchi operation and was manned by about 250 soldiers. On 6 July, 1987 about 50 LTTE cadres attacked the camp while an explosives laden truck crashed in through the gate, driven by the LTTE's first suicide bomber 'Captain Miller' and exploded, flattening one of the buildings. Around 18 soldiers died and 21 were injured in the attack. The LTTE was desperate to salvage their self respect in the wake of the Vadamarachchi operation. The year before, Prabhakaran had boasted during an interview with N.Ram of *The Hindu* that the LTTE had managed to halt the army offensive of May 1986 and that support for the LTTE among the people had increased on account of that. If that was true, then the fact that they had fled in the face of the army onslaught of May 1987 would mean that support among the people for the LTTE would have come down.

The day after the Nelliady attack, the LTTE launched mortar attacks on the army camps in Vasivilan, Kurumbasetty, Jaffna Fort and Palaly. As mid-July approached, fighting erupted in the Vadamarachchi town when around 200 LTTE cadres tried to take it back. The fighting spread all over the north and even the Kilinochchi and Mulleitivu districts were placed under a 24 hour curfew. It was while all this was going on that Prabahakaran was taken in an Indian helicopter from the Duriappah stadium in Jaffna to New Delhi on 24 July to discuss the Indo-Lanka peace accord with Rajiv Gandhi, but even the day after that, the LTTE was still firing mortars into the Jaffna Fort. After the Vadamarachchi operation was halted, the 1st Gajaba Battalion was withdrawn to its Saliyapura headquarters where they held an exhibition of weapons captured from the LTTE which included a 'Pasilan' mortar - an LTTE invention.

The Indo-Lanka Peace Accord (ILPA)was signed in Colombo on 29 July 1987. According to the terms of this accord and subsequent exchange of letters between Prime Minister Rajiv Gandhi and President Jayewardene, Sri Lanka created the provincial councils system to decentralise political power, and for its part, the Indian government agreed to prevent Indian territory from being used by Sri Lankan terrorists and to disarm all Tamil terrorist groups. After the Indo-Lanka Peace Accord had been drafted, all terrorist groups were invited to New Delhi for talks with Rajiv Gandhi, but it was to the LTTE that the Indians talked most, with Rajiv Gandhi meeting the LTTE leader several times to get his consent to the accord.

Obviously, this was not the kind of settlement that the LTTE had been fighting for. Initially, due to unrelenting Indian pressure the LTTE made a pretence of acceding to the accord and even put on a show of surrendering arms. But within days of the ILPA coming into force, the LTTE was actively working to undermine it. Barely two weeks after the accord was signed, on 15 August 1987, Prabhakaran told the Indian magazine *India Today* "*This was totally unacceptable to us. It is called the Indo-Sri Lankan friendship agreement but it deals with the Tamil ethnic question. And it was drafted without consulting the Tamil representatives. So we rejected it.*"

Prabhakaran also argued in this interview that there were 200 army camps in the north and east and that if they lay down their arms the Tamil people will be left with no protection. And that unless an arrangement is in place to ensure the security of the Tamils, the question of disarming does not arise. On 12 August 1987, defence secretary Sepala Atygalle reported that only 381 weapons had been handed in by the tigers. The LTTE mobilised friendly politicians in Tamil Nadu to whittle down Indian resolve. On 17 August 1987, less than three weeks after the accord was signed, V.Gopalswamy then a member of the upper house of the Indian parliament, the *Rajya Sabha* was saying sarcastically, "*Our Honourable prime minister described this accord as unprecedented in the 20th century. Yes I concur with him. It is an unprecedented accord because this is an accord between the mediator and the aggressor. It is not an accord between the aggressor and the aggressed. I am shocked to know that the militants were not taken into confidence and they did not give their consent to the accord.*"

After the Indo-Lanka accord, the LTTE did not want any of the other Tamil terrorist groups to come into Jaffna. The Indian peace keeping force (IPKF) also played along because they did not want to upset the LTTE. The thinking was that everything would turn out well if the LTTE was kept happy. IPKF brigade commanders would sometimes wait two hours to meet the LTTE deputy leader Mahattaya. Dinners, lunches and gifts were exchanged by both sides. The Indians bent over backwards to please the LTTE. Originally all the Tamil terrorist and political groups were to be represented on an equal footing in the interim administration for the combined northern and eastern provincial council. But because the LTTE kept insisting that they were the only representatives of the Tamils, the Indians agreed to give fifty percent of the Tamil slots to the LTTE and all other groups including the TULF would get the remaining 50%.

Finally, it came to a stage where in the 12 member council, the LTTE was to have 6 seats, the TULF 2, the Muslims 2 and the Sinhalese 2 representatives. One of the TULF members and one Muslim member would be appointed by the LTTE. Other Tamil groups such as the EPRLF, PLOTE, TELO and the TULF were all to be represented by the single TULF nominee on the council – and the leader of the world's largest democracy agreed to this outrageous arrangement. Bowing down to such intransigence was a sure-fire way of inviting even more intransigence. Through this policy of abject appeasement, the Indians set the stage for what was to follow.

By the first several weeks of the ILPA, only a few thousand Indian troops had been inducted into the north and east, and with the Sri Lankan army largely confined to their camps, the LTTE had almost complete freedom of movement. During this period, they massacred over 100 members of rival Tamil terrorist groups who were cooperating with the Indians. This first started as sporadic attacks on members of rival groups in places like Vavuniya, Kilinochchi, Mannar and Trincomalee. This was then followed by a major massacre in Batticaloa with several dozen killed in just one day. After killing members of rival terrorist groups, the LTTE started a fast unto death by one of their members Thileepan, and put forward a list of demands to the Indians. By 20 September 1987, the Indian government put out a statement accusing the LTTE of fomenting violence in the north and east and trying to place the blame on the Indians for this situation.

By the last week of September 1987, the LTTE and the Indian government were clearly on a collision course. Prabhakaran and J.N.Dixit had a six hour discussion on 23 September 1987 at the Palaly headquarters of the IPKF with a view to ironing out their problems but it was clear at the press conference that followed, that no problems had been resolved. There was an exchange between Prabhakaran and Dixit where Prabhakaran said that he had been given various assurances by the Indian government, such as establishing the interim administrative council with a clear majority for the LTTE, the admission of the LTTE to the north-eastern police force which was to be established and the confining of the Sri Lanka army to their barracks and the vacation by the army of the schools they had occupied - none of which had been fulfilled.

Dixit then asked Prabhakaran whether he will give up the agitation and Thileepan's fast if the Indian government meets these requirements. Prabhakaran's answer was that 'they would see' when that happens. An incredulous Dixit asked Prabhakaran whether even in the event of a satisfactory response, they will make a decision only afterwards? A furious Dixit gave the LTTE an ultimatum. He said that he had requested that the agitation be withdrawn and if it was not, the LTTE would have to take the consequences. Dixit's impatience was understandable. During the six hour discussion that had preceded that joint press conference, Prabhakaran had made five demands,

1. *The immediate cessation of all state aided colonization,*
2. *Immediate cessation of all rehabilitation work,*
3. *All police stations in the north and east be closed down,*
4. *The home guards be disarmed*
5. *The army be withdrawn from the north and east.*

Dixit had responded to these demands as best as he could. He had explained to Prabhakaran that all Sinhalese who had lived in the north and east had to be resettled in their homes. Rehabilitation could not be stopped as all displaced people had to be resettled. The police stations were necessary to maintain law and order and the home guards were being disarmed and as for the Sri Lankan army, their camps had to remain so that the writ of the Sri Lankan government ran in those areas. But the LTTE leader stubbornly stuck to his guns. This was the day that even the pretence of an understanding between the Indian government and the LTTE ended.

The very next day, on 24 September 1987, the LTTE organized a demonstration by Tamil civilians in front of an IPKF camp in Mannar. Taking cover behind the civilians, LTTE cadres had pelted the Indian soldiers with stones. They had subsequently tried to storm the IPKF camp, forcing the Indians to open fire. The Indian government put out a statement saying that *"It is reprehensible and cowardly to use women and children in this manner in incidents in which the LTTE intends to incite violence."* And they warned that the IPKF will have to adopt stronger measures if this kind of provocation occurs. The LTTE response to the Indian warning was to step up their campaign of violence by killing at least two hundred Sinhalese mainly in the Trincomalee district ostensibly in response to the suicide of 12 of their senior cadres who had been in the custody of the Sri Lankan government.

Chapter 28

The Second JVP Insurrection

The JVP had commenced its second insurrection on 15 December 1986 by killing Daya Pathirana the leader of the Independent Students Union of the University of Colombo. This was followed up with the killing of several other left wing activists. A highlight of this early period was the attack on the Pallekele army camp in Kandy on 15 April 1987 where thirteen T-56 assault rifles and some other items had been removed by the JVP. Several weeks later, when the attention of the whole country was focused on the Vadamarachchi operation and the Indian air drop of food over Jaffna, the JVP launched simultaneous attacks on the Katunayake air force base and the Kotelawala Defence Academy on 7 June 1987. Both attacks failed.

The JVP insurrection really got off the ground only with the signing of the Indo-Lanka peace accord and the anti-government riots that accompanied it. The JVP with its anti-Indian rhetoric emerged as a force which could harness the emotion running high in the country. About a week before the Indo-Lanka Peace Accord was signed the 1st Gajaba Battalion had been posted to Colombo and played a part in containing the riots that erupted with the signing of the ILPA. Gōta also came to Colombo with the battalion and was for a while working with Brigadier Wimalaratne to secure Colombo against the JVP. The 1st Gajaba Battalion would be in Colombo until October 1987 when it was posted to Trincomalee where they remained until May 1989.

In the meantime, in December 1987, Gōta was given a staff appointment at army headquarters in Colombo. After he returned from staff college in India at the end of 1983, he had not been given the customary staff appointment but had to take up duties with his unit in operational areas. The belated staff appointment that he was entitled to, came in the army headquarters training branch. Gōta became staff officer under Col C.H.Fernando the then director of training. While he was a staff officer at army headquarters, he applied for an eight month advanced infantry officer training course at Fort Benning, Georgia USA and was selected for the programme. When he applied for this course, there was a regulation which said that those who had gone to staff college would not be eligible to apply for this course. Gōta presented the case to his superiors that this regulation was unfair because selection to staff college was based on a competitive exam. If he had not gone to staff college early, he could have gone to Fort Benning and then gone on to staff college.

Col. Fernando agreed with Gōta's point, and changed this regulation to enable those who had attended staff college also to apply for the advanced infantry officer's course in Fort Benning. Gōta went to the USA in 1988. When he left for the USA, he sent his wife and son to live with his in-laws in the USA. He went to Fort Benning as a Major and was promoted to Lt Colonel while he was in the USA. The Fort Benning course concluded on 20 January 1989. After his return, he continued for a while in his staff appointment at army headquarters. On 1 May 1989, with Colonel Wimalaratne being promoted to the rank of Brigadier, Gōta was made the commanding officer of the 1st Battalion of the Gajaba Regiment. This was now a permanent appointment unlike the temporary command he held during the Vadamarachchi operation.

With this promotion, he was posted to Matale as the district coordinating officer tasked with bringing the JVP under control. The 1st Gajaba Battalion, which had been in Trincomalee for nearly one and a half years, was brought down to Matale. Lieutenants Shavendra Silva, Jagath Dias and Sumedha Perera were among his company commanders in Matale. When Gōta was appointed coordinating officer of the Matale district, the ruling party politicians of that area had complained to the powerful deputy defence minister Ranjan Wijeratne that Gōta was Mahinda Rajapaksa's brother and that they had no faith in him.

At that time, Mahinda Rajapaksa was back in parliament after an interval of 12 years and was a vocal critic of the manner in which the UNP government was handling the JVP insurrection. At that time Brigadier Wimalaratne was director operations of the Joint Operations Command. He had told Ranjan Wijeratne that it was up to the government to decide whom to appoint as the coordinating officer for Matale. However he had pointed out that Gōta was serving in Matale as the commander of the 1st Gajaba Battalion and that he could not be removed from the position of battalion commander because he was a good officer who was committed and professional in his work. Brigadier Wimalaratne had explained to Wijeratne that Gōta had fought in Vadamarachchi and given him details of other operations that he had carried out. Wijeratne had agreed that Gōta should not be removed from his position.

Later, Wijeratne came to Matale and Gōta organized a conference for him and he explained what he was going to do to secure the district against the JVP terrorists. After the conference, Wijeratne told him that the politicians of the area don't want him because he is Mahinda Rajapaksa's brother but that his commander says he is a good military officer that he has earned the command of the battalion. Wijeratne had added, *"I don't want to change you, you get on with the job and if any of the politicians give you trouble, tell me."* After Gōta took over the Matale district, detachments were posted in every strategically important location.

During that period, among some suspected JVP activists arrested in Matale was a person who happened to be a relation of Mahinda Wijesekera's wife. Wijesekera, who had played a major role in getting Mahinda elected to parliament in 1970, was now himself a member of the SLFP and a parliamentarian representing the Matara district. Wjesekera had come to Matale to plead with Gōta to release his relative. Having himself been a leader of the JVP, Wijesekera told Gōta that Matale is an important region for the JVP and that Rohana Wijeweera had been talking about this area even during the 1971 insurgency and there was a strong possibility that he was hiding somewhere in an inaccessible place in the district.

Wijesekera had also given him the tip that Wijeweera was extraordinarily security conscious and that he would never sleep in the most obvious place - on the bed – but somewhere else, on the floor or behind a table so that if an attempt is made on his life, he would at least have some warning. Wijesekera's recommendation to Gōta was that if his men were carrying out raids in the night, he should instruct them not to go for the most obvious place but to look elsewhere.

174

While the 1ˢᵗ Gajaba Battalion was in Matale, the 3ʳᵈ Gajaba was deployed in the Kurunegala district. There were three detachments in Mahawa, Galgamuwa and Kuliyapitiya. Lt Sahampathi Ekanayake was in charge of the Mahawa detachment. About a month after being posted to Mahawa, Lt Ekanayake was relaxing after lunch one day when the police asked him for help to defuse what they suspected to be an improvised landmine. A police patrol had come across a group of men who had been hauling a box along the road and they had taken to their heels on seeing the police.

Lt Ekanayake rushed to the spot in his Toyota Land Cruiser with some men in an armoured personnel carrier and defused the mine. This was a time when troop movements took place mainly in armoured personnel carriers because of the ever present threat of landmines. The Sinhala south was fast becoming what Jaffna had been in 1984. When they were returning to base, Lt Ekanayake's Land Cruiser sped on ahead and the armoured personnel carrier fell behind out of sight. On a lonely stretch of the road, there was a patch of fresh sand clearly visible near a culvert they were about to pass. An officer accompanying Lt Ekanayake wondered aloud whether there could be more of those landmines and the driver in his anxiety applied the brakes as the vehicle was about to pass the patch of fresh sand. With that there was a deafening blast and Lt Ekanayake felt his vehicle going up in the air, and turning over. The next thing he knew was that he was sitting upside down in the vehicle. He groped around for the others, his shouts not getting any response. Then he heard shots being fired outside. He grabbed a weapon and crawled out of the Land Cruiser and began firing in the direction the gunfire.

He knew that if he did not show signs of life the JVP attackers would come closer and pick off the survivors at close range. Then he heard one of his soldiers who had crawled out from the back, also firing at the JVP. The Land Cruiser was now lying upside down in a crater in the middle of the road. Just then their troops in the armoured personnel carrier and another vehicle with police Special Task Force personnel arrived on the scene and they too fired into the surrounding undergrowth to chase away JVP cadres who had been waiting to pick off survivors. Lt Ekanayake had survived with nothing more serious than a gash on his forehead. No one in the Land Cruiser had been seriously hurt because the engine had taken the full force of the blast. It was the timely application of the breaks that had saved their lives.

The JVP's second insurrection was very different to their earlier attempt at grabbing power in 1971. They were now prepared to wage

175

a protracted war against the state. The method they adopted was individual terrorism with hit men killing their victims in surprise attacks just as the Tamil terrorists did in the north in the late 1970s and early 1980s. The JVP however carried out such attacks with much greater frequency than the Tamil terrorists. They labelled all those who supported the Indo-Lanka Peace Accord - the ruling UNP and opposition left wing parties such as the LSSP, SLMP and the CPSL and many other left wing trade unions and student organizations - as traitors and declared death sentences on all of them. As unarmed people we either shot or hacked to death by JVP death squads, a fear psychosis gripped the country. By the end of 1987, the JVP could order the closure of shops, offices and business establishments by just slipping a note under the door or by giving an anonymous phone call.

What the Tamil terrorists had taken years to do, the JVP had done in as many months. If the security forces arrested any JVP suspects, the JVP was able to get the ordinary public to stage demonstrations against 'state repression'. As the terror spread, the general public and even civil society organizations would under JVP prodding, protest all the more loudly against 'state repression'. From this, the JVP graduated to landmines in 1988 and made it difficult for the armed forces to move about. Even during Gōta's stint as coordinating officer for Matale, one officer and several men were killed in two separate landmine blasts. The land mine peril seriously affected the mobility of the security forces.

Had this situation continued, there's no telling which way things would have gone. But around August 1989, the JVP in a foolhardy attempt to fast-track things, issued an ultimatum to all police and armed forces personnel that they should resign *en masse* failing which their families would be done to death. No member of the armed forces could resign in a hurry even if he wanted to, and the ultimatum left them with little choice, especially after the JVP followed through with their threat and started killing the family members of security forces personnel. The families of armed forces personnel had to be accommodated in hotels to prevent them from falling victim to JVP death squads.

It was after this that the armed forces really began going after the JVP. Up to that time, many members of the armed forces were against the presence of the IPKF in the country and since the JVP too was of the same mind, there was no enthusiasm to rein in the JVP. But now, the ordinary soldier and policeman had no way of guaranteeing the safety of his own family except by defeating the

JVP. By this time, the disruption of transport, the closure of hospitals and the general disruption of public life not to mention the gruesome killings perpetrated by the JVP had turned the public against them as well. In the latter half of 1989, the JVP was wiped out in a determined crackdown with only one member of the JVP politburo - its present leader Somawansa Amarasinghe - escaping death.

The Rapid Deployment Force started in 1987 by Colonel Wimalaratne played a major role in ending the JVP insurrection by capturing the JVP leader Rohana Wijeweera on 13 November 1989. Fighting the JVP was simply a case of gathering intelligence and going after individual JVP members. They never operated in groups except when they attacked police stations or military installations for which they would assemble at a place close to the target, and after the attack they would blend into the population. Gōta remained the security coordinating officer of Matale until the end of the second JVP insurrection. In January 1990, he applied for three months leave and went to the USA to see his family.

Chapter 29

India Outmanoeuvred

On 3 October 1987, the navy arrested seventeen LTTE cadres in a boat on the seas off Mulleitivu - a group which included Kumarappa the LTTE's eastern commander and his deputy Pulendran. They were caught red handed transporting weapons into Sri Lanka, which was banned under the peace accord. The captives were brought to the Kankesanthurei harbour by the navy and Major Kapila Hendavitharana of military intelligence took charge of the captives. As mentioned earlier, this was the time the Indians thought humouring the LTTE was the way to avoid problems and Brigadier Fernandez of the IPKF was very keen to see the captives freed but Hendavitharana refused.

As Indian pressure mounted on him, Hendavitharana consulted his superior officer Col. Jayantha Jayaratne, who confirmed his decision. This Brigadier Fernandez was close to the LTTE, having even attended Kumarappa's wedding. The captives were then taken to Palaly and kept in a hangar. The next day, due to immense pressure from the Indian authorities, the captives were allowed to see visitors and receive food and clothes. The army knew that along with the clothes and the food, cyanide capsules had been smuggled to the detainees. The minister of national security Lalith Athulathmudali was insisting that they be brought to Colombo. Hendavitharana told Athulathmudali that moving them to Colombo would be inadvisable as they possessed cyanide capsules and that interrogation of the LTTE cadres was best done in Jaffna.·

But Athulathmudali persisted and on 5 October, a special plane was waiting on the Palaly tarmac to take the captives to Colombo. Elaborate plans were made to transfer the captives from the hangar to the plane. The military hospital had been alerted to stand by and ambulances and trucks to take the captives to hospital were brought to the vicinity of the hangar. When Col Jayaratne announced to the captives that they will be taken to Colombo, Pulendran who was standing in front of the group slunk back to the rear, and he looked agitated and worried. The Sri Lankan authorities knew that he was the main culprit behind the Aranthalawa massacre of Buddhist monks in June that year and Pulendran obviously knew what was in store for him in Colombo.

As the announcement was made, the plan was for some brawny soldiers to rush into the hangar, and grab each of the captives before they could bite their cyanide capsules. But the captives were too quick for the soldiers and the army could save only about four of the captives, all the others including Kumarappa and Pulendran died. That night, the LTTE went on the rampage. They first killed eight soldiers they had been keeping in captivity for a considerable period of time. The parents of these soldiers had been allowed to see them in March 1987. They were now all shot dead in cold blood and their bodies dumped in the Jaffna town. Two senior executives of the government owned Cement Corporation who had come to Jaffna with a view to re-commencing operations at the Kankesanthurei cement factory, were among the Sinhalese the LTTE killed in retaliation.

Even by the second week of October 1987, the IPKF had only a little more than 8000 soldiers in the entire north and east – numbers insufficient to keep the LTTE in check. The LTTE went on the rampage against Sinhalese in the east, in Batticaloa and Trincomalee with dozens of Sinhala residents in these districts being gunned down. On 9 October, Gamini Jayasuriya, a cabinet minister in the UNP government was to state indignantly in parliament that the Sri Lanka army had been confined to barracks, but that weapons had not been surrendered by the terrorists. He said that all that he could see was an escalation of hostilities and not a cessation of hostilities.

He said that it was with the utmost restraint that the Sri Lankan armed forces stationed in the north and east were witnessing the butchery of Sinhalese civilians virtually on their door steps and stomaching the insults of a foreign army patrolling the streets. Minister Jayasuriya said that the Eelam flag had been hoisted in the vicinity of

Sri Lankan military camps while the IPKF turned a blind eye to all these goings on. The BBC reported that nearly 200 Sinhala civilians had been massacred by the LTTE in the east. The pressure was building up on the Indians to take more resolute action to rein in the LTTE.

As the IPKF moved to crack down on the LTTE following the events of early October 1987, a mighty caterwaul of protest was raised in Tamil Nadu. On 6 November 1987, a Tamil legislator during a debate on Sri Lanka in the upper house of the Indian parliament, expressed shock at the fact that the Indian army was killing Tamils. Another legislator V.Arunachalam said that the Indian government had now taken the place of J.R.Jayewardene.

It was clear that the Indians had no idea about who they were dealing with. Before the hostilities commenced, the Indian army chief General K.Sundarji had confidently said that the Indian army could wipe out the LTTE in two weeks. Yet when the hostilities did commence, it was the Indian army that faced the threat of being wiped out in two weeks, not the LTTE. Jaswant Singh, a future Indian defence minister, then an opposition politician, speaking in parliament at the debate held on 6 November 1987, about three weeks after the IPKF offensive against the LTTE started, said that the Indian army had suffered more than a thousand casualties already - the dead, injured and missing - in their clashes with the LTTE and described this as the highest casualty rate ever suffered by the Indian army - higher than in any of the wars they had fought against Pakistan and China in 1948, 1962, 1965 or 1971.

On 25 December 1987, the LTTE's mentor in Tamil Nadu, M.G.Ramachandran died. But by this time, supporting the Tamil Eelam cause had become a part of Tamil Nadu politics. Rajiv Gandhi had discovered to his dismay that Ramachandran continued to help the LTTE even after the IPKF commenced operations against them. An Indian chief minister was helping a foreign terrorist movement that was fighting the Indian army and there was nothing that the central government could do about it. Several months into the hostilities between the Indian army and the LTTE, on 21 March 1988, all the opposition parties in the Indian parliament signed a petition to the government calling for an immediate ceasefire in Sri Lanka. On the same day, the Indian government issued a statement from New Delhi denying that they were hunting for Prabhakaran. This was ironic because this is precisely what they should have been doing.

Dixit says in his memoirs that LTTE cadres injured in clashes with the IPKF were brought to Tamil Nadu and treated in government hospitals there. In a sense one could hardly blame the Tamil Nadu establishment for helping the LTTE when Rajiv Gandhi himself followed the strange policy of fighting the LTTE through the IPKF while maintaining a line open to them through RAW. That sent confusing signals to everybody. The IPKF was in the meantime suffering grievous casualties. By the end of March 1988, in less than six months of fighting, they had over 400 men killed with another 1000 injured. The Indian answer to the unprecedented challenge being posed by the LTTE was to induct more and more troops to Sri Lanka.

A little over a year after the signing of the ILPA, by August 1988, the Indians had more than 100,000 military and para-military personnel in the north and east of Sri Lanka. The idea was to saturate the two provinces with troops thus restricting the ability of the LTTE to move around. By this time, Jaswant Singh was talking about an 'Indian military failure'. He told the Indian upper house of parliament that despite the presence of the IPKF, it is still the writ of the LTTE that runs in Jaffna and that the LTTE's supply routes from Tamil Nadu had not dried up even though India was fighting the LTTE.

Thus the Indian central government was cornered on their own soil by the LTTE. In February 1989, president J.R.Jayewardene retired from politics and R.Premadasa who had won the presidential election held in December 1988, became president. Premadasa had always been anti-Indian and it did not take long for the LTTE to form a link with Premadasa against the Indian presence in Sri Lanka. Within a few weeks of Premadasa assuming office as president, in April 1989, talks between the LTTE and the government commenced. Shortly thereafter, government owned newspapers began publishing negative stories about the IPKF. Now the Indian central government and the IPKF was being opposed by both the government of Sri Lanka and the LTTE at this end, and by Tamil Nadu and the Indian opposition at that end. In a policy as short sighted as that followed by the Indians earlier, president Premadasa cosied up to the LTTE and Sri Lankan government communiqués soon began to echo the views of the LTTE.

TULF leaders A. Amirthalingam and V. Yogeswaran were shot dead by the LTTE in Colombo on 13 July, 1989, ending an era in Tamil politics. They had long since ceased to count in the politics of the north, but the TULF was still preferred by the Indians and the LTTE may have feared that the purpose of the IPKF operations in the north and east was to eliminate the LTTE and restore the TULF to their former position.

The manner in which the LTTE worked on the IPKF can be illustrated by a statement made on 23 August 1988, by the spokesman

181

of the Indian external affairs ministry; *"Two IPKF patrols were operating in the crowded market place in Velvettiturei at 10.00 hours on the 2nd August, when they were fired upon by the LTTE. Approximately 40 LTTE militants had taken position for this ambush in houses and shops in the marketplace. They used weapons which included AK-47s, rocket launchers, grenades and improvised explosive devices. In making this attack, the LTTE militants showed callous disregard for the safety of 800 civilians who were present in the market at the time. The IPKF suffered 6 killed and 10 wounded in the initial burst of fire. They were forced to return fire in self defence and this exchange went on for about an hour. Five LTTE militants were killed and unfortunately, 24 civilians died in the crossfire. It is quite clear that civilian casualties are entirely the result of a deliberate policy of the LTTE to fight in densely populated areas using human shields in order to inhibit the IPKF from returning fire."*

An official statement of the Indian external affairs ministry issued on 17 August 1989 stated the following: *"A group of LTTE militants under cover of darkness sneaked into a civilian hospital in a heavily populated area of Mannar, broke open the windows of the main hospital building and in utter disregard for the patients opened fire on an IPKF picket which was in the vicinity of the hospital for security and policing duties. The LTTE used rocket propelled grenades, rocket launchers and machine guns against the IPKF. But the IPKF soldiers in deference to the inmates of the hospital, did not use heavy weapons to retaliate. As a result, 24 IPKF soldiers were killed and a portion of the hospital along with a temple in the vicinity were damaged. The hospital was one of the biggest in the northern province and had 200 beds. It had 89 patients and a large number of staff at the time of the incident."*

"The hospital was used with total disregard of the 89 patients within. Since the IPKF could not retaliate, they suffered heavy casualties There is a clear political motive to disrupt the IPKF and to bring it into disrepute, to demoralize the civilian population and to jeopardize ongoing Indo-Sri Lankan talks."

With all this going on, the Indian government was still describing the LTTE as 'militants' in their official communiqués and not as 'terrorists' obviously in deference to public opinion in Tamil Nadu. In December 1989, Rajiv Gandhi lost the elections in India and a government led by V.P.Singh was installed in New Delhi. With regime changes having taken place both in Sri Lanka and India during the year 1989, the stage was set for the withdrawal of the IPKF. Earlier, on 1 June 1989, a few weeks after he commenced talks with the LTTE, president Premadasa had in a speech at the Chittavivekaramaya Temple in Battaramulla, called for the complete withdrawal of the IPKF by the end of July 1989 – ie. within a period of eight weeks.

There was a sharp deterioration in Indo-Lanka relations during the latter half of 1989, with Premadasa at one point even giving arms, ammunition, and money to the LTTE to fight the IPKF. Perhaps Premadasa saw this as a way of hoisting the Indians with their own petard as a few years earlier, it was the Indians who had trained and armed the Tamil terrorist groups to fight against the Sri Lankan state. With Rajiv Gandhi's defeat at the end of 1989, the fate of the IPKF was sealed.

By the end of March 1990, the IPKF had withdrawn completely from Sri Lanka. On 1 April 1990, Prabhakaran issued a statement gloating: *"We have successfully foiled the Indian military intervention. Now the Indian occupation forces have completely withdrawn from our homeland. The termination of the Indian intervention is a grand victory to our struggle. The Indian forces were sent here specifically to crush our liberation struggle and to annihilate our organization. It is for this specific reason India unleashed a fully fledged war against us. This war is a monumental event in the history of the world. For more than two years, we fought a relentless war shedding our blood against a formidable military force, against a mighty power in Asia. The supreme sacrifice made by our fighters and by our people in this armed conflict has become a historic epic of heroism and courage. Our victory in this war has set an excellent example that the legitimate struggle of an oppressed people and their yearning for freedom could not be crushed by military force however formidable it may be."*

Altogether 1155 Indian soldiers sacrificed their lives in Sri Lanka and 36 had been permanently disabled. This brief, unsuccessful engagement in Sri Lanka was a military, diplomatic and political debacle for the Indians. Rajiv Gandhi was assassinated by the LTTE in Tamil Nadu on 21 May 1991. As Subramanian Swamy was to say later in the *Rajya Sabha*, the assassination of Rajiv Gandhi was *"Not just an assassination of a political leader of India but an insult to our national honour and a challenge to our national sovereignty."* The worst ignominy of all was that for over two decades, the Indian army was not able to commemorate their fallen comrades in Sri Lanka, for fear of inflaming public opinion in Tamil Nadu. This situation changed only after the defeat of the LTTE in 2009. In 2010 the Indian army chief on a visit to Sri Lanka was finally able to lay a wreath at the memorial erected in Battaramulla to commemorate the Indian soldiers who laid down their lives in Sri Lanka in the fight against terrorism.

Chapter 30

The Resumption of War

When Gōta went to the USA on overseas leave, Mahinda thought he may not come back, and he confided his fears in Brigadier Wimalaratne. The latter was on good terms with Mahinda and whenever he went down south, he would stay at Mahinda's residence in Tangalle town. Mahinda had good reason to think Gōta may not want to come back. From the day he had got married, he had been out in the operational areas and was under pressure from his family to leave the army and take up residence in the USA. Apart from his wife's family, Gōta's younger sibling Dudley also lived in the USA. Mahinda knew the pressures that were building on Gōta. Brigadier Wimalaratne did not relish the idea of losing a good officer and he wrote Gōta the following letter.

Sri Lanka Army Headquarters, P.O.Box 533, Colombo

30 mar 90

My Dear Gota,

I trust that you and Ioma are packing your bags to come back. You may have heard that the country is back to normal with the south peaceful and the N & E almost normal now. The movement of Saturn has been very good for the world. So Ioma need not worry. I am also planning to post you to Colombo by the end of this year after Sivali (Wanigasekera) and Lawrence (Fernando) return from Staff (College).

We are raising another battalion each. Gajaba will have 4 permanent camps in Kandy (Dharmaraja Hill) Nalanda (Matale)

Saliyapura and Vavuniya. The Motherland awaits the return of their illustrious son of Ruhuna. The Gallantry Awards list was finalized with GR (Gajaba Regiment) topping the list.

Please convey our fond regards to Ioma, Manoj, Lucas and Padma Peiris. I am sure you will find our Pol Sambol and Bath far better than American beef and corn. Awaiting your arrival. Pl let me know if anything is required. May the blessings of the Devas be with you all.

Yours sincerely,
Brig Vijaya

Gōta came back soon afterwards and was posted to Welioya. The brigade commander in Welioya at the time was Janaka Perera. Gōta was at the Sinhapura army camp while Perera was at the main camp at Welioya. When the IPKF left at the end of March 1990, the LTTE was quick to return to the Jaffna peninsula which the IPKF had vacated. By mid-June 1990, The LTTE was once again surrounding government military installations exactly as they had been before the IPKF arrived in July 1987. When the IPKF was in the north and east, only small groups of Sri Lankan military personnel were in the camps in those areas. Most troops had been deployed in the south to quell the JVP insurrection. The government had not really thought of the scenario after the Indian army leaves and there was no plan to dominate the territory vacated by the IPKF.

It was in Batticaloa that hostilities really commenced on 11 June 1990. The LTTE found a pretext to launch all out war when a Muslim youth who was a supporter of the LTTE was arrested by the Batticaloa police over an altercation with a Sinhala man. The Batticaloa police station was surrounded by the LTTE who ordered the police out until 'investigations' into the incident were completed. In a simultaneous move police stations in Valachchenai, Kalawanchikudy, Eravur, Akkaraipattu and Kalmunai were also surrounded. While this was going on, army troops in a truck on their way to Kalmunai to purchase provisions were fired upon killing ten soldiers. A reporter from the *The Island* who phoned the Batticaloa police station to find out what was happening, was answered by an LTTE cadre at the other end.

It was not just the police who were in trouble. The army camps in Kalawanchikudy, Kiran, Vellaveli, and Kalmunai were also surrounded. Meanwhile, the policemen in Batticaloa, Kalkudah, Valachchenai, Samanthurei and Akkaraipattu were already in LTTE captivity and details of one of the worst atrocities in the entire war, were already beginning to surface. A police sub-inspector by the name of Ranaweera who had escaped from the LTTE revealed that the policemen who had been abducted by the LTTE had been shot dead. They had also taken 400 guns and more than 165,000 rounds of ammunition from the police stations that had surrendered.

The LTTE had begun taking over police stations in the north as well starting with the Pt Pedro police station and by the second day of hostilities, the police stations in Mankulam, Murunkan, Vavuniya, Velvettiturei, Kankasanthurei and Jaffna had been taken over by the LTTE. Things happened fast during the first few days. By the third day, nothing was known of the 600 or so policemen who had fallen into the hands of the LTTE in the east and had been taken in buses to Tirukkovil. The suspicion was that they had already been massacred. Retired senior police officer Tassie Seneviratne, who has done a study of these events, says that the police stations of the Batticaloa Division had caved in immediately to the LTTE demand because of a standing order from the government not to confront the LTTE whatever the cost. Around 300 policemen had fallen into the hands of the LTTE as a result of this surrender. The police stations of the Kalmunai Division in the Ampara district – in Kalmunai, Akkaraipattu, Samanthurei and Potuvil resisted, but were forced to surrender to the LTTE by the Premadasa government.

Seneviratne says that the then IGP Earnest Perera had been flown to Batticaloa with specific orders from President Premadasa to get the resisting policemen of the Kalmunai Division to surrender. So instead of receiving reinforcements, what they got was an order to surrender. Around 324 policemen led by ASP Ivan Botheju had surrendered under protest. None of them were heard of again. On making inquiries later, a Tamil farmer had told Tassie Seneviratne that the captured policemen had been made to lie face down on the ground with their arms tied behind their backs in a long line, and they were sprayed with bullets after which the bodies were heaped up, doused with patrol and set alight. The Tamil farmer who narrated this incident to Seneviratne had been one of those tasked with burying the charred bodies afterwards. More than 600 policemen died at the hands of the LTTE in this manner.

The Kilinochchi army camp was attacked on 14 June and the Jaffa Fort siege of which we will read more in subsequent pages, had begun. The army camps in Vellaveli, Kalkudah, and Kalmunai were abandoned. By the fourth day, the Kiran, Kalawanchikudy, and

Kinniya camps were still under attack. The Kalawanchikudy army camp was located about 20 km south of Batticaloa, just opposite the police station. The LTTE surrounded the place and demanded surrender. The policemen surrendered but the army camp which had only 48 men and three officers, refused. Ten policemen refused to surrender and went into the army camp with their weapons. The Kalawanchikudy camp held out for four days against a 300 strong LTTE force until the Rapid Deployment Force was able to relieve them. In the meantime, the defenders who had no food had eaten an unlucky bull that had strayed into the camp.

The Kiran army camp which was also besieged, held on for eight days against all odds. They too had no food, and no cattle came straying anywhere near their camp. So they ended up eating boiled unripe papaya and whatever else they could find, until the Vijayaba Regiment was able to relieve them. During the last week of June and the first week of July, Gōta's battalion, the 1st Gajaba participated in a major operation to clear the area to the south of the Trincomalee bay covering Kinniya, Kattaparichchan and Sampur. After the Kiran camp was secured, the focus shifted from the east to the north with Palaly and the Karainagar naval base coming under LTTE fire. The Jaffna Fort also came under heavy fire after which leaflets were air dropped around the fort telling civilians to leave the area to avoid getting caught in the crossfire. While all this was going on, the Muslims living in Jaffna were given three hours to pack their belongings and to leave the peninsula. Around 30,000 Muslim inhabitants of the Jaffna district were turned into internally displaced persons overnight.

In the middle of these hostilities in mid-June 1990, Rajiv Gandhi, now out of power and in the opposition, was to write to J.R.Jayewardene, now retired, *"The agreement which you and I concluded in July 1987, was expressly designed to preserve the unity and integrity of Sri Lanka…Anyone with the least acquaintance with the LTTE could have foretold the rapid breakdown of the accommodation of convenience arranged between the LTTE and the Sri Lankan government. But perhaps even the most pessimistic prognostications could not have envisaged so quick and complete a collapse. Sri Lanka has been plunged once again into an agonizing civil war. As I write this letter, it would appear from newspaper reports that the unity of Sri Lanka is facing its most serious challenge ever."*

J.R.Jayewardene wrote back to Rajiv at the end of June 1990 saying *"I agree with you that the withdrawal of the IPKF without adequate Sri Lankan security replacements created a vacuum which was filled by the LTTE. Sri Lanka is now back at 'square one' as far as the North-East problems are concerned. While talking peace with the Premadasa government, the LTTE was preparing for war..."*

One of the army camps surrounded by the LTTE as the IPKF left was the Kokavil camp which at the time had 48 soldiers of the 3rd Sinha (Volunteer) Battalion led by Lt S.U.Aladeniya. The task of the Kokavil camp was to protect a TV transmission tower. Its vulnerability was that the water supply was located outside the precincts of the camp. When the LTTE surrounded the camp they were cut off from their water supply. The besieged camp could not be supplied even by air as helicopters would have been shot at. Fixed wing aircraft had dropped food, blocks of ice (for water) and ammunition but from that height there was no possibility of ensuring that they fell into the small area held by the detachment and much of it had fallen into enemy hands. The camp valiantly held on for one month before being overrun.

On 10 July, the LTTE brought in bulldozers which had been modified with armour plating and prepared a final assault. Lt Aladeniya was instructed by his superiors over the radio, to withdraw to a safe location but he refused saying that most of his men had been wounded. That night, the LTTE launched an all out assault with their improvised Arul and Baba mortars, and the camp was overrun. Only two soldiers and a cook managed to escape alive. Because most regular units had been deployed to quell the JVP insurrection, most camps in the north were manned by volunteer troops and even that in very small numbers. Even the vital Elephant Pass camp was manned at the time by just one volunteer company and the total area of the camp was not more than 300X300 meters in extent. It was commanded by an officer who was a schoolmaster by profession. The camp was under siege for about eight weeks until troops were inducted by air to relieve it.

On 3 August 1990, in what may have been a move to terrorise and chase the Muslims out of the east as well in a Jaffna style ethnic cleansing operation, the LTTE massacred 142 Muslims in a mosque in Kaththankudy. The Jaffna Fort was also surrounded by about 400 LTTE cadres. The LTTE now had control of the Telecommunications building which adjoined the Jaffna Fort and they could prevent supplies from coming into the fort from Mandativu Island. The LTTE had taken over Mandativu and Kayts islands as well so no supply was possible in any case. It was estimated that around 150 LTTE cadres were on Kayts Island. The LTTE had also taken up position in the abandoned police quarters opposite the Jaffna Fort. LTTE attacking parties had even managed to scale the ramparts but had been beaten back with air support.

An operation was launched to rescue one officer and 51 soldiers of the 6th Sinha Battalion and one assistant superintendant of police, 6 sub-inspectors and 112 constables (about 172 men in all), who were under siege in Jaffna Fort. There was no land route into the Jaffna Fort. Food, water and ammunition was supplied by air dropping the goods over the fort in gunny bags from a Chinese built Y12 transport aircraft. For the sake of accuracy, the plane would go into a steep dive and then pull up after releasing the cargo so that the bags would also take the same trajectory downwards as the plane. The SIAI Marcetti attack aircraft would dive on either side of the Y12 with their guns firing at the periphery of the fort so as to draw fire to themselves instead of the unarmed transport plane. The fort was kept supplied but soldiers inside were dying and there was no way to evacuate the injured.

When the Jaffna Fort was under attack, night missions were flown to attack the perimeter of the besieged camp. The SIAI Marcettis always carried out missions in pairs mainly because of the minimal armaments they carried necessitating two planes to meet the firepower requirement. The pilots could communicate directly with the fort on army compatible radios. Once the SIAI Marchetti got to the scene the ammunition would be over in five to ten minutes. It could carry only around 150 rounds of .50 ammo in each gun. The rockets carried on the SIAI Marchetti would have had the same effect as an RPG. Hence the SIAI Marchettis would have to do several sorties a night to help the besieged fort with those below calling constantly for more support.

As the situation in the Jaffna Fort became more desperate, Major General Kobbekaduwa summoned Gōta to his Vanni headquarters and told him that the soldiers and policemen in the Jaffna Fort could not be allowed to die and that they had to be rescued somehow. He added that they may lose more troops in the rescue operation than the number in the Jaffna Fort, but that it had to be done nevertheless because if the Jaffna Fort falls and the people in there lose their lives, it will have a catastrophic impact on morale within the whole army and will convey the impression that if any army camp is surrounded, they will face certain death with no prospect of rescue. Kobbekaduwa told Gōta that he had selected the 1st Gajaba and Sarath Fonseka's 1st Sinha Battalion to mount the rescue operation.

Chapter 31

A Hundred Mirrors

The two battalions were accordingly taken to Palaly. The plan was to land in Kayts, make their way to Mandativu and from there, cross the lagoon and fight their way into the fort. The rescue party had to first fight their way to Karainagar from Palaly because the Karainagar naval detachment had also been surrounded and was under intermittent attack. From Karainagar, the next step was to establish a foothold on Kayts Island. (See maps 1 & 2) Troops left from Palaly at around midnight to prepare for a silent landing on Kayts. At dawn, General Kobbekaduwa came on the radio and asked Captain Deepal Subasinghe of the 1st Gajaba Battalion whether he was sure wanted a silent landing, or whether they should shell the place first before landing.

The navy had a Dvora gunboat on standby for close support for the beach landing and the air force kept on standby, two helicopter gunships and two fighter aircraft for the same purpose. But Capt Subasinghe insisted on a silent landing in the night. The gamble paid off and he was able to land and make his way into the interior, coming almost up to Kayts town without being noticed. Kayts Island had flat open terrain with scattered built up areas. The LTTE realised that a landing had taken place only when the choppers started coming in. Then the army fought their way down through the length of Kayts. By the time they had secured the island, it was late afternoon and the LTTE had begun firing upon the advancing troops from the adjoining Mandativu Island.

Gōta and Fonseka took Mandativu in a two pronged attack and the LTTE was surrounded. Around 80 LTTE cadres were killed and weapons recovered and the whole of Mandativu was cleared. To kill such a number of terrorists and to recover so many weapons was a rare achievement those days. The 1st Sinha Battalion suffered only two dead and 25 injured in the operation. Shavendra Silva who was one of the company commanders in Gōta's battalion recalls that for the first time the army came across seven or eight members of what would later come to be known as the LTTE's baby brigade - boys below the age of ten years in LTTE uniforms. The boys were fed, shown to Gōta and sent back to their parents.

As Mandativu was cleared, the LTTE thought the army would cross the Pannai causeway and come to the fort without halting. The LTTE cadres who were manning the beachfront positions on either side of the fort disappeared in expectation of an army onslaught. The rescue party on Mandativu got radio messages from the besieged fort saying that the LTTE cadres were running away. At this point, Major Gen Kobbekaduwa made a crucial mistake. Through an excess of caution, he decided that they would consolidate their positions in Mandativu and then go into the Jaffna Fort. Brigadier Wimalaratne who was then the director operations of the Joint Operations Command, kept asking Gōta why they were not going into the fort, but there things stood.

During this hiatus in operations, the deputy minister of defence Ranjan Wijeratne visited the newly captured Mandativu. Kobbekaduwa told Gōta to prepare a briefing for the deputy minister and also to display the weapons they had captured. Ranjan Wijeratne by that time, had become very fond of Gōta. The deputy minister arrived, toured Mandativu and was given a briefing. After the briefing, Major Gen Kobbekaduwa, Sarath Fonseka and Gōta took Wijeratne to view the captured weapons. When they went to an old school building where all the weapons were on display, Gōta found that the officer he had placed in charge of organizing the display had got only Gajaba soldiers wearing T-shirts with the Gajaba logo standing by the captured weapons.

The operation had however been carried out by the Sinha and the Gajaba battalions together. Gōta knew immediately that Fonseka would be upset by this and he apologized and immediately got the Gajaba soldiers to move away out of sight. For his part, Fonseka had not said anything about it at that time. But it was going to resurface in the relations between these two soldiers two decades later. One of the acts of heroism during this lull in the operation was that Captain P.J.G.Fernando of the 1ˢᵗ Sinha Battalion volunteered with five other soldiers, to join the soldiers under siege inside the fort and they went into the Jaffna Fort in a hazardous helicopter ride piloted by a young air force pilot Lasantha Waidyaratna.

When helicopter landings at Jaffna Fort were made, diversionary tactics were used with other helicopters and SIAI Marcettis firing at the LTTE positions around the fort and the chopper flying in low from Mandathivu to land inside Jaffna Fort. The LTTE had positions on the beach on either side of the Jaffna Fort. They could not completely surround it because there was no space on the beach immediately outside the fort. The troops inside Jaffna Fort started firing at the LTTE positions outside the fort on the beach to keep them busy. This was accompanied by artillery fire on the LTTE positions from Mandathivu, all aimed at drawing LTTE fire away from the approaching helicopter. Another such landing was made in the fort to drop off two 120mm mortars with ammunition and to evacuate casualties. The chopper that landed inside fort with the mortars was piloted by Senaka Darmawardhana a young flying officer at that time.

Certain limited operations were done such as evacuating the injured by helicopter, but the troops did not cross over. The crossing over operation was perilous. Three kilometres of open sea had to be crossed in dinghies and when they got closer to the beach they would have to get off the dinghies and run onto the beach. This was the first amphibious operation attempted by the army, and they had to rehearse before the operation was carried out. There was also the need to study the tides, before attempting the crossing. When the attack finally began, the left flank of the attack was led by Sarath Fonseka and the right by Gōta.

Over 90 were killed in Gōta's battalion alone in the landing - an unprecedented casualty rate in those days. A similar number died in Fonseka's battalion. Among those under siege in the fort, only six were killed and had been buried inside the fort. Major Gen Kobbekaduwa's prediction that there would be more casualties in the rescue attempt than the total number in the fort was coming true. Once they landed, Gōta was supposed to fight his way to the town and Fonseka was to secure the Telecom building and the Pannai causeway. The rescue parties went into the fort but couldn't do much else. They were not able to break out into the Jaffna town or capture the Pannai causeway as planned.

Both Gōta and Fonseka tried their best, but both failed. In Gōta's opinion, this was the price they had to pay for delaying the operation. Had they effected the landing on the same day that they had captured Mandativu, in his opinion the disarray in the ranks of the LTTE would have reduced the number of casualties and also enabled them to advance beyond the fort. This experience would provide Gōta with a valuable lesson in the need to maintain momentum and pressure on the enemy, which would stand him in good stead later. In October 1990, the Jaffna Fort was abandoned and troops evacuated but the army continued to hold Kayts and Mandativu.

After the failed Jaffna Fort operation, Gōta went back to Welioya with his battalion. Immediately afterwards, came another disaster. The Mankulam camp in the centre of the Vanni was one of the most isolated army camps in the country with the Elephant Pass camp being 28 km to the North and Vavuniya 30 km to the south with nothing in between. This camp had been held by a detachment of the 3rd Gajaba Battalion and had been under siege continuously from June to November 1990 and was dependent on air drops of food and ammunition. Since many other camps faced the same problem, reinforcements could not be sent to Mankulam. At the time of the siege, the total extent of the Mankulam camp was about 400 by 400 meters and was held by about 200 men.

During the siege of Mankulam, helicopters made risky landings to take away casualties and dead bodies. Senaka Dharmawardhana, was one of those who did flying missions into the Mankulam camp. He remembers that the bodies that were removed from that camp were several days old and in an advanced state of decay. The choppers had open doors and for the force of the rotor blades, the flesh would be torn off the bodies and at times particles of human flesh would land on the front windscreen of the chopper.

Some bodies would have limbs stripped to the bone by the force of the rotor blades by the time they got to Vavuniya. At that time, morale would have gone down if the dead were not sent home for burial. So choppers would land even under heavy enemy fire for no other reason than to remove dead bodies. By the end of November 1990, the situation was becoming untenable due to increased pressure from the LTTE. On 23 November 1990, the troops in the Mankulam camp slipped out of the LTTE cordon with a view to making their way to Vavuniya on foot. The troops had withdrawn from the camp by the time the LTTE launched their final assault which featured a 'Nelliady style' explosives laden vehicle as well.

All communication with Vavuniya was lost after the troops left the Mankulam camp. At this point Dharmawardhana had taken a chopper and flown over the thick jungle between Mankulam and Vavuniya when he suddenly saw what looked like a hundred mirrors flashing at him from the jungle. Later he found that these were not mirrors but ration tins that the soldiers who had managed to escape from the besieged camp were flashing in the sunlight to attract his attention. This was about five kilometres south of the Mankulam camp. He flashed the landing lights of his chopper to show that he had identified them. They were later picked up from the jungles by helicopters. It was raining in the Vanni at that time, and many of the solders including their commanding officer Major Lalith Daulagala had rotten feet after marching for days in the mud. Of the 200 troops in the camp about 140 to 150 troops had made it to Vavuniya after retreating through the Vanni jungles.

A group of about 15 stragglers had to be picked up a little distance away from the main party and the chopper crew was not sure whether they were LTTE or army. But the soldiers in their desperation were holding up their joined palms in the gesture of supplication and entreaty, literally begging the chopper to pick them up. Dharmawardhana landed the chopper and the soldiers were instructed by hand signals to drop their weapons and come forward with their hands up and to show their identity cards. It was only after that that they were allowed to get into the chopper. One problem was that with 15 passengers on board, the chopper was overloaded. But nobody would get off once he had got in. Fortunately the Bell 212 choppers were relatively new at that time and they could lift off even when overloaded.

Following fast upon Mankulam came another blow. Brigadier Lucky Wijeratne was a popular officer in the army holding the position of area commander of the Trincomalee district which lay to the south of the special administrative region of Welioya beyond the Yan Oya river. On the morning of 18 December 1990, there was to be a security coordinating meeting between him and Brigadier Janaka Perera the area commander of Welioya. Lunch had been prepared for those arriving from Trincomalee and everything was in readiness when the news came over the radio that Brig Wijeratne had *en route* to the meeting, been killed in a massive landmine blast.

In 1990, the main factor that hampered the military was the lack of manpower. The army did not have the capacity to take on the LTTE from several fronts, and the same battalion was sent from one place to another to fight battles. When war broke out with the LTTE again, Gōta was in Welioya and he had to conduct operations first to secure the Welioya area. Then his battalion was sent to relieve the Jaffna Fort. After that he was sent into the Vanni to clear the LTTE from the Mannar area. From there he was sent to Trincomalee to capture the 'Baskaran' base of the LTTE in the Upparu jungles. Gōta's 1st Gajaba Battalion and the 3rd Gajaba Battalion were deployed under Brigadier Janaka Perera for that operation.

Gōta's battalion went to Trincomalee and from there to Nilaveli, marching in the night. They took the Baskaran base in the morning. What they did not know was that there was not just one, but a series of LTTE camps in these jungles. About 18 vehicles stolen from government officials were recovered from this camp. The troops captured the camp early in the morning and they made the mistake of just waiting there without exploring the jungles further. At 5.00 pm the LTTE mounted a counter attack. They started firing mortars followed by small arms fire. In the thick jungle, nobody could see where the firing was coming from. Fortunately, the 3rd Gajaba Battalion came to the rescue of Gōta's party. The first to come on the scene was Capt Deepal Subasinghe with his company. Gōta withdrew under cover of darkness.

Then they were given another target in the Vanni in Paraiyanlankulam which is the turn off to the famed Madhu Church on the Vavuniya-Mannar road. Once again it was Gōta's battalion and the 3rd Gajaba with Janaka Perera commanding the Brigade. All this was in a matter of weeks and months. It was the same battalion going from one area to the next resulting in battle fatigue and demoralization. Perhaps nothing illustrated this better than the fact that the troops that had come to Vavuniya after enduring a six month siege at the Mankulam camp were soon afterwards deployed to relieve the besieged Elephant Pass Camp.

It was at that time, a useless war with one area being captured and the LTTE withdrawing elsewhere only to come right back to where they were once the army was gone. The army did not have enough troops to hold the areas they captured. An example of such an operation was the *Vanni Vickrama I* operation conducted in the jungles to the north of Vavuniya to attack the LTTE deputy leader Mahattaya's 'Yankee' base. The army estimated the presence of about 250 to 300 LTTE cadres in Mahattaya's complex. This operation concluded on 14 May 1991, but Mahattaya survived to be killed by the LTTE itself later. Operation *Vanni Vickrama II* was launched in June 1991 to destroy terrorists in the general area of Madhu in the

Mannar district. But the Madhu area always remained an LTTE stronghold until its liberation in 2008.

It was no wonder that battle hardened soldiers like Gōta left the army to do something more useful. At that time, there was no overall plan to destroy the LTTE completely and only piecemeal operations to capture, defend or destroy were carried out. By the end of 1990, Gōta had obtained married quarters at the Summit Flats in Colombo which was opposite the apartment occupied by Brigadier Wimalaratne. His wife would keep telling Wimalaratne to release Gōta because they wanted to go to the USA. It was during this period that the *Sunday Island* carried a front page news item with the title, "Lt Col Gotabhaya Rajapaksa to retire". It had been Brigadier Wimalaratne who had given that piece of information to the press. Ranjan Wijeratne had seen this and phoned Mahinda to ask him why he was trying to get his brother out of the army. Mahinda had said that he has nothing to do with it and that he did not want Gōta to leave the army either.

Gōta was in Welioya at that time and one day, Ranjan Wijeratne had visited his headquarters along with Major Gen Denzil Kobbekaduwa. After the usual briefings followed by lunch, minister Wijeratne had a one to one chat with Gōta under a tree in the compound of the brigade headquarters and wanted to know why he was trying to leave the army. Gōta explained that he had not made a decision yet, despite the report in the *Sunday Island*. Wjeratne told Gōta that he was doing a good job and that since he has been in the operational areas throughout, he would like Gōta to take a break in Colombo. Gōta said he was quite happy commanding his battalion, but Wijeratne had insisted that he should take up an appointment in Colombo. On minister Wijeratne's orders, he was posted to the Kotelawala Defence Academy (KDA) as the deputy commandant at the end of 1990. Several weeks later, on 2 March 1991, Ranjan Wijeratne was assassinated in a massive bomb blast just meters from his private residence in Colombo. It was after the charismatic deputy defence minister was assassinated that Gōta put in his papers for retirement. He retired from the army on 1 November 1991. Looking back at this period, Gōta says *"A lot of good officers left because they thought the way the war was conducted was an exercise in futility. The LTTE would be cleared from one place only to return the moment the army withdrew. There was no driving factor to remain because nothing worthwhile was happening".*

Chapter 32

The Decade of Darkness

In the year 1991, everything seemed to be going against Sri Lanka. When the government sought to purchase jet attack aircraft to meet the increased threat from the LTTE, no country wanted to sell aircraft to Sri Lanka. Finally, the Chinese agreed to sell some attack aircraft to Sri Lanka. What Sri Lanka wanted to buy from China were Fantan A-5s which could carry a payload of around 8,000 kilos – even more than the MiG-27s and could travel a distance of 500 km and back. At that time, the Fantan A-5 was used by Pakistan and Bangladesh as well. But due to pressure from the West, the Chinese said that they could sell only Chengdu F-7s to Sri Lanka. Since no other country was offering Sri Lanka even that, the government decided to go in for F-7s.

The Chinese had the requirement that a pilot should have 250 hours of jet flying experience to get into this plane. At that time Sri Lanka did not have any jet military aircraft nor did it have any jet pilots. Harsha Abeywickrema then a propeller driven fixed wing aircraft pilot was assigned as one of the first pilots to be trained by the Chinese instructors. He was taken to China for the initial training and his first impression of flying a jet was that 'everything happened faster'. The six Sri Lankan pilots who were subsequently trained by the Chinese instructors at Katunayake in an FT-5 jet trainer were not taught any combat manoeuvres. The Chinese instructors had explained to the air force that while they were authorized to teach them to fly the jets, they were not authorized to teach ground attack manoeuvres. Later, Harsha Abeywickrema and two other pilots had

197

to make a visit to Pakistan to learn ground attack manoeuvres in a jet.

On 19 March 1991, the LTTE launched a massive attack on the Silavathurai camp in the Mannar district. After three days of intense fighting, the LTTE attackers were beaten off by Kamal Gunaratne, the second in command of the 6th Gajaba battalion with 125 terrorists dead and seventy six T-56 assault rifles, 12 light machine guns, three RPG launchers and a stock of ammunition captured by the army. This was one of the few victories for the army after 1990 – the victory being mainly that the camp was not overrun by the LTTE. During the siege, helicopters would land inside the Silavathurai camp and take off in less than a minute. In such circumstances, it was only the walking wounded who could be evacuated.

The seriously wounded were never evacuated because nobody could be found to take the stretcher to the chopper under fire for fear that they would become casualties themselves. It was a brutal, every-man-for-himself scenario. Triage was practiced in reverse. Usually, the walking wounded would be looked at later and those that are either unconscious or immobile will be looked at first. But during the siege of Silavathurai, it was the walking wounded who managed to rush to the helicopter as soon as it landed and elbow their way in and the stretcher cases remained on their stretchers in the camp. This was now a demoralized and defensive army after the string of defeats in 1990. If the seriously wounded managed to live, it was only because the LTTE was not able to overrun the camp.

On 22 April 1991, the helicopter landing site of the Elephant Pass camp came under LTTE mortar fire. This important camp was kept supplied by air as were all other camps in the north and with just a few mortar rounds, the LTTE succeeded in creating a major crisis for the government. Following the mortar attack, air force pilots refused to land at Elephant Pass and keeping this isolated camp supplied became a major issue. By June 1991, the Elephant Pass camp was surrounded by the LTTE. The camp had about 600 men and was besieged by an estimated 3000 LTTE cadres and there was no way to induct troops by land. Food was supplied through air drops. As water could not be dropped from a height, it was blocks of ice in bags that was dropped from the planes into the lagoon. Everything that was dropped on the ground came in powdered form. Sacks of dhal that were dropped had instantly turned into dhal powder due to the impact. Bags of fresh food like chicken and vegetables were dropped into the lagoon, from where the soldiers fished them out. At times bags of supplies would fall outside the defence lines and on such occasions, the troops would use ropes and hooks to pull the bags into the camp.

On 10 July 1991, a massive attack on the camp commenced. On the third day, at around 7.00 pm, the LTTE began firing mortars and RPGs at the camp and a terrorist contingent several hundred strong, began to advance behind a specially built armoured bulldozer designed to withstand both small arms fire and RPGs. As the modified bulldozer crashed through the army defences and the LTTE cadres coming behind it engaged the soldiers in close quarter combat, infantryman Gamini Kularatne of the 6th Sinha Battalion had clambered up the steel ladder of the armoured bulldozer and lobbed two grenades in through the open hatch, killing the operator inside. But Kularatne himself was cut down by LTTE fire, giving rise to a legend. With their bulldozer destroyed, the LTTE was forced to withdraw by midnight.

Operation Balavegaya was launched by Brigadier Vijaya Wimalaratne to relieve the besieged Elephant Pass camp. Gōta was at this time, Deputy Commandant of the Kotelawala Defence Academy and was not involved in the Elephant Pass operation but his battalion was. Troops were landed on the Vettalankerny beach to the east of the besieged camp in what was at that time the largest amphibious landing attempted by the Sri Lankan armed forces, and they had to fight their way to the target. The 1st and 4th Gajaba Battalions were sent for the seaborne assault. The troops assembled in ships and barges off the coast of Vettalankerny while about 45 dinghies were prepared for the initial landing. Fifteen of them were to secure the beach head, and the other 30 were to bring in the main force.

It was a primitive, brutal war. There would be 12 soldiers in each dinghy and the rule was that no one could turn back unless more than six of the 12 men had been hit by enemy fire. Only if the seventh was injured, could any boat turn back. Eight boats made it to the shore through withering enemy fire. After establishing a foothold on the beach, troops quickly cleared an area and then the barges brought the rest of the troops and the armoured vehicles. At this time, the army did not have any tracked vehicles and all armoured vehicles ran on tyres. The distance from the Vettalankerny beach head to the Elephant Pass camp was about 18 km. It took over three weeks for the two battalions that landed to fight their way to the camp through tough LTTE resistance. All along the route, the LTTE had Vietnam-style single man fox holes which they used with devastating effect on the advancing troops. The troops in fact had to crawl much of the way on their bellies, using their helmets to scoop out depressions in the sandy soil to take cover. Twenty six soldiers killed during the siege had been cremated inside the Elephant Pass camp. Fifty two had been injured. Later, in an interview with BBC correspondent Chris Morris on 1 September 1991, Prabhakaran would claim that the LTTE had now graduated from being a guerrilla force into a conventional force with the siege of Elephant Pass.

* * * * *

The nature of naval warfare was to undergo a radical change from 1990 onwards. In the 1980s, the LTTE never confronted the navy on the sea. Moreover the navy's strategy of using large command and surveillance ships with sophisticated radar systems in the Palk Straits as mother ships for the smaller fast attack craft, had also been successful. But from 1990, a deadly new weapon was added to the LTTE arsenal - the suicide boat. Thus the Sri Lankan navy became the first navy in the world to face suicide attacks on the sea. On 16 July 1990, the command and surveillance ship SLNS *Edithara*, commanded by Lt Commander Sarath Weerasekera had seen a cluster of boats moving out into sea from Velvettiturei at around 10.30 in the night and had gone to investigate.

Usually, LTTE boats would try to escape when confronted. But this time, to the surprise of the crew on *Edithara*, the LTTE boats came straight at the naval vessels. Three suicide boats had attacked while two other boats provided covering fire for the suicide boats to dash at the navy vessel. All three LTTE boats were destroyed in cannon fire from the naval vessel but the third exploded just yards from the *Edithara* which sustained serious damage as a result. Only one naval crew member was killed, but the ship had been spattered with human flesh from the last suicide boat.

Because the LTTE had targeted the command and surveillance ship, the fast attack craft now had to act as escorts for their mother ships instead of going out in search of terrorist boats. By this time, LTTE boats had also improved. Earlier in this narrative, when an LTTE boat was destroyed for the first time in 1984, it had only two 40 horse power engines. But on 21 July 1990, the navy destroyed an LTTE boat with two 225 horse power out board motors plus three more 55 horse power OBMs on standby and in addition was armed with two mounted .50 calibre machine guns. With this kind of speed and firepower combined with explosives laden suicide boats, the sea tigers had come into their own.

The LTTE soon added another dimension to their modus operandi on the sea. In earlier days, stealth was the key word and the LTTE tried to avoid being detected. Then it changed to head on confrontation. To this was added deception. In the early 1990s the LTTE's suicide boats still could not match the speeds of the naval fast attack craft and they could not launch suicide attacks on a moving vessel. They had to use various ruses to get close to the naval vessels by for example, pretending to be fishermen in distress, and exploding themselves when the Dvora comes close. On 4 May 1991, another command and surveillance ship the *Abheetha* was blasted and badly damaged by a suicide boat which pretended to be a smuggling boat. When taken alongside to be searched, the sea tiger cadres exploded their boat, tearing a gaping hole in the hull of the *Abheetha*. Seventeen navy crewmen died in that attack.

Another LTTE strategy in the early 1990s was to attack ships at anchor. At that time, most such suicide attacks were carried out in the night. The navy vessels were larger and easy to spot whereas the LTTE boats were smaller and more difficult for the navy to spot. The Dvoras had radar but the radars were useless in the night. In the late 1990s, the navy went in for thermal cameras. The thermal cameras gave the navy the upper hand once again and LTTE boats were not able to sneak up on them at night. Over the years, the LTTE's operational ability on the sea would keep improving. The navy had a hard time keeping up. At the initial stages, the fast attack craft were equipped mostly with 20mm guns and the larger offshore patrol vessels with 37mm cannon. Later the LTTE too began to fit their boats with the same high calibre guns.

* * * * *

In 1990 began a decade of darkness. Between 1990 and 2001, the army launched many ground offensives of which only one or two would have a lasting impact on the LTTE. The 50th anniversary publication of the Sinha Regiment listed the major operations launched by the army against the LTTE as follows.

1990: OP Gajasinghe – To reinforce Elephant Pass and evacuate the Kilinochchi camp.
1990: OP Trivida Balaya – To relieve Jaffna Fort
1991: OP Vanni Vickrama I – To destroy LTTE bases in Mannar
1991: OP Vanni Vickrama II – Same as above
1991: OP Balavegaya I – To relieve besieged Elephant Pass camp
1991: OP Asakasena – To divert LTTE from Elephant Pass
1991: OP Akunupahara – To destroy LTTE camps in jungles of Welioya
1992: OP Sath Bala – To capture Alampil (a sea tiger base)
1992: OP Balavegaya II – To link Elephant Pass with Vettalankerny
1995: OP Thunder strike – To clear launching pad for the Riviresa operation.

1995: OP Riviresa I – To liberate Jaffna town
1995: OP Riviresa II – To liberate Tennamarachchi
1995: OP Riviresa III – To take over Vadamarachchi
1996: OP Sathjaya I,II,III – To capture Paranthan and Kilinochchi
1996: OP Edi Bala – To link Mannar-Vavuniya road with Cheddikulam
1997/98 OP Jayasikurui – To open a land route to Jaffna
1998 OP Rivibala – To capture the Oddusudan area
1998: OP Ranagosa I – To expand western army defence line in the Vanni
1998: OP Ranagosa II – To capture Madhu
1998: OP Ranagosa III – To capture Palampiddy
1999: OP Bunker Buster – To destroy enemy bunkers in Elephant Pass and
Paranthan
1999: OP Ranagosa I (Continued)
1999: OP Ranagosa II (Continued)
1999: OP Ranagosa III (Continued)
1999: OP Ranagosa IV – To secure coastline south of Vedithaltivu.
1999: OP Ranagosa V – More operations in the Mannar district.
1999: OP New Year Strike – To hit enemy points beyond Paranthan.
1999: OP Team Spirit – Same as above
1999: OP Whirlwind – Same as above
1999: OP Side Thrust – To destroy enemy defence lines on the western flank
1999: OP Ralapahara I – To secure Kandavilai eastern flank
1999: OP Ralapahara II – To destroy enemy defence lines on the eastern flank.
1999: OP Watershed I – To capture east of Ampakam
1999: OP Watershed II – To consolidate hold over Ampakam
2000: OP Rivikirana I, II – To capture Ariyalai and outlying areas
2000: OP Kinihira I – To capture Chavakachcheri area.
2000: OP Kinihira II – To capture Sarasalai-Madduvil area
2000: OP Kinihira III – Same as above
2000:OPKinihira IV – To capture Madduvil and Chavakachcheri areas.
2000: OP Kinihira V – Same as above
2000: OP Kinihira VI – Same as above
2000: OP Kinihira VII – To secure Ariyalai Gamudawa site
2000: OP Kinihira VIII – To capture Muhamalai
2000: OP Kinihira IX – Same as above
2001: OP Agnikheela – To recapture Elephant Pass.

This is by no means an exhaustive list. There were dozens more bearing various names such as *Bhoomi Kampa* (1992), *Bambara Chakara* (1994), *Quick Strike* (1996), *Royal Flush* (1996) etcetera. All the operations conducted by the army against the LTTE are too numerous to mention here. None of these operations really had the aim of destroying the LTTE. Any gains made were always soon lost. The only offensive of lasting value was the *Riviresa* operation launched to capture the Jaffna peninsula. The rest were exercises in futility. The only purpose they served was to provide combat experience for the army.

Chapter 33

A Failing Military

When Lt Gen Cecil Waidyaratne who led the crack outfit that crushed the second JVP insurrection became commander of the army on 16 November 1991, he took over a demoralized outfit. In his unpublished memoirs, he observed that between mid-1990 and the time of his taking over as commander, the army had suffered the following major setbacks.

* *Complete overrunning of the Kokavil army camp with the entire cadre of over 70 men massacred.*

* *Attack on the Mankulam camp and the camp completely destroyed.*

* *The abandoning of the Jaffna Fort. The rescue operation was delayed for over two weeks due to heavy resistance from the LTTE.*

* *The siege of Elephant Pass base camp for over six weeks with many of its defensible positions overrun. Reinforcements were kept at bay by the LTTE thus starving the camp of supplies and food for over a month until the task force launched from Vettalankerny linked up.*

* *The killing of 50 elite commandos in Kattaparichchan.*

* *Attack and siege of the Mulleitivu camp.*

* *Daily attacks on camps and convoys.*

* *Ambushing of entire road clearing patrols.*

Waidyaratne wrote *"Thus when I took over as Army Commander I had to face a situation where terrorists had the upper hand within the north and the east and Army morale was at a low ebb..."* and he was right. The army was in dire straits. This could be gauged from the fact that Brigadier Wimalaratne described the *Balavegaya* Operation launched to relieve the Elephant Pass camp in July 1991, in an official army document as "The greatest victory achieved by the Sri Lankan armed forces." If the prevention of an army camp from being overrun by terrorists is the greatest victory that the army has won, that in itself was a major problem.

In the early 1990s, the situation was such that even inspired soldiers like Wimalaratne could not conceive of anything better than simply holding on to what the armed forces already had. Even this holding operation had to be done amidst many shortcomings. Officers involved in this 'greatest victory' (the operation to relieve the Elephant Pass camp) noted the lack of 60mm and 81mm mortar ammunition. At that time, for the army 'artillery' meant mostly mortars and the lack of mortar ammunition meant that they did not get sufficient covering fire. Lt Col Lawrence Fernando, the commanding officer of the 1st Gajaba Battalion after Gōta left the army, was to note that there was a need to provide adequate vehicles, radios and flak jackets for the troops as well as adequate infantry training. It had become an aimless war fought by ill equipped troops.

It was with Cecil Waidyaratne that thought first began to be given to an overall strategy to defeat terrorism conclusively. Waidyaratne was not a flamboyant and inspired field commander like Wimalaratne, but he was a good military theoretician. In 1989, Waidyaratne led the Operations Combine, a separate command structure with powers over the army, police navy and air force, set up to crush the JVP insurrection which he achieved in record time. Even the crack unit that Wimalaratne created - the RDF - was deployed in Colombo under Waidyaratne's command. On 29 June 1991, some months before he became commander of the army, and was still the army chief of staff, Major Gen Cecil Waidyaratne submitted a proposal to Prime Minister D.B.Wijetunga who chaired meetings of the security council. He wrote:

"We have been fighting this current war now for over a year with a winning position clearly not in sight. On the contrary the LTTE has gained territory in the north. In the north, damage to private and government property, loss of life and limb of our soldiers and countrymen far outweigh our military successes whatever they may have been. We should not get carried away by dramatized propaganda. Therefore the entire programme needs reassessment of why we have failed....It is essential that we do not underestimate the enemy. We must realize that the LTTE is no pushover

204

force. They are fighting.., a protracted revolutionary war and their ability to sustain it needs no elaboration. Their performance on the international scene to obtain support for this war is also commendable."

Basing himself on this assessment, Waidyaratne recommended that the main theatre of operations be shifted from the north to the east. He argued that if the LTTE loses the east, the Eelam concept is dead. A well coordinated political and military strategy can bring normalcy to the east. The security forces did not have the resources to take the north and east together to conduct two major campaigns simultaneously. He said that the east should be tackled first because there were large liberated areas in the east already, and it was more feasible to strike first where the enemy was weakest. After taking over the east, the government forces could move with 'overwhelming force' to the north.

This finally is what happened between 2007 and 2009 – taking over the east first and then moving with 'overwhelming force' on the north. General Waidyaratne was in that sense right in his assessment of what had to be done. But the 1990s was not the time his plan was going to be implemented. Waidyaratne died in 2001. It was eight years after his death that his vision was to pay off. Gōta himself rates Waidyaratne among the best in the army at making 'military appreciations'. Even though Waidyaratne was a military visionary and was ruthless enough to fight a ruthless enemy, his tenure as commander was to prove an ill-fated one. He held the post of commander for barely two years. He took over in the midst of an unprecedented string of humiliating defeats for the army and during his tenure, the downward slide not only continued but grew in intensity.

The first army operation to be launched under Waidyaratne's command was operation *Hayepahara* with Brigadier Rohan Daluwatte as the Brigade commander, which ended on 31 March 1992. Ironically, even though it was Waidyaratne who for the first time conceived of an overall plan to defeat the LTTE, the first operation even under his command was of a similar nature to the others that had been carried out earlier. Operation *Hayepahara* was meant to destroy as many terrorists as possible in the general area of Kokkutuduwai, a coastal town to the north of Welioya. The army ended up with 42 fatalities and 154 injured and had precious little to show for their efforts. The claim was that over 200 terrorists had been killed but what really happened is evident from the recommendations made by the brigade commander who led the operation. "...*The temptation to panic when a leader is hit should be avoided. The next in line should take over command and continue with the offensive. Pausing or turning back even for a short time can be disastrous...More training has to be carried out together to build up mutual trust...*"

After Waidyaratne became army commander, he set about trying to infuse professionalism into what was then clearly a failing army. The director of operations of the army issued circulars to commanders at all levels from time to time outlining what went wrong in incidents where the army suffered losses, so that commanders could take remedial action. On 6 July 1992, Brigadier Lucky Algama the then director of operations issued such a circular to all commanders, basing himself on two incidents. He made the following observations:

Sinhapura Incident 29 - January 1992 (Attack on patrol, 13 troops killed)

* *Troops had not carried out proper route clearing but moved 'non-tactically' along the road.*
* *Troops not caught in the initial fire fight ran away without regrouping for counter attack.*
* *The Non-Commissioned Officer in charge of the patrol had been the first to run away.*
* *Troops had not been alert but had been laughing, joking and singing when leaving the camp on patrol.*
* *Senior officers at the Sinhapura detachment had not made any attempt to attack terrorists after the attack.*

Thoppigala Incident - 27 February 1992 (Attack on clearing operation, 20 troops killed)

* *Troops had been moving in open country through paddy fields but not tactically.*
* *At the time of the attack, troops had been enjoying a meal sitting in the open without any sentry points.*
* *Terrorists accepted the easy target offered and attacked inflicting the maximum casualties.*
* *After terrorists engaged troops there had been no command and control - the officers had run in one direction and the troops in another.*
* *The body of troops that went out on this march did not have a proper command and control structure with some being administrative personnel and others had just returned from leave or other non-combat appointments.*

On 2 May 1992, about six months into his tenure, Waidyaratne issued a circular through the directorate of operations of army headquarters titled *'Measures to improve the operational capability of troops, to prevent casualties and to improve level of morale'*. In this circular issued to all commands, Waidyaratne wrote –

"I have always stressed the need for training and it is nothing but training that will minimize own casualties and equipment losses. I have also stressed that training is the 'best welfare' for the soldier and every effort must be made to find time to train the soldiers during off hours in the detachments."

"It is once again reiterated that certain precautionary measures and steps have to be taken on various aspects to ensure that the casualties to own troops and loss of equipment are prevented or minimized"

"It has been observed that a large number of casualties occur when own troops are on fighting patrols, moving in vehicles for routine admin runs and securing the forward defence lines. The steps and measures indicated would give a definite improvement in avoiding our own casualties and improve the general standard of all the troops."

Among the measures ordered by Waidyaratne were the following

* *Reducing routine admin movements outside the detachment to the minimum by stocking up on rations for long periods.*
* *When any movement takes place outside the detachment, adequate resources to cover such movement should be ensured if necessary with help from the Divisional headquarters.*
* *The Divisional commanders must check the rolls of the battalions to ensure that the strengths are accurate and the platoons and companies are formed properly.*
* *Divisional and Brigade commanders must speak to the troops regularly and motivate them.*
* *Commanding officers of battalions must stay on a rotational basis in the detachments of his battalion and should examine among other things, the defence layout, offensive operations, training programmes leave, duty, food, welfare etc.*
* *Infantry should be trained to operate with armour and they should be taught that it was not necessary to 'hug armour' in order to be supported by armour. Armoured units should be educated that their biggest enemy was the rocket propelled grenade (RPG) and infantry must be arranged to protect the tanks.*
* *RCLs (A reference to recoilless heavy calibre anti-tank guns) and machine guns are long range weapons and should not be carried with the forward most troops.*

* Commando and Special Forces troops must be able to conduct small group operations. Their actions must always be daring in keeping with their training. If a 4 man team meets a terrorist group of 12 they must be able to destroy the terrorists without calling for reinforcements.

* All troops must rest during the day and dominate all areas by night. Although this has been explained clearly and passed down to everyone, this does not seem to happen. The terrorist gets a chance of infiltrating because we are not alert by night.

* There is a tendency to carry out operations with large numbers of troops and thereby we become targets. We must plan to operate with small numbers such as platoons or sections so that the enemy can be taken by surprise. Large numbers of troops moving about the jungles makes a lot of noise and own troops may be taken by surprise as a result. Operations carried out with a small force could achieve surprise and will give better results.

* Change around of troops must be carried out particularly in difficult areas to ensure that the troops' morale is maintained.

* Route clearance and fighting patrols and ambushes must be conducted to dominate all areas and especially the roads.

* The carrying of large quantities of ammo by troops on patrols and ambushes leads to restriction of movement and fatigue. Kit and equipment should be carried depending on the nature and duration of the operation.

* Commands from divisional to battalion level should carry out investigations into losses, failures and heavy casualties and report to the army commander through the Divisional commanders. No effort should be made to cover up faults as this is 'dangerous and counterproductive'.

A similar circular was issued to all commands two days later on 4 May 1992 also under the signature of Lt Gen Waidyaratne with the title 'Protective measures and counter-action in the defences'. In this circular Waidyaratne wrote -

"In the recent past, there have been a fair number of incidents where the FDLs (defence lines) have been attacked by the terrorists resulting in casualties to our own forces and loss of weapons and equipment. In most of these instances the terrorists have escaped without losses. My own observations are that the defences are not organized properly in some places and the defence routine is not carried out properly to ensure that attacks by the terrorist are repulsed with confidence."

Waidyaratne adduced several reasons as to why the terrorists had been successful in attacking the army defence lines, the foremost among them being that troops tended to fall asleep at night due to fatigue. The lethargic attitude of the troops, not dominating the area in front of the defence lines, and not constructing obstacles in front of the defence lines along with reasons like poor visibility on dark or misty nights were adduced by him as reasons for the success of the terrorists. He proposed the following remedial action.

* Construction of a proper trench system on the defence lines with good fields of fire and observation. Bunkers must be properly constructed and have a field of fire of at least 100 meters.

* A good obstacle belt around the defences with mines, concertina wire, trip flares, punji pits etc should be constructed to make it difficult for terrorists to launch attacks and these should be regularly inspected by commanders.

* The no-man's land should be dominated up to 200 meters from own line with aggressive ambushes and patrols every night.

* Troops in bunkers must be 100% alert.

* Alternative bunkers must be available for troops as well as dummy bunkers with dummies.

* Routine movements must be avoided when the enemy can observe such movements.

* Grenades are hardly being used by the troops. They should be educated in the use of grenades to destroy the enemy.

* Positioning of long range weapons and indirect weapons such as mortars must be to the rear of the bunkers to ensure the maximum kills.

* Excess arms and ammo should not be kept in the bunkers.

* Trench systems with communication trenches should be organized.

* Counter attack plans must be planned and rehearsed so that troops will know what to do when under attack.

* A system for the replenishment of ammo must be organized.

* Bunker lines must not be held thinly but in depth.

* Commanders at all levels must think three to four levels below them when inspecting the defence layout of the detachments.

* Commanders must visit defence lines irregularly during the day and at night to ensure alertness at all times. Close supervision is essential at all times.

Chapter 34

On the Verge of Collapse

On 5 August 1992, Brigadier Lucky Algama, director of operations of the army, issued a comprehensive 70 point check list to all commanders with the title *"Check list for troops on holding role including aspects pertaining to defences, operations, training, administration, logistics and welfare"*. Brigadier Algama issued specific instructions in a covering letter that was sent with this check list. *"Defences must be checked as per this check list and the assessment must be marked by the detachment commanders and then submitted to the battalion commanders who in turn would make his assessment and forward it to the brigade command. The brigade commander must make an assessment and take necessary action to remedy any shortcomings immediately."* Among the things to be checked and confirmed were the following:

* Bunkers should be able to resist mortar, RPG and machine gun fire and should be able to support one another.

* Bunkers should have a clear field of fire of at least 100 meters.

* The enemy should not have any cover around the detachment to approach the defence line.

* Reserve troops should be earmarked to meet contingencies and trenches should be available to enable reserves to take up position.

* Two thirds of the detachment should be out at night dominating the area around the detachment.

* Will the detachment be able to hold on until reinforcements arrive in the event of an attack?

* Does the detachment have adequate support weapons like machine guns and mortars?
* Adequate stocks of ammunition?
* Can the detachment withstand simultaneous attacks from at least three directions?
* Are sentry points able to support one another?
* Are communication trenches available?
* Does the detachment have a casualty evacuation plan?
* Is adequate medical support available in the detachment?
* What proportion of troops are on leave and how have cover up duties been arranged?
* What percentage of troops are on the sick list?
* Is the storage system for weapons secure?
* The water supply into the detachment... etc.

In addition to the above, another such circular was issued to the troops by Brigadier C.S.Weerasooriya on 29 September 1992. Brigadier Weerasoriya had replaced Algama as the army director of operations by this time. Weerasooriya's circular was titled *"Security of equipment and war-like stores in operational areas"*. This circular set out in detail the measures that had to be taken with regard to armoured fighting vehicles and other specialized vehicles and heavy guns etcetera. The instructions were as follows.

* Areas where such vehicles or equipment are parked or stored should be declared high security zones and sentries posted day and night.
* When not in immediate use, a key component (such as the rotor arm in vehicles) should be removed.
* Such assets should never be left unattended day or night and electronic or mechanical alarm systems must be affixed.
* Obstacles should be constructed in the vicinity to cut off escape or prevent entry.
* The optical instruments of artillery guns should be removed and stored separately when not in use. The breech blocks and firing pins of guns should also be removed when not in use.

Even after all these instructions were given, Brigadier Weerasooriya had to issue yet another circular on 15 October 1992 titled *"Measures to be adopted for prevention of casualties due to ambushes and terrorist attacks."* He was to write ruefully, *"A study of the eyes only reports of the recent terrorist ambushes in Welioya and Trincomalee*

211

has revealed that the main causes are mostly common to all incidents. Instructions have been issued from time to time from this directorate and it appears that troops initially comply and after a period of time, tend to throw caution to the winds and act in a complacent and irresponsible manner. Some of the mistakes committed are careless and unpardonable and this results in the terrorists who keep watching us all the time getting an opportunity to strike when least expected. Therefore an awareness of the threat should be constantly emphasized to all ranks down to the last soldier." Brigadier Weerasooriya had mentioned three instances where non compliance with instructions given earlier had led to serious setbacks for the army.

Attack at Palampattaru on 9 September 1992.

* *In this instance an ambush laid for the LTTE was ambushed by the LTTE.*
* *The ambush was led by a staff sergeant and not an officer*
* *Excessive and wasteful use of ammo by firing without aiming caused a shortage of ammo at the latter stage of the confrontation.*
* *Induction of troops had been poor as the enemy had been able to locate the ambush.*

Ambush on 9 September 1992 on Nelumwewa-Ehetugaswewa road

* *In this instance a platoon was moved to a position beyond the defence lines as backup in case of an attack. The practice is to take up position in the evening and withdraw at first light. However this platoon withdrew with all personnel mounted on a tractor and was ambushed at 6.30 am.*
* *Troops had taken it for granted that it was safe when withdrawing after guard/patrol duties.*
* *There had been no night movement to dominate the gaps in the defence lines.*
* *Civilian intelligence on a possible terrorist ambush had not been taken seriously.*
* *Considering grey areas as completely safe, and relaxing.*
* *The route clearing party had been travelling in the tractor along with the other troops thus violating instructions regarding movement of troops in vehicles in vulnerable areas.*
* *Troops tend to stick to routine and operate in a relaxed manner which are capitalised on by the terrorists.*

212

Blasting of Kiliveddy ferry with an underwater mine 10 September 1992

* *The ferry was destroyed by a wire controlled under water mine when a vehicle carrying troops and some civilians were travelling on it. Twenty two troops and six civilians were killed.*

* *Troops frequently used the ferry but those responsible for its security had not maintained vigilance in the area so terrorists had been able to infiltrate and plant the under- water mine.*

* *Normal civilian activity was taken as a sign that there was no terrorist activity.*

* *Staggered use of the ferry by sending small groups across would have prevented the entire platoon being caught up in one explosion.*

* *Troops made the mistake of not getting off the vehicle even after it had been loaded on to the ferry.*

* *The mine was activated on a holiday when very few Tamil civilians would be using it. The LTTE did not mind a few civilians getting killed if they could kill more soldiers. But this point was not taken into consideration by the commanding officer.*

It appeared that despite any instructions that may emanate from army headquarters, careless mistakes continued to be made. The worst and most unforgivable such mistake was made by none other than the most senior officers conducting the war – Major General Denzil Kobbekaduwa and Brigadier Vijaya Wimalaratne. While on a pre-operational inspection on Kayts Island in the Jaffna peninsula, on 8 August 1992, in a clear breach of security instructions, Kobbekaduwa had got Brigadier Wimalaratne, and several other officers into one vehicle which ran over a landmine killing all except one soldier in the vehicle. Three other contemporaries of Gōta in his Sinha Regiment days in 1975/76, died in that single blast – Colonels G.H.Ariyaratne, Neomal Palipana and H.R.Stephen.

The stage was thus set for a series of major debacles that would bring Sri Lanka to its knees by the end of the decade. The two worst debacles in Sri Lanka's military history up to that time, took place during Waidyaratne's tenure as commander – the attacks on the Janakapura and Pooneryn army camps. The Janakapura army camp in Welioya along with three other satellite camps in the area was attacked on 23 July 1993 by the LTTE in commemoration of the 10th anniversary of the July 1983 riots. Twenty three soldiers lost their lives in the attack and around 30 were reported missing. Later the LTTE exhibited the bodies of 18 soldiers killed in the Janakapura attack.

213

Well over 50 million Rupees worth of arms and ammunition was taken by the LTTE after flattening the camp with the army's own bulldozers. This was officially declared to be the worst defeat ever suffered by the army at the time.

On 27 July 1993, a furious Waidyaratne wrote a letter reprimanding the divisional commander under whose command the Janakapura camp functioned pointing out that the army had lost a large number of men as well as considerable quantities of weapons and ammunition in the Janakapura debacle and that this incident was 'a serious reflection on the level of alertness maintained by the detachments under his command'. He fumed that the debacle was demoralizing to the army and totally unacceptable when the circumstances under which the camp fell are examined. Waidyaratne observed that proper supervision of the Janakapura camp defences had not taken place and the fundamentals spelt out in the defence line check list issued through the army directorate of operations on 5 August 1992 had not been adhered to.

The Pooneryn army camp was located on a long thin sliver of land that stuck out into the Palk Straits just below the Jaffna peninsula. To the north was the Jaffna lagoon, to the west was the Palk Straits and on the east was the town of Nallur. The sprawling camp was six kilometres from west to east and about 2 km from north to south. On 11 November 1993, Capt Sampath Karunatilleke the adjutant to the officer commanding of the 1st SLLI battalion was in a mortar point in the camp when at around 1.30 am, he heard the sound of small arms fire in the distance. He went to the radio room to see what was going on and he learnt that an attack was in progress in the western part of the Pooneryn defence lines known as Koma Point. The Jaffna town was just across the lagoon from Koma Point. Unbeknownst to those in the battalion headquarters, the Koma Point defence lines had by then already been infiltrated by the LTTE and while attackers coming across the Jaffna lagoon had engaged the army lines from the front, the infiltrators had engaged them from the rear. Capt Karunatilleke reckons that at least 150 infiltrators had been inside the camp when the attack commenced. The army defence lines were overrun and five to six hundred LTTE cadres poured into the breach.

The LTTE attackers swept everything before them as they converged on the two battalion headquarters located in close proximity to one another at the eastern end of the camp. As the company bases fell, radio communication was lost. At some bases, soldiers and LTTE cadres had been fighting hand to hand. In addition to the group that had broken through the Koma Point defence lines, another attacking party had come across the Jaffna lagoon from Chavakachcheri and had engaged the north eastern defence lines as well. By 6.30 am they had taken over the entire camp including the 3rd Gajaba battalion headquarters, and the Armoured Corps yard from where the LTTE drove away two T-55 main battle tanks.

The survivors in the camp were now restricted to the 1st SLLI battalion headquarters. The soldiers had thought the LTTE would use the battle tanks against them but they had for some inexplicable reason simply driven them away without using them in the ongoing battle. The defenders in the 1st SLLI headquarters had heavy calibre armour-penetrating vehicle mounted recoilless guns referred to in the Sri Lanka army as RCLs, ready to use on their own tanks if they entered the battle. The LTTE also took a heavy duty 120 mortar. But the 1st SLLI support company was able to counterattack and prevent more artillery from being removed. Small groups of soldiers had been retreating to the 1st SLLI battalion headquarters from other parts of the camp.

A ring of defences was set up around the battalion headquarters and the defenders managed to hold out till reinforcements landed at Koma Point in an amphibious operation. In the meantime the defenders also got air support. Ammunition for the T-56 assault rifles and medical supplies were air dropped but as is usual in such instances, much of it fell into enemy hands. The last patch of land controlled by the defenders around the SLLI headquarters was about 500X500 meters and making accurate air drops into such a small area was not easy. The defenders used their mortar rounds very sparingly, firing only when absolutely necessary. Even T-56 rounds had been rationed.

On the day that the attack commenced about 800 to 900 troops had been deployed on the defence lines. In Capt Karunatilleke's reckoning, on the first day over 300 soldiers lost their lives. The medical facilities in the camp were inadequate to cope with the number of casualties coming in. There were only four medical orderlies to treat all the wounded. The defenders managed to maintain radio communication with Palaly throughout the attack and they had to fight continuously day and night for three days. When reinforcements arrived at Koma Point on the fourth day, pressure on the defenders had come down palpably. It took about a week to clear the camp of the LTTE completely. The LTTE had evacuated their casualties from the beachhead they had established just across the lagoon from

Chavakachcheri. Of the 1000 or so men who had been in the camp only about 500 remained by the time reinforcements arrived.

Tell-tale signs of an impending attack had been around for some time. About three months before the attack, the army had detected two LTTE infiltrators inside the camp. A little to the east of Koma Point, there had been a refugee camp with about 30 to 40 Tamil families. The refugees had provided these two infiltrators with food. On some days, search parties would find rigifoam floats used by infiltrators to swim across the lagoon into the camp. On the day of the attack, infiltrators had used rigifoam floats which had been neatly wrapped in dark coloured cloth to swim across the lagoon. After everything was over, army reinforcements had found over two hundred such rigifoam floats strewn all over the beach. The LTTE attacking party had used cellophane bags to prevent their weapons from getting wet while crossing the lagoon.

The LTTE knew that the defences of the huge encampment were weak because troops were spread out too thinly over a large area. Capt Karunatillke reckons that if the camp was to be defended effectively, they would have needed at least 2000 troops. But there were only half that number in the camp at the time of the attack. Karunatilleke had in fact, informed his superiors that troop numbers were inadequate.

In this unpublished memoirs, Waidyaratne was to write later, *"In the wake of the Pooneryn attack, I decided to resign from the post of commander of the army. The debacles at Janakapura and Pooneryn had occurred despite all the steps taken by me to retrain and re-equip the army. The subsequent courts of inquiry into these incidents revealed that there had been gross negligence at all levels on the field...Armoured Corps officers had failed to adhere even to the most basic precautionary measures for armoured vehicles in operational areas. I decided that if this level of negligence and irresponsibility was possible after I had retrained a large part of the army, the responsibility was entirely mine."*

"Even while the rescue operations were being planned, at a conference held for this purpose, I openly expressed my desire to retire from the army as soon as Pooneryn was recovered from the terrorists and stabilized. Not only was I appalled at the number of troops killed, as a former Armoured Corps officer, I was also ashamed that battle tanks had fallen into enemy hands and all this was due to nothing but simple negligence. Upon my return to Colombo, I spoke to the president and expressed my desire to retire immediately on the basis that I accepted full responsibility for all that happened at Pooneryn..."

Sri Lanka had seen nothing like this up to that time. The second in command of the 3rd Gajaba Battalion was killed and this single battalion had 149 dead and another 115 disappeared and presumed dead. Altogether, the army death toll was around 500. However a small group held out, and as the Gajaba Silver Jubilee publication says, 'saved the self respect of the 3rd Battalion and the Gajaba name'. The remnants of the 3rd Gajaba Battalion were withdrawn to Palaly on 23 November to be 'reorganized'. What was meant by this was replacing the dead and disappeared with fresh recruits. This would be the first of many occasions before the war was over, that an entire battalion had to be 'reorganized' following massive losses in LTTE attacks. The army claimed that nearly 500 LTTE cadres had also died in the battle for Pooneryn, but that was hardly any consolation for what had happened.

Major T.T.R.de Silva of the 1st SLLI Battalion was given a field promotion for preventing the camp from being overrun by the enemy. Pooneryn also represented a major debacle for the Sri Lanka navy. There had been naval detachments in Senguppidy, Nagasivanthurei, and Pooneryn which were also attacked. These detachments were for the purpose of patrolling the Jaffna lagoon. Five inshore patrol craft were destroyed and 105 naval personnel lost their lives – the highest naval death toll in a single engagement during the entire war.

Chapter 35

Another False Peace

At the parliamentary elections held in August 1994, the UNP which had ruled the country for 17 years was voted out, and an SLFP led coalition, the Peoples' Alliance came into power under the leadership of Chandrika Kumaratunga. Like the Premadasa government before it, the Kumaratunga government also went in for peace talks with the LTTE. As soon as the PA was installed in power, they lifted the restrictions on the transport of certain items to the north as a goodwill measure. The LTTE for their part welcomed the election of the PA to power and expressed their willingness to have unconditional talks. After much discussion, an agreement for the cessation of hostilities was signed on 7 January 1995 after which the LTTE commenced the usual routine they followed during ceasefires.

On 18 February 1995, they held a massive demonstration in Jaffna where they read out eight demands to be presented to the government. Among the eight demands made, was the removal of the Pooneryn camp so that the Tamil people could use the Senguppidy passage 'without fear'. Another demand was that the army should vacate the areas they had 'forcibly occupied' and army check-points removed. They also wanted the restrictions on fishing lifted. Later, the LTTE would complain that even though the restrictions on the transport of certain items to Jaffna had been lifted, only a fraction of those items were actually making their way to Jaffna because the goods could not be taken beyond the Vavuniya checkpoint. The ceasefire between the LTTE and the Kumaratunga government did not last more than a few months.

The government may have wanted a ceasefire but the LTTE clearly did not. Just before mid-April 1995, the 3rd Gajaba battalion was holding a line on the eastern perimeter of the Palaly camp when two soldiers had been shot dead by the LTTE. Senior officers had been insisting that the commanding officer not say that the LTTE had attacked and killed the soldiers. The story given out was that the two soldiers had committed suicide. The government and even the army top brass were engaging in desperate self-deception about the true intentions of the LTTE. However they would come face to face with the reality within a matter of days.

Four large Chinese built 40 meter gun boats *Ranasuru, Ranaviru, Sooraya* and *Jagatha* were moored abreast at a jetty in the Trincomalee harbour on 19 April 1995, the outermost being the *Ranasuru*. Somatilleke Dissanayake was the commanding officer of the *Ranaviru*. That night, Dissanayake was on a routine inspection of the security illuminations around the vessels moored there and he was on the *Ranasuru* trying to adjust one of the flash lights when it was hit by a massive explosion. The blast was so powerful that the rear end of the vessel broke off completely and flew over the two other gun boats to land on the front part of the fourth vessel *Jagatha*. Dissanayake was left in the other half of the *Ranasuru* and fell into the sea when it tipped over. Twelve naval personnel lost their lives in the blast. Dissanayake managed to rescue one officer who was in the water.

The moment he got out of the water and stepped onto the pier, the *Soorya* also exploded. This time, the ship was completely obliterated with nothing but debris remaining. Dissanayake could see a shower of debris falling all around him but miraculously, nothing landed on him. The mast of the *Soorya* was found on the adjoining jetty. Strangely, Dissanayake's own ship the *Ranaviru* and the *Jagatha* suffered relatively little damage. These were huge barrel bombs that LTTE divers had brought under water to explode right under the ships. It is believed that each of the bombs would have had more than one hundred kilos of C-4 explosives each. The bodies of four LTTE suicide frogmen were found later.

Sarath Weerasekera was the commanding officer of the Trincomalee naval base when the two gun boats were destroyed in 1995. The Trincomalee bay covered a vast area and frogmen could be launched from any point along the coast. One of the methods adopted to counter the LTTE frogman threat was to explode grenades or gelignite sticks under water throughout the day and night at irregular intervals to force any frogmen who may be below, to surface. These were called 'scare charges'. Despite the name, the intention was not to scare any enemy frogmen but to kill or at least disorient them, by creating underwater shock waves. During the ceasefire, they did not explode scare charges in this manner and the LTTE made good use of that to launch this surprise attack. The navy did possess sonars but they were of the 'fish finder' type and not very effective.

Just over a week after the Trincomalee attack, on 28 April 1995, Major Dudley Weeraman of the Sri Lanka Engineer Corps was relaxing after lunch in his quarters on the outskirts of the Palaly military base Jaffna. He had been on an early morning operation in the Madagal area and had just got back to base and had his midday meal. He was listening to a complaint being made by one of his subordinates 2nd Lt S. Anthonyz who was complaining that the Engineers' Corps corporal who had been assigned to the Palaly airport to coordinate seating arrangements for their unit had not allowed him to get on the plane that was just about to leave from Palaly to Anuradhapura. The system at that time was that soldiers going on leave were allocated seats on the basis of the units they belonged to.

Each regiment had a corporal to represent them at the airport and it was this corporal who allocated seats to those in his unit going on leave. Major Weeraman was trying to pacify the irate junior officer who had been denied a seat on the flight that had just left, when they suddenly heard a loud noise and there were cries heard from outside that the plane had fallen. They all ran out. Major Weeraman commandeered a bicycle and rode as fast as possible to the scene of the crash. The plane had hit the ground a little distance away from the security forces headquarters within the Palaly complex soon after taking off and there were no survivors. At that moment everybody thought the plane had come down due to a technical defect. That night, another plane came in from Anuradhapura to take away the remains of those who had died.

The next morning, on 29 April 1995, Major Weeraman was taking a wash with other officers outside his quarters in the small camp he was billeted in, when somebody said that he just saw another plane coming in to land at Palaly fall. Major Weeraman had not believed it, but before long, he got the news that a plane had indeed fallen in Atchuveli, an area outside the army's control. Wing Commander Shirantha Gunatilleke had been on his way from Colombo to Palaly to inquire into what had happened to the other Avro. Even though many had seen the second plane falling, nobody had gone to check the wreckage because it was outside the control of the army and if there were any casualties among the party that goes out, there would have been no way of taking them out of Jaffna. Sea transport to Trincomalee would have taken too long.

At the Anuradhapura air force base, pilots had begun suspecting that both planes had been downed by missiles and they were up until 2.00 am discussing the situation. Wing Commander Kolitha Gunatillake too had joined the discussion. One of the pilots told him that they suspected that the planes had been brought down by surface to air missiles and that they would no longer be able to fly. Gunatilleke had barked, *"What do you mean you can't fly? Do you mean to say you can't get into an aircraft and go to Colombo?"* He then got all the pilots to write down all that they had been doing on a daily basis. They were to tick off functions they could continue to perform. If they couldn't perform a particular function, they should specify what they need to enable them to continue doing it.

By the next day, the pilots were able to tell air force headquarters that they could not perform certain functions unless protective devices such as anti-missile systems were provided. In any event, after this the transportation of troops and goods by air to Palaly was drastically curtailed. Jaffna was now supplied only by sea. What this meant was that soldiers could not go on leave except by sea. Senior officers would also visit Palaly by sea. The operation of the SIAI Marchettis by the air force came to a halt as these planes did not have a pressurized cabin or oxygen. This limited the height they could fly to about 10,000 feet. The range of the SA-14 and the SA-7 missiles which the LTTE was suspected to have, would be about 18,000 feet.

At the end of 1992 four Pukaras, an Argentinian produced twin engine ground attack aircraft had been introduced to the air force. While the SIAI Marchetti could carry only 14 rockets, the Pukara could carry around 75 and it could carry 18 bombs compared to the two carried by the SIAI Marchetti. It had two .50 and 7.62 calibre forward firing guns as well. The Pukara had a pressurised cabin and could operate at higher altitudes. In bombing missions, the Pukaras would go over the target at 5000 feet and go into a steep dive down to 1500 feet and release the bombs and pull up back to 5000 feet again. This could not be done now because the missile range was 18,000 feet. Hence, a method was developed to drop a bomb from 20,000 feet without any aiming devices. Because of the inaccuracy of this method, it was used only on jungle targets.

It was after the missile threat emerged that the air force needed jets for the first time. The air force had six Chinese built F-7 jets bought in 1991. These had a very low carrying capacity as mentioned in a previous chapter, but they were jets and could operate out of missile range. The Sri Lankan air force had actually entered the jet age as far back as 1971 when Soviet Russia had donated five MiG-17s to Sri Lanka in the wake of the first JVP insurgency. However by about 1980, all the pilots trained to fly the MiG-17s had retired. The planes too had become obsolete and had been grounded. These MiG-17s were then mounted on stands and used for ornamental purposes in various air force installations. In addition to switching to jets, anti-missile self protection systems were fitted onto the fixed wing aircraft as well as the helicopters. The way the self protection system worked was to emit flares in all directions to 'confuse' the heat seeking missiles.

It was not just the air force that was having problems. The mid-1990s was probably the worst period for the navy as well. First came the Pooneryn debacle with the death of over a hundred naval personnel. Then came the sinking of the offshore patrol vessel *SLNS Sagaravardhana* which was rammed by an LTTE suicide boat off Mannar on 19 September 1994. This was the LTTE's welcoming gift to the Chandrika Kumaratunga government which had come into power on a peace platform about a month earlier. A few months later, came the destruction of the *Ranasuru* and *Soorya*, in April 1995. On 17 October a large fishing trawler used by the navy to transport food from Trincomalee to Kankesanthurei was destroyed by underwater saboteurs in the Trincomalee harbour. The powerful blast broke the ship in two.

On 30 March 1996, the LTTE tried to attack *MV Nagoroma* which was transporting service personnel from Kankesanthurei to Trincomalee. A cluster of LTTE attack craft and suicide boats launched from Chalai tried to engage and ram the *Nagoroma* but was destroyed by the two naval vessels escorting it. Thereupon, another four LTTE boats entered the fray and a fast attack craft with the pennant number P-458, which was on tow, disconnected the line and confronted the LTTE boats in order to save the *Nagoroma*. The P-458 was rammed by a suicide boat and sank with only one rating surviving. Its commanding officer J.A.D.L.Wijayatunga was posthumously conferred Sri Lanka's highest gallantry award.

The only bright moment during this period of gloom for the navy was the destruction of an LTTE gunrunning vessel, *MV Horizon* on 14 February 1996. But even for this, the navy cannot really take the credit because this vessel was first intercepted by the Indian navy and handed over to the Sri Lankan navy and it was destroyed only when it tried to escape captivity by speeding off as the convoy neared the Mulleitivu coast.

Chapter 36

The Capture of Jaffna

Even though both the air force and navy were reeling from unanticipated losses, 1995 was going to be a good year for the army. Auspicious signs began manifesting themselves early on. On 29 July 1995, the LTTE launched simultaneous attacks on army detachments in Jayasinhapura, Kokkuthudwai and the brigade headquarters in Parakaramapura in Welioya. The troops repulsed the attacks and over 350 LTTE cadres were killed in one night. The Welioya area was commanded by Brigadier Janaka Perera and the 4th Gemunu Watch manned Jayasinhapura and Kokkuthuduwai. Up to that time such a large number of LTTE cadres had never been killed in a single confrontation.

By the time the LTTE recommenced hostilities in April 1995, the area held by the government forces in the Jaffna peninsula extended from Kankesanthurei in the west, to Thondamanaru in the east with Vasivilan and Telippalai as the southernmost positions. The total land area held by the government was around 10 km long and 4 km wide. About four to five battalions held this patch of land. Major Deepal Subasinghe was the commander of the 9th Gajaba Battalion in Telippalai. At this time all troop movements and supplies to this beleaguered patch of land was by sea and air as the LTTE controlled the land routes into the peninsula. The government held only this small area around Palaly, the Kayts/Mandativu islands and the Elephant Pass camp in the south, with nothing in between these three points.

Dry rations like rice, pulses, sugar, etc would come once a month by sea. Fresh produce such as vegetables and meat was brought daily by air. Soldiers could go on leave only once in three months. Some soldiers had to wait for days at the Palaly airport to get a flight back to Colombo. Even this was disrupted when the flights stopped coming in after the downing of the two Avros in April 1995. With the missile attacks on planes, the supply of fresh produce stopped.

After that a few risky flights did come into Palaly using a certain flying technique. The planes would come into Palaly from the sea side, flying at tree top level. There was a minimum angle at which surface to air missiles could be fired and they could not be used when the planes came in so low. But at that height, the planes became vulnerable to small arms fire. So gunboats from Karainagar and Pt Pedro would secure a corridor about a kilometre wide on the sea along which the planes would approach Palaly. But even this was not foolproof. On one occasion during the operation to take Jaffna, a sea tiger infiltration team managed to get into the corridor and bring down a Y-8 cargo plane with a rocket propelled grenade.

The government felt that in this situation, it was only a matter of time until the LTTE made an attempt to overrun Palaly and Elephant Pass. The deputy defence minister Anuruddha Ratwatte's view was that the whole Jaffna peninsula had to be brought under government control. When the battalion commanders in Jaffna were sounded out about the plan to capture the entire peninsula, the reaction had been negative. Major Subasinghe's view was that if they capture the rest of Jaffna, they may require about ten times the present number of troops to hold the peninsula. Then there would be a lot of civilians to look after as well and the question would arise how the civilians were going to be fed. In a situation where even the small area held by the government could not be kept supplied, how were they going to keep the whole Jaffna peninsula supplied?

Soldiers were entitled to a meal with five curries which included fish, meat or eggs. But at that time in Jaffna, troops never got their entitled meal because fresh produce could not be brought in, and there was always something missing. Then the soldiers started cultivating vegetables on the lands in proximity to their camps. Virtually every detachment had a hectare or two under cultivation. Major Subasinghe's view was that it would be better to hold what they had in Jaffna, and to fight their way northwards from Vavuniya. Another reason why Col Subasinghe opposed the taking over of Jaffna was that so long as the population was under the LTTE's jackboot they would put up with their privations, but the moment they were liberated, they will be asking for water, electricity, medical facilities, houses, etc and Subasinghe didn't think the government forces could handle such demands since it would be the army that would have to take over the civil administration.

Besides, even the troops were not confident that an operation to clear Jaffna would succeed. The navy chief of staff had to come to Palaly and address the troops and tell them that all the logistical support would be given by the navy in the form of transporting troops and armaments and other supplies. The move to capture Jaffna was preceded by Operation Thunder strike on 1 October 1995, to expand the government held area beyond Thondamanaru and to secure a launching pad for the main operation. Troops of the 53rd Division led by Janaka Perera broke out of the Palaly-Vasivilan defence lines in a south-easterly direction to capture Puttur and the Pt Pedro-Jaffna road. The mission was accomplished with 96 LTTE dead bodies recovered by the army which for its part, suffered only 24 fatalities.

Operation *Riviresa* to push the LTTE out of Jaffna was launched on 21 October 1995. Before the offensive commenced, leaflets were air dropped over Jaffna instructing civilians to congregate at certain locations like kovils and schools. A good part of the population that had family members in the LTTE went into the Vanni mainly out of fear of reprisals if the army captured Jaffna. The army broke out of their defence lines on two fronts with a simultaneous diversionary attack launched on the Jaffna town from Mandativu Island. Operation *Riviresa* was led by three Brigadiers, P.A.Karunatilleke, Niel Dias, and Janaka Perera. When the offensive commenced, the 51st Division advanced southwards along the Palaly-Jaffna road while the 52nd Division advanced along the Pt-Pedro-Jaffna road from the newly captured launching pad in Puttur. (See map 2)

All along the route, kovils and schools were being used by the LTTE as defensive positions. The LTTE tried to demoralize soldiers by threatening gas attacks and vehicle bombs. In these heavily built up areas, armour manoeuvrability was poor. The guns of the tanks could not take ground level targets. However the saving grace was that LTTE rocket propelled grenade fire at these armoured vehicles were also not accurate as they fired not at specific targets but in the general direction of the sound or dust clouds generated by the armoured vehicles. The advancing troops met with stiff resistance in Kopay, and Urumpirai, but the LTTE failed to stop the advance. On the border of Jaffna town, Janaka Perera's 53rd Division was launched through the line held by the other two formations to take over the Jaffna town.

The retreating LTTE cadres regrouped and launched a counter attack at Tirunalveli but they were pushed back losing around 400 cadres in the process. This set back had been one of the main reasons for the LTTE to leave the Jaffna peninsula. The LTTE gave the advancing troops the maximum resistance up to the capture of Jaffna town. The army suffered the highest number of casualties during this phase of the operation with 167 troops killed. The number of injured was nearly 1500. There was a fight up to the Jaffna hospital after which LTTE resistance just collapsed and they gave up and decamped. In capturing the entire Jaffna peninsula in stages, the 51st, 52nd and the 53rd Divisions of the army, suffered a total of 408 fatalities with 2,906 wounded in battle.

After the LTTE lost the Jaffna town and the western part of the peninsula to the government, the LTTE heroes' day celebrations on 26 November 1995 were held in a sombre mood. The Jaffna peninsula had been up to this time, the main theatre of operations of the LTTE. With the loss of Jaffna, they would now be restricted to the Vanni. In his heroes' day message that year, a rattled Prabhakaran was to say:

"Today, the war of aggression against our land by the enemy has reached a phenomenal scale. Having mobilized all its military power and having utilized all its national resources, the enemy has launched a massive invasion of the Jaffna soil...The intense shelling that rains down has wiped out the face of Jaffna. The fundamental objective of this war of aggression is to destroy the economic resources and cultural heritage of Jaffna thereby uprooting the national life of the people...The strategy is the encirclement and occupation of the densely populated vital area of the Tamil homeland and to proclaim to the world that Jaffna society is 'liberated'. But this strategy of Chandrika's government, has turned out to be a disaster since the people of Jaffna city and the Valigamam region have evacuated the area before the encirclement by the army. This massive exodus has demonstrated the fact that the people of Jaffna, in a unanimous stand, have expressed their opposition to the government war effort and the absurd reasons attributed to it. This mass exodus has impressed upon the Sinhala nation and the world that the people and the LTTE could not be separated..."

It is clear that Prabhakaran was shaken as never before by the capture of Jaffna by the army. He tried to put a positive gloss on the LTTE's retreat by telling the Tamil people in his heroes day speech:
"The Sri Lankan army has over-stretched its feet on the Jaffna soil. It is not a difficult task to conquer territories by mobilizing large formations of troops.

226

But it will be a difficult task to hold the territories captured. This is the historical reality faced by the aggressive armies all over the world. The Sri Lankan army will soon learn this historical truth."

Operation *Riviresa* was undoubtedly the most successful operation ever launched by the army before the final operations that wiped out the LTTE. Not only did the army evict the LTTE from the peninsula, they held it for nearly fifteen years until the LTTE was finished off on the banks of the Nandikadal lagoon. A year after the *Riviresa* operation, the 10th Gajaba Battalion which was still in Jaffna would describe their presence in Jaffna as 'internal security services'. Yet this was an area that had been enemy territory for the previous ten or more years, with the army not being able to come out of their camps.

Another significant fact was that after the army captured the Jaffna peninsula in 1995, the LTTE was not able to hide among the general public and conduct guerrilla operations. Small LTTE groups had been operating in areas like Anaikoddai, Manipay, Vadukkodai, Araly, Uduvil and Kokuvil areas. In April 1996, an operation had to be launched to clear these areas, and 78 LTTE guerrillas were killed in the process. In October the same year a similar operation was launched in the Valikamam south area. The 3rd Gajaba Battalion established detachments in the area and launched a public relations campaign organizing *sramadanas* (voluntary community work) with the people and repairing kovils, churches and schools that had been damaged in the war.

As the public warmed up to this approach, information about LTTE activity came in leading to the arrest of more than three dozen LTTE operatives and the recovery of weapons and explosives. The 3rd Gajaba battalion held the area for more than three years. The army was no longer under siege in the peninsula, there were no landmines and they could move about freely. The people were no longer with the LTTE and infiltrators were not able to do any major damage from this point onwards.

In December 1995, Prabhakaran was to issue a special statement to the people of Tamil Nadu. He wrote: *"The waves of sympathy that sweep across Tamil Nadu whenever the Eelam Tamils are repressed has always been a deterrent to our ruthless enemy and a great source of hope and relief to our aggrieved people. It also impresses upon the world that Eelam Tamils are not alone and without support....Having assembled a formidable force in a single battle front, it has occupied the historic city of Jaffna and has raised the Sinhalese national flag over our soil. The Sinhalese*

227

nation is celebrating this tragic event soaked by the tears of five hundred thousand displaced Tamils...In these circumstances, Tamil Nadu should continue to voice our plight and express support to our legitimate cause. This is what the people of Tamil Eelam fervently expects from the people of Tamil Nadu."

The second phase of the *Riviresa* operation was launched in April 1996 to liberate the Tennamarachchi area. The army advanced on Chavakachcheri and Kilali. Once Kilaly was secured, many of the people who had left their houses in the Valikamam sector began returning to their homes. The Vadamarachchi area was captured virtually without any resistance and most of the people who had gone with the LTTE returned to their homes. (See maps 1 & 2) After the capture of the Jaffna town, LTTE resistance went down drastically and the army lost only 10 men in capturing the Velvettiturei-Pt Pedro area. Brigadier N.R.Marambe was to report that capturing Kilaly to the south-east of the Jaffna Peninsula was done 'without effort' as the terrorists had fled the area.

By the end of June 1996, President Chandrika Kumaratunga was able to report to the heads of foreign missions at a conference in Colombo, that about 450,000 people had returned to the Jaffna peninsula. The loss of the Jaffna peninsula on the one hand and the return of civilians to the government held areas was a body blow to the LTTE. Up to that time, the conventional wisdom was that Jaffna could never be taken by the Sri Lanka army because the casualty rates among troops and civilians will be too high for the international community to countenance a move to take the peninsula. Now what had been deemed impossible had actually happened.

Chapter 37

Disaster in Mulleitivu

After the Jaffna peninsula had been cleared, three isolated camps were left in the Vanni which could face a retaliatory attack from the LTTE. Mulleitivu, Pooneryn and Mannar. (See map 3) The idea was to abandon these camps and to withdraw the troops to prevent them from being surrounded and attacked. The Pooneryn camp was evacuated. One of the LTTE's main demands during the 1994/95 peace talks had been the dismantling of the Pooneryn camp. The navy had opposed the plan to evacuate the Mulleitivu camp for the reason that if it was withdrawn, the government would not be holding any east coast territory between Trincomalee and Elephant Pass and that would give the sea tigers a free run of the coast.

Capt D.K.P. Dassanayake of the navy says that the loss of the Mulleitivu army camp was a major factor which strengthened the sea tigers as a large stretch of the coast was left completely in their hands. With control over this stretch of land gone, the navy could not destroy the sea tiger bases from the sea as the sea tigers hid their boats in the jungle and could not be seen or destroyed from the sea. However other naval officers expressed a different view saying that the Mulleitivu camp was a burden to the navy and it was not serving any purpose. The navy had to keep the camp supplied by beaching their landing craft under fire during the off monsoon periods. The army presence in Mulleitivu did not help reduce LTTE activity along the coast either as they did not move out of the camp. Even before the camp fell, the LTTE still had a free run of the coast.

Before the *Riviresa* operation commenced, Major Gen Daluwatte had visited the Mulleitivu camp and told the then commanding officer Brigadier Kumban Bohran to prepare plans to withdraw. If the navy was unable to help in the withdrawal, the instructions were that they should try to fight their way either north to the Elephant Pass camp or south to Welioya.

Despite the isolation of the Mulleitvu camp, it need not have fallen. The Mulleitivu debacle, highlighted the fact that the Sri Lankan military was still a sick institution despite the victory in Jaffna. The attack on the Mulleitivu camp commenced at 1.00 am on 18 July 1996. The area held by the army was 2.8 km in length and 1.2 km in width. At the time of the attack, there were 1,200 troops belonging to the 9th Sinha and the 6th Vijayaba battalions in the camp. They had two 122 mm artillery guns with 610 rounds of ammunition, and two 120 mm mortars with 377 rounds. There were 5 General Purpose Machine Guns and forty one 60 mm mortars and fifteen 81 mm mortars and there had been no shortage of food or ammunition as stocks had been replenished.

Moreover, unlike in the case of other such attacks, reinforcements began arriving on the very day of the attack with the 1st Special Forces Battalion being inducted to a point to the south of the Mulleitivu camp by helicopter. The operation to reinforce Mulleitivu by air in 1996, was a precision operation. The LTTE knew that reinforcements would arrive either by air or sea and were fully prepared. Air force jets bombed the beachhead minutes before the landing. Then the landing helicopters would arrive escorted by the Mi-24 attack helicopters. The Mi-24s would then overtake the personnel carriers and with just 30 to 45 seconds before the landing, would unleash another barrage of rocket fire on the beachhead to enable the troop carriers to land.

Despite all this, when the choppers landed they found LTTE cadres still on the beach in trenches immobilized due to the sand storm churned up by the helicopters and they had to be picked off by the special forces troops as they landed. Over the next few days there were over 1100 reinforcement troops from the Special Forces as well as regular infantry at various places close to the Mulleitivu camp. Yet the Mulleitivu camp had fallen to the LTTE within 7 hours of the battle commencing and the fight was now not between the camp and the LTTE but between the LTTE and the reinforcements. The camp was attacked at 1.00 am on 18 July and the LTTE had overrun it by 8.00 am.

The first line of defence had fallen within the first 20 minutes as well as the 9th Sinha battalion headquarters and the artillery gun positions. A disorganised group of soldiers had gathered at the 6th Vijayaba battalion headquarters but even this was overrun by the LTTE by 5.00 pm the next day. Over 1200 men died in this debacle with all the weapons and equipment in the camp falling into the LTTE's hands – two battalions wiped out in a matter of hours.

While the LTTE attack on the Mulleitivu army camp was on, there was a parallel battle on the sea between the navy and the sea tigers off the cost of Mulleitivu. After the attack on the Mulleitivu camp commenced, the first naval craft to reach the scene had been a Dvora fast attack craft commanded by Lieutenant Commander M.Jayasooriya. They confronted a sea tiger cordon that had been laid off the coast to prevent the besieged camp from being relieved by sea. This was around 5.00 am on 18 July. Even by this time, the navy was unable to establish communication with the Mulleitivu army camp. It was late afternoon the next day when the navy managed to induct 450 troops of the Air Mobile Brigade into the besieged camp. The sea conditions had slowed down the transfer of troops into dinghies for the landing.

When the landing party neared the shore, the LTTE launched more than 25 boats along with five suicide boats to prevent the landing. The landing party was turned back while the navy confronted the LTTE flotilla. Two suicide boats rammed a fast gun boat, the *Ranaviru* and it sank with two officers and 34 men on board. The amphibious landing was abandoned. The next day however, two mechanized landing craft managed to make a landing after successfully destroying the LTTE boats sent out against them. They came under heavy mortar fire from the LTTE. By this time however, the Mulleitivu camp had fallen to the LTTE and all that the landing party could do was to evacuate some stragglers. This operation was concluded by 22 July 1996.

A small group of about eight men from the 6th Vijayaba Battalion had hidden in the water tank of the Mulleitivu camp and had been there for about a week, coming down in the night to forage for scraps of food. After about a week, the LTTE had left the area and they had walked southwards through the jungle towards Welioya. Among those who lost their lives trying to relieve the besieged Mulleitivu camp was Major Fazly Lafir who was married to Gōta's maternal cousin Anoma Wickremasuriya. Commodore Ravi Wijegunaratne of the navy remembers Major Lafir with respect. When the navy's elite commando force modelled after the navy seals of the USA was started in 1993, it was Lafir who had instructed the naval personnel in the land based component of their training in Maduruoya.

The inquiry into the Mulleitivu debacle revealed that there were no contingency plans or any strategy for counterattack. When the attack commenced, troops had just run around like disorganized rabble and got killed in the process. LTTE infiltrators had got inside the camp and had neutralized several bunkers simply by lobbing grenades into them. Many soldiers had died while trying to withdraw from one defence line to another because there had not been any communication trenches between the defence lines. On the night of the attack the brigade commander Brigadier Lawrence Fernando was in Colombo to testify before a government appointed commission and the commanding officer of the 9th Sinha Battalion was on leave.

Only the commanding officer of the 6th Vijayaba Battalion had been in the camp. By the time of the attack, the 6th Vijayaba troops had been deployed in Mulleitivu for over four years. When a unit has been in the same area for so long without incident, complacency sets in. It was this same negligence and complacency that had given the LTTE victories in Pooneryn and Janakapura as well earlier. The terrorists could attack at a time of their own choosing. What was surprising was that the troops in the Mulleitivu camp had not been more alert because thousands of desperate LTTE cadres who had been pushed out of Jaffna were converging on their area and there was the distinct possibility that the LTTE would try to claim some victory to assuage their grief and shame over Jaffna. But officers in Mulleitivu failed to recognize this danger and to take the necessary precautions. This negligence was the bane of the 1990s.

Following the Mulleitivu debacle, the government decided to push further south from the Jaffna peninsula and capture Kilinochchi in retaliation. After the LTTE lost Jaffna, they had made Kilinochchi their main centre of administration. Troops commanded by Janaka Perera captured Kilinochchi in two stages in the *Sathjaya* operations, first moving to Paranthan, a few kilometres south of the Elephant Pass camp and then onwards to Kilinochchi by August 1996. The loss of Kilinochchi was as much a loss of face for the LTTE as the loss of Mulleitivu was to the army. So by the end of 1996, the LTTE and the army were more or less even.

Chapter 38

The Highway of Death

Then began a disastrous adventure that would bring the entire military campaign and the government itself to its knees. After capturing Kilinochchi, the next priority that presented itself was to clear a land route to Jaffna to keep the troops supplied. Supplies for the troops in the entire Jaffna peninsula were being transported by sea and air. This supply issue had been foreseen by Lt Col Deepal Subasinghe and other battalion commanders in Jaffna before the operation to take over Jaffna had been launched. The political authorities did not think of the supply issue when they went into Jaffna. But now, with the months dragging into years, the government was beginning to feel the strain. In this situation, they thought the only solution was to open an overland supply route to Jaffna.

Operation *Jayasikurui* was launched in March 1997, to open a land route from Vavuniya to Jaffna along the A-9 road. In the original plan, the projection was to fight their way from Vavuniya up the A-9 road to Mankulam in just four days. Troops advanced from the outskirts of Vavuniya town to Omanthai a town further up the A-9 road and consolidated their power in the area. (See map 3) The LTTE tried to retake Omanthai in a counter-attack, but the attempt failed and the LTTE retreated having lost a significant number of cadres. The LTTE was determined not to allow the government to open a land route to Jaffna via Kilinochchi and offered stiff resistance. It took more than a year for the army to fight its way to the outskirts of Mankulam in the centre of the Vanni.

The terrorists had surveyed the path the army would take and marked it with wooden pegs demarcating targets for their artillery. When the advancing troops came across a little yellow wooden peg in the ground, they knew they were standing on an LTTE bull's eye and they would flee for their lives before the mortar came whistling through the air. During the monsoon season, the entire Vanni would turn into a massive marsh. The roads that had been cleared through the jungles would be churned into rivers of thick mud by the wheels of hundreds of tractors used to transport supplies to the advancing troops. After some time even tractors would find it impossible to move on these roads with the rear wheels sinking deep into the viscous mud. Food, ammunition and equipment then had to be carried to the frontlines on the backs of the soldiers, all of which slowed down progress considerably.

Despite the stiff resistance that the LTTE was putting up, Karuna Amman says that Prabhakaran had at first believed the army would capture the A-9 highway and he had made contingency plans by assigning Tamilselvam and Theepan to handle the territory to the west of the A-9 road and Karuna to handle the eastern half of the Vanni under Prabhakaran's personal command. But subsequently, the LTTE was able to turn the tables on the army. Even before the army took Mankulam, they were acutely aware that the LTTE had infiltrated the areas under army control in large numbers and that they will attack the army defence lines in force once the latter were stretched out. Warnings to this effect were issued in the operational order for the capture of Mankulam.

The *Jayasikurui* operation which began as an offensive operation ultimately ended up becoming a defensive operation in its last stages. It was Major Gen Lakshman Algama a former chief of staff of the army who labelled the project to open a land route to Jaffna 'the highway of death'. Appearing on several TV talk shows, he pointed out that it was not feasible to open a route to the north with enemy territory on both sides of the road. It would be impossible to hold for any length of time. On 8 June 1998, while the *Jayasikurui* troops were stalled in Mankulam, the LTTE launched an operation to regain Kilinochchi which they had lost in 1996.

The army wanted to link Mankulam with Kilinochchi and complete the capture of the A-9 road to Jaffna. The LTTE wanted to prevent that at all costs. Karuna says that in his battlefield experience the Kilinochchi defences were the strongest he had seen, with concrete bunkers every 30 meters or so. But the army was holding only a narrow stretch of land about ten kilometres long and just two kilometres wide along the A-9 road from Elephant Pass to Kilinochchi manned by around 2000 troops. It was the narrowness of the strip of land which stuck out from Elephant Pass into Kilinochchi that finally proved to be the army's undoing.

On one occasion, Prabhakaran had tried to recapture Kilinochchi through sheer firepower, firing 10,000 mortar and artillery rounds at the defences but they failed to dislodge the army except from a two square kilometre area at the southern extremity of the Killinochchi defences – so strong were the army positions. It is after this that plans were made to cut off Kilinochchi from Paranthan by capturing a segment of the long narrow sliver of territory held by the army. The LTTE had trained for three months with a specially constructed mock up of the Kilinochchi defences and planned meticulously for the operation.

About 1400 LTTE cadres were inducted to a point above Kilinochchi town in the night and within 15 minutes, two 200 man teams had stormed the defences and separated Kilinochchi from Paranthan. Within two hours, the LTTE cadres who had gone in equipped and prepared to dig in, were so well entrenched that no counter attack could dislodge them. The army was completely unprepared for this attack because Karuna had chosen to attack on a day that the LTTE did not customarily launch attacks - 26 June 1998. The LTTE assault started at midnight and continued into the day and the following night. At around 3.00am in the early hours of 28 June, the army decided to withdraw. The Air Mobile Brigade was deployed in the rescue operation to extricate those caught in the LTTE encirclement of Kilinochchi. The army fell back to the Paranthan junction.

In this debacle, the army lost hundreds of men. The 4th Sinha Battalion alone suffered 132 fatalities with 286 troops suffering injuries. Similarly, the 10th Sinha had 121 soldiers killed and 184 injured. Karuna Amman who commanded the LTTE forces that took Kilinochchi, says that 420 LTTE cadres died and over 700 were injured in the battle to take Kilinochchi.

Thus in one fell swoop, the LTTE turned the army's offensive into a defensive action. By October 1998, the army was planning operations to prevent Paranthan from falling to the LTTE. The next phase of Jayasikurui was to prevent Mankulam from falling to the LTTE and as the operational order itself put it, 'to defend the areas captured by *Jayasikurui*'. As the army did not have sufficient troops to hold the area captured, navy, air force and police special task force personnel were also deployed to man the defence lines. The eastern defence lines were on the Oddusudan road from the Mankulam junction and the western defence lines on the Thunukkai road.

On 6 September 1998, in an interview with the Sunday Leader, Tamilselvam was to gloat: *"...Operation Jayasikurui becomes decisive in two ways. First Jayasikurui has provided us with an opportunity to decide upon the life span of the government. Secondly the operation has transformed the LTTE which fought as a guerrilla organization into a combat army that could fight face to face. It was not we but the government that brought about such a situation.... Whether one likes it or not, it is we who decide upon the duration of this war and the lifespan of this government. One cannot get away from that reality."*

Even Prabhakaran's heroes' day speech of 26 November 1998 echoed the same triumphalistic mood. He said *"Chandrika's military project has crumbled and failed to achieve any of its strategic objectives...the LTTE has not been defeated but has grown immensely in strength acquiring wider experience in the art of modern warfare and turned out into an invincible force. The Vanni battles caused a series of debacles and massive casualties to the Sinhala armed forces. The Jayasikurui battle which was undertaken with the grand design to open the road to Jaffna has been prolonged for more than a year and a half and reached an impasse with the fall of Kilinochchi."*

For about another year, until the last quarter of 1999, the government forces were able to hold on to the defences they had built along the A-9 road. They had fought their way to Mankulam, but could advance no further especially after the fall of Kilinochchi in late 1998. While they were thus in a situation of stalemate, the government made a crucial mistake. The year 1999 was to be an election year, and they wanted to clear the Madhu Church area in order to please the Roman Catholic voters in the north western province. The reserve division that was kept on standby to meet any contingencies was assigned the task of capturing Madhu. By 3 August 1999, the 53rd Division was able to capture Periyamadu, Mallavi and the Madhu church area. When the government wanted to take over the Vavuniya-Mannar road, Karuna advised Prabhakaran not to try to prevent it, but to allow the army to take over that area so that thousands of troops would be tied down in holding the area, thus preventing them from being deployed in the operations to take over the A-9 road.

The army was now overstretched, holding the A-9 road as well as the Madhu area, and had no reserve division to deploy in case of an emergency. In October 1999, the LTTE struck, attacking the army defence lines in Oddusudan, Kanagarayankulam, and Nedunkerny. (See map 3) While the Oddusudan defence line was at the northernmost point that the army offensive had reached, Kanagarayankulam was a point on the A-9 road to the south of Mankulam and the Nedunkerny defence lines were even further to the south-east. If the LTTE broke through the Kanagarayankulam and Nedunkerny defence lines, the troops in Mankulam would have been surrounded.

Hence within two days, the army withdrew from Mankulam and retreated to Omanthai while they still controlled the A-9 road. Thus in November 1999, all the gains of the *Jayasikurui* operation were lost in a matter of two days. During this period the morale of the army hit rock bottom. Looking back at these events Anuruddha Ratwatte says that if they had just three more fighter/bomber planes, they could have kept the LTTE at bay, but the government did not release the funds. Understandably, Prabhakaran's heroes' day speech of 26 November 1999 was one of the most truimphalistic speeches ever delivered by him. He said:

"Our massive offensive campaign in the Vanni code named 'Unceasing Waves 3' has effectively demonstrated to the world the extraordinary growth and development of the Tiger fighting forces in the art of modern warfare. The speed of our strikes, the ability of rapid deployment, the unified command, the high discipline, the spectacular offensive tactics, and the tremendous courage displayed by our fighting formations have astounded the world military experts...Swept by the 'Unceasing Waves' of the Liberation Tigers, Chandrika's military project crumbled as a house of sand built on the seashore. The spectacular military victories that we gained in this current offensive campaign have turned the balance of military power in our favour. The massive effort made by Chandrika over the last five years to weaken the LTTE and to achieve military hegemony was shattered by us in a matter of a few days."

The now triumphant LTTE felt confident enough to release over the Voice of Tigers radio on 26 December 1999, figures of the number of casualties they had suffered. The total number of LTTE cadres killed over the past 17 years, was given as 14,335. Of this 9,598 cadres had been killed during the five years of the PA government's rule. The highest number of cadres killed in any year during UNP rule had been in 1990 with 1,613 deaths. During PA rule the highest number of 2,146 had been killed in 1997, in countering the *Jayasikurui* operation.

237

Chapter 39

The Fall of Elephant Pass

If the beleaguered government thought they would have some respite after the LTTE pushed their troops back to Omanthai, they were wrong. The worst was still to come. The Elephant Pass camp was a whole complex of military installations with the 54th Division commanding the whole area. There were over 5000 troops stationed in this complex of military installations and with good reason, because this was the southern flank of the government held Jaffna peninsula.

The southern-most point of the Elephant Pass complex was the defence line in Paranthan. Beyond this lay a huge swathe of land controlled completely by the LTTE. The next government held position to the south of Paranthan was Omanthai which was about 65 km away. The territory in between Paranthan and Omanthai from north to south and from the Bay of Bengal in the east and the Palk Straits to the west, was completely dominated by the tigers. The LTTE administrative centre of Kilinochchi was located just 4 km to the south of Paranthan. By December 1999, this uneasy arrangement had been in place for one year since the LTTE wrested Kilinochchi from the army in late 1998.

Guarding the southern defence lines of the Elephant Pass complex in Paranthan were three battalions, including the 8th Gajaba. The eastern flank of the complex on the beach front at Vettalankerny was held by the 2nd Gemunu Watch. In December 1999, the LTTE made a sea landing on the beachfront at Vettalankerny and engaged troops of the 2nd Gemunu Watch. After a few days, they infiltrated the army defence line under cover of darkness and occupied the scrub

238

jungle between the beach and the 54th Divisional headquarters. At this point, commandos were sent in to engage the tiger infiltrators. After some days of skirmishing, the LTTE inducted more fighters through the Vettalankerny breach (See map 2).

After a certain point, it was no longer possible for small commando teams to engage the LTTE infiltrators. So the eastern defence line was withdrawn and a new line formed covering the Iyakachchi junction. While this was going on in the eastern flank, the LTTE opened up another front in the south in Paranthan. One day in December, the LTTE started bombarding the Paranthan defence lines at around 2.00 in the afternoon. The officer commanding the 8th Gajaba battalion Major Sahampathi Ekanayake and his brigade commander Colonel Percy Fernando were present at the Paranthan junction when the shelling started. There was nothing unusual in the LTTE firing at the army defence lines, but what worried Major Ekanayake and Col. Fernando was that an LTTE armoured vehicle was also involved in the bombardment.

At that time, the 8th Gajaba battalion had about 500 men with over a hundred being away on leave. The troops on the front lines put up a stiff resistance in the face of the LTTE bombardment. Supporting artillery fire was provided from the brigade headquarters behind the Paranthan chemicals factory. The bombardment that started at 2.00 pm in the afternoon continued throughout the night and day for the next three days. The LTTE threw everything they had against the Paranthan defence line. In the first day of the bombardment, the 8th Gajaba alone suffered more than 150 dead. There were brief respites in the night between 1.00 and 3.00 am and it was during these breaks that soldiers were able to have a hurried meal and clean the guns and prepare for the next offensive. By this time several army radio sets had fallen into the hands of the LTTE and they were jamming the airwaves. The troops had been given multiple frequencies to use just for such a contingency and they had to keep switching from one frequency to another to keep in contact with the battalion headquarters.

After just two days of fighting, the 8th Gajaba Battalion was so short of men that the commanding officer sent even the civilian employees like the orderlies, with guns to man the bunkers. Major Ekanayake who commanded the 8th Gajaba Battalion says that throughout the battle, it was Colonel Percy Fernando the deputy divisional commander who came on the air waves and gave them guidance and instructions. Major Gen K.B.Egodawela was unreachable. Major Ekanayake asked for more reinforcements to hold the Paranthan line. When no reinforcements came, preparations were made to withdraw. Major Ekanayake took his brief case and a diary from the battalion headquarters and fired several bursts at the TV and other equipment in the battalion headquarters and came onto the Paranthan road. By this time, it was virtually impossible to induct any more troops to reinforce the front lines. The surviving troops of the 8th Gajaba withdrew under cover of darkness and in the confusion, many soldiers were left behind. The withdrawal was to another line to the south of the Paranthan junction. Within 10 minutes, the withdrawing troops could hear the LTTE inside the battalion headquarters.

They had withdrawn to the brigade headquarters which was near the Paranthan chemicals factory. At this point, the 3rd SLLI Battalion under Major Ralph Nugera arrived to reinforce the second line. Later the brigade headquarters and the Paranthan chemicals factory were abandoned and a new line of defence formed. This line held, but at night there was heavy infiltration of the army line by the LTTE. Some infiltrators were dressed in army uniforms and spoke Sinhala. This spread consternation throughout the front line because the soldier next to you could be a tiger in disguise. By this time, soldiers had been without food for two or three days. All rations had been distributed and fresh supplies were not coming through.

It was pitch dark at night and soldiers monitored the goings on outside the bunkers using night vision goggles. This state of confusion prevailed for some days on the Paranthan front. In the meantime, there was a sea landing by an LTTE contingent from Pooneryn to the west of the elephant Pass complex. Now there were three fronts around the Elephant Pass camp – the Vettalankerny front, the Paranthan Front and now the Pooneryn front. By this time the 8th Gajaba Battalion was down from 500 to between 200-300 men. Major Ekanayke asked to be withdrawn from the frontline to regroup and reorganize his decimated battalion. Accordingly, the 6th SLLI Battalion was sent to the Paranthan line and the remnants of the 8th Gajaba withdrawn to the Vettelankerny line which had been holding steady up to that time.

After the 8th Gajaba was posted to the Vettalankerny line, another massive attack was launched on this line by the LTTE with supporting artillery fire from Pooneryn. There were civilians living within the defence lines in this sector and the army's suspicion is that the civilians may have guided the LTTE mortar batteries. The LTTE's artillery and mortar fire proved to be deadly accurate. Commando reinforcements that were rushed to the Vettelankerny sector were brought back in fertilizer bags. Orders were coming from the top to hold the eastern flank at all costs. But as the LTTE attack progressed relentlessly, all the radios were destroyed in mortar and artillery fire. An artillery shell had fallen directly on the command bunker and completely destroyed it. There were no rations or water either. Major Ekanayake and a group of about 26 soldiers were stuck in the trenches. The group included the second in command of the 2nd Sinha Battalion who had got detached from the rest of his unit in the prevailing confusion.

At this point, Major Ekanayake told the rag tag band that had survived that they would not last another night in the trenches and that they should break out under cover of darkness. Major Ekanayake told his men to withdraw without waiting even to pick up casualties and that even if he were to fall, they should leave him and make good their escape. That night the entire party slipped out of the trenches and met at a predetermined spot. All 26 individuals had managed to get out alive. Later Major Ekanayake had done a head count of those remaining from his battalion which had more than 500 when the attack started. There were only 94 left.

In April 2000, the LTTE contingent that broke through the Vettelankerny line, was able to batter their way through all resistance and capture the Iyakachchi junction and the wells that supplied water to the divisional headquarters in Elephant Pass and the brigade headquarters in Paranthan. A desperate attempt was made to recapture the wells. Two battalions the 9th Gajaba and the 1st Sinha were airlifted to Palaly from Vavuniya and arrived in Elephant Pass by road. When they reached the Iyakachchi junction, the LTTE had already formed two lines of defence around the wells. The divisional headquarters had been trying their best to break through to the wells from the west but all attempts had failed. The rescue party was told to launch an attack from the north and try to capture the wells. The 9th Gajaba and two companies of the 1st Sinha, broke through the first line of defence early in the morning. Having come from Vavuniya, they did not know the realities of the ground situation and they thought they would be able to complete the operation by ten in the morning.

Due to the fear the new troops may not want to fight, they had deliberately been misled into underestimating the gravity of the situation. When they were briefed at Palaly, they were told that the LTTE had captured the wells and the terrorists should be evicted from the area. They had not been given any idea of the ferocity and magnitude of the LTTE attack. After breaking through the LTTE lines,

241

the battalion commander realized that the situation was much more serious than they had been led to believe. Because of this realization, he left two detachments to guard the breach they had made in the LTTE lines and moved into a Palmyra grove to the east of the wells. Breaking in through the LTTE's first line of defence had been easy. But once inside, things changed. From there, try as they might, they could not break through the second LTTE defence line to get at the wells.

In the meantime, they came under attack from an LTTE supply base behind them. Under attack from both sides and after taking hundreds of casualties in about four hours, the commander of the 9th Gajaba tried to contact the detachments he had left to guard the breach but there was no answer. The LTTE had wiped out both detachments and closed the breach. The rescue party was now trapped and in need of rescuing themselves. They spent the night in this no-man's land and everybody thought the 9th Gajaba Battalion had been wiped out in the LTTE encirclement. That evening a small group of the 1st Sinha Battalion under the leadership of its commanding officer Major Mudannayake managed to break through the LTTE lines and link up with the 9th Gajaba troops.

Fighting continued sporadically throughout the night and the trapped troops were running out of ammunition. The LTTE meanwhile was addressing them over loud hailers telling them to surrender and that fighting was useless. They promised to give the troops food and to look after the wounded and to send them home to their families. They even said that they know that only a few of them were still able to fight. But the encircled troops were determined to break out without surrendering. They asked divisional headquarters for a heavy bombardment of the LTTE lines to open up a breach and then separating the survivors into small groups of eight so as not to present an easy target for mortar and small arms fire, they came out of the encirclement from multiple points under cover of darkness.

Everybody was asked to leave their backpacks behind, taking only ammunition and a water can. Each able bodied man had to help two casualties when retreating. Even the walking wounded had to drag out one casualty each. The number of casualties was appalling. By the time the troops were able to break out of the encirclement, over seventy 9th Gajaba soldiers were dead and nearly 600 were wounded. The 9th Gajaba which had gone in with 800 men had been reduced to just a hundred odd men in less than 18 hours.

Chapter 40

Jaffna Under Siege

When the attack on Elephant Pass was on, army commander Lt Gen Srilal Weerasooriya sent Major Gen Seevali Wanigasekera to Jaffna to check out the situation. Wanigasekera had several of his Gajaba Regiment battalions in Jaffna at the time, and he visited his battalions and came back and reported to Weerasooriya that the situation was much worse than he had expected. Weerasooriya had wanted to know why the army couldn't fight when there are 30,000 troops in the peninsula. Wanigasekera had pointed out that having 30,000 men will not help because the troops are demoralized and there is no proper command. Wanigasekera recommended sending another division to Jaffna to give confidence and strength to the troops there.

The army commander told Wanigasekera that senior officers were reporting sick and that there was no one to send. Wanigasekera thereupon volunteered to go to Jaffna. In March 2000, four months after the attack on the Elephant Pass complex began, Wanigasekera went to Jaffna with the 55th Division. The troops were either air lifted or taken by ship from Trincomalee. It took about a month to get his troops to Jaffna. By this time, complete chaos reigned in Elephant Pass. Soldiers were shooting themselves, so that they would be removed from the frontlines as casualties, and senior officers were returning to Colombo and getting themselves admitted to hospital. The siege of Elephant Pass had been on for months, starting in December 1999 and still continuing in April 2000. In the meantime, Sarath Munasinghe who was the security forces commander for Jaffna had put in his papers for retirement and had been replaced by Lionel Balagalle.

243

With Elephant Pass on the verge of collapse, president Chandrika Kumaratunga ordered a change in command and Major Gen. Janaka Perera was made the overall operations commander and Sarath Fonseka the security forces commander Jaffna. What finally precipitated the withdrawal of troops from Elephant Pass was the prospect of being cut off completely from the rest of the Jaffna peninsula in the LTTE encirclement.

On 18 April, both Janaka Perera and Fonseka came to Wanigasekera's divisional headquarters, which was a medium sized bunker in Muhamalai just behind the Palai-Soranpattu defence line that his troops were holding. From Wanigasekera's bunker Janaka Perera issued instructions to Major Gen K.B.Egodawela about the withdrawal from Elephant Pass and special emphasis was placed on the five artillery guns with a range of 15 to 25 km, and the eleven 120mm mortars that had a range of 6-7 km. Perera personally gave strict orders to both Major Gen Egodawela, the divisional commander and his artillery commanding officer Col. Franklin Rodrigo that explosives should be packed into the barrels of the guns and blasted. He asked the officers whether they had sufficient explosives to make the charges. He also ordered that soldiers should bring their weapons and ammunition and to destroy everything that cannot be brought with them.

The withdrawal was scheduled for 20 April. On the night of 19 April, Wanigasekera heard the sound of firing from the side of Elephant Pass. Contrary to all orders, someone had tried to get the guns across to the government held area. The LTTE had ambushed the convoy transporting the guns. It was the sound of this confrontation that Wanigasekera had heard. Janaka Perera sent the commandos to retrieve the guns. They had fought till morning, but the guns fell into the hands of the LTTE.

There was a gap between the Elephant Pass camp and the Soranpattu-Palai line held by the army, and in between was the LTTE contingent that had been inducted across the lagoon from Pooneryn. Hence, the withdrawal from Elephant Pass had to be done through enemy dominated territory. About 300 troops are believed to have died and another 500 or so injured in the withdrawal. The withdrawal began at 5.00 pm on 20 April 2000, and by 6.00 pm Major Gen Egodwela had got into a tank and come ahead of his troops. Col Percy Fernando his deputy who opted to accompany his troops was killed during the withdrawal. Major Lalith Daulagala who was also among those in the retreat from the Elephant Pass camp said: *"It*

244

was the worst experince of my life. I had to walk past the bodies of my men. Mortars were exploding all round, there was nothing to do but to look down and keep walking. If you were lucky you will escape death."

As the Elephant Pass camp fell, the LTTE moved in to take over Jaffna as well, with an incursion across the Jaffna lagoon into Chavakachcheri which was held by Major Gen Parami Kulatunga's troops. They broke through the army defences, advancing up to Sarasalai, a few kilometres to the north of Chavakachcheri. Wanigasekera was listening in on LTTE radio communications with the help of a Muslim soldier who understood Tamil, when LTTE front ranker Sornam came on the air waves. The Elephant Pass front was commanded by Karuna and Theepan and the Chavakachcheri front was commanded by Sornam from Pooneryn and he was on the radio speaking to his fighters who had overrun the army lines.

He was answered by female LTTE cadres now in Chavakachcheri. Sornam was asking them, "Where are the horses?" The female cadres replied, "We can see them ahead of us." After a while Sornam came back on air with instructions to set up two machine guns and to fire on the army defence line. After a few minutes, Wanigasekera could hear the sound of machine gun fire from the LTTE side as per the instructions. Then Sornam came back on the radio asking his cadres what was happening now. The female cadres reported back saying "The horses are running." The LTTE referred to the army as 'horses' because government troops were so fleet of foot! One day a Tamil man who had seen the LTTE offensive in Chavakachcheri told Wanigasekera that about 25 LTTE female cadres had come to Chavakachcheri via the lagoon and about a thousand soldiers had fled at their approach.

That was how demoralized the army was at that time. Soldiers would run the moment they came under fire and started taking casualties. Fortunately says one officer, the soldiers did not have an extensive hinterland to flee into, and were constrained to remain in the Jaffna peninsula. It was at this point that soldiers had begun shooting themselves so as to leave the war zone as casualties. Even though the LTTE appeared invincible at this point in time, Karuna says that during the battles of 1998-2000 that pushed the army back, he had only around 15,000 fighting cadres under him in addition to another 15,000 temporarily conscripted civilians of all ages who had to compulsorily report for duty for a certain period of time and were given two weeks weapons training before they were deployed to man the bunkers, and as service cadres for the fighters.

After the withdrawal of troops from Elephant Pass, a new frontline was formed at Soranapattu about six kilometres northwest from Elephant Pass. (See map 2) Later this line was pushed back further to Muhamalai. The Gajaba Regiment silver jubilee publication writes of this retreat *"For several days from April 19, 2000, the Soranpattu and Palai forward defence lines were bombarded by the LTTE and the army sustained severe casualties. This led to the defence line being abandoned and all infantry battalions were withdrawn. So high was the rate of casualties in this battle that the 16th Gajaba battalion was disbanded and amalgamated with the 10th battalion."* For a battalion to be disbanded and amalgamated with another, both battalions should have lost half their men through death and injury.

Major General Sarath Fonseka was later to write of the Elephant Pass debacle and the subsequent events in the following words – *"...After the enemy attack on Elephant Pass, I was appointed as the Commander Security Forces (Jaffna) to muster and hold troops without withdrawing further towards Jaffna. A large number of heavy guns, mortars had fallen into the hands of the enemy and the morale of the troops was declining. They had lost many of their colleagues, some were wounded and also they did not have the opportunity to evacuate the dead bodies of their comrades. With the rapid disorganization which occurred, they were not in a position to execute their assigned tasks. Troops lacked superior fire power and they requested the support of multi-barrel rocket launchers which were not seen on the battlefront. They fought till death with their morale at the lowest ebb. In contrast, the morale of the LTTE cadres had risen to the highest level with the capturing of Elephant Pass..."*

"...The terrorists however continued their onslaught, broke through the temporary defence line at Palai and forced the troops to withdraw to the Muhamalai area. There too the enemy launched several severe attacks against our troops... the enemy launched disastrous assaults against our troops in Ariyalai and Tanankilappu areas. Subsequently they occupied not only the above 02 areas, but also Navatkuli, Kaithadi and Kolombuthurei areas. Security forces retaliated the enemy attacks from the temporary defence line they had established at Chavakachcheri. At this juncture, face to face fighting continued between the enemy and the security forces. The distance between the enemy and the security forces was less than 75 meters..."

"...The continuous onslaught of the terrorists on the defence line at Chavakachcheri which went on for many hours left our troops with no alternative but to withdraw abandoning the Chavakachcheri defence line and the town. In this situation, suspicion arose among many personnel as

to whether the strength of our troops would suffice to defend strategic areas such as Varani, Kodikamam and Sarasalai and troops were called to defend these strategic points. Further, it was a rather uphill task to defend the Sarasalai area through which there were a number of roads leading to...Varani and Kodikamam areas which were always vulnerable to enemy attack..."

The lowest point in this battle to save Jaffna was reached on 5 May 2000, when Major General Fonseka signed a withdrawal plan in case the entire Jaffna peninsula had to be abandoned. Only nine copies of these withdrawal orders were signed and circulated to the commanders of various formations in Jaffna. The plan was to establish four lines of defence across the narrow 'neck' of the peninsula behind the existing front line at Muhamalai so that troops could progressively retreat from one line to the next as the LTTE advanced giving time for the rest of the troops to escape through the Palaly airport or the Kankesanthurei harbour. The idea in establishing the four lines of defence was just to delay the LTTE's advance. These defence lines were established across the seven kilometre width of the neck of the Jaffna peninsula starting from Muhamalai in the south to Nagarkovil in the north. The second line was from Kilali in the south to Nagarkovil in the north. The third line cut across the peninsula with Murusuvil as a centre point. The fourth line was to cut across the peninsula with Varani as its centre point (See map 2).

Major Gen Fonseka had laid down in detail, the order in which each unit would fall back when their lines were breached by the advancing LTTE. There were four 'contingency situations' envisaged by Fonseka for the phased withdrawal centered on the four lines of defence that were to be established. The distance between the first and the fourth lines was around 15 kilometres. Writing about contingency four, the fall back to the final line of defence on the Varani axis, Fonseka had written that with the fall back to this last line of defence, Palaly the only airport on the peninsula would be threatened. There was no contingency situation five. Fonseka had ominously written that the capture of the last line of defence at Varani would isolate Palaly – which meant in effect that the trapped troops would be facing a massacre.

Chapter 41

Teetering on the Brink

Fonseka's withdrawal order never had to be implemented due to the turnaround achieved in Sarasalai. In any case, this withdrawal order envisaged the LTTE advancing along the land route from Elephant Pass and did not provide for the LTTE attacking across the Jaffna lagoon from Pooneryn and capturing the Chavakachcheri, Tanankilappu and Navatkuli area, which is what they actually did. Had the LTTE in fact managed to move upwards to Varani via Chavakachcheri, as they seemed bent on doing, they would have not only encircled the troops on the front line in Muhamalai, but also isolated Palaly and the Kankesanthurei harbour, trapping over 30,000 troops in the peninsula in a military debacle of unimaginable proportions.

As the LTTE stood poised to take over the Jaffna peninsula, the government of Sri Lanka was appealing to India for help. They even took the extreme step of asking for military help, but the Indians after their IPKF experience, were wary of getting involved in Sri Lanka. One Indian legislator Swaraj Kaushal explained why India should not get involved. Referring to the IPKF experience he said, "*Although we had gone at the invitation of the Sri Lankan government, when we returned, we were unwelcome guests in Sri Lanka and also in Chennai.*" Another senior legislator Pranabh Mukherjee said in a more conciliatory manner, "*We share with anguish our concern about the developments in Sri Lanka.*" But India would only be concerned, not involved.

With the unfolding crisis in Sri Lanka, the parliament of the European Union adopted a resolution on 19 May 2000, making reference to the assassination over 20 democratic politicians from both the Tamil and Sinhala communities by the LTTE and urging them to accept the offer of talks by the Sri Lankan government. In this grave situation, president Kumaratunga in an interview with *The Hindu* correspondent in Colombo Nirupama Subramaniam, said; *"What we are worried about is the Jaffna population. They are pleading with us not to leave them at the mercies of the LTTE in case the army has to withdraw...They fear they will all be killed by the LTTE because they came into government controlled areas when we invited them despite the LTTE trying to keep them back."*

The US government also showed its concern by sending Undersecretary of State for Political Affairs Thomas R.Pickering on a visit to Sri Lanka. He stated at a press conference on 29 May 2000, *"The USA has long supported the territorial integrity of Sri Lanka...the USA does not envision or support the establishment of another independent state on this land nor do we believe other members of the international community would support it."* Gamini Weerakoon, the editor of *The Island* who was present at this meeting, asked Pickering the question: *"You stand against a separate state here. But what happens if it is created?"* Pickering gave a very categorical answer: *"I think it is quite clear that it will receive no recognition from anyone...It is the international community that is arbiter of who becomes states and who do not become states through a process of recognition and establishment of relations."*

When the Chavakachcheri line fell to the LTTE, Janaka Perera gave command of Major Gen Parami Kulatunga's division to Major Gen. Wanigasekera. In the meantime the LTTE had broken through into the Colombothurei area a few kilometres to the east of Jaffna town. If Colombothurei fell, the troops on the eastern part of the peninsula would have been cut off so Wanigasekera sent Col Jagath Dias to hold Colombothurei which he did successfully. It was here that the relentless advance of the LTTE was first stopped. Wanigasekera also assigned another of his officers Col. Sumedha Perera to the Sarasalai area where an LTTE offensive commenced at about 4.00 in the afternoon and raged on until noon the next day. Reinforcements were rushed in and for the second time since the failure of Operation Jayasikurui the year before, the army was able to repulse an LTTE attack. About a 100 bodies of LTTE cadres had been recovered after the battle of Sarasalai.

By this time, two multi barrel rocket launchers that had been ordered form Pakistan had arrived in Kankesanthurei on 15 May

2000 and they were used in the battle of Sarasalai. The tide turned thereafter and with the added firepower of the Pakistani MBRLs, the army was able to recapture some of the lost territory. Later summing up how the relentless advance of the LTTE was halted, Major Gen Fonseka was to write – "*In the true sense of the word, the only support weapon in this battle was the words of command given by the officers who fought shoulder to shoulder with the brave soldiers in the war front. If not for their conspicuous bravery, the whole of the Jaffna peninsula would have fallen into the hands of the separatist terrorists.*"

From mid-July 2000 onwards, the troops began to claw back territory from the LTTE on the peninsula. In a series of operations code named *Rivikirana* and *Kinihira*, government troops recaptured territory they had lost in Chavakachheri, Tanankilappu, and Ariyalai. With this army offensive, LTTE contingents that had broken into the Chavakachcheri area were finding it difficult to keep their cadres supplied from Pooneryn across the Jaffna lagoon. In December 2000, the LTTE declared a unilateral ceasefire to prevent the army from regaining even more territory, and thus the new defence lines were established on a line of control extending from Muhamalai to Nagarkovil.

This frontline would remain the border between tiger country and government held territory for nearly a decade. The fall of Elephant Pass was the LTTE's greatest military triumph and the government's biggest embarrassment in the four decade long conflict. This represented the peak of the Tamil separatist war. The year 2000 was the most disastrous year in the army's history. The loss of men through death and injury was so serious that in the Gajaba Regiment several battalions were disbanded and amalgamated with other battalions to form proper units. On 18 September 2000, the 8th Gajaba Battalion was disbanded and amalgamated with the 1st, the 9th with the 4th, 12th with the 6th and the 16th with the 10th.

The year 2000 was the closest Sri Lanka ever came to the creation of a separate state. Even as late as 1 July 2000, when the advance of the LTTE had been halted, Anton Balasingham was telling the London based *Tamil Guardian*, "*The LTTE controls over 70% of the land mass in the Tamil homeland...we have already instituted a de facto state in the territories under our control. We run a permanent administration there.*" Balasingham betrayed resentment against the international community for taking the Sri Lankan government's side when the LTTE stood poised to take over Jaffna. He said in this interview, "*Insofar as the ultimate solution to the Tamil question is concerned, it is not the American superpower nor the Indian regional power or the Sri Lankan state power that have the power of determination. It is our people, the people of Tamil Eelam who will ultimately determine their political status and identity."*

This same attitude was echoed by Prabhakaran in his heroes' day speech of 26 November 2000. *"The western governments want peace and a negotiated settlement through peaceful means. They insist that the Tamil conflict cannot be resolved by war. It is precisely for this reason that Chandrika has been making subtle propaganda statements to placate the western nations using the categories of peace, negotiations, devolution and constitutional reforms...The entire world rushed to help Sri Lanka with emergency military assistance when Chandrika raised the alarm of an impending military disaster claiming that the lives of thirty thousand troops was in danger...It was the same world which closed its eyes and observed a studied silence when Jaffna was invaded militarily by the Sri Lankan army and ...half a million Tamils were uprooted and displaced...*

In late April 2001, the army launched Operation *Agnikheela* to take back the territory between Muhamalai and Elephant Pass. But four days after the operation was launched, *The Island* stated editorially. *"...the fact remains that the military has fallen short of capturing...Palai... And the reason given... is the heavy resistance put up by the terrorists firing... barrage after barrage of artillery. The high casualty figures have been attributed to the mines the terrorists had laid in the area. This brings us to the much vaunted firepower of the military which once so effectively halted the LTTE's 'Unceasing Waves'... The firepower of the Army was... enhanced immensely at tremendous cost to the public... For the first time perhaps, there have been no allegations of lack of armaments for the troops. Nor is it claimed that the Generals were denied a free hand. But today we hear of the military once again being driven back by the LTTE..."*

Up to this point, we have dealt primarily with LTTE confrontations with the military. Attacks on civilian targets may have received only cursory mention if at all in these pages. However attacking civilian targets was an integral part of the LTTE's strategy to break the will of the government in Colombo. Over the decades, the LTTE had carried out many attacks on civilians and civilian targets, some of which have been mentioned in previous chapters. One such attack on a civilian economic target was the bombing of the Central Bank in Colombo Fort which killed 91 people and injured another 1400 of which at least 100 were believed to have lost their eyesight. The lorry that was rammed into the Central Bank building was believed to contain at least 200 kilos of C-4 explosives.

Then there was the 15 October 1997 bombing of the Colombo World Trade Centre twin towers, which took place soon after the towers were opened. A truck laden with explosives which had gained access through the car park of an adjoining hotel was exploded near the twin towers causing serious damage to the building as well as the Colombo Hilton and the Galadari Meridien Hotels located nearby. Around 23 people died, and of the 100 or so injured, about two dozen were foreigners. The most devastating attack on an economic target was the attack on the Katunayake air base and international airport. On 24 July 2001, at around 1.15 am a group of about 15-20 terrorists infiltrated the defences of the Katunayake air force base and the international airport. They completely destroyed eight air force aircraft and three civilian craft belonging to Sri Lankan airlines. A further three civilian jets were severely damaged in an attack which lasted around four hours.

The air force was primarily responsible for the security of their own air base as well as the Katunayake international airport but after the attack began there was absolutely no counter action taken by the air force and the terrorists had a free run of both the air base and the civilian airport, destroying aircraft at leisure. It was two and a half hours into the attack, at around 3.40 am that the terrorists were identified and fired upon on the tarmac where the helicopters and Kfir jets were parked. There was a team of army commandos in the airport to be deployed in anti-hijack operations. However they were armed only with Heckler and Koch short-barrel, low-velocity weapons meant for close quarter combat such as hijackings. They also had only stun grenades instead of the usual explosive grenades.

Yet it was this team of commandos along with other army commandos who had finally cleared the terminal building by killing the terrorists. The civilian airport was handed back to the air force at around 2.00 pm on 24 July. The impact this fiasco had on the war, the minds of the public and on the beleaguered government of president Chandrika Kumaratunga is indescribable. This was something that could easily have been prevented if only the air force personnel guarding this vital installation had had been a little more alert. Civilian intelligence tip offs that suspicious characters were seen around the air port were ignored, as was information provided by an air force sergeant about suspicious movements in the vicinity.

The air force had more than 2000 troops in the complex but they had been effectively neutralized by 15-20 terrorists with only small arms who moved about freely destroying aircraft at will. The end result was the biggest civil aviation disaster in world history. This was eclipsed only by the September 11 attacks in the USA the same year. This saw the driving up of international insurance premiums for Sri Lanka, a dip in tourist arrivals and all round economic mayhem in addition to having a good proportion of the air assets of the air force completely destroyed. The air force assets destroyed included two Kfirs, two Mi-17 transport helicopters and four F-7 jets.

Chapter 42

The Ceasefire Agreement of 2002

In the midst of unprecedented military debacles and economic collapse, the Chandrika Kumaratunga regime lost the parliamentary election of December 2001 and the UNP formed a government headed by Prime Minister Ranil Wickremesinghe. The new government immediately went in for a Norwegian brokered ceasefire with the LTTE. The defence establishment was not happy with the ceasefire agreement at all. According to the provisions of the ceasefire agreement that came into force in February 2002;

* All hostilities between the signatories on land, air and sea would cease. The rather incongruously drafted article 1.3 of the CFA expressly stated that the Sri Lankan armed forces shall continue to perform their legitimate task of safeguarding the sovereignty and territorial integrity of Sri Lanka without however, engaging in offensive operations against the LTTE.

* Each party would continue to hold the territory it held as of 24 December 2001.

* Tamil paramilitary groups were to be disarmed by the government within one month of the ceasefire coming into effect. The government had the option of absorbing these members into its armed forces but they would not be allowed to serve in the north and east.

* Unarmed government troops would be allowed freedom of movement along the A-9 highway between Vavuniya and

Jaffna. Combatants of either party would be allowed to visit family and relatives in the territories held by the other party.

* Up to 90 unarmed LTTE members would be allowed to enter the government held areas for political work.

* All places of worship occupied by the armed forces of either side shall be vacated. Even such places within high security zones had to be vacated and maintained by civilian workers. School buildings occupied by armed forces also shall be vacated and returned to their normal use.

* Checkpoints in densely populated areas would be reviewed with a view to setting up systems to prevent harassment to the civilian population.

* Non-military goods except for non-military arms and ammunition, explosives, remote control devices, barbed wire, binoculars, telescopes, compasses, and penlight batteries, will be allowed to flow freely. Diesel, petrol, cement and iron rods would be sent only in restricted quantities.

* The A-9 road would be open for non-military goods and passengers. The Trincomalee-Habarana road was to be kept open on a 24 hour basis.

* All restrictions on fishing were to be removed within 90 days except in an area within 2 nautical miles of security forces camps on the coast and fishing will not be permitted near the approach to harbours.

* Search operations and arrests under the Prevention of Terrorism Act will not take place.

* A ceasefire monitoring mission named the Sri Lanka Monitoring Mission (SLMM) would be set up headed by Norway and will establish a presence in Jaffna, Mannar, Vavuniya, Trincomalee, Batticaloa and Amparai.

* The SLMM will be given access to places where ceasefire violations have taken place.

* The SLMM will take immediate action on any complaints made by either party to the agreement and inquire into and assist the parties in the settlement of any dispute that may arise in connection with such complaints.

Less than two weeks after it was signed by Velupillai Prabhakaran and Ranil Wickremesinghe, a presentation on the ceasefire agreement was made at the Joint Operations Headquarters with the commanders of the army, navy and air force and the police chief present. The presentation was tellingly titled *"Eelam through negotiations"*.

In this presentation it was argued that the goal of the LTTE was a separate state and that there was nothing to indicate that this aim had changed. They had been trying to achieve their goal both through terrorism and through negotiations. The September 11 attacks had tilted world opinion against terrorism and the LTTE now had no option but to rely on negotiations to achieve their aim.

The presentation warned that the government must be alive to the danger that the LTTE will try to gain full control of the area claimed by them in stages. They will first ask for the withdrawal of troops from schools and places of worship, then the removal of checkpoints, followed by a stop to all searches and patrolling on the grounds that such activities are a hindrance to the public. They would also ask for the withdrawal of the military from all civilian areas, towns and villages for the same reason. The final step would be to demand that all airports and seaports be handed over to civilian control. Another warning issued was that the LTTE would seek freedom of movement throughout the north and east for itself but deny the armed forces access to areas held by them.

The next step would be to expand the control the LTTE already has over the government administrative machinery in both their own territory as well as the government held areas by negotiating for more control by some formal arrangement with the government. Then they would try to acquire the trappings of sovereignty by sitting at the negotiating table as an equal of the government of Sri Lanka. The LTTE's demand that they be de-proscribed before the talks commenced was also interpreted as a reflection of this desire to be on an equal footing with the government. It was also said that the LTTE would at the same time try to portray themselves as different to other terrorist outfits in that they possess armed forces, and a civilian administration necessary to run a sovereign state. It was urged that the government of Sri Lanka should be able to 'see through' the LTTE demands and the presentation pointed out that the government had not been professional in the manner they were dealing with this matter. The warnings of the military fell on deaf ears.

Shanaka Jayasekera, then a senior official of the Secretariat for Coordinating the Peace Process (SCOPP) the body set up under the ceasefire agreement to coordinate the peace process from the Sri Lankan government side, told the present writer that one of the main weaknesses of the SLMM was that they maintained a presence only in the government held areas of Mannar, Vavuniya, Trincomalee, Batticaloa, Ampara and Jaffna. But they did not have a presence in the LTTE held areas except for a liaison office in Kilinochchi. So the SLMM was in effect monitoring only one party to the conflict. When officials of SCOPP contacted the SLMM about violations of the ceasefire in LTTE held territory, they came back with the excuse that their mandate does not extend to those areas.

Another weakness was that the LTTE was allowed to establish offices all over the cleared areas. The LTTE used this to get their intelligence operatives into the government held areas. During the ceasefire, LTTE cadres who had been arrested by the navy and detained under the Prevention of Terrorism Act had to be released. The released tigers had gone away triumphantly after threatening the navy personnel present in courts saying, *"We'll see about you later"*. Some had even raised their sarongs to the military as they went. When unarmed LTTE cadres had been allowed to go into the Jaffna peninsula for 'political work' through Muhamalai, the first LTTE cadres had gone in cheering and singing, as if they had won the war, and the military was humiliated. The officers had to prevail upon the soldiers to be patient.

Commodore Sarath Weerasekera, the then head of the northern command of the navy bluntly told Prime Minister Ranil Wickremesinghe when he was on a visit to the Karainagar naval base in 2002 soon after the peace accord was signed, that the LTTE was using the ceasefire as an instrument of war. Weerasekera had pointed out that the LTTE was collecting millions of Rupees per day through various 'taxes' imposed on the people. In addition to that, they were also trying to forcibly recruit at least one member from each family in Jaffna so that the entire Tamil community would automatically be involved in the fight for Eelam. Weerasekera reminisces that a common sight at Muhamalai those days was that of distraught Tamil mothers peering into vehicles moving into the LTTE held area to see whether their abducted children were being taken into the Vanni by the LTTE.

After the ceasefire agreement was signed, one of the main demands of the LTTE was that they should be de-proscribed if they were to come to talks. But in a rare instance of acting in the national interest, the Wickremesinghe government did not de-proscribe them because they thought a de-proscription in Sri Lanka would have a domino effect on the proscriptions that some Western countries had imposed on the LTTE. So the government adopted a compromise measure by suspending the proscription of the LTTE.

There was a great drama enacted by the LTTE even to have the first round of talks. The purpose was to show the Tamil people, the Sri Lankan public and the world at large that they could make the government dance to their tune. When the first peace talks were to be held, Balasingham said that he could not come for the talks without consulting Prabhakaran but he refused to come to Sri Lanka via the Katunayake airport and wanted to fly in direct to 'Eelam' from overseas. This was to stress the fact that there were now two territories on the island. He flew to the Maldives, and then came in a chartered sea plane which landed at the Iranamadu tank and Prabhakaran received him with much fanfare. The then government bent over backwards to assist in this LTTE propaganda stunt by sending an official of the Immigration and Emigration Department to the Maldives with a seal so that he could stamp Balasingham's passport before he got on to the seaplane to come to Iranamadu!

After this drama, the first peace talks were held in Satahip Thailand in the third week of September 2002. Anton Balasingham and V.Rudrakumaran, led the LTTE delegation. The Sri Lankan delegation was led by cabinet ministers G.L.Peiris, Milinda Moragoda, Rauff Hakeem, and defence secretary Austin Fernando. The Sri Lankan team had studied Balasingham's modus operandi at previous peace talks and they went prepared. The LTTE's strategy was to raise minor issues like removing checkpoints, bringing in more food, reducing restrictions on fishing and avoid going into core issues. They had done this during the 1995 peace talks with the Chandrika Kumaratunga government. The SL delegation checkmated the LTTE by agreeing to ease all restrictions. Items going into the Vanni were checked but there were no restrictions except for a very few items like 'penlight' batteries. So Balasingham could not do the filibustering act that he did earlier.

Jayasekera reminisces that Solheim always emphasised the parity of status of the two parties. At the inaugural talks, Balasingham was even addressed as 'Your Excellency'. When the next round of talks was held about six weeks later in Narkorn Pathom, Thailand at the Rose Garden hotel, the government asked for executive suites for its three cabinet ministers, Peiris, Moragoda and Hakeem, but Solheim turned down the request saying that the LTTE delegation too was given only one executive suite. Another instance when the Norwegians tried to establish this parity of status, was in the workings of the Sub-

Committee for Immediate Reconstruction and Humanitarian Needs (SIRHN) which was set up after the ceasefire was signed.

This body was to comprise of LTTE and government representatives. Money for reconstruction was to come in from donor countries and a mechanism had to be worked out to decide how it was to be handled. Solheim undertook the task of drafting a proposal for the two sides to consider. The first proposal that he sent in, was to have a representative of the department of external resources of the treasury and a representative of the finance department of the LTTE, on the committee. This proposal was however dropped due to objections from the Sri Lankan government.

At the third round of talks held in Oslo, the government and the LTTE signed a document which became known as the Oslo Declaration. In this joint statement, Balasingham said that *"The LTTE was agreeable to explore a solution founded on the principle of internal self determination in areas of historical habitation of the Tamil speaking peoples, based on a federal structure within a united Sri Lanka"*. Balasingham was encouraged to sign the Oslo declaration by Karuna, Dr J.Maheswaran from Australia and also by Adele Balasingham. Those who opposed it were Rudrakumaran and Tamilselvam. The latter had held that they should consult Prabhakaran before signing the declaration, but Karuna had said that there was no point in asking Prabhakaran because they knew what his answer would be.

Balasingham signed the Oslo declaration in good faith, but Prabhakaran never had any intention of settling for a federal solution. Kumaran Pathmanathan says that by this time, Prabhakaran was surrounded by subordinates who would find out what he liked to hear and tell him exactly that without expressing their own thoughts freely. The overseas Tamils also reinforced Prabhakaran's thinking because they were as much out of touch with the reality as Prabhakaran himself. So the synergy between the LTTE and the overseas Tamils resulted in mutually reinforcing each other's delusions and the realism that Balasingham had tried to bring into the equation was brushed aside. In the midst of all this hostility, Balasingham himself was to repudiate the Oslo declaration later.

Chapter 43

Whistling in the Wind

The ceasefire agreement of 2002 had no reference to the sea or the air. The air force continued to carry out UAV (unmanned aerial vehicle) reconnaissance and the SLLM described this as 'unhelpful' and not something that would conduce to building trust. Moreover, the sea tigers could not operate freely as the ceasefire did not apply to the sea. The SLMM head Tryggve Tellefsen came up with a suggestion to the government peace secretariat that a stretch of the coast off Chalai, three kilometres into the sea and five kilometres wide, be designated as a 'training area' for the sea tigers - a proposal which was furiously rejected by the navy.

During the ceasefire when Sarath Fonseka was the security forces commander Jaffna, Shavendra Silva was his principle staff officer and he accompanied Fonseka on the regular discussions with the LTTE in the no man's land in Muhamalai between the army and LTTE lines. A tent would be set up in the no man's land and army and LTTE delegations would meet. A game of one-up'manship between the army and the LTTE was played out even here. The LTTE delegation would arrive with much fanfare, the sirens on their vehicles blaring, and they would be dressed in smart uniforms. At times they would be sporting accessories such as belts that had clearly been taken from the army. If an army officer had a pointer, the LTTE delegation would also bring a pointer the next time.

Of the LTTE leaders who came for the monthly talks, Karuna Amman the Batticaloa-Amparai leader was quite moderate and

260

understood the concerns of the military side recalls Shavendra Silva. But he would say apologetically that his 'national leader' as he referred to Prabhakaran, had a different view and he was answerable to him. Theepan the Jaffna commander was much more of a hardliner who always wanted only his own way. During the talks, Karuna would always lead the discussions and Theepan, Jeyam and others would make an appearance depending on whose area it was. At times during the discussions, Theepan or Jeyam as the case may be, would get highly agitated and speak animatedly to Karuna but most of the time, they were quiet and observant.

One of the main issues discussed during these meetings between the armed forces and the LTTE was the dismantling of the high security zones. Without the high security zones, the terrorists would have been within small arms range of all military installations including the Palaly airport and the Kankesanthurei harbour - a situation that would have been suicidal for the military. So this invitation to commit suicide was always politely turned down by the army. Sarath Fonseka then the security forces commander Jaffna, had drawn up a plan linking the dismantling of the high security zones to the decommissioning of the LTTE's long range weapons – a very sound and reasonable approach.

From day one, the Sri Lanka Monitoring Mission was monitoring only reported violations by the government and not those committed by the LTTE. On 20 June 2002, two LTTE 'political workers' in Kayts complained that they had been assaulted by eight men, two in army uniform, one in navy uniform and five masked civilians. The SLMM actually wanted no less than an 'independent special commission' reporting directly to the prime minister to probe this relatively minor incident. In reaction to this single incident, they even established a point of contact in Kayts with an SLMM monitor present on a regular basis. They however never showed the same concern over complaints made against the LTTE by the government. Referring to the killings by the LTTE that had taken place since the ceasefire came into operation, United Nations Special Rapporteur on Extra-Judicial Killings, Phillip Alston observed after his December 2005 visit to Sri Lanka, that the most disturbing aspect of this was that these killings were being used to control the Tamil population. He observed that even though governments and even armed guerrilla groups usually have to respect the rights of the people in order to retain popular support, the LTTE was largely exempt from this because they depended for financial and political support on the 800,000 strong Tamil diaspora living in the West.

Alston recommended that all Western countries with a significant Tamil population should initiate a dialogue with the Tamils living in their countries with a view to bringing pressure on the LTTE to reign in the violence in Sri Lanka. According to the figures of the government, the LTTE had carried out 363 killings from the time the ceasefire agreement was signed in February 2002, up to the end of September 2005 - a figure that Alston accepts. Alston was also critical of the Sri Lanka Monitoring Mission that had been set up under the chairmanship of Norway. His criticism was that the SLMM did not investigate the various killings that were reported to it. He also noted that there was a conflict of interest in that Norway was the facilitator of the peace process as well as the head of the SLMM. Alston held that the desire to keep the broader peace process on track would inhibit any desire to investigate violations of the ceasefire properly for fear that it would upset the LTTE.

Individual military officers did what they could to safeguard the integrity of the country within the space left to them under the ceasefire agreement. The then director of military intelligence Major Gen Hendevitharana, says that one of the things that his department did was to update their maps of the north and east, some of which were inaccurate. Satellite images had shown for example, that the Palai junction on the military maps was about 700 meters away from the actual location. The locations of the LTTE's camps, fuel and ammunition dumps, training facilities and sea tiger bases were also collected during this period. The air force in particular remained busy during the ceasefire with aerial surveillance and training at their range in Kalpitiya to practice bombing dives. It was this that enabled the air force to improve their accuracy in taking targets during the final war.

Sri Lanka would be led by three leaders during the period of the ceasefire agreement, Prime Minister Ranil Wickremesinghe from February 2002 to April 2004, President Chandrika Kumaratunga from April 2004 to November 2005 and president Rajapaksa from November 2005 to July 2006. Of them, both Wikremesinghe and Kumaratunga proved to be inept at handling the LTTE. They both seemed to believe that appeasement was the only way left. The LTTE for their part did exactly as they pleased. As the SLMM maintained a presence only in the government held areas, the LTTE was able to carry out their war like preparations in the areas under their control, without any hindrance.

On 1 May 2002, just weeks after the signing of the ceasefire agreement, three navy fast attack craft accosted a suspicious trawler which was blown up by its crew as the navy drew close. At the same time, LTTE boats hiding among a cluster of fishing boats nearby had started firing at the naval craft. SLMM observers came to the scene to investigate the incident. An examination of the wreckage of the trawler resulted in the recovery of 15 boxes of 120mm mortars, two boxes of 81mm mortars and RPG launchers. In another incident on 6 February 2003, two naval craft with two SLMM staff aboard went to examine a trawler that was being towed by two sea tiger craft off Delft. Upon examining the trawler, the navy found one 23mm anti aircraft gun and explosives. The sea tigers aboard then set fire to the trawler and exploded themselves. The two Scandinavian SLMM observers narrowly escaped death by jumping overboard.

Karuna, the renegade LTTE field commander says that Prabhakaran had told them to keep the ceasefire going for five years during which period, the LTTE would stock up on arms and make preparations for the final war. In the two years between the time the ceasefire was signed and he broke away from the LTTE, Karuna said that 11 shiploads of weapons had been brought into Sri Lanka and LTTE trawlers were bringing in weapons even in the daytime whereas earlier weapons shipments came into Sri Lanka only in the night.

Rear Admiral Wasantha Karannagoda was appointed the eastern commander of the navy in January 2003 and served in that post for a little over one year. After taking over the command, Karannagoda found that despite the clause in the ceasefire agreement which prohibited the setting up of new camps, the LTTE was in fact setting up new camps in Illankanthei in the Sampur area just south of the mouth of the Trincomalee harbour. When the LTTE's first movement of 170 cadres going 'on leave' from Mulleitivu to Vakarai took place on 18/19 August 2002, on the return journey from Vakarai to Mulleitivu, the LTTE had in fact stopped over in Illankanthei as well. This was outside the agreed route, and was typical of the way the LTTE always tried to force the military into giving into their demands so as to humiliate them.

On 16 February 2003, Prime Minister Ranil Wickremesinghe and the defence minister Tilak Marapone came to Anuradhapura and held a meeting with senior military officers. Karannagoda had come from Trincomalee and when it came to his turn to speak, he reported that there was an LTTE build up in Illankanthei, Sampur. Wickremesinghe took this as a joke. He had asked Karannagoda with a sarcastic smirk, "Why can't you fire at them from the sea?" Karannagoda had explained that he can't see the target from the sea and that in any case, the guns possessed by the navy were not big enough for the purpose. He stressed that a land operation had to be launched to clear Sampur and that the LTTE should not be allowed to set up bases there because it posed a direct threat to the Trincomalee harbour.

The intelligence officer in the eastern naval command at that time was a young officer by the name of D.K.P. Dassanayake and it was he who had gathered information about the eleven new LTTE camps. The army divisional commander of that area also had officially reported 17 camps, including the older camps the LTTE had. The navy's information was provided by a mole they had deep in the LTTE set up, a school teacher who was in personal contact with Sornam the Trincomalee leader of the LTTE. The intelligence reports had been confirmed by satellite images. When the ceasefire accord was signed, the idea was for the two sides to control the areas they already had. While the line of control was well defined in the north, it was not so in the east. Things were better defined in the Batticaloa district than in the Trincomalee district where there were always disputes as to who controlled what.

Prime MinisterWickremesinghe took no notice of Karannagoda's warnings. About three months after the Anuradhapura briefing, Karannagoda got a call from the then navy commander Admiral Daya Sandagiri telling him that President Chandrika Kumaratunga wanted a briefing from him about the Trincomalee harbour. The president was no longer the head of the government as that role was now being played by Wickremesinghe, but as the commander in chief of the armed forces, she had the right to summon and question members of the armed forces. Karannagoda made the presentation in the presence of the three service commanders and the former foreign minister Lakshman Kadirgarmar. President Kumaratunga had been at the presentation for a short while but she had left half way, because she had to attend the funeral of a close relative. Thereafter Kadirgarmar had chaired the meeting.

Karannagoda showed that around a dozen new LTTE camps had come up to the south of Trincomalee in the Sampur area including Illankanthei. Several days later, the defence secretary Austin Fernando telephoned Karannagoda and asked him whether he had made a presentation to the president. Karannagoda had answered in the affirmative. Fernando had asked him, *"Who gave you permission to do that?"* To this Karannagoda's answer was that his commander had asked him to do it. Fernando had then told him to make the same presentation to the defence minister Tilak Marapone. What had raised the ire of the UNP government was that soon after listening to Karannagoda's presentation, Kadirgarmar had gone to India and said at a gathering there, that there was an LTTE build up south of the Trincomalee harbour.

This had been reported in the Indian newspapers and had by that means come to the attention of the Sri Lankan government. When this matter was brought to the notice of the prime minister directly by Karannagoda, he chose to ignore it, but when the same issue bounced back through the Indian media, the government evinced some interest in it. A few days later, Karannagoda repeated to defence minister Marapone and defence secretary Fernando, the same things he had told the prime minister in Anuradhapura a few months earlier. Once again, the three service commanders were present. One useful thing about these repeated lectures was that the other branches of the armed services were also educated about the danger of allowing an LTTE build up in Sampur.

Chapter 44

The Policy of Appeasement

One of the few things that president Kumaratunga did well, was to oppose her opponents and the disquiet in the military over what was going on in the name of the ceasefire agreement, was exploited by her to the maximum. Even though she made use of this disquiet for political purposes, once she was back in power after April 2004, she too followed much the same policy of appeasement that the Wickremesinghe government had followed. That however was still in the future. By the time the Wickremesinghe government came around to paying any attention to what the navy was saying about Sampur, over four months had lapsed between February and July 2003 and Karannagoda had already destroyed two LTTE vessels on the eastern seas.

On 10 March 2003, an LTTE vessel suspected to be carrying arms was detected off Mulleitivu. When the SLMM was informed by SCOPP that an LTTE ship had been detected 185 nautical miles off Mulleitivu, the SLMM chief Tryggve Tellefsen contacted the navy commander and requested that the navy keep the vessel under close observation, maintain a distance from it, and avoid confrontation until an SLMM representative got there. The navy commander however informed the SLMM head that a fire fight had already broken out between the two vessels. The vessel had been detected, and the identification details given had discrepancies and it was not flying a national flag or displaying a visible name.

The crew on the LTTE ship had for their part, contacted the SLMM and said they were in international waters and that their vessel was a 700 ton tanker 61 meters long and that they were sailing in the direction of India with a legal cargo of diesel. The ship was fired upon and sunk 195 nautical miles off Mulleitivu. On 14 June 2003, Karannagoda was able to destroy another LTTE arms vessel. That day at around 6.30 am, the head of the SLMM Tellefsen was informed by Austin Fernando that two LTTE vessels had been intercepted about 100 nautical miles off Mulleitivu. Once again the LTTE too was in contact with the SLMM and was giving a different story. According to the LTTE, the vessel intercepted was MT Shoshin a tanker which was in international waters 266 nautical miles from Sri Lanka.

The navy had asked the tanker for its identification and when the details were checked, they were found to be false. They had then wanted to board the tanker to inspect it, but the tanker did not stop. Three warning shots were fired and the response to this was small arms fire. Thereupon the navy had fired upon the LTTE tanker and sank it. The SLMM ruled that that navy had not violated the ceasefire by intercepting the vessel because the law of the sea gave the navy the power to inspect the tanker. They also declared that the LTTE had violated the ceasefire agreement by not flying an appropriate flag or having any visible form of identification. That day, Karannagoda was asked both by Marapone and Austin Fernando, who had given him instructions to destroy that ship. They had wanted to know whether he had spoken to the president. Karannagoda had simply said that he had acted in his capacity as the eastern area commander of the navy.

Karannagoda had to take extraordinary precautions to prevent news of impending operations from leaking out to the LTTE. In October 2003, there was a controversy about an SLMM officer having tipped off the LTTE about an impending interception of an arms ship. The government had wanted the navy to carry a representative of the SLMM when they went out on operations. On one occasion when the SLMM representative was on board, he had spoken to somebody over his satellite phone and the intended target did not appear. The suspicion was that the LTTE was tipped off by the SLMM. President Chandrika Kumaratunga wrote to the Norwegian government asking them to remove the head of SLMM Teleffsen.

The latter had admitted later in a conversation with a US diplomat in Colombo that a member of their staff had indeed contacted the LTTE and wanted to know whether they had a ship in the eastern waters and that this was not a case of 'tipping off' the LTTE. He had however admitted that the issue was badly handled. This conversation was reported to Washington in a confidential cable from the US Embassy in Colombo and was made public by Wikileaks in 2010. Be that as it may, after this incident, the navy did not take members of the SLMM on their ships. Karannagoda held that operational secrecy would be compromised if the SLMM personnel were on board. Up to 2003, LTTE arms ships used to come close to Sri Lanka to unload their goods into trawlers. But after the navy sank two LTTE ships in 2003, shipments had stopped for a while.

Then the LTTE arms vessels began staying further away, and multi-day trawlers would go further out into deep seas to collect the goods. Some of these weapons and munitions would be taken to Mannar, and from there, overland in trucks to the Vanni. The LTTE trawlers operating from Arippu in Mannar were registered in the name of a Sinhalese owner. Most of the items transported through Mannar were shells and ammunition. One 152mm artillery gun was transported to Vedithaltivu and the trawler transporting it was brought right up to the quay and a crane was used to unload the heavy gun. At times, if a crane was not available, backhoes would be used to unload heavy cargo from the trawlers.

The LTTE preferred to use trawlers from Mannar because there were no trawlers in Mulleitivu and in any case, any trawler seen in those waters would immediately be suspect. Moreover, hundreds of trawlers went out to sea from the Mannar coast and the LTTE boats could blend in with bona fide fishermen and move with relative ease. The navy also did not patrol the western coast with the same intensity as the Mulleitivu coast.

The entire LTTE arms smuggling operation was based in Indonesia. The LTTE did not buy weapons from that country but obtained all non-military supplies for the ships and other goods like medicines from Indonesia. Even outboard motors for the LTTE boats were brought from Japan to Indonesia and then loaded onto the ships to be brought to Sri Lanka. Communication equipment was brought from Malaysia to Indonesia by air and from there loaded into the LTTE ships. The repair and maintenance of all LTTE ships was done in Indonesia. The LTTE had sufficient stocks of arms and ammunition to take on the regular army of a state which obtained supplies from several different countries. The LTTE got their stocks of arms and ammunition from North Korea and their cargo ships would collect the goods direct from North Korean harbours. The North Korean munitions factories sold the goods to the LTTE through an agent on a 'cash and carry' basis.

268

The LTTE cargo vessels collected the goods from North Korea, and then transferred the cargo to small tankers in mid-sea near the equator where the sea was usually calm enabling such transfers to be made without much difficulty. It was these tankers that brought the munitions closer to Sri Lanka to be offloaded into trawlers. The LTTE used tankers to transport their weapons closer to Sri Lanka because the hulls of the cargo ships were high whereas the tanker at the lowest point was only three to four feet above sea level and that made it easier to transfer cargo from the tanker to the trawler in mid sea. The tanker could take about 50 tonnes of cargo. When the tanker offloads its 50 tonnes, they would go back to the mother ship for more.

By this means, not only was the mid sea transfer of weapons made easier, it also enabled the LTTE to safeguard the precious cargo ships. Even if a tanker was hit by the navy, they would lose only the tanker and around 50 tonnes of munitions. If a cargo ship had been hit however they would have lost a much larger vessel as well as over 1200 tonnes of munitions. The passports and seaman certificates of the sea tigers working on these ships were Bangladeshi and the ships they were working in were registered for the most part in Panama.

When the seas were rough, the Dvoras could not be put out to sea but the trawlers that the LTTE used to smuggle arms could operate in rough seas. The trawlers had displacement hulls which cut through the water and therefore could operate in rough seas whereas the Dvoras had planing hulls that skimmed over the water. They were built for speed but could not operate in rough seas. Hence much of the LTTE arms smuggling was done during the north-eastern monsoon when the seas were rough and the navy's fast attack craft could not be put out to sea.

Tilak Marapone the UNP defence minister listened to Karannagoda's presentation about Sampur in July 2003. It appeared that the UNP government was unwilling to accept that the ceasefire was being violated by the LTTE. By this time, the UNP defence authorities had got down a report from the army divisional commander of Trincomalee to the effect that there were no such camps in the Sampur area. Karannagoda however was not outdone. He had with him a report by the previous army divisional commander in the area confirming his story that there were new LTTE camps coming up in Sampur.

Unable to get Karannagoda to drop the Sampur issue, the UNP government launched a media blitz against him. The state owned ITN news channel accused him of providing a confidential report on

Sampur to the former foreign minister Lakshman Kadirgarmar before it was submitted to the prime minister, and that Kadirgarmar had used this report to criticize the government. The ITN news broadcast also said that Karannagoda was prone to panicking needlessly and that on one occasion he had mistaken a whale for an enemy submarine and ordered his gunners to open fire, killing the whale. With the media blitz against him, Karannagoda had told the navy commander Daya Sandagiri that with that kind of propaganda being carried out against him by the state owned media, he would find it difficult to command his men. Sandagiri had told the president about it. President Kumaratunga then wrote to Prime Minister Wickremesinghe saying that the Trincomalee harbour was being threatened by the LTTE and the eastern navy commander was being harassed by the government owned media and that this should stop.

This letter was leaked to the newspapers. A few weeks later, on 4 November 2003, the president seized control the media, defence and finance ministries, claiming among other things that national security was under threat and that the government owned media was being used to bring down the morale of the armed services. By that time, Karannagoda had filed action in courts against *ITN*, and he would later win the lawsuit. The UNP led parliamentary government of December 2001- April 2004, mishandled the whole ceasefire from the very beginning. Their attitude differed only marginally from that of the SLMM, with the emphasis being on preserving the ceasefire at all costs by endlessly appeasing the LTTE. When military officers reported that the LTTE was violating the ceasefire, the first instinct of the government was to try to silence the military, instead of taking account of what they said.

In fact during that October 2003 controversy about the SLMM having tipped off the LTTE about the navy's hunt for their arms vessel, the US Embassy had been told by the Sri Lankan defence minister Tilak Marapone that the SLMM's action had been 'inadvertent'. The UNP government did not support President Kumaratunga's call for the removal of the SLMM head Teleffsen over the tipping off scandal because they felt that the president's initiative was putting the peace process at risk.

Chapter 45

Karuna Amman Defects

However, if the armed forces thought they had in Chandrika Kumaratunga someone who could stand up to the LTTE, they were soon to be disappointed. In March 2004, towards the final days of the short-lived UNP government, Karuna Amman, the eastern commander of the LTTE broke away in what was undoubtedly the most damaging split that the organization had ever suffered. The split proved to be an embarrassment for the UNP government which was intent only on appeasing the LTTE. Phillip Alston estimated that Karuna took about a quarter of the LTTE's cadres with him. A problem that the UNP government was confronted with was that if Karuna had indeed taken a good part of the LTTE cadre with him, then they would come under pressure from the public to support Karuna, and that would have antagonized the LTTE.

So the solution the UNP came up with was to simply write off Karuna as an insignificant factor. There was one glitch however. The director of military intelligence Major Gen Hendevitarana was insisting that Karuna had taken a very significant number of cadres with him when they split and his opinion was that the government should support Karuna against the LTTE. Unable to get the army officer to toe their line, the UNP government resorted to the same tactic they adopted earlier with Karannagoda. They launched a media attack on Hendavitharana using the private media this time, because they did not have control over the state media. The next day, a pro-UNP private newspaper reported that Hendavitharana had been pulled up by the prime minister for giving him half baked information.

In April 2004, the UNP government was defeated at the parliamentary elections and Chandrika Kumaratunga once more had complete control over the government. Karuna now became Chandrika Kumaratunga's problem. She was as perplexed by Karuna as Wickremesinghe was, and she did not know what to do with him. The politicians tended to be obsessed with appeasing the LTTE and keeping the ceasefire going. The ceasefire was more than just the absence of gunfire. With it went the whole edifice of relations with the West and economic aid and all governments after 2002 - including initially even the Rajapaksa government - were keen to see it continued. President Chandrika Kumaratunga may have found the spats between the UNP government and the military leaders useful in clawing her way back into power, but once restored to her former status, she too found Karuna a vexing and unwanted sideshow.

In contrast to the politicians who wanted to humour the LTTE, the military leaders instinctively tended to see Karuna as the enemy of their enemy and therefore their friend. Even the Norwegian government appointed team tasked with evaluating their peace efforts in Sri Lanka were to observe retrospectively in 2011, that the Karuna split altered the military balance in a fundamental way. The military recognized the advantage of having Karuna out of the LTTE and on their side. Nimal Leuke a former senior officer of the elite police Special Task Force says that of all the LTTE leaders the east had starting with Bashir Kakka, Aruna, Kumarappa, Karikalan, Karuna, and Ramesh, Karuna was by far was the most formidable military commander who did a lot of work for the LTTE in the northern operations, even though he could not do much in the east. Not only was Karuna one of the best military commanders in the LTTE, he could drive a wedge between the Tamils of the east and the north in a way that no one else could. In fact it is after Karuna's emergence that the eastern Tamils had a leadership of their own. Up to the time Karuna and his protégé Pillaiyan emerged, the eastern Tamils had always been under the political tutelage of the north.

The split was some time in the making. Karuna's thinking had changed with the ceasefire and in the midst of emerging differences, Pottu Amman had come to Batticaloa to conduct an inquiry into the finances of the eastern command and Prabhakaran summoned Karuna to the Vanni for an inquiry. The latter refused to turn up and a tense standoff ensued. When Karuna ordered the Batticaloa cadres serving in the north to come down to Batticaloa with their weapons, Prabhakaran countermanded the order. During this period Karuna was in the Toppigala jungles with about 600 of his cadres and army intelligence had established contact with him over satellite phone. Two of Karuna's close aides had been picked up from Tivuchenai in the Batticaloa district, and brought to Colombo for talks.

The army wanted Karuna to fight the LTTE and pledged to provide all the backing they needed. Hendavitharana however says that by that time Karuna had lost the desire to continue fighting and even though he pledged to hold the area, he kept the best cadres around him without deploying them to hold vital areas such as the north of Vakarai. The cadres who were deployed there could not stop the LTTE from coming into the Batticaloa district because they did not have proper leadership. Initially, Karuna did put up a fight. His cadres killed seven Vanni LTTE cadres in Batticaloa on 25 April 2004 and two more in the Thannamunai area on 6 May 2004. By 15 June, the LTTE had replaced Karuna as the commander of Batticaloa and Ampara with 'Colonel' Ramesh.

By the end of June, Karuna simply gave up fighting and disbanded his cadres. He then came to Colombo in a vehicle belonging to a UNP parliamentarian from the east, Ali Zahir Moulana and stayed at the JAIC Hilton. His cadres and their families were put up at a hotel in Colombo. Military intelligence re-established links with the fugitives and provided them with a safe house. Konesh, the second in command of Karuna's breakaway group was shifted to this safe house with some other cadres on 14 April. After a while, however, some of them moved back to Tivuchenai saying they could live there without any problem. Then despite army warnings not to have safe houses anywhere else in Colombo, in July 2004 Konesh, Castro and some of the best fighters in that group moved out to a safe house in Kottawa about 18 km from Colombo.

While at this safe house, they were first put to sleep with food laced with a drug by an LTTE infiltrator among them and then shot by an LTTE operative about whom we will hear again later in this narrative. That it was an inside job was clear by the fact that there were no signs of a struggle and these seasoned fighters had been killed where they slept. That night they had been playing cards and sipping a hot sago drink and the sleeping tablets had been introduced into the sago drink. The infiltrator was an LTTE cadre who had lost a leg in battle and who had done the cooking for the Karuna cadres in the safe house. It was this man who always prepared the hot sago drink for them and on the night in question they had drunk the preparation without any suspicion. After this, Karuna sent his brother

Reggie back to Tivuchenai and reopened a camp in the Thoppigala jungles. So long as Lt Gen Lionel Balagalle was the commander of the army, the army had no problem in helping Karuna because Balagalle understood the importance of Karuna's split from the LTTE. But Balagalle retired in June 2004 and Shantha Kottegoda became army commander, after which the situation had changed.

After Chandrika Kumaratunga came back to power in April 2004, she too did not help Karuna for fear that it might antagonise the LTTE. She even wanted the Karuna group to stop attacking the LTTE. If the LTTE killed a member of the Karuna group there was no issue. But if a Karuna cadre killed an LTTE member that was a problem. Kumaratunga had even tried to prevail upon Hendavitharana to cut down on military intelligence operatives by half, a gesture which amply demonstrates that her commitment was to appease, not to combat the LTTE. Karuna had provided valuable information to the intelligence services about Prabhakaran's weaknesses, his cadre strength etc. Besides, Karuna's breakaway had considerably weakened the Tigers. None of this however was of any consequence to Chandrika Kumaratunga. In order to curry favour with the LTTE, president Kumaratunga told Hendavitharana to send Karuna out of the country. Seeing that he was no longer welcome, Karuna went to India in August 2004. He entered India through Nepal, coming down into West Bengal overland and then moving southwards.

As it turned out, Kumaratunga was no less an appeaser than Ranil Wickremesinghe. After the Asian Tsunami on 26 December 2004, she entered into an arrangement with the LTTE which was perhaps worse than the ceasefire agreement of 2002. This was the Post-Tsunami Operational Management Structure better known by its acronym P-TOMS which was signed by the Government of Sri Lanka and the LTTE on 24 June 2005. The P-TOMS arrangement was to facilitate post-tsunami reconstruction and development in the six districts of Ampara, Batticaloa, Jaffna, Kilinochchi, Mulleitivu and Trincomalee. What counted in this arrangement was the committee that would have complete control over deciding what the relief and reconstruction priorities were in those six districts, and approving, managing and monitoring the projects. Besides, this committee was to be permitted to receive foreign funds direct from donors. It was to comprise of two nominees of the government, five nominees of the LTTE and three Muslim representatives. One of the LTTE nominees would chair the committee. Two representatives from donor countries were also to sit on this committee as observers.

274

The office of this committee was to be located in Kilinochchi. The JVP which was now a member of the ruling coalition filed a fundamental rights suit in the Supreme Court against P-TOMS and the judgement delivered in July 2005 was that the government could not transfer its powers of financial management to a non-governmental committee. This put an end to P-TOMS. That a president of this country was willing to hand over control of foreign aid coming into Sri Lanka to a body dominated by a terrorist organization was the probably the lowest point reached by the Sri Lankan state.

While Karuna was in exile in India, members of his group still in Sri Lanka had their moment of revenge when they carried out an ambush in Batticaloa on 7 February 2005 that killed among others, Kaushalyan the LTTE eastern political wing leader and Ariyanayagam Chandranehru, former TNA parliamentarian from the Ampara district. The police were to find out later that it was Chandranehru who had in fact taken away the weapons after the killing of Konesh, Castro and other Karuna group seniors in Kottawa in August 2004. During the period February 2002 to July 2006, the LTTE killed off whoever they wanted at will. These attacks extended even to senior army intelligence officers like Col. Nizam Mutaliph and Col. Tuan Meedin. The attack that killed Kaushalyan and Chandranehru was the only worthwhile hit made against the LTTE.

The government of President Chandrika Kumaratunga was so keen to appease the LTTE that even an attempt to maintain law and order was taken as an attempt to scuttle the ceasefire agreement. On Wesak day in May 2005, the trishaw drivers in Trincomalee town replaced a small Buddha statue in the town with a larger one. The LTTE closed down the entire town in protest. The banks, shops, government offices and schools were closed. On the second day a grenade was lobbed at the Buddha statue damaging it. On the third day a Sinhalese youth who opened a shop was killed in a grenade attack. The police and the army stood by paralysed not knowing what to do. Any attempt at restoring law and order would have been seen at that time as an attempt to undermine the ceasefire agreement.

At that time, Sarath Weerasekera had just been appointed eastern commander of the navy. His tenure was to be the shortest ever, in that position. As things got out of hand in the Trincomalee town, Weerasekera stepped in to provide security to the Buddha statue. Then the navy set about breaking the LTTE enforced *hartal* by using commandeered CTB buses to commence transport services.

They also started pumping fuel with naval ratings manning the petrol stations. These measures effectively broke the *hartal*. Weerasekera was removed from the position of eastern naval commander on 19 June 2005. He however argued that if the Buddha statue in Trincomalee town had been destroyed, the Sinhalese would have retaliated by destroying kovils, leading to riots spreading to other districts. Seeing the logic behind this, president Kumaratunga relented and appointed Weerasekera as the deputy chief of staff of the navy in compensation for his hasty removal from the east.

The LTTE used the ceasefire to kill off their opponents within the Tamil community and the most high profile murder of this kind during the ceasefire was that of the former minister of foreign affairs Lakshman Kadirgamar who was shot by an LTTE sniper while taking a swim at his official residence in Stanmore Crescent on 12 August 2005. The house next to his was occupied by a Tamil man named Talaisingham who was an alcoholic and his wife was a bedridden invalid. The LTTE had obtained a key to the sprawling house from the caretaker. The three man LTTE team had set up a sophisticated sniper gun on a tripod in the bathroom overlooking Kadirgarmar's house. Kadirgarmar had 100 army commandos for security, in addition to the ministerial security division personnel from the police, but in an unforgivable security lapse, they had not checked the neighbouring houses. They probably thought it was not necessary because of the ceasefire.

On one occasion, the LTTE sniper had seen Kadirgarmar pointing in the direction of this bathroom window, and saying something to his security personnel. Thinking he had been discovered, the would-be assassin had fled the Talaisingham residence and had gone all the way to Mannar. After a few days he realized that he had not been discovered and the assassin came back and took up position again. (It later transpired that Kadirgarmar had been pointing at a bird's cage.) The sniper gun was still on its tripod just as he had left it. It was twenty days after this incident that the sniper finally pulled the trigger on Kadirgarmar. At the moment he had been shot Mrs Sugandi Kadirgarmar had been sitting near the pool as Kadirgarmar took his customary swim. She had heard no noise at all and had thought her husband was having a heart attack when he collapsed. The LTTE had used a sophisticated silencer and subsonic ammunition for the operation.

The first breakthrough for the police in this case came with the discovery of the key used by the LTTE sniper in the caretaker's overalls.

But they were not able to uncover anything beyond that. Nearly four years later, in May 2009, as the war reached the final stages, the State Intelligence Service managed to arrest a key LTTE operative called 'Aiya' who was responsible for directing and facilitating operations in Colombo. It was through Aiya that the remaining parts of the story had been pieced together. It was he who had taken the LTTE sniper to and from the house next door. A Peugeot car that Aiya used was also recovered. After shooting Kadirgamar, Aiya and the assassin had gone to Wellawatte with the sniper gun in the boot of the car, had tea and had leisurely set off for Mannar.

Periamban, the senior LTTE cadre who had coordinated the whole operation on the orders of Pottu Amman, had given strict instructions to them to get rid of the sniper gun but they were taking it along in the car as a souvenir. While they were on their way to Mannar, Periamban began bellowing abuse at them over the phone and unable to face his wrath, they had broken the sophisticated optical sights on the gun and thrown it by the wayside on the road to Mannar. Aiya told the SIS where they had thrown the weapon and took them to the spot. By that time, the gun had been recovered by the local police without knowing that that it was the gun that had been used in the Kadirgamar assassination. The LTTE knew the weakness of the police. The moment they heard of Kadirgamar's assassination, the top brass had all been at the scene of the crime. Had they cordoned off the area and searched all vehicles moving out, they would have caught the assassins on the same day as they were in a car with the sniper gun.

Chapter 46

The 2002 US Defence Dept. Report

During the ceasefire in 2002, a comprehensive assessment of both the Sri Lankan armed forces and the LTTE was carried out by the US Defence Department at the invitation of the Ranil Wickremesinghe government. In later years, this report would inspire many of those who played a key role in the defeat of the LTTE. A team of specialists from the US Pacific Command were deployed in Sri Lanka to carry out this assessment. On 26 November 2002, Peter Rodman, Assistant Secretary of Defence/ International Security Affairs of the US Defence Department signed a voluminous report containing the findings of the Pacific Command team which was then sent to the government of Sri Lanka. What follows are verbatim extracts from this report.

During almost 20 years of conflict, the AFSL (Armed Forces of Sri Lanka) has been unable to defeat the LTTE despite greatly outnumbering them. The political and military shortfalls that contributed to this situation will take time and investment to correct. However, the assessment team believes that the situation in Sri Lanka is one of the most promising in South Asia.

The Sri Lankan military is populated with many bright and articulate officers who are proud of their services and their contribution to society. All whom the team met were eager to expand their knowledge of professional military education and wanted to take the best practices from all sources in order to develop a workable system for Sri Lanka.

The military has not received sufficient political guidance on what it should do. That is, there are no overtly stated national objectives or strategy. The military leaders have interpreted and extrapolated to develop their own perception of a national strategy, but in so doing, have run the risk of guessing wrong. Guidance from civilian leaders is absolutely necessary to the accomplishment of national strategic objectives.

Due to a lack of a national security strategy, the country has not focused all of its instruments of national power against the threat posed by the LTTE. During the military's rapid expansion, the AFSL did not develop the long range planning and integrated systems needed to effectively prepare and employ forces and to support the larger structure. This is explained in part by the country's limited resources and engagement in deadly battle. However it is also due to the influence of partisan politics and a lack of initiative at higher levels.

The high morale and fighting spirit of the AFSL service members despite years of hardship is evident throughout the force. Small unit proficiency and confidence in their fellow service members is impressive. Officers at all levels were able to identify and propose solutions for current shortcomings. However it appears that much of the possible internal reform is squelched in a system where promotions are based almost entirely on longevity. One of the top recommendations of the assessment team and many Sri Lankan officers were to establish a merit based promotion system and service limits for senior personnel.

North and south of the LTTE controlled area in Jaffna, the army has deployed across the width of the island in single-line trench and bunker positions. Due to manpower shortages units are spread very thinly and do not possess reserves to counter enemy attacks. In the eastern districts the lines of control are not clearly delineated and the army is deployed in a line of isolated, company sized bases. Since these units cannot support each other due to the distance and a severe lack of trucks Army-wide, their only real value is presence. However, the LTTE can easily breach or destroy AFSL positions designed in this manner.

Up to 50% of soldiers in some units are lacking such basic items as uniforms, helmets, protective vests, and sleeping mats. Taking care of these soldiers is not only important for morale; it sends an important message to the LTTE that this is a well-equipped, well trained force that they should avoid. It also sends a message to the Sri Lanka public during a difficult recruiting period, that their sons and daughters will be well cared for if they decide to serve their country in the military.

The SLA has impressive soldiers and a decisive advantage in manpower, equipment and facilities, yet has failed to defeat the LTTE because *of failures in leadership, long range planning and failure to adopt combined arms operations.*

The strength of the Army is undoubtedly their impressive soldiers who endure tremendous hardship while maintaining a fighting spirit that has prevented more drastic defeats. They have an impressive training programme using Special Forces and Commandos to improve their individual and small unit training.

The army is also suffering from a lack of long term or strategic planning and programming. Its organizational structure and troop strength have been developed in reaction to enemy actions and not from a deliberate, analyzed effort to defeat the enemy. Its equipment is procured solely on the basis of what is available cheaply. The results of this short sighted process are an inefficient Army structure that wastes manpower and an eclectic mix of equipment that is over burdening the spare parts logistics and maintenance systems.

The Sri Lanka Army is actually conducting three types of counter-insurgency warfare. In the Jaffna peninsula and the northern area called the Vanni, full manoeuvre warfare is conducted in an area where the majority of the population supports the LTTE. The eastern sector where the population is split between LTTE and government support, classic counter guerrilla operations are being conducted. The remainder of the country, including Colombo, operations are primarily counter terrorism oriented.

* * * * *

While much smaller than the army, the Sri Lanka Navy (SLN) plays a key role in the country's defence. Our assessment team and senior officers from each Sri Lankan service component agree that the LTTE's centre of gravity is its resupply of arms by sea. Stopping this flow must be among the highest priorities. While the SLN has pushed the arms transfer points from coastal waters to mid-ocean channels, the AFSL must possess long range surveillance aircraft and maritime interdiction vessels capable of stopping the transfers. SLN vessels need a deck gun with greater standoff range and accuracy than the LTTE suicide boats. The SLN fast attack craft (FAC) units must change their tactics to reduce their target signature. Finally, the government of Sri Lanka and the AFSL must develop rules of engagement that support the actions of local commanders who board suspicious ships to confiscate smuggled arms and ammunition.

The fundamentals of the Sri Lanka Navy are sound with a level of pride and professionalism evident from the deck plate sailor through the area commanders.

In the event of a resumption of hostilities, the Jaffna peninsula would quickly become an untenable position for the Sri Lanka Army without an extensive sea-supply effort and capability from the SL Navy. The SLN does not have the lift resources to conduct a complete resupply effort for 3 Divisions of troops in Jaffna or sufficient control of the sea space to ensure contract resupply ships would safely reach the peninsula.

The LTTE vessels are not designed for multiple or prolonged use. As such they are smaller and more manoeuvrable and tend to have a main gun that is larger than the boat could support in the long run creating a localized parity with the SLN. Recommendation: Retrofit the DVORA class with 30mm guns to replace the 23mm currently employed to create an 800 meter range advantage over the LTTE.

* * * * *

The Sri Lankan Air Force (SLAF) has an adequate military structure, but faces some critical operational shortfalls. Its four intelligence, surveillance and reconnaissance (ISR) aircraft are inadequate for the country's requirements. While its transport aircraft pilots are very experienced, the service has essentially withdrawn from combat actions due to the perceived air defence threat. To execute the joint fight, the SLAF must develop the ability to fly at night, suppress enemy air defences, and accurately hit point targets. The Air Force needs to invest in spare parts, night vision goggles, upgraded avionics, and guided weapons, rather than adding new, expensive aircraft to its inventory. Finally, it must expand its pilot training programmes.

No new aircraft other than (ISR) should be acquired until all current, operationally required aircraft are serviceable. The aircraft fleet should be streamlined to as few types as necessary and spare parts and upgraded weapons should be obtained. After ISR platforms, the priority aircraft for acquisition should be more Mi-24s.

Night combat capability is vital for the SLAF to counter the current threat. Night vision goggles (NVGs) and associated training should be a priority for the SLAF. Helicopter crews must receive NVGs first, followed by transport crews and then fighter pilots.

The SLAF requires a comprehensive plan to defeat its enemy. A four phased operational air campaign is recommended. First ISR assets must identify and define the enemy. Second an air interdiction campaign should be conducted with appropriately equipped aircraft attacking targets based on acquired intelligence. Third, after degrading the enemy with air interdiction, an air mobile/airborne assault in the heart of enemy-held

281

territory should be executed. The attack should be supported with CAS and sustained with aerial resupply. Fourth, the SLAF should prepare to conduct a joint, on-going operation against the small enemy elements that survive the main attack.

The SLAF has poorly managed its limited resources. A case in point is the heavy airlift squadron, where neither of the two C-130s is flyable and only two of seven AN-32s are...In every unit, the primary reason for unserviceable aircraft is a lack of spare parts. Furthermore, SLAF purchases of additional types of aircraft have diverted logistical support from the existing fleet. For example, buying two MiG-27s drained resources that could have been used to maintain, arm and upgrade the Kfirs.

The Man Portable Air Defence Surface to Air Missile (MANPADS) threat to the SLAF is formidable, making daylight flying extremely hazardous. In order to successfully conduct an air campaign, the SLAF must fly combat missions at night.

SLAF and army personnel relayed many incidents of aircraft being unable to destroy targets in combat. Video was observed of a Kfir attack on a bridge in which targeting was extremely poor. Currently, SLAF Kfirs and MiG-27s carry only high explosive unguided or 'dumb' iron bombs. Mi-24s are armed with machine guns and rockets. Many of the targets engaged by aircraft are un-armoured area targets such as artillery pieces or personnel. Recommendations: Cluster Bomb Units should be purchased for un-armoured area targets. Guided weapons should be purchased first for the Mi-24s then for the Kfirs.

One of the most significant concerns for the assessment team was the lack of useful, timely, exploitable intelligence. While the AFSL have a good understanding of the capabilities and operating methods of the LTTE, some senior officers stated that they had never had warning of an impending enemy attack.

A national level intelligence agency does not exist, degrading joint coordination, nested focus and functionality among sister service intelligence directorates. Additionally, sister service intelligence agencies and elements are not linked into a common information sharing system.

In an environment of constrained resources, Sri Lanka must develop a truly joint operations headquarters (JOH), where there have been half-hearted efforts and political squabbles thus far.

The AFSL currently uses conventional defensive operational concepts and tactics that leave their forces vulnerable to LTTE attack and are not designed to defeat a counter-insurgency threat. Political pressure to hold terrain is part of the reason. The AFSL also tends to throw manpower at the problem rather than using more effective tactics and equipment. With *many frontline infantry units near 60% of authorized strength, the Navy and Air force supply large numbers of ground troops and Special Forces/ Commando units have often been used as regular infantry. The AFSL needs to develop improved defensive plans to reduce its vulnerability and manpower requirements and improve its effectiveness. It must prepare plans for offensive operations to ensure it is ready if the peace does not hold.*

Before conducting any offensive operations, the Sri Lanka Air Force must have a clear and comprehensive understanding of the LTTE's disposition and activities. This understanding can only be gained through an extensive and on-going ISR effort. ISR activities should begin in earnest now, focusing on the LTTE leadership and supply routes.

As the SLAF increases its knowledge of the LTTE, it should begin attacking the enemy's logistics. As Sri Lanka is an island almost all supplies are imported by sea. Working closely with the Navy, the SLAF should initially focus its interdiction efforts on ships and boats resupplying the LTTE.

After degrading the enemy through interdiction, the Sri Lankan military should attack the heart of LTTE territory with the enemy's leadership as its primary target.

The Armed Forces of Sri Lanka has established very strict rules of engagement and demonstrated great restraint in the face of small-scale incidents and provocations. However we cannot assume that peace is inevitable.

Chapter 47

US Defence Dept. on the LTTE

The US Defence Department report of 2002, also made an assessment of the LTTE, and what follows are their observations on the terrorist organization the Sri Lankan armed forces were fighting. These too are verbatim extracts.

The LTTE has an approximate strength of 16,000 individuals consisting of 'hard core' cadre (e.g., terrorists, extortionists and child forced recruitment) and dedicated support personnel. It is capable of conducting conventional manoeuvre warfare, guerrilla warfare and terrorist operations on land and sea. Relying on sea lanes of communication for external supply, the LTTE has a diverse array of small arms, indirect fire assets, suicide maritime craft, and various ground and sea transport vessels. Communications capabilities range from VHF and UHF to commercial satellite and cellular phones.

Since signing the MOU (CFA) with the government of Sri Lanka, the LTTE has increased political presence within AFSL controlled territory and actively repositioned, re-equipped and retrained combat forces. As a result of these activities, the LTTE has improved its ability to affect civilian popular opinion, interdict AFSL lines of communication and seize control of additional territory.

The LTTE is taking advantage of the ceasefire to strengthen its position politically and militarily through strong recruiting, public relations efforts, establishment of political cells in government controlled areas, training programmes and weapons resupply. Due to a variety of challenges, particularly economic shortfalls and operational inefficiencies, the AFSL have made only limited improvements. This situation threatens to place the government of Sri Lanka in a precarious position at the negotiating table or on the battlefield if hostilities resume.

Due to the lack of a national security strategy, and thus a national military strategy, the country has not effectively focused all of its instruments of national power against the threat posed by the LTTE.

The Liberation Tigers of Tamil Eelam (LTTE) or the Tamil Tigers as they are commonly known, is considered one of the most ruthless terrorist organizations in the world.

Previously, the LTTE was viewed by most Tamil civilians as the legitimate defender of the Tamil cause. Much of its funding came from Tamil expatriates as well as the Indian government. However in recent years, the LTTE has lost much support from Tamil civilians and resorted to tactics that instil fear in order to control the Tamil community.

Tamil civilians are also weary of Sri Lanka's ethnic conflict. Thousands of Tamils have suffered at the hands of both the Sri Lankan armed forces and the LTTE. Tamil parents have had their children forcibly abducted by LTTE recruiters to be indoctrinated and trained by Tamil militants. In addition, hundreds of thousands of Tamil civilians have been displaced from their dwellings to makeshift refugee camps by the fighting between the armed forces and the LTTE.

Until the 1990s, most Tamil civilians genuinely lent their support to the LTTE which was seen as the legitimate champion of the plight of Tamils who were discriminated against in a Sinhala dominated society. However the tide began to turn when the LTTE was perceived as protecting its own interests rather than those of the Tamil people. As support by Tamil civilians slowly waned, the LTTE resorted to fear tactics to control the Tamil population, further alienating its support base.

Though a significant number of Tamils continue to support the LTTE, a larger number find themselves alienated from both the LTTE and the Sri Lankan government.

The leader and founder of the LTTE, Velupillai Prabhakaran is often described as a megalomaniac. He is practically worshipped by Tiger cadres, who have been inculcated with Tamil nationalist propaganda. Prabhakaran has insisted that all LTTE soldiers wear a cyanide capsule around their necks maintaining that it is better to commit suicide than be captured alive by the enemy. Though Prabhakaran is aware that the United States publicly condemns the LTTE's terrorist campaigns, he continues his efforts to win sympathy from the United States. For this reason the United States has some leverage with him. However if the perception of the United States as a direct supporter of Sri Lanka's armed forces against the LTTE persists, Prabhakaran's susceptibility to US influence will decrease or vanish completely.

In Tamil dominated areas in the North and East, the government continues to lose popular support. Government officials/agencies have been run out of these areas by the LTTE, leaving local populations with no government representation. As a result locals are beginning to feel abandoned by the government. The major issue with the non-combatant population is the total destruction of civil infrastructure resulting from the war. Whichever side can demonstrate the ability to provide for the public in this respect will win the 'hearts and minds' battle.

Prabhakaran reportedly was very tense and nervous about operations and could not accept defeat. He developed a reputation for losing control if things did not go his way. Even when engaged in friendly physical contests, if Prabhakaran felt that he was losing, he would resort to viciously biting his opponents.

Prabhakaran's local propaganda and recruitment efforts are directed at children and adolescents.

Tamil youths in particular, are attracted to Prabhakaran's image as a folk hero. A supernatural image has been created of Prabhakaran and tales abound of the numerous instances where he narrowly escaped death. These escapades and the fact that he has never seen the inside of a jail cell continue to impress youths who stand in awe of Prabhakaran's achievements in the Tamil struggle for independence.

Relentless indoctrination is a powerful tool utilized by Prabhakaran to ensure that a cadre is not forced into battle, but willingly chooses to enter the fray and very likely lay down his or her life for the sake of Tamil Eelam. Prabhakaran rarely visits training bases, but studies videos to improve the curricula. Prabhakaran thoroughly examines military successes and defeats so that he may repeat the successes and develop new mechanisms for overcoming failures.

Prabhakaran does not favour democratic processes. Though there is a central committee of the LTTE on paper, Prabhakaran's word is decisive. Prabhakaran continues to neutralize all competing Tamil groups and individuals both moderates and militants who pose any challenge to his leadership and to the LTTE as the sole representatives of the Tamils.

Since Prabhakaran feels that the main threat to his survival comes from within the LTTE, he is obsessed with his personal security. He is known to sleep with a revolver under his pillow. In addition, the only member of the LTTE allowed to carry a firearm in Prabhakaran's presence is Soranam, the trusted commander of his bodyguard contingent. When Prabhakaran plans to visit a place, he ensures that extensive preparations are taken for his protection. Over a hundred bodyguard cadres (who do not interact with other cadres) are assigned to protect him. It is reported that there are three rings of 40 bodyguards each surrounding Prabhakaran upon his arrival at a particular destination.

Prabhakaran has gradually created a culture where dissent is absent. His close associates are Tamil Chelvam, head of the political branch; Pottu Amman, head of intelligence; Karuna head of Batticaloa-Amparai commands; Balraj, military commander; Soranam, bodyguard commander; Shankar head of Air Tigers, Soosai head of Sea Tigers; Jeyam special group commander; and Kumaran Padmanathan head of procurement. They all merely hold executive posts and carry out Prabhakaran's dictates.

Prabhakaran is an innovator, improviser and a technophile. His macabre creativity is reflected in the human bombs, suicide boats, projectiles and mines the LTTE has been producing over the years. Irrespective of the cost, he orders the best equipment for himself and his men. LTTE cadres have used night vision goggles and rocket propelled grenades (RPGs) to engage Sri Lankan troops. If the desired equipment cannot be procured, Prabhakaran will order improvisation using existing equipment for the designated purpose. He also uses satellite communications with LTTE ships and LTTE cells around the world.

Prabhakaran uses deception as an integral part of his modus operandi. In many cases he has arranged to visit subordinates or extended olive branches to political targets to lull them into a sense of false security just prior to their assassination. In tactical operations, Prabhakaran would conduct deception manoeuvres to draw attention away from an intended target. LTTE duplicity often factors into the organisation's public posture. Deceptive guidelines are given to LTTE cadres on how best to answer questions posed by the public and the media. Carefully worded guidelines are even provided to the Tamil diaspora over the internet on how best to respond to questions on the conflict posed by non-Sri Lankans. These guidelines are designed to portray LTTE cadres as freedom fighters pitted against a hostile and ruthless government.

. Prabhakaran's mindset has been proactive and rarely reactive. Prabhakaran realizes the advantage of seizing the initiative in battle, always exploiting the element of surprise.

Some analysts believe that his actions are also driven by a desire for revenge. The ordered assassination of former Indian prime minister Rajiv Gandhi is a case in point. Most analysts believe that Prabhakaran perceived a future threat emanating from Gandhi (the redeployment of Indian troops to Sri Lanka to disarm the Tigers) and therefore had him assassinated as a pre-emptive measure. However Prabhakaran also felt a deep sense of betrayal from Gandhi for reversing India's policy towards the LTTE which points to revenge as a motive. Another example of revenge as a possible motive is the January 1998 bombing of a revered Buddhist shrine in Kandy. This LTTE action was rumoured to be Prabhakaran's retribution for the Sri Lanka army's mass destruction of LTTE gravesites.

Prabhakaran's long term goal is to break the will of the Sinhalese led government and thus lead it to accede to his demand for a Tamil homeland. To achieve this end, any and all means are justified in his mind. Prabhakaran is likely to continue assassinating political and military leaders as well as bombing key targets in the economic infrastructure. He views the high political and economic costs his actions impose on the government as doors that lead to negotiations. Prabhakaran uses negotiations as a ploy for the LTTE to rearm and regroup, especially after a series of battlefield defeats.

Chapter 48

Gōta Returns to Sri Lanka

By 2005, Gōta was doing well in the USA. He was employed as a Unix systems administrator at the Loyola Mount Mary Law School in California. When his brother Mahinda became the presidential candidate of the UPFA in 2005, Gōta obtained three months leave to help his brother with the election campaign. He coordinated Mahinda's security arrangements and also campaigned for him in the Kurunegala district. At the height of the election campaign, there was a function in Hambantota to hand over some houses constructed by the Kelaniya Raja Maha Viharaya to tsunami victims. Mahinda in his capacity as the incumbent prime minister was to declare open the housing scheme.

Gōta accompanied his brother to the meeting and as they were being taken in a procession to the venue, he saw his old army colleague Sarath Fonseka standing under a tree watching the procession along with another mutual friend Padmasiri Hapangama. Instead of sitting on the stage, Gōta went over and spoke to his old friends. Hapangama had been at Ananda College with Gōta and he was now a member of the Kelaniya temple board of trustees. Fonseka was then the chief of staff of the army and due to retire from the army in December that year. After he left the army and went to the USA, Gōta had met Fonseka once when the latter came to Los Angeles on a tour organized by the Royal College of Defence Studies UK. The two were meeting now after several years. Fonseka told Gōta during their conversation that he is due to retire that year, but that he would like to be army commander obviously on the calculation that if Mahinda wins the

289

elections, Gōta would be in a position to influence his brother's decisions.

At that time Gōta's intention was to help his brother in the election campaign and go back to his job in the USA. The morning after election day, all the results were in except for the results of the Amparai district. There was much tension at the prime minister's official residence Temple Trees, from where the election campaign was run as this was the closest fought presidential election ever. In the morning, Mahinda Rajapaksa came down to the operations room and he called the coordinator of his campaign in the Amparai district and was told that the result had been finalized. This was the confirmation that Mahinda Rajapaksa had won the presidential election. As the victorious president-elect came out of the operations room, he saw Gōta standing in the corridor chatting with some lawyers. He told them that the election result was finalized and that he had won. And the next thing he told Gōta was *"You must take over as secretary defence."*

That was the first thing that Mahinda Rajapaksa did as the new president-elect. Gōta had by that time been living in the USA for over a decade and he had a house that he had bought on a mortgage. His son had graduated and just started working. Relocating to Sri Lanka was thus a major operation. His wife rented out an apartment for their son and they sold the house and moved to Sri Lanka. By the end of 2005, there was in fact a separate state in everything but name. In 2005, during the presidential election campaign, when Mahinda's wife, Shiranthi Rajapaksa had gone to Vavuniya for a ceremony, they had not been allowed to hoist the national flag by the LTTE who said that if the national flag was being hoisted, the LTTE flag also had to be hoisted. In fact, Mahinda Rajapaksa himself had not been able to attend his final rally at Campbell Park due to concerns over an assassination plot by the LTTE.

At the time Gōta took over as defence secretary, the air force was commanded by Donald Perera, the navy by Wasantha Karannagoda and the army by Shantha Kottegoda. Gōta knew all of them very well. After he became defence secretary, Fonseka had been calling Gōta wanting to be appointed army commander. Shantha Kottegoda still had eighteen months to serve. But Fonseka had more like eighteen days to retirement. President Mahinda Rajapaksa had no particular reason to cut short Kottegoda's tenure and appoint Fonseka. So his only chance was to use his old friendship with Gōta to get the job. At that time, there was no war anywhere in sight and

290

simply to give an old friend the chance to command the army before he retired, Gōta told the president that Fonseka should be given an opportunity to command the army.

Gōta says that if his old friendship with Fonseka had not been revived in Hambantota, he may never have decided to give the position to Fonseka. When it became known that Fonseka was going to be made commander, Shantha Kottegoda asked Gōta why he was being removed from the position of army commander and said that whatever task the government wanted the army to do, he was equally capable of fulfilling it. But by that time however, Gōta had decided to give that opportunity to Sarath Fonseka. The president called Kottegoda to his office and told him that he wants to appoint Fonseka as the army commander but that he would appoint Kottegoda as the Ambassador to Bazil. The president had explained to the crestfallen Kottegoda that he wants to give Fonseka an opportunity to command the army otherwise he would have to retire as chief of staff.

A lot of people had opposed the appointment of Sarath Fonseka. Foremost among those opposing the appointment were ex-army officers who were close to Gōta as well as the president. The main point they put forward was that he was very untrustworthy. It was not his military ability that people questioned but the other aspects of his character. Even after he was appointed commander, Fonseka could have been retired at some stage, and the command could have been given to Mallawarachchi who was the chief of staff. But at that stage Gōta had not taken that decision because Fonseka had been injured in an attempt on his life even before the war had begun.

After the war commenced, Gōta's view was that there was no need to make any changes in midstream. Things were going the way he wanted so there was no major reason for change. Sarath Fonseka was a very thorough officer. When he was security forces commander Jaffna, he would visit even isolated detachments and walk the length and breadth of the camp inspecting the company bases, the platoon bases and at times even inspect bunkers and check whether they were positioned properly to meet the threat from terrorists. He would even check whether the visibility from the bunker was adequate. Then he would want to know how guard duties were allocated, how the troops ate, went on leave and all other details. Gōta conceded to a question posed by this writer, that of the three choices he had for the position of army commander at the end of 2005 - Shantha Kottegoda, Sarath Fonseka and Nanda Mallawarachchi, the most ruthless was Fonseka.

After they assumed office, president Mahinda Rajapaksa and Gōta literally walked into a minefield. The LTTE did not give the new government any respite – not even the brief respite they had given president R.Premadasa in 1989/90 and president Chandrika Kumaratunga in 1994/95. Mahinda Rajapaksa assumed duties as president on 19 November 2005. There had been killings, abductions and various other ceasefire violations perpetrated by the LTTE from the time the ceasefire agreement had been signed. But just days after Mahinda was elected to power, the LTTE attacks increased in intensity.

The very day after the presidential election, a naval rating was abducted in Jaffna. On 24 November, a grenade attack on an army truck in Puloly Jaffna killed one soldier and injured four. On the same day, there was a grenade attack on an army checkpoint in Trincomalee injuring two soldiers and six civilians.

With these sporadic acts of violence in the background, Prabhakaran delivered his heroes day message on 26 November 2005. He said that the LTTE will wait until next year to see how the new president handles things. He described Mahinda as a "realist" committed to "pragmatic politics" while saying in the same breath that president Mahinda Rajapaksa has not grasped the fundamentals, the basic concepts underlying the Tamil national question. He also stated ominously that *"As far as the Tamil people are concerned, the concepts of peace, ceasefire and negotiations have now become meaningless"*.

Even though the LTTE supremo said they would wait till 'next year' to see how the new president fares, they would not be waiting inactively. The LTTE was to soon begin 'educating' the new president on the 'fundamentals of the issue at hand' so that Mahinda Rajapaksa would be able to look at the situation 'pragmatically and realistically'. Their intention obviously was to soften up the new president so that he would be inclined to look favourably upon their demands. Starting in December the LTTE was to ratchet up hostilities to a level never before seen during the ceasefire. On 2 December 2005, the LTTE killed the Muslim divisional secretary of Kaththankudy in the east. There was a *hartal* in the east as Muslims protested.

On 4 December a soldier was shot and killed at the army checkpoint in Neerveli. On the same day, a claymore mine blast in Kondavil killed seven soldiers who had been travelling in a tractor. This was the most serious attack on the armed forces since the ceasefire came into effect in February 2002. This was followed up with another claymore mine blast on 6 December in Nallur in Jaffna which killed another seven soldiers. In tandem with these attacks, school students were made to stage protests outside army camps in Jaffna. UN Special Rapporteur Phillip Alston was in Sri Lanka between 28 November and 6 December 2005, and he captured the mood of the times in the report he filed about this visit.

In Alston's own words, he was in Sri Lanka at a time when the ceasefire agreement was under 'unprecedented stress'. He further observed that the last days of his visit saw the deadliest attacks on government forces since the ceasefire came into effect in 2002 and that even deadlier attacks had taken place after he left Sri Lanka. Between the time of his visit to Sri Lanka and the writing of his report which was finalized on 27 March 2006, he estimated that 78 Sri Lankan armed forces personnel had been killed by the LTTE. That the LTTE was clearly preparing for war, was quite obvious. When Alston met the head of the LTTE's political wing Tamilselvam, he had stressed the need for the LTTE to unequivocally condemn and reject acts of violence, the latter's argument was that the LTTE was a movement of the Tamil people and that they could not condemn the actions of pro-LTTE civilians.

Alston observed that civilians living in government controlled areas had been ordered by the LTTE to report for 'civil defence training' in the areas controlled by them, and he did not rule out the possibility of recently trained civilians having had a hand in these attacks. He characterized this tendency to use civilian surrogates as a dangerous escalation of the conflict. By this time, even the Norwegian headed Sri Lanka Monitoring Mission was commending the Sri Lankan armed forces for restraint in the face of provocation.

Chapter 49

Squaring With India

With the situation in Sri Lanka clearly careering out of control, the deputy spokesman of the US Department of State Adam Ereli expressed concern about the persistent violations of the ceasefire and specifically condemned the LTTE attack in Jaffna which killed seven soldiers. But the LTTE carried on regardless. Grenade attacks in Vavuniya and Talaimannar in the second week of December killed one and injured 21 policemen. In the third week of December the abduction of a senior PLOTE member S.Ganeshalingam led to a massive protest in Vavuniya town. Three policemen attached to the Child Protection Authority were detained by the LTTE when they entered LTTE held areas in search of a British paedophile.

The actions of the LTTE became increasingly provocative. On 22 December, several LTTE boats had surrounded two naval fibre glass dinghies off Mannar and three naval ratings had been abducted. A grenade attack was also carried out in Nallur injuring four policemen and two civilians. On 23 December there was a claymore attack on a naval bus in Mannar killing 15 naval ratings. Thus as the eventful month of December went into its fourth week, the LTTE appeared to be surpassing themselves with each attack marking a new high in the escalation of hostilities.

On 25 December 2005, Joseph Pararajasingham parliamentarian of the pro-LTTE Tamil National Alliance was gunned down at St Mary's cathedral in Batticaloa as he attended Christmas midnight mass. The very next day, the LTTE killed Tirupan Master a senior cadre of PLOTE. On 27 December, 11 soldiers were killed in a claymore mine explosion in Jaffna. On the same day, another claymore mine weighing six kilograms was discovered in Jaffna. It was in the middle of all this mayhem that president Mahinda Rajapaksa made his first visit as head of state to India, accompanied by Gōta. They went armed with a comprehensive briefing document for the Indians.

This document was titled *"Military assistance required from the government of India."* The newly elected Sri Lankan president, barely six weeks in office was squaring very frankly with the Indians and telling them that the LTTE was preparing for all out war and that the government of Sri Lanka had to be prepared for any eventuality. The document the Rajapaksas submitted to the Indian government, provides a glimpse of the government's assessment of the strength of the LTTE at that point in time. They had estimated that the LTTE had 12,000 fighting cadres with about 250 new cadres being recruited monthly. Added to this was the training the LTTE had given civilians to be used as a 'force multiplier'.

The LTTE was thought to possess well over 700 heavy weapons of various description including fifteen 107mm multi-barrel rocket launchers, twenty 122mm Howitzers, and four 152mm artillery guns. The LTTE was also believed to possess 10 Stinger surface to air missiles, a dozen SA-14 missiles and at least 40 Ack Ack guns. The strength of the Sea Tigers was estimated at 1,250 cadres with about 8 cargo ships, 30 fast attack craft, 20 transport boats, an unknown number of fibre glass boats and suicide boats and at least 50 radars. Even though no LTTE air raids had taken place at that time, the report stated that a runway had already been established in Iranamadu and that a number of LTTE cadres had obtained training in private flying schools in Europe and returned to the Vanni. The LTTE was also thought to possess 2 micro light aircraft, 2 light aircraft and even two R44-ASTRO helicopters.

In the event of an outbreak of hostilities, the Indians were informed that attacks were expected in the Jaffna peninsula and on the Trincomalee harbour. In Jaffna the government anticipated a heavy attack on the Muhamalai forward defence lines with a simultaneous amphibious attack across the Jaffna lagoon from Pooneryn. They also expected a seaborne attack on Palaly and also the possibility of an LTTE aircraft flying into Palaly on a suicide mission. In Trincomalee, they expected an attack on the harbour from the LTTE stronghold of Sampur just south of the strategically important harbour. In the light of all this, the Sri Lankan government held that they had to be prepared and military assistance was sought from the Indian government to meet such an eventuality.

The Sri Lankan government's wish list was long and comprehensive. They wanted ten MIG-27 jets, four Antonov -32 transport aircraft, five Mi-24 attack helicopters, twelve Mi-17 transport helicopters, three unmanned aerial vehicles (UAVs) for reconnaissance purposes, 10 laser target designators, 24 battle field surveillance radars. On the naval front, the Sri Lankan government asked for two Indian offshore patrol craft. In addition to that they requested the sharing of actionable intelligence on terrorist logistic vessels, and coordinated surveillance patrols in the Palk Straits, as well as similar patrols off the eastern coast of Sri Lanka, about 150-200 nautical miles out in the deep seas. There was also a request for 6 Indian field guns with ammunition, protective gear for troops such as 13,000 sets of body armour, 19,500 flak jackets, and 30,000 helmets.

During this trip to India, president Rajapaksa had a one-to-one discussion with prime minister Manmohan Singh first and then they called Gōta in to deliver the defence briefing at which M.K.Narayanan the Indian national defence advisor was also present. Following this visit and the appeal for aid, the Indians would provide a radar system and ack ack guns as well as two Mi-17 helicopters for the air force and two off shore petrol vessels for the navy. The two helicopters were returned to India after the war was over as was one of the OPVs. Even as the president was on his three day visit to India, the LTTE continued to wreak havoc in Sri Lanka. On 29 December, 12 LTTE cadres attacked the Kodikamam police station with hand grenades and small arms fire. The gun fight had continued for around 45 minutes after which the attacking party had withdrawn. On the same day, a similar attack had been launched on an army bunker in Inuvil Jaffna but this too had been repulsed successfully. Yet again on the same day, landmines were discovered in Vavuniya and in Madhu.

When Mahinda was elected to power, the ceasefire was still in place, at least on paper and the Sri Lanka Monitoring Mission was also functioning though its impartiality was much in doubt. Once in power, Mahinda decided to revive the stalled peace talks. Both Mahinda and Gōta had been convinced from the beginning that the LTTE was not sincere. Indeed the SLMM had announced that between February 2002 and December 2005, there had been 3,827 ceasefire violations by the LTTE as against 348 by the armed forces. Any person of average intelligence could see that this ceasefire was not meeting its objectives. Even in the run up to the 2005 November presidential elections, a Toronto datelined news item in *The Island* reported that the LTTE had stepped up collecting funds among Tamils living overseas for the final war. Tamil businessmen in Canada had to contribute 25,000 US$ and individuals 2000 US$. The World Tamil Movement had announced a target of 5 million US$ by the end of November 2005. The violence on the ground and the collection of funds overseas were sure signs that war was inevitable.

Despite these signs, Mahinda would not be the first to commence hostilities. He told the security council that he will be restarting the peace talks but that the military would not have anything to do with that process, and that they should be prepared for any eventuality. At the time Mahinda became president, the military was in a very somnolent state due to the lack of any government direction. He found that the security forces commanders and the LTTE leaders used to meet on a monthly basis to iron out problems. The president put a stop to these meetings and said that the LTTE should talk only to the politicians. The president was very clear that while he would give peace a chance, he would take military action where necessary. Previous governments had made the mistake of completely neglecting the military when going in for peace talks.

As one ceasefire violation was followed by another, each transgression being worse than the one preceding, Gōta met officials of the SLMM to complain that they were not doing their job and that they were only reporting and no action is being taken about these outrages. The issue that he had with the SLMM was identical to that raised Phillip Alston earlier. Neither Alston's biting comments nor Gōta's fulminations made the SLMM change their ways. Unsurprisingly, none of the many discussions Gōta had with the SLMM were pleasant or cordial.

On 24 March 2006, presidential secretary Lalith Weeratunga went to Arippu in Mannar on a secret mission to meet LTTE leaders in an attempt to iron out outstanding problems. He went to Arippu in a vehicle belonging to an NGO called Sevalanka. He would have claimed to be an employee of Sevalanka if he was stopped and questioned at checkpoints. After his vehicle entered LTTE territory, he was escorted to the rendezvous by gun-wielding LTTE motorcycle outriders. Weeratunga had a discussion over lunch with a senior LTTE functionary by the name of Poovannan and came back to Colombo. Nothing concrete came out of this discussion. The most important thing that Weeratunga had to report back to Colombo was that his vehicle was not checked at all during the entire journey to and from Mannar, which highlighted how lax the security arrangements were. What this clandestine visit showed was that if there was a way forward through negotiations, the president would have taken it.

Chapter 50

Tolerating the Intolerable

Sri Lanka began the year 2006 with war on the horizon. On 5 January 2006, a navy gunboat was sunk off the eastern coast after an LTTE suicide boat rammed it, killing 15 crewmen on board. The suicide boat had been lurking among a flotilla of fishing boats. This was the biggest loss to the military both in terms of men and equipment since the ceasefire began in February 2002. Night fishing off the eastern coast was banned after this incident. During this period, army and police patrols kept discovering claymore mines set up to take military and police targets. On 10 January US Ambassador Jeffery Lunstead warned the LTTE that a return to war would cost them dearly and that they should stop the violence and go back to talks. The LTTE took no notice of the warning.

On 12 January, a claymore mine attack on a navy bus killed 10 navy personnel and injured seven more on the Cheddikulam-Medawachchiya road. A few days later, another navy bus was ambushed in Trincomalee. A bicycle bomb meant for the bus had exploded but the bus had managed to escape the full impact of the blast. However the LTTE hit team had opened fire and injured 12. During this period, there were frequent grenade attacks and claymore mine blasts that killed several and injured dozens of police, army and navy personnel. Despite all this, the president called a press conference on 21 January and declared that he would not be provoked to war. The intensity of the LTTE's provocations during this period can be gauged from the fact that in just one day, 8 claymore mines were found by the Ampara police alone. The US Undersecretary of

State for Political Affairs Nicolas Burns who was on a visit to Sri Lanka said that the LTTE should stop the violence and get back to talks.

One of the methods adopted by the navy and army to protect their troop convoys from LTTE mines was to use an electronic jamming device developed by the Centre for Research and Development set up by Gōta in the defence ministry. This device caused the remote control devices used to detonate the claymore mines to malfunction. These jamming devices were effective up to a range of anything between 150 to 300 meters, and a convoy would have several such devices so as to provide protection to all the vehicles. This piece of equipment was carried in a back pack by the operator. In addition to this, the buses were protected with steel plates between which was a layer of sand, to minimize the impact of the blast. There were also bags of sand placed inside the bus for the same purpose. Only 20 security forces personnel were allowed on a bus and the seating arrangements were also such as to minimize casualties in the event of a blast.

With international pressure mounting on them, the LTTE spokesman Daya Master declared that these claymore mine attacks were not carried out by them but by civilians who had received arms training from the LTTE. By the fourth week of January, Erick Solheim managed to get the LTTE to agree to a round of peace talks with the Rajapaksa government and Geneva was fixed as the venue. The LTTE also released one of the three Child Protection Authority policemen they had been holding hostage, as a goodwill measure. Yet, even as the government negotiating team left for Geneva on 19 February, three claymore mines weighing 7 kg each, were found in Thalpadu, Mannar

The government prepared for the peace talks very professionally. Mahinda Rajapaksa was going to make good on his pledge to the Indians that he was going to try his level best to come to a negotiated settlement with the LTTE. Central Bank governor Ajith Cabraal, brought down a team of experts from Harvard University to train the government negotiating team in the art of negotiation. All officials and ministers who were to participate in the peace talks were made to attend a workshop conducted by these experts. The negotiators were given briefings on the shortcomings of the ceasefire agreement, experiences of past peace negotiations and so on.

Even foreign minister Mangala Samaraweera had to attend these workshops. Thus when the Sri Lankan government team went to the peace talks, they were very well prepared. Dossiers had been prepared on every possible topic that could come up at the negotiations so that the moment the relevant topic came up, the negotiators had plenty of reference material at hand. In Geneva, on the first day of the negotiations, things had gone generally well. Opening statements had been made by both sides, and they had talked. During the breaks, everybody went out to the far corners of the garden and made their calls because they thought the chateau in which the discussions were held may be bugged. The government had been keen to discuss core issues like the extent of devolution and a so on, but the LTTE was interested only in militarily important matters such as the dismantling of the high security zones.

A bit of comic relief was provided by police chief Chandra Fernando, who had said to his LTTE counterpart, Nadesan "I know your wife. She was a woman police constable, and she worked under me. You were a Sergeant no?". Nadesan had been highly embarrassed at this reminder of his lowly antecedents in the Sri Lanka police force. Everybody else however had had a good laugh at his expense. It was clear that the LTTE was not serious about the peace talks, and were only making a pretence just to keep the Western powers happy. On the second day after making the usual calls during the morning break, Anton Balasingham said he is not feeling well, and suggested the talks be postponed for the next day. That was the end of the talks. The dossiers on various topics that had been prepared, had hardly been used.

Just as they brought the first round of peace talks with the Rajapaksa government to an abrupt halt in Geneva, the LTTE began a war exercise in the jungles of Kanjikudichchiaru in the east. Mortars, RPGs and light machine guns were used in a mock attack on an army camp. In the meantime, Human Rights Watch reported that the LTTE was collecting funds in Western countries for the final war. Foreign minister Mangala Samaraweera expressed concern at these reports and took the matter up with the British Minister of State for the Home Department Tony McNulty.

On 8 April 2006, Canada banned the LTTE as a terrorist organization. The LTTE responded to the Canadian ban by stepping up their attacks. On 9 April a claymore mine in Mirusuvil, Jaffna killed seven including five soldiers. The SLMM rejected the LTTE's claim that a third force (other than the LTTE and the government) was behind these mine blasts. Two days later, another claymore attack in Thampalakamam killed 11 including 10 naval ratings. The following day, a bicycle bomb in the Trincomalee vegetable market killed one soldier and nine civilians. In a separate incident two policemen were killed in a landmine blast in Kuchchuveli also in the Trincomalee district. The government expressed dissatisfaction at the SLMM for failing to name the perpetrators.

The SLMM's insipid response to these outrages was: *"We are making inquiries into all three attacks (in Mirusuvil, Tamapalakamam and Trincomalee) but will refrain from making any further comments regarding the perpetrators and possible motives until further inquiries have been done."* This was a classic example of the malady that Phillip Alston identified in the SLMM - the fear of carrying out effective investigations into violations of the ceasefire for fear that it would 'upset' the LTTE and jeopardize the second round of peace talks that was now on the cards.

While the negotiators were reluctant to upset the LTTE, the latter were not worried about upsetting anybody. They did just as they pleased. On 16 April one soldier was killed and another injured in a claymore attack in the Tennamarachchi area of Jaffna. The STF caught two LTTE cadres in the very act of planting claymore mines. On 17 April, four soldiers were killed and 10 others injured in a claymore mine blast on the Mannar-Vavuniya road. In another incident on the Batticaloa district, three airmen were injured in a mine blast. In the middle of all this mayhem, the Australian foreign minister Alexander Downer praised the Sri Lankan government for not retaliating to the violence and continuing to call for a negotiated settlement.

With the second round of peace talks in Geneva scheduled for 24 April 2006 the LTTE refused to go for the peace talks unless their leaders were airlifted to meet Prabhakaran. They wanted a helicopter to take the area commanders to and from locations like Sampur and Thoppigala to Kilinochchi and back. H.M.G.S.Palihakkara, then the secretary to the foreign ministry brought up this issue of a helicopter for the LTTE in the security council. Gōta vehemently objected and the president also agreed with him. Some however thought that the request should be allowed and that it was not a major issue and that if they are demanding a chopper ride, the government should let them have it, to get them to come for the talks.

Gōta however held that the LTTE wanted a helicopter ride just to ridicule and demoralize the military and to show that they can demand anything and get it. So he stood his ground, arguing that the government did not provide helicopters even to their own divisional commanders to come to Colombo and if helicopters were provided to the LTTE's area commanders, that would send the wrong message to the armed forces. Gōta however agreed to provide helicopters for the LTTE delegation to come from Kilinochchi to the airport. Later, he was to issue a press statement about the incongruous situation where the LTTE was demanding a ride on a military helicopter while at the same time directing claymore mine attacks on them on a daily basis.

Indeed even as these issues were being discussed, soldiers in Maduruoya came under a claymore attack and small arms fire. In Trincomalee airmen exchanged small arms fire with the LTTE. In Vavuniya terrorists fired at soldiers injuring one. A hand grenade was thrown at the Batticaloa police station by a lone LTTE cadre injuring one sub-inspector and killing two constables. In another incident in the Batticaloa district, soldiers came under small arms and RPG fire but no one was injured. On 24 April, at a press conference at Temple Trees president Mahinda Rajapaksa declared, *"No other president would have acted the way I have in a situation like this."* Nothing could be truer. No head of state anywhere in the world would have tolerated anything even remotely resembling what he had to tolerate in the first few months of his presidency. Any one of the many of the incidents that had occurred since his election would have been enough to declare open war. But the worst was yet to come.

Chapter 51

Suicide Attack on Fonseka

On 25 April 2006, Gōta was seated in his office in the defence ministry building some time past noon, when he had heard a loud blast from inside army headquarters in the adjoining compound. This was the attempt to assassinate army commander Sarath Fonseka inside army headquarters. A Tamil woman who had obtained a pass to attend maternity clinics at the army hospital within the army headquarters had come in with the bomb belt concealed under her maternity clothing. What this incident showed was that despite the daily attacks that had been occurring since December 2005 on the armed forces, the army was still in a ceasefire frame of mind.

The State Intelligence Service head Keerthi Gajanayake had in fact been sounding warnings that an attack could take place inside army headquarters because security arrangements were so lax. To illustrate the point they were making, they had sent an SIS woman police constable whose husband worked in the army hospital inside army headquarters with two mangoes hidden on her person to demonstrate how lethargic the security personnel were. But the warnings fell on deaf ears. It was not just the army headquarters that was being targeted. The intelligence agencies had warned that the president, Gōta and the three service commanders were also being targeted by the LTTE.

The president had immediately given everybody instructions to obtain bullet proof vehicles. In the meantime, Gōta and the three service commanders had been given bullet proof vehicles from the president's pool while the new ones were on the way. However on the day of the blast, Fonseka was going from his office to his residence within army headquarters to lunch, a distance of about 200-300 meters. Hence he did not use his bullet proof vehicle but had gone in his soft skin official car. He had to pass the military hospital on the way to his chalet and it was here that the suicide bomber had struck. Gōta had rushed to the hospital to see Fonseka.

The doctors informed him that despite serious injuries, Fonseka's chances of survival were good. After receiving treatment for a while in Sri Lanka, Gōta sent him for further treatment to Singapore along with Mrs Fonseka and some security personnel. Everything was arranged at the other end by the Sri Lankan High Commissioner in Singapore. Gōta also saw to it that Fonseka's two daughters who were students in the USA were paid a stipend from the president's fund, which would continue till the end of 2009. Army chief of staff Nanda Mallawarachchi overlooked the duties of the army commander during Fonseka's convalescence. Following the attack on the army commander, the government for the first time, ordered retaliatory air attacks on LTTE targets in Sampur in Trincomalee.

The area where the government was most vulnerable was in Sampur with the LTTE controlling the southern part of the Trincomalee harbour mouth. These retaliatory attacks were aimed at dislodging the LTTE from their positions in Sampur without however provoking a return to all out war. On 27 April, foreign minister Mangala Samaraweera, reiterated the government's commitment to the ceasefire despite LTTE provocations. Ceasefire violations continued unabated, even though the second round of peace talks was now overdue. On 4 May 2006, the government once again turned down the demand for a helicopter to airlift LTTE area commanders to Kilinochchi for consultations with Prabhakaran. In Kebithigollewa, five sand miners were killed by the LTTE and schools in the area were closed. As the situation deteriorated, the government closed the A-9 road and road travel between Jaffna and the south came to a halt. A pitched battle took place in Sampur between the Karuna faction and the LTTE. On 9 May, the army found seven claymore mines weighing 10 kilos each and 45 kilograms of plastic explosives in various locations in the north and east.

On 11 May 2006, there occurred an incident which was to change the whole trajectory of naval engagements with the LTTE. A passenger ship, the *Pearl Cruiser* carrying 710 officers and soldiers was sailing from Jaffna to Trincomalee escorted by four Dvora fast attack craft when the LTTE tried to sink it. The modus operandi for suicide attacks at sea which the LTTE had perfected in the 1990s was to attack in clusters with several attack boats which would engage the enemy while two to three suicide boats would try to ram their prey. At times, anything up to five such clusters would attack a single naval vessel. The LTTE attack boats knew when the naval guns needed to be reloaded. It took at least one minute to reload the guns and it is in that interval that the suicide boat makes its dash.

To meet this threat, the navy began moving only in convoys of two or three fast attack craft or gunboats. Another method was to draw the LTTE boats out to sea when they attack. The LTTE boats were fast but could carry only a limited amount of fuel and did not go too far out to sea as they would not have enough fuel to get back. When the *Pearl Cruiser* was attacked, the Dvoras engaged the LTTE suicide boats while the passenger ship moved off into deep seas beyond the reach of the LTTE boats. The confrontation ended with the loss of one Dvora which went down with two officers and 15 naval ratings. This was by far the most serious incident that had taken place since the ceasefire agreement came into effect in 2002. Had the LTTE succeeded in their objective of sinking the *Pearl Cruiser* with its 710 armed forces personnel, the consequences would have been unimaginable.

It seemed that the audacity and arrogance of the LTTE knew no bounds. The day after the attempt to sink the *Pearl Cruiser*, the LTTE ordered the SLMM, which was supposed to be monitoring the ceasefire, not to board navy vessels, and the SLMM meekly obeyed. Following these outrages, the USA urged the European Union to list the LTTE as a terrorist organisation. As Donald Camp a senior official of the US State Department explained, the LTTE was 'very deserving of that label'. The EU had been debating a ban on the LTTE for some time and the events since December 2005 had helped bring about a consensus among the 27 countries of the EU on this matter. With the EU ban now virtually a certainty, Anton Balasingham tried to forestall it through blackmail and threats. He issued a statement saying among other things that: *"The more the international community alienates the LTTE, the more they will be compelled to tread a hard-line individualist path."*

In other words, the LTTE ideologue was warning the world that if the ban was motivated by the LTTE's conduct, implementing it would only motivate the LTTE to persist in the behaviour that caused the ban. The LTTE undoubtedly was a very difficult customer to deal with. Even the looming EU ban did not result in a scaling down of ceasefire violations by the LTTE. On 25 May, the LTTE blasted an army tractor killing three soldiers in Cheddikulam. A 10 kilo claymore mine was found in Nelliady Jaffna. In Colombo, there was a bomb scare at the World Trade Centre. A landmine blast in the Wilpattu national park killed 6 local tourists and a wild life department tracker.

The European Union banned the LTTE on 30 May 2006. Mangala Samaraweera was the foreign minister at that time and he claims the banning of the LTTE by the EU as a personal diplomatic victory. At that time there were 25 countries in the EU and only 17 were in favour of banning the LTTE. Seven countries were not in favour and the EU needed unanimity to make a decision. The responsibility of persuading these seven countries fell on Samaraweera as the foreign minister. The sales pitch adopted was that the government wants the LTTE listed as a terrorist organization not as an end in itself, but as a means to an end to get them back to the negotiating table. Even Benita Ferrero-Waldner the external affairs commissioner of the European Commission was not in favour of listing the LTTE as a terrorist organisation. Samaraweera met her personally to persuade her to agree to ban the LTTE.

Samaraweera had managed to enlist the help of the Americans to persuade the reluctant EU countries to agree to the ban. The Secretary of State in the Bush administration Condoleeza Rice had been very sympathetic to Sri Lanka at that stage. Nicholas Burns, her deputy in the State Department came to Sri Lanka on a number of occasions and he had persuaded the seven EU countries to support the ban on the LTTE. Samaraweera had met Rice twice, and the Indian Prime Minister Manmohan Singh four times to get them to bring pressure on the Europeans to ban the LTTE. Rice had also taken the initiative in setting up a Sri Lanka 'contact group' in the State Department with the help of the FBI and the involvement of Vietnam, Thailand Cambodia, and Malaysia. This was an informal intelligence gathering group to monitor LTTE arms procurement from South East Asia. The FBI also started a new unit with 41 full time staff to monitor LTTE activities in the USA.

The LTTE's response to the EU ban was to massacre 13 civilian irrigation workers in Welikanda. Attacks were also launched on home guard bunkers, precipitating an exodus of civilians from the Welikanda area. Even the EU had to face reprisals from the LTTE in the wake of the ban. On 8 June 2006, the LTTE ordered Sweden, Denmark and Finland - all members of the EU, to withdraw their ceasefire monitors from the north and east as they could no longer guarantee their safety. Following this order, the Co-Chairs had a hastily arranged meeting between the government and the LTTE in Oslo. This was supposed to be the long overdue second round of talks with the Rajapaksa

306

government. Even though the LTTE did go to Oslo, no negotiations took place because they refused to sit down to talks. The Western nations involved in the Sri Lankan peace process had clearly lost control of things.

It was in this deadlocked situation that the LTTE carried out the worst atrocity since the signing of the ceasefire agreement. A claymore attack was carried out on a crowded civilian bus in Kebithigollewa killing 64 passengers, many of them women and children and injuring 86 others. President Mahinda Rajapaksa himself rushed to Kebithigollewa with Gōta. When they arrived by helicopter, there were black flags of protest all over and tyres burning on the roads. The people were in an ugly mood. The presidential chopper had landed near the hospital where the bodies had been brought and there were thousands of people milling around. The atmosphere was tense, the people hostile. The president saw for himself the carnage wrought by the LTTE and spoke to the injured in the hospital wards. From the hospital he went to the Kebithigollewa police station and discussed the security situation in the area with the army and police.

The hostility of the people towards a government they felt was failing to ensure their physical security was barely disguised. When Basil Rajapaksa went to Kebithigollewa the next day, the people told him that for over two years, they had been asking for a bulldozer to build some bunkers but had always been fobbed off with excuses. But after the bomb blast, the government had miraculously provided earth moving equipment within two hours, to dig the mass graves to bury the victims of the bomb blast.

After this attack, special arrangements were made to strengthen the defence lines in the area with new bunkers and road clearance patrols, and the deployment of police commandos in the area. Following the Kebithigollewa outrage, the government once again launched artillery attacks on LTTE positions in the Sampur area along with air strikes on targets in Kilinochchi and Mulleitivu. War now seemed a foregone conclusion, but still the government held back. The LTTE did not. On 18 June, a police water bowser was blasted killing three policemen. On 26 June, Major Gen Parami Kulatunga, deputy chief of staff of the army was killed in a suicide attack in Pannipitiya, a town 17 kilometres from Colombo.

Chapter 52

The Wretched of the Earth

In early July 2006, Palitha Kohona, the head of the government peace secretariat expressed disappointment that the international community was not taking cognizance of the fact that the LTTE was continuing to train civilians in armed combat. He revealed that the LTTE had trained over 6000 Tamil civilians in the Muttur area alone. Even with these signs of an impending war plainly visible, President Mahinda Rajapaksa appeared on the Indian NDTV news channel and invited Prabhakaran to help Sri Lanka evolve a peaceful solution. In the first week of July 2006, the government showed its flexibility by facilitating a visit to Sri Lanka by Martin McGuiness the deputy leader of Sinn Fein the political wing of the Irish Republican Army. Despite the fact that McGuiness had opposed the EU ban on the LTTE, he was provided with a government helicopter to go on a tour of the north.

By this time, the LTTE was in an upbeat mood. The new confidence was reflected in *Tamilnet* reporting that the LTTE political head S.P.Tamilselvam had ruled out negotiating for devolution based on Sri Lanka's unitary constitution. He was reported as having said that the Tamils had rejected the unitary constitution decades ago. In the meantime, the killings continued. In the first half of July 2006, 14 security forces personnel were killed in separate incidents in Mannar and Batticaloa. The outgoing French Ambassador in Colombo, Jean Bernard de Vaivre said that violence and terrorism cannot achieve anything and that it was high time pretexts were set aside and a dialogue resumed. As the second week of July ended, claymore blasts occurred in Jaffna and Trincomalee killing four armed forces personnel and injuring 12. Another claymore mine attack on a bus killed three army personnel.

War was looming over the horizon but public opinion at that time was still against a war. The people had long since lost confidence in the ability of the military to tackle the terrorist problem. Many thought it was not possible to win the war against the LTTE because over the years, military action had consistently proved to be unsuccessful. Repeated defeats over the years and decades had taken their toll. The public had absolutely no reason to believe that the Rajapaksa government would be any different to the governments that had preceded it when it came to the success or otherwise of military operations.

At this point in time, the soldiers who had fought to maintain the integrity of the country were not seen as heroes. There were many in the armed forces too who did not see themselves as heroes. Hamilton Wanasinghe, the last army commander that Gōta served under before retiring, gave an interview to the *Sunday Leader* on 29 July 2007, which was published with the defeatist title "No war can be won militarily". This was after the LTTE attacks in Mavilaru, Muttur, Selvanagar, Kattapararichchan, Muhamalai, Kayts and other places had been repulsed and the LTTE dislodged from Sampur, Vakarai, Batticaloa, Amparai and Thoppigala. The entire east had been cleared and the army was clearly on a winning streak, and yet even an ex-army commander like Wanasinghe refused to accept the fact that the army he had once led, could win the war. During this interview, apart from stressing that no war can be won militarily, Wanasinghe also said that "Problems have to be finally solved through discussions" and further that "there are no winners in any war - all are losers."

That was a whipped, beaten and cowed army commander speaking. In his view, the military had no role to play in dealing with terrorism and the only way it could be dealt with was though negotiations. This despite the fact that all negotiations with the LTTE had consistently failed with the LTTE breaking off negotiations when it suited them. To talk of negotiations even in such a context was a case of going for negotiations as a supplicant and in a state of surrender. Wanasinghe was at the time of the interview, the President of the Sri Lanka Ex-Servicemen's Association. With ex-army commanders holding such opinions even after the army started chalking up victories, one can imagine what the situation was prior to July 2006, when no victories had yet been won, and there was only defeat and ignominy in the background. That was the attitude of mind that Gōta had to start changing before he could get things rolling.

As recounted earlier, Prime Minister Ranil Wickremesinghe who signed the ceasefire agreement of 2002, was inclined to treat the armed forces with open contempt. President Chandrika Kumaratunga who wrested control of the government after April 2004, may not have treated the armed forces with contempt, but she was not willing to rely on the armed forces to contain the LTTE. She too thought appeasement would be the safer option. This negativity with regard to the armed forces was reflected in popular culture as well. For some reason, the war never featured prominently in Sinhala novels, short stories, poetry, stage drama or television dramas but it did feature to some extent in cinema where almost invariably, the soldier was cast in a negative light.

Commodore Sarath Weerasekera had come to Gōta's notice while he was still in the USA because the former had running battles in the newspapers with some Sinhala film directors over the portrayal of military personnel in their films. The first film director that Weerasekera, a movie buff, locked horns with, was Asoka Handagama who produced *Me mage sandai* in the year 2000. A young Tamil woman seeks shelter in an army bunker during a confrontation and the soldier inside spares her life in exchange for sex. Afterwards, she follows the soldier and goes with him to his village where he deserts the army. When the military police come in search of him, the young Tamil woman offers herself to them in exchange for her life, suggesting that she has got conditioned to exchanging sex for her life with uniformed personnel. Ultimately, the middle-aged Buddhist monk in the village elopes with her leaving his robe on a bush.

The issue that Weerasekera had with this film was that while killing Sinhala, Muslim and even Tamil civilians with impunity, the LTTE was still able to tell the world that the Sinhalese were barbaric and uncivilized because films like this tended to reinforce that impression in the world. The idea conveyed in the film was that Tamil women were being kept as sex slaves by Sinhala soldiers.

These were not mainline films that were screened in Sri Lanka with any degree of success but they won awards at foreign film festivals and the impression conveyed even to those limited foreign audiences and foreign critics would be that this was a correct portrayal of the situation in Sri Lanka. Weerasekera while still a serving naval officer had an exchange of letters in the press with director Asoka Handagama even calling him a 'terrorist' for producing such a film. He drew attention to Indian movies like 'Mother India' and 'Border' which upheld patriotism and depicted the manner in which soldiers fight and lay down their lives for their people and their country. Weerasekera wrote that directors who produce films on war situations, should have lived with the soldiers on the frontlines to see what kind of lives they led in the bunkers, not knowing when they would be attacked and the hardships they put up with on a daily basis, at times even having to go without water and food.

Weerasekera declared war against three movies in particular - the afore mentioned *Me mage sandai* and *Sudu kalu saha alu* (2004) by Sudath Mahadivulwewa and *Sulanga enu pinisa* (2005) by Vimukthi Jayasundara all of which portrayed the soldier in a negative light. The film *Sulanga enu pinisa* for example, depicts the wife of a home guard in a border village as a promiscuous nymphomaniac who sleeps with her husband's colleagues. Weerasekera took strong exception to this. He complained that the commitment of soldiers' wives, the way they hold *bodhi poojas* for the safe return of their husbands, the way they bring up the children on their own, and the constant uncertainties they live with, are not depicted in these films.

The three film directors were not mainline commercial film directors but artistic types who dealt with topics like repressed sexuality and combining sexual themes with soldiers fighting a war was the surest way of bagging an international award in a situation where due to LTTE propaganda over three decades, the West had got used to thinking of the Sri Lankan soldier as an oppressor who raped and violated Tamils. At a certain point, President Chandrika Kumaratunga instructed Wasantha Karannagoda who had by then become navy commander, to stop Weerasekera from writing to the press. The navy commander thereupon instructed Weerasekera to show him any articles he writes in future before sending them to the newspapers.

That put an end to Weerasekera's role as a film critic but his lone battle had not gone unnoticed. The issues raised by Weerasekera were of grave concern to Gōta. As a former soldier himself, he knew that no nation can fight a war with a negative perception of soldiers prevalent among the public. And with an all out war clearly on the cards, this negative perception had to be changed if public support for the war was to be forthcoming. These three films were in one sense a monument to the openness of the Sinhalese. However they

311

did exemplify the lack of self esteem in the Sinhala people especially with regard to matters military. Perhaps it was no accident that these films came out between 2000 and 2005 when the military had hit rock bottom after a decade of debacles.

That was a period when defeatism was the order of the day among the Sinhalese and such films probably reflected the mood of the times. Gōta was to change the whole trajectory of Sri Lankan thinking on this matter. At the time the LTTE began stepping up their attacks on the military in December 2005, most politicians on both sides of the divide including senior government ministers like Mangala Samaraweera, did not believe that the war could be won. The defence analysts in the newspapers were also uniformly negative about the prospect of the military ever being able to defeat the LTTE. Unsurprisingly, Western governments and international organisations were always talking about the LTTE's military capabilities and their strengths. Their advice was against even thinking of a military option. Everybody said that the military option had been tried out and that it had failed and that the LTTE was too strong.

Eric Solheim had a meeting with president Mahinda Rajapaksa in late March 2006 where he told the president that Prabhakaran was a military genius and that it would be suicidal to take him on and that the best thing the president could do is to negotiate with him as fighting will not succeed. To this the president had said that he comes from the south and that southerners will not succumb that easily. Mahinda had told Solheim "You think he is a jungle boy from Mulleitivu, well I am a jungle boy from the south! We'll see what happens". Gōta was to have a similar exchange with the SLMM head Jon Hansen Baur and Norwegian Ambassador Hans Brattskar on 6 April 2006. When the two Norwegians asked Gōta whether he thinks the problem in Sri Lanka can be solved by military means, Gōta had answered YES!

The entire focus was on a political settlement and avoiding confrontation with the LTTE at any cost. Yet, Gōta could not simply go along with the conventional thinking on this matter as it was clear that the LTTE was going to wage war and the military had to be prepared. In the middle of all this negativity regarding the Sri Lankan armed services, the one beacon of light was the 2002 US Defence Department report quoted extensively earlier. The American defence authorities alone seemed to believe that the Sri Lankan armed forces could do what they were supposed to do.

312

Preparing to meet the LTTE challenge had two components, acquiring the necessary military hardware and recruiting more people into the armed forces. That the Rajapaksa government was seriously looking for military hardware within weeks of being elected to power was seen in the wish list they presented to the Indian government. The next problem that Gōta had was recruitment. A public that had lost faith in a military solution could not provide recruits for the armed forces in the numbers required. Given the past track record of the military, there was also the widespread feeling that joining the armed forces was the surest way of getting to an early grave. Thus the perception of the soldier was of an unfortunate, condemned creature. Many were thought to join the armed forces due to the lack of better employment opportunities and this impression lowered the self-esteem of the armed forces and their status among the general public.

Recruitment had become an endemic problem for the armed forces from the 1990s onwards and if war broke out again, Gōta knew that this would be the biggest problem the government would confront. There was a dire need to change the mindset of the people and get them thinking positively about the armed forces. Gōta called in Dilith Jayaweera of Tri Ads, whom he had got to know during the presidential election campaign and told him that the perception of the military had to be changed and the people have to start thinking of armed forces personnel as their own brothers and sisters and their own people. The *Api wenuwen api* campaign designed by Tri Ads turned out to be a watershed in the advertising and public relations industry.

Never has any advertising campaign brought about such an immediate change in public attitudes. Of course they were helped along by changes in the public mood due to events on the ground. While the people may not have believed that a military option was possible, the abject capitulationism of the UNP government of 2001-2004 irritated the voting public no end, and that was one of the main reasons for the ignominious defeat of that government just 30 months after being elected to power. The people resented the way the UNP bent over backwards to accommodate the LTTE. After the Rajapaksa government came into power, the intolerable provocations and outrages that the LTTE perpetrated brought things to a state where the people individually and collectively came to the conclusion that enough was enough and this issue had to be decided either way, once and for all.

Chapter 53

Combating Defeatism

Thus when the *Api wenuwen api* campaign was launched, it immediately struck a responsive chord among the people. The timing of the launch of the campaign may also have had much to do with its success. It was just after the army had beaten off LTTE attacks in Mavilaru, Muttur, Kattaparichchan, Selvanagar, Pahala Thoppur, Muhamalai and Kayts (events described in the following chapters) that *Api wenuwen api* was launched in mid-August 2006. The security forces had the upper hand and were upbeat. All of a sudden military service began to be seen as an honourable duty to the nation.

More than a decade ago, when the army took over the Jaffna peninsula in the *Riviresa* operation in 1995, Brigadier Hiran Halangoda of the Air Mobile Brigade observed that the LTTE had taken great pains to construct special cemeteries and memorials for their dead cadres and that not having similar methods to motivate the soldiers of the armed forces was a 'glaring shortcoming'. He also observed that the LTTE had put up posters motivating youngsters to join the LTTE outside every school – again another practice that was absent in the south. These shortcomings observed by Halangoda were to be addressed only a decade or more later after Gōta took over the military establishment. He was ably assisted in this matter by his younger brother Basil, who looked after the civilian administration aspects of the war.

Basil Rajapaksa recognized quite early on that the reason why people were so willing to flee threatened villages was because there was nothing to keep the people in such areas. Very often, they had nothing but a house. Because other facilities like water, electricity, roads, schools, and even employment was not available, people thought nothing about fleeing their abodes. The government stared repairing the roads, building houses, providing electricity, and building schools and providing teachers so as to give people more to lose and a reason to stay. The government employed one member of each family in the home guard unit (later called the civil defence force) so that they would have employment. Doctors were provided for hospitals. Pickup trucks were bought with the help of private donors and distributed to temples in these areas, so that the villagers would be able to transport casualties to hospital in the event of an LTTE attack.

During this period, the government got together the trade unions to seek their help in maintaining industrial peace and keeping the essential services functioning. Even anti-government trade unions were generally cooperative during this period. This was probably due to the recognition that the reaction from the public would have been negative if the trade unions were seen to be sabotaging the war effort. There was also the fact that there would have been little support from among the union membership itself for industrial action during this period. When hostilities started, steps were taken to protect certain installations such as the pumping station in Ambatale which provided drinking water to Colombo. At the time, this vital installation did not even have a protective fence. Some of the guards had shotguns, but no ammunition. The government sought to ensure the security of such places, with the help of the trade unions and the employees.

Another matter that was looked into was the situation that would arise when dead bodies of soldiers came back to the villages. A team of ministers was appointed to attend these funerals and all local government authorities were instructed to provide the tents and chairs and other paraphernalia that were needed for a village funeral. Local political activists were also mobilized to put up decorations etc, so that the family of the serviceman would not be left feeling abandoned in their bereavement. A separate office was set up to deliver a wreath from the president and to deliver his message to the bereaved family. When civilian deaths and injuries took place, compensation was paid promptly, sometimes, while the victims were still in hospital.

When the Rajapaksa government was elected into power, compensation for terrorism victims had not been paid for the past five to six years. All such arrears were also paid off. In the event of a massacre of civilians, the administrative set up led by the Government Agents and Assistant Government Agents (Divisional Secretaries) was mobilized to see to all the needs of the victims. The government was acutely aware of the possibility that resentment at such massacres could be channelled against the government as the president himself had seen and experienced in Kebithigollewa.

With his background in information technology, Gōta took the initiative to start www.defence.lk, the armed forces website to counter the LTTE run *Tamilnet*. He realized that a lot of people and not just Tamils, but journalists, politicians, foreign governments, the diplomatic missions and many members of the general public read *Tamilnet* and they believed most of the news that appeared on that website. Apart from *Tamilnet* there were the defence columns in the newspapers which were mostly negative. Thus the international community, the general public and the members of the military themselves were on an intellectual diet of negativity. This propaganda was believed by decision makers and even members of the military who read them.

The purpose of www.defence.lk was to counter all this negative propaganda. Gōta got together a small number of army and air force officers who had some knowledge of information technology and had the necessary writing and graphics skills. What he wanted was a website that would convey the other side of the story to the public.

The new website became a huge success because there was a market opening up for the 'other side of the story'. By the time www.defence.lk got off the ground, the LTTE's provocations and outrages had created an appetite for non-defeatist news and opinions. Later, when the war did start and the military began chalking up successes one after the other, this appetite would become an obsession. By early 2009, before the war ended, Gōta was able to tell the public in a TV interview that the most widely read news media in the country was www.defence.lk. This website acted as the counter-propaganda arm of the government when the military suffered setbacks like the Muhamalai incident of 2006, the Anuradhapura air base attack of 2008, the several air raids carried out by the LTTE on Colombo in 2007/2008 and the mounting number of armed forces casualties as the war progressed.

Apart from trying to improve the self-esteem and morale of the troops through ideology and propaganda, the conditions under which the soldiers served was also improved. Shortcomings in the kit and equipment of soldiers were sorted out. Another issue that had affected the soldiers serving in the Jaffna peninsula, was transport between Kankesanthurei and Trincomalee. There were about 40,000 troops in the Jaffna peninsula and because of LTTE domination of the Vanni, the only connectivity was through air and sea. Not many troops could be transported by air, and movement was mainly by sea. For many years, troops were transported in cargo ships which had no toilets and the defenders of the nation were reduced to urinating or even defecating into plastic bags on their way between Jaffna and Trincomalee.

None of this was contributing to morale. Even the UNP government of 2001-2004 had tried to do something about the situation. Milinda Moragoda who had been a minister in the UNP government, had told Gōta that they had gone to see how the soldiers were being transported between Jaffna and Trincomalee and that conditions were really bad.

The then UNP government had even set up a ministerial committee to go into the matter of transporting the troops. But nothing concrete had been achieved. This long standing issue had been sorted out by Gōta who had leased out the *Jetliner*, a cruiser from Indonesia, in which 3000 troops could be carried comfortably. With this, a long standing problem was solved, helping to improve the morale of tens of thousands of troops guarding an isolated and vulnerable part of the country.

The attention paid to such matters went a long way towards convincing the troops that they had not been abandoned by the government. The manner in which the army, navy, air force and police personnel in Jaffna were transported to and from their stations had a knock-on effect on the whole defence establishment and the acquisition of the *Jetliner* contributed directly and significantly to armed forces morale. The *Jetliner* was ten years old when acquired by the navy in July 2006 and it was brought with an Indonesian crew of 22 including the captain who were contracted to serve with the navy for three months. Ambassador Janaka Perera serving in Indonesia at the time, also played a part in the negotiations.

The vehicle holds of the ship were converted into passenger areas and air conditioned, TVs were also installed and the ship could carry over 3000 passengers with ease. In addition to the numbers transported and the level of comfort, another advantage that the *Jetliner* offered was speed. The *Pearl Cruiser* which did the ferrying of passengers earlier, could carry only around 700 men and it did only 11 knots and took one and a half days to go to Jaffna. The *Jetliner* despite its size, was a much faster ship and enabled the trip to the north to be made in about seven hours.

Another change that took place after 2005 was that arms and supplies procurement for the military establishment was brought under one government owned procuring agency called Lanka Logistics and Technology Ltd which operated under the defence ministry. Under previous regimes, there had been widespread allegations of racketeering in arms deals and the new set up eliminated private arms dealers. Having himself been a soldier on the battlefield, Gōta knew how rumours about racketeering in arms deals and military supplies could demoralize the armed forces and starting a government procuring agency was meant to eliminate both the abuses as well as the stories that would filter down to the soldiers on the frontlines.

Lanka Logistics & Technologies Ltd began operations around March 2007, and it eliminated middlemen in arms procurements by dealing directly with the manufacturers. Earlier there had been many private arms dealers registered with the defence ministry to supply various military items. One problem was that when a procurement was to be made, calling for tenders ensured that the news went out to the LTTE as well. The LTTE knew exactly what was being purchased and in what quantities. This too was eliminated by the defence ministry doing the procuring themselves and calling for tenders not from local arms dealers but from foreign manufacturers.

Most of Sri Lanka's military purchases were made from China, Pakistan, Russia, Ukraine, Israel and to a lesser extent Brazil. China had an umbrella organization called COSTIND (Commission of Science, Technology and Industry for National Defence) which dealt with arms sales under which there were about eleven large manufacturers and the Sri Lankan government dealt directly with about eight of these manufacturers. In Russia there was one umbrella organization, RUSPORM which the Sri Lankan government dealt with. In Brazil, Lanka Logistics dealt directly with the individual companies to purchase ammunition and spares for the NATO standard weapons that the air force needed. At one time, the Chinese firm NORINCO was the sole Chinese supplier of weapons to Sri Lanka. Later, another Chinese firm called Poly Technologies also began supplying arms.

Sri Lanka purchased short shelf-life ammunition during the war as it was used almost as soon as it reached Sri Lanka. Buying such ammunition reduced the cost. When requisitions were made by the various branches of the armed services, the tenders would be called by Lanka Logistics and put to the technical evaluation committees of

318

the various service branches and finally to the standing committee of the cabinet on arms purchases. Lanka Logistics was a small organization with just 21 employees in total including two drivers and one accountant, with its offices located at the BMICH complex in Colombo.

Obtaining arms and ammunition was not just a case of paying the money and getting the items across the counter. There were at times other barriers. The military had to match the firepower of the LTTE and in this, the demands coming in from the Artillery Corps and the air force were especially intense. There was a time during the Beijing Olympics in China when arms shipments were held up. China faced a blitz of Western propaganda about human rights violations. Tremendous pressure had also been brought on the Chinese ambassador in Colombo by the heads of Western missions not to send arms and munitions to Colombo. President Mahinda Rajapaksa had to personally use his good offices with the president of China and the president of Pakistan to obtain the necessary arms shipments.

During the war, Udaya Perera director of operations of the army, maintained constant contact with Gōta and kept him updated about the ammunition stocks. When Gōta was told of the requirement, he would go to the president. On one occasion, the president had to phone president Musharaff of Pakistan in the night to organize the purchase of emergency supplies.

Apart from these measures at the governmental level, Gōta personally looked into the state of preparedness of the armed services. On 15 July 2006, while Sarath Fonseka was still convalescing after the attempt on his life, Gōta went on a tour of Jaffna with Nanda Mallawarachchi the acting commander of the army and he stayed overnight in the peninsula, visiting places like Muhamali where he addressed the soldiers of the 55th Division stressing the need to be prepared for any eventuality. Jaffna and particularly Muhamalai was one place where LTTE attacks were expected. He also addressed the navy at the Kankesanthurei harbour and troops at Palaly as well during the two day visit. As it turned out, this visit was almost a premonition of things to come. Just days later, the LTTE closed the Mavilaru anicut heralding the resumption of hostilities.

* * * * *

On 14 August 2006, the Pakistani High Commissioner in Colombo Bashir Wali Mohamed's motorcade came under a trishaw bomb attack in the heart of the city. High Commissioner Mohamed was a former chief of military intelligence in Pakistan. Four Sri Lankan army commandos were killed on the spot and eight others seriously wounded. The High Commissioner's wife and daughter were also with him when the attack took place. Mohamed's first reaction was to blame the attack on the Indian intelligence agency RAW. Some thought the LTTE would have done it to ingratiate themselves with the Indians. Then there was also the theory that the LTTE may have tried to assassinate the Pakistani High Commissioner because Pakistan was one of the principal arms suppliers to Sri Lanka.

But the real explanation was much simpler. This was a case of mistaken identity. That day, an LTTE hit team had tried to blast the motorcade of a minister with a trishaw packed with explosives and operated by remote control. They missed the motorcade of the minister because the remote control device malfunctioned. Then they had taken the trishaw to the Liberty Plaza car park and repaired the faulty circuit and it was brought right back to where it had been. The LTTE operative on the ground had hit the Pakistani High Commissioner's motorcade because with an army commando escort, it looked like a ministerial motorcade. Aiya, the previously mentioned LTTE operative in Colombo who is now awaiting trial for other hit jobs, had told his interrogators that he had been verbally abused and given the telling off of his life by his LTTE superiors over this incident.

Chapter 54

The LTTE's Fatal Error

It was in July 2006 that the LTTE finally overstepped their mark. The final war with the LTTE would not have broken out if not for an incident that occurred on the border of the Polonnaruwa and Trincomalee districts. The Mavilaru anicut is located 5 km to the south of the Kallar army camp. This anicut had three sluice gates and provided irrigation water for the areas of Kallar, Dehiwatte, Thoppur, Seruvila and Serunuwara in the Trincomalee district. The irrigation engineer in Kallar was responsible for maintaining the anicut and the irrigation channels radiating from it. On 21 July 2006, villagers reported an unusual reduction in the water flow to the Kallar irrigation engineer. When he went to investigate, he was stopped by the LTTE about one kilometre from the anicut. This situation was reported to the Sri Lanka Monitoring Mission but they took no action.

·   The villagers began to stage protests because the crops were without water at a crucial time and further delays in the release of water would have damaged the whole crop. They tried to march on the anicut to open it themselves. Because of the unfolding situation, the government was forced to ask the army to mount a limited operation to open the Mavilaru sluice gates. At 5.00 am on 26 July 2006, army commandos began to move southwards from the Kallar army camp followed by the 8th Gemunu Watch and the 5th SLLI battalions. They advanced to within 800 meters of the anicut under heavy mortar and artillery fire from the LTTE. By 31 July, the army had advanced to within 100 meters of the main sluice gate but progress was slow due to improvised explosive devices and anti-personnel mines. The LTTE was occupying bunkers and trenches all along the route.

When the Mavilaru attack started, the Divisional Secretary (Assistant Govt. Agent) for Seruvila had disappeared as had most of the government servants except the medical officer of the area and his wife. The government had to appoint the Labour Dept. Officer of Trincomalee as the Acting Divisional Secretary for Seruvila during the crisis. People of the area were kept supplied with food by lorries that went around the villages throwing bags of rice, flour, onions, dhal etc, into residential compounds so that the civilians cowering inside their houses would not starve. Money was also distributed among the villagers to build bunkers.

By this time, Sarath Fonseka had recovered and he resumed duties as army commander at the end of July 2006. When it seemed as if the Mavilaru sluice gate was on the verge of falling to the army, the LTTE opened up another battlefront. It started on 1 August 2006, with an attempt to sink the *Jetliner* which was bringing 1200 servicemen to Trincomalee from Jaffna. The *Jetliner* was escorted by no less than 12 fast attack craft. But this did not deter the LTTE. It was just the forth run of this ship which had been acquired only about a month earlier. At that time the Indonesian crew was still operating the ship. Just as it was entering the harbour, about a dozen LTTE boats came at it from the Sampur coast, while artillery was fired at it from Sampur. The Indonesian captain who had not known what to expect in Sri Lanka, had been trembling in fear. Commander Noel Kalubowila who was in charge of the ship, ordered the Indonesian captain to increase the speed. The *Jetliner* sped into the harbour and berthed at the Ashroff Jetty unharmed despite the artillery fire from the shore. The hull of the *Jetliner* was of aluminium alloy, lightweight and built for speed, and the ship could not have withstood a direct hit. Navy fast attack craft managed to beat off the attackers with the help of Mi-24 helicopter gunships. Five naval personnel were killed and 12 injured in the confrontation. Even worse was to follow.

The very next day, on 2 August 2006, at around 10.00 am, the LTTE began shelling the navy dockyard complex located on the other side of the harbour mouth from their stronghold in Sampur. The first shell fell near the naval academy. Five shells were fired and the fifth fell into the sea right in the centre of the mouth of the Trincomalee harbour proper. The LTTE gun was zeroed in on the centre of the harbour mouth. The navy realized that the LTTE was preparing to blockade the harbour. The *Jetliner*, the only means the navy had of transporting troops from Jaffna was anchored in the Trincomalee harbour at the time, having itself come in under fire on the previous day and the priority was to get it out of the harbour before it was too late. At 11.30 that night, even without informing the eastern area commander, Karannagoda took a call to Commander Kalubowila, the officer in charge of the Jetliner and told him to start the engines right now, and get the ship out of the harbour without telling anyone.

Kalubowila confiscated the mobile phones of all the personnel on board and nobody was told about the movement. At midnight they sailed out. Even the crews of the two Dvoras patrolling outside the harbour had been surprised to see a massive blob moving out of the harbour in total darkness but they knew that anything that big could not belong to the LTTE. The *Jetliner* sailed to the Galle harbour to await further instructions. Once in Galle, the panic stricken Indonesian crew abandoned ship *en masse* saying that they could not die in somebody else's war. Commander Kalubowila and his crew had to take over the ship even though they had not been trained to operate a ship of such sophistication and size. Soon after the *Jetliner* was taken out of the Trincomalee harbour, the LTTE launched an attack on the Muttur naval detachment followed by attacks on the army camps in Kattaparichchan, Selvanagar and Pahala Thoppur (See map 4).

Because of these unexpected attacks the 8th SLLI battalion had to be withdrawn from the Mavilaru operation and deployed to save Muttur. As it turned out, Mavilaru had been only a diversion. The real target of the LTTE was the southern belt of the Trincomalee harbour. The Muttur naval detachment in the vicinity of the Muttur town, had a beach head of about one kilometre and the whole camp would have been around one square kilometre. The Trincomalee bay is a huge area, and its southern part was almost completely dominated by the LTTE. Only Muttur and Kinniya were under government control. Even during the ceasefire, the LTTE would fire upon passing ships with small arms from Sampur. The excuse they gave the SLMM was that they were doing 'firing practice'. Thereafter the navy too was constrained to have 'firing practice' on the sea near the southern belt of the harbour.

All the ships moving in and out of the Trincomalee harbour were well within LTTE artillery range and the only reason why the LTTE did not use artillery to block access to the Trincomalee harbour was because it was very difficult to hit a moving target on the sea. Muttur was located on the south of the harbour mouth which was about six kilometres across. If Muttur fell, LTTE guns and suicide boats would be deployed to blockade the harbour and supplies and troop movements to and from Jaffna would have come to a halt. Despite the importance of the Muttur jetty, only about 120 men manned it because the army was in control of Muttur town. By the second day of the attack on Muttur, the army detachment had been overrun, and by about 10.00 o'clock in the morning, the first line of defence in the naval detachment fell.

By 2.00 pm in the afternoon, half of the second line of defence had also fallen. The police station was adjacent to the navy detachment but they were holding on. Muttur town was in the hands of the LTTE. The embattled navy sought the help of the army and the next day, 65 army commandos were ferried across by the navy under fire, but after they got to Muttur, they had said that their task was to protect the police station and the navy was back to square one. At this point, Captain Udaya Bandara, one of Karannagoda's staff officers, remembered that when he was accompanying the navy commander on an inspection tour, he had seen a multi barrel rocket launcher which had been parked at the naval dockyard by the army.

Upon inquiring from the officers there, Bandara had learnt that it was under the command of the navy so long as it was in their premises. He suggested to Karannagoda that they use this to fire right across the mouth of the harbour at LTTE positions in the Sampur area. There was an artillery officer in charge of the MBRL and Karannagoda spoke to him over the phone and gave him the positions of the LTTE in Sampur. The MBRL kept firing salvoes across the mouth of the harbour intermittently until morning. It was with the fire power of this MBRL that the Muttur jetty was held by the navy. Over the next couple of days, the navy ferried across about 700 naval patrolmen to reinforce the jetty. The Navy lost 14 men in the battle for Muttur. It took four days of fighting to dislodge the LTTE from Muttur.

Over 40,000 people, mostly Muslims were displaced as a result of the fighting in the Trincomalee district. Even as late as 19 August, Muslims were fleeing the Thoppur area and coming into Kantale with some reporting that Muslim youth had been detained en route by the LTTE and later killed. It was in this confused situation that reports began to circulate about the killing of 17 Tamil workers attached to a French NGO called Action Against Hunger (Action Contre la Faim). The army was accused of having carried out the massacre. Suddenly, everybody's focus shifted from the gross violations of the ceasefire agreement that the LTTE had been perpetrating over the past many days, to the massacre of the 17 Tamil aid workers. The LTTE was always adept at this kind of manoeuvre and had mastered the technique of throwing red herrings across the trail with the Western community of nations unfailingly going after the herring.

While the battle for the Muttur jetty was on, there were simultaneous attacks on several army camps to the south of the harbour. The 7th SLLI battalion was headquartered in Pahala Thoppur, with detachments in Selvanagar, Pansalwatte, the 64th Mile Post, and Kattaparichchan. About three days after the operation to recapture the Mavilaru anicut had been launched, troops at the Selvanagar camp had noticed an unusual boat movement in the lagoon and they had observed the LTTE taking their 152mm artillery guns along the road towards Sampur. The boats had been picketing the lagoon to facilitate the movement of the two guns. That was on the very day the Jetliner was attacked. Tell tale signs of an impending attack had manifested itself in the past few days with some civilians moving out of the Tamil village located near the 7th SLLI battalion headquarters.

The next night, just past midnight, a report came in from the Kattaparichhan camp to the east, that sentries posted at the bridge near the camp had been attacked and some soldiers injured. At the time of the attack the camp was manned only by about 45 men. Some of the men were in Muttur manning strong points in the town. Lt Col Senaka Wijesuriya the officer commanding the 7th SLLI Battalion, placed all the camps under his command on red alert. Then came a message from the Selvanagar camp saying that the nightly patrol that went out from the camp was being attacked. The Selvanagar camp was manned at that time by about 60 troops. The patrol had accosted an LTTE contingent moving towards the Selvanagar camp and a confrontation had taken place. The next morning, several dozen LTTE bodies had been recovered. Two soldiers were killed in the ambush and seven injured.

Then the Kattaparichchan camp was attacked and in the initial assault, eight bunkers fell to the LTTE. Gōta was in touch with officers at all levels in the army and the detachment commander of Kattaparichchan had in fact informed Gōta that his camp had been surrounded. Lt Col Wijesuriya then asked the Pansalwatte detachment consisting of about 45 men to take all their weapons and move immediately to the Kattaparichchan camp. By dawn, the strength of the Kattaparichchan camp had been beefed up. Wijesuriya then spoke to individual corporals and privates in the camp whom he knew were aggressive fighters and impressed upon them the need to hold the camp at all costs. By dawn they had managed to recapture the eight bunkers that had fallen to the LTTE. In the meantime, the 64th mile post detachment was also under fire and by about 4.00 am, the Pahala Thoppur battalion headquarters also came under fire.

Lt Col. Wijesuriya however did not tell the detachments that the battalion headquarters was also under attack, as that would have caused a collapse of morale. One problem was that the detachments were located too far away for any supporting fire to be given. The battalion headquarters had 81mm mortars but their effective range was about four kilometres and all the detachments were located farther than that. The Kattaparichchan camp was 12 km away, and Selvanagar 7 km from the battalion headquarters. The situation was turning desperate in Kattaprarichchan with 11 soldiers killed and more than 20 injured.

At around 7.00 am the next day, Wijesuriya got a call from Gōta who wanted to know whether the Muttur police station had been overrun. Wijesuriya had told him that he was in communication with the police station and that it had not fallen and that it was the army camps in Kattaparichchan and Selvanagar that were under siege. Gōta had been under the impression that the Muttur police station had been surrounded and all the policemen captured alive by the LTTE. On the morning after the first attack, the casualties in the Selvanagar camp were removed in trucks by Muslim villagers who were supportive of the army. Wijesuriya had the casualties in the Kattaparichchan camp taken in a commandeered tractor to the navy pier in Muttur by a shortcut. Terrorists were seen near the navy hospital, and the casualties had to be taken to the pier by a different route. On the night of the second day the attacks had resumed on the besieged camps.

Communication between the Pahala Thoppur battalion headquarters and the Kattaparichchan camp failed on the second night and communication was maintained through cellular phones. The numbers of the phones being used were given to a soldier at the Panagoda army cantonment located 20 km away from Colombo and he kept topping up the credit on the phones from a night kiosk nearby. In that manner communication was maintained with the Kattaparichchan camp until radio communication was re-established. In the meantime, the Kattaparichchan camp ran out of ammunition and ammo had to be air dropped into the camp from a Bell 212 helicopter. Mi-24 helicopters were also used to attack LTTE positions around the besieged camps. The single multi barrel rocket launcher located at the naval dockyard saved the day yet again by supporting the Kattaparichchan camp with a barrage of fire from the other side of the harbour mouth.

After the attempt to capture Muttur failed, the Norwegian Ambassador Jon Hansen Bauer tried to broker a ceasefire with the LTTE agreeing to open up the Mavilaru anicut if the army would withdraw to the Kallar army camp and discontinue the air strikes. *Tamilnet* quoted S.P.Tamilselvam as saying that *"Any future Sri Lankan military offensive involving air attacks, artillery attacks and limited operations will be interpreted as a declaration of war."* This seemed to suggest that in the eyes of the LTTE, all that had been going on during the past several days was not war.

The Muslim community leaders of Muttur were brought to Colombo for a discussion at the presidential secretariat and they had said with one voice that they could not go back to live in Muttur so long as there were LTTE heavy guns in Sampur which could easily bombard Muttur. It was with the Muttur crisis that the Rajapaksa government was confronted for the first time with the problem of internally displaced people (IDPs). The Muttur IDPs were resettled within a period of 45 days. The UN High Commission for Refugees office in Sri Lanka had objected to this resettlement and the UNHCR head in Trincomalee had even tried to obstruct the buses that had been brought to transport the IDPs back to Muttur. However, all 40,000 people were taken back to Muttur and resettled.

Chapter 55

The Hunters Hunted

The government rejected the LTTE's conditional offer to open the Mavilaru anicut. At the height of the hostilities in Trincomalee, two LTTE cadres had been arrested in Bentota in the south while travelling in a lorry which had a concealed compartment with no less than 30 five kilo claymore mines, 50 kg of C-4 explosives, 15 hand grenades, among other things and it was clear that the LTTE was preparing for anything but peace. After repulsing the LTTE's surprise attacks on Muttur, Kattaparichchan, Selvanagar, and Pahala Thoppur, the operation to recapture the Mavilaru anicut resumed on 11 August.

On the same day, the LTTE launched a full scale attack on the Muhamalai defence line in Jaffna, at around 5.30 pm. They carried out a simultaneous bombardment of Kayts and Mandativu islands from Kalmunai Point. While Muhamalai was under attack, military intelligence intercepted a radio message about a seaborne landing in the Jaffna peninsula.

All possible sites for a seaborne attack such as Kayts and Point Pedro were placed on red alert. Gōta summoned the commanders of the army, navy, air force, the chief of defence staff and president's secretary Lalith Weeratunga and coordinated the defence of Jaffna with the three service commanders working together in one room. That night, LTTE boats were detected trying to make a landing at Kayts at around 8.45 pm. When it was confirmed that the LTTE landing was to be in Kayts, reinforcements were rushed in and the

LTTE plan thwarted. The hostilities in Jaffna continued for four days. The crisis in Jaffna was over by 5.00 pm on 13 August 2006. By 15 August, the LTTE had been beaten off in Muhamalai. Army commandos had been deployed in Kayts against LTTE infiltrators and helicopter gunships had thwarted the LTTE's plan to land reinforcements in Kayts in 50 boats. Between 11 August and 6 September 2006, no less than 221 army personnel were killed and 900 soldiers injured in the defence of Muhamalai and Kayts.

In the Trincomalee district too, the army had captured the head sluice gate of the Mavilaru anicut and the LTTE had withdrawn by 14 August, but they continued to direct mortar and artillery fire into the area. Eighteen soldiers had been killed and 84 wounded in the battle to regain control of the Mavilaru anicut. If one looks at the sequence of events in July/August 2006, the LTTE's grand plan seems to have been to first sink the Jetliner killing 1200 troops in one go. With bodies of soldiers going to every district in the country, demoralization would set in, which they would use to capture the Muttur jetty and consolidate their power south of the harbour mouth in Trincomalee. Thereafter they would blockade the harbour and stop all troop movements and supplies to Jaffna. Then they would attack Jaffna and take over the peninsula.

If this grand plan had worked, the LTTE would have had their separate state. The LTTE had launched a major operation after a long time, and it had been successfully repulsed. These initial battles in the north and east made the government war machine fall into place. It was at this time that certain practices were established that would last till the end of the war. The security council began meeting every Wednesday at 10.30 am, and would at times go on till evening. The president participated in all the security council meetings. When there were incidents there would be extra meetings. Comprehensive debriefings were done about all operations and the progress achieved, the number of casualties, the areas captured, the present location of troops etc. No notes were taken at security council meetings. Everything was done by word of mouth.

Whatever happened, the president was always in the picture and what he was hearing was the unvarnished truth, not sunshine stories designed to keep him happy. Even as the LTTE attacks in the east and the north were being successfully repulsed, similar victories were being chalked up in Colombo, that other main theatre of operations of the LTTE. On 13 August, the police discovered in Wattala, a town between the city of Colombo and the International

329

airport, a cache of arms including 8 claymore mines, 15 hand grenades, three T-56 assault rifles, two pistols and hundreds of rounds of ammunition.

When the LTTE broke ceasefires in the past in 1990 and 1995, they managed to send the government reeling by the sheer magnitude of the attacks. But in 2006, they could not overrun even small army and naval detachments manned at the most by a few dozen men. It would be interesting to dwell on why things turned out that way. One obvious explanation is that the LTTE seriously underestimated the state of preparedness of the military this time around. Another theory that Gōta adduces with his experience of the battlefield, is that it takes time for any fighting force to get into the trend of things. Because of the long ceasefire, the LTTE had not been able to get into the fighting mode fast enough.

In 1990 and 1995, the difference was that the ceasefire did not last more than a few months or weeks. But by 2006, the absence of manoeuvre warfare and pitched battles had gone on for a few years, and both the armed forces and the LTTE were not battle ready. This is why it took the army so long to dislodge the LTTE from Mavilaru and why the LTTE was not able to overrun even small camps in the Trincomalee district. Both sides may have been training, but there is always a difference between training and actually doing it on the battle field. That is Gōta's take on the matter. Kumaran Pathmanathan, the senior most member of the LTTE left alive, has his own ideas about why the LTTE offensives failed in July/August 2006 which can be summarized as follows:

* During the long ceasefire from 2002 to 2006, the mindset of the LTTE middle rankers and fighting cadres had changed and they had got used to a normal life. The middle rank commanders of the LTTE had grown soft, leading comfortable lives in big houses. Pathmanathan says he was surprised to find that in Kilinochchi and Mulleitivu many big houses were owned by LTTE higher-ups. Thus the fighting spirit of the organisation had dissipated. Pathmanathan who had studied other struggles, says that you have to be poor to have the stomach for a fight.

* Because of the ceasefire, Prabhakaran himself had become more of a political leader, talking on a regular basis to representatives from the Tamil diaspora with dinners and meetings. He couldn't avoid these meetings and his lifestyle changed even without him noticing it. "It was like running a government" said

Pathmanathan. The military in contrast, especially after the Rajapaksa regime came in, was in the field, not in the conference room.

* The top military leaders of the LTTE were ageing and were past their prime and no longer able to do what they were able to do in their youth.

* The LTTE tried to function as the government and a state power with police stations, courts, prisons, a system of taxation and emigration and immigration regulations etcetera. This was a recipe for disaster as a government that wields power, loses popular support as time goes on, and at a certain stage may even be seen as oppressive. "Why do people change governments every five years in a democracy?" asks Pathmanathan and says that this law of diminishing popularity applies to all those who wield power including organizations like the LTTE.

Be that as it may, the attacks that took place in August 2006, showed clearly that the warnings that Wasantha Karannagoda had been sounding since 2003 about the LTTE's plan to disrupt shipping from the Trincomalee harbour and to isolate Jaffna, were absolutely accurate. After the LTTE attack on Muttur and the army camps to the south of the harbour were beaten back, Karannagoda wanted the Sampur area cleared of the LTTE arguing that the August 2006 situation could recur if that was not done. The army however said that they do not have enough troops for such an operation. (This was before the recruitment drive and *Api wenuwen api* had been launched.) Karannagoda then asked the army to give the navy some heavy guns and that they will clear Sampur themselves. The army was not agreeable to that either, because this was a land operation. At this point president Mahinda Rajapaksa told Fonseka that Sampur should be cleared.

With this, the army commenced search and destroy operations in the areas of Muttur, Kattaparichchan, Selvanagar and Thoppur. The operation to clear Sampur commenced in the pre-dawn hours at around 3.00 am on 24 August 2006. The Sampur area up to Foul Point was cleared by 4 September 2006, thus securing the southern belt of the Trincomalee Bay. The 22nd Division suffered only two fatalities in capturing Sampur while 166 had been wounded in battle. The clearing of Sampur was followed by an operation to clear the Manirasakulam area during the first week of October 2006. Special Forces teams along with troops from the 7th and 8th SLLI Battalions completed the takeover of Manirasakulam with no fatalities among the troops.

After Mavilaru, there was no real break in military operations until the end on the banks of the Nandikadal lagoon. Even if there were no infantry manoeuvres there would be Special Forces, commando and SIOT operations going on somewhere. The LTTE suffered another setback when the navy and air force in a combined operation destroyed one of their arms ships off Batticaloa on 17 August 2006. The very next day, in what was probably a revenge attack, the LTTE killed 11 Muslim irrigation workers in Potuvil. The operation to clear Sampur began in October 2006 with the induction of Special Forces and 'special infantry operational teams' (SIOT teams of which we shall hear more later) into the LTTE held areas. Brigadier Daya Ratnayake points out that up to that time, the LTTE had well trained small groups to carry out disruptive attacks and the army was constrained to deploy a large number of troops to contain the activities of these small LTTE groups in the eastern province.

When the operation to clear Sampur was launched, this usual pattern was turned on its head with the army deploying small groups and the LTTE being constrained to deploy large numbers of cadres to combat the activities of the army's small groups. Brigadier Daya Ratnayake explained that Special Forces operating in small groups could advance 20 km a day whereas conventional infantry would be able to advance only 5-6 km. At any given moment during the Sampur operation, 40 such Special Forces small groups and SIOT teams were kept on the field and the objective was to target the LTTE's cadres and restrict vehicle movement. The target was to kill at least 300 LTTE cadres and wear them down before the infantry moved in. Sampur was thus cleared with the Special Forces and SIOT teams dominating the area ahead of the defence line and the infantry following, a pattern that was to be followed throughout the war. The whole area from the south of the Trincomalee harbour up to the Verugal Aru river was cleared in this manner.

When the LTTE found it difficult to hold Sampur, they withdrew to Vakarai taking with them the entire civilian population of Sampur – about 30,000 people. The LTTE was clearly on the back foot and once again tried to extricate itself from this mess of its own making by making an announcement to the international community through Eric Solheim that they were willing to resume peace talks. But by this time, the government was no longer interested.

Thus Sri Lanka entered the last quarter of 2006 in an upbeat mood. The armed forces had beaten off LTTE attacks, an aggressive recruitment drive had begun, and the army had even begun advancing on territory held by the LTTE in Sampur. However, it was not all going one way. The Sri Lanka army celebrated its 57th anniversary on 10 October 2006. The very next day, there occurred an incident in Muhamalai that nearly halted the war before it even began. After the government managed to recapture the Mavilaru anicut and beat back the simultaneous LTTE offensives in Muttur, Kattaparichchan, Muhamalai and Kayts, the plan then was to clear Sampur. There certainly was no plan to open up a battle front in the Jaffna peninsula. Yet on the morning of 11 October 2006, the army launched a surprise attack across the Muhamalai defence line.

This operation turned out to be the closest thing to a military debacle that the Rajapaksa regime had to face. Within two hours of the operation having commenced, the army had been beaten back to where they had started. The defence specialist of *The Island* Shamindra Ferdinando placed the number of troops killed at 130 and the number of injured at over 300. The military hardware lost had included six armoured fighting vehicles, four Czechoslovakian built T-55 battle tanks and two Russian BMP infantry fighting vehicles. One of the tanks had fallen into an anti-tank ditch. The others had been disabled by anti-tank mines and artillery. The national security council was as taken by surprise by this attack as everyone else. By afternoon the same day, the Media Centre for National Security was trying to do damage control by portraying the whole episode as a case of the army having beaten back an LTTE attempt to overrun the army defence line in Muhamalai.

Air force jets had bombed and strafed LTTE positions in Muhamalai at around 11.15 am, after the army offensive had been beaten back. A senior officer of the ICRC had told *The Island* that 74 bodies of soldiers killed in Muhamalai had been sent to Omanthai, the southern border between government and LTTE held territory. The LTTE released photographs of the destroyed battle tanks and the bodies of dead soldiers to the media and this caused a great deal of embarrassment to the government. According to a report in *The Island*, Sarath Fonseka was later to admit in a discussion he had with US Undersecretary of State Nicholas Burns that 300 soldiers had lost their lives in Muhamalai. The victory at Mavilaru, Kattaparichchan, Selvanagar, Pahala Thoppur and Jaffna had been wiped off the slate in one fell swoop. Now what everybody was talking about was not the victory of the army in Mavilaru but the victory of the LTTE in Muhamalai. Lalith Weeratunga says that in the security council, the president was very clear about the need to take the east first. Sarath

Fonseka's thinking however had always been that the army should come down through Muhamalai. Not a word had been discussed in the security council before the October 2006 attack on Muhamalai was launched by the army.

This was Gōta's worst moment in the entire war. This seemed for all the world, like one of the numerous military debacles of the disastrous decade of the 1990s. All the components were there – the high death toll, the high number of injured, the loss of military hardware, and most galling of all – the handing over of dead soldiers by the LTTE to the ICRC. This single incident was enough to create public opinion against any resumption of hostilities. In fact Gōta's worry at that time was that this incident would turn opinion within the cabinet against going through with any plans to conduct offensive operations against the LTTE. The UPFA cabinet had experienced at first hand in the late 1990s, what botched military operations could do to a government.

Most politicians thought at that time that the military was incapable of prevailing against the LTTE. Now the army appeared to have proved once again that they could not face the LTTE even with superior firepower. It was perhaps only the faith he had in his brother that gave President Mahinda Rajapaksa the confidence to stay the course. There was also the fact that unlike almost all the presidents before him, Mahinda Rajapaksa was in on the details. He understood the ground situation well enough to realize that this was an unplanned attack which was nowhere in the overall plan for the offensive against the LTTE. In the Security Council, Sarath Fonseka explained that the Muhamalai offensive had been done hastily and that was why it had failed. However it was pointed out that no damage had been done that the security forces could not recover from. Battle tanks and lives had been lost, but not territory and the defence line itself had not been pushed back.

Chapter 56

Gōta Survives Suicide Attack

Despite the fully fledged war that had been going on in the Trincomalee and Jaffna districts, the ceasefire had not been repudiated by either party and was still in force at least on paper. The possibility of having peace talks was still being discussed by the peace mediators. The government agreed to have peace talks even at this late stage on three conditions namely; that Prabhakaran should personally guarantee a specific time frame to begin and end talks, he should guarantee that no acts of violence took place during the talks and that no arms would be smuggled in during that period. The talks were to be held in Geneva at the end of October 2006. In the meantime, the LTTE managed to chalk up another victory by carrying out the Digampatana truck bomb attack, killing 105 naval personnel on 16 October 2006.

At the end of October 2006, the final round of peace talks commenced in Geneva with Eric Solheim announcing that there will be no support from the international community for a military solution. This was a thinly disguised warning aimed directly at the government. As with all other talks, nothing concrete was achieved. The LTTE went to Geneva in a situation where they were on the back foot militarily. To make things worse, the prestigious International Institute for Strategic Studies in London announced that the LTTE and *Al Qaeda* were cooperating with one another in drug trafficking and the exchange of technical knowhow. This last piece of news would have jeopardized the relationship that the LTTE had with the Western powers and they needed a red herring to deflect attention from themselves and to put the government in the spotlight.

The outspoken Tamil National Alliance parliamentarian Nadarajah Raviraj was assassinated in the heart of Colombo in a daring attack in broad daylight on 9 November 2006. Suspicion immediately centered on the government and once again, as in the case of the 17 aid workers during the Muttur attack, the spotlight was on the government and not on the gross ceasefire violations of the LTTE. The LTTE was a past master in the art of manipulating Western opinion. The attackers who killed Raviraj had left behind a travelling bag with the weapon used in the assassination. It later transpired that this attack had been carried out by the LTTE. The Inter-Parliamentary Union which went into the Raviraj case was later to observe that the motorcycle the assassins escaped on had been traced. It had been sold to a certain Arul by two brokers, one of whom was called Ravindran.

The house at which Arul had been living had been found and the landlord, one S.T.K.Jayasuriya (a Sinhalese) had been arrested. This Jayasuriya had admitted that Arul was a member of the LTTE. Both Ravindran and Arul had fled to the LTTE controlled areas after killing Raviraj. The Scotland Yard team investigating the Raviraj killing had commended the local police for the work done, and the travelling bag with the weapon used had been tested for DNA samples to identify the assassins. After the war, the CID had even scoured the IDP camps in search of the elusive Arul and Ravindran. What the Raviraj episode showed was that the LTTE would not hesitate to sacrifice one of their own if the killing directs suspicion on the government and helps the LTTE by gaining them international sympathy.

On 1 December 2006, as the army consolidated its hold over Sampur, the LTTE made an attempt to assassinate Gōta by ramming a trishaw packed with explosives into his motorcade as he passed the *Pitthala* Junction in the up-market Cinnamon Gardens area of Colombo. Three of his personal bodyguards were killed in the explosion and the entire motorcade was wrecked. At the time of the attack, Gōta was using the old bullet proof BMW that the president had given him. The bomb used on Gōta was far more powerful than that which had been used on Sarath Fonseka a few months earlier. In Fonseka's case, the bomb was carried on the person of a suicide cadre and the only reason why Fonseka sustained injuries was because he was not using his bullet proof vehicle to travel about within the army complex. In Gōta's case, the bomb was 25 kilos of C-4 explosives packed in a trishaw.

There were only two routes that Gōta could take to work from his official residence and despite the attendant security threat, there was a route that his motorcade regularly took for the sake of convenience. All traffic would be stopped at certain places and the road cleared for the motorcade to pass, but there was no prohibition on being on the lane going in the opposite direction to that taken by the motorcade. The LTTE suicide cadre had positioned his trishaw on the other side of the road.

On the day in question, Gōta could remember approaching the Red Cross junction as usual and the motorcade took the opposite side of the road, as it approached the *Pitthala* Junction, there was a loud bang and he remembers being thrown to the other side of the rear seat. He had been sitting on the left side. He could not see anything around him because of the smoke. "What happened" he had asked in Sinhala thinking they had met with an accident. The security man on the front seat said "We're under attack". Gōta could vaguely see through the front windshield that something was burning on the middle of the road in front. It was the remains of the motorcycle with an armed outrider that had been travelling on his left. The motorcycle had taken the full impact of the blast and had been thrown high up in the air to fall in front of Gōta's car in the middle of the *Pitthala* junction.

Most of the damage to Gōta's car had been towards the front. Had the suicide bomber delayed the blast by just a second, the impact of the blast would have hit exactly the spot where Gōta was seated. His bodyguards used crowbars to force open the jammed doors of Gōta's car and he was transferred to another vehicle and taken straight to Temple Trees, the president's official residence. At the time of the incident, President Mahinda Rajapaksa had been at a meeting and on hearing the blast, he had told his security personnel that this was the time that Gōta went to office and to see what had happened. Gōta escaped unscathed from the attempt on his life. As was usual with such assassination attempts, it was only much later in February 2008 that any breakthrough was achieved in the police investigation, and that too by accident.

On 16 March 2008, an LTTE suspect was arrested in Dehiwala, a suburb of Colombo in connection with a different investigation. In interrogating the suspect, the police were able to ascertain that he had been directly involved in the plot to assassinate Gōta. On information elicited from him, another suspect 'Arunan' was arrested. From Arunan, sleuths were able to ascertain that the LTTE intelligence chief Pottu Amman and another senior intelligence cadre called Kapil Amman had personally given him the assignment to assassinate Gōta. They had shown him a map of the *Pitthala* Junction and explained exactly how the operation had to be carried out. Arunan had been given Rs 200,000 to rent a safe house in Colombo by one Paramadevan, a high ranking member of the LTTE intelligence set up. A separate safe house to fit the bomb on the trishaw was rented in Modera, a low-income area of Colombo.

The bomb, weighing 25 kilos had been brought from the Vanni in a double cab belonging to CARE International. The driver of this vehicle, one Thambirajah Yogarajah was an LTTE activist. The bomb had been concealed in the fuel tank of the vehicle. It was removed from the fuel tank in Wellawatte, Colombo and transported to the safe house in Modera in a trishaw driven by the suicide cadre, one Balasingham Vijayakumar who was posing as a Muslim by the name of Mohamed Lathif Mohamed Fareed. He had been taught the rudiments of Islam and Muslim customs so that he would be able to pass off as a Muslim in Colombo. A trishaw for the suicide operation was purchased for Rs 300,000 once again by Arunan, and the bomb was fitted on to this newly purchased trishaw at the safe house that had been rented for the purpose in Modera.

* * * * *

No discussion of the separatist war in Sri Lanka would be complete without a word on the suicide cult. In one sense, the whole LTTE was a suicide outfit because every fully fledged LTTE cadre wore a cyanide capsule around his or her neck. Every LTTE cadre was expected to bite the cyanide capsule in the event of capture. The LTTE did not look after their cadres who were unfortunate enough to get caught. A Tamil lawyer who appeared for LTTE detainees in custody told the present writer that the LTTE did not provide any back up support for their cadres who had been arrested. The blanket order given to all LTTE operatives was never to get caught alive. If they for some reason failed to bite the cyanide capsule in the event of capture, then they had to look after themselves from that time onwards. LTTE detainees did not have anyone to provide them with even basic needs such as soap or a change of clothing.

We saw how even important leaders like Kumarappa and Pulendran were expected to commit suicide when they were captured in 1987. How then does an ordinary LTTE cadre differ from a suicide cadre? The difference appears to be mainly in the deployment. An LTTE cadre with a gun in the Vanni is an ordinary cadre while one with an explosives jacket in Colombo is a suicide cadre. What motivates suicide cadres to volunteer for what they do is a much discussed question in this era of a global terrorist threat. Fanaticism is certainly the main motivating factor. Other reasons like isolation, lack of family ties, poverty, the lack of a future to look forward to, and various personal psychological issues could also be motivating factors. Not many suicide cadres have been captured alive. Of those who have been captured, fewer still have provided details about themselves.

One of the few complete personal accounts of an LTTE suicide bomber was that provided by Nagarajah Rajeshwari who was tried and convicted. To the Western mind, her story would have all the ingredients necessary to turn an ordinary person into a human bomb. Rajeshwari was born in 1980, and her mother was killed by her father when she was three years old. Thereafter she was brought up by her paternal grandmother. When she was seven years old, her father had raped her at the grandmother's house. Thereafter, she had been sent to live with her maternal aunt and her husband. They had a son called Ramesh. Rajeshwari had studied up to the General Certificate of Education (Ordinary Level) and then stayed at home. In the meantime, her maternal grandmother had deposited Rs 115,000 in her name in the bank.

In addition to that all her grandmother's lands had been written in Rajeshwari's name. The grandmother died in 1998. At that time, Rajeshwari had a love affair with a youth and her maternal aunt and her husband had got her to transfer all her lands and money to them for safe keeping saying that they will arrange a marriage with her lover. During this period, the LTTE issued an order stipulating that one member from each family should be handed over to them. In October 2000, her aunt had handed Rajeshwari over to the LTTE. She was taken to an LTTE training facility in Visuamadu and had undergone training for seven months with 150 other girls. During this period, high ranking LTTE female cadres like Vidhusha, Durga and Tamilini, among others had visited the training camp.

After completing training, her first assignment was to the intelligence division of the LTTE. She was tasked with monitoring the Tamil press. On the LTTE heroes day 26 November 2003, Pottu Amman the LTTE intelligence chief had come their camp had said that if there were any volunteers for suicide missions, to apply to him and that it was not necessary to apply to Prabhakaran (as was the practice earlier) and that the national leader had given him the authority to recruit suicide cadres. Rajeshwari and another girl by the name of Vasuki had applied to become suicide cadres. Rajeswari says that she volunteered to join the suicide squad as she had no family and nothing to live for. Some months later, in July 2004, she had got the letter asking her to join the suicide unit.

She and Vasuki had been taken to a suicide cadre training facility in Mulleitivu. There were 10 women and 20 men being trained at that facility. All of them had to wear face masks at all times when training so that one cadre would not recognize the other. Only the trainers were allowed to see their faces. They were trained in intelligence gathering techniques, communicating in code words, and to conceal cyanide capsules in their mouths and move around wearing the suicide vests etc. They were even taught the mode of dress and hairstyles that would be suitable for Colombo. In addition to this they were told about previous suicide operations carried out in Colombo and the commitment shown by the suicide bombers who had made the supreme sacrifice. Pottu Amman and a senior female leader called Manimekala had delivered lectures on this subject.

Later Rajeshwari was taken to Kilinochchi and placed in a house with eight other suicide cadres. She was trained to attack Prime Minister Ratnasiri Wickremenayake's motorcade in Nugegoda. The plan was that a contact would bring the suicide jacket to a clothing store at the Nugegoda junction and she would put it on in the toilet. She had been shown detailed maps of the Nugegoda junction as well as photographs of other Colombo landmarks such as the parliament, the presidential secretariat, the central bank, and other such places to familiarize her with the city. Later, she was given training to target an army bus transporting troops from Homagama to Colombo using a van packed with 50 kilos of C-4 explosives.

Before she was dispatched to Colombo, she had a felicitatory meal of chicken biriyani and ice cream with Pottu Amman and some other leaders of the black tiger unit. They had also posed for a photograph. (Usually, this felicitatory meal and photo opportunity would be with Prabhakaran himself.) Pottu Amman had told Rajeshwari that in the recent past, they had experimented with remote controlled explosions but that they were not successful and that the only way to ensure the accuracy of a hit is to make it a suicide attack. Later, she had been given a forged national identity card giving her a false name, with an address in Championpattu, Jaffna. Her excuse for being in Colombo was that she had been married with two children and that her husband and children had died in the December 2004 tsunami and that she had come to Colombo to go overseas. She was given two mobile phones. One was for her day to day use and the other was a dedicated phone to communicate with her handler in Colombo.

Once she was in Colombo, she was assigned a handler who would call her often telling her not to be distracted from her mission by what she sees of life in Colombo. Her mission was to detonate an explosives laden van targeting army troop transport vehicles. As the van explodes, a can of petrol placed near the front seat would ignite setting everything on fire so that no evidence would be left. On 10 September 2009,Rajeshwari had gone to the Vijerama Junction as usual, done the reconnaissance and informed her handler about what she had seen. Then she had taken a bus and come to the Nugegoda junction where she waited to board the 176 route bus that would take her to Kotahena. She was checked on suspicion at the bus stand by two soldiers. She had told them that she had come to see a patient at the Maharagama cancer hospital and that she was on her way back to Kotahena. The soldiers had handed her over to the Nugegoda police. She was later tried and convicted.

It should be noted that not all stories of suicide cadres is this picture perfect. Not many suicide bombers were raped by their fathers or cheated by their close relatives and handed over on a platter to the LTTE to be used as cannon fodder. Most had no other reason than simple fanaticism to want to die for the cause.

Chapter 57

Using the Aid Agencies

After the LTTE took the population of Sampur with them to Vakarai, the Rajapaksa government and the army were confronted with the problem of IDPs once again. Gōta's achievement was in the marshalling of men and material towards the objective of defeating the LTTE. He marshalled the international aid agencies as well towards this purpose. The presence of these Western organizations in the war zone was a nuisance to the government. But it was only these aid agencies that could go into the LTTE held area with supplies and therefore the government needed them. After the hostilities commenced, Gōta set up a body known as the Consultative Committee on Humanitarian Assistance (CCHA). This body was chaired by the then minister of disaster management and human rights, Mahinda Samarasinghe. It met for the first time on 14 October 2006, at the height of the Sampur operation.

Among those present at the first meeting of the CCHA were; the Head of Delegation of the European Union Julian Wilson, the Ambassador of Germany Juergen Weerth, the UN Acting Resident Coordinator Humanitarian Affairs Amin Awad, the Representative to the UN High Commission for Refugees Toon Vandenhove, the Head of Delegation International Committee of the Red Cross Jeff Taft-Dick, the Country Director, World Food Programme Valentin Gatzinski, the Head of Office, UN Office for the Coordination of Humanitarian Affairs Ms Joanna Van Gerpen and the Country Security Advisor UN Department of Safety and Security, Chris du Toit.

Later, US Ambassador Robert Blake would join this committee as the representative of the 'Co-Chairs'- the international body made up of the USA, the EU, Japan and Norway which presided over the ceasefire agreement and the peace process in Sri Lanka. Throughout the war the CCHA would meet regularly every fortnight at the defence ministry premises to coordinate humanitarian assistance for the north and east. Detailed minutes were maintained of the decisions taken at each meeting and the progress of follow up action was discussed at the subsequent meeting. This was a body that discussed the nuts and bolts of the relief operation and Gōta played a central role in the proceedings.

At the first CCHA meeting, one of the issues discussed was the chartering of a ship to ferry relief supplies to the conflict areas by sea. Toon Vandenhove the ICRC Head said that they were trying to charter a ship for the transport of relief supplies and passengers and was appreciative of the government's efforts to assist them in this matter. Minister Samarasinghe said that the cabinet has decided to charter three ships. But the deputy commissioner of essential services who was present, said that only one ship had agreed to sail to Jaffna due to security concerns. This ship had sailed under the flag of the ICRC but the LTTE had refused to guarantee the safety of the international and national crew. The ICRC had cause to be concerned. The LTTE had a history of having deliberately targeted ships transporting food to the north.

In October 1995, a ship chartered by the ICRC the *MV Sea Dancer* sank after being hit by a sea mine laid by the LTTE. Then *MV Mo Rang Bang* a North Korean owned cargo vessel which was transporting food to Jaffna was attacked in July 1997. Another ship *MV Princess Cash* which was transporting provisions for civilians was hijacked, looted and run aground in August 1998. This was followed by a suicide attack on *MV Mercs Uhana* in June 2000. A merchant tanker *MT Dunhinda* carrying much needed fuel to Jaffna was attacked off Point Pedro in October 2001. The LTTE was well aware that the efficient delivery of humanitarian assistance was one way the government would wean the civilian population away from them and they lost no opportunity in obstructing all such attempts. At this first CCHA meeting, the ICRC chief said that naval protection will be needed for the transport ships.

The A-9 road had been closed on 8 May 2006 due to attacks by the LTTE and there was no security for vehicles travelling on the road. The LTTE was trying to force the government to reopen the A-

343

9 road by blockading Jaffna. The government in fact made an offer to reopen the A-9 with an arrangement whereby food convoys to Jaffna would be checked by representatives of the Catholic Bishops of the north in Omanthai and once again at Muhamalai to ensure that what is passing through LTTE territory is only food for the civilians and not military supplies. This scheme was however turned down by the LTTE. Over 4000 retail shops in Jaffna had been forced to close by the LTTE. Only some 200 odd cooperative stores were distributing food and other essential items. One cooperative store manager was killed by the LTTE in an attempt to force the closure the cooperative stores as well.

The government went to remarkable lengths to keep Jaffna supplied, even air lifting eggs to Jaffna for Christmas. At that time, eggs were not available even in Colombo and what was sent to Jaffna were eggs that had been earmarked for the armed forces. In another instance, due to the spread of dengue fever in Jaffna, ten tones of mosquito coils were airlifted. At one point, there was no poonac for the livestock in Jaffna and this too had been sent. The World Food Programme country director said that his organisation had sent 1300 metric tonnes of food to Jaffna and that there was wheat flour in Trincomalee and that supplies could be sent if a ship was provided. Gōta observed that even items like tooth paste and soap was in short supply in Jaffna. One TNA parliamentarian had informed Gōta that the main shortages in the north were groceries, oil and spices.

No one was willing to provide a ship to transport food to Jaffna. It was T.Maheswaran, the UNP parliamentarian who came to the government's rescue by giving them his ships to transport goods to Jaffna. Maheswaran however, had wanted a letter from the government to the effect that his ships had been acquired by the defence ministry so that the LTTE could be told that he no longer had control over his ships. Gōta had thought it was inadvisable to issue such a letter as it could lead to other problems since Maheswaran was an opposition parliamentarian and Basil Rajapaksa had to prevail upon Willie Gamage an additional secretary to the defence ministry, to issue the letter. This however did not prevent the LTTE from killing Maheswaran later.

Gōta took good care to keep the discussion focused on material assistance to those in the conflict zone. In what would be a rare foray into anything but the physical needs of civilians, Gōta at the first meeting of the CCHA, said that there was a widespread belief in the country that the UN was working against the state, and one of the reasons could be because 90% of the UN's local employees were Tamil. He said that there could be problems when Tamil UN employees are sent to work in predominantly Muslim areas like Muttur.

The advisor to the UN Department of Safety and Security explained that most relief organizations work in the north and east and that the majority of those applying for these jobs were Tamil and that in any case Sinhalese were not comfortable working in those areas. The UNICEF country representative said that when working in un-cleared areas it was necessary to be in contact with the LTTE in order to provide relief to civilians. In the light of what was soon to happen, this exchange about the local staff employed by foreign relief agencies was almost a premonition. It was barely six weeks after this discussion that the attempt to assassinate Gōta was made. As we saw in the previous chapter, the bomb used in the operation had been brought to Colombo from the Vanni by a Tamil driver working for CARE International.

The CCHA was a nuts and bolts operation. The UNICEF country representative said that two flights a week to Jaffna were being made on a private domestic airline with health personnel, and three metric tonnes of high protein energy biscuits. These UNICEF biscuits would become a major bone of contention in the CCHA later because even the army special forces used high nutrition biscuits when they were out on operations and Gōta had the justifiable concern that if high nutrition biscuits fell into the hands of the LTTE, it would be used as food for their cadres during combat operations.

The aid agencies had to be handled carefully. While providing some material assistance for the civilians, they were doing everything they could to stop the war. Sparring went on between the government and the Western powers even within the CCHA. One of the ways that the West sought to force the government to stop the war was to cut off aid. Germany took the lead in this. At the 3 November 2006 meeting of the CCHA, minister Samarasinghe tabled a letter sent by the Sri Lankan Ambassador in Germany, informing him that funding had been withdrawn from German sponsored projects in Sri Lanka due to access issues. The German Ambassador Juergen Weerth explained that German organisations were having many problems in working in the north and east.

Citing an example, he said that the German government had an MOU with the ministry of education to reconstruct 14 schools in the Mulleitivu district but that not one had got off the ground due to the lack of cement and steel and donors were questioning the pile up of funds. Gōta pointed out that before 16 August 2006, there were no problems in transporting cement and steel and movement to Jaffna was not restricted. So it couldn't be due to the six week old war that the German projects had been delayed. At this point the UNICEF country representative had come to the German ambassador's rescue by saying that the construction of schools had begun but that they cannot be completed because contractors and workers were not willing to stay in the area.

That however was very different to saying that these projects had not got off the ground because of the restrictions on the transport of cement and steel to the north. The heads of aid agencies and Western heads of mission sitting on the CCHA, knew that they were perceived by the general public to be handmaidens of the LTTE. The EU head of delegation Julian Wilson timidly suggested that it would perhaps be timely for the government to issue a statement to the effect that the INGOs are doing a good job, particularly Medicines Sans Frontiers. Gōta, never a man to mince his words, said that MSF had made a mistake but that the government had decided to overlook it adding that it was not the organization that was in question but certain individuals. Two weeks earlier, the government had announced that it would be suspending the activities of MSF France, MSF Spain, MDM France and Doctors of the World USA for promoting LTTE activities. MDM France had been displaying a banner on their vehicles with the wording "Department of Health services of the LTTE".

Some CCHA meetings were attended by various highly placed visitors to Sri Lanka. For example the 25 February 2008 meeting was attended by UN Assistant Secretary-General for Political Affairs Angela Kane, The Deputy Head of Operations for South Asia Udo Wagner and the Deputy Director of Operations ICRC Dominik Stullheart. Minister Samarasinghe was marketing the CCHA as a model of best practice that can be emulated in other countries in similar conflict situations. Angela Kane said that she was indeed impressed by the CCHA mechanism and said that this was an example of how practical humanitarian issues could be solved through dialogue and cooperation, and that though there may be temporary setbacks and difficulties, this experiment in Sri Lanka with international aid agencies working together with the government in areas where a fully fledged war was in progress, was probably unique in the world.

Chapter 58

Vakarai and Thoppigala

After the LTTE moved out of Sampur taking the entire population with them, a tense standoff between the army and the LTTE ensued in Vakarai with the LTTE holding the civilian population hostage. With 30,000 civilians forcibly brought into Vakarai by the LTTE, the population had swelled from 15,000 to 45,000. Around 2000 LTTE cadres were now in Vakarai, a 600 square km area of which about 400 square kilometres was thick jungle. The army adopted the strategy of taking over the jungles first. The operation to capture Vakarai commenced on 30 October 2006 and went on for the better part of three months until the third week of January 2007. The first reconnaissance patrol went out on 29 October followed by the induction of about two dozen more into the jungles of Vakarai. Daya Ratnayake, who was then the commander of the 23rd Division which led the operation to take over Vakarai says that when the SIOT teams first went in, the jungle tracks in Vakarai were 'like the Galle road', with a great deal of vehicle movement by the LTTE. Within a week of the SIOT teams commencing work, all LTTE vehicle movement in the jungle stopped.

Usually, it was the LTTE that did such things to the army. This was the first time that the tables were turned. Army SIOT teams saw to it that LTTE cadres in the jungles were even deprived of cooked food by attacking LTTE logistics bases and cook houses just as the food was to be taken for distribution. There were various ruses adopted to draw the LTTE out, such as for example pretending to have an army tractor bogged down in the mud. The LTTE hearing about it would close in for the kill only to be ambushed by other teams laying in wait. In the old days, if news came that an army vehicle was stuck in the mud on a jungle track, the vehicle was genuinely stuck. But now the LTTE could not be certain as it could just as easily be a trap.

It did not take long for the LTTE to be dislodged from the Vakarai jungles and restricted to the towns and villages. The besieged LTTE then started preventing food supplies from reaching the swollen civilian population with a view to creating international pressure on the government to stop the offensive. When the government tried to send food into Vakarai, the LTTE attacked the food convoy and forced the lorries to turn back. They had prevented even the ICRC from sending food. The Tamil National Alliance raised a hue and cry in parliament about a 'blockade' of Vakarai stating that it was the army that was preventing food from reaching the civilians. One day, in the midst of the agitation launched by the TNA, the chief government whip Jeyaraj Fernandopulle phoned Brigadier Daya Ratnayake to ask him to explain matters to R.Sambandan, the TNA leader. Ratnayake told the TNA leader to come to Vakarai and see for himself the efforts that the army was making to send in food supplies.

After a standoff lasting about six weeks, the army managed to send in a convoy of vehicles with food. Even that was made possible only because the ICRC had managed to hammer out a deal with the LTTE. On 30 November 2006, the Batticaloa government agent S.Punyamoorthy confirmed that 117 lorries of food supplies had reached Vakarai. The goal of the army however was not to keep the civilians supplied and fed and in LTTE control, but to get them out. Following on the success of the small teams waging a war of attrition in the jungles, a fully fledged infantry offensive was launched on 6 December 2006. Troops of the 23rd Division moved out of the Kajuwatte camp into Vakarai. The final thrust to complete the clearing of Vakarai was launched on 16 January 2007. The 22nd Division which controlled the Trincomalee district also contributed to the takeover of Vakarai by inducting troops to the north of Vakarai through Mahindapuram during the final phase of the offensive on 17 January 2007.

With the commencement of the infantry offensive, civilians began crossing over into government held territory. Reception centres were set up for civilians and those coming over were treated well with soft drinks, buffet meals and Tamil films for entertainment while awaiting transfer to an IDP camp which the army called 'welfare centres'.

Sinhala and Muslim village folk from Welikanda would take turns to cook in the field kitchens. With people crossing over in organized bodies, the LTTE was not able to prevent the civilian exodus. When LTTE intelligence cadres came along with the IDPs, the army would get the tip off. By the end of December, over 23,000 civilians had crossed over to the government side.

Conditions in the IDP camps was at times better than what the IDPs had back home. The Veddah population in Ichchilampattu were also in these IDP camps and a Veddah chief was later to complain to the president that their people had got used to habits such as bathing every day in the IDP camps which had pipe borne water whereas water was scarce in Ichchilampattu and the returnees had some difficulty trying to adjust to the old conditions. The Vakarai operation had ended by the end of January 2007. The army captured vast quantities of weapons including over 170,000 rounds of T-56 ammunition, 312 T-56 assault rifles, two 152mm artillery guns and one 120mm mortar from Vakarai. Never before had LTTE weapons been recovered by the army in such quantities.

The two 152mm guns were undoubtedly the most eye-catching items recovered from Vakarai. Three such guns had been brought in by the LTTE in one cargo ship. Two were taken in trawlers to Trincomalee while one was taken to Veditaltivu on the west coast. The LTTE cargo ship transporting these three artillery guns among other items, was caught in a storm and they had to put into Sumatran waters to take shelter. At this point an Indonesian naval vessel had appeared and the LTTE crew had panicked thinking their vessel would be checked. But the Indonesian navy passed by without checking the ship. These guns had been transferred in mid sea and brought into Sri Lanka in 50 foot trawlers operating out of Negombo.

With the fall of Vakarai, the writing seemed to be on the wall for the LTTE. Completing the dismal picture, the LTTE's long time theoretician Anton Balasingham died in December 2006. As the army advanced from Vakarai into Batticaloa, the LTTE withdrew into the Thoppigala jungles, burying their weapons as they went. In a departure from past practice, the army kept going during the monsoon season as well. Many LTTE bunkers were under water and could not be manned, which meant that the terrorists had to be on the run. President Mahinda Rajapaksa visited Vakarai on 3 February 2007, soon after the area had been cleared. This was the first time that a head of state had visited a war zone. This ready willingness to visit the war zone despite the risk of attacks from infiltration teams was what gave the armed forces the feeling that this was a president to whom the war was a national priority and not just a regrettable necessity. Mahinda posed for a historic photo with the Special Forces troops who had cleared Vakarai. A Hindu priest who had garlanded the president when he visited a kovil in Vakarai, was shot dead by an LTTE hit team a few days later, highlighting the fact that the president had visited an area not yet cleared of the LTTE completely.

Following the capture of Vakarai came the operations to clear the remainder of the Batticaloa district (See map 4). The operations to clear Thoppigala to the west of Batticaloa began on 20 February and went on till 11 April 2007. It was at the height of the operations to clear the Batticaloa district that a group of VIPs including American Ambassador Robert Blake, Italian ambassador Pio Mariano, the German Ambassador Juergen Weerth and minister Mahinda Samarasinghe came under 120mm mortar fire by the LTTE soon after their helicopter landed at the Weber stadium in Batticaloa. The mortar attack had been launched from Vavunativu, an LTTE stronghold. It was estimated that around 400 to 500 LTTE cadres were in the Batticaloa area with small arms, mortars and a 12 barrel rocket launcher.

By the second week of April, Batticaloa too had been cleared and the LTTE had withdrawn into the Kanjikudichchiaru jungles of the Amparai district further south. The STF took over the clearing of the Tirukkovil-Kanjikudichchiaru area in the Amparai district while the army commandos were redeployed in the jungles of Thoppigala which was also cleared by10 July 2007, thus completing the clearing of the east. One of the highlights of the final push in Thoppigala was that government troops for the first time captured an LTTE multi-barrel rocket launcher with 12 barrels. The entire eastern province was now under army control. All this had started with the closing of the Mavilaru anicut. A story that circulated among LTTE cadres fleeing the eastern province, was that sea tiger leader Soosai had told Trincomalee commander Sornam's wife to tell her husband never to close even a tap again!

The total number of commandos killed in the clearing of the eastern province was 24. The number wounded was 266. In an interview with the Sinhala weekly *Silumina*, Gōta would claim later, that not a single civilian had died in the operations to clear the east. Even though no civilians had died, the IDPs who had been left behind by the retreating LTTE had to be resettled and in this, one of the biggest stumbling blocks turned out to be the international aid agencies

350

working in the east. As in the case of Muttur earlier, they seemed to be intent on not allowing the IDPs to return to their villages. This was the subject of a headline story in *The Island* of 24 March 2007. Responding to a query by a reporter, a UN spokesperson Orla Clinton had admitted that they had indeed distributed a leaflet titled "Returning home" to educate IDPs about their rights. According to Daya Ratnayake, the basic message conveyed by this UN agency was that the people should remain in the camps as it was unsafe to go back to their villages.

In this situation, Brigadier Ratnayake called the international aid agencies together and asked them how long they think it would take to resettle the 15,000 IDPs in Vakarai and all of them had said that it would take anything between one to two years. Ratnayake had then shown them a copy of the UN resettlement guidelines and told them that the resettlement will go forward on the basis of the UN guidelines and that it will be done within one month. Before the resettlement took place, de-mining was completed, electricity was provided, and the roads were repaired. Then one village at a time, the chief occupants of the houses were taken to identify their houses and soldiers helped them to clean and repair their houses prior to settlement.

The SLMM, UN, ICRC and other international agencies in the east all tried to undermine the army at every turn. On one occasion, a senior LTTE cadre was killed in an ambush and the police took custody of the dead body and reported the matter to courts. The Valachchenai magistrate ordered that the body be handed over to the family members who had come to claim it. The army carried out the court order. Then the Batticaloa ICRC representative had met Daya Ratnayake and said that the LTTE was asking for the body. Ratnayake told him that it has been handed over to the family. The ICRC man had then gone to the funeral house and told the bereaved family that the LTTE wanted the body and he had taken it, coffin and all, in his own vehicle to Thoppigala. Soldiers at an army checkpoint had reported to Ratnayake that an ICRC official was taking a dead body in a coffin into Thoppigala. The ICRC official Abhas Geha, was reported to the defence ministry and he was immediately expelled from Sri Lanka

UN agencies went to incredible lengths to help the LTTE. In April 2007, *The Island* exclusively reported that the UN had hushed up the abduction of two members of its staff by the LTTE. They had not reported it to the UN headquarters or the government of Sri Lanka.

The Acting UN Resident Representative Jeff Taft-Dick was summoned to the foreign ministry for a dressing down for not reporting the abductions. Even though the UN did not even report the matter when the LTTE abducted their workers, if the government arrested any of their employees it was another story. After the war around July 2009, two UN workers, one from the UNHCR and another from UNOPS was arrested for having been involved in transporting explosives to Colombo.

When they were taken in, their families had been issued receipts to say that they had been arrested and all the procedures of a formal arrest had been carried out. One employee of Save the Children Fund was also arrested in the same operation and a micro pistol was recovered from the drawer of his desk in his office. Despite all this, UN secretary general Ban Ki Moon's office issued a statement saying that two aid workers had been 'abducted' and two UN officials were sent from Geneva to Colombo to investigate. The police had however placed on the table the evidence against the two suspects and said that they were to be indicted. The LTTE had systematically made use of Tamil UN employees to transport arms and explosives to Colombo. Pottu Amman had an operative by the name of 'Alagan' working in the UN system to handle the aid workers.

As more and more territory in the east was brought under government control, the scope of the Consultative Committee on Humanitarian Assistance expanded and they established five sub-committees on education, health, logistics and essential services, resettlement and welfare, and livelihood. The last named sub-committee looked into the employment issues of the newly liberated people of the east. They prepared comprehensive district by district profiles for the livelihood situation in the districts of Jaffna, Kilinochchi, Batticaloa, Ampara and Trincomalee. Among the issues they identified in the Batticaloa district was a shortfall of good quality seeds for the upcoming cultivating season, the lack of paddy storage facilities and the lack of breeding animals for livestock development.

Among the problems identified by the livelihood sub-committee in the Trincomalee district was that fishing was permitted five days of the week, but only during daytime and the distance they could go out was restricted to 5 km and as a result the incomes of fishermen had gone down. Discussions with the security establishment had quite understandably not resulted in any relaxation of the restrictions. The LTTE used fishing flotillas as cover for their arms smuggling operations and also as cover to surprise naval craft in the vicinity.

After the entire east was brought under government control, the post-conflict plan for the east was discussed in detail. On security issues, it was decided that the police should take over the maintenance of law and order and that more local Tamils should be recruited to the police force. As an interim measure, interpreters were to be placed at police stations.

It was also decided to facilitate civil administration in the east by the provision of identity cards, birth certificates, title deeds for lands and the like and provision of basic services like schools and hospitals. (Many children born in the LTTE held areas of the east did not have birth certificates.) The UN Under-Secretary General for Humanitarian Affairs John Holmes was also present at this meeting of the CCHA. By January the following year, the Government Agent for Batticaloa was able to report to the CCHA that a batch of 150 Tamil police officers and 50 policewomen had been recruited and that another batch was being recruited but that there were very few applicants.

Whenever the LTTE was on the back foot, they would try to make a comeback with a devastating attack elsewhere. As they lost ground in the east to the army, the LTTE tried to score victories elsewhere. On 14 April 2007, Captain Piyal Silva of the navy was told that the LTTE had laid some sea mines off Nayaru and he was rushed to the place with a team of divers. What they found was an improvised sea mine with a fibre glass body containing about 25 kilos of C-4 explosives, and the detonator was made of an ordinary light bulb. When the bulb hits the hull of the ship, it shatters and sea water gets in. This sea water would act as the conductor of the electricity current to complete the circuit that detonates the mine.

The mine was attached by a line to a weight on the bed of the sea. By a miscalculation, the LTTE had laid it at high tide and at low tide, the tip of the mine was over a foot above the water. The LTTE had also placed some floaters to warn their own craft to keep away. An alert sailor had seen one of these contraptions in the water and raised the alarm. The officers on the boat had then fired upon this device with small arms and ruptured the bulb. With the sea water going in, it exploded thus confirming that it was indeed a mine. Captain Silva's team of divers recovered 24 such mines that day. Lines were secured to the weight of the mine on the sea bed by divers and a dinghy was used to tow them to the shore. As an additional security measure, a cap was placed on the bulb to prevent it from rupturing and any sea water getting in. All this was done manually by the divers. This was the first and the last time the navy came across such mines.

Just days later, on 18 April 2007, Captain Silva was told that a boat patrol had seen something unusual attached to a commercial ship transporting clinker to the cement factory at the Mitsui pier in the Trincomalee harbour. The device on the merchant vessel *MV Tabernacle Grace* turned out to be an improvised limpet mine. Capt Silva had the left side of the ship ballasted, so that it tilted to the left. The bottom of the right side came up revealing two limpet mines. As the ship tilted to the side, the mines slid down the hull. So long as the mine was in the water, its weight was neutralized by the water. But when it comes out of the water, the magnetic field is not sufficient to hold its weight, and it slides down. This told Capt Silva that there was no anti-removal device on the mine because an anti-removal device would have caused the mine to explode at the slightest movement.

Ropes were hooked to the mines and after the divers moved away, Capt Silva pulled the mines and they came off. Once they were in the water, they were weightless again and they were towed away by a dinghy. These mines contained 15 kilograms of C-4 explosives each. They were defused later. Capt Silva says admiringly of the LTTE's skill that the buoyancy of the mines in the water was perfect, even though it was only an improvised device. At that time, the navy never admitted that these were real mines. Even the police were not told the truth. The story given out to the world was that the LTTE had attached dummy mines to commercial ships to create the impression that even commercial shipping was not safe and to have insurance premiums for shipping bumped up. The navy even prepared a dummy mine to the same proportions of the actual mines and that was what was given to the police and put on display for the media. The world fortunately believed this story and insurance premiums did not go up.

Chapter 59

Revamping the Intelligence Setup

If the LTTE failed to deflect attention from its defeats in the east in 2007, that was not for the want of trying. The LTTE's luck just seemed to have run out. Every attempt they made to launch 'shock and awe' hits in areas outside the north and east failed. June 2007 was the month in which the biggest ever improvised bombs made of C-4 explosives were discovered. In no other country in the world has such large quantities of C-4 explosives been found packed in a single bomb. On 1 June 2007, a lorry packed with over 1052 kilos of C-4 explosives was discovered in Kotavehera in Kurunegala. The lorry had been stopped for a routine check. It had been transporting a load of coconuts at that time. When an alert policeman tapped the sides of the lorry, the hollow noise had aroused his suspicions.

A further search had yielded 47 flat packages of explosives which had been connected to the dashboard with wires, ready to be detonated. The driver and cleaner of the vehicle were promptly arrested. The police Sergeant D.H.M.Prematilleke who made the detection at the checkpoint was promoted to sub-inspector as was constable S.Herath who was promoted to sergeant. Several others including the OIC of the Kotavehera police station received financial rewards. Then on 29 June 2007, the biggest ever truck bomb with around 1120 kilos of C-4 explosives, was seized by the navy in Trincomalee following a tip off received from a mole in the LTTE. It was a freezer truck used to transport fish to the St John's market in Colombo and it kept doing its usual rounds even with the bomb wired and ready. Upon interrogation of the driver, the navy found that the explosives had been packed in a hidden compartment so cleverly made that looking into the back of the truck revealed nothing. They had to measure the outside and the inside of the truck to find that the inside was shorter than the outside.

The vehicle was then towed to the naval dockyard in Trincomalee where the defusing was done. The removal of the panels at the back of the truck revealed that the explosives were packed in steel canisters placed one above the other, with about 20 kilos of C-4 explosives in each canister. There were 56 such canisters and because of the way the explosives were packed, the full force of the explosion could be focused in one direction. Capt Piyal Silva of the navy who carried out the sensitive defusing operation thought there was the possibility of a pressure release mechanism which could detonate the bomb and elaborate precautions were taken in removing the canisters.

A system of pulleys and lines with a clamp was set up and the clamp would be placed manually over one canister at a time by navy personnel and they would then move to a safe distance before the lines were pulled to raise the canister. Once the canister was raised and no explosion had taken place, it would be taken down. Each canister had to be brought down in this manner as a pressure release mechanism could have been installed under any one of the canisters, and it had taken more than four tense hours for the whole operation. Each of these two mega bombs packed over five times the explosive power of the Central Bank bomb of 1996.

While the east was being cleared and preparations were being made for the Vanni campaign, the LTTE's usual attacks on civilians in other parts of the country continued unabated. In the first four months of 2007, bus bombs in Nittambuwa, Hikkaduwa, Ampara and Vavuniya had killed over 45 and injured over 140 civilians. The LTTE expended a great deal of effort on attacks carried out outside the north and east. Attacks on economic targets also had spin offs like crippling insurance surcharges which also helped the LTTE. Hence, protecting Colombo was a vital consideration. All victories in the north and east could be vitiated by just one successful attack in Colombo.

After the war commenced in 2006, Gōta brought all the different intelligence services in the country under one coordinated command. Past experience showed that intelligence services tended to work in closed compartments with little or no sharing of information and this had a seriously debilitating effect on efforts to combat terrorism. The Terrorism Investigation Department (TID), Criminal Investigation

Department (CID), the Colombo Crimes Division (CCD), the State Intelligence Service (SIS) the Police Special Branch, the Western Province Intelligence Division (WPID) the Director Army Intelligence, Director Naval Intelligence, Director Air Intelligence were working independently. Gōta created the position of Chief of National Intelligence to which he appointed Major Gen Kapila Hendavitharana. This was a cabinet approved post with direct line authority over all intelligence agencies.

Furthermore, Gōta got all these agencies to meet regularly every Tuesday at a meeting presided over by him personally. He insisted that all information should be shared and details of every incident and every investigation be discussed at such meetings. The arrests made, the progress of interrogations and so on also had to be reported. Apart from the sharing of intelligence, these coordinating meetings between intelligence agencies were forums where chinks in the security set up in the areas outside the main conflict zone, were dealt with. Gōta went down to the nuts and bolts of security issues and he made spot decisions on issues raised by the representatives of the various intelligence agencies. Examples of matters discussed and decisions made at these meetings would be as follows:

* Important private sector institutions such as the World Trade Centre were to be persuaded to increase searches of their premises and to purchase walk-through metal detectors and explosives detectors and other security equipment so as to enhance the security of their establishments.

* Garages and houses that had welding equipment had to be monitored closely to prevent the fitting of bombs onto vehicles.

* The identity cards of the Colombo port could easily be forged and the LTTE could obtain seaman licenses which would then provide authority to access ships anchored in the Colombo harbour. Gōta promptly ordered the navy to inform the civilian authorities responsible for issuing seaman licenses to ensure that the identities of the recipients were thoroughly checked and made available for screening by the intelligence agencies.

* The gas collection point at the Shell gas complex at ˌKerawalapitiya is located too close to the storage tank and it should be shifted further away from the storage areas. Gōta also ordered that the checkpoints for bowsers at the Sapugaskanda oil refinery as well as the Kerawalapitiya Shell gas complex be shifted one kilometre away from the present location.

* Large quantities of fuel, batteries, ball bearings, and cement were being smuggled into the un-cleared areas through Veditaltivu as there were no roadblocks to monitor the goods going from Colombo to Mannar which had enabled Veditaltivu to become a transit point. Gōta immediately gave the Vavuniya police the authority to establish the necessary roadblocks to prevent the smuggling of banned items to LTTE held areas by land. The director naval intelligence admitted that these banned items were moving to Veditaltivu by sea as well, with some fishermen using their boats to take the contraband into LTTE held areas.

* The police chief reported that earlier, LTTE suspects had been released because of the lack of Tamil speaking interrogators at police stations. He said that specially trained teams of interrogators had been assigned to some police stations now and that more such teams would be deployed in due course.

Gōta made the observation that a large number of policemen and soldiers were seen standing along the roads when VIPs move in those areas but that they did not know what to look for in their immediate vicinity so as to really secure the route. The police chief was told to instruct all officers in charge of police stations along such routes to be personally present on the scene and to instruct their men to check the shops, pedestrians and houses along the route. It was this kind of attention to detail that prevented the LTTE from launching attacks on economic and civilian targets in Colombo as they lost in the east.

* * * * *

Soon after clearing the east, moves were made to re-establish representative government in the province by holding elections to several local government bodies including the Batticaloa Municipal Council. Provincial council elections were also held in the eastern province. With this, the Karuna group transformed itself into a political party. Gōta had first established contact with Karuna before the 2005 presidential election when the latter was in exile in India. It was K.Wasantha, a member of the Jathika Hela Urumaya who later became a member of the Eastern Provincial Council who had first arranged a meeting between Gōta and Karuna's deputy Pillaiyan at a house in Colombo.

At that time, it was purely to get Karuna's support for the election. Pillaiyan arranged for Gōta to meet Karuna in India. Karuna was then staying in a hotel in Kerala with his wife and two children.

358

It was with good reason that Gōta had sought Karuna's help. The differences between the Jaffna Tamils and the Batticaloa Tamils was well known. In Gōta's reckoning, if Karuna's support could obtain some votes for Mahinda from Batticaloa, that would help counterbalance the overwhelming Tamil vote that would go to Ranil Wickremesinghe. Every vote counted in what was the closest fought presidential race ever. After Mahinda Rajapaksa won, Karuna came back to Sri Lanka. Gōta had always felt that the previous governments had not used the Karuna group the way they could have.

By the time Gōta got Karuna back to Sri Lanka, the group had lost their cadres and their weapons and were in a bad shape. He helped them to reorganize and establish a few camps in the east. Even though the Karuna group could not be made use of militarily, still they could look after a certain area, and obtain information and so on. Money was given by the defence ministry to maintain around 700 cadres. Karuna had come to Sri Lanka having sent his wife and children to live in Britain. After spending some time in Sri Lanka, Karuna had wanted to be with his children in London, and against Gōta's advice, he went. In Britain, he was jailed for some months for violating British immigration laws.

It was while Karuna was languishing in a British jail that the eastern provincial council elections were held. Gōta thought the Karuna group should contest elections, and Pillaiyan was encouraged to contest on the UPFA ticket. During a visit to India earlier, Gōta had discussed the Karuna group with the Indian external affairs secretary Shivshankar Mennon. He had explained that the Karuna group had not played a significant role in the military operation, but the fact that he was not with the LTTE had helped. Gōta also told Mennon that while Karuna was away, his group had split into no less than nine groups based mainly on allegations of use of funds for personal use. He also stressed that military intelligence officers had been trying to wean them away from activities like extortion and kidnapping for ransom and that the Karuna group has now got to get used to the political process.

Gōta knew that the problem will never end if there are military groups and his belief was that they should be transformed into political organizations. A political party was formed for the Karuna group to contest elections. At first they wanted to contest independently, but Gōta had vetoed the idea. The new party the *Tamil Makkal Viduthalai Puligal* or TMVP first contested the local government elections and won the Batticaloa municipality. Then they contested the provincial council elections that followed under the UPFA banner and won. By the time Karuna had managed to get out of jail in the UK, Pillaiyan was the chief minister of the east. Karuna himself was appointed to parliament on the national list and made a non-cabinet minister after he returned to Sri Lanka.

The Ranil Wickremesinghe and Chandrika Kumaratunga governments had treated Karuna so shabbily that many LTTE renegades who left with him may have felt that they would have been better off remaining with the LTTE. Karuna and the formidable fighters in his group were actually penalized for breaking away. Both Gōta and Mahinda wanted to send a completely different message to those in the LTTE, by demonstrating that those who defect from the LTTE and join the mainstream would be treated well.

Chapter 60

The Navy in Transition

Over the years, the sea tigers had tried on several occasions to destroy vessels used to transport servicemen between Trincomalee and Jaffna. Such attempts started with the attack on SLNS *Ranagaja*, a mechanized landing craft carrying 170 army personnel in October 1995. The battle lasted for ten hours and a fast attack craft managed to tow the landing craft to safety, but not before 20 army and navy personnel on board had died and another 76 were injured. This was followed by an attack on a merchant vessel *MV Nagoroma* also carrying service personnel in March 1996. In February 1998, the *SLNS Pabbata* another mechanized landing craft and a passenger ferry, the *Valampuri* were actually sunk off Pt Pedro killing 50 navy and army personnel and wounding another 15.

It was finally the attempt to sink the *MV Pearl Cruiser* in May 2006 with over 700 servicemen on board which has been recounted in a previous chapter, that convinced the navy commander Wasantha Karannagoda that an unconventional solution was called for, to meet the threat posed by the sea tigers. At that stage, the LTTE could put out to sea three times the number of craft put out by the navy and Karannagoda realised that the LTTE would keep targeting the troop carriers so long as they had the capacity to do so. For one Dvora to be out at sea continuously, they had to have three such vessels, one out at sea, one that was preparing for the next patrol and one that had just returned and was being refuelled and cleaned up. The navy at that time had only 45 Dvoras in all. So the maximum number that could be deployed at any given time was about 12, throughout the entire country.

Dvoras always patrolled in pairs. The LTTE's modus operandi would be to move their small boats along the coast to the point where the attack would be launched and suddenly, 25 to 30 boats would dash out against the two navy fast attack craft. Among the LTTE cluster would be about five suicide boats and the two Dvoras had to hold them off until reinforcements came. The reinforcements immediately available would be those already out at sea but for these vessels to reach the scene would take over one hour from either direction. Some boats could be low on fuel and unable to sustain a battle for long. Being surrounded by smaller LTTE craft, there was always the danger of one small suicide boat slipping through and ramming the Dvora. The LTTE had craft with four 250 horse power out board motors which gave these boats tremendous speeds.

The navy decided that they could not face the LTTE boats in a head on confrontation and the only hope of survival in such an attack would be to use evasive manoeuvres to tire out the LTTE attackers first by drawing them further out to sea and exhausting their fuel supply. The LTTE boats ran on petrol and could accelerate much faster than the diesel driven Dvoras. However the Dvoras were faster, being able to do 48 to 49 knots whereas the LTTE boats were slower with a maximum speed of 35 to 38 knots. Besides, the Dvoras were more stable platforms and the guns were more accurate. The Dvoras would attack and withdraw alternately without confronting the LTTE boats direct.

When the LTTE boats began to run out of fuel and started withdrawing, the Dvoras would move in for the attack. Another ingenious improvisation to meet the LTTE clusters was the fitting of a few Dvoras with multi-barrel rocket launchers. Initially, when these were fired, it shattered the windshields of the boats. Then they installed aluminium plates to prevent the windscreens from shattering. Even though there had been fears that the tremendous recoil from the MBRLs would damage the equipment in the boat, that did not happen.

The navy found that when these MBRLs were fired on land the recoil is much greater because they are fired off a hard surface, whereas on the sea the water absorbed the recoil much better. The MBRLs which are area weapons, were not accurate but the rate of fire and the air-burst shells which exploded in mid air sending down a shower of deadly shrapnel acted as a deterrent to LTTE boat clusters. After dispersing the cluster, with an MBRL salvo, the Dvoras could pick off LTTE boats one by one with everybody firing at one boat before going on to the next one. Another expedient was to keep the Dvoras continuously on the move without remaining stationery so as to avoid low profile LTTE suicide boats which may sneak up on them without being noticed in the darkness.

At one point the LTTE and the navy both had 23mm guns on their boats. This stalemate was broken only after 2006 when some old 30mm guns were installed on some Dvoras. This was followed by fitting of new 30mm Bushmaster guns bought from the USA which arrived around September 2007. Despite all these new manoeuvres and innovations, two Dvoras were lost in a single sea battle off Pt Pedro on 9 November 2006 in an attempt to defend the *MV Green Ocean*, a passenger ferry which happened to be transporting 300 civilians. After those two Dvoras were lost in a single battle, much discussion took place in the navy about how to face the LTTE's 'swarms'. Altogether, no less than six fast attack craft were lost by the navy in the year 2006. This, combined with the Digampathana truck bomb that killed over 100 naval personnel made 2006 the worst year for the navy ever.

Clearly a new approach was needed. By using suicide boats against the Dvoras the LTTE tried to break the backbone of the navy. The navy could not purchase replacements for these fast attack craft easily. They were not available ex-stock. Even if new boats were ordered it would take at least two years to build and deliver one Dvora. An Offshore Petrol Vessel will take even longer. So the navy could not afford to lose these boats. Losing fast attack craft in direct confrontations was one problem. The operational limitations of these fast attack craft was another important issue.

The LTTE brought their arms supplies into Sri Lanka in trawlers. The Dvoras had been specifically instructed by naval headquarters not to allow trawlers to come alongside as the LTTE would blast the trawler taking the Dvora down with it. It was on very rare occasions that LTTE trawlers had been caught smuggling arms into the country as the Dvoras tended to avoid them. The procedure laid down was that if a trawler was to be checked, a distance of at least 25 meters should be maintained between the two vessels, the crew had to get into a boat and move away from the trawler while two of the occupants had to swim across to the naval craft to be questioned. At times, one or two navy personnel would swim across to the trawler to search it.

Even though fishing was banned in many sensitive areas, the LTTE took full advantage of the Indian fishing trawlers that used to come close to the Sri Lankan coast poaching in the absence of Jaffna fishermen and the LTTE would hide among these Indian fishing craft. The LTTE in fact encouraged the Indian fishermen to come into Sri Lankan waters so as to provide cover for their smuggling activities. There was no military or naval presence on the coast between Pooneryn and Mannar on the western coast and this facilitated the smuggling of weapons and other material. Locating LTTE smuggling vessels among the swarm of Indian trawlers was almost impossible. On 29 July 2008 however, two LTTE boats were detected trying to come into Sri Lanka with the Indian poachers. The next day, Indian fishermen found two 120mm mortars still in their casing, which had fallen overboard when the munitions were being transferred into the trawlers to be brought into Sri Lanka.

Another problem was that the Dvoras could not operate in rough seas. There are sea states from zero to six, with 'zero' denoting a mirror calm sea and sea states five and six denoting very rough seas. A Dvora fast attack craft can operate at the most at sea state three, but not at five. One of the reasons for this was that the Dovras had planing hulls which meant that at speeds of about 20 knots, the hull emerges above the water. To operate in rough seas, ships needed a displacement hull which could cut through the waves. But a displacement hull would mean that the vessel would be slower. Dvoras found it difficult to operate in the rough seas during the monsoon season.

But the LTTE's multi-day trawlers could operate even in the roughest sea conditions because they had a deep draft, and with a heavy load, the stability of the vessel was that much better. Hence, the navy could not stop the flow of weapons into the country. The navy was not geared to handle this situation. They had to have bigger vessels with displacement hulls like offshore patrol vessels to operate in rough seas. Moreover, the LTTE had the advantage of being able to choose the time and place to smuggle in arms. They even used radars from the shore to locate the Dvoras and to find gaps between naval patrols so that their arms smuggling trawlers could come in undetected. The Dvora squadron was the backbone of the navy but they were no longer able to control LTTE activity on the seas.

The most radical decision made by Karannagoda during his tenure as navy commander was to reduce reliance on the Dvoras and other fast attack craft and to have a large number of small craft so as to outnumber the LTTE on the sea. This decision to establish numerical superiority over the sea tigers saw the navy going in for an ambitious small boat building project. The navy already had the capacity and the technology to build boats. They were already building inshore petrol craft at the rate of about five a year. Naval engineers were instructed to design a small craft modelled on the LTTE boats but which could carry a bigger gun, and had greater manoeuvrability and speed. After a process of trial and error, the navy finally settled for 250 horse power out board motors.

Prototypes were built and tested until Karannagoda found them satisfactory. Captured LTTE boats were also used in designing the naval craft. Two kinds of small boats were built. There were the 40 foot inshore patrol vessels which had 23mm guns on board and the smaller 23 foot 'Arrow boats' with 14.5mm guns. The production of these small boats began from December 2006 and they began to be deployed on the seas from April 2007 onwards. The inshore patrol craft were manned by 8 men while the Arrow boats had a five member crew.

The personnel to handle these craft were chosen from among the applicants to the navy's commando arm. This was the elite force of the navy comparable to the special forces of the army and were required to have very high physical standards, which meant that in any batch of trainees about a half would drop out during the one year of special training they had to undergo. These were highly motivated men whom Karannagoda formed into a new unit styled Rapid Action Boat Squadron. And these men were given training to man the new boats. After the small boats were stationed off Point Pedro, the problems that the navy had with LTTE boats harassing vessels approaching the KKS harbour stopped.

An ingenious improvisation that the sea tigers came up with to combat this new challenge of small boats were 'bottle mines', which consisted of two 1.5 litre PET bottles one packed with C-4 explosives with a fuse-well, and another similar bottle filled with sawdust and linked together with a line. When in the water, the weight of the C-4 explosives would ensure that the unit will be submerged and barely visible. About 15 to 20 such units would be linked together in a long line with a unit every 15 meters. These were laid targeting the approach routes of the navy's new small boats. The detonators were set to explode upon vibration. When the line gets entangled in the propeller of the small boat, it gets pulled in with a jerk and that jerk was the vibration that would set off the mine. The whole bottle mine set up was towed to the shore by one end of the line, and destroyed by navy explosives experts.

Karannagoda's mission was to change the entire way in which the navy did things. One of the several benefits of getting the *Jetliner* was that it released the navy from troop transport duties and provided them with more time for offensive operations. The difference was that the *Jetliner* could carry up to 3000 passengers whereas the ships used earlier, could carry only a few hundred men. *The Pearl Cruiser* for example, could carry only around 700 men. The navy had to escort it to and from Jaffna everyday and that was taking a heavy toll on their operational capacity as they could not do anything other than escorting this ship. *The Pearl Cruiser* was a slow vessel which took about one and a half days to get from Trincomalee to Jaffna and the return journey would take the same time. Because the carrying capacity of the vessel was small, more runs had to be done and consequently, *the Pearl Cruiser* was always on the move, tying up the navy in guarding it.

Karannagoda's plan was to get one massive ship which could carry a large number of passengers so that the passenger run could be reduced to just one per week, releasing the navy for other operations on other days. Many officers had objected to this plan saying that if the *Jetliner* was sunk with 3000 troops, the loss would be too much for the nation to take. The danger was that if it was hit by a suicide boat, there were dinghies and life vests, but there was no vessel in Sri Lanka that could rescue 3000 men and bring them ashore. But Karannagoda was adamant saying that the full strength of the navy should be deployed to carry the 3000 in one go, so that the navy would be freed for other operations.

So each weekly run of the *Jetliner* resulted in much tension at naval headquarters. When it was on the move, nobody went to sleep until it was safe in the harbour. Around 20 to 25 Dvoras and other fast attack craft would be used to guard the route the *Jetliner* would take. The vessel was kept 30 nautical miles off the coast. It had a maximum speed of 28 knots. Whenever LTTE boats put out from the coast, the *Jetliner* would go further out into the sea, beyond the reach of the LTTE boats. The *Jetliner* had been turned into a floating gunship with ten 14.5 guns and twelve .50 guns installed on the decks. There were also 50 light machine guns on board – all meant to be last resort defences against suicide boats.

Chapter 61

The Year of the Navy: 2007

One of the most important recommendations made in the US Defence Department report of 2002, was that the Sri Lankan navy had to develop the capacity for deep sea operations in order to halt the flow of arms to Sri Lanka. The navy did not have corvettes, frigates, destroyers or battle ships which could carry out operations in the deep seas. As explained in a previous chapter, the LTTE's modus operandi was to bring the arms in large cargo ships to the equator, where they were offloaded onto smaller tankers. The tankers would then bring the cargo closer to Sri Lanka and multi-day trawlers would collect the goods in mid sea in international waters. The LTTE arms smuggling vessels destroyed by the navy in 2003 were both tankers and not cargo ships which meant that the navy was reaching only up to the middle of the LTTE weapons smuggling chain. The weakness of the navy lay in that they tended to wait for LTTE ships to come to Sri Lankan territorial waters before taking them on.

Another LTTE arms smuggling tanker was destroyed 240 km to the east of Batticaloa on 17 September 2006. The navy was helped by the air force in that operation. At that stage, it was by monitoring LTTE satellite phone conversations that the navy got information about arms shipments. When the LTTE tanker comes around 300 nautical miles off the coast of Sri Lanka, they inform the LTTE by satellite phone and then the trawlers move out to collect the cargo. The directorate of military intelligence could tap satellite phones and they monitored the conversations and found out exactly where the operation was taking place. The technology was available to trace the origin of the call and map its exact location on the global positioning system.

But one day, a certain newspaper revealed that military intelligence was monitoring LTTE satellite phone conversations to obtain information about arms shipments. After this, the LTTE stopped using satellite phones from their arms vessels. The navy was furious. Many naval officers say that the information was deliberately leaked to the newspapers by a certain group in the army who were well known to be antagonistic to the navy. The army had complete control over the information flow because the monitoring was done by army intelligence. The navy was now totally in the dark about LTTE weapons shipments. They had got some information from the crews of two captured LTTE trawlers and the sea tiger survivors of some other confrontations, but that was far from being specific actionable data.

It was a well known fact that the LTTE brought in arms to Sri Lanka in multi-day fishing trawlers, but only a very few were apprehended over the years. One difficulty was that the LTTE trawlers were indistinguishable from genuine civilian trawlers. As Commodore Ravi Wijeguneratne explains, about 3000 fishing trawlers went out to sea from the south, and there were about 8000 Indian trawlers also moving about in the Palk Straits. Checking all these vessels was not possible. The only way to stop the smuggling was to strike at the LTTE's bulk ships instead of looking for trawlers, needle-in-haystack fashion. The navy knew that unless these mother ships were destroyed, there was no way to really stem the flow of arms to the LTTE.

With information about LTTE arms shipments suddenly being blacked out due to the LTTE giving up the use of satellite phones, Karannagoda spoke to the then American ambassador in Sri Lanka and impressed upon him the threat that the LTTE poses as an international terrorist organization. He stressed that the LTTE was the only terrorist outfit in the world that had arms smuggling ships and that given their expertise, and their contacts with *Al Qaeda*, they posed a global threat. After about two weeks, four Americans turned up at naval headquarters headed by a lady, who met Karannagoda and his intelligence officers and took notes and collected all the information they could about the LTTE's maritime operations.

About a month after that, the defence attaché of the US Embassy turned up at naval headquarters with a black and white satellite image on which stationary ships appeared as white dots and ships on the move were indicated by dots with a little white tail. He pointed to some dots on the photograph and told the navy that these were the ships the navy was looking for. When the locations were plotted on the map, the navy found that the LTTE ships were about 3000 kilometres away from Sri Lanka. In desperation, Karannagoda asked the defence attaché whether the Americans could not do anything about the LTTE ships, to which the defence attaché replied that exchanging information was the maximum they could do.

Karannagoda consulted the engineers of his offshore patrol vessels and they were confident that their vessels could do the trip. The problem however, was refuelling in mid-sea. When the suggestion came that they should use the 1066 tonne P520 as a logistics ship to carry fuel for the combat vessels, Karannagoda had been sceptical about this 44 year old ship with a single engine being able to do the job. It had once been an ocean going trawler which was donated to Mahinda Rajapaksa when he was the prime minister by the Sri Lankan community in France. It had been earmarked to be scrapped but was still usable. Mahinda had given the ship to the navy. One engineer assured Karannagoda that the single engine despite its age, would keep running and not conk in the middle of the sea. This ancient vessel, which could do only 8 knots at full speed was then converted into a logistics ship with fuel and water tanks and cold rooms to store food. It was not just the P520 that caused concern. The other five vessels were also ancient.

Among them were two offshore patrol vessels, one of which was from the US coast guard and was 36 years old. The biggest vessel the navy had was a 105 meter offshore patrol vessel purchased from India, which was 19 years old. This ship had a World War II Borfors gun as its main armament. Then there was a 47 year old merchant vessel the navy captured while she was engaged in human smuggling. This was impounded by the courts. The navy paid a deposit to the courts and took it and converted it into another logistics vessel. The two logistics vessels refuelled and re-supplied the other four that went to destroy the LTTE ships in mid sea, both on the onward and return journeys.

Medical teams were in two vessels because not all ships could carry additional personnel. If there had been an exchange of fire, there was no guarantee that medical personnel could be transferred to the ship where they were required. Besides, no other nation had been informed of the operation and they could not seek help from any other country in case of an emergency. It would take seven to eight days to get to back to Sri Lanka. If any deaths occurred, there were no freezer compartments on board and the dead would have to be given a sea burial. It was with all these risks that the navy undertook its first deep sea operation and what was probably the strangest engagement in the annals of naval warfare.

Capt Piyal Silva was the skipper of the *Sayura* an offshore patrol vessel that participated in this deep sea operation. When they set out, what the crew was told was that an arms ship for the government was coming from China and that they were going out to escort the vessel. It was only after they were 200 nautical miles from land that the crew were mustered and told what their real mission was. The mission commander Capt T.L.Sinniah also sailed on the *Sayura*. The two logistics ships had sailed from Galle earlier to the equator and waited on standby to fuel the gun boats. It took about six days to sail to the location. Combat drills and emergency exercises were also carried out en route.

On 16 September 2007, the first LTTE ship to be sighted was a small tanker. What raised the suspicions of the navy was that it was floating way off the established sea lanes. The LTTE crew on the tanker had first thought they were being challenged by the Australian navy as they never expected the Sri Lanka navy in those waters. When asked for their identification, the LTTE vessel provided wrong information. They did not display a flag and spoke in an unmistakable Tamil accent. Besides, the details they provided were not on the automatic identification system (AIS). The navy ordered the crew of the LTTE ship to abandon ship, prior to a team from the navy boarding it. The LTTE crew refused.

The navy then told them that they knew who they were. At that point the LTTE tanker had broken off radio communication. Then the navy fired warning shots over the tanker. The LTTE fired back with small arms. A confrontation ensued during which two arrow boats were also launched from the naval vessels and they went close to the LTTE tanker and fired RPGs at the waterline, sinking it. While this was going on, another LTTE ship was detected, this time a bulk carrier. The navy went through the same identification procedures and a call to surrender followed by an exchange of fire which sank the second ship. Then a third ship was detected and engaged by the offshore petrol vessel *Samudura*. The LTTE ship was trying to make a getaway. The other naval vessels rushed to the scene and darkness had fallen by the time they managed to destroy the third ship.

The LTTE crew in the third ship put up a desperate fight as they were aware that the other two ships had been destroyed. LTTE cadres were firing heavy calibre mortars from the deck of the ship at the pursuing naval vessels. But finally the third ship was also destroyed in a huge explosion. The offshore patrol vessel *Suranimala* had an RCL anti-tank gun which is what got the ship. A fourth ship was detected but with the long drawn out struggle to sink the third vessel, the fourth managed to get away. By this time, the Sri Lankan naval contingent was running out of fuel and Karannagoda ordered them back without pursuing the fourth ship.

When the four naval vessels, *Samudra, Shakthi, Sayura* and *Suranimala* returned to Trincomalee after having destroyed these three ships in Sri Lanka's first deep sea operation, a grand ceremony was held to receive the returning heroes at the Trincomalee naval base. President Mahinda Rajapaksa, Gōta and several cabinet ministers were present on the occasion. Later the navy came to know the whereabouts of the fourth vessel that had escaped and it was destroyed on 7 October 2007. Once again, the *Sagara, Sayura* and *Suranimala* went out of Trincomalee and the two logistics vessels were waiting at the equator to refuel the combat vessels. The LTTE cargo vessel was detected, they failed to identify themselves, and were fired upon and sunk.

What was significant was that none of the ships that were fired upon by the navy escaped. Sinking a ship is no easy task. Ships have water tight compartments and if damaged, water gets in only to that compartment. To sink a combat craft, about a third of it would need to sustain damage. The cargo ships and small tankers used by the LTTE being civilian craft, did not have the same water tight integrity as combat vessels. However, even civilian vessels are not easy to sink. One of the factors that helped was that the LTTE ships too were carrying explosives which exploded aiding in the navy's task. The last of the four LTTE ships was the one that put up the most resistance. For nearly 12 hours the navy was chasing the ship and the LTTE was firing 81mm mortars from their deck at the pursuing naval vessels. They were essentially firing their cargo at the navy. But with all the rolling and pitching at sea, the mortars were not as accurate as on land. However, it did compel the navy to maintain their distance.

The naval gunboats also used land based multi barrel rocket launchers in these sea battles. Platforms were built on the decks and eight barrels of the usually 40 barrel MBRL were detached and fixed on to the platforms. The MBRL had worked very well on the seas. If fired on a trajectory, the MBRL has a range of 20 km. But on the high seas, the navy fired the MBRLs at the LTTE ships horizontally, in direct fire like a cannon. So the chances of hitting a ship was that much greater. There were also snipers on board the navy vessels and on one occasion a sniper hit a gas cylinder on an LTTE ship's deck and that set the ship ablaze. The destruction in the latter part of 2007 of the LTTE's gun running vessels depleted their stocks of mortars and artillery rounds and was one reason why the army progressed so rapidly after mid-2008. G.V.Ravirpiya, who commanded a brigade under Jagath Dias before becoming commander of Task Force 8, confirms that the tigers were using artillery rounds very carefully throughout the Vanni operations and that they were not firing the same way the army was.

In discussing the LTTE's arms smuggling operations, a logical question that needs to be asked is why air force jets could not be used to attack LTTE gun running boats on the high seas. One issue was the low endurance of the combat aircraft. A Kfir could not move beyond 200 km off the shores of Sri Lanka. Another limitation was that all jets could operate only from Katunayake with no other airfield capable of accommodating jets on the eastern coast. So that too limited the outreach of the jets which had to fly across the country to get to the eastern seas where most of the arms smuggling took place.

During the three decade long war, 28 naval vessels were destroyed by the LTTE, almost all of them in head-on encounters. The vessels lost were all fast attack craft or larger vessels which could be anything from 45 to 60 tonne seagoing craft. The Dvoras were crewed by 18 men. The smallest vessel in the list of naval craft destroyed by the LTTE below is the Z 142 which was an Arrow boat crewed by five men. The naval vessels lost were as follows.

P 143 - Destroyed by sea mine near Karainagar in 1991.

P 116 - Stolen by LTTE divers from Mandativu pier 30 August 1992.

P 115 - Destroyed by suicide boats, 26 August 1993.

P 121   - do -

P 464 - Sunk by LTTE, 29 August 1993.

SLNS Sagarawardhana - Sunk off Mannar, 19 September 1994.

SLNS Ranasuru - Destroyed in Trincomalee harbour, 19 April 1995.

SLNS Soorya   - do -

A 512 (cargo vessel) - Destroyed in Trincomalee harbour, 17 October 1995.

P 458 - Sunk in suicide attack off Chalai, 30 March 1996.

SLNS Ranaviru - Sunk off Mulleitivu, 18 July 1996.

P 452 - Sunk off Kokilai, 18 October 1997.

SLNS Pabbatha (mechanized landing craft) - Sunk off Point Pedro, 22 February 1998.

SLNS Valampuri (troop transport vessel)   - do -

P 498 - Sunk off Mulleitivu, 30 October 1998.

P 497 - Sunk off Mulleitivu, 21 March 2001.

P 251 - Destroyed off Trincomalee harbour, 3 September 2001.

P 476 - Destroyed in suicide attack off Trincomalee harbour, 6 January 2006.

P 431 - Sunk off Mannar, 25 March 2006.

P 418 - Destroyed off Point Pedro, 11 May 2006.

P 461 - Destroyed off Point Pedro, 9 November 2006.

P 416   - do -

P 132 - Sunk off Silavathurei, 6 April 2006.

P 413 - Destroyed off Delft, 26 December 2007.

P 438 - Destroyed off Nayaru, 22 March 2008.

A 520 (logistics ship) - Destroyed in Trincomalee harbour, 19 May 2008.

Z 142 (Arrow boat) - Destroyed on 1 November 2008.

P 434 - Destroyed off Mulleitivu, 19 January 2009.

P 020 - Sunk off Mulleitivu, 4 May 2009.

No other navy in the world had suffered as much damage due to terrorism.

Chapter 62

The War Behind the Frontlines

One of the things that Gōta had learnt well from Brigadier Wimalaratne was the importance of motivation. This was a principle he applied not just to the military but the police as well, especially those serving in the intelligence gathering units. Knowing that the security of Colombo depended on these police personnel, Gōta made it a point to summon all members of these intelligence units down to the last reserve police constable and talk to them about the importance of the job they were doing and why their contribution was essential to orchestrate the war to a victorious conclusion. During these meetings, he would at times ask even reserve police constables to explain what he as an individual, had done when bombs went off in Colombo.

One thing that Gōta was acutely receptive to was negative publicity regarding the war. He knew that negative publicity could stymie the entire war effort and negative publicity tended to be generated more when an attack took place in Colombo than when lives were lost in the north and east. He knew that the key to keeping the war on track in the north was to keep Colombo and other parts of the country free from terrorist activity. Whenever the LTTE carried out a bombing in Colombo, Gōta would immediately call the CID, TID, NIB, WIPD and all other intelligence and investigative units of the police and the military and ask them why nothing was being done to stop these incidents. He kept the pressure on them to deliver. As the coordination between the various intelligence arms and the police improved, their ability to crack cases also improved.

Despite the desire of the intelligence services to gather information about LTTE activities, at the initial stages of the final war, they were mainly groping in the dark. The biggest obstacle to gathering information was the language barrier. While many Tamils knew some Sinhala, the Sinhalese were largely ignorant of Tamil. The LTTE made it impossible for Tamil recruits to join the police force. Throughout the 1970s they killed mainly Tamil policemen and ensured that no Tamil will ever think of joining the police force. Because of the lack of Tamil speaking police and intelligence operatives, it was always difficult to obtain information about what was happening within the large Tamil speaking community in Colombo.

The inability to penetrate the LTTE network led to some desperate measures. On 7 June 2007, as the government completed the clearing of the east and commenced the Vanni operations with the launch of the 57th Division to the east of Vavuniya, police and army units surrounded the numerous 'lodges' in Colombo city where Tamils coming from the north found cheap accommodation, screened the occupants and those thought suspicious were put on buses and sent off to Vavuniya. There was an immediate outcry at this, with the press, human rights groups as well as opposition political parties crying foul. M.A.Sumanthiran, a lawyer petitioned the supreme court an obtained an order calling for an immediate halt to the expulsions.

Apart from the ordinary civilians who managed to flee the north and east, many LTTE operatives and suicide cadres coming from the north also stayed at these lodges. Even Rajeswari the suicide cadre whom we wrote about in a previous chapter, stayed at one of these lodges when she first arrived in Colombo. As the military operations intensified in the north and east, more and more people had come to Colombo and this was raising concerns among security personnel. This in fact had been the main topic of conversation at the western province security conference held on 4 June 2007. It was at this conference that it was decided that those who could not come up with a proper reason for being in Colombo, would be sent back. The police had even held a discussion with the owners of these 'lodges' to seek their cooperation in this matter.

It was after this that 376 individuals who could not explain what they were doing in Colombo had been provided transport to go back to the north. They were transported up to Vavuniya at state expense. This was probably the most unpopular, and most universally condemned action taken by the security forces in the course of the last war. Gōta was to explain later in an interview on *Derana TV* in August 2007 that this was not a case of evicting innocent Tamils from lodges in Colombo but that when suicide cadres came from the north, they usually took up residence in these lodges and that they had taken in suspicious individuals, who had been questioned at length and only the most suspicious who could not adduce a valid reason for being in Colombo were asked to go back.

For many years, the war in the north was an ever present, but low intensity conflict for those living in Colombo. They became aware of the war only when the LTTE carried out an attack in Colombo, but the initial excitement would soon die down until the next bomb went off. Things had gone on like this for years and decades, and people had come to assume that everything could be normal in Colombo while the battle was being fought in the north and east. Looking back at the reaction to the expulsion of the 376 suspicious individuals from Colombo, Gōta says that this highlighted the difficulties that the security forces had to face - the LTTE was sending suicide bombers to Colombo, but the defence establishment was prevented from giving priority to security concerns.

This was followed by an even more serious crisis. A fundamental rights case had been filed in the supreme court by a Sinhalese man who had been arrested at a security checkpoint in Colombo on the grounds that he did not have a valid driving license. In the judgement of the supreme court delivered on 3 December 2007, the chief justice Sarath N.Silva ordered the dismantling of all permanent road blocks and checkpoints saying that they violated the freedom of movement. During the hearings, the chief justice issued another order saying that no household should be searched between 9.00 pm and 6.00 am, unless it was absolutely necessary, and the local police should be present when the search is carried out. Given the all out war that had been launched against the LTTE, such rulings would seem daft, and indeed, they were.

Minister Jeyaraj Fernandopulle, the outspoken chief government whip in parliament, lashed out at this supreme court ruling at a discussion on *Isuru Radio* where he said, "*Police cannot search houses in the night, Lodges cannot be searched, Roadblocks have been removed. Now the tigers have been given a free visa to infiltrate Colombo and kill anyone...*" Gōta was rattled by this ruling as it could have jeopardized the entire war effort by leaving the whole of the south open to LTTE vehicle bombs and suicide bombers. In the immediate aftermath of the supreme court ruling, some check points were removed, but the checking continued nevertheless, this time, security forces personnel designated as 'mobile units', were checking vehicles in exactly the same place where the old permanent checkpoints had been.

When the supreme court ordered the removal of permanent road blocks, and banned night time searches, that was at a stage of the war when this kind of protective measures were absolutely necessary. As the pressure mounted on the LTTE in the Vanni, they were going to step up attacks in Colombo. Gōta explained to his colleague the secretary to the ministry of justice Suhada Gamlath, why such measures were necessary. Gamlath had thereupon had a discussion with Sarath N.Silva and arranged for Gōta to see him in his chambers. During this meeting, Gōta explained matters to him and certain compromises were worked out, such as the shifting of some road blocks, and not having permanent barriers and so on.

It was easy enough to circumvent the ban on night searches of houses. The requirement was that if such a search is being carried out, a member of the local police force had to be present. This was not difficult as most of the police units such as the Western Province Intelligence Division for example, had five policemen attached to every police station. As the war escalated in 2008, these two bizarre rulings of the chief justice were forgotten by everybody, including Sarath N.Silva himself. What this showed however was that there was a large constituency in Colombo that expected a normal life in the middle of a war against terrorism.

Road blocks were an integral and indispensable part of Gōta's plan for the defence of Colombo. At one security coordinating meeting, he had told those present that that when he went to Israel, the Israeli army had told them that the main way they prevented suicide bombers from getting to Tel Aviv was by thoroughly checking all traffic coming in from the Gaza strip and the West Bank into Israel at permanent road blocks. Thus, the main checkpoints in Medawachchiya, Hathares Kotuwa on the Trincomalee-Habarana road and at Manampitiya on the Batticaloa-Polonnaruwa border were absolutely essential for the security of the rest of the country. Thorough checking of goods being brought from the north and east was done at these checkpoints with the entire cargo unloaded, checked and loaded once again. The vehicles too were thoroughly checked and kept overnight at the checkpoint for the purpose.

There was no doubt that these arrangements had a deterrent effect on the LTTE's arms and explosives transfers to Colombo. Nothing was left to chance. There were State Intelligence Service sleuths working undercover among the naatamis (labourers) with some even suffering back injuries as a result of the unaccustomed heavy lifting. The head of SIS would call together these hard working sleuths and give them a good meal just to show them that their labours were not unappreciated. The SIS also compiled a booklet for security forces personnel with instructions on what to look out for at checkpoints, giving real examples of the methods used by the LTTE to smuggle explosives and armaments into Colombo and other areas of the south.

Such methods included false panels on lorries, smuggling items in fuel tanks of vehicles, depressions carved out in school text books, depressions carved out in shoes and sandals, tiny cyanide capsules in the hairdo of female suicide cadres, explosives hidden in children's toys, inside the audio set ups in trishaws, in the upholstery of vehicles, etc. Probably the most bizarre method used was to transport explosives inside coconuts that had been drained of water. Another thing that security personnel were asked to look out for was the 'suicide bra' worn by women. A fully fledged suicide vest in its own right, the suicide bra would look like an ordinary padded bra from the outside. It was one of these that was used in the attempt to assassinate minister Douglas Devananda on 28 November 2007, probably the only instance in the world where a suicide bomber was caught on camera in the act of exploding herself.

Ironically, it was just after the above mentioned rulings by the chief justice that the US Federal Bureau of Investigation declared in January 2008, that the LTTE was the world's deadliest terrorist organization, outranking even *Al Qaeda*. In fact the FBI would have been quite amazed to learn that there were people in Sri Lanka who actually expected the government to combat such an organization without permanent checkpoints on the roads or night searches of suspected terrorist locations and without removing suspicious persons from sensitive localities. Fortunately however, the ability of the police to detect LTTE activity in Colombo improved phenomenally and several intelligence breakthroughs prevented the city from becoming a killing field for the LTTE.

On 4 June 2008, an improvised explosive device was exploded on the railway tracks as the Panadura-Colombo train approached the Dehiwela station, injuring 22 commuters and causing some harm to a railway carriage. The Western Province Security Coordinating Conference was in session when this incident occurred and Gōta immediately got the police to follow it up. A woman in the vicinity had seen a man pressing the remote controller and had raised cries at which a passing trishaw driver had confronted and grappled with the suspected terrorist. The LTTE cadre had wrestled free and had fled, but in the melee he had dropped his wallet, in which was a parking permit which had his passport number. Using the passport number, the police obtained a photograph of the terrorist from the department of immigration and emigration.

The police then traced his workplace through the number of a motorcycle on the parking permit in his wallet. The motorcycle belonged to an air conditioning maintenance company which handled the Bank of Ceylon headquarters building air conditioning system. The police also found that the bomber had a colleague named Kanagarajah at the same workplace who lived in Bambalapitiya. The vehicle permit that gave him away had been given to him to enable him to park his motorcycle near the Bank of Ceylon headquarters in Colombo Fort, which was located in a high security zone. The address given by the bomber to his workplace had been a house in Hekittha, Wattala. When police raided his house, they found nobody at home.

But they were told by neighbours that the occupant's wife had been taken away by one of his workplace friends whom they identified as Kanagarajah. The Police then obtained Kanagarajah's address from the workplace and went to his house in Bambalapitiya. They found the bomber's wife at this house but there was no trace of Kanagarajah. The bomber's wife had her husband's telephone number and the police immediately had the number traced. The bomber's phone was switched on, and through the global positioning system that is a standard feature of all mobile phones, they could trace where he was headed. He was on a bus that was passing through Kurunegala on his way to the Vanni. All the checkpoints along the route, were alerted and the photograph of the bomber faxed to them.

The bomber was identified at the Irattaperiyakulam check point. The Dehiwela explosion occurred at 7.15 in the morning. By 8.00 the same night, the bomber was in police custody. He had a hideout on 36th Lane in Wellawatte and by 11.00 pm the same night the police recovered 10 kilos of C-4 explosives, one micro pistol and other items from this hideout. The Sri Lankan intelligence services had come a long way since the days when incidents occurred and nobody had a clue as to who had done what.

Chapter 63

Terrorists in the Skies

Even as far back as 1995, in the operational instructions signed by Major Gen Rohan Daluwatte for Operation *Riviresa*, he specifically warned that the LTTE is believed to have acquired light air craft for suicide missions. From 1998 onwards the intelligence agencies had been issuing warnings that the LTTE had purchased aircraft. Soldiers had reported sightings, but they were not taken seriously. After assuming duties as defence secretary, Gōta asked the then air force chief Donald Perera what was being done in terms of air defence for Colombo. Perera had said that as of that moment, there was no air defence system in the country even though he had submitted a report to the government earlier stressing the need for such a system.

The then government of President Kumaratunga, made arrangements to obtain the radars from China, but India had objected saying that they would supply the radar system. Subsequently, India had done a survey in Sri Lanka to ascertain what was really required but no air defence system had yet been set up. Gōta got the stalled process started again and spoke to the Indian high commissioner Mrs Nirupama Rao and made arrangements to get the air defence radar systems and the ack ack guns. In December 2005, a team from the Sri Lanka air force led by the then director of air operations Roshan Gunatilleke visited India on a study tour to observe how radars were used by the Indian military for air defence. The Indian radars came after the visit made to India by the new president Mahinda Rajapaksa and Gōta at the end of 2005.

The Indians gifted two Indra Mark II, two dimensional radar units to Sri Lanka. The air force team from Sri Lanka had observed how these units were in use in the conflict zones of India. One was installed in Katunayake, the other in Vavuniya. After the air defence system was set up in early 2006, the air force had a rehearsal in the night. Both Gōta and President Mahinda Rajapaksa were personally present at the Katunayake air force base for the rehearsal. The new president observed how the warning was received, how the MiG-27s and helicopters were scrambled to meet the threat, the use of illumination flares etcetera. By being personally present at the first rehearsal, the president gave the air force the feeling that air defence was a national priority and not just a sideshow.

The Indian Indra Mark II radars were land based, 'gap filler' radars designed to operate within a larger air defence system. They were mounted on three vehicles and were purpose built to detect aircraft flying low at an altitude between 35 to 3000 meters. Each radar unit could cover a range of 90 km around it. However even these radars were meant to detect low flying fighter aircraft like the F-7s, Kfirs and MiG-27s and not the single engine light aircraft that the LTTE used. India sent experts to train Sri Lanka air force personnel in the maintenance and use of the radars. The 40mm anti-aircraft guns also provided by India were installed in Katunayake and other air force bases and important civilian installations such as the Colombo harbour.

These were trailer mounted cannon which could be towed to locations where they were needed. The anti-aircraft guns played a major deterrent role because the LTTE planes did not attack the same place twice. This radar set up ensured that every time the LTTE planes came in, the armed forces had advance warning. The first time however, the LTTE was able to attack the Katunayake air force base without anybody coming to know of their approach. The LTTE used Czechoslovakian made Zlin 143 single engine planes which could carry four bombs on improvised mounts. All air defence systems were designed to deal with fighter aircraft, not small, slow moving, low flying aircraft with improvised explosives that come only at night. The reflection registered on the radars by these planes was minimal.

Elaborate precautions had been taken to secure the Katunayake air force base. Troops were deployed to dominate a five kilometre radius around the Katunayake air base. The area around the air base and international airport was declared a high security zone. Civil defence committees had been set up within the high security zone with hotlines so that people could report suspicious movements. Air force personnel had gone from house to house in the high security zone to obtain the people's support for these measures. They even took houses on rent and families of 'spies' were settled in them with instructions to be on the lookout for any suspicious goings on in the area.

Wing Commander Kolitha Gunatilleke was the commandant in charge of the Katunayake air force base at the time of the LTTE's first air borne attack on Colombo. On 25 March 2007, he was asleep after midnight in his quarters when he was jolted awake by a loud explosion. He knew that the long awaited LTTE attack had finally come. Even though the air force and the government had installed an air defence system, since no LTTE planes had yet been seen, they expected a ground attack like the one in 2001. Wing Commander Gunatilleke started radioing his defence lines to locate the breach, but much to his surprise, he found that the defence lines were intact. Then a naval officer who lived in the vicinity of the Katunayake airport rang Gunetilleke with the theory that an LTTE attacking party may be firing mortars into the air base from a distance.

It took a while for people to realize that this had been an air attack. The three LTTE bombs that had exploded had hit the hangar housing the helicopters and the engineering hangar. Anti-aircraft gunners had in fact seen the aircraft and were firing in the direction of the sound of the plane engine. One of the improvised bombs dropped by the LTTE had failed to explode. Despite the heavy anti-aircraft fire from the ground, the LTTE planes went back unscathed. Three airmen died in the attack while 14 were wounded. An LTTE spokesman had told the LTTE website *Tamilnet* that their target had been the newly acquired MiG-27s and the Kfirs which operated out of the Katunayake air base. The entire military establishment was shaken by this attack. Due to sheer luck, the LTTE planes had failed to find their target. If they had been successful, this would have been a war-terminating event and all the gains after Mavilaru would have been wiped out at a single stroke.

The LTTE always counted on master strokes of this kind to regain their public standing as well as the military upper hand after suffering a setback. But this time, even though they had the element of surprise on their side, luck failed them. After that initial attack Gōta had a meeting to which he even invited a former air force commander Jayalath Weerakkody to discuss how to counter this new threat. Initially, the air force was perplexed because this was the first experience ever of being attacked from the air. Following the LTTE's first air raid, steps were taken to import a more sophisticated three dimensional radar system from China. The three dimensional radar system was active from November 2007 and used mainly for the protection of Colombo. Unlike the Indian radars which were gap filler units to be used within a bigger system, the Chinese radar was a self contained unit with an operational range of about 70 kilometres. The main advantage that it offered was that the altitude the enemy plane was flying at was also shown, making interception that much easier. Detection however was not the end of the story. Bringing down the LTTE planes was another matter entirely.

Firing at the LTTE planes from the ground was not a practical proposition as the target moves laterally and vertically while accelerating, so it is very difficult to manually hit a moving plane. This advantage that the LTTE now had, was previously enjoyed by the air force. The LTTE fired at the air force aircraft from the ground, but missed almost all the time. Even ack ack guns operate on the basis that if you keep firing in the direction of the target, you could chance upon a hit. The MiG-27s and Kfirs were too fast to intercept the LTTE planes. The air force was forced to think a few levels down. They even toyed with the idea of getting the turbo propeller driven SIAI Marchettis out of the museum because they could move at speeds similar to the LTTE's planes. The LTTE moreover flew only at night making both the detection as well as the interception of their planes that much more difficult. When an LTTE plane was detected, the slow moving helicopters were scrambled, but the LTTE planes were too small to be targeted in the night even by the helicopters.

In the early hours of 24 April 2007, an LTTE plane carried out another air raid on the Palaly air base in the Jaffna peninsula. Two bombs were dropped close to the Myladdy beach and six soldiers were killed. It was a coordinated operation with LTTE artillery guns in Pooneryn shelling Palaly, forcing the troops to take cover in bunkers while the LTTE plane flew in for the attack. A week later, on 29 April as Sri Lankans stayed indoors glued to their TV screens watching the 2007 cricket world cup final between Australia and Sri Lanka, the LTTE carried out another air raid on the Kolonnawa oil refinery and the Kerawalapitiya Shell Gas complex. Once again no real harm was done except some damage to a Shell Gas complex building.

On 26 August, 2008, the LTTE carried out a raid on the Trincomalee naval base. According to the navy, one of the two bombs dropped failed to explode and four naval ratings were injured in the attack. On 9 September 2008, the LTTE attempted another ground and air combined attack on the Vavuniya armed forces complex shared by the army, police and air force. The air defence radars were also located in this complex. A group of ten LTTE infiltrators were to attack from the ground while LTTE planes would bomb the facility from the air. However the infiltrators were detected early and even though the LTTE planes came and dropped a few bombs no damage was done. However 11 armed forces personnel were killed in the confrontation and 31 injured.

In another attack carried out on 28 October 2008, an LTTE plane had dropped two bombs on the Thallady army camp in Mannar and then proceeded to the Kelanitissa power station in Colombo to drop two more bombs which caused extensive damage to the power plant. One of the F-7G interceptors that had been purchased from China earlier that year had been scrambled to take on the LTTE plane but the air-to-air missile system on the F-7 failed to lock on to the LTTE plane. This sent shockwaves through the air force as the entire country was now with no defence against the LTTE planes.

Six Chengdu F-7G interceptors with air to air missiles had been acquired from China in early 2008 to shoot down the LTTE's planes. These were a different model to the F-7s already in use by the air force. The air to air missiles on the F-7Gs also needed a heat source to lock on to. However, the LTTE had used some method which the air force can only speculate on, to cover the heat source. On the Zlin-143 light aircraft used by the LTTE, the engine is in front and for a missile attack, a head on engagement would help the missile to lock into the heat source. However, coming at the target from the front reduces the time for engagement and if the target is passed, it takes time to double back. Pursuing the target from behind gives more time for engagement but from behind the only heat source is the exhaust which could either be covered by insulating material and the outlet extended so that the heat gets dissipated to an extent that the heat seeking missile does not lock on to the plane.

An extension nozzle just one foot in length attached to the exhaust of such a plane could cut heat signature by nearly half, which is why the air to air missiles on the F-7Gs failed to lock on to the LTTE planes. Moreover for the F-7Gs to operate at a low altitude in the night was risky as a jet could hit the ground in just a matter of seconds. With the new threat, Gōta brought down air defence experts from India, Pakistan, and the USA, but all of them said that there is no readymade solution to the problem of the LTTE planes and the only option was to improvise. The LTTE air threat came in for a great deal of scrutiny internationally too, as visions of small, single engine planes laden with explosives and flying at tree top level in the night, piloted by fanatics, gave Western defence authorities sleepless nights. Air attacks using this kind of aircraft was perhaps the LTTE's third major innovation bequeathed to the international terrorist community after the suicide jacket and the suicide boat.

Since all options had failed, the defences around what could be assumed to be the LTTE's main targets like the harbour, airport, the various army camps, the oil refinery, and Temple Trees, had to be directed to use ground fire. So every time the LTTE planes got past the defences, the guns in all these establishments would fire continuously into the air, preventing the planes from coming into that air space. There were no precedents for what was happening in Sri Lanka and no lessons that the air force could use from other such instances anywhere in the world.

In the absence of any guarantee that the LTTE planes could be intercepted and destroyed in the skies, the only available option was to ensure that they would not be able to take the intended target on the ground. A coordinated plan was put into place between the air force and the Colombo security apparatus to knock off the electricity supply the moment the approach of an LTTE plane was notified. On 4 May 2007, a major security coordinating conference was held with the participation of the CEOs and other top officials of leading banks, hotels and private sector business houses in the city of Colombo along with senior officers of the Kelanitissa power station and the Kolonnawa oil refinery complex.

The conference was presided over by Gōta. The main item discussed was what to do during air raids by the LTTE. Gōta explained that plans had been made for a total blackout during LTTE air raids so that it would be more difficult for the LTTE pilots to identify targets. The overall operations commander of Colombo complained that some hotels and banks did not adhere to the total blackout plan when the LTTE planes attacked the Kolonnawa oil refinery and the Kerawalapitiya Shell gas complex. William Costley, the General Manager of the Colombo Hilton outlined the difficulties they had in observing a shutdown of electricity supply, because elevators, fire and security alarm systems and the communication systems had to function and their standby generators had to be operational during a blackout.

At this meeting Gōta stipulated that private sector establishments could switch onto standby generators to keep computers, ATM machines, elevators and fire control systems functioning but no illumination should be visible to the outside. As such, signboards, anti-collision beacons on top of tall buildings and lights, should not come on when the stand by generators take over during a blackout. He stipulated that hotel guests should be given appropriate instructions on arrival. The overall operations commander Colombo requested the cooperation of all private sector organizations in mounting ack ack guns on top of tall buildings to meet the LTTE threat.

It would be logical to ask whether the air force couldn't go down to the LTTE's level the same way the navy did with their small boat concept and have dozens of small planes with one pilot and one gunner to locate and destroy the LTTE aircraft in the air in a re-enactment of world war one dogfights. Some air force officers say this may have been a successful strategy in the daytime but not in the night. The two dimensional radars could provide the location but no indication as to the altitude the target was flying at. Moreover, locating the LTTE planes in the skies in the night would have been a problem as it was not easy to keep a plane in the air while looking around for the target and trying to engage it.

One air force officer pointed out that even in world war one, there were hardly any dogfights in the night because it was not possible to shoot effectively in pitch darkness. Even the moonlight was not helpful because the LTTE attacked during the waning half when there was not much moonlight. Using night vision goggles did not help because it changes depth perception and makes targeting difficult. On 20 February 2009, as the war neared its end, the two LTTE planes were used in a kamikaze style attack in Colombo but both were shot down. One plane targeted the multi-storied air force headquarters in Colombo, but hit the Inland Revenue Department building instead. The air force speculates that anti aircraft fire from the ground would have hit the pilot causing the crash. The other plane which flew to the Katunayake air base, was shot down by ground fire and the plane was found with the body of the pilot and the explosives intact. This marked the end of the air tiger saga.

Chapter 64

The Expansion of the Military

Until the Rajapaksa government took office, the military never had the necessary troop strengths to be able to combat terrorism effectively. Lt Gen (Ret.) Gerry Silva a former army commander was quoted in the 50th anniversary publication of the army as having said that various studies had recommended increasing troop strengths threefold if the war is to be won. Silva also pointed out that the Sri Lanka army is the only army in the world which had its entire 'bayonet strength' continuously deployed in operations and that this was a fighting force that has not had the time to rest, recuperate, relax and retrain in a normal cycle of military life enjoyed by most armies in the world.

Furthermore, he pointed out that the capture and holding of ground absorbs large manpower resources. In his view politicians were reluctant to expand the military firstly, because of the cost involved, and secondly because politicians are always wary about large armies. Silva reminisced that a former minister in charge of defence when asked for additional forces, announced to a body of frustrated service chiefs, "*I invite you to come and convince my cabinet colleagues if you can!*" The Rajapaksa government however, was prepared to expand the armed forces to whatever extent necessary. After the recruitment drive began towards the last quarter of 2006, defence ministry processes were speeded up facilitating the raising of new battalions in the army.

Earlier, the procedure of writing to the defence ministry and awaiting approval would take at least six months. After 2006, approvals came almost immediately. Expansion was not just a case of recruiting men. Each new battalion raised had to have a commander, a second in command, company commanders, platoon commanders, and a quartermaster to manage the equipment and a regimental sergeant major with a service of at least 12 years, experienced sergeant majors and sergeants, corporals with about 2-3 years experience and lance corporals.

When experienced personnel are withdrawn from other units to form the new battalions, the resulting vacancies in the old battalions had to be filled up and this was a huge administrative task. Experienced personnel could not be arbitrarily withdrawn from the older battalions because the fighting qualities of each battalion differed due to the experience gained on the battle field. So each battalion had to be studied before their personnel were withdrawn for the new battalions. While there was a rapid expansion of the army from mid-2006 onwards, it was mostly the infantry that was expanded and not support elements like armour and artillery. In a conventional army, there should be a unit of armour and a unit of artillery for every infantry brigade. Conventionally, the formula is that if you have 200 battalions of infantry, they should have the support of roughly 70 units of armour and 70 units of artillery.

But throughout the war, there were only five units of armour and five units of artillery for the entire army. Brigadier Udaya Perera was the director of operations of the army from August 2006 to April 2009. The army directorate of operations coordinated the distribution of arms, ammunition, communication equipment and manpower etcetera to the divisional commands. Managing the limited armour and artillery support was a major issue at army headquarters during the final offensive in the Vanni. The armour and artillery units could not be expanded at the same rate as the infantry.

Each artillery regiment had to have a certain number of guns, and each armoured regiment had to have tanks and armoured fighting vehicles. At any given time on the Vanni front at least four divisions were fighting with an average of around 15 battalions each. Assessing the need and distributing the armour and artillery around was one of the tasks that Udaya Perera had to handle. In the east, where operations were conducted mainly by the special forces and the commandos, issues of artillery and armour support did not crop up in the same manner as during the Vanni operations. Any field commander would like to neutralize the enemy before sending the infantry in, and in order to do that there has to be the proper ratio of artillery and armour to infantry which the army did not have due to the sudden expansion of the infantry.

This was an infantry war and not one fought on the classic model where you use air power first, followed by artillery and armour, with the infantry walking in at the end of it all. The other major issue during the Vanni operation was ammunition. Once again there was no ammunition problem during the eastern operations because the ammunition that was in stock was used. But as the level of stocks went down, more had to be imported. There were lean periods as during the Beijing Olympics in 2008, when China was under pressure from the West. So the ammunition levels went dangerously low during the Vanni operations. Even buying new assault rifles for the infantry suddenly became a problem.

Hence the Sri Lanka Electrical and Mechanical Engineer regiment (SLEME) was assigned to repair whatever old equipment they had - even old T-56 rifles. At the point that the army started expanding, they had around 60 infantry battalions both regular and volunteer. Between 2006 and 2009 at least another 100 infantry battalions were raised and in this expansion, they had to provide the newly raised battalions not only with small arms but support arms as well. The difficulties that the operations directorate had on the logistics front were not shown to the ground troops and in the reports submitted by field commanders, they expressed satisfaction about the flow of equipment during the operations.

The rapid expansion of the army meant that by the time the war ended, a good number of recruits were men who had been recruited just for the Vanni operation. By 2006 July when the war started, most of the soldiers were experienced men and this situation lasted into the latter part of 2007, when new recruits started coming in large numbers. By the time the war came to a close in 2009, the proportion of new recruits would have been something like 75% of the army. After the basic training of three months, they were given further battlefield training. One way in which this was done, was to establish new training camps in the recently liberated areas like the Thoppigala jungles, and the jungles of Vavuniya that had been Tiger territory until recently.

The establishment of these battlefield training centres in the newly liberated areas also helped to dominate those areas. The conditions in these areas couldn't have been any closer to the real thing and the raw recruits were given training with live ammunition in these newly established camps before being launched into the actual operational areas. Between 2006 and 2009, the army alone had taken in no less than 121,141 new recruits. The new recruits did not all go to raising new battalions as the existing battalions had to be replenished as the casualty rate depleted their numbers. Despite this unprecedented expansion, the army was still short of troops. By the latter part of 2008, the army was getting the help of the navy and air force as well to man the newly liberated areas.

The A-9 road up to Mankulam was manned by the air force and police. Parts of the Trincomalee and Ampara districts were also being held by navy and air force troops. Even the injured were deployed to hold territory. At the latter stages, entire battalions were raised from among the injured who were leaving hospital. Soldiers who could walk, see and use both arms, were assigned new duties. Every infantry regiment raised up to three such battalions of slightly injured soldiers to man the roads captured in the 'belly area' of the Vanni. These soldiers did not have to move around much and had to clear only a few meters around their bunker to keep the road clear. While about 6000 injured men were employed in this manner, another 2000 to 3000 were used as administrative personnel for the fighting units.

The slightly injured who were pronounced fit enough to go to the war zone but not to fight, were assigned to the administrative companies of operational battalions so that they would release the able bodied for battle field duties. Those who had passed their GCE O/Ls and above were made clerks. Each battalion needed about ten clerks and these were recruited from among the injured. Some others had been given a crash course in typing and turned into typists. Some were even retrained as cooks and barbers. Besides this, about 100 injured men without an arm or a leg were used in Colombo and the outstations for surveillance duties. They were given mobile phones and functioned as the eyes and ears of the military intelligence set up. Some even travelled in buses and trains for surveillance duties.

One of the duties the armed forces had was to protect villages under threat - meaning Sinhala and Muslim villages straddling the borders of the northern and eastern provinces claimed by the LTTE as the Tamil homeland. These villages had been subject to many attacks by the LTTE over the two and a half decades since 1983. Gruesome stories and images of these massacres got wide publicity through the mass media and contributed significantly to demoralizing the general public. Apart from this, the Sinhala and Muslim people in those threatened villages tended to abandon their lands and to migrate to other parts of the country in fear of their lives thus leaving even more territory open to the terrorists.

There were such threatened villages in seven of the 22 districts in Sri Lanka viz. Puttlam, Anuradhapura, Vavuniya, Trincomalee, Polonnaruwa, Ampara and Moneragala and if the army and police had been deployed to protect these villages, they would have been doing nothing but that. Besides, such deployment was not the most effective way of preventing LTTE attacks on these villages. Major Gen Daya Ratnayake said that in 2006, two battalions under his command had been deployed to guard 63 threatened villages in the Batticaloa district. They were deployed in groups of 10 to 20 and were only giving the villagers a false sense of security as there was nothing that a small contingent of soldiers could do to stop or even deter an attack. Soldiers were scattered, guarding things and waiting to be attacked by terrorists giving the latter the initiative. Ratnayake argued for the freeing of soldiers from guard duties and making them available for offensive operations. He explains that about 60% of the army was being used to defend the rear against a handful of LTTE cadres trained to carry out infiltration attacks.

A 'home guard' system had been in place since the mid-1980s to guard the threatened villages. Originally, they were merely unpaid volunteers. Later they were organized as a unit under the supervision of the police department and paid a daily wage. By early 2006, there were 19,200 home guards serving under the police in those respective areas. Known pejoratively as '*gambattas*' (Short for '*gramarakshaka bhataya*') they were not very effective in preventing LTTE attacks on the villages. The 2005 film *Sulanga enu pinisa* by film director Vimukthi Jayasundera which has been referred to in a previous chapter, depicted the humble village *gambatta* as a cringing, oppressed wretch, treated as an object of derision even by the army. The film begins with a group of soldiers in a truck getting a '*gambatta*' drunk and then leaving him stark naked and clutching his 12-bore shotgun by an irrigation canal.

In early 2006, Gōta set about knocking the home guards into shape. The first thing he did was to rename them as the Civil Defence Force to be run as a separate department under the Defence Ministry and separate from the police. Then he appointed the then serving chief of staff of the navy Rear Admiral Sarath Weerasekera, as the head of the force - an unusual appointment – assigning a naval officer to command a land based force. The CDF was divided into 17 commands in the vulnerable districts and each command was placed under either an army or police officer in that district. Weerasekera was handpicked to lead the outfit because of demonstrated ability to do what it takes to maintain the morale and patriotism of the men under him and Gōta considered him the ideal person to improve the morale and self-esteem of the demoralized home guard outfit.

The repeater shot guns used by the *'gambattas'* were replaced with T-56 assault rifles and their shabby uniforms changed into smart 'desert storm' style camouflage uniforms and army boots. Weerasekera in the meantime did a survey of the threatened villages in the vulnerable districts along with the army and police. He studied the previous attacks carried out by the LTTE in those areas and submitted a report to Gōta, who took the decision to double the number of CDF personnel. Over the next three years, the force would expand to 41,500. The training regimen also changed and the former home guards were re-trained by army and navy instructors for four weeks. The shabby and comic looking *gambatta* depicted in *Sulanga enu pinisa* in 2005 had disappeared by the end of 2006.

The CDF's role was in defence. But around 400 members of the CDF were given a ten week commando style training in carrying out limited offensive operations so that they could lay ambushes on the approach roads to the villages to deter LTTE death squads. Army commander Sarath Fonseka had not been happy about giving CDF personnel commando style training because they were civilians and not bound by special legislation applying to the military proper. Be that as it may, the net result of these developments was that the LTTE was not able to effectively terrorise people in the threatened villages in 2007, 2008 and until the end of the war in 2009. The CDF carried out clearing operations along the 55 kilometre Trincomalee-Habarana road and many main roads in the Anuradhapura, Polonnaruwa and Ampara districts which would otherwise have to be held by the army, tying up personnel who were better deployed in offensive operations. Towards the latter stages of the war, 3000 CDF men had been absorbed into the army overnight and deployed in the Vanni thus freeing up more regular soldiers for the final operations.

Chapter 65

The Vanni Operation Begins

The contiguous administrative districts of Vavuniya, Mulleitivu, Mannar and Kilinochchi are referred to collectively as the Vanni (See map 3). The A-9 road cuts through the centre of this vast, remote, sparsely populated swathe of land to connect the Jaffna peninsula with the main population centres in the south. With the entire eastern province and the Jaffna peninsula now under government control, the Vanni was the last LTTE stronghold.

Army formations under several separate commands, were inducted into the Vanni one after the other over a period of about eighteen months, gradually taking over and holding territory the LTTE had controlled for years. It was the way the Indian army operated in Sri Lanka during the late 1980s, that had given Gōta the idea of saturating the entire Vanni and ensuring that the LTTE could not come back into the areas that had been cleared. The Eastern Province which had just been cleared, was also completely dominated by government forces with the police, navy, air force, the police commando unit and the newly reorganised civil defence force all chipping in to dominate cleared territory so as to release the army for offensive operations.

The Vanni operation began even before the eastern operations ended. The first formation to be launched into the western Vanni was the 57th Division through the government defence lines 15 kilometres to the west of Vavuniya town. Beyond that was a stretch of LTTE held territory going right up to the Mannar coast. On 25

March 2007, three brigades were launched in the direction of Mannar from this defence line, but they were beaten back. Resistance was fierce because this was the only battlefront in the Vanni and the LTTE was able to concentrate all their forces to beat back the offensive. After this initial assault failed, Brigadier Jagath Dias was posted as the commander of the 57th Division. Dias observes that the mistake made in the first foray, was that the army advanced along roads without dominating the areas between the advancing columns. The LTTE infiltrated the areas between the advancing columns and inflicted heavy casualties on the troops, forcing a retreat.

The east had almost been completely taken over by the army by that time and the LTTE now knew that the government will not be sitting on their laurels after the east but coming straight into the Vanni without giving them any respite. Around three weeks after the first foray in the Vanni, in April 2007, the army began clearing the last stronghold of the LTTE in the east - the jungle bases of Thoppigala which was completed by mid July 2007. While mopping up operations to destroy small pockets of LTTE resistance were still going on in the east, another thrust was made through the western Vavuniya defence line with three brigades once again moving towards LTTE held targets in the Mannar district, this time, under the command of Jagath Dias. The latter's first task after he took over the 57th Division had been to retrain and infuse confidence into the troops demoralized by the failure of the first offensive in March that year. Dias had to move among his troops and talk to the lowest foot soldier to get them into a mood to fight again.

This time however, the 57th Division moved forward in a broad front with a baseline that would be lifted and taken forward when the troops ahead were able to establish domination over the territory. The strategy of establishing a baseline and advancing on a broad frontage with a large number of infiltration teams waging a war of attrition against the LTTE had been suggested by Gōta at a security council meeting. By the third week of July 2007, public attention had shifted from the eastern province to the Vanni. This new theatre of operations to the west of the A-9 road in the Mannar district, consisted mostly of scrub jungle with open patches interspersed with thickets. Progress was excruciatingly slow given the stiff resistance of the LTTE and the nature of the terrain. In addition to this was the fact that the whole area was heavily mined.

Around the last quarter of 2007, the Monsoon set in, and no advance was possible and the soldiers had to dig in until the rains were over. During the monsoon rains, the entire area changed into one huge marsh. The method of warfare adopted was not to move forward in mass formations as had been done during previous military operations, but to deploy 8 man teams ahead of the base line. These small teams were tasked with the duty of dominating the area ahead for 48 hours after which they would be relieved by another team. The domination teams were tasked with killing at least one terrorist a day. The troops on the base line would act as a reserve force for the domination troops. The 57th Division advanced by lifting the base line and re-establishing it further ahead as the domination troops cleared the area ahead. This represented a radical departure from previous practice.

The army had learnt the hard way during the 'decade of darkness' in the 1990s that moving in large formations presents an easy target for LTTE artillery and that their target signature had to be minimized. After assessing where they went wrong in past operations, the army stopped operating in traditional formations like platoons, companies and battalions and split up instead into small groups, the eight man team being the norm. The new formation was called Special Infantry Operational Teams (SIOT). Originally, these were conceived as small specialized units within each battalion. But as the war progressed the entire army adapted to the new way of fighting.

The army was able to take stock of things after the ceasefire of 2002 and it was during this period that the idea of operating in small groups was germinated. Chagi Gallage and Ralph Nugera both middle ranking officers at that time, were in the army training centre in Maduruoya where small group training began. Nugera had got the inspiration for SIOT teams from the example of the *Selous Scouts* of Rhodesia of the 1970s, who were described as highly trained small groups of 'bush fighters' who inflicted the maximum damage on the enemy with minimum casualties to themselves. Several incidents in the past had convinced these young officers that that even ordinary soldiers who did not have Special Forces training could not only survive behind enemy lines, but pass through successive enemy lines and get back to base.

In the failed *Agnikheela* operation of 2001, for instance, several soldiers who had gone missing behind enemy lines had managed to come back to base. There was also the realization that instead of throwing mass formations of soldiers at the LTTE lines, the more effective method would be to deploy teams that could penetrate enemy lines and engage them from the rear causing the enemy line to collapse. Training SIOT teams had begun in 2005 and each infantry battalion was asked to send up to sixty men to be given training in communication, demolition, directing air support, marksmanship, direction of artillery fire, night fighting, etc. Thus, when hostilities commenced in earnest in 2006, every infantry company had about 6-8 SIOT trained soldiers. Initially, SIOT teams were made up of troops specially trained for the purpose, but later as ordinary troops were assigned to SIOT teams to take the places of casualties, they too learnt the ropes while on the job and in that manner, the concept seeped down to the whole army. SIOT teams had been extensively used in the eastern operations as well, and by the time the Vanni operations began, the army had got accustomed to this way of fighting.

The realization that this method reduced casualties was one of the main reasons why ordinary soldiers were quick to adapt to the new system. The largest number of casualties among the ground troops was caused by LTTE artillery fire and operating in small groups reduced target signature. If not for this new way of fighting the final casualty figures would have been much higher. The difference between SIOT teams on the one hand and Special Forces and commandos on the other was that the former moved only one or two kilometres ahead of the base line whereas the latter moved much deeper into enemy territory. After the SIOT team establishes domination ahead of the defence line, the base line could be lifted and taken forward. This was slower and less dramatic than throwing mass formations of soldiers at the LTTE positions. But it reduced casualties, made the war more sustainable and destabilised the LTTE much more than the conventional mass formations.

Jagath Dias instructed each battalion to have a minimum of eight SIOT teams ahead of the baseline with another eight on standby waiting to take over when the others return. In the first six to seven months of the brutal war of attrition in the Vanni jungles, the original SIOT teams took a lot of casualties and Dias had to call for volunteers from among ordinary soldiers to take the place of the fallen SIOT members. Special short courses in administering advanced first aid to combat casualties was given to members of SIOT teams by military doctors so as to minimize losses of SIOT members wounded in the jungle. Jagath Dias never had commandos or special forces placed under his command and he relied almost exclusively on these SIOT teams.

While Jagath Dias's troops were advancing slowly in the hinterland of the western Vanni, Task Force 1 was launched at the end of August 2007, under the command of Brigadier Chagi Gallage to take over the coastal belt of the western Vanni. The first target they took was the coastal town of Silavathurei which lay to the south of Mannar. Silavathurei was a coastal town used mainly for logistical purposes by the LTTE. Around 50 to 75 sea tiger cadres carried on smuggling operations with the help of civilian partners and were engaged in transporting smuggled goods into the LTTE held areas from Silavathurei. This was an important target because it was the sea tiger base closest to the Colombo harbour and could be used to stage attacks on the country's very lifeline. Moreover, the army had to clear and secure their rear if they were to advance further up north into the Vanni. The navy commander had also been stressing the need to clear Silavathurei because of the LTTE arms smuggling operation that was going on there.

Task Force 1 started off with two brigades. After capturing the coastal towns of Silavathurei and Arippu to the north of the Wilpattu national park which was done without much difficulty, Gallage's formation moved northwards into a vast paddy cultivating area known appropriately as the Mannar 'rice bowl' irrigated by the Yoda Wewa (Giant's tank). From the Mannar rice bowl onwards, Brigadier Gallage was replaced by Brigadier Shavendra Silva as the commander of Task Force 1. The latter would command the formation until the end of the war. Even though both Jagath Dias and Shavendra Silva were operating to the west of the A-9 road in the Mannar district, the terrain that each formation had to pass through could not be more different. The Mannar rice bowl, approximately 80 sq km in size, consists mainly of paddy fields and wide open spaces. The ground was soggy even during the dry season. Three main LTTE centres in the rice bowl had to be captured - Adampan, Anandakulam and Parppakadaththan, the last of which was an abandoned town about 4 km to the east of Anandakulam.

From the last week of September 2007, three brigades began advancing simultaneously on Adampan, Anandakulam and Parappakadaththan. Each brigade commander commanded up to six battalions including the volunteer troops. The advancing troops encountered heavy mortar and artillery fire from the LTTE. Progress was excruciatingly slow. The army had to advance only a few kilometres to get to their targets in the rice bowl. The total distance that had to be traversed in the case of Adampan was 4.5 km, Anandakulam, 6 km and Parappakadaththan 7 km. But it took Shavendra Silva's troops over nine months from September 2007 to the end of June 2008 to traverse these few kilometres and complete the capture of the rice bowl.

On some days, the troops were unable to advance even 25 meters. Less than 500 terrorists were keeping over 7000 trained soldiers at bay by using the terrain to their advantage. In the rice bowl, no movement was possible in the day time because the terrain was so open. Even when troops moved in the night, there were no points to occupy. The only available places to occupy in that vast stretch of open land, were the LTTE's own bunkers which they had constructed on the few patches of dry land available. As the army advanced and captured the few vantage points the LTTE left behind, the LTTE fired mortars and artillery upon what had been their own bunkers a while earlier in the certainty that the army would be in those locations.

It was a case of moving forward a few meters a day, and constructing safe points and consolidating before moving on again. Soldiers moving forward would use wooden railway sleepers to give themselves temporary cover from LTTE artillery and small arms fire. Each soldier was given two railway sleepers to provide cover. If he advanced in the night, the soldier had to dig a depression in the ground about two feet deep to take cover in during the day. After the sun rose, they would have to stay behind these railway sleepers the entire day for fear of being picked off by LTTE snipers. It became safe to raise their heads only after darkness fell. There were at times houses or thickets in the open paddy fields. But these were invariably mined or booby trapped because the LTTE knew that the army would have to seek cover in such places as they advanced.

The terrain was so flat and open, that the troops could see a kilometre ahead clearly. The problem was that the LTTE also had the same field of vision and knew exactly where to direct their fire. The LTTE had also deployed a large number of snipers to make maximum use of the open terrain. Even though the terrain was flat, very little use could be made of armour because of the soggy ground conditions. At night, any sound could be clearly heard over a long distance and whenever armoured vehicles started up, that would precipitate a barrage of LTTE artillery fire in the direction of the noise.

Troop movements were very predictable as they had only a limited number of places to advance to, and the maximum use was made of anti-personnel mines and booby traps. Anti-personnel mines had been scattered so liberally in this area by the LTTE that a large number of livestock, had been killed in mine blasts. The advancing troops could see dozens of dead cattle ahead of them and the air was heavy with the stench of rotting animal carcasses. The sight of the dead animals gave an indication to the troops about the sheer quantity of anti-personnel mines that had been scattered in the area and that had a negative impact on morale. Bangalore torpedoes could not be used effectively to clear paths in the minefields because the engineers had to go into the minefield to use the torpedoes and nobody knew where the mine fields were as they had not been laid methodically but simply strewn all over by the LTTE and someone had to step on one to know that the area was mined. However when they were approaching specific targets such as LTTE bunkers, they would clear a path with Bangalore torpedoes before approaching such locations.

Bangalore torpedoes were explosive devices made by the field engineers of the army. What was used were two inch PVC pipes into which was stuffed explosives with a detonation cord. The lengths of pipe used were usually six feet and could be joined together to form much longer charges. A bullet shaped tip was fixed to one end so that it can be pushed forward even through thick undergrowth. When exploded, the shock waves make any anti-personnel mines along the path of the explosion go off and a path about two and a half to three feet would be cleared in this manner. Booby trapped locations had to be dealt with by exploding an improvised explosive device near it to make any explosive devices go off. Bangalore torpedoes and improvised explosive devices had to be extensively used by the army as the LTTE had anti-removal devices placed even on anti-personnel mines.

When troops were bogged down in the Mannar rice bowl and unable to move forward, the target was brought down to each battalion having to cause just one LTTE fatality a day. Since there were about twenty battalions deployed in the rice bowl, that would be an attrition rate of twenty terrorists a day. From the intelligence gathered by the army, only about 400-500 LTTE cadres were holding the rice bowl. So killing 20 a day would have meant that in one month there would be no LTTE cadres left to defend the rice bowl. The fact that the rice bowl could not be cleared for nearly ten months means that even this target was not met.

One difficulty was that the ground in the rice bowl was always soggy, rain or no rain, and some LTTE bunkers that were captured by the advancing troops could not be occupied because they were water logged. There was always water inside the boots of soldiers and at times entire companies and even battalions had to be withdrawn due to troops suffering from rotting feet. Needless to say, the long delay in the rice bowl and the western Vanni was causing a great deal of anxiety in Colombo. Gōta had discussed a strategy to break the stalemate with Shavendra Silva and the army director of operations Brigadier Udaya Perera among others and had come to the conclusion that a division should be withdrawn from the Jaffna peninsula and tasked with cutting across Jagath Dias's front line in the hinterland, to the coastal town of Vedithaltivu which was well to the north of the rice bowl.

To help in the encirclement, a simultaneous amphibious operation to take Vedithaltivu would be launched from the sea. With such a manoeuvre, the terrorists defending the rice bowl would have been surrounded and their supply lines cut off. Even if the LTTE had withdrawn before the encirclement could take place, that too would have been advantageous to the army as that would have hastened their advance. Gōta had suggested the move to Sarath Fonseka, but Fonseka thought it was too risky. He preferred to go slow than to quicken the pace with the attendant risks – amphibious operations were always fraught with risk. Fonseka also did not want to withdraw a division from Jaffna and Gōta had not pressed him on the matter because there were both pros and cons in withdrawing troops from Jaffna.

Shavendra Silva's travails in the rice bowl were paralleled by the experiences of Jagath Dias in the hinterland of the western Vanni. One of the fiercest confrontations between Dias's troops and the LTTE took place in Periyatampanai, a small town to the north of the Vavuniya-Mannar road, leading directly to the Madhu Church. A massive LTTE counterattack took place in Periyatampanai around November 2007, and nearly overwhelmed Dias's troops. His troops took around nine months to capture the famed Madhu church which was finally secured only in April 2008 - a distance of around 20 km from their starting point to the west of Vavuniya. The going was slow until Dias's troops captured Madu, Periyamadu and Palampiddi. After this, progress was rapid until they got to the Tunukkai-Mallawi complex further up north. Dias's troops managed to get to Thunukkai before the LTTE managed to complete building the ditch-cum-bund they had been building in the area.

The LTTE was holding the army back despite the fact that the best trained troops the army had were deployed against them. The army Special Forces had three battalions numbering about 1500 men in all. The entire 1st Special Forces Battalion and half of the 2nd SF Battalion as well was operating in the hinterland of the western Vanni ahead of Jagath Dias's troops, while the entire army Commando Brigade with about 2000 men, was with Shavendra Silva in the Mannar rice bowl. It was while the army was bogged down in the western Vanni making minimal progress, that another challenge arose which could have derailed the entire war effort.

Chapter 66

Keeping the War on Track

By the last quarter of 2007, Gōta was publicly declaring the aim of destroying the LTTE completely. One of the first occasions when he mooted this idea was at the reception held in Trincomalee for the returning heroes after the navy's first deep sea operation in September 2007. One thing Gōta knew well from personal experience was that if such an aim was to be achieved, the whole country had to be on a war footing, the people had to support the war, the armed forces have to be properly equipped and led, and most importantly, the political will of the government to finish the war had to be maintained no matter what. He knew that he was fighting a deadly enemy that could give good account of itself and he knew that it would not always be smooth sailing. He had to have the ability to withstand the rough patches that were invariably going to come.

At any moment, the LTTE could launch an attack of such proportions that would make half the cabinet rise up against the war. Then again, there could be a military failure that would prompt even ordinary people to have second thoughts. Gōta had a foretaste of this with the Muhamalai debacle of October 2006. One member of his brother's government who came in for much scrutiny by Gōta was Mangala Samaraweera, then the Minister of Ports, Civil Aviation and Foreign Affairs. Samaraweera, a close protégé of president Chandrika Kumaratunga had joined Mahinda Rajapaksa and played a major role in his election campaign of 2005. After Mahinda became president, Mangala expected to be given the position of prime minister, but Mahinda appointed Rathnasiri Wickremanayake instead.

Mangala was given the ministries of foreign affairs, ports and aviation, powerful ministries that no one else had held concurrently. The ports and aviation ministries in particular would have spearheaded many of the development projects planned by the Rajapaksa regime. Even though Mangala did not have the title of prime minister, he was the visible second in command in the Rajapaksa government. It was however a resentful Mangala who served under the Rajapaksas. By mid-2006, a cold war had commenced between Samaraweera and the Rajapaksas. This mainly took the form of *Maubima* a weekly Sinhala newspaper started by one of his supporters Tiran Alles which directed scathing attacks on the government.

Samaraweera always denied that he had anything to do with *Maubima*. In February 2007 after president Rajapaksa sacked him from the cabinet, Samaraweera wrote in his open letter to the president saying among other things: *"Many people claim that there is some sort of a connection between Maubima newspaper and me. Apart from the fact that Maubima publisher was the head of Colombo airport which is under my ministry, and my coordinating secretary works as an editor at Maubima, and my sister worked at Maubima's sister paper, the Weekend Standard, I don't have any connection with Maubima. Even prior to this, several interested parties have attempted to create a connection between Maubima and me in order to discredit me in your eyes. This is a completely baseless allegation...Even though I don't agree with many articles that are published in the newspaper, I admire their efforts in being truly independent..."* This was a denial that would not have rung true even to the most sympathetic listener.

During these months, it was Mangala's set up that directed the most effective attacks on the Rajapaksa government and even the most vociferous external opponents of the government were overshadowed by the internal opposition. Military matters came in for special scrutiny by Mangala's media group much to the fury of Gōta. His concern was that when the war effort was being criticized in this manner by elements within the government, he was going have a difficult time convincing the public that the military would be able to prevail over the LTTE.

After it became obvious that the president would finally have to settle for a military option, Mangala Samaraweera became a problem for the government. It was well known that he had never supported military action against the LTTE. At a workshop which was held in preparation for the second round of peace talks with the LTTE at which both Gōta and Samaraweera were present, the issue of the disappearances that had been occurring in Colombo, came up for discussion with somebody saying that this issue will come up at the peace talks. Gōta had told the gathering that while certain incidents had taken place, and people were putting the blame on the military, it was not the military that was doing this but various Tamil groups and that measures had been taken to minimize such occurrences.

At this point Mangala had snapped that minimizing is not acceptable and that it has to be eliminated completely. The tone and manner in which Mangala had spoken, had indicated in no uncertain terms his attitude towards the war effort. Gōta could see two camps emerging within the cabinet over the war effort. His worst nightmare was coming true. In his open letter to the president after his sacking, Samaraweera was to write: *"It is no secret that disappearances, abductions, kidnappings, and killings keep happening on a daily basis in Sri Lanka. We have absolutely no arguments against defeating the LTTE completely. But the human rights violations that occur within the country have become a hindrance to defeating terrorism. By becoming known as a government that violates human rights we are allowing LTTE to build a case against us among the international community. Responding to terrorism with even more terrorism is not the act of a responsible government..."*

Samaraweera had in fact opposed the war even in the 1990s under the Chandrika Kumaratunga government, and the last thing that Gōta wanted was a repetition of that. While the Chandrika Kumaratunga government was engaged in mortal combat with the LTTE, Mangala Samaraweera started the *Sudu Nelum Movement* which organized anti-war activities including a travelling show called *Thawalama* which staged anti-war street drama. The SNM also inserted anti-war advertisements on TV. One advertisement that the present writer remembers featured four women representing mothers, grandmothers sisters and wives carrying the bier of a soldier dressed in army green on their shoulders to the sound of mournful music conveying the impression that joining the army means death. Another such advertisement featured a scene of a herd of deer crossing a river and crocodiles ravenously devouring them. No doubt was left in the minds of the viewer that the deer represented soldiers and the crocodiles represented the LTTE.

As Mangala recounts, a few days after the LTTE broke the ceasefire in April 1995, president Chandrika Kumaratunga asked him to come to Temple Trees one morning. When Samaraweera went to see her, she had been in a pensive mood and had said that the LTTE has now unilaterally broken the ceasefire, and the military will have to wage a war against them and that when the war drums start beating, people can easily be misled and some of the more racist elements could create problems in the south. Her concern was that another July 1983 should not take place and she said that a programme has to be designed to educate the Sinhalese and not the Tamils, about the need for a negotiated settlement in order to meet the justifiable grievances of the Tamil people.

Samaraweera's brief was to ensure that the Sinhalese people should not see the LTTE and the Tamil people as one entity but as two distinct groups. Samaraweera says that it was with this objective that he started the *Sudu Nelum Movement*. The war was marketed as a war for peace. This saw Sinhala politicians going to Sinhala villages to talk about the genuine grievances of the Tamil people and also of the ruthlessness and unacceptability of the LTTE. Over the years, the *Sudu Nelum Movement* would hold over 700 seminars, and street theatre programmes. Buddhist monks were also involved in the movement. Samaraweera claims that the success of the *Sudu Nelum Movement* can be gauged from the fact that there was no repetition of July 1983 - despite a series of bombings carried out by the LTTE, no Tamil was harmed in Colombo.

By 1998, when the war was reaching a critical stage, the then deputy minister of defence Anuruddha Ratwatte had complained to president Kumaratunga, saying that the SNM was one of the main causes for the poor response to recruitment drives by the military. Samaraweera however says that the SNM had a programme to look after the families of military personnel, which included a scholarship programme for the children of servicemen and even a small housing programme. He says that the lack of recruits to the military would have been more due to the lack of a coordinated drive for recruitment. Under pressure from Anuruddha Ratwatte and the heads of the armed services, president Kumaratunga had summoned Samaraweera and requested him to scale down the work of the SNM which ceased to function after 2000.

Samaraweera, says in defence of his project that the SNM helped prevent riots in the south and therefore, the army was free to fight the war in the north without being diverted to the south from time to time to quell ethnic riots. At the root of his supporting an anti-war campaign in the middle of a war, was a deep rooted belief that the LTTE could not be defeated militarily. Samaraweera says that even though Anuruddha Ratwatte said that the LTTE would be defeated in a matter of months, he and some others in the cabinet were of the opinion that the most that could reasonably expected from the war was to compel the LTTE to come to the negotiating table. Thus opinion within the government was divided.

It did not help at all that the leader of the government was Chandrika Kumaratunga the daughter of the woolly headed and impractical S.W.R.D.Bandaranaike who was squarely responsible for most of these problems anyway. His daughter was no less impractical in government and it was hardly surprising that Sri Lanka suffered the worst military debacles under her stewardship. The difference after 2006 was that president Mahinda Rajapaksa knew what he was doing, Gōta knew what he was doing, and everybody, the politicians, the military, the police and the people were all mobilized to win the war. Previously, when Anuruddha Ratwatte was waging war, Mangala Samaraweera and by association Chandrika Kumaratunga, was waging a war against the war.

On 9 February 2006, president Mahinda Rajapaksa made his move. He sacked Mangala Samaraweera and Anura Bandaranaike from the cabinet and Mangala's sidekick Sripathy Sooriyarachchi from his position as the non-cabinet minister for ports and shipping. Gōta says that he can't imagine what would have happened if the president had not taken that decision to remove Mangala Samaraweera from the cabinet. He says that Mangala would have definitely formed a group within the ruling party and worked against the war effort. While a lot of people did support the war effort, there were some military setbacks like the Muhamalai debacle, the attack on the Anuradhapura air base and the LTTE aerial bombing of Colombo. Gōta says that if there was a bloc within the government opposing the war, when the setbacks came, there was no telling which way things would have tilted.

At that time, the ruling party was in a minority in parliament and every individual mattered. In such a situation, getting rid of people like Mangala and Sripathy Sooriyarachchi was a major political decision. What gave the government the leeway to sack Mangala Samaraweera, Anura Bandaranaike and Sripathy Sooriyarachchi was the fact that 18 dissident UNP parliamentarians had joined the government and swelled their numbers. The removal of Mangala Samaraweera from the government brought everybody together into one agenda. The cabinet, the government and the whole country was now focused on one task. Mangala however did not go quietly. On

16 February 2007, he published in *The Island*, the aforementioned open letter to the president, outlining all the problems that he had with the Rajapaksa administration. Among other things, he complained that he had been kept out of security council meetings even though the foreign minister should have been present in the security council. Samaraweera ascribed his exclusion to Gōta's influence.

Chapter 67

The Political Crisis of 2007

When Mahinda Rajapaksa became president in November 2005, he inherited a parliament in which the ruling coalition was in a minority. The core of the ruling alliance was the Sri Lanka Freedom Party. In 1994, the SLFP had entered into a coalition with the LSSP, the CPSL, the SLMP, and some smaller parties like the *Desha Vimukthi Janatha Peramuna*, *Bahujana Nidahas Peramuna* and the Democratic United National Front to form the People's Alliance to contest the parliamentary elections of that year. In April 2004 this pre-existing coalition entered into another coalition with the JVP, and it was renamed the United People's Freedom Alliance (UPFA) which name it retains to this date.

By entering into a coalition with the former PA, the JVP improved their political fortunes enormously. They had only 16 members in the parliament of 2001, but after entering into the UPFA coalition in April 2004, their representation in parliament went up to 39. Every voter has three preference votes and the JVP voters cast their preference votes only for JVP candidates. When this combined with preference votes going to JVP candidates from voters of other parties in the coalition, the result was that in most districts, the three candidates who got the highest number of preference votes on the UPFA list happened to be members of the JVP. The UPFA won the 2004 parliamentary election with 45.6% of the popular vote and got 105 seats in parliament in a situation where 113 seats were needed to have a clear majority in the 225 member parliament. The breakdown was as follows:

UPFA - 105
UNP – 82
ITAK – 22
JHU – 9
SLMC - 5
Up-country People's Front -1
EPDP - 1

The UPFA in fact could not even get a speaker appointed to this parliament. The nominee of the opposition UNP, W.J.M.Lokubandara won with 110 votes to 109 in a secret ballot amidst manhandling, fisticuffs and chaos in the well of the house. Despite this set back, president Chandrika Kumaratunga managed to cobble together a government with the help of the SLMC, UPF the CWC, the EPDP and the 'tolerance' of the JHU. The SLMC had in addition to the five seats they won on their own account, four seats on the UNP national list and one more MP elected on the UNP list in the Vavuniya district. The CWC's 8 MPs were all elected on the UNP list.

It was this shaky government that Mahinda Rajapaksa inherited in November 2005. By the time he took over however, the JHU had become a steadier ally by entering into an agreement with him. So the UPFA (which included the JVP), JHU, SLMC, CWC, UPF and EPDP together had a working majority in parliament. Later, many members of the UNP proper, apart from the minority party members who had contested the 2004 April election on the UNP ticket, also joined the Rajapaksa government, which meant that by November 2007, they had a good majority in parliament. But this was a majority only on paper.

In June 2005, the JVP had opposed president Chandrika Kumaratunga's proposed P-TOMS arrangement with the LTTE to distribute Tsunami funds in the north and east as mentioned in a previous chapter. The JVP went to the supreme court and got the P-TOMS arrangement declared unconstitutional. The three JVP ministers in the UPFA cabinet also resigned in protest, and from that time onwards, they remained a separate entity in parliament. In 2005, the JVP played a crucial role at the presidential elections and was a major factor that ensured Mahinda Rajapaksa's victory. However after Mahinda's victory, they opted to continue sitting as a separate entity in parliament without joining the government.

The JVP contested separately at the local government elections of February 2006. By the end of 2007, the UPFA and the JVP had

409

reached the parting of ways. The influx of UNP dissidents into the UPFA government had diluted the influence of the JVP and they resented that. The estrangement of the JVP was what gave the opposition UNP the courage to attempt a parliamentary coup against the Rajapaksa government. One JVP MP Nandana Gunatilleke was sitting separately and would subsequently support the government. When the 38 MPs that the JVP now had were removed from the UPFA, they were down from 105 seats to just 67. Of this, Samaraweera and Sooriyarachchi had been sacked, bringing their numbers further down to 65. The UPFA was now totally dependent on their allies to remain in power. The UNP dissidents had brought in 21 MPs. The JHU had 9 MPs. Of the minority parties in the ruling coalition, the SLMC controlled 10, the CWC, 8 and the UPF 2 bringing the total up to 117 MPs. (One of the JHU monks, Ven. Uduwe Dhammaloka was sitting separately, but he has been counted as an MP who would vote for the government.) If the minority parties broke away from the Rajapaksa regime, the government would have fallen.

Throughout the year 2007, the UNP had been holding public rallies to whip up support for their plan to topple the Rajapaksa government at the vote on the budget. Once the government loses its majority, a parliamentary election will have to be called and the UNP hoped to win the ensuing parliamentary election with the help of the minority parties. Despite the elaborate preparations made by the UNP, the government won the vote at the second reading of the budget on 19 November 2007 with 118 voting for and 102 against. The JVP voted against the budget but until the last moment, they kept mum about their decision and this lack of information about what the JVP would do prevented those who wanted to defect from jumping the gun. All the constituent members of the ruling coalition, the UPFA, the UNP dissidents, the SLMC, CWC, UPF and the JHU voted with the government.

After the JVP voted against the government at the second reading, those planning to defect were emboldened. The government now had a slim majority of only six votes in parliament. This made the final vote on the third reading of parliament on 14 December 2007, a crucial and decisive matter. Conspirators went into overdrive, trying to buy off MPs from the government. Four members of the SLMC including its leader Rauff Hakeem voted against the budget. Anura Bandaranaike and Wijedasa Rajapakse abstained. Politically, the end of 2007 was the most dangerous moment for the Rajapaksa government.

No other government would have survived after having lost 41 members of parliament, (38 JVP members, plus Mangala, Anura and Sooriyarachchi) but the UPFA survived, thanks to the reverse flow of defections from the UNP. At the third reading of the budget on 14 December 2007, the JVP abstained from voting. The ruling UPFA's votes in parliament went down to 114 with the defection of Anura Bandaranaike and the earlier defection of SLMC leader Rauff Hakeem with three others. Ven Uduwe Dhammaloka voted for the government as did Nandana Gunatilleke the dissident JVP parliamentarian. December 2007 was a close call for the Rajapaksa government. The parliamentary coup against the government was mounted in a situation where the government had not really convinced the electorate that it was winning the war.

The east had been cleared and some sensational recoveries of LTTE weapons and artillery guns had been made, but the east had been cleared in the early 1990s by the UNP government as well, but the army had soon lost control of the area, and there was nothing to show that things would be any different this time. In what seemed to be a confirmation of the UNP's claim that the government was not getting anywhere with the war, the army was stuck in the western Vanni with little or no progress to show for months of fighting. In this gloomy scenario, the worst possible blow to the government was the Anuradhapura air base attack which took place in the early hours of 22 October 2007, just weeks before the crucial budget vote. The maximum propaganda advantage was derived by the LTTE by making this a combined ground and air operation. Like all the other military debacles that the Sri Lankan military has had to face, this too could have been avoided if the air force been just a little more vigilant. The LTTE knew the weaknesses of the Sri Lankan military and this was one instance where they used it to the maximum.

This air base was located well outside the conflict zone, and conditions therefore, were more relaxed. It was not located in Colombo, where the state of alertness would be higher. Finally, Anuradhapura was not a major launching pad for offensive air operations. It was mainly a training facility. The air force training school had been shifted from China Bay in Trincomalee to Anuradhapura in the late 1980s. The only militarily important task carried out from the Anuradhapura air base was air surveillance. Due to all these reasons, the LTTE knew that the state of alertness at the Anuradhapura air base would be lax.

The LTTE chose a night on which the air base would be even more relaxed than usual. The previous day, an annual motoring event, the Gajaba Super Cross had been held at the Saliyapura complex of the Gajaba Regiment in Anurdhapura which is located in the vicinity of the air base. About a 100,000 people had converged on Anuradhapura to witness the event. The night after an event like this would make everybody relax even more. A contingent of 21 black tiger cadres had assembled in a coconut plantation adjoining the air base and the pre-dawn attack on Monday had started at around 2.30 am. The attacking party had cut through the protective fences and had inexplicably got through the electrified fence as well. The electrified fence had not been connected to the power grid at that time.

The 21 member attacking party also got through the minefields without stepping on any of them, which may show that they had a map indicating the mine distribution. Inside help obviously would have been available to them. Once they were inside, two LTTE planes took off from the Vanni and were detected by the radar and the electricity supply was cut off in Colombo, Anuradhapura and other towns in the path of the planes. The bombs the planes dropped did no real damage, but the LTTE squad on the ground in an attack that continued till late morning, destroyed the Beechcraft that the air force had owned since the 1980s, two Mi-24 attack helicopters, one Mi-17 transport helicopter, two trainer jets, one Cessna 150 used for training, and a Bell-212 helicopter, while another ten aircraft including three jet training aircraft were damaged.

A Bell-212 helicopter that went in pursuit of the two LTTE planes crashed some distance away in Mihintale. The theory is that it could have been hit by friendly fire aimed at the LTTE planes. The air force was deeply embarrassed. However several days later, on 2 November 2007, the air force managed to salvage their self respect by carrying out a spectacular bombing raid that killed the LTTE political-wing chief S.P.Tamilselvam.

Two aircraft took part in the Tamilselvam attack, a MiG-27 and a Kfir. They took off before dawn and reached Kilinochchi just as the sun was rising. The planes could not circle overhead for long lest it alerted the target and they had to take the target just as they arrived on location. As the LTTE political wing chief slept in his bomb-proof concrete underground bunker, the two aircraft above unloaded a total of 4000 kilos of bombs over Tamilselvam who never woke up again.

In the middle of the budget vote crisis, Gōta pleaded with JVP leader Somawansa Amarasinghe and their parliamentary leader

Wimal Weerawansa not to defeat the government at the budget vote and that the war can be won if they are given one more year. Weerawansa always unequivocally gave Gōta the assurance that they will see to it that the government will not fall. Amarasinghe however was evasive. He would say they have 'other issues' which are 'political matters'. By which he implied that Gōta was not a political person who could understand such things. Gōta would argue that other issues were not important and that the most important issue was to defeat the LTTE. However, Amarasinghe had remained doggedly evasive.

There had been a long drawn out debate raging within the JVP central committee about what trajectory its relationship with the UPFA government should take from late 2005 to mid-2007. The JVP had decided to support Mahinda Rajapaksa's candidacy at the 2005 presidential elections in the midst of this debate. In fact even though the JVP supported Mahinda's candidacy, they opted not to join his government and remained a separate force in parliament. So while the JVP was with the government, they were not of it and Gōta never knew what they would do. What was most disconcerting to Gōta was that JVP leaders like Somawansa Amarasinghe did not appear to have the confidence that the government could win the war. It was in this unpromising scenario that the budget vote crisis of 2007 came up. Following this crisis, Wimal Weerawansa defected to the government with 12 JVP parliamentarians. From that time onwards, the UPFA never had a problem about their parliamentary majority.

Chapter 68

The Murky World of Colombo

In the north and east, the fight was for the most part straightforward. The LTTE was uniformed and the military was uniformed, and they shot at each other on sight. But in the murky world of Colombo, nothing was clear cut. The LTTE was mixed up with the Colombo underworld, members of the police force, intelligence operatives, businessmen, politicians and even prostitutes. The easy and casual relationships that existed between the LTTE suicide cadres and their contacts in Colombo are a study in themselves. The LTTE could not have operated with impunity in Colombo unless they had contacts with the Colombo underworld and even the police.

In early 2008, the Western Province Intelligence Division had come into contact with a Sinhalese woman 'Mallika', who ran a prostitution ring in Colombo. She happened to know a Tamil woman in the same trade who brought Tamil women to Colombo to work as prostitutes. Mallika told the police that this Tamil woman 'Gowri', looked after LTTE suicide cadres who came to Colombo. The police traced Gowri to a house in Modera on 26 February 2008 and she was arrested and brought to the Borella headquarters of the WPID. Unaware that she was under arrest her customers kept calling on her phone and the police let Gowri talk to them. Among the many calls she got, was one from a youth 'Nagesh' who wanted to know where she was.

On prompting from the police Gowri told Nagesh that she was in police custody on a prostitution charge. Nagesh wanted to know whether she would get police bail and Gowri had answered in the affirmative. Unsuspectingly, Nagesh had come to the Borella police station to bail her out. Despite being an LTTE suicide cadre, he had thought nothing of coming to a police station. It was not just the military that became complacent and lowered their guard. It happened to the LTTE as well, and this was one good example. Nagesh too was arrested and sent off to the Grandpass police station.

There had been a certain Muslim police inspector at the Maligawatte police station 'Abdul' who had been transferred out due to various suspicions. One day, the Grandpass police phoned Superintendent of Police Ravi Seneviratne the head of the WPID and said that Inspector Abdul had come to see Nagesh claiming that the latter was his informant. Seneviratne had told the Grandpass police to ask Inspector Abdul to stay right there until he comes, and he had immediately set off for Grandpass, but the Inspector had vanished by the time Seneviratne arrived. Alarm bells were now ringing in Seneviratne's mind as Abdul had been transferred out of Maligawatte due to suspicions that he was in league with the LTTE.

Several months earlier, Inspector Abdul had claimed to have discovered a Claymore mine which had been set up targeting Seneviratne who lived in the police flats in Maligawatte. Seneviratne had asked Inspector Abdul how he had come upon this Claymore mine. To this Abdul had said that he had received the information from an informant who had been drinking in a bar when he had heard that a Claymore had been placed in such and such location targeting a police intelligence officer. Seneviratne was aware that at the time the mine had been recovered, it had been armed which meant that the operator had been in the vicinity, waiting with a remote controller to explode it. Seneviratne had told Abdul at that time, to follow the standard procedure in such cases and deploy sniffer dogs to see where the track led. But Inspector Abdul had failed to use police dogs. When asked why he did not use sniffer dogs, the excuse had been that other people had also touched the Claymore mine and that he did not use sniffers on that account. This had raised Seneviratne's suspicions. Thereupon he had wanted to know whether he could meet his informant who had told him about the Claymore mine. Inspector Abdul had readily agreed but he never brought the informant to see Seneviratne. When he was next asked about the informant, Abdul had said the informant had taken the reward money for the Claymore mine and gone to Kilinochchi.

What had raised Seneviratne's suspicions even more was that one day, Inspector Abdul had casually told him, that two more

Claymores had been brought from the north and that he will have them brought to a spot near a certain budget shop in Maligawatte and for Seneviratne to take the two Claymores and to recommend him for a reward. Suspicious about this ready flow of information that Abdul seemed to have about Claymore mines, Seneviratne had told him, "If you have any information about Claymores, tell me where they are, and I will recover them. What is the point in having them brought to the Maligawatte budget shop?" Seneviratne suspected this to be a trap and brushed off the offer. He then sent a confidential letter to the Senior DIG Colombo to transfer Abdul out of Maligawatte. The latter was then posted to the Galle Face police post. Seneviratne objected to this as well, because this was in proximity to Temple Trees, the presidential secretariat, the defence ministry and army headquarters. Thereupon he was posted to the Police training school in Kalutara.

Now when he heard that that Inspector Abdul had come to see Nagesh, Seneviratne knew his suspicions were justified. When he arrived at the Grandpass police station, Abdul had given him the slip. Seneviratne had then taken Nagesh out of his cell and wanted to know how he knows Inspector Abdul. Nagesh claimed that he was Abdul's informant. Seneviratne wanted to know what kind of information he had been giving Abdul. During the conversation, the Maligawatte Claymore mine was also mentioned. Seneviratne had wanted to know how he (Nagesh) had come by the information that there was a Claymore mine there. Nagesh had said that he had been drinking in a bar in Panchikawatte when he had overheard two people discussing that a Claymore mine would be set up in such and such place. Nagesh also claimed that he had had a drink with Inspector Abdul at P.D.Sirisena grounds in Maligawatte that night, but he had not been able to explain at what time in the night he had got to know that the Claymore had been set up. Seneviratne had thereupon told Nagesh that the LTTE can't be operating in such a slipshod manner, having discussions about laying Claymore mines in bars and that he does not believe a word of that story.

Upon further interrogation, Nagesh admitted that he himself had set up that Claymore mine targeting Seneviratne. At this point, police recovered the cyanide capsule Nagesh had kept up his rectum. He revealed that he had first met Inspector Abdul with 'Charles' the deputy to Pottu Amman. Inspector Abdul had met Charles in the Vanni twice. He had gone to Mannar and taken a boat to Vedithaltivu and from there travelled overland to Kilinochchi. At the first meeting, Abdul had been given Rs. 300,000 and a gold necklace. Later they had bought a Mitsubishi Hi Ace van for him and the LTTE had paid the instalments. The target he had been given was president Mahinda Rajapaksa. In the meantime, Nagesh had been circumcised, given a Muslim name and sent to Colombo to work with Inspector Abdul who was tasked with enrolling him in the police force as a Tamil speaking recruit. There was then a recruitment drive on for Tamil speaking policemen after the east had been cleared. When Nagesh came to Colombo, accommodation was found for him by Gowri, the Tamil 'madam' mentioned earlier.

Though months passed, Inspector Abdul and Nagesh were not delivering anything. Under pressure from Charles, they decided to take an easy target which was SP Seneviratne of the WPID who lived in Maligawatte. Abdul came on night rounds to Maligawatte and one day he had brought Nagesh on his police motorcycle and shown him Seneviratne's car and quarters. The hit was planned for 8 June 2007. Abdul had gone to Modera to an LTTE safe house and brought the Claymore mine and kept it in the police station. That night he had taken a drink at P.D.Sirisena grounds with Nagesh and the latter had planted the Claymore mine on the road taken by Seneviratne. The latter would go past that spot at around 6.45 to 7.00 in the morning. As he passed, Nagesh had pressed the button on the remote controller, but the Claymore failed to explode. What had gone wrong was that he had wrapped some cello-tape around the remote controller and it was obstructing the sensor.

Nagesh now in a state of panic, had gone to see Inspector Abdul, and told him that the Claymore failed to explode. Abdul, a cool operator, had told Nagesh to go home and he had gone to where the Claymore mine had been set up at around 8.30 am and taken it away as if he had just received information about it. This claymore had been produced as a 'recovery' and Abdul had even claimed a reward from the police department for it. As Nagesh spilled the beans, Seneviratne started looking for Abdul. He found that from the Grandpass police station, Abdul had gone straight back to the police training school and had taken leave and was on his way to Akkaraipattu. Seneviratne then spoke to Nimal Leuke the STF commandant who had Abdul arrested at a check point in Aranthalawa in the Ampara district. He was brought to WPID headquarters in Borella and under interrogation, had confirmed the story that Nagesh had related. The LTTE had roped in Abdul when he was the Officer in Charge of a police post in Tirukkovil in 2002.

After the arrest of Abdul, Nagesh was interrogated again and a massive haul of weapons was recovered from his house in Modera, among which were two 20 kg Claymore mines. Four 8 kg Claymores, two suicide jackets - one of them having five kilos of C-4 explosives and ball bearings, five kilos of C-4 explosives, four hand grenades and even the remote controller that failed to work in the abortive 8 June 2007 operation with the obstructing cello tape still covering the sensor. Most chillingly, Nagesh had revealed that during the short period that Abdul had been at the Galle Face police post, the two of them had watched the president's movements, his motorcades, the vehicles he travelled in, and the level of security etc. They had come to the conclusion that a conventional suicide attack could not be carried out on the president's motorcade and that there would have to be an RPG or Claymore attack to stop the motorcade first, before carrying out the suicide attack.

In the meantime, Nagesh had applied to join the police force through Abdul's good offices. Through a Colombo ruling party politician, the latter had got himself a posting to the Norwood police station in Nuwara Eliya. When asked why he wanted to go to Norwood, Abdul had explained that when the president goes to Nuwara Eliya, the policemen on duty on the roads were drawn from the Nuwara Eliya police division, and the OICs of the various police stations were given sections of the road to guard. The suicide cadre then would be in police uniform and wearing the suicide jacket underneath and in that manner, a direct hit on the president's car can be achieved. A micro pistol and a claymore mine were recovered from Abdul.

When the police checked Nagesh's email, they came across the name of one Vijayan who lived in Modera. When Seneviratne and another senior police officer Jayantha Kulatilleke went to Vijayan's house, the latter knowing that he was surrounded, exploded a Claymore mine and killed himself inside his house. A search of the premises of the late Vijayan yielded a SIM (Subscriber Identity Module) card. The details on the SIM card led to two other LTTE cadres. It was through one of these two cadres that a breakthrough was finally achieved into the plot to assassinate Gōta. The Sinhala 'madam' Mallika who provided the police with this breakthrough was paid a reward by the police and still runs a prostitution ring. Inspector Abdul, Nagesh and Gowri (not their real names) are awaiting trial. There is a common misconception that the 'war zone' was in the north and east. As far as the LTTE was concerned, there was no such demarcation. For them, the whole country was a war zone. There were many attacks on civilian targets outside the north and east during this period. The frequency and the intensity of the attacks can be gauged from the following list:

* 24 July 2007 – Claymore mine attack on Medawachchiya-Mannar road at Settikulam, 9 soldiers killed.
* 28 November 2007 – Assassination attempt on Minister Douglas Devananda by a female suicide bomber wearing a 'bra bomb'.
* 1 January 2008 - Opposition UNP parliamentarian T.Maheswaran shot dead by a lone LTTE gunman at a Hindu temple in Colombo.
* 2 January 2008 – Bus carrying wounded army personnel attacked at Slave Island Colombo, 4 killed, 28 injured.
* 8 January 2008 – Minister D.M.Dassanayake killed in Claymore mine attack in Ja Ela.
* 17 January 2008 – Claymore attack on bus in Moneragala, 32 killed. The LTTE hit team shot dead five farmers on their way back. On the same day, 10 more civilians were killed in Hambegauwa and Tanamalwila.
* 2 February 2008 – Bus bomb in Dambulla kills 20, fifty injured.
* 3 February 2008 – Claymore attack in Welioya kills 12 civilians and injures 17.
* 10 February 2008 – Bomb discovered at the Anuradhapura weekly fair.
* 23 February 2008 – Bomb left on bus discovered in Mt Lavinia.
* 10 March 2008 – Time bomb explosion near Roxy Cinema in Wellawatte injures four school children.
* 6 April 2008 – Minister Jeyaraj Fernandopulle and 12 others killed in bombing.
* 16 May 2008 – Two police buses targeted by a suicide bomber on a motorcycle, seven policemen killed, 85 injured.
* 24 May 2008 – Time bomb with 1.2 kilos of C-4 explosives found on crowded bus in Kirillawela.
* 29 May 2008 – Claymore attack in Vavuniya kills three policemen.
* 6 June 2008 – Claymore attack on bus in Katubedda kills 22 and injures 60.
* 11 July 2008 – LTTE infiltration team fires at a bus on the Kataragama-Buttala road killing 4.

Chapter 69

Breakthrough in the Vanni

Sri Lanka began the year 2008 with a stalemate in the western Vanni. In January 2008 in an interview with the Sinhala weekly, *Lankadeepa*, Gōta admitted that a time frame could not be set for the war and that all that can be stated is that the government had the resolve to destroy the LTTE, even though it is not possible to predict when the war will be over. The strategy favoured by Gōta was to tax the LTTE to the maximum by opening up more and more battle fronts. Fonseka had argued against Gōta's suggestion that another division be deployed to capture Vedithaltivu on the west coast as recounted in a previous chapter. The strategy then changed to opening up another front on the east coast so that the LTTE will be forced to divide their fighters and resources between two separate theatres of war located far apart on either side of the country.

In the special administrative region of Welioya, on the border of the Mulleitivu jungles, Brigadier Nandana Udawatte, an Armoured Corps officer, was busy raising a new infantry division to make a direct incursion into the LTTE's heartland in the eastern Vanni. The 59th Division of the army, started off with just two battalions, the 11th Gemunu and 14th Sinha, neither of which were seasoned, battle hardened units. Later more battalions were added to the new division including seasoned fighting units like the 1st Sinha. On 7 January 2008, Brigadier Udawatte advanced on the LTTE's frontline on the border of the Mulleitivu jungles. The LTTE had a well fortified defence line extending from Kokkuthuduwai on the coast, to Kambiliwewa in the interior with strong points every 300-350 meters and bunkers every 100 meters (See map 3).

About 325 LTTE cadres were thought to be manning this defence line which marked the border between government and LTTE held territory in the eastern Vanni. They were backed by artillery and the areas in front of their line were heavily mined and strewn with improvised explosive devices. Brigadier Udawatte's troops established their line as close as possible to the LTTE defences and commenced the offensive. This was now the third major battlefront that the LTTE had to face. It took over six weeks for Udawatte's troops to wear the LTTE down and breach their front line on 22 February 2008. After entering LTTE held territory, the troops had to stay dispersed over a wide area to avoid providing a target for LTTE artillery fire. This was very different terrain to that in the western Vanni. There were large swathes of canopied primary forest interspersed with wide open cultivated areas.

Once through the LTTE frontline, the next major obstacle that Brigadier Udawatte's troops faced in the jungles of Mulleitivu was the LTTE's 'One-Four Base' a huge complex of camps and underground bunkers in the Andankulam forest reserve. This base had never been taken by the Indian or Sri Lankan armies and had always functioned as the LTTE's last place of retreat. For the next several months, the 59th Division would be laboriously taking over one LTTE installation after another in the One-Four Base. The opening of the eastern Vanni front showed results. With the mounting pressure on their men and resources, The Madu Church fell in April 2008 to Jagath Dias's troops and Shavendra Silva captured Adamapan, one of the LTTE strongholds in the Mannar rice bowl in May 2008.

As Udawatte's troops fought in the LTTE's very backyard, in mid-June 2008 the pressure on the LTTE was ratcheted up further with another front being opened up in the central Vanni. Task Force 2 under the command of Brigadier P.M.R.Bandara made up of 11 battalions was launched to fight their way up the A-9 highway from Omanthai to Kanagarayankualm and to capture a T-shaped piece of territory extending to the town of Mundimuruppu in the western Vanni and a point to the south of the A-34 Mankulam-Mulleitivu road in the eastern half of the Vanni. Within a few weeks after Brigadier Bandara's columns started moving up the A-9 highway, LTTE resistance in the rice bowl crumbled and they fell back to the town of Vedithaltivu several kilometres to the north. The LTTE could not take the pressure on the west, east and now the centre as well. The strategy of taxing the LTTE by opening up multiple battlefronts was working well. Breaking through the rice bowl, which was the strongest point the LTTE had in the western Vanni, was a major event. Both the army and the LTTE knew that nothing could now stop the army from advancing right up to Pooneryn.

An elated Gōta visited Shavendra Silva's field headquarters in Mannar along with army commander Sarath Fonseka to commend the troops for the landmark breakthrough. The visit by Gōta and Fonseka boosted the morale of the troops no end. This was not an achievement that was cheaply obtained. In the ten months of fighting to capture this 80 square kilometre patch of land, Shavendra Silva's troops had suffered an appalling casualty rate with 248 men killed and 1,308 injured. The casualty rate of the army was thus well over three times the total number of LTTE cadres who were thought to have been holding the area. After Gōta's visit, the town of Vedithaltivu fell to Shavendra Silva's troops on 16 July 2008. A special forces contingent led by Col. Nirmal Dharmaratne made an incursion from Periyamadu through the 57th Division line across to the north of Vedithaltivu and captured a village called Attimodi and the LTTE defences in Vedithaltivu collapsed due to the threat of being surrounded.

In many ways the final war was a technology driven war. Many improvements were made in the equipment and armaments available to the armed forces. In late 1998, during the *Jayasikurui* operation, some ancient artillery locating radars (manufactured in 1973), were bought for the ground troops. These were replaced around August 2007 with brand new Chinese built radars which had been brought to Sri Lanka on an experimental basis. There was some doubt whether the Chinese radars would work in the humid conditions in Sri Lanka as the humidity levels here were much higher than in China. These radars function by picking up the sound of the enemy artillery fire and then plotting the location of the enemy guns. However, even the slightest rain could affect the interdiction of the sound waves.

The moisture levels in the air also affected the accuracy of the radars. The Chinese sent the expert who had designed these radars with around 20 others to Sri Lanka and they stayed here for some weeks. After much experimentation, they finally managed to adjust the machines to function even at Sri Lankan levels of humidity. By around October 2007, these artillery locating radars were fully functional and playing a part in the Vanni operations. These radars were supposed to be effective up to a radius of 32 kilometres, but their actual range was about twice that and they were deemed to be exceptionally good pieces of equipment by the army. The four radars were distributed to the various Vanni fronts as they opened up.

Whenever Gōta went around to the field headquarters of the fighting formations in the Vanni, the first thing he would look into would be the battalion strengths. He always replenished the manpower lost as a result of casualties. He knew that unless the battalion strengths were maintained, the momentum of the advance would falter. The LTTE used small group infiltration attacks, withering mortar and artillery fire and even poison gas attacks to stop the advance of Brigadier Bandara's troops into the eastern Vanni. When the army came under gas attacks in the eastern Vanni, they were not ready for such a contingency. The available gas masks were rushed to the Vanni, but were not sufficient for the task at hand. Gas masks cost a lot of money and were not produced in large quantities. So the director of medical services of the army together with a local company, Hayleys Ltd produced a disposable gas mask using charcoal as the filtering agent.

After some experimentation, the medical services director had advised that it should be a full face mask because problems could ensue if the gas particles touched the skin. Each of these masks would last only two or three minutes so each soldier was given two or three masks to give him enough time to leave the contaminated area. A total of around 50,000 of these improvised gas masks were produced for the army. There were casualties as a result of gas attacks, but no deaths. When the gas attacks came, the army had two options, they could publicise the matter and tell the world that the LTTE was using chemical weapons. Or they could keep quiet about it and try to meet the challenge as best as they could. They chose the latter course of action because the moment this talk of chemical weapons went out, recruitment into the army would have dried up.

There was also the fact that complaining to the outside world would not have stopped the LTTE from using such weapons. As with many other things, the LTTE had an ingenious chemical weapons delivery system. They put the chemical substance encased in wet clay into an ordinary mortar round. When fired, the mortar would explode on impact and the chemical would be released. But because of the wet clay, the release of the poison would take place very slowly and could last up to one or two days. The outer part of the wet clay casing would be burnt and crusty due to the explosion, but the core would be wet, and retaining the chemical agent. Brigadier Bandara's Task Force 2 would secure a total of 860 square kilometres in the central Vanni with 111 men losing their lives in the process.

Brigadier Udawatte's troops in the Mulleitivu jungles were also finally able to dislodge the LTTE from the 'One-Four Base' by the end of July 2008. After this, the army formations in the western Vanni found the going much easier and they were able to link up and form one front in Periyamadu about 15 kilometres to the south east of the town Vedithaltivu. How rapid the progress of the army now was can be gauged from the fact that Jagath Dias's division which captured the Madu Church in April 2008, was assaulting the LTTE defences in Thunukkai and Mallawi, two important towns in the Vanni about 30 kilometres to the north, by July the same year.

Once out of the rice bowl, the terrain changed to the usual sandy soil with scrub jungle that was characteristic of much of the western Vanni. The ditch-cum-bund earth defences which were such a familiar feature of the battles in the Vanni, were not to be seen in the rice bowl. The LTTE probably never really expected the army to cross the rice bowl. Once they did, movement was very rapid firstly because unlike in the rice bowl, the troops had plenty of points to capture, which would provide cover for the advancing troops. The Engineers would blast the buildings first before troops advanced so as to avoid any harm to troops as a result of booby traps. It was a destructive process and the advancing troops were told by their commanders to minimize damage to government owned buildings like schools and hospitals.

There was close coordination between the two advancing formations in the western Vanni, with each looking after the other's flank. Troops were deployed along the coast to prevent a seaborne attack by the LTTE as well. As the troops advanced, the LTTE retreated northwards taking the civilian population with them. The first time that Jagath Dias's troops came across the LTTE's ditch-cum-bund defences in the hinterland of the western Vanni was in Periyamadu. These were broad anti-tank ditches about ten feet deep combined with a bund made of the excavated earth which was about as high as the ditch was deep. These were not pre-existing defences in the Vanni, and were being built by the LTTE as the army advanced, in a desperate effort to stop or at least slow their advance. The air force bombed and strafed the LTTE cadres and earth moving equipment engaged in building these earthworks and it was in the midst of air attacks and artillery strikes that these defences were built all over the vast Vanni plain.

Thunukkai, an important junction in the western Vanni, held by 150-200 terrorists with the usual earth bund defences and anti-tank ditches, was captured by Jagath Dias's troops by the third week of August 2008. Once past Vedithaltivu, Shavendra Silva's troops found a five kilometre long ditch-cum-bund in Vellankulam on either side of the A-32 road along which they were advancing, held by about 200 LTTE cadres. Even though the LTTE cadres would have literally broken their backs building these huge earthworks at short notice, they were perhaps worth the effort because it is only with such defences that a couple of hundred cadres could even hope to delay the advance of several thousand well trained and well equipped battle hardened troops.

After this came the LTTE's equivalent of the great wall of China, a huge ditch-cum-bund that went half way across Sri Lanka from Nachchikudah on the coast, up to the Akkarayankulam tank and from there across the A-9 road up to the Iranamadu tank in the eastern Vanni, a distance of about 30 kilometres. This bund was held by a force of around 1000 cadres. The Nachchikudah-Akkarayankulam-Iranamadu earth bund posed a particularly difficult obstacle. Both army formations led by Shavendra Silva and Jagath Dias were stopped by this bund. G.V.Ravipriya who was a brigade commander under Jagath Dias says that the Akkarankulam bund was unlike anything they had come across earlier. Even in Thunukkai, the bund they had come across had not been a continuous structure as in Akkarayankulam.

The bund was constructed in L shaped segments. When troops broke through one part, the LTTE would engage them from the remaining part. Hence the breaching of the bund in one place did not result in the entire line falling to the army. Shavendra Silva's troops took the bund from the Nachchikudah end and Jagath Dias's troops assailed it from the Akkarayankulam-Iranamadu end. Because of the height of the bund and the deep anti-tank ditches in front of it, in addition to the improvised explosive devices and the strong points on the bund, not to mention the wide open space in front, it was a difficult obstacle to take. The LTTE was amazingly resilient. If a bunker on their bund was destroyed in artillery fire, they would repair it in the night. It took Shavendra Silva's troops two months to capture the Nachchikudah end of the bund which was finally achieved towards the end of October 2008. Shavendra Silva lost 153 soldiers in breaching his end of the bund.

Brigadier Udawatte's troops moving northwards in the Mulleitivu district came up against a major bund about 12 km in length between the Nayaru lagoon and the town of Tannimuruppu in the interior. This was well defended with a wide open space of 800- 1500 meters in front of it which was mostly abandoned paddy land. This made approaching the bund a very hazardous exercise.

Udawatte's troops were now faced with the situation that Shavendra Silva's troops were confronted with in the rice bowl earlier.

The field of vision available to the enemy made it impossible to advance in the daytime and troops could advance only at night. Digging infiltration trenches to get troops close enough to charge the bund was the method adopted by Udawatte. The LTTE kept firing mortars but the probability of taking a direct hit on a narrow trench was low because the army too used mortars and artillery and snipers to keep the LTTE busy. It was the 7th Gemunu battalion that had finally breached this bund capturing a two kilometre stretch. Udawatte's troops were most of the time deep inside a primary forest and with the monsoon rains came a plethora of diseases like Chickengunya and Malaria and there was a high sick rate among troops.

In the meantime in the western Vanni, with two divisions assailing the Nachchikudah-Akkarayankulam bund, Lt Col Senaka Wijesuriya of the 57th Division took the eastern extremity of this bund. His troops had taken Kokavil, a town on the A-9 highway and then turned their attention to the Iranamadu extension of the bund, which was taken without much difficulty but the two SLLI battalions occupying it had to face a withering counterattack with around 400 mortars being fired at them in the course of a single day. The LTTE managed to recapture a part of the bund and at one point it appeared that the LTTE would prevail. The army was fired upon by LTTE boats in the Iranamadu tank as well. Captain Narangoda, a company commander of the 10th SLLI was injured and captured by the LTTE. His body was later handed over to the army by the ICRC. This was probably one of the last occasions that the ICRC would deliver dead bodies of soldiers to the army.

Once the Nachchikudah end of this bund was breached, Pooneryn was left wide open to Shavendra Silva's troops. As Pooneryn was being assailed by the army, on 21 November 2008, troops in Muhamalai attacked the LTTE's first line of defence and captured it as a diversionary tactic to prevent the LTTE from concentrating their forces and military assets on defending Pooneryn. As the army took over Pooneryn, a good number of civilians who were in LTTE captivity managed to escape across the Jaffna lagoon in boats to the peninsula. The fleeing civilians waved shirts and white cloths to the troops to stop them from firing on the boats thinking they were LTTE. With the capture of Pooneryn, the possibility of LTTE artillery fire into Jaffna and incursions across the lagoon was eliminated, releasing the troops in Jaffna for offensive operations.

Chapter 70

The Understanding with India

The most important country with regard to the Tamil question in Sri Lanka was India. An important development in this regard was the setting up of the troikas - committees of three key officials from both sides who would have unfettered access to one another, circumventing the usual protocol. After Gōta accompanied president Mahinda Rajapaksa to India in late December 2005 soon after they assumed office, he made yet another visit to India on 15 May 2006. This time, Gōta travelled alone. On this trip, he met Vijay Singh the defence secretary, and the commanders of the Indian army, navy and air force and the Indian defence advisor M.K.Narayanan. It was the new Indian High Commissioner Alok Prasad who had arranged the visit because the relationship between the two countries was still not on a good footing even after the president's visit in December 2005.

When Gōta met Narayanan, he knew that there still was a problem because Narayanan was talking about the 13th Amendment to the constitution and saying that the LTTE problem could not be dealt with militarily. After this round of talks in India, Gōta came back and informed the president that there still were outstanding issues. Soon after he returned to Colombo, High Commissioner Alok Prasad came to Gōta's office for a discussion because he realized that even Gōta's trip had not succeeded in ironing out the outstanding problems. At this meeting it was Gōta who had suggested to Prasad that there should be more interaction between the two countries at the level of officials so that any outstanding problems could be dealt with at that level, before it goes to the politicians on both sides.

Alok Prasad got the nod for this arrangement from the Indian side. President Mahinda Rajapaksa appointed his brother Basil Rajapaksa as the head of the troika with Gōta and Lalith Weeratunga being its other members. From the Indian side it was the external affairs secretary Shivshankar Menon, the defence secretary Vijay Singh and the national security advisor M.K Narayanan. High Commissioner Alok Prasad coordinated the whole process. Soon after this, the Sri Lankan troika visited India to meet their Indian counterparts and a line of communication was established. The arrangement was that any member of the troikas on both sides could contact anyone on the other side at any time of the day or night, with no need to go through protocol. This was a ground breaking arrangement and probably unique in the annals of bilateral diplomatic relations, at least in South Asia.

From the time the troika arrangement was put into place, there were no major problems between the two nations. Basil Rajapaksa kept the Indian government informed about what exactly was going on. By 2007, the relationship was on a good footing. Gōta visited India in late May 2007 and held discussions with the heads of the Indian army, navy and air force. The matters discussed related mainly to military cooperation, especially naval surveillance beyond Sri Lankan waters. The Indian navy chief assured Gōta that Indian resources would continue to be diverted for surveillance duties as and when requested by the Sri Lankan navy.

During his meeting with Shivshankar Menon, Gōta explained that so long as the moderate Tamil leaders continue to entertain any hopes of the LTTE achieving something militarily, their desire to engage in constructive discussions will be diminished. He also explained to Mennon that the president was of the opinion that the people had lost confidence in the provincial councils system and decentralisation based on the district would be the most useful method as the president himself had experienced as a member of parliament in the early 1990s. Gōta had also stressed that it was necessary to think beyond the LTTE and that political processes should not be guided solely by considerations related to the tigers. Mennon warned Gōta that the perception that the Sri Lankan government is not serious on devolution is spreading among other countries.

During this visit, Gōta explained to the Indians that Sri Lanka turned to other countries, (meaning Pakistan and China) for military supplies only when India was unable to supply the material needed due to sensitivities in Tamil Nadu. He explained that Sri Lanka had to pay for supplies from Pakistan and China. Despite this link that had been established behind the scenes, in the public domain, India kept on issuing statements which stressed that there could be no military solution and that negotiations were the only way. This was the public position taken by India throughout the early stages of the war - through Mavilaru, Sampur, Vakarai, Thoppigala, Silavathurei, and the initial part of the Mannar operations.

The Indians were kept informed about the ongoing operations in the Vanni as the year 2007 rolled into 2008. In mid-February, 2008, Gōta visited India again and held talks with Shivshankar Menon, Vijay Singh, and the Indian defence minister M.K.Anthony. This was during the period that Shavendra Silva and Jagath Dias were stuck in Mannar. At this meeting, Shivshankar Menon said that if the army was able to clear the north western stretch of the coastline, that would be a significant achievement. Menon had also complimented Gōta saying that what had been achieved in 2007 was 'very impressive'. Mennon said that the LTTE will break at some point with the pressure on them. Gōta however sounded a word of caution by saying that the LTTE was still very strong in Kilinochchi and that they derived strength from supporters overseas.

Mennon agreed with this view saying that he had met a Tamil man who was a mayor of a town in the UK and that he had articulated views similar to that of the LTTE. In Menon's view the overseas Tamils could only be won over when they hear from their own people back home about the way the LTTE led them on the path of destruction and for that it was important for the Tamil people in Sri Lanka to feel that they were being offered a fair deal. Gōta had explained that was exactly what they were trying to show by the implementation of the provincial councils system and the holding of elections to the eastern province.

Gōta also had discussions with the Indian defence secretary Vijay Singh two days later. At this meeting he had said that Sri Lanka would like to obtain supplies of ammunition from India. The Sri Lankan high commissioner in New Delhi Romesh Jayasinghe said that the ability to procure arms from India would remove the irritation resulting from the media highlighting instances when Sri Lanka was constrained to obtain supplies from other countries. The supremely pragmatic Vijay Singh said that in the situation that Sri Lanka finds itself in, such equipment should be purchased from whoever is able to supply the required items. Among the matters discussed with his Indian counterpart was the possibility of extended training for newly recruited Tamil policemen in India, which however could not be implemented due to the lack of Tamil speaking instructors in their police academies.

Even at the height of the war, one matter that loomed as large as the Tamil issue in Indo-Lanka relations was the issue of Indian fishermen straying into Sri Lankan territorial waters. This too was a main topic of discussion on Gōta's trip to India. He was accompanied by Wasantha Karannagoda the navy chief who had with him, radar screen images of large clusters of Indian boats within Sri Lanka's territorial waters and some very close to the shore and vital security installations. Gōta pointed out to the Indian defence minister M.K.Anthony that when Indian boats are detained as a deterrent they are released expeditiously through the Indian High Commission and that the navy is under instructions to treat Indian fishermen in a humane manner.

At one of these troika meetings held in India, there was an exchange which highlighted the increasing understanding of the issues facing both countries. M.K.Narayanan, Shivshankar Mennon, Vijay Singh, Gōta and others were present when Narayanan brought up the subject of giving police powers to the chief ministers of provinces. Gōta told Narayanan that giving police powers to the provincial councils is disadvantageous even for the minorities. He pointed out that in Sri Lanka the provinces are very small and the chief minister will know each and every police officer in his region and the police force will become his own private army.

Gōta also pointed out that a Tamil chief minister can be guaranteed only in the northern province. But that Tamils were a minority in the east and this time the chief minister ship was given to Pillaiyan only on the president's personal intervention and in the face of opposition by the Muslim ministers in the province. If there is a Muslim chief minister in the east with police powers, the eastern Tamils are not going to be happy. He also pointed out that the Central province has a large Indian Tamil population and Arumugam Thondaman, their leader does not want police powers given to the chief minister as the chief minister of the central province will always be a Sinhalese. Gōta said that giving police powers to the chief ministers is a very dangerous thing because they are merely second tier politicians.

Narayanan was taken aback by what Gōta said. He had then turned to Vijay Singh the Indian defence secretary and asked him what his opinion about this was. Singh said without batting an eyelid, *"I agree one hundred percent with what Gōta said"*. And he added that even India was having problems with police powers being vested in the chief ministers. After this, Narayanan had never brought up this question of police powers again.

It was only after October 2008 following a visit to India by Basil Rajapaksa that the Indian stance seemed to change completely and they dropped all mention of negotiations and peace talks even from their public statements on Sri Lanka. The last time the Indians said there was no military solution to the LTTE problem was on 18 October 2008. The Indian ministry of external affairs press release following a telephone conversation between president Mahinda Rajapaksa and Prime Minister Manmohan Singh went as follows: *"Prime Minister Dr Manmohan Singh further mentioned that the rights and the welfare of the Tamil community of Sri Lanka should not get enmeshed in the ongoing hostilities against the LTTE. He reiterated that there was no military solution to the conflict and urged the president to start a political process for a peacefully negotiated political settlement within the framework of a united Sri Lanka."*

On 22 October 2008, Indian external affairs minister Pranab Mukherjee expressed much the same sentiments in a statement made in the Indian *Lok Sabha*. That was just before Basil Rajapaksa visited India. In October 2008, as the troops closed in on Pooneryn, and pressure was being brought on the Indian central government by Tamil Nadu to stop the offensive, the Indian high commissioner Alok Prasad went to see president Mahinda Rajapaksa and he recommended that Basil Rajapaksa be sent to India to talk to the Indian government. Basil went the very next day. The foreign ministry had advised him not to agree to issue any joint statement because the wording used by the Indians would restrict the Sri Lankan government's freedom of action. Before he left for India, Basil met chief justice Sarath N.Silva, to get some advice about the kind of terminology that should be used if he cannot avoid agreeing to a joint statement.

On 26 October 2008, following Basil Rajapaksa's visit, the tone of the joint statement put out to mark the visit was distinctly different. India had expressed the usual concerns about the humanitarian situation in the north and the need for a negotiated political settlement. But at the same time it said that *"both sides agreed that terrorism should be countered with resolve"*. Most importantly, the idea that there was 'no military solution to the conflict' which had been the centrepiece of earlier Indian statements on Sri Lanka, had been dropped. From this time until the end of the war, the Indians never again said publicly or privately, that there was no military solution to the conflict.

Chapter 71

The Fall of Kilinochchi

The Long Range Patrol (LRP) units in the Special Forces were started in 1996, modelled on the British Special Air Service (SAS) and were for operations more than 50 km into enemy territory. At that time, the LTTE was threatened only on their frontlines and not in their rear whereas the Sri Lankan state was threatened both on the frontlines and in the rear. The LRP units within the commando and Special Forces units of the army were set up to force the LTTE to deploy a part of their strength to guard their rear and also to restrict the movements of LTTE leaders. The claymore mine was the preferred strike weapon of the LRPs because they often had to hit a moving target and could not afford to miss the first time. If the Claymores missed the target, they would use the disposable RPGs they carried with them as a back-up weapon.

An LRP operation takes a great deal of preparation. First a reconnaissance patrol selects an ambush site. Then supplies are stocked in the vicinity for the use of the attack party. This is then followed by the attacking party moving into the area and waiting for their target over a number of days. They survive on the stockpiled rations. High-nutrition biscuits and water is the usual fare but the men do need occasional meals, so ration caches have to be built up. Then they have to carry several claymore mines for the ambushes. The mines are always laid in clusters to ensure that the target they hit is annihilated. Concealing the claymores, wiring them, and waiting for the right moment all require a great deal of skill.

During the Vanni operation, military red tape was cut down to the minimum. The LRP teams out the field led by a corporal could talk direct to the director operations of the air force - an Air Vice Marshall - over their satellite phones. It was from the air force that even the officers in the Special Forces got to know that a target was taken on information provided by an LRP team.

The most spectacular operation carried out by a special forces LRP unit was the hit on the LTTE air wing chief, Shankar in July 2000. He was killed at a location two kilometres to the south of Puthukudiirippu town by an LRP team led by Captain Lalith Jayasinghe. The killing of the LTTE air wing chief just two weeks after the LTTE's spectacular attack on the Katunayake air base and international airport added significance to the operation. Shankar would have been a prime target in any circumstances but just after the Katunayake attack, his importance was enhanced tenfold and the hit was brought forward as a matter of priority. Shankar used a black Mitsubishi Pajero which was noted by the LRP teams stalking him. At that time LTTE leaders had not been targeted behind their own frontlines and they went about quite confidently without switching vehicles.

The LRP team that killed Shankar had entered the Mulleitivu jungles from Welioya. The whole operation from start to finish took two weeks - for the LRP team to trek through the jungle to Puthukudiirippu, carry out the hit, and make their way back to base. Shankar died in a simultaneous blast of three claymore mines weighing 5 kilos each. Lalith Jayasinghe was killed in action later while on a similar operation in 2008.

During the Vanni offensive of 2007-2009, the most spectacular hit by an LRP team was that carried out on the deputy head of the LTTE intelligence wing Charles, who was killed to the north of Mannar on 5 January 2008. It was ironic that Charles who specialized in fixing hit jobs on VIPs behind the army's front lines, had to die himself in a similar hit job by the army behind LTTE lines. As we saw in an earlier chapter, it was Charles who was working on a hit job to take out president Mahinda Rajapaksa himself. As Shavendra Silva's troops were inching their way forward through the Mannar rice bowl, Charles was one of the LTTE leaders sent to oversee the operations in that sector. By this time, LTTE leaders did not use conspicuous vehicles for fear of LRP teams. The hit on Shankar in the very centre of LTTE territory had changed the way the LTTE leaders travelled.

However, even though they now used less conspicuous means of transport and changed vehicles frequently, when LTTE leaders travelled about there were tell tale signs that the LRP teams had learnt to recognize. There were signs like an advance party that may check the road that the LTTE leader would travel on. An LRP team that had marked out a site had been observing the area for twelve days before the hit team took over. The surveillance teams would often film the goings on digital cameras so that the hit team would know what to expect. The hit team itself had to lie in wait for Charles to turn up. His vehicle was first seen by a member of the four man LRP hit team who was up on a tree looking out for approaching vehicles.

In an article penned after his death, journalist D.B.S.Jeyaraj said that Charles held three leadership positions in the LTTE. He was the head of 'military intelligence', the head of 'external operations' (meaning terrorist attacks in Colombo) and in addition to the above, he was in charge of a special combat unit in Mannar. It was the latter job that exposed him to the LRP team. Jeyaraj wrote *"Charles was a protégé of Pottu Amman the dreaded intelligence chief of the tigers. He was an able deputy of Pottu Amman and in later life became near equal to his mentor."* Jeyaraj also reported Soosai the sea tiger chief as having said at a memorial meeting for Charles in Putukudiirippu that the high profile attacks masterminded by the low profile Charles had captured global attention.

According to Jeyaraj, it was Charles at the age of 19, who had masterminded the assassination of UNP strongman Ranjan Wijeratne in March 1991, the bombing of the Joint Operations Command headquarters in Colombo, the killing of navy commander Clancy Fernando in 1991, Lalith Athulathmudali and Ranasinghe Premadasa in 1993, and the Totalanga Bombing of 1994 that caused the deaths of the leader of the opposition Gamini Dissanayake, and UNP parliamentarians G.M.Premachandra, Weerasinghe Mallimarachchi, and Ossie Abeygunasekera among scores of others.

He had also had a hand in the central bank bombing, the attack on the Kolonnawa oil refinery, the 24 July 2001 attack on the Katunayake airport, the Anuradhapura air base attack of 2008 and many other LTTE operations. The list appears endless. In a fitting end to such a career, Charles and three other senior LTTE cadres died in a massive simultaneous explosion of five, seven and a half kilo claymore mines. He was given a grand funeral in Kilinochchi by the LTTE with a schoolgirl band and eulogies by Sooai among others.

Walking through the jungles did not pose much of a problem for the LRP teams as the jungles were not mined. The jungles were hardly patrolled by the LTTE and it was only the routes used often by them that were guarded heavily. The LRP teams would themselves be dressed in LTTE uniforms and would be mistaken for LTTE cadres even if they were seen by Tamil civilians. Once the hit takes place and their cover was blown, the difficult part of the operation was to get back to base alive. When LRP teams were coming back, the entire army front line had to be alerted to look out for the returning heroes who would be in LTTE uniforms. Since 1996, the Special Forces LRPs suffered only six fatalities. The commando LRP teams got away with injuries but no deaths. The LRP units did not exceed ten percent of the total strength of the Special Forces and the commandos. No member of an LRP team was ever captured alive by the LTTE.

* * * * *

In November 2008 as Jagath Dias's troops and Brigadier Bandara's Task Force 2 cleared the vast 'belly' area of the Vanni, and Shavendra Silva's troops swept on towards Pooneryn, yet another front was opened by launching Task Force 3, consisting of six battalions through Dias's frontline. Task Force 3 led by Brigadier S.D.T.Liyanage crossed the A-9 road and captured the Mankulam town on 17 November 2008 in a surprise attack. Pooneryn had fallen to Shavendra Silva's troops two days earlier. They then moved further east and captured the Olumadu junction and the area to the north of the Mankulam-Mulleitivu A-34 road. By this time, Brigadier Bandara's Task Force 2 was assailing the area to the south of the A-34 road. Brigadier Nandana Udawatte's 59th Division was by this time, about 10 kilometres away from Mulleitivu town. Task Force 3 did not encounter any LTTE defences as such but the terrorists used the terrain, the open patches, streams and tank bunds to delay troops. They also used small groups to infiltrate the front lines of the army and take opportunity targets. Task Forces 2 and 3 were now operating in the heartland of the LTTE in the eastern Vanni.

Since this was the height of the monsoon season, rain, mud and floods made advance arduous. Even tractors could not move on the dirt tracks to the north of the A-34 road. Supplies came in by helicopter and were transported on the backs of troops to the baseline 5-6 km from the helipad. Heavy machine guns could not be used because of poor visibility in the thick jungle. This was very different terrain to the scrub jungle to the west of the A-9 road. The eastern Vanni was mainly canopied primary forest. Artillery was also not effective due to the muddy condition of the ground. One of the issues that had to be dealt with was the question of soldiers being in wet clothing throughout the day and night during the monsoon rains. This was an issue right from the beginning of the Vanni operation in mid 2007. The soldiers operating in the western Vanni had to confront this problem in a particularly virulent manner in the rice bowl which was water logged to begin with and even the dry scrub jungle in other parts of the western Vanni turned into a marsh during the monsoon rains.

Gōta instructed Udaya Perera, director of operations of the army, to send dryers for the troops to dry their clothes in. The latter summoned the electrical and mechanical engineering unit in the army and told them to devise a dryer that could be dispatched to the operational areas. Army engineers first experimented by fixing floodlights inside a 20 foot container to dry the clothes and boots of men but that failed. It was Major Gen Palitha Fernando who suggested that perhaps the method used in tea factories to dry tea leaves may work. Using this principle, about ten large containers were converted into dryers. A 500 kilo watt generator was needed to power the dryer. So the whole unit was mounted on two trailers, one for the dryer unit and another for the generator and sent to the battlefront. When putting the uniforms into the dryer, each piece of clothing had to be identified and that in itself was an administrative nightmare.

After the capture of Pooneryn, Shavendra Silva's column turned east towards Paranthan and Kilinochchi. The victorious troops who had swept everything before them, now came up against another huge LTTE earthwork from Sinnaparanthan, a town several kilometres to the west of Paranthan proper, right up to the Iranamadu Tank in the south-east. The Sinnaparanthan-Iranamadu tank was about 11 km long. The number of terrorists holding it was estimated to be around 225. Once again, Shavendra Silva and Jagath Dias had to take this long bund from the north and the south respectively. The bund was breached in a joint night operation by both army formations, which left the towns of Paranthan and Killinochchi open to the army. Shavendra's formation suffered 77 fatalities in taking this bund.

While Shavendra Silva and Jagath Dias were at the Sinnaparanthan- Iranamadu bund and Brigadier Bandara's troops and Task Force 3 were fighting in the eastern Vanni on either side of the A-34 road, yet another front was opened across the Puliyankulam-Nedunkerny road by launching Task Force 4 led by Brigadier N.D.Wanniarachchi consisting of four battalions in mid-December 2008. The LTTE was now fighting on five different fronts, a situation they had never had to face. The LTTE now could not stop the army from advancing. All they could do was to delay the troops, using small infiltration groups, booby traps, mortar fire and high density anti-personnel mines.

The shrinking LTTE held territory was heavily infiltrated by commando and Special Forces long range patrol teams. On 26 November 2008, the last LTTE heroes day commemorated in the Vanni, LRP teams declared an unofficial curfew in the LTTE held area, by carrying out 14 ambushes within a 48 hour period in the LTTE held area on 25 and 26 November 2008. Nobody came out to commemorate *Mahavir* day that year.

The army field commanders fighting on the various Vanni fronts had to call Fonseka once in the morning and again in the evening to report everything that was happening. Fonseka could remember everything that was discussed in the previous telephone conversation and he would ask follow up questions to ensure that instructions given by him had been followed. While Fonseka kept in touch with army operations in that manner, Gōta had a similar system for all armed services, whereby he kept abreast of what everyone, the army, navy, air force, police, the police Special Task Force, and the intelligence services were doing, especially in the flash spots. It was not just the commanders of these services that Gōta kept in touch with. When necessary, Gōta went several levels down. For example, the naval northern commander had to call Gōta at 7.45 in the morning. The eastern naval commander at 7.50 for routine reports. Anything extra would be discussed later. Gōta spoke to officers in the army right down to the battalion commander level to keep abreast of what was happening.

After Shavendra Silva's Task Force 1 entered Paranthan, they were declared a fully fledged Division and named the 58th Division in recognition of outstanding performance. The symbolically important town of Kilinochchi was occupied in a combined operation between Shavendra Silva's and Jagath Dias's troops on 2 January 2009. Once the town was captured, President Mahinda Rajapaksa together with Gōta visited Kilinochchi in triumph.

Chapter 72

A Newspaper Editor Murdered

After the eviction of the LTTE from Kilinochchi, the next piece of news to shake the nation was the brutal killing of Lasantha Wickremetunga, the editor of the *Sunday Leader* on 9 January 2009. Wickremetunga was a bitter critic of both the Rajapaksa regime and the war. But towards the latter stages, he had mended fences with Mahinda Rajapaksa and was meeting him on a regular basis. On that fateful day, the assassins had followed Wickremetunga on two motorcycles for some distance before overtaking him and forcing him to stop. As he sensed he was being followed, Wickremetunga phoned Eliyantha White, a native healer who was one of President Mahinda Rajapaksa's personal physicians and told him he was being followed by suspicious persons on motorcycles.

White had arranged several meetings between president Rajapaksa and Wickremetunga and was his link to the president. Wickremetunga was once close to Mrs Sirima Bandaranaike and he and Mahinda Rajapaksa had known each other for many years on that account. Wickremetunga had come to the conclusion that after the elections of 2010, there has to be a UPFA-UNP national government. He told the present writer several months before his death that if there was no national government by 2010, he would go off to live in Australia.

By renewing his contacts with his old friend Mahinda, Wickremetunga was obviously positioning himself to negotiate for that national government. His direct link to the president did not help him on this day. The assassins on motorbikes overtook him and blocked his path forcing him to stop. The two pillion riders alighted, smashed the windows of his car and hit Wickremetunga on the head with what is believed to be a steel club like instrument used to kill livestock in some Western countries. A single blow drives a pointed spike into the skull and smashes the bone structure. Wickremetunga died in hospital. The brutal killing shocked the nation and a pall of gloom descended on the victory in Killinochchi. The UNP of which Wickremetunga was an ardent backer, immediately blamed army commander Sarath Fonseka for the killing.

The leader of the opposition Ranil Wickremesinghe made a statement to that effect in parliament. The view he held on this matter was that this was done by a hit team directly reporting to Fonseka. This placed Gōta in a quandary. The war had reached a point of no return and the LTTE was teetering on the brink of defeat, and at this very crucial moment comes this unwanted controversy over the killing of a newspaper editor.

While the blame game was being played out in the public arena, the victory in Kilinochchi was forgotten temporarily. Gōta had one thing in mind, to keep the war effort on track. If there was a public backlash against the army commander at this crucial moment, it would have affected morale down the line in the army just when the war was coming to its most crucial stage. It was easy to clear the western half of the Vanni. But the real LTTE heartland was the heavily forested eastern part of the Vanni which the army now stood poised to attack as the Wickremetunga killing eclipsed everything else. Army commander Sarath Fonseka had had a running battle with the opposition for some time. Mangala Samaraweera had become a vocal critic of the way the war was being conducted and this brought him into direct confrontation with the military and especially with Fonseka.

The latter was in fact a favourite target of Wickrematunga as well. One thing that his newspaper would do was to add up the numbers of LTTE dead that the army would release from time to time and match this figure with projections that Fonseka gave in the past about the cadre strength of the LTTE, pointing out that the number of LTTE casualties was beginning to exceed their total strength. Baiting the government and the military over the war effort was in fact the mainstay of the opposition at that time. The opposition never believed that the LTTE could be defeated. Ranil Wickremesinghe and some others in the UNP had come to that conclusion a long time ago. Mangala Samaraweera held much the same view.

439

Hence, it was with immense confidence that they lampooned the government's war effort and all those involved in it. They saw the war as a foolhardy and immature project which was definitely going to explode in the government's face. Up to this point, there was nothing remarkable in what the government had achieved either. The east had been cleared by the UNP government as far back as 1993, but those gains had been lost again. Even Kilinochchi had been captured by the PA government in 1996 and held for over two years till 1998 but that too was lost. So as far as the opposition was concerned, these military operations were exercises in futility costing billions of rupees and thousands of lives for no purpose. Usually, when a country was at war, the democratic opposition would be circumspect and would always try to identify with the national interest. But in Sri Lanka, the opposition was so certain that the government would fail to prevail over the LTTE, that they went out on a limb against the war effort.

Among the best remembered jibes directed by UNP politicians at the war effort is the comment by Ravi Karunanayake made in parliament in mid-November 2008, that the army claimed to be going to Alimankada (Elephant Pass in the north) but was actually going to Pamankada (A suburb of Colombo) and then again that the army claims to be going to 'Killinochchiya' but was actually going only up to Medawachchiya (in the Anuradhapura district). Another such jibe was by Kandy district parliamentarian Lakshman Kiriella who said during a press conference, that "Any ox can wage war!" Ranil Wickremesinghe became famous for brushing off the capture of Thoppigala in the east by saying that it was 'just a patch of jungle'. Technically, he was right – it was in fact a jungle but it was the LTTE's main centre of operations in the east and the capture of this base marked the end of the eastern operations.

Needless to say that this attitude on the part of the opposition placed them on a collision course with the military. Following a sarcastic comment made by Fonseka to the effect that those who had learnt to sew women's undergarments were in no position to criticize the way the war was being conducted, (the reference to sewing undergarments was a reference to Samaraweera's past as a fashion designer before he became a politician) a furious Samaraweera summoned a press conference on 27 November 2008 and said that Sarath Fonseka had approached him in 2004-2005 when Chandrika Kumaratunga was the president begging to be promoted army commander but that he had not been promoted because he had no vision to hold the post. It was at this press briefing that Samaraweera said that in his view, army commander Sarath Fonseka was not fit even to be the commander of the Salvation Army!

Continuing his broadside against Fonseka, Samaraweera said that Fonseka had been commissioned in 1971 and had been in the army for over 30 years and that during this entire period no army commander had recommended him for the *Visita Seva Vibhusanaya* but that the moment he became commander, he recommended himself for the award. He also said that Sarath Fonseka had been penalized on disciplinary grounds in 1975 in a court of inquiry headed by then Col. Cyril Ranatunga. During this broadside Samaraweera had also darkly hinted that *"These persons handle death squads on behalf of the Rajapaksas."* This was the kind of exchange that was taking place between the members of the opposition and the serving heads of the military as the army was fighting their way into the LTTE strongholds in the Vanni.

Samaraweera's November 2008 broadside could be dismissed as a tit for tat reaction to what Fonseka had said about him sewing women's undergarments, but Gōta could not ignore the open accusations that Fonseka was responsible for Lasantha Wickremetunga's killing. No less a person than the opposition leader himself was directing accusations against Fonseka under parliamentary privilege and there was nothing that Fonseka could do about it. Five days after Wickremetunga's killing, Gōta appeared on the government owned *ITN* news channel and in the course of a wide ranging interview, he came to the defence of the beleaguered army commander by telling the public that the Indian defence advisor M.K.Narayanan had told him that Sri Lanka had the best army commander in the world.

Gōta countered the negative propaganda against the army commander by praising him in public, in the highest possible terms. In this interview, Gōta paid glowing tributes to the commanders of all three services, the army, navy and air force, saying that their experience and knowledge was what was turning the tide against the LTTE. He spoke of the strategies and tactics used against the LTTE this time by the army and said that fighting the war on multiple fronts, the use of small groups and Special Forces and commando teams had been introduced, leading to the successes that had been achieved. He also said that the navy had developed the small boat squadrons and that the LTTE would not be able to put out any boats to sea in the future.

Gōta further said that when he went to Indonesia, the president and the defence minister and service chiefs had all been full of praise

441

for Sri Lanka for being a trail blazer and showing that terrorism could be defeated. When he went to Israel, the Israeli navy commander had wanted to have a separate chat with the Sri Lankan director of naval operations to find out how the Sri Lankan navy faced the suicide boat phenomenon.

The high casualty rate in the war was one of the opposition's favourite sticks to flog the government with. Their argument was that these deaths were in vain. In his January 2009 interview over *ITN*, Gōta had an argument for this as well. He said that by 1977, when the UNP came into power, not a single soldier had lost his life, and the army and police could go anywhere in the north and east and there was no special presence of police or army personnel in those areas. But by the time the government changed again in 1994, some 7,174 military and police personnel had lost their lives. These lives had been lost while losing huge swathes of territory to the terrorists.

Gōta also took Mangala Samaraweera to task, pointing out that Samaraweera had been a powerful member of the PA government for 11 years and during that time, the number of casualties had been as follows.

1995 - 1,221

1996 - 2,120

1997 – 1,662

1998 - 1,063

1999 - 700

2000 - 2,248.

Once again, Gōta pointed out that these people died while suffering unprecedented debacles and losing key military installations in Mulleitivu, Kilinochchi, Mankulam and Elephant Pass. In contrast to this dismal record, he pointed out that after the Rajapaksa government took over, 3,703 army, navy, air force and police personnel had died in three years but that none of these deaths were in vain and that the government had established control over the entire eastern province, Mannar, Pooneryn, Killinochchi, Paranthan, parts of Mulleitivu, Oddusudan and other areas and the LTTE was now confined to a small area in the Mulleitivu district.

Chapter 73

Breaking the Muhamalai Jinx

Despite all that had been going on in the Vanni, a good part of the troops, armoured vehicles and artillery assets of the army were in Jaffna having no part of the action. The LTTE also had a concentration of forces and heavy guns in Muhamalai. Both sides had tried to push the other beyond Muhamalai for nearly a decade and both had failed. In the year 2000, Muhamalai was the place where the army managed to halt the advance of the LTTE. When the army tried to break through this line in the *Agnikheela* operation in 2001, they had failed. Even the second attempt to breach the Muhamalai line failed in October 2006 at enormous cost in terms of both men and material. Both sides appeared to be jinxed in Muhamalai.

The decade long jinx was partially broken in November 2008 when the two divisions stationed in Jaffna, the 55th and the 53rd, under Brigadiers Prasanna Silva and Kamal Gunaratne respectively, carried out a diversionary attack on the LTTE defences across the Muhamalai-Nagarkovil frontline just as Shavendra Silva's troops were poised to take Pooneryn. The operation to take the LTTE's first line of defence in Muhamalai lasted a week from 15 to 21 November 2008. The LTTE defences fell to this diversionary attack – the biggest victory the army had achieved on this front in a decade. It was from Pooneryn that the LTTE fired artillery into the Jaffna peninsula. Back in January 2008, a plane carrying Gōta and Sarath Fonseka had not been able to land in Palaly because of LTTE artillery fire coming from Pooneryn. This was also a staging area for sea borne attacks on the peninsula.

When Pooneryn was taken by Shavendra Silva, the security threat to the Jaffna peninsula diminished and the troops in Jaffna were free to concentrate on Muhamalai.

The operation completion report submitted by the 55th and 53rd Divisions after this limited operation stated that at the time of the offensive, the terrorists were demoralized and communication intercepts indicated that they were not telling their superiors the realities of the situation. Another observation made by the troops in Jaffna was that the LTTE was not firing as many mortar and artillery rounds as they used to on earlier occasions. The army was able to overrun the LTTE line in Muhamalai with just 11 soldiers killed and 127 injured in stark contrast to what happened in October 2006.

The strategy to take Muhamalai changed after the experience of October 2006. Instead of a headlong attack, the army now maintained a war of attrition on the LTTE defence line, wearing them down. The army would attack the LTTE lines with RPGs and artillery on a daily basis. Narrow infiltration trenches were dug so that attacking parties could sneak up on LTTE bunkers and launch surprise attacks, at times even dragging away the LTTE dead bodies. This was on the one hand, a way of weakening the LTTE in this sector while at the same time keeping the LTTE busy in Jaffna while their territory was being taken over in the Vanni.

After the towns of Pooneryn, Paranthan and Kilinochchi had been taken by the army, Prasanna Silva's and Kamal Gunaratne's troops attacked the LTTE's second line of defence in Muhamalai on the night of 5 January 2009. The troops used infiltration trenches to plant improvised explosive devices and claymore mines on the LTTE bunds which were exploded to facilitate the army offensive. In the meantime, Special Forces teams had infiltrated the LTTE lines through the Kilaly lagoon. By 6.00 pm the next day, the army had captured the LTTE's second line as well - which put an end to LTTE resistance in Muhamalai. Troops then started moving down towards Elephant Pass via Palai, Soranpattu and Iyakachchi. They met with some resistance in Palai which was soon repulsed. The most number of casualties was suffered by the Jaffna troops in breaching the LTTE's second line of defence in Muhamalai – resistance to which was personally led by Theepan.

Parallel to the move towards Elephant Pass, another offensive was launched by the Special Forces and the commandos along the coast from Nagarkovil to Vettalankerny. On this axis however, they encountered little or no resistance. The troops moving down from

Muhamalai were in Elephant Pass by 9 January, and the other column moving down the coast was in Vettelankerny by 10 January 2009. The Muhamalai-Nagarkovil defence line was the main theatre of conflict between the army and the LTTE for nearly a decade and the ease with which it fell in January 2009, shows that the LTTE was in an advanced state of collapse by that time. After Elephant Pass and Vettelankery, Prasanna Silva's 55th Division on its own, advanced along the coast to Puthumathalan.

After coming down to Elephant Pass, Kamal Gunaratne's 53rd Division was redeployed in the Mankulam area to support Task Forces 2, 3 and 4 in carrying out limited operations in the 'belly' area and also to act as a reserve force. This arrangement made perfect sense because if the LTTE leadership managed to break out of the encirclement in the Mulleitivu district, they would try to sneak into the belly of the Vanni, which was a vast, sparsely populated area where they could have gone into hiding.

In the meantime, Shavendra Silva's troops had begun going down the A-35 road from Paranthan towards Mulleitivu. They faced pitched battles with the retreating LTTE in places like Dharmapuram, and Visuamadu. In Suthanthirapuram, the advancing army found huge stores of food - rice, sugar, dhal and other foodstuffs obtained from the World Food Programme, which had been left behind by the retreating LTTE. A little distance further down the road, in Devipuram, they came across a large stock of chemicals in 25 litre containers. As the 9th Gemunu Watch passed that location, the LTTE rained mortar fire on them, apparently aiming at the stock of chemicals but they could not hit the stockpile. By this time, Nandana Udawatte's troops of the 59th Division had broken through the Tannimuruppu-Nayaru bund and by the second week of January had captured the road from Oddusudan to Puthukudiirippu which linked the A-34 and A-35 roads. On 25 January 2009, they captured the strategically important town of Mulleitivu without much difficulty even though there had been around 200 to 300 LTTE cadres defending it.

As February 2009 began, three divisions of the army, led by Shavendra Silva, Jagath Dias and Nandana Udawatte had converged on the Puthukudiirippu area and LTTE was getting hemmed in. On 7-9 February, Udawatte's 59th Division had to face a heavy LTTE counterattack in the area between Puthukudiirippu and the Nandikadal lagoon and they suffered heavy casualties in the three day, non-stop battle. When the attack commenced, Udawatte was in Colombo on leave. He was air lifted to the battle front and assumed command of the troops. The fighting raged for three days with the LTTE using four or five explosives laden vehicles and even motorcycles in suicide missions. During this counterattack, the 53rd Division which had been deployed in the belly area was redeployed in Puthukudiirippu to contain the desperate LTTE offensive.

Task Force 8 was also hurriedly set up to meet the LTTE offensive, and Colonel G.V.Ravirpiriya was placed in charge. The new command functioned as a part of the 53rd Division under Kamal Gunaratne and was made up of two brigades with the same troops of the 59th Division that had faced the LTTE counterattack. The new task force advanced north from the 59th Division line, hugging the bank of the Nandikadal lagoon. The advance was excruciatingly slow. Movement at times was only about 100 meters a day and the daily casualty rate could be as high as 20 dead and over 30 injured and that was just in Task Force 8. Containing the desperate LTTE counterattacks was not easy and the army had to dig ditches across all the by-roads in the area and bury land mines to prevent the LTTE's explosives laden vehicles from reaching their targets.

By the end of February 2009, Jagath Dias's troops had swept through the Iranamadu area and was operating to the west of the Puthukudiirippu junction. During its trek from Vavuniya to Puthukudiirippu, the 57th Divisison had captured 1296 sq km of LTTE territory and in the process the division suffered a death toll of 962 with a further 40 reported missing and presumed dead. The total number of injured was 5,630. To capture that territory, they had fired over 202,000 artillery and mortar rounds. The 57th Division which pioneered the Vanni operation, taking the brunt of the LTTE's counterattacks in 2007, would at this point cease its advance and hold the ground it had captured. Just as Jagath Dias's troops were about to conclude their advance, the LTTE carried out an unconventional attack which was experienced by the 58th and 57th Divisions in different ways.

In Visuamadu, the LTTE blasted the bund of the Kalamadukulam tank (See map 3) which was swollen due to the rains with the hope of drowning the advancing troops. The water from the tank flooded an area of 15 square kilometres and the troops of the 11th SLLI Battalion which was under Shavendra Silva were caught up in the flood. Their ammunition and even the clothes of some soldiers had got washed away in the flood but many managed to climb trees and save themselves and there were no fatalities as a result of the flooding. But for 8 hours all communication between the

446

11th SLLI and the rest of the Division ceased and confusion reigned. Some of Jagath Dias's troops who faced the same inundation were luckier because they had prior warning.

When the 19th Sinha Battalion under Jagath Dias was in the vicinity the Kalmadukulam tank, a skirmish broke out with the LTTE and in the confusion, the army inducted an eight man SIOT team into the LTTE held area. The next day, the corporal leading the SIOT team inside LTTE territory reported over the radio that he heard a blast and that there was now the sound of running water. On receiving this message, Lt Col Wijesuriya quickly ordered his men to withdraw about 600 meters to higher ground. It took about fifteen minutes to effect the withdrawal. The 58th Division which was in the area was also warned but they could not act on the information with the same speed. Within about 20 minutes of the SIOT team leader's warning, the tank bund gave way and a wall of water several feet high, swept through the jungle.

The initial blast had opened up a small breach and it took several minutes for the pressure to build up and for the bund to give way. Fortunately for the army, only two of the multiple charges that the LTTE had laid had exploded, thus giving them time to move to higher ground. After inundating the area, the LTTE launched six boats and went around firing at the trees to kill any soldiers who may have climbed them escape the surging waters. A few soldiers who had in fact climbed trees had been killed in this manner. Despite the prior warning that Lt Col Wijesuriya had got, the volume of water that came had been unexpected. In some places the water had been high enough to go over a single story house and the A-35 road had become completely impassable.

As the LTTE drove the civilians ahead of them, the latter took along their most valued possessions and this included fishing boats. All along the path of retreat, even deep in the centre of the Vanni were many abandoned boats which the civilians had not been able to take with them anymore. These boats were collected by the advancing troops and used as water containers to store bath water for soldiers on the front lines. In the nights, soldiers would bathe in the water that was pumped into the boats from bowsers. Each soldier was given five buckets of water before soaping, and five more afterwards. Now even when the Kalamadukulam tank was breached, it was these same abandoned boats that had been of use to the troops to mount rescue operations to save stranded soldiers amidst the swirling waters.

After the army captured Kilinochchi in early January 2009 and started coming down the A-35 road towards Mulleitivu, a demilitarised zone was declared to the east of the A-35 road at Suthanthirapuram. At this point, the area controlled by the LTTE was around ten times bigger than the demilitarised zone. However, instead of leaving the civilians behind in the demilitarised zone as they were supposed to, the LTTE forced them to move to the coast. The government then declared the actual area where the civilians were being held by the LTTE, a demilitarised zone in mid-February 2009. This was a long sliver of land of 14 square kilometres extending from Puthumathalan in the north to Vellamullivaikkal in the south.

Everybody knew that the LTTE had large numbers of civilians with them, but nobody knew how many. On 28 January, 2009, the Indian external affairs minister Pranabh Mukherjee in an official statement to the media estimated that the number of civilians held by the LTTE was around 150,000 plus. The Indian government had intelligence on the ground in the north and east of Sri Lanka and that was their estimate. Gōta's own estimate had been something in the range of 100,000. By mid-February 2009, in an interview with the *Lankadeepa*, Gōta said that since over 30,000 IDPs had escaped, there would be only around 70,000 IDP's still held by the LTTE. The Vanni had been out of government control for a quarter of a century and nobody knew the exact number of people living there. The last time a census had been carried out in these areas was in 1981.

The coastal front that Prasanna Silva's 55th Division was advancing on from Vettelankerny to Puthumathalan was only one and a half kilometres wide and consisted of sandy soil. This division had to cross several bodies of water along their route. By 14 January, the 55th Division was in Chundikulam. The LTTE had built a sand bund on the other side of the lagoon mouth. The width of the body of water varied with the tide. At times it was only 25 meters, at other times over twice that. In Chundikulam, the Pakistani MBRLs were used with devastating effect on the LTTE's sand bund by positioning the vehicles on which the MBRLs were mounted, in such a manner as to enable the rockets to hit the LTTE defences direct, after the fashion of cannon. Firepower was used to the maximum to reduce army casualties.

At one point, when the army was stuck to the north of Chundikulam, the sea tigers assembled a flotilla of about 50-60 boats with a view to attacking the 55th Division from the rear in an amphibious operation. Prasanna Silva had ordered the loading of two salvos into the MBRLs while monitoring the position of the sea tiger boats and just when they were getting into formations, he ordered the firing of the MBRLs with air burst rockets. After that there were no more attempts at making seaborne attacks. The MBRLs are usually long range weapons, but in these battles, they were used to take targets just 500 meters away. At short distances, the practice was to fire a limited number of rounds instead of a full salvo.

At night, the banks of the Chundikulam lagoon were lit up by dozens of powerful flashlights powered by mini generators to prevent LTTE infiltration. The other side of the lagoon had not yet been cleared and the danger was that the LTTE's small teams would infiltrate through the lagoon and plant claymore mines in the army held area. Army drivers would be very vigilant about possible infiltrators. They would watch out for footprints and other such tell tale signs that infiltrators were in the area. Every such report was followed up even if they ultimately turned out to be false alarms.

Chundikulam was the 55th Division's most difficult call. They tried to induct commandos on to the LTTE side in dinghies. But the LTTE fired on the landing party from an abandoned coconut plantation, and the commandos had to be withdrawn because they were taking too many casualties. A few days later, the 1st SLLI Battalion stormed the coconut plantation and dislodged the LTTE. Heavy firepower was used to soften up the enemy lines. On some days over 2000 mortar rounds would be fired at the LTTE defences.

Another point at which the LTTE offered stiff resistance to Prasanna Silva's troops was the major sea tiger base of Chalai where they were held up for over one week. Once again, a sand bund 450 meters in length had been built on the approach to Chalai. On 28 February, troops moved along infiltration trenches to approach the lagoon and sea. They were launched across the lagoon mouth on logs and other improvised floating devices at around 8.45 in the night. The LTTE counter attacked and despite a one and a half hour battle, and ten other counter attacks into the late morning the next day, the troops had breached the bund by 11.00 am on March 1. Chalai had for a long time been the main base of the sea tigers. In nearly four months of fighting, 55 men including three officers in the 55th Division had been killed, with 204 injured. Between the mouth of the Chundikulam lagoon and Chalai, the LTTE had no less than 6 earth bunds and between Chalai and Puthumathalan there were another seven of the same.

Chapter 74

Air Support in the Vanni

What made a major difference for the air force in the final war, was the ready access to information and the vastly expanded use of UAVs to gather intelligence. In the mid 1980s, when bombing raids were first carried out by the air force, pilots got targets that were drawn by hand on pieces of paper. They had to place the target against the grid map to get their bearings. There would be indications given such as 'a white building with a parapet wall around it'. But the colour of the building and the parapet wall will not be visible from 15,000 feet up in the air. The person giving them the target would need to visualize how the target would look like from above. But this was not possible and that seriously handicapped the air force.

When the pilot gets there, he would see a patch of jungle or a paddy field with no terrorists to be seen. The targets given to the air force looked like cadjan huts or small bunkers from the air. Some pilots say that they themselves had doubts about how worthwhile those targets were. The LTTE at that time did not have established bases and were always on the move. They did not have the personnel to man any permanent bases. The bombing raid would be carried out, but with little or no effect on the LTTE. There were instances when pilots were instructed to fly over LTTE held areas just so that the terrorists hear the noise in the belief that they would be more defensive if they heard air force jets flying overhead! When pilots were called upon to support ground troops, they were given only a grid reference and told the approximate positions of the army and the enemy on the grid reference.

Later in the late 1980s, the air force began using aerial photographs taken by the survey department which has an aircraft with a camera fixed to the undercarriage. The air force photographed certain critical areas using this plane and used those images to improve target location. By the late 1990s, they began using satellite images which the ground forces also had and it was made easier to pin point the targets. Unmanned aerial vehicles (UAVs) were acquired for the first time by the Sri Lankan air force from Israel in 1996. However at that time, the video footage would not be available to the pilots for about 48 hours. The film was transferred to a VHS cassette and taken to air force headquarters and headquarters sends it to the squadron which in turn gives it to the pilots. The pilots watch it on the screen a couple of times and then go on the mission. The information loop thus took too long.

A major innovation during the final Vanni operation was the use of digital technology to link the cameras on the UAV live to air force headquarters and simultaneously to the squadron as well so that the headquarters and the pilots were watching the same images at the same time. The same link was made available to the divisional commanders of the army on the ground as well so that everybody was watching the same images at the same time and spot decisions were being made by the ground forces and the air force together enabling the pilots to take the target in a matter of minutes. What this meant was that they could take even moving targets minutes after detecting the movement. When the army came up against the LTTE's earth bunds in the Vanni, they could now see what was going on the other side. This enabled the army to direct the air force to targets on the other side of the bund as well. In 2007, four Blue Horizon UAVs were bought from Israel to augment the air force's surveillance capability. Altogether the UAVs flew 900 mission hours during the Vanni operations.

There was also an improvement in the bombing accuracy of the pilots. In the late 1990s, when the air force took a target, they would ask the ground troops to be one to two kilometres away from the target they were taking. As accuracy improved and the targets were also better defined, the air force could bomb just the target and not all around it. As the accuracy of air force bombing improved, the army too built up the confidence to remain closer to the target. There were also situations in the final Vanni operation where the army could not withdraw for the air force to carry out a bombing raid because the LTTE could have seized that moment to grab back ground they had lost. So the army had to remain where they were and the LTTE line still had to be bombed. In such cases, the air force jets would approach the target parallel to the army line without flying over or across it to reach the target, so that even if the target was missed, the bomb would still fall on the LTTE line and not outside it.

The LTTE's anti-aircraft strategy was to wait until the plane commences the dive and they start shooting in the same path, or across its path with several anti aircraft guns at the same time. It is always difficult to hit a plane with ground fire because of its speed but they keep firing in its direction with the hope of chancing upon a hit. On a couple of occasions, the MiG-27s were hit but were not crippled. In 1995, as we recounted in a previous chapter, the biggest threat to the air force were the surface to air missiles of the LTTE. The anti missile system that was available to meet this threat involved the emitting of flares generating more heat than the engine so that the heat seeking missile will be directed elsewhere.

To counter this, the anti-aircraft missiles were programmed to detect stable heat sources instead of short lived and diminishing bursts of heat as in flares. In Sri Lanka, the air force never had to go beyond the first generation anti-missile system because the LTTE used only SA-14s, an older and less sophisticated heat seeking missile. Shooting off flares as an anti-missile measure by air force planes was not completely foolproof. The flares did not go off automatically and had to be manually activated by the pilot. Since the engine of the plane was located at the back the LTTE had to fire the missile at the heat source at the back of the plane when it was retreating and not head on to the front. So a precaution taken often by pilots was to emit flares during the recovery after a dive when the engine was exposed to the ground as the plane pulled up to a higher altitude. Each plane would have enough flares for two or three attack runs.

Surface to air missiles were not as much a problem during the final war as it had been over a decade earlier. While the LTTE may have initially got SAMs from Afghanistan in the mid-1990s, the availability of such sophisticated weapons had decreased after 9/11 as all countries manufacturing such weapons had stricter controls on who they sold such armaments to. Western intelligence agencies were keeping tabs on these illegal international arms deals and that made it harder for the LTTE obtain fresh supplies of SAMs. On 19 August 2006, just as the final war started, two LTTE operatives were arrested in an FBI sting operation in the USA while they were trying to purchase twenty SA-18 surface to air missiles, and ten missile launchers among other weaponry. (They would later be sentenced to 25 years in prison.)

There was also an additional problem that the SAMs had to be stored properly in a cool place and the battery life would last only a few seconds upon activation. A lock on to the target had to be obtained within the first few seconds before releasing the missile. In the event of a failure to lock on, the battery expires. For these and other reasons, the LTTE did not use SAMs much during the final war. However they did have missiles to the very end. Even in the final battles in Puthukudiirippu, a Kfir pilot had seen two missiles being fired. But these were older heat seeking missiles which were easily 'misled' by the flares emitted by the air force planes. Had the LTTE got access to the newer SA-18 SAMs they had been trying to buy, the air force would have had a serious problem on their hands.

The MiG-27s were the most formidable aircraft in the possession of the air force. The first MiG-27s were bought in June 2000 and they came with Russian mercenaries to fly them. The Russian pilots left after the hostilities ceased in late 2001. When the Rajapaksa government came into power, of the original six planes, three had been destroyed in war. The remaining three were grounded and unusable as their guarantees had expired. Later the Rajapaksa government added four more to the fleet of MiG -27s and the three older planes were given a complete overhaul, bringing the MiG-27 fleet to seven. The advantage of the MiG-27s was that they could carry a bigger payload than the Kfir. MiG-27s could carry a payload of 4000 kg. The aiming devices in the Kfir jets however, were in general more sophisticated than those available in the MiG-27s.

The MiG-27s were available for a reasonable price whereas Kfirs would have cost much more. Moreover, Kfirs were not readily available to be bought ex-stock. By the time war broke out again in 2006, about 15 pilots had been trained to fly the MiG-27s. The MiG-27s were also used for night operations. The pilots were gradually introduced to night flying by being trained to fly at twilight and then in the moonlight and finally in darkness. The targets taken in the night were mostly area targets, and not ones that required great precision. When night operations were carried out, one aircraft would fire powerful flares which would illuminate the target for about 20 seconds.

During the Vanni operations, the Mi-24s were used as ground attack aircraft to provide close air support to the advancing ground troops. Of the fixed wing aircraft, the old F-7s, the Kfirs and the MiG-

27s were used in operations. As in the case of the navy, the Sri Lankan air force too has suffered more losses than any air force anywhere in the world ever has, to a terrorist organization. After the blasting of the Air Ceylon Avro in 1978, the LTTE was not able to destroy any government owned air assets until 1990. The air assets destroyed as a direct result of terrorist actions are as follows. This does not include air assets that were lost due to accidents or mechanical failures during the war or the civilian air assets destroyed by the LTTE.

1. *Siai Marchetti SF 260 fighter/bomber, Palaly, Jaffna, 13 September 1990.*
2. *Bell 212 helicopter, Vavuniya, 16 June 1991.*
3. *Shaanxi Y-8 transport plane, Palaly, 2 May 1992.*
4. *Avro passenger/transport aircraft, Palaly, 28 April 1995.*
5. *Avro aircraft, Palaly, 29 April 1995.*
6. *Pucara IA-58 fighter/bomber, Palaly, 14 July 1995.*
7. *Shaanxi Y-8, Palaly, 18 November 1995.*
8. *Antonov 32 passenger/transport plane, Palaly, 22 November 1995.*
9. *Mi-17 helicopter, Palaly, 22 January 1996.*
10. *Harbin Y-12 transport plane, Palaly, 20 January 1997.*
11. *Harbin Y-12, China Bay, 3 May 1997.*
12. *Mi-24 attack helicopter, Mulleitivu, 19 March 1997.*
13. *Mi-24, Kokavil, 11 October 1997.*
14. *Bell-212, Vavuniya, 25 November 1997.*
15. *Mi-17, Olumadu, 1 February 1998.*
16. *Mi-24, Irattaperiyakulam, 26 June 1998.*
17. *Antonov AN-24, Iranativu, 29 September 1998.*
18. *Mi-24, Kilaly, 17 December 1999.*
19. *Mi-24, Meesalai, 24 May 2000.*
20. *Mi-24, Nagarkovil, 19 October 2000.*
21. *Mi-17, Katunayake, 1 July 2001.*
22. *Mi-17, Katunayake, 1 July 2001.*
23. *MiG-27, Katunayake, 1 July 2001.*
24. *Kfir C-722, Katunayake, 1 July 2001.*
25. *Kfir C-722, Katunayake,1 July 2001.*
26. *Karakorum K-8 trainer, Katunayake, 1 July 2001.*
27. *Karakorum K-8 trainer, Katunayake, 1 July 2001.*
28. *Karakorum K-8 trainer, Katunayake, 1 July 2001.*
29. *Bell 212, Anuradhapura, 22 October 2007.*
30. *Pratt & Whitney PT-6 trainer, Anuradhapura, 22 October 2007.*

31. *Karakorum K-8, Anuradhapura, 22 October 2007.*
32. *Mi-24, Anuradhapura, 22 October 2007.*
33. *Bell 206 helicopter, Anuradhapura, 22 October 2007.*
34. *Beechcraft aerial surveillance plane, Anuradhapura, 22 October 2007.*

* * * * *

With the advent of the small boat units of the navy, the LTTE stopped using clusters and swarming tactics in sea battles. From using numerical superiority, the LTTE went back to stealth. From early 2008, a new danger manifested itself in the seas - low profile LTTE suicide boats which hardly registered on the radars or thermal cameras of the fast attack craft. It would appear on the radar only as a minute dot which too would be seen only intermittently. Because of this new threat, of the 18 crewmen on board the fast attack craft, about half were always on watch in the night with about four having night vision devices, and the gunners were always at their stations. These flat low profile suicide boats, which were only about two feet high were not visible even on the radars and thermal cameras when it was raining and during the pre-dawn hours.

However, even if the radars and thermal cameras were not able to detect such craft, the wake of the low-profile suicide boats would be visible to the naked eye at around 300 meters. In early 2009, powerful searchlights were fitted onto the fast attack craft to meet the threat of these low profile suicide boats. Those on the deck also had assault rifles and machine guns as they were the most effective weapon against an enemy boat at very close quarters. Towards the end, the LTTE suicide boats had around 350 kilograms of C-4 explosives each. The lorry bomb with which the LTTE had tried to bring down the World Trade Centre in Colombo was thought to contain 350 kilos of high explosives. What this meant was that an increasingly desperate LTTE had deployed on the sea, suicide boats packing the same destructive power as the biggest vehicle bombs ever used on land.

Chapter 75

Rescuing the Civilians

Why the LTTE insisted on taking the entire civilian population along with them as they retreated, is an inexplicable enigma. Even during the operation launched to clear Jaffna in 1995, the LTTE took much of the population with them as they fled into the Vanni. By clearing large areas of the Jaffna peninsula of civilians, the LTTE actually made it much easier for the army to capture Jaffna. If the civilian population had remained in their houses, the army would have had to be very cautious and would not have been able to simply come barrelling down the road to Jaffna town. Besides, if the LTTE allowed the civilian population to remain as they were, and conducted guerrilla operations against the army then the going would have been very slow and the international outcry and especially the pressures emanating from Tamil Nadu may even have prevented the operation from ever being concluded.

But instead the LTTE removed the civilian population from their homes and cleared the path for the army to simply hammer their way down to Jaffna town in record time with the full assurance that no non-combatant Tamil would come to any harm in the process. Until 1995, the conventional wisdom was that the Jaffna peninsula could never be taken by the army because the casualty rates among civilians and combatants alike would be too high to risk such an operation. Yet when the Chandrika Kumaratunga government did launch this risky venture, the LTTE took the population of Jaffna with them and made the advance of the army much quicker and cleaner and far less complicated than anticipated. After the army had completed the takeover of the entire Jaffna peninsula, the people who had gone into the Vanni with the LTTE came back to their homes. Thus the LTTE ended up losing both the peninsula and the population.

Despite that experience, the LTTE did the army the same favour once again in 2007 in the east, by taking the civilian population of Sampur into Vakarai as the army advanced. With this strategy, the LTTE again lost the territories of Sampur, Vakarai and the population as well when the latter came *en masse* into the government held area as recounted in an earlier chapter. Despite this very recent lesson about taking civilians with them, the LTTE took the population of Mannar and the entire Vanni with them as they retreated. The army could always fire at will because there was nobody but LTTE cadres within range. Besides, with the LTTE literally keeping the population under arrest, they could not go to India as refugees either. That too made things much easier for the government.

We can only speculate on why the LTTE adopted this policy of taking the Tamil population with them as they retreated. One reason of course would be to show the world that the Tamil people were with the LTTE. Another obviously was that the LTTE needed a captive population for recruitment. With the people of Jaffna and the eastern province in government control, recruitment from those sources dried up and the only population left to them were the people of the Vanni. Moreover, if the government got control over a part of the Vanni population, they would normalize things, hold elections and in that manner score a propaganda victory over the LTTE.

Some may wonder why the LTTE did not allow the government to take over the Tamil population centres and then launch guerrilla attacks on the military while living among the people. Such a strategy however, had long since ceased to be practicable. Even in Jaffna, the people were quite ready to give information to the army about LTTE operatives and a guerrilla campaign was no longer feasible. The era when Tamil civilians helped the terrorists voluntarily had long since ended and the Tamil population was now being controlled only through terror. All these considerations were perhaps at the root of the LTTE's decision to take the Tamil population with them as they retreated.

The LTTE policy of removing civilians from the path of the advancing army and going forward to meet the advancing troops head on, may also have been due to excessive confidence in their capacity to fight a conventional war. Indeed it has to be said that the

LTTE did keep the army bogged down in one place for over nine months all on their own by utilizing the terrain to their advantage. But once the army broke through and the LTTE started running, they fled right across the island from the west coast to the east coast and all that while, the first glimpse the advancing army had of Tamil civilians was after the capture of Pooneryn when troops saw civilians who had escaped from the LTTE moving across the Jaffna lagoon in boats. After this, as the army advanced into the Mulleitivu district, they began to encounter small groups of civilians who had escaped from the LTTE and were coming into the army held area.

The LTTE did everything they could to discourage the civilians from escaping. On 9 February 2009, an LTTE suicide bomber who had tagged along with escaping civilians exploded herself inside an IDP reception centre in Dharmapuram, killing 23 and injuring 64.

* * * * *

In the Vanni battles, the LTTE used a weapon which the army did not possess. The term used by soldiers to describe this piece of equipment was 'pedal gun'. These were actually naval guns mounted on trailers. Naval guns have a much faster rate of fire than conventional artillery guns as boats had to fire from an unstable platform which will always be pitching and rolling even in the best of conditions, and they had to depend on the rate of fire to be able to hit a target. The 'pedal' part of it came from the fact that all naval guns are operated by foot controls. It was this pedal gun that had the greatest psychological effect on the government troops – with its distinctive sound and rapid rate of fire.

The LTTE put up a desperate fight in the eastern Vanni, fighting every inch of the way. A general indication of the ferocity of the fighting can be obtained from the casualty figures of Shavendra Silva's 58th Division as it moved down the A-35 road to Mullitivu. In the battles around Visuamadu, 92 soldiers were killed, this was followed by 55 in Suthathirapuram, 45 in Puthukudiirippu West, 80 at the Puthukudiirippu Junction, and no less than 135 in Iranapalai (a location close to Puthukudiirippu). The 58th Division suffered the highest number of casualties in capturing the final few kilometres of LTTE held territory from Puthumathalan to Vellamullivaikkal - with a staggering 459 fatalities and 2,499 troops wounded in battle. Thus this narrow sliver of land cost more lives than the entire Jaffna peninsula in 1995 and these were the casualty figures of just one of three divisions operating in the area. The experience of Nandana

Udawatte's 59th Division which was the first to start fighting in the eastern Vanni, was no different. To advance 28 kilometres into the enemy heartland and capture 425 square kilometres of territory, 579 soldiers laid down their lives while 3372 men were wounded in battle. Two officers and 65 soldiers were also reported missing in action.

The fiercest pitched battles in the Vanni operation took place in the vicinity of Puthukudiirippu. The Puthukudiirippu town was captured by the end of February 2009. There was a major battle in Iranapalai to the east of Puthukudiirippu town on 4 and 5 April 2009, where over 600 LTTE cadres had been killed including important commanders like Theepan, Gaddafi, Nagesh and leadership level female cadres likeVidusha and Durga. The advancing troops of Task force 8 had linked up with Shavendra Silva's troops thus encircling the LTTE contingent led by Theepan. The latter, a fighter to the last, counterattacked and died fighting.

Among the items captured in Iranapalai, were three 130mm heavy artillery guns. After the battle of Iranapalai, the LTTE had no more territory left, and they were now in the Puthumathalan demilitarised zone along with the civilians.

With the clearing of the Puthukudiirippu area, the next obstacle that the 58th Division encountered was the earth bund constructed by the LTTE on the other side of the Puthumathalan lagoon. During the standoff at the Puthumathalan bund, army intelligence operatives kept interviewing the few civilians who managed to escape the LTTE. One such informant called Srikanthan, a fisherman who could speak Sinhala, told them that if the army manages to capture even a part of the bund, the civilians on the other side were in readiness to storm the gap despite anything the LTTE may do to stop them. So it was due a synergistic desire for the army to break in, and the civilians to break out, that the last bund was breached. Even before the army captured the Puthumathalan bund, nearly 3000 civilians escaped by sea and gave themselves up to the navy on 18 April 2009.

The Indian journalist B.Muralidhar Reddy writing to *Frontline*, the fortnightly Indian magazine said: *"For the Sri Lankan government, the final phase of the war against the Liberation Tigers of Tamil Eelam (LTTE) is proving to be tougher, trickier and nastier than anticipated. None had thought the Tigers would last long after the fall of their main garrison town Mulleitivu on January 25, but 10 weeks later, they are still fighting, much to the agony of the civilians trapped in the war zone, and the rest of the world...The presence of a large number of civilians in the war zone is one of the main reasons for the prolonged war. Estimates of their number vary from 70,000 to 150,000..."*

At Puthutmathlan, the army was faced with three obstacles - there was the Puthumathalan lagoon, and beyond that a patch of mangroves, then there was the bund itself. Because of the nature of the obstacle that had to be overcome, it was the 1st Commando Battalion and the 1st Special Forces Battalion that were assigned to breach the bund. The first thing that had to be done was to gauge the depth of the narrow lagoon and fix a path to be taken through the water because the depth differed at certain places. Once this was worked out, on 20 April 2009, a joint commando and Special Forces attacking party along with eight SIOT teams from the 9th Gemunu Watch crossed the lagoon wading through water up to their chests in a night operation and secured the western side of the bund by about 2 am.

Rafts made of plantain tree trunks, sealed PVC pipes and even empty plastic 81mm mortar casings were used as floating aids to get the troops across. A stretch of about 2 km was secured by the attacking party with the commandos and Special Forces on either side and the SIOT teams in the middle. Immense acts of bravery were seen in this assault. The fighting continued for about three hours with the LTTE directing barrages of mortar fire at the troops. Hearing the gunfire and knowing that the army was on the other side of the bund, the civilians were preparing to flee but the LTTE was beating them back.

At around 5.00 am, Captain Ajith Gamage a squadron leader of the 1st Special Forces Battalion had clambered up the bund with some troops and all of them had bellowed at the tops of their voices in Tamil 'Enga waanga!' (Come here) giving an indication to the civilians on which stretch of the 3 km long bund they were. About 800 civilians had come rushing over the bund at his call. There was chaos at the first rush with people tumbling down the bund and children and old people being trampled underfoot. Then there was a lull and no more people came. Then Capt. Gamage went to the top the bund to see what was going on. He was promptly shot through the head by an LTTE sniper. Two other soldiers were also killed by snipers.

By first light, the people on the other side were able to stampede their way over the bund and for a few hours the LTTE lost control. Over 33,000 people escaped from 6.00 am up to around 10.00 am on 20 April. This was watched live at air force headquarters by president Rajapaksa and some Western diplomats who had been invited to witness the world's biggest rescue operation live through UAV images relayed to Colombo. The president and the invitees saw live, how the

LTTE was trying to prevent the civilians from fleeing by shooting them. Then there was the sound of three blasts and a lull as the LTTE managed to beat the civilians back.

At first the army commandos had thought the LTTE had fired mortars at the civilians. But a Tamil civilian who had just come over and spoke Sinhala told them that it was not a mortar attack but three suicide cadres blasting themselves. Seventeen civilians died and nearly 400 were injured in those explosions as well as due to LTTE small arms fire. After around 10.00 am, there was no movement. Throughout the day the army teams that had crossed the Puthumathalan lagoon lay against the side of the bund, taking cover from LTTE fire. From morning till night, the bodies of Capt Gamage and the other two special forces men lay at the top of the bund and the army made no attempt to retrieve them because if there was a firefight, many civilians would have got caught in the crossfire.

Over the next few days, a further 100,000 people would escape the clutches of the LTTE. The government launched a massive public relations exercise in tandem with the rescue operation. The distance between the Puthumathalan bund and the beach was less than one kilometre and Shavendra Silva's troops cut across to link up with Prasanna Silva's 55th Division on 22 April 2009. Prasanna Silva as recounted earlier, had fought his way down from Vettalankerny to Puthumathalan some time earlier. This thrust by Shavendra Silva's troops bifurcated the 14 sq km demilitarised zone and the LTTE was pushed into Vellamullivaikkal to the south of Puthumathalan.

A large group of foreign journalists were taken to the Puthumathlan front to see the situation for themselves. Reddy, the *Frontline* correspondent quoted earlier who was in this group of foreign journalists, was to report of the rescue operation in the following words *"The breaking of the three meter high embankment in the early hours of April 20 resulted in a flow of 1.15 lakh civilians in to government controlled territory over the next six days. It began as a trickle but turned into a flood within hours and grew into an avalanche over the next four days...Of those pouring in from the NFZ were shrunk and sick old men and women with little children clinging to them. Barefooted and empty handed, they could hardly walk...they appeared dazed and bewildered, Presumably, they had not had a decent meal in weeks if not months. Living under the constant fear of death for nearly two years, they looked like walking corpses..."*

Writing in the same issue of Frontline, the eminent Sri Lankan academic Michael Roberts formerly of the University of Adelaide

Australia, wrote as follows: "... *today, we know that the commando operation was one for the text book; it resulted in relatively few non-combatant deaths and created a path for streams and streams of Tamils to cross the lagoon... This for me was better than the tale of Moses crossing the red sea....*"

A point that has to be noted is that even though the government tried to have certain areas declared de-militarised zones, the LTTE never agreed. In terms of the international law of armed conflict, demilitarised zones can be established only through the mutual consent of the warring parties. Once a demilitarised zone is established the forces of the belligerent parties cannot remain inside it. The LTTE's consistent refusal to acknowledge any demilitarised zone meant that there were never any demilitarised zones anywhere in Sri Lanka even though people continued to refer to a so called 'no fire zone'. In fact after the battle of Iranapalai, there was a bizarre situation where there were no terrorists anywhere in Sri Lanka except inside the area referred to incongruously by many people as a 'no-fire-zone'. The presence of thousands of terrorists along with their heavy weapons inside this so called no-fire zone meant that at the last stages, there was no firing taking place anywhere in Sri Lanka except inside the 'no-fire zone'!

Chapter 76

Pressures from the West

During the final months of the war, tremendous pressure was brought on Sri Lanka by certain Western countries to halt military operations. One of the means adopted by the West to bring the Sri Lankan government to heel was by exerting economic pressure. In the years 2008 and 2009, every country in the world was economically vulnerable because of the world economic recession of those years which was widely regarded as the worst since the Great Depression of the 1930s. The year 2009 was the worst possible year for any country to be embroiled in a war. When the global recession hit, there was a flight of capital from Sri Lanka because the investors were having problems back home. In this situation it appeared that Sri Lanka's foreign exchange reserves would not be sufficient to meet even day to day needs. This is the classic situation in which the IMF was supposed to come in and assist member countries. They are the lender of last resort to countries that are having balance of payments problems. As a member of the IMF, Sri Lanka was entitled to that help.

But the IMF delayed the stand-by facility by more than five months. The application for the funding was made at the end of February 2009. In March that year central bank governor Ajith Cabraal and senior presidential advisor Basil Rajapaksa went to the IMF headquarters in Washington and met the managing director and he had told them that they were happy to consider Sri Lanka's application. Everything had been finalized and the money should have come by the end of March or at least the beginning of April 2009. But the money never came. As a result of this, capital continued to flow out of treasury bills and treasury bonds. The foreign currency held in treasury bonds came down from 800 million to 17 million USD.

When Cabraal went to the regular IMF meeting in mid-April 2009, he realized that the money was still not on the way. Something had to be done fast, or the Sri Lankan economy would have collapsed and the war would have come to a grinding halt. Cabraal phoned President Mahinda Rajapaksa from Washington and informed him of the situation. The American government had a lot to do with delaying the stand-by facility to Sri Lanka with Hillary Clinton openly saying that this was 'not the best time' to give that loan to the Sri Lankan government. Voting power in the IMF depended on economic strength and the US, the EU and other Western powers opposing the war effectively controlled the IMF.

President Mahinda Rajapaksa then spoke to Libyan leader Muammar Gadaffi over the phone and arranged for a bilateral loan of 500 million US$ and Cabraal flew straight from Washington to Tripoli to meet his Libyan counterpart and finalise arrangements for the funding line. In Libya, Cabraal had told the news channels that he was negotiating a loan and this was flashed all over the world by the newswires. This had helped stabilise the markets in Sri Lanka because of the impression that the government had somehow got the money. If the impression had been created that there was going to be a balance of payments crisis with no one coming to Sri Lanka's aid, then the markets would have panicked. Thus, due to some deft footwork on the part of president Mahinda Rajapaksa, Sri Lanka survived the financial crunch that was almost upon the country just as the war entered its final stages.

While the Western powers conspired to deny Sri Lanka a badly needed stand-by facility by using their voting power on the IMF board, India came to Sri Lanka's rescue with the Indian representative on the IMF board Adrash Kishore, a former finance secretary of India telling them on the express instructions of prime minister Manmohan Singh, that if the IMF was not going to give Sri Lanka the money that they were entitled to, India would provide the funds themselves. At this, the Western powers backed down and allowed the loan to go through. The IMF bureaucracy had been scandalized by what was happening and they had said privately to Sri Lankan officials that they had never experienced such attempts to politicize the IMF before. The IMF money finally came only in July 2009 when the war was over, and Sri Lanka was already on its way to recovery with money flowing in again.

On 16 April 2009, Vijay Nambiar the chief of staff to the UN Secretary General Ban Ki Moon, came to Sri Lanka trying to broker a ceasefire. He had a meeting with Gōta who ruled out a ceasefire point blank on the grounds that it would only help the LTTE and prolong the suffering of the civilians held hostage. Gōta explained to Nambiar how the demilitarised zone that the government had declared, had to be changed to a different location because the LTTE sent the civilians into Puthumathalan to prevent them from going over to the government side. Gōta had also explained that there was no road access to the second demilitarised zone and that food and medicine was being provided by ship. Nambiar wanted to send a UN fact finding team into the demilitarised zone. But Gōta pointed out that was not a practical proposition because the army will have to cease operations for the UN team to go there.

The president had a one to one meeting with Nambiar the next day, but there was no change in the government's stance. On 24 April 2009, as the great hostage rescue was in progress in Puthumathalan, US State Department spokesman Robert Wood at the department's weekly press briefing, called upon the LTTE to stop holding civilians and putting them in harm's way and to lay down their arms and surrender to a third party. This call by the USA for the LTTE to surrender to a third party, raised many an eyebrow in Sri Lanka. On 27 April, the *Sunday Island* reported in a headline story that the government has ruled out any deal for the LTTE to surrender to a third party. A senior defence ministry official was quoted as having said that the ongoing offensive would not be stopped, and that there could not be any third party involvement in this matter, and that the government was not going to give up its right to destroy the LTTE militarily.

Even after all this had been said, French foreign minister Bernard Kouchner and British foreign secretary David Milliband came to Sri Lanka on 29 April 2009, in a bid to prevail upon the government to halt the war. At a meeting with the two visiting foreign ministers at which the Sri Lankan foreign minister Rohita Bogollagama, foreign secretary Palitha Kohona, and attorney general Mohan Peiris were present, Gōta categorically rejected Kouchner's and Milliband's call for a ceasefire and told them point blank that the government will continue military operations until Prabhakaran is captured dead or alive.

During this meeting, Milliband had been the more agitated of the two, sitting on the edge of his chair while making his case for a halt to the war. Gōta told both Kouchner and Milliband that these 'humanitarian concerns' they were talking about was only a ploy to extricate Prabhakaran and his top leaders from the situation they were now in. And he told them in no uncertain terms that the military was under orders to kill Prabhakaran if they are unable to capture him alive. Gōta told Milliband that over 200,000 civilians had been rescued from the LTTE clutches and that over 100,000 had been rescued in the days prior to their arrival in Sri Lanka. He told him that visuals of the whole rescue operation had been relayed live over the news services worldwide.

At this point, Milliband who was in an agitated state had said that Britain had information that civilians had been harmed due to army shelling. To this Gōta had said that the Birtish foreign secretary should not be misled by LTTE propaganda and that even the BBC was broadcasting LTTE propaganda material without verification. The visibly flustered Milliband had said that he was not being influenced by BBC reports but by credible reports from people inside the no-fire zone. To this Gōta had said that anybody who knew the LTTE would not believe that reliable information would come out of a population under its control. All communication into and out of the area under their control was completely in LTTE hands and only those whom they permit, will have access to the outside world.

Gōta pointed out that the stories coming out of the area of LTTE control are all doctored to elicit the most favourable response from the Western community of nations and the international media. Knowing that they were not getting anywhere with calls for a ceasefire, Kouchner had finally said that their concern was for the civilians and he requested the government's permission to visit the LTTE held area to talk to the LTTE and to get them to agree to release the remaining civilians. Gōta however had turned down this request saying that it was too dangerous and that the LTTE may even take him hostage. To this Kouchner had replied that he was willing to risk his life if necessary on behalf of the civilians. Gōta shot back that his concern is not about what would happen to him (Kouchner) but that operations will have to be halted to facilitate such a visit and that through that, the opportunity to get at Prabhakaran may be lost.

President Mahinda Rajapaksa was on that day in Embilipitiya for a function and was staying in a guest house on the banks of the

Chandrika Wewa. Kouchner and Milliband were air lifted to Embilipitiya from Vavuniya after visiting the newly set up IDP camps to meet the president. Just half an hour before they arrived, the president ordered his staff to get a place ready for a meeting outside by the side of the lake under a tree. The president, Rohita Bogollagama, Lalith Weeratunga, Palitha Kohona, Kshenuka Seneviratne, and the British and French ambassadors were present. Milliband started by saying that they were representing the international community and that "This massacre of Tamils must stop". The president had flown into a towering rage at this. "What do you mean massacre of Tamil people?", he had asked. "We have to free these people from the LTTE". He also told Milliband not to think that Sri Lanka was still a British colony. The president told him, that even if the entire international community comes to Sri Lanka he couldn't care less, and that he will stop the war only after terrorism is eliminated. Kouchner, striking a conciliatory note had said "Look Mr president, we are here to help you. We are your friends". To this the president had shot back that he knows who his friends and enemies are. He said "For you people, what happens here is news, but for us, its agony!".

Milliband and Kouchner went back without having achieved anything. A Norwegian government commissioned report on Sri Lanka was to observe later that overseas aid workers in Sri Lanka had regarded the visit of the duo as 'a joke'. Just days before he arrived in Sri Lanka, according to an AFP report, Kouchner had said in a radio interview that civilians fleeing Puthumathalan by boat had been drowning in the sea and that French and British boats could be deployed to help the IDPs. This comment made it to the headlines of *The Island* on 23 April 2009. The navy hotly denied that any IDPs had drowned in the sea and that all those who escaped by boat were being looked after by the navy and that the vast majority of the IDPs had waded across the shallow lagoon and escaped by land. With that kind of pre-arrival press, it was not surprising that both Kouchner and Milliband were summarily brushed off by the Rajapaksas.

An interesting sequel to this fiasco was that Tim Waite, the British foreign office team leader on Sri Lanka had told Richard Mills a political officer of the US Embassy in Colombo that the reason why the British foreign secretary David Milliband and the Labour government in Britain were lavishing so much attention on Sri Lanka was because of the 'very vocal' Tamil Diaspora in the UK numbering more than 300,000 who had been camping in front of the British parliament since 6 April 2009. Waite had told Mills that with the UK elections on the horizon and many Tamils living in labour constituencies with slim majorities, the labour government was paying particular attention to Sri Lanka. Waite had also told Mills that Milliband had told him that he was spending 60% of his time on Sri Lanka at that moment. A few days later, Mills was to report this conversation to Washington in a routine communiqué.

This communiqué was among the US government documents that were published on the Wikileaks website in November 2010 and was reported in a story in the British newspaper *The Telegraph* by Gordon Rayner. What this reveals is that Milliband sought to put pressure on the government of Sri Lanka to halt the war due to considerations pertaining to British politics. Therefore the manner in which both the president and Gōta brushed him off was fully justified. The very notion that a sovereign nation combating the world's deadliest terrorist organization should halt the war so that the British Labour party could win elections, was absolutely preposterous.

The grand finale to all this was that the UN secretary general Ban Ki Moon also wanted to come to Sri Lanka just as the war was entering its final few days. However, Mahinda Rajapaksa was in Jordan at the time, and he told Ban that he shouldn't come, because he (Mahinda) would not be able to receive him. To this, Ban had said that it is quite all right even if His Excellency is not there to receive him as he can always talk to the prime minister. But Mahinda insisted that if no less a person than the UN secretary general was coming to Sri Lanka, the head of state should be there to receive him and to postpone the visit until he gets back to Sri Lanka. By the time Ban finally got to Sri Lanka, Prabhakaran was dead and the war was over.

Chapter 77

Black Tigers Fail in Colombo

One area of anti-terrorist activity that needed luck as much as anything else was in either preventing or investigating a black tiger attack. At times spectacular success or abject failure for both the terrorists and the government may hinge on just a fortuitous event. As the war drew to a close in 2009, the president himself had a very close shave. After 2008, the intelligence services and the police generally became more adept at tracking down the operatives and networks behind the terrorist strikes that the LTTE did succeed in making. The disruption of the LTTE's networks in Colombo with such breakthroughs was the urban equivalent of the gains being made in the Vanni. As the US Defence Department report of 2002 observed, the LTTE fought three kinds of war with the government. In the eastern province they fought a guerrilla war, in the Vanni they fought a full scale conventional manoeuvre war and in Colombo they launched classic terrorist attacks.

During the year 2008, there was a spate of bombings in the greater Colombo area aimed at undermining the war effort by taking on the adversary from the rear and breaking the will of the public to support the war. Among the attacks that took place in 2008, were the following.

2008 February 03 – Suicide attack at Colombo Fort railway station, 11 killed (mostly schoolboys) and over 100 injured.

2008 April 25 – Bus bomb in Piliyandala, 24 killed, 40 injured.

2008 May 16 – Suicide bombing near the presidential secretariat, 11 killed, over 100 injured.

2008 May 26 – Bomb at Dehiwela railway station 8 killed, 62 injured.

2008 June 4 – Blast on railway tracks in Dehiwala, 24 injured.

2008 June 6 – Bus bomb in Moratuwa, 20 killed, 90 injured.

2008 Oct 6 - Anuradhapura suicide bombing , Janaka Perera and 27 others killed, 80 injured.

A series of breakthroughs achieved in the investigations into some of these incidents laid bare and disrupted the LTTE's network in Colombo, crippling their capacity to carry out such attacks. By February 2009, with the LTTE facing imminent defeat in the north, Gōta was able to congratulate the security forces at the Western Province Security Coordinating Conference held on 12 February 2009, for having been able to maintain an incident free environment during the independence day celebrations, the *Deyata Kirula* development exhibition, the *Navam Perehera* in Colombo and the India-Sri Lanka cricket matches all of which took place in the month of February 2009. That was made possible because of a series of breaks that the intelligence services got in 2008.

The suspects in the 3 February 2008 bomb at the Fort railway station which killed nine schoolboys - members of the D.S.Senanayake College baseball team - were apprehended as a result of the intelligence dragnet over Colombo. The State Intelligence Service visited police stations in the city and interviewed people routinely brought in by the police for questioning. On 13 June 2008, they came across a suspicious individual at one of these interviews and under intense interrogation he had admitted that he was a suicide cadre. Acting on information provided by this suspect, a Tamil shopkeeper was taken into custody the very next day.

It was from this shopkeeper that the SIS had obtained a lead about the suicide bombing at the Fort railway station. Under interrogation the shopkeeper admitted that it was he who had transported the female suicide member to the Fort. It was in his shop at Kotahena that the woman had donned the suicide jacket. The shopkeeper had locked his shop from the outside to allow the woman to put on the suicide vest. She had actually been deployed in front of Lake House to attack troops rehearsing for the independence day parade to be held the next day on 4 February 2008. The suicide cadre had entered the Fort railway station through the rear entrance because

470

people were being checked on the streets, and she thought that in the railway station, she would be able to blend into the crowd.

Usually, it was those going into the railway station who were checked, but that day, the SIS had deployed about 50 operatives to check people who came out of the station, so as to search those coming into Colombo. So the suicide cadre could go in without anybody stopping her, but she could not come out without being checked. Hence she blew herself up right inside the station, near the best looking target – the D.S.Senanayake College baseball team. A search of the shopkeeper's premises yielded cyanide capsules, a small quantity of C-4 explosives, several hand grenades, detonators, ball bearings etc. All the suspects in this case are now awaiting trial.

The day before the Piliyandala bus bombing of 25 April 2008, which killed 24 people and injured 40, the government had announced the capture of the Madhu Church, one of the holiest Roman Catholic shrines in the country - a landmark achievement in the ongoing Vanni operation. The bombing in Pliyandala was the LTTE's way of trying to save face. That day, as usually happens after a bomb explosion, the police carried out a routine cordon and search operation and brought 29 individuals to the Piliyandala police station for questioning. Then an SIS officer got a call from a certain Tamil prison guard he knew who wanted him to intervene and save his brother who had been among those arrested in the round up.

This prison guard had another brother who was a police officer attached to the Kollupitiya police station located in close proximity to Temple Trees, the residence of the president. The anxiety of the prison guard aroused the suspicions of the SIS and they sent a team to the Piliyandala police station and interviewed this individual who had been standing around in the police station compound waiting to be questioned. After the interview, the SIS sleuths knew they had a lead and they made a formal arrest. Upon interrogating the suspect, they found that it was the suspect himself who had planted the bomb. All this occurred on the very day of the blast. The newly exposed LTTE operative even showed the SIS sleuths the open drain into which he threw the remote control device. That too was recovered even though it had been carried some distance with the rainwater.

In May 2009, as the war came to a close, the SIS made a major breakthrough. Through a foreign source of information, the SIS got the number of a dedicated mobile phone used by the LTTE. The LTTE always used dedicated phones for operations after which the SIM (Subscriber Identity Module) card would be discarded. The LTTE was able to get an inexhaustible supply of SIM cards because each LTTE operative had several bogus national identity cards, which could be used to apply for SIM cards. Upon receiving this telephone number from a foreign source, the SIS had tried to trace the owner of the mobile number but had come up against a blank wall because it was still in the name of the dealer who had issued it. This particular dealer had issued 192 SIM cards without registering the owner's details with the service provider.

Besides, the SIS guessed that even if the owner's details had been registered, that would not have been helpful because the details would all be bogus. The free availability of bogus national identity cards was one of the biggest loopholes in the security system and it was never properly addressed until the end of the war. Very often when the police check back with the Registrar of Persons, they find that the identity card is genuine, but the details given are false. Only two documents were needed to obtain a national ID card - a birth certificate and the *Grama Niladhari's* (village headman's) certificate both of which could easily be forged.

Be that as it may, this phone number that the SIS had, had been used to receive and make calls to a foreign country – about 75 calls in all, both ways. Just four missed calls had been made to two local numbers. One of them turned out to be due to a genuine dialling error. The other three were made to an employment agency and had remained unanswered because the owner was overseas. The SIS went to extraordinary lengths to follow up on the lead provided by this telephone number. They waited until the employment agency owner returned from overseas and arrested him at the airport. Then they made him return the call to the mobile phone number telling the person at the other end that he was returning the calls he had received while he was abroad. The employment agent was told to call back on another number.

That was a giveaway sign that this was indeed an LTTE operational phone which could not be used for private matters. When they traced the tower locations, the SIS found that the recipient of the call was in the Negombo area. The LTTE operative at the other end told the employment agent that there were two men to be sent off for employment overseas. They arranged to meet in Negombo to discuss the deal. The LTTE operative was arrested and he admitted that he was a black tiger. He also told the SIS that he was in contact with a certain army officer whom he referred to as 'Army Uncle'. The suicide cadre said he had met Army Uncle but did not know his rank. As luck would have it, minutes after his arrest, this suicide cadre got a call from Army Uncle and with SIS officers breathing down his neck, he spoke to the army officer without raising the latter's suspicions. The entire conversation which was in Tamil, was recorded by SIS officers on another mobile phone. During the conversation, Army Uncle had said that 'Periyappa' (meaning the President) was going to Jordan and that something could be done on the way to the airport. This trip to Jordan was the one made by the president just days before the end of the war. The army officer involved was a fluent speaker of Tamil.

After recording that conversation, they continued interrogating the suicide cadre, who revealed that his handler was in the UK and that he would receive calls from the UK telling him when and where to meet Army Uncle. He also revealed that there was another contact person in Colombo known only as 'Aiya' (meaning elder brother) whom he was in regular contact with. The SIS got him to make an appointment to meet 'Aiya' at the a car park in Bambalapitiya. *Aiya* turned up and he too was arrested. This Aiya turned out to be one of the best catches ever made by any intelligence organization in the country. He was a key operative who had been involved in among other hit jobs, the assassination of Lakshman Kadirgarmar.

Aiya's arrest took place on 10 May 2009. This Aiya was a smart young man driving a flashy car and playing the part of a well to do upper-class youth always in tie, designer clothes and shoes and gold cufflinks, and just looking at his turnout, no one would ever suspect him of being an LTTE operative in Colombo. It was the Tamil hoi polloi who carried out dangerous missions for the LTTE and even at checkpoints, his being a Tamil was not a problem because he looked the part of a hot shot executive. After his capture, he had told the police that he had transported suicide jackets under the seat of his car because his car was never searched at checkpoints. With Aiya in the bag, the SIS turned its attention to Army Uncle and the tower location of the latter's phone was checked and they found that most calls were taken between Ratmalana and Homagama. He was identified as Lt Col Ranjith Perera and arrested.

The plan Aiya and Army Uncle had was to attack the president when he arrived for the *Deyata Kirula* exhibition which was due to commence on 4 February 2009. What prevented the attack from taking place was an order stipulating that only those above the rank of Brigadier could take their vehicles into the venue. Army Uncle was a Lt Colonel and therefore could not take his vehicle into the venue. He was to take the suicide cadre into the *Deyata Kirula* exhibition grounds dressed as a soldier. He had even got an army uniform tailored especially for the suicide cadre. The plan was that if the first attack at the exhibition failed, another suicide cadre would strike when the injured president was taken to the accident ward at the Colombo general hospital.

More suicide cadres had been assigned to Aiya to ensure that the job was completed. He had been told that the mission has to succeed, even if he too has to die in the process because the situation was so precarious in the north. Upon further interrogating Aiya, the SIS was told that some suicide jackets were in a flat at Sunflower Court on 37th Lane, Wellawatte. When the police went to the flat, its occupant Satish Kumar Sujindan leapt off the seventh floor balcony and committed suicide. He was the brother of Aiya's handler in the UK. One of the four suicide jackets discovered in the Sunflower Court flat weighed 15 kilos, the biggest suicide jacket ever found and this could have been the one that was to be worn for the *Deyata Kirula* attack.

Those who knew Army Uncle well, say he was a capable officer. The reason why he was fluent in Tamil was because he hailed from Bandarawela where many up-country Tamils live. He was a hard drinker and with his colleagues, he would often talk about visiting Karoke bars which in Sri Lanka, are mainly brothels. These plans were foiled at the last moment due to the discovery of a single phone number which the LTTE operative had in a moment of indiscretion, used for a private purpose and that was what led to the unravelling of the whole plot.

The need to protect Colombo became ever more pressing as the LTTE struggled for survival in the north. Another breakthrough towards the very end of the war came with a police informant recognizing a key LTTE hit man in Colombo handled by LTTE intelligence wing leader Vinayagam who had been overlooking operations in Colombo after the death of Charles. The Western Province Intelligence Division had arrested this hit man on 21 March 2009 but he kept insisting that he was not the man the police thought he was and that it was all a case of mistaken identity. The police however had been able to confront him with evidence that he was living under a stolen identity and that the real individual who went by the name he had given had been traced.

This highly skilled hit man spoke fluent Sinhala and posed as a Sinhalese. When confronted with this information, the hit man had admitted his real identity. He was a top operative who had worked with Pottu Amman and Vinayagam closely and had been responsible for among other operations, the spectacular killing of eight of Karuna Amman's best cadres at a safe house in Kottawa on 1 July 2004. After the Kottawa killings, the guns used had been taken away by a TNA parliamentarian at the time, Ariyanayagam Chandranehru in his vehicle with his two police guards.

It had also been Chandranehru who had introduced the Muslim police inspector 'Abdul' (mentioned in an earlier chapter) who had been assigned to assassinate the president, to the LTTE in Amparai. Chandranehru would unsurprisingly be killed in a Karuna group ambush while he was travelling with Kaushalyan the LTTE's political wing leader for Batticaloa-Ampara on 7 February 2005. He was no longer in parliament by that time. Upon further interrogation, this LTTE hit man had taken the police to his house in Mattakkuliya where in a compartment in his water tank, were over 280 kilos of C-4 plastic explosives, 28 rocket propelled grenades, 30 hand grenades, and nearly 700 rounds of T-56 ammunition. This was the largest haul of explosives in Colombo. The explosives were for an attack on the Colombo harbour. The plan of the LTTE had been to attack the harbour and ram an explosives laden van into the army warehouse in the harbour which stocked the artillery shells and other munitions coming from Pakistan and China for the war. A hit like that would have brought the war to a halt until fresh stocks were brought in.

The last successful suicide bombing by the LTTE took place at a festival of the Godapitiya Mosque in Akuressa on 10 March 2009, killing 14 and injuring 35. Among the injured was Mahinda Wijesekera who had helped Mahinda in his 1970 election campaign and was at the time of the incident, a member of the cabinet. He was permanently disabled as a result of his injuries.

Chapter 78

The Tamil Nadu Factor

The Indian external affairs secretary Shivshankar Mennon visited Sri Lanka in mid-January 2009, as fighting raged in the eastern Vanni and in the statement put out to mark this visit, what was stressed was the need to move on rapidly from military successes to a political solution. Mennon also stressed the need to prevent civilian casualties. Once again there was no mention of the old refrain that there was no military solution to the conflict nor was there any call to halt the hostilities. The Indian emphasis after the end of October 2008, shifted to providing humanitarian assistance such as food and medicine to the IDPs and minimizing civilian casualties. This was a time when the Indians worked very closely with Sri Lanka. Just days after Mennon's visit, The Indian external affairs minister Pranabh Mukherjee himself was in Sri Lanka on 27 January.

Among the matters discussed by Mukherjee in Sri Lanka was the declaration of a safe zone for civilians so that the LTTE would be able to release the civilians into those areas. On 29 January 2009, at Mukherjee's request, the government declared a 48 hour period for the LTTE to release the civilians in their control. But this call was ignored by the terrorists. According to the Indian government's estimates at this point, the LTTE had with them about 150,000 civilians and this was the figure that Mukherjee mentioned in the Indian parliament. This was a period when tremendous pressure was brought on the Indian central government by politicians on both sides of the divide in Tamil Nadu to intervene in Sri Lanka to stop the war.

But the Indian central government took the flak and shielded Sri Lanka. As we saw in an earlier chapter, the 16th Amendment to the Indian constitution made it impossible for any political party in India to advocate separatism openly. As a result of this, Tamil separatism in India began to find expression as support for Tamil separatists in Sri Lanka. This was a way of being Tamil nationalist and separatist without breaking any laws in India.

President Mahinda Rajapaksa told Mukherjee during his visit that Tamil Nadu politicians like M.Karunanidhi and Jeyaram Jeyalalitha were welcome to visit the conflict zone in Sri Lanka. On 18 February 2009, Mukherjee made a statement to the Indian parliament that the LTTE had now been restricted to an area of 150 sq km and that the government had gained control of Kilinochchi, Elephant Pass and Mulleitivu. Once again his concern was with providing relief to the civilians. He reported that in the two weeks preceding, about 35,000 Tamil civilians had escaped the LTTE and come over to the government side.

As the war ground to a close, the pressure from Tamil Nadu on the Indian Central government intensified. The ruling party of Tamil Nadu, the *Dravida Munnethra Kazagam* was a member of the ruling coalition at the centre as well and the central government could not possibly ignore a demand made by a constituent of the ruling coalition. The Congress Party led government in India during the final war in Sri Lanka was a minority government with the Indian Congress Party holding only 145 seats in a 552 member parliament. They had to scrape together a coalition that included the *Dravida Munnethra Kazagam* which had 16 seats in the *Lok Sabha*. Once formed, the ruling coalition had 335 members in parliament and could easily survive even if the DMK pulled out.

But given the fragile nature of the coalition they would not have wanted to rock the boat. All Indian governments since 1991 had been reluctant to antagonize the Tamil Nadu establishment and their position on the Sri Lankan issue was coloured by that paramount consideration. On the evening of 23 April 2009, Gōta got a call on his mobile phone from Shivashankar Mennon. He explained to Gōta that his government was coming under pressure from Tamil Nadu, and that he and Narayanan wanted to come to Sri Lanka urgently to deliver a message from the Indian government to the president. Gōta called the president immediately and got an appointment for Mennon the next morning. Mennon and Narayanan got on a special flight that night and arrived in Colombo.

Mennon and Narayanan were at Temple Trees by 9.00 am on 24 April 2009. Alok Prasad and Vikram Misri the Indian deputy high commissioner were also present from the Indian side. President Rajapaksa, Lalith Weeratunga and Gōta were present to hear what the Indians had to say. The Indians explained that in Tamil Nadu, people believed that Tamils were being massacred, but that the Indian central government knew it was not so. The president said that the LTTE was now cornered and weaker than it ever was and that this was an opportunity to end the war. The president then wanted to know, what he could do to help the Indian central government get over its predicament in Tamil Nadu.

The discussion then turned to the limiting of the use of heavy artillery. The president said that he will place the matter before the security council on Monday and get back to them. It was Alok Prasad and Lalith Weeratunga who drafted the joint statement that was to be issued regarding the non-use of heavy weaponry. The message they put out after their return to India on 24 April was cryptic and non committal.

"We were received by H.E. the President of Sri Lanka. We conveyed the concerns of the government of India on the evolving situation in Northern Sri Lanka, especially the casualties caused among Tamil civilians as a result of ongoing operations."

"We also expressed the government of India's concerns about the humanitarian situation as a result of nearly a hundred thousand Tamil civilians coming out of the conflict zone since early this week."

"The President of Sri Lanka was receptive to our concerns."

"We are hopeful of a positive outcome."

* * * * *

The crossing over of the civilians to the government side in the third week of April 2009, was a disaster to the LTTE but a great boon to the government. It represented the very essence of the victory of the government over the LTTE. The pro-LTTE Tamils living in the West were beside themselves with fury. S.Manoranjan, a Tamil media personality now living in Canada told the present writer that when the Tamil civilians started moving onto the government side, furious Tamil demonstrators on the streets of Toronto had shouted over the loud hailers *"Don't send them one red cent, they're all traitors!"*

After the capture of the Puthumathalan bund, the link up with Prasanna Silva's troops of the 55th Division on the Puthumathalan beach and the liberation of a large number of the civilian hostages, the next task of Shavendra Silva's 58ᵗʰ Division was to fight their way southwards along the beach and to capture *MV Farah III*, a Jordanian ship that had been hijacked earlier by the LTTE and run aground 5 km south of Puthumathalan. This Jordanian ship with a largely Egyptian crew was transporting a consignment of rice from India to South Africa when it developed engine trouble and drifted towards Sri Lanka. While anchored off the coast of Mulleitivu, the ship was boarded by the LTTE and the crew taken hostage. Then the ship was run aground at a point between Puthumathalan and Vellamullivaikkal. The 175 meter long and 15 meter high vessel was thereafter used as a sea tiger command centre and after the fall of Chalai to Prasanna Silva's troops, the wreckage of *MV Farah III* became the last sea tiger base.

After the LTTE was cornered in a part of the Mulleitivu district, the navy deployed barrier lines on the sea to prevent the escape of the LTTE leaders. After the Puthumathalan bund was breached on 20 April, the small boat squadrons of the navy were also deployed off the Mulleitivu coast. There were now four barrier lines on the sea, the Arrow boats and inshore patrol craft about one nautical mile off the coast, two Dovras about another nautical mile away, a line of other fast attack craft about 5 nautical miles away, and beyond that were the offshore patrol vessels. The last barrier line was to prevent any vessels from getting in, rather than out, because of the fear that the LTTE leaders would be picked up on the sea by vessels coming from outside.

Those manning the barrier line on the sea were as confident in the night as in the daytime, because the thermal cameras on the fast attack craft could pick up the image of even a dog on the beach. They could see the number of civilians escaping by boat under cover of darkness, the number of engines on the boat and the number of adults and children and all other details as if it was day. Towards the last stages, these thermal cameras were fitted even on to the locally built inshore patrol craft, with a little compartment made of plywood for the sophisticated equipment which was air conditioned with car air conditioners.

The last sea battle was on 9 May 2009 when the LTTE attacked the navy barrier line in force in front of *MV Farah III*. It is a testimony to the effectiveness of the Arrow boats that even though they were the first line of defence against a desperate LTTE, only one Arrow boat was destroyed between the time they were first introduced and the end of the war. During this last desperate sea battle, two low profile suicide boats had penetrated the Arrow boat line and these were taken by the Dvoras commanded by Commander Sujeewa Seneviratne. One of the suicide boats was destroyed and another captured after firing at it with a 30mm Bushmaster gun, killing the two cadres on it. With that the sea tiger saga came to an end.

Shavendra Silva's troops were joined by Kamal Gunaratne's 53rd Division, in the southward move from Puthumathalan. Both columns were moving southwards on a front that was less than two kilometres in breadth with the 58th moving down the sea side and the 53rd on the lagoon side. Usually, if an operation was started in the morning, it would stop in the evening or vice versa. During the last week of the war however, Shavendra Silva's troops were moving down a narrow frontage which could be held by a single battalion. By this time, the 58th Division had plenty of troops and the battalions were rotated on the front line so that the division was fighting 24 hours a day – a thing the LTTE had never experienced before.

Even though the LTTE was now on its last legs, the ferocity of fighting did not diminish. Besides, the army was now fighting with one arm tied behind its back, being unable to use heavy weapons to neutralize enemy fire because of the presence of civilians on the other side. The LTTE however could fire everything they had at the advancing army. The army took over the last piece of territory held by the LTTE with wave after wave of infantry and small arms. As we mentioned in an earlier chapter, death rate in capturing this last piece of land was appalling. The 58th Division alone lost 224 men in crossing the Puthumathalan lagoon, capturing the LTTE bund, and cutting across to the beach to tie up with Prasanna Silva's troops of the 55th Division. In the final push southwards to secure Vellamullivaikkal, another 225 of Shavendra's troops were killed. Of all the fighting formations in the Vanni, the 58th Division suffered the most number of casualties. This was to be expected given the extended duration of their operation and the distance covered. By the end of the war, they had suffered 1,397 fatalities with a further 33 missing and presumed dead and a total of 7,113 men wounded in battle.

Even though the entire LTTE had been cornered into an ever shrinking patch of land, nobody really expected the war to end soon. The fact that army commander Sarath Fonseka saw it fit to leave on an extended tour of China on 11 May indicates that even at the highest levels of the government there was no real conception of when the war would end. Kamal Gunaratne's troops stopped their advance after the capture of *MV Farah III*, but the 58th Division kept moving southwards and tied up with the 59th Division on 16 May 2009 thus sealing off the beachfront. After this, in what can be described as a 'lawnmower' kind of manoeuvre, the 58th Division began going north again clearing the remaining narrow strip of land between the Nandikadal lagoon and the beach front that they had just captured

* * * * *

These events had not gone unnoticed in India and Tamil Nadu. From the last week of April until the war ended, the Indian central government was involved in a game of political brinksmanship in Tamil Nadu. Three days after Mennon and Narayanan returned to India after their meeting with president Rajapaksa which was recounted earlier, the crisis in Tamil Nadu came to a head. On 27 April 2009, the 85 year-old Tamil Nadu Chief Minister M.Karunanidhi went on a fast unto death, calling for an immediate ceasefire in Sri Lanka. This was probably the worst moment for the Indian central government. All this was happening with a general election in progress. Because of the sheer size of the world's biggest democracy, polling is conducted in five phases with various Indian states going to the polls in an order decided on by the election authorities. Polling began on 16 April 2009 in several states and 'union territories' including Delhi. Phase two of the Indian election was on 22 and 23 April, the third phase on 30 April, phase four on 7 May and phase five on 13 May. Sri Lanka's communal problem attracts attention only in Tamil Nadu and it so happened that the elections in Tamil Nadu were held only in the last phase on 13 May 2009.

It was with around two weeks to the Tamil Nadu round of polling that Karunanidhi went on hunger strike. The Sri Lankan Security Council was meeting at that very moment at president's house in Colombo Fort. Indian high commissioner Alok Prasad was sitting tensely in Lalith Weeratunga's office waiting for the outcome of the Security Council meeting. The moment the joint statement they had written three days earlier on the non-use of heavy weaponry by the army was approved, Weeratunga rushed back to his office and gave the statement to Prasad. From the presidential secretariat, Prasad read the statement out to the Indian external affairs ministry. It was this statement that was rushed by the Indian central government to Karunanidhi who gave up his fast on the assurance of the central government that the use of heavy weaponry would be stopped.

This was politics on the edge of a kind never before seen in this part of the world. When Karunanidhi was on his fast, Prabhakaran issued a statement saying that Karunanidhi was a hero for standing

481

up for the Tamil cause in Sri Lanka. The Sri Lankan government, using contacts in Tamil Nadu, managed to prevent this statement from being given to Karunanidhi before he met Indian external affairs minister Pranabh Mukherjee and gave up his fast. The Sri Lankan government feared that if Karunanidhi saw Prabhakaran's message, he may have wanted to play hero for a while longer.

The joint statement issued by India and Sri Lanka on 27 April stressed that *"The government of Sri Lanka has announced that combat operations have reached their conclusion and that the Sri Lankan security forces have been instructed to end the use of heavy calibre guns, combat aircraft and aerial weapons which could cause civilian casualties. Sri Lankan forces will now confine their attempts to rescue the civilians who remain and give topmost priority to saving them."*

Polling took place in Tamil Nadu as scheduled on 13 May. Ironically, the Sri Lankan Tamil issue did not affect any political party in Tamil Nadu adversely because all political parties held much the same view on the Sri Lankan issue. The results of the Indian general elections was announced on 16 May 2009. The ruling DMK won yet again getting 18 seats in the *Lok Sabha* as against the 16 they had earlier. The state of Tamil Nadu contributed 39 of the 543 members of the *Lok Sabha*. The ruling Congress Party led United Progressive Alliance got a total contribution of 28 seats from Tamil Nadu with the *Dravida Munnethra Kazhagam* contributing 18, the Indian National Congress 9, and a small party the *Vidutalai Chirutaigal Kachchi* one seat. The victory of the DMK-Congress Party combination in Tamil Nadu wiped out any hope the LTTE may have had of their supporters in Tamil Nadu being able to force the central government to intervene and stop the war in Sri Lanka.

Chapter 79

The End at Nandikadal Lagoon

On the night of 16 May 2009, after the dramatic link up of the 58th and 59th Divisions on the beach, Lt Col Senaka Wijesuriya had got a call from the Vanni Commander Major Gen Jagath Jayasuriya telling him that radio intercepts indicated that there would be a plan to break out and link up with LTTE groups still operating in the hinterland and to watch his sector carefully. Wijesuriya was at the time commanding a Brigade of the 59th Division which held a part of the bank of the Nandikadal lagoon. That the army had surrounded the last stronghold of the LTTE did not mean that there were no terrorists behind the army lines. The LTTE had small groups of three to five cadres operating in the areas that the army had captured such as Oddusudan, Mankulam and Kanagarayankulam, who had caches of supplies like dried meat, dried coconut, rice flour etc which would have last lasted several weeks.

Several such groups had been encountered and killed by the special forces and army commandos in the 'belly area' of the Vanni, well behind the army lines. So an attempt to break out and link up with their small groups operating in the hinterland had in fact been anticipated and multiple counter penetration lines had been formed. Chagi Gallage who had been commanding operations of the 59th Division until the last few days, even had battle tanks driven into depressions in the ground so that the guns would be able to fire direct at the LTTE boats that were expected to come speeding across the Nandikadal lagoon in an effort to break out of the encirclement.

483

Infiltrators were present within the army lines till the very end. On one occasion, LTTE infiltrators had come up to the tack headquarters of the 1st Sinha battalion of the 59th Division. Nandana Udawatte the then commander of the 59th Division who had gone to inspect the scene had a narrow shave, with a few terrorist infiltrators coming within 10 meters of him. A fire fight ensued with Udawatte caught in between the enemy and his own soldiers. Infiltrators often wore army type uniforms and it was almost impossible to tell them apart from a soldier. Only an experienced eye could observe the way they carried themselves, or through differences in the accessories, like the pouches they wore. Often being able to identify infiltrators was just a case of sheer luck. Udawatte managed to escape death that day because he wore no insignia and the infiltrators could not identify him. The presence of LTTE infiltrators near the 1st Sinha battalion headquarters had been detected only because two of them had panicked and taken to their heels when spoken to.

So the twin horrors of breakouts and infiltration were always on the minds of everybody as the army advanced relentlessly. Army commander Sarath Fonseka operated from Colombo. Once a week, he would arrive in Vavuniya by helicopter, and when it lands, an armoured personnel carrier would take him to the Vanni headquarters and from there back again to the chopper for the flight back to Colombo. During these routine visits, one of the main concerns discussed was the possibility of breakouts. At one of these routine conferences, after examining the troop deployment of the 55th Divison which was then in Chalai, Fonseka had found that the counter penetration lines were inadequate. He had bellowed at the officers of the 55th Division saying that the war was not over yet and that if the LTTE managed to break out of Chalai, they would come right up to Elephant Pass and that three counter infiltration lines should be established to the south of Elephant Pass, starting from the Puthumathalan-Visuamadu area. Breaking a line was not too difficult. If heavy firepower is concentrated on a few bunkers, a gap could be opened up without much difficulty which is why more than one counter infiltration line was needed. The long anticipated attempt to break out of the army encirclement came on the night of 17 May. As narrated below, it was experienced differently by the various army formations that were surrounding the area.

On the night of 16 May, at around 8.30 pm, two LTTE boats came about two kilometres towards the 59th Division line and stopped, apparently surveying the army defence lines. The Nandikadal lagoon is a large body of water, about 5 kilometres wide. The two LTTE boats were watched tensely by the troops on the other side. Lt Col Wijesuriya who commanded the line approached by the boats issued orders not to fire upon the boat even if fired upon. This was to prevent the enemy from taking note of where the army's gun emplacements were. One of the boats then came closer to the army line and stopped. But with no reaction coming from the army, both boats withdrew at around 11.00 o'clock in the night.

The following night, on 17 May, two boats emerged again from the LTTE held area at around 7.40 pm. By 11.00 o clock, there were four boats on the water. As on the previous night, two boats came forward and one boat came within a kilometre of the army line and opened fire, and the army responded with a few mortar rounds which hit the boat and sank it. Then several boats that were on the water came speeding towards the army lines. Loud blasts were heard and Lt Col Wijesuriya could see firing going on within the 59th Division line. The blasts they had heard were suicide cadres exploding themselves in two bunkers killing all the soldiers inside.

Over the radio, he was able to ascertain that three bunkers had fallen to the LTTE and a gap had opened up in the army line. However, when the LTTE's main attacking party came across the lagoon, they walked right in between two 12.7 machine gun emplacements and were cut down in a hail of bullets. With their plans going awry, a group of the attackers went towards the part of the line held by Task Force 8 of the 53rd Division. The gap in the 59th Division line was closed by daybreak and in the morning around 120 LTTE bodies were recovered on the banks of the lagoon. The attackers were heavily armed with night vision goggles, light machine guns, general purpose machine guns, and everybody wore suicide jackets as well. An examination of the numbers on their dog tags indicated that these were the most senior cadres of the LTTE.

While this battle was going on, the 59th Division had also detected an LTTE eight man team talking to the attacking party from within their lines. This team had come to receive the LTTE leaders when they broke through. An area of around two square kilometres was boxed off and by the afternoon of 18 May, search parties managed to locate and destroy the eight man team as well as a couple of stragglers from the previous night's attack.

The experience of Task Force 8 was different. On the evening of 17 May, around 100 civilians had surrendered to them. In the early hours of 18 May, at around 1.30 am, Col G.V. Ravipriya received a call from one of his officers saying that a group of civilians had come to surrender. Ravipriya had issued strict instructions that civilians should be taken in only during the day. His officers were telling him that the civilians were standing in the water with screaming children in their arms and that the civilians were pleading that they can't be in the water with the children. Ravipriya flatly refused to allow the civilians to come in and told his troops to tell them to wait until morning. When they knew they would not be allowed in, about twenty of the supposed civilians opened fire simultaneously with a variety of weapons and overran two bunkers manned by the 12th Gemunu Watch.

Due to the counterattack by Task Force 8, some of the attackers were forced to retreat into a mangrove swamp on the banks of the lagoon and this was where Sornam, Soosai and others were killed in a hail of army small arms and RPG fire. Pottu Amman had been killed a short while earlier. By 5.30 am the breach had once again been sealed but some infiltrators had got in. About 40 bodies had been found near the breach. Then commandos were inducted into the area to deal with the infiltrators. On the evening of 18 May, mopping up operations had halted for the day with no trace of Prabhakaran.

The 58th Division also played a role in containing this final offensive by the LTTE. By 7.00 pm on that night of 17 May, Shavendra Silva found that the LTTE was restricted to a tiny patch of land. They were surrounded on three sides from the north, south and east, with only the lagoon front remaining open. He then halted operations for the night at the request of the field commanders who told him that the troops were exhausted after fighting continuously. Besides, it was pitch dark and every inch of the remaining patch of LTTE held territory was full of tents and terrorists and other obstacles and to clear that without being able to tell troops and terrorists apart in the darkness would have resulted in unnecessary casualties.

After halting operations, Shavendra went back to his divisional headquarters in Kilinochchi which he reached at around midnight and he was in the operations room for a while watching the footage captured by a UAV that was flying over the last patch of LTTE held territory. He had just retired to his room for a wash and to get some sleep when he got a call from the operations room saying that they could see some firing in the line held by the 53rd Division. Shavendra rushed back to the operations room. The UAV was still up in the air but it was running out of fuel and would soon be flown back. He listened to the 53rd Division radio transmissions and realized that the line had been breached.

This meant that the terrorists would now be in his sector. Shavendra immediately informed the commanding officer of the 7th Sinha battalion who was in charge of the sector closest to the breach, that the LTTE may try to break out and to be prepared. Behind the 7th Sinha was the 6th Gemunu Watch which was also placed on alert. He was rushing back to Puthukudiirippu, when an intelligence officer told him that Prabhakaran and Pottu Amman were among those who had broken out of the 53rd Division line and that they had commandeered an army ambulance and were trying to make a getaway. He then gave instructions that all movements including the moving of casualties should stop immediately within his area of control. After breaking through the line held by the 53rd Division, the LTTE party had ended up in the patch of land that was being cleared by the 58th Division and the LTTE group was now trapped in a cul de sac with Shavendra's troops to the north, the south and the east as well. Shavendra gave instructions to the 7th Sinha that if they see an ambulance on the move, they should destroy it.

After some time, he got a call from a 7th Sinha officer that they have spotted an ambulance and that they are going to open fire. Shavendra gave the go ahead and the troops fired and reported back to him that the ambulance was burning. Shavendra then instructed the troops to check who's inside. An officer reported back that there was a tall guy, a fat guy and another person burning inside the vehicle. This was at around 3.00 am. The immediate thought that had come to Shavendra's mind was that the 'fat guy' was Prabhakaran and the 'tall guy' was Pottu Amman.

While he was half way towards Puthukudiirippu, army commander Sarath Fonseka called Shavendra on his phone and asked him whether he is aware that the 53rd Division line had been breached. Shavendra answered in the affirmative. Fonseka had returned to Sri Lanka only a few hours earlier after a visit to China from 11 to17 May with his wife, two daughters, son in law and an entourage of army personnel at the invitation of the Chinese arms manufacturing firm NORINCO. Fonseka was furious. He thought that all was lost with the LTTE leadership making their getaway. Shavendra however had assured Fonseka that his lines cannot be breached and that the LTTE leaders would not escape.

Shavendra went to the 53rd Division headquarters at Puthukudiirippu junction and by 5.00 am. all the other divisional commanders had also come to the 53rd Division headquarters. In the meantime, Charles Anthony, eastern commander Ramesh and others, had come in through the 53rd Division line and had moved about a kilometre into the no-man's land being cleared by Shavendra's troops. Charles Anthony had been on foot when he was shot dead. LTTE front liners Nadesan, Pulidevan, and Illango, the LTTE 'police chief' were among the others killed in this confrontation. By first light, things were under control again. The LTTE's breakout plan was a failure.

The government thought Prabhakaran too had been in the hijacked ambulance and on 18 May, the end of the war was announced. The Indian government reported to parliament that Prabhakaran was dead and that the war was over. The Indian external affairs ministry put out a brief message which said among other things, *"In a telephone conversation with External Affairs Minister Shri Pranab Mukherjee earlier today, the President of Sri Lanka confirmed that armed resistance by the LTTE has come to an end and that LTTE leader Velupillai Prabhakaran is dead."* The president however had not publicly announced that Prabhakaran was dead and the show was not over yet.

On the afternoon of 18 May, troops of the 59th Division accosted a group of LTTE cadres led by Bhanu and Jeyam and killed all of them. At dawn on the morning of 19 May, the 4th Vijayaba battalion under Task force 8, sent in their first SIOT team into the last un-cleared patch of land, a belt of mangroves by the banks of the Nandikadal lagoon around 800 meters long and 20 meters wide. There was a confrontation here with a group of LTTE stragglers and Ravipriya was told that about 20-30 weapons were heard firing from inside the patch of mangroves. He then inducted two more SIOT teams into the mangrove belt where they captured three individuals who revealed that Prabhakaran was in the Mangroves with around 30 men. Upon hearing this, troops had fired into the mangroves until there was no more returning fire. Thereafter, troops had been sent in to search the mangrove swamp, and Prabhakaran's body was found by a SIOT team leader.

His body was still warm when found indicating that he had just been killed. He had not shaved that morning and the faintest white stubble was visible on his face. His corpse was borne aloft on the shoulders of 4th Vijayaba soldiers and brought for the senior officers to inspect. Brigadiers Jagath Dias, Shavendra Silva, Chagi Gallage, and Kamal Gunaratne were all there to inspect the corpse of the terrorist who had led the world's deadliest terrorist organization.

Hundreds of delirious soldiers had been clambering on top of one another to catch a glimpse of the corpse. Later in the day, the former LTTE spokesman Daya Master and Karuna Amman were flown from Colombo to identify the body. Daya Master identified Prabhakaran's body not by looking at his face, but a blackened scar on his thigh – the result of the bomb explosion in Velvettiturei in 1971 which was mentioned in a previous chapter. Thus ended nearly forty years of Tamil terrorism in Sri Lanka.

On 19 May, president Mahinda Rajapaksa made an address to the nation at 9.30 in the morning and he declared that the LTTE had been defeated, but he did not make any mention of Prbahakaran's dead body being found. By that time no confirmation had been received that it was indeed him and not one of the many doubles the LTTE supremo is said to have had. It was army commander Sarath Fonseka who officially announced that Prabhakaran's body had been found, a couple of hours later. The honour of making that announcement was given by the president to Fonseka. The latter had in fact told Gōta that the proper thing would be for the president to announce it. But Gōta told Fonseka that the president wanted him to make the announcement. The last formal meeting of the troikas between India and Sri Lanka was held in New Delhi on 26 August 2010 fifteen months after the war, and Shivshankar Mennon now the national defence advisor summed up things by saying that 'these troika meetings have achieved things that others may think impossible'.

Epilogue

The death of Prabhakaran was met by unprecedented rejoicing in Sri Lanka. This was a victory that amazed the entire world. In January 2008, the US Federal Bureau of Investigation had officially declared the LTTE to be the deadliest terrorist organization in the world barring none. Even *Al-Qaeda* which posed a direct threat to the USA was ranked below the LTTE. Yet by May 2009, this formidable terrorist organization lay completely annihilated - its leader dead with a bullet clean through the head.

This was not a victory cheaply achieved. Over a period of nearly 30 years, the army had suffered 23,391 deaths. The number of army deaths in the final war against the LTTE from July 2006 to the end of May 2009 alone was 5,876. During the 30 year war, the navy had suffered 1,142 fatalities and the air force 404. The commando unit of the police, the Special Task Force lost 430. This is without mentioning the policemen and home guards/civil defence force personnel and civilians who lost their lives in the war. As we saw earlier in this narrative, at the very early stages, it was the police that bore the brunt of terrorist attacks.

After this unprecedented victory, the dream team that achieved it, split up with army commander Sarath Fonseka going his own way and ending up as a bitter political rival of his own former commander in chief Mahinda Rajapaksa. Differences began emerging just days after the end of the war. At the first Security Council meeting after the death of Prabhakaran, Sarath Fonseka wanted a doubling of the size of the army. No country would ever double the size of the armed forces once a war was over. The tendency would rather be to demobilize. The president responded saying that the war was now over and that he had now to develop the country and that the resources allocated to the war had now to be diverted to development and that expanding the army was out of the question.

Another claim made at this first Security Council was that ninety five percent of the credit should go to the army. At this point, Wasantha Karannagoda had said that the army was able to kill Prabhakaran because the navy had prevented him from escaping by sea, and moreover that it was the navy that stopped the LTTE from bringing in arms shipments. The question he had posed was, if the 95% of the credit was to go to the army, what were the navy, air force and police supposed to have been doing?

Inter-service and intra-service rivalries are a part of the armed forces culture of any nation and there is nothing surprising in one General being against the other and the navy having problems with the army and so on. But in Sri Lanka during the final war, these rivalries were taken to ridiculous lengths. In addition to all the problems that the president and Gōta had to handle, the international pressures, the financial headaches, the coordination of the operations between all the forces, and the media front, there was the running battle between Sarath Fonseka and Wasantha Karannagoda to contend with.

When the navy wanted to establish a base for the small boat squadrons in Chalai, the army objected to this and the president had to intervene personally to get the navy its base. This was a vital need as the small boats had been deployed to form a barrier line on the sea to prevent the escape of the LTTE leaders by sea and these boats needed to be provisioned and rest provided for the crews. When the navy could not be prevented from putting in at Chalai, instructions went out not to provide the navy with any food or supplies and most importantly, not to allow any naval craft to be beached, because the land does not belong to the navy but to the army. Steel rails were planted on the sea bed to moor the small boats and even this was objected to, but it was pointed out that anything beyond the water line belonged to navy.

Naval personnel from the boats had to moor their craft out at sea, swim ashore, use the toilet, eat and relax and to get back to duty, they had to swim across to their boats. Naval officers did not even bother to complain about this to headquarters but made do as best as they could to prevent inter-service friction. The army and navy officers on the ground however, cooperated with one another regardless of the bizarre orders emanating from army headquarters. Another odd and very harmful order that army units received was to prevent the navy from operating in the lagoons. The navy was not permitted into the Chundikulam lagoon when Prasanna Silva's troops were passing it, even though it would have been natural to hand over the securing of water bodies to the navy. The 55th Division had to have the entire lagoon floodlit in the nights to prevent LTTE infiltration. That would not have been necessary if small naval craft had been deployed to secure it.

When it came to the crossing of the Nandikadal lagoon, some army officers had wanted to get the support of the navy but this too had been vetoed. To the very last, the LTTE had a completely free run of the Nandikadal lagoon and there was no barrier line of naval craft to prevent them from launching an attack on the army line across the lagoon. If navy small boats had been in the Nandikadal lagoon, the attack of 17 May described earlier in this narrative would never have taken place.

In the old days, it was the field commanders like Denzil Kobbekaduwa, Vijaya Wimalaratne and Janaka Perera who would get the credit for fighting the war. Today, nobody remembers the names of the army commanders that Kobbekaduwa and Wimalaratne served under. There were attempts to prevent that from happening this time around. One of the young field commanders who had gained much popularity was Brigadier Shavendra Silva, because of his epic long march from Mannar to the banks of the Nandikadal lagoon. At around 7.30 in the morning, on 18 May after the LTTE's breakout had been contained and only the final mopping up operation remained to be done, there was an attempt to make Shavendra Silva hand over the command of the 58th Division to Brigadier Prasanna Silva.

Shavendra however had held that he had commanded the division for two and a half years and that it was unfair to ask him to hand over command to another officer for the last two hours of the war. When Fonseka left for China, the troops of the 59th Division directly opposite the last LTTE stronghold were commanded by Chagi Gallage. In the last ten days of the war, Gallage was transferred out to the 55th Division and was in Putumathalan when the war ended. Major General Nandana Udawatte, the officer who raised the 59th Division from scratch, was transferred out a little more than a week before the war ended and sent to Anuradhapura. Hence he too was not present on the battle field when the war ended.

Gallage, the former commander of the 59th Division had just before being transferred out, sent commandos and Special Forces

492

across the Nandikadal lagoon to reconnoitre the opposite side to check the location of LTTE bunkers, minefields etcetera and a crossing had been planned. The lagoon had been nine feet deep at the point chosen for the crossing. Some boats had also been prepared for the crossing with sand bags and mounted weapons. However Army HQ had objected to this plan to attack across the lagoon and had packed Gallage off to the 55th Division and sent Brigadier Prasanna Silva to the 59th Division, to dig trenches to get close to the LTTE defences. It appears that there was an attempt to ensure that all those field commanders who had led the various Vanni fronts would have been 'displaced' by the time the war ended and no field commander left to harvest the credit for having led the army to victory except the institutional head.

The signs of future problems were to be seen even while the war was still being fought. When *Sunday Leader* Editor Lasantha Wickremetunga was killed in January 2009, the UNP accused Fonseka of the killing as recounted earlier in this narrative, and high ranking members of the UNP told the present writer at the murdered Wickremetunga's funeral that even president Mahinda Rajapaksa was not safe. The feeling was that there was now a power centre in the country that the politicians had no control over.

Earlier on in May 2008, Keith Nohyer the deputy editor and defence correspondent of the English language weekly *The Nation* was abducted and brutally assaulted by assailants Nohyer himself was too afraid to name. Later in July 2008, two other media persons, Namal Perera and Mahendra Ratnaweera were set upon and attacked by assailants who had followed their vehicle in the heart of Colombo. This was followed by an attack on Upali Tennakoon, the editor of *Rivira*, a Sinhala weekly, in January 2009 around two weeks after the killing of Lasantha Wickrematunga. Suspicion did not centre on politicians for any of these incidents. Even media organizations held the government only 'indirectly responsible' for these attacks. These were the indications to the outside world that something was out of control in the government set up.

In the middle of the deteriorating relations between Fonseka and the Rajapaksas, in June 2009, a large shipment of munitions from China arrived, which the government turned away saying that they had not ordered any munitions from China after the war had ended. Sarath Fonseka did not agree with this move. He was later to say during the presidential election campaign, that China helped us to win the war by giving us arms on credit and this is the way the government repays Chinese generosity. As the tensions between Fonseka and the government worsened, one day Gōta had phoned Lalith Weeratunga and told him that there was a move to have Major Gen Jagath Jayasuriya arrested. By this time, the government had become intensely suspicious of Fonseka and deemed it necessary to remove him from the position of army commander.

However, the hitch was that the only position Fonseka could be given was that of Chief of Defence Staff, but it was Wasantha Karannagoda who was entitled to that position as the senior most among the service commanders. If Fonseka was to be given the position of CDS, Karannagoda had to be taken out of the navy. Thus to move Fonseka into the position of CDS, several other movements had to be done simultaneously.

Presidential secretary Lalith Weeratunga called Sarath Fonseka on the night of 11 July 2009 which was a Saturday and informed him that the president wanted to promote him to the position of CDS. Fonseka had wanted to know when that would happen. Weeratunga had told him that he did not know the time frame that the president had in mind. Fonseka had complained that the position of CDS was a nominal post. Weeratunga reminded Fonseka that he himself had played a role in drafting the CDS Act and that under the new legislation the position was different. The position of Chief of Defence Staff under the CDS Act No: 35 of 2009, was modelled on the Chairman of the Joint Chiefs of Staff of the USA and the powers wielded were almost exactly the same.

The following morning, Fonseka was appointed CDS, Jagath Jayasuriya was made army commander, Karannagoda was made an advisor to the president, Tisara Samarasinghe was made the commander of the navy, and everything was over by 10.00 am on Sunday morning. Only the president , Gōta and Lalith Weeratunga knew of the operation. G.A.Chandrasisri the army chief of staff and Fonseka's chosen successor, was asked to come in civvies and to bring his wife along as well. Chandrasiri was sworn in as the Governor of the Northern Province. The serving Governor of the North, Dixon Dela Bandara was taken out and given an ambassadorial post.

Fonseka would have had to retire from the army anyway, and the position of CDS was the next logical step for him – that of the first soldier in the country. Fonseka however was not happy with the new position and he asked Gōta for powers to command two levels down. But Gōta had pointed out that such powers would see an army officer commanding air force squadrons and naval fast attack craft in addition to army divisions and that no such practice exists anywhere in the world.

As Fonseka's differences with the government snowballed and became public knowledge, opposition parties lost no time in fishing in troubled waters and by the last quarter of 2009, they had managed to work out a deal between all opposition parties including the pro-LTTE Tamil National Alliance to field Fonseka as the common candidate of the opposition at the presidential elections scheduled for January 2010. As Mangala Samaraweera, the estranged SLFP strongman now a member of the UNP explained this decision to the present writer, they needed to field a representative of the dominant pattern of thinking in the country if they were to have any hope of defeating Mahinda Rajapaksa.

When rumours began circulating that Fonseka was going to contest the presidency, the well known Buddhist monk Uduwe Dhammaloka had gone to see Fonseka to tell him not to contest against Mahinda and create a split in the patriotic camp. Fonseka had complained about the way he had been treated by the Rajapaksas and in the course of his tirade, had related the story of the Mandativu incident of 1990 where during Ranjan Wijeratne's visit, the weapons captured from the LTTE had been displayed with only Gajaba soldiers in the background thus denying any credit to Fonseka. He had related this story and said "This is what he did to me even at that time." Ven Dhammaloka later told Gōta about this conversation and said that he fears for Gōta's life if Mahinda fails to win the elections.

The presidential election campaign of 2009/10 was undoubtedly the most acrimonious election campaign in living memory. Hate and venom spewed forth from the opposition stage in a manner the people of this country had never seen. When he won, the opposition candidate promised to give his opponents bones to lick (*katu levakanna*), and get them to wear 'jumpers' (prison garb worn by convicts). Fonseka lost the presidential elections of 26 January 2010 with a huge margin of 1.84 million votes. Being a political neophyte, he had no conception of the spectacle he made, contesting as the common candidate of the UNP which ridiculed the war effort and of the pro-LTTE Tamil National Alliance. The Rajapaksas in contrast, had promoted him, and provided everything he needed and defended him when the UNP accused him of murdering Lasantha Wickremetunga. The incongruity was not lost on the electorate, as the election result showed. Today, Fonseka languishes in prison, convicted of tender irregularities in the purchase of equipment for the army and of spreading false rumours which is a punishable offence under the emergency regulations. Thus the victory that amazed the entire world, ended with disunity and acrimony within the dream team that achieved it.

Looking back, Gōta observes that the political authorities in the past were reluctant to appoint certain officers to the position of army commander because of the fear of a military takeover of the country. He told the present writer that if one looks at what happened in the end, in a way, the apprehensions the previous leaders had, were justified.

Despite claims to the contrary from certain quarters, Generals only carry out the will of the political authorities. Gōta himself experienced the primacy of the political factor at first hand in 1987 when they had to halt the Vadamarachchi operation on the orders of the J.R.Jayewardene government. Whether the Generals go forwards or backwards is decided by the political authorities. Fonseka himself fought against the LTTE under Chandrika Kumaratunga and parleyed with them under Ranil Wickremesinghe. Despite the open enmity and acrimony between members of the team that achieved what was long thought to be impossible, after forty years of war and unrest, the country was at peace at last.

Postscript:

The Satanic Agenda

D.P.Sivaram was the foremost commentator on Tamil politics in this country. He was the editor of the LTTE website *Tamilnet* when he was abducted and killed in April 2005, by members of a rival Tamil group. The present writer met him just two days before he was killed and in the course of the wide ranging discussion we had, Sivaram said that to him, Prabhakaran was like Satan in John Milton's *Paradise Lost*. He said that in *Paradise Lost*, Satan is portrayed as a heroic figure, a brave and audacious rebel unbowed by the blows of adversity, trusting above all else, in the strength of his own indomitable will.

In Milton's epic poem, Satan, recently defeated by God and cast down from heaven, surveys the infernal realms into which they had been banished, and seeing another fallen angel Beelzebub lying next to him, says,

What though the field be lost?

All is not lost; the unconquerable will,

And study of revenge, immortal hate,

And courage never to submit or yield:

And what else is not to be overcome?

Thus the condition of 'not being overcome' is deemed to consist of 'the courage never to submit or yield', 'the zeal for revenge', 'immortal hate' and 'the unconquerable will'. When addressed thus by Satan, Beelzebub has his reservations at first. He suggests timidly,

497

But what if he our Conqueror, (whom I now
Of force believe Almighty, since no less
Than such could have o'erpow'r'd such force as ours)
Have left us this our spirit and strength entire
Strongly to suffer and support our pains,
That we may so suffice his vengeful ire,...

Beelzebub thus suggests that God triumphed over them only because he was truly the almighty and that the reason why he left them their indomitable spirit even in defeat would be to make them suffer torment all the more acutely. But Satan disdainfully interrupts Beelzebub laying down the agenda for the future in the following words;

Fall'n Cherub, to be weak is miserable.
To do aught good never will be our task,
But ever to do ill our sole delight,
As being the contrary to his high will
Whom we resist. If then his Providence
Out of our evil seek to bring forth good,
Our labour must be to pervert that end,
And out of good still to find means of evil;

If God hoped to bring forth good by defeating the Satanic multitude, their future purpose would be to do what it takes, to subvert that very aim. In the post war scenario, Sri Lanka does seem to be confronted with just such a Satanic agenda on the part of the Tamil Eelamist lobby as well as the Western powers supporting them. What made the LTTE and by extension the Tamil Eelamist lobby in general such a formidable enemy was their sophistication, ingenuity and adaptability and this Satanic stubbornness that Sivaram so admired. The ignominious defeat of the LTTE and the death of Prabhakaran has not diminished the Satanic stubbornness of the overseas LTTE lobby.

The LTTE groups in the West would have known that their military organization in Sri Lanka was finished at least from the end of 2008 onwards, and they were well prepared with plan B by the time the end came. Since terrorism had failed to achieve anything, the next phase was to reinvent themselves as victims of oppression and do through the sympathy of Western powers what they failed to

498

do through terror. Plan B went into operation the very day that images of Prabhakaran's dead visage was flashed around the world by the international news channels.

The day after Prabhakaran's dead body was found, on Wednesday 20 May 2009, an article with the title, *"Tamil leaders 'killed as they tried to surrender"* by Andrew Buncombe appeared in the British newspaper *The Independent*. The allegation in this article was that as LTTE front rankers B.Nadesan and S.Pulidevan tried to surrender to the army by coming out with a white flag held high in the early hours of 18 May, they had been shot dead by the army. Buncombe wrote:

*"Sometime between midnight on 17 May and the early hours of the next morning, the two men were shot dead. **LTTE officials overseas** claim the two men were killed by government troops as they approached them bearing a white flag."*

*"**The pro-LTTE website TamilNet yesterday reported claims from rebel officials outside Sri Lanka** that Mr Nadesan and Mr Pulidevan had been shot dead by government troops as they advanced towards them carrying a white flag, as they had been instructed to do. The report claimed informed sources said what happened in the early hours of Monday was "a well-planned massacre of several unarmed civil officers of the LTTE with the aim of annihilating its political structure".*

Thus in one master stroke, the LTTE rump overseas had reinvented themselves as a political organization demanding justice and human rights. The only hitch was that the article in *The Independent* had revealed the sources they had got their news from. Four days later however, Marie Colvin of *The Sunday Times* London, well known to be a friend of the LTTE, came to their rescue by publishing another article on the same subject on 24 May 2009 with the title, *"Tigers begged me to broker surrender"* which gave a personalised account of how Nadesan and Pulidevan had asked her to broker a surrender. Instead of admitting that it was the LTTE rump overseas that had first announced on 19 May that Pulidevan and Nadesan had been shot while trying to surrender, Colvin claims to have got the details from an unnamed aid worker.

"A Tamil who was in a group that managed to escape the killing zone described what happened. This source, who later spoke to an aid worker, said Nadesan and Puleedevan walked towards Sri Lankan army lines with a white flag in a group of about a dozen men and women. He said the army started firing machine guns at them."

"Nadesan's wife, a Sinhalese, yelled in Sinhala at the soldiers: 'He is trying to surrender and you are shooting him'. She was also shot down."

Despite the attempt to disguise it, Colvin's story follows the same LTTE line which found expression through Buncombe's article in *The Independent* four days earlier. The line was that Nadesan and Pulidevan were civilian officials of the LTTE and they were killed while trying to surrender because the army wanted to destroy the political structure of the LTTE. Colvin has much the same refrain in her article.

"Nadesan and Puleedevan favoured a political solution to the conflict. Had they lived, they would have been credible political leaders for the Tamil minority".

Prabhakaran and Pottu Amman were demonized by everybody, so no international sympathy could be whipped up over them. It was the same in the case of LTTE commanders like Theepan and Jeyam. Nobody has shown any interest in how such individuals met their end. It was easier to whip up sympathy for individuals like Pulidevan and Nadesan who had received much exposure internationally during the peace talks and by interacting with the Western embassies in Colombo. The LTTE was always adept at putting cadres with toothy smiles to interact with the Western community. Their strategy was to invoke fear in Sri Lanka but sympathy overseas. So the scowling cadres fought with the army and the smiling cadres interacted with the foreigners.

Interestingly, the 58th Division also claims that Nadesan and Pulidevan were among many others killed by their troops – not however while trying to surrender but in the final LTTE offensive in the early hours of 18 May. We have described the events of that night in a previous chapter and there could have been no question of anyone trying to surrender in the middle of that final pitched battle fought in pitch darkness. One of the reasons why Shavendra Silva had stopped operations for the night was because it was too dark to tell friend and foe apart. The red herring that the LTTE threw on the path of the Western community of nations with the issue of Nadesan's and Pulidevan's deaths, had its desired effect. Many Western countries, smarting from the snubs they received from Sri Lanka's leaders to their repeated calls for a halt to the offensive against the LTTE, were only too happy to make use of this LTTE propaganda to flog the Sri Lankan government with.

Thus the focus shifted to allegations of war crimes and civilian deaths rather than the fact that Sri Lanka is the only country in recent times to decisively defeat terrorism. Several reports emanating from the West dealt with this allegation of civilian deaths in the final days

500

of the war. The first report to take up the issue of civilian deaths was the European Commission's Interim Report on Sri Lanka published on 19 August 2009 just three months after the end of the war. At that early stage, the European Commission said in all honesty that *"The casualty figures for those killed and injured are not known. Owing to the refusal to grant access to journalists, it is not possible to obtain accurate figures. Without knowing what was targeted and why, it is difficult to establish whether the security forces breached their obligations under human rights law as interpreted in the light of (law of armed conflict and international humanitarian law) LOAC/IHL."*

The European Commission published their final report on Sri Lanka two months later on 19 October 2009. In the final report however, they stated that the number of civilian casualties may be as high as 20,000. Their source was a single article in *The Times* London published on 29 May 2009. This newspaper report, based wholly on undisclosed 'UN sources' and 'leaked' UN documents, stated that 7000 civilians had been killed from the beginning of January to the end of April 2009 and then from 1 May, to 18 May 2009 there had been a further 13,000 deaths at the rate of around 1000 deaths per day bringing the total to 20,000.

In October 2009, at around the same time that the European Commission put out their final report, the American State Department also put out a report titled : *"Report to Congress on Incidents During the Recent Conflict in Sri Lanka."* The American report has an exhaustive list of the all the reports the American Embassy in Colombo had got from various sources on *"Harms to civilians and civilian objects"* from the beginning of January 2009, to the end of the war on 19 May. The American Embassy was a focal point for all western diplomatic missions in Colombo, as well as organizations like the UN and the ICRC, and they collected information from all these sources. The US report lists 172 allegations of causing harm to civilians and civilian objects attributed to the army.

But the number of deaths mentioned in the American report certainly come nowhere near the figures mentioned in *The Times* and the European Commission report – certainly not the 1000 deaths per day figure between 1 to 19 May 2009. The American embassy could not have possibly missed a civilian death rate of 1000 per day for an unbroken two weeks. On the question of the number of civilian casualties, the UN Secretary General Ban Ki Moon's advisory panel report of 2011 says that according to figures collected by the UN Country Team, the total number of casualties from August 2008 right

501

up to 13 May 2009, was 7,721 killed and 18,479 injured. After 13 May, they had been unable to count the number of casualties.

However the UN has never made these figures public as they cannot verify the authenticity of their sources. The fact that they have been mentioned in Ban Ki Moon's advisory panel report does not give it official status because this report is not a formal report of the UN. Not being constrained by the usual UN requirements, Ban Ki Moon's advisory panel report says, *"The number calculated by the United Nations Country Team provides a starting point but is likely to be too low, for several reasons. First, many casualties may not have been observed at all. Second after the United Nations stopped counting on 13 May, the number of civilian casualties likely grew rapidly."* And further that *"A number of credible sources, have estimated that there could have been as many as 40,000 deaths"*. Who or what these 'credible sources' are has not been revealed anywhere in the 214 page report. The language used in the Ban report in relation to the number of civilian casualties is that of speculation, with terms like 'could have been' 'may not' 'likely' being used.

Even though figures on civilian deaths are supposed to have been collected by the UN country team, the Ban Ki Moon report does not give any indication of how the UN country team differentiated between civilian casualties and LTTE casualties. A curious fact that one notices in all the western reports that have come out so far, the European Commission's Interim Report of 19 August 2009, their Final Report of 19 October 2009, the US State Department report of October 2009, the International Crisis Group Report of May 2010, and the Ban Ki Moon advisory panel report of April 2011, is that not a single observer reporting on the war to the Western embassies and aid agencies, has ever seen any LTTE injured or any LTTE dead bodies. Everybody had seen and reported only civilian casualties.

After reading this kind of material, future students of history may be left with the impression that the Sri Lankan army won the war not by killing LTTE fighters, but by leaving the terrorists untouched and killing only Tamil civilians. The LTTE's control over information going out of their areas was almost water-tight. The US State Department report has around 45 incidents of causing harm to civilians ascribed to the LTTE. However this does not mean that there was a free flow of information from LTTE areas and that people were free to complain about the LTTE to outsiders. Most of those negative reports about the LTTE had gone to the Americans through civilians who had just escaped from LTTE control. On close examination of the US report, only one adverse report on the LTTE seems to have actually originated from within LTTE territory.

The lengths to which Western nations would go in their witch hunt against Sri Lanka was revealed in an event that took place in January 2011. The American defence attaché in Colombo Lt Col Laurence Smith hosted parties from time to time, and one such party was held on 20 January 2011, in honour of a high ranking officer from the US Pacific Command who was on a visit to Sri Lanka. The morning after the party, Major Gen Prasad Samarasinghe, the former army spokesman had come rushing to see to see Gōta in an agitated state and told him that at the party the previous night, Dr Paul Carter, the head of political affairs of the American Embassy had told him that they know that his sons are in the UK but that American education is much better and that the US government will give Samarasinghe and his entire family permanent residency in the US and look after them if he is willing to testify to certain allegations.

Dr Carter had then given Samarasinghe a piece of paper on which were several accusations, alleging among other things that it was Gōtabhaya Rajapaksa who ordered the eviction of Tamils from Colombo and also that it was Gōta who was responsible for covert operations. There were three allegations against the navy as well. On hearing this, Gōta had been livid. He had told external affairs secretary Romesh Jayasinghe about this incident and Jayasinge had said that this was not a matter to be taken lightly – offering bribes and inducements to a serving army officer to testify against his superiors. At 10.30 am the same day, American Ambassador Patricia Butenis arrived at Gōta's office for a pre-arranged appointment. Gōta had first discussed her business and at the end of that discussion, he had told the Ambassador that he has something to else to discuss. From the ambassador's facial expression, Gōta realized that she knew what the issue was.

Major Gen Samrasinghe was also called in to the room at this stage and in his presence, Gōta told the American Ambassador what Samarasinghe had told him. Butenis had tried to explain it away by saying that it was all a big misunderstanding. What she told Gōta, was undoubtedly the strangest and most convoluted story ever to be told in the annals of Sri Lankan foreign relations. She explained that what Dr Carter had actually meant was that that in the future, there would be some more US embassy documents put out by Wikileaks and that among the leaked documents will be a cable from the US embassy in Colombo to the State Department saying that Brigadier

Prasad Samarasinghe had revealed to the US Embassy that Gōtabhaya Rajapaksa and the navy had been responsible for certain incidents.

The US ambassador told Gōta that Samarasinghe had not in fact provided that information to the embassy but that his name had been mentioned in the embassy communiqué by 'mistake'. The Ambassador said that Dr Carter's concern was that when this information comes out in Wikileaks, the government will punish Samarasinghe and since he will be penalized for a mistake made by the US Embassy, Dr Carter had told Samarasinghe not to worry and that they will look after him, and take him to the USA. There is no reason to believe a word of what Butenis said by way of explanation. This was nothing but an attempt by the US government to fix Gōta on trumped up charges with witnesses who have been given inducements to testify falsely. This shows the lengths to which the West will go to persecute the Rajapaksas who defied their diktat and ended Sri Lanka's four decade long agony.

Select Bibliography

Alston, Phillip – *Report of the Special Rapporteur, Mission to Sri Lanka (28 November to 6 December 2005) United Nations Economic and Social Council E/CN/2006/53/Add.5*

Bhasin, Avatar Singh (Ed) – *India-Sri Lanka Relations and Sri Lanka's Ethnic Conflict Documents 1947-2000, Volumes I, II, III, IV & V, India Research Press, New Delhi, 2001*

Chandraprema, C.A. – *Sri Lanka: the Years of Terror, The JVP Insurrection 1987-1989, Lake House Bookshop 1991.*

Checklist for TPS on Holding Role Including Aspects Pertaining to Defences, OPS, TRG, Admin, LOG and Welfare, Directorate of Operations, Army Headquarters Colombo, 8 August 1992.

Ceylon Daily Mirror, 1956-1982

Ceylon Daily News, 1956-1982

Convening Order, Court of Inquiry into the incident at Pooneryn Camp on the night of 10/11 November 1993

Dewaraja, L.S – *The Kandyan Kingdom of Sri Lanka 1707-1782, Lake House Investments Ltd, Colombo 1988*

Dinamina (Sinhala Daily) 1956-1958

Dias-Bandaranaike Lakshmi – *FDB (Felix Dias Bandaranaike Commemorative Volume) Colombo, 1994.*

Dixit, J.N. *Kolomba Bhoomikawa (Sinhala translation of Assignment Colombo) Vijitha Yapa Bookshop, Colombo 1998.*

Gajaba Regiment 25ᵗʰ Anniversary Publication

Hansard, Parliament of Ceylon, 1956, 1957, 1958, 1960, 1961, 1971, 1974

Hendavitharana, Sujeewa (Air Force Aviation Engineer) statement given to the Mt Lavinia District Courts in Case No: 6036/08/M

Hoole, Rajan – *Sri Lanka, The Arrogance of Power: Myths, Decadence and Murder, University Teachers for Human Rights (Jaffna), Wasala Publications Nugegoda 2001.*

Jagathchandra, Nihal Mahayaye Kathawa (A biography of General Anuruddha Ratwatte) S.Godage & Brothers, Colombo 2007

Kumarasinghe, Jayanath (Air Force Aviation Engineer) statement given to the Mt Lavinia District Courts in Case No: 6036/08/M

Major Incidents in 2 Div TAOR, Directorate of Army Headquarters, Colombo, 27 July 1993.

Measures to improve the OP capabilities of TPS to prevent casualties and to improve level of morale, Directorate of Operations Army Headquarters, Colombo 2ⁿᵈ May 1992.

Measures to be Adopted for Prevention of CAS due to Ambushes and TERR Attacks, Directorate of Operations, Army Headquarters, 15 October 1992

Minutes of the Western Province Security Conference December 2006-August 2010.

Mistakes Made by Own TPS Resulting in Loss of Life and Equipment, Directorate of Operations, Army Headquarters, 6 July 1992.

OP Completion Report - Operation Liberation (Vadamarachchi Operation) Sgd. Lt Col C.L.Wijayaratna, 25 June 1987

OP Completion Report – Operation Balawegaya, Sgd. Brigadier Vijaya Wimalaratne, 31 October 1991

OP Completion Report - Operation Hayepahara Sgd. Major Gen R De S Daluwatte, 5 May 1992

OP Completion Report – Operation Thunder strike Sgd. Col. G.Hettiarachchi, 24 May 1995

OP Completion Report – Operation Riviresa (51ˢᵗ Division) Sgd. Brigadier P.A.Karunatilleke, 13 October 1995

OP Completion Report – Operation Riviresa (52ⁿᵈ Division) Sgd. Brigadier H.N.W.Dias, 26 Dec 1995

OP Completion Report – Operation Riviresa Stages II, III & IV (53ʳᵈ Division) Sgd. Brigadier K.J.C.Perera, 24 December 1995

OP Completion Report – Operation Riviresa (Artillery Brigade) Sgd. Brigadier H.N.W.Dias, 15 June 1996

OP Completion Report – Operation Riviresa Stage II, (Armoured Brigade) Sgd. Brigadier N.R.Marambe, 7 April 1996

OP Completion Report – Operation Kinihira (53rd Division) Sgd. Major Gen S.Wanigasekera, 26 September 2000.

OP Completion Report – Operation Kinihira II, Sgd. Major Gen K.J.N.Senaweera, 5 October 2000.

OP Completion Report – Operation Agnikheela I, Sgd Major Gen A.E.D.Wijendra, 7 May 2001

OP Completion Report – Operation Rivikirana, Sgd Major Gen A.E.D.Wijendra, October 2000

OP Completion Report – Mavilaru, 3 April 2007, Sgd. Brigadier M.P.Peiris

OP Completion Report – Sampur, 24 August to 4 September 2006, 22nd Division, Sgd Brigadier M.P.Peiris GOC.

OP Completion Report – Manirasakulam, 1 to 10 October 2006, 22nd Division Sgd. M.P.Peiris GOC

OP Completion Report – Vakarai, 23rd Division, 30 October 2006 to 21 January 2007, Sgd. Brigadier R.M.D.Ratnayake

OP Completion Report Vakarai, 22nd Division, 13 to 20 January 2007, Sgd. Brigadier M.P.Peiris

OP Completion Report – Operation to Liberate Batticaloa West (Thoppigala) 20 February to 11 April 2007, Sgd. Brigadier W.P.D.B.Fernando

OP Completion Report – Batticaloa District, (Commando Brigade) 30 September 2007, Sgd. Brigadier C.P.Gallage.

OP Completion Report – Peraru, (22nd Division) 7-10 March 2007, Sgd. Maj Gen M.P.Peris GOC.

OP Completion Report – Silavathurei (Special Forces Brigade) 23 September 2007, Sgd. Col. N.A.Dharmaratne

OP Completion Report – LTTE Attacks on Kattaparichchan, Selvanagar and Mahindapuram Army Detachments 2 to 7 August 2006 (22nd Division) Sgd. M.P.Peiris GOC

OP Completion Report – LTTE Attacks in Jaffna 11 to 13 August 2006 (51st Division) Sgd. Brigadier C.B.R.Mark

OP Completion Report – Task Force 4, 20 June 2009, Sgd. Major W.S.N.Perera for TF Commander (Brigadier N.D.Vanniarachchi)

OP Completion Report – 57th Division, 25 June 2009, Sgd. N.A.J.C. Dias, GOC

OP Completion Report – 58th Division, July 2009 (Brigadier Shavendra Silva, GOC)

OP Completion Report – 59th Division, 23 July 2009, Sgd. Col. G.J.L.Waduge for GOC

OP Completion Report – Task Force 2, 24 June, Sgd. Brigadier P.M.R.Bandara TF Commander

OP Completion Report – Task Force 3, 30 June 2009, Sgd. Brigadier S.T.D.Liyanage TF Commander

OP Completion Report – Commando Brigade, 1 July 2009, Sgd. Col R.A.Nugera

OP Completion Reports – Special Forces Brigade, 15 March 2009, Sgd. Brigadier N.A.Dharmaratne (February 2007 to February 2009) Col. A.A.Kodippily (February-May 2009)

OP Completion Report – 55th Division, 28 June 2009, Sgd. Brigadier P.P.De Silva for GOC

OP Completion Report – 53rd Division, 24 June 2009, Sgd. Major Gen. G.D.H.K.Gunaratne GOC

Operation Completion Report, OP Sathjaya III, Air Mobile Brigade, 2 October 1996, Sgd. Brigadier Seevali Wanigasekera

Operational Order, Operation Jayasikurui, Air Mobile Brigade 11 May 1997, Sgd Brigadier Seevali Wanigasekera

Pawns of Peace: Evaluation of Norwegian Peace Efforts in Sri Lanka, 1997-2009, Norwegian Ministry of Foreign Affairs, September 2011.

Peiris, Janadasa - Jathika Getaluwa: Gothriya Rajyaye Sita Goleeya Rajya Dakwa, Appendices, Colombo, 2007

Protective Measures and Counter-Action in the Defences, Directorate of Operations, Army Headquarters, 4th May 1992.

Ranatunga, Cyril Genaralwarayakuge Kathawa, Vijitha Yapa Bookshop, Colombo, 2010.

Report of the Secretary General's Panel of Experts on Accountability in Sri Lanka, United Nations, March 2011

Report on the Findings of the Investigation with respect to the effective implementation of certain human rights conventions in Sri Lanka, European Commission, October 2009

Report of the Presidential Commission of Inquiry into the Terrorist Attack that Took Place at the Air Force Base and the Bandaranaike International Airport Katunayake, 21 October 2002.

Roberts, Michael (Ed) – Collective Identities, Nationalisms and Protest in Modern Sri Lanka, Marga Institute, Colombo 1979.

Security of Equipment & War-Like stores in OP Areas, Directorate of Operations, Army Headquarters, 30, September 1992.

Seneviratne, Dhammika (Ed) Discussions with the Electronic Media and Press over Two and a Half Years by Defence Secretary GStabhaya Rajapaksa, S.Godage & Brothers, 2009

Silva, K.M de & Howard Wriggins, J.R.Jayewardene of Sri Lanka: A Political Biography, Volume II From 1956 to his retirement in 1989, J.R.Jayewardene Cultural Centre, 1994

Silva G.P.S.H. de, A Statistical Survey of Elections to the Legislatures of Sri Lanka 1911-1977, Marga Institute, Colombo, 1979.

Sinha Regiment 50th Anniversary Publication (2006)

Sivarajah, A The Federal Party of Sri Lanka: The Strategy of an Ethnic Minority Party in Government and Opposition 1949-2002, Kumaran Book House, Colombo, 2007

Sri Lanka Army 50th Anniversary Publication (1999)

Police Special Task Force – 26 Weni Ranaviru Guna Samuruwa 1 September 2010.

Pupurana Dravya Pareekshawa Sandaha Upades – State Intelligence Service booklet, 2008

The Island, 1982-2009

The Implementation of Certain Human Rights Conventions in Sri Lanka (Interim Report) European Commission, August 2009.

Tiranagama Rajini, Rajan Hoole, K.Sridharan, Daya Somasundaram - Bindunu Thalruka (Sinhala Translation of The Broken Palmyra) Colombo, 1993

The Ceylon Daily News Parliament of Sri Lanka, 1977.

University of Ceylon History of Ceylon Volume III, University of Peradeniya, 1973

US Department of State, Report to Congress on Incidents During the Recent Conflict in Sri Lanka, 2009

US Department of Defense Assessment of the Armed Forces of Sri Lanka, 2002 Sgd. Peter Rodman

---

Interviews:

Interviews were conducted with the following individuals. This is by no means a comprehensive list of those who were interviewed and the names mentioned here are of those who provided core interviews for this book.

Gotabhaya Rajapaksa – *Defence Secretary*
Basil Rajapaksa – *Senior Advisor to the President*
Chamal Rajapaksa - *Speaker of Parliament*
Lalith Weeratunga – *Secretary to the President*
Anuruddha Ratwatte - *former Deputy Defence Minister*
Mangala Samaraweera – *former Minister of Foreign Affairs*
Austin Fernando – *former Defence Secretary*

Army
Shavendra Silva
Chagi Gallage
Jagath Dias
G.V.Ravipriya
Kapila Hendavitharana
Mahinda Hathurusinghe
Milinda Peiris
Lalith Daulagala
Chandana Weerakoon,
Seevali Wanigasekera,
Sampath Karunatilleke
Sahampathi Ekanayake
Senaka Wijesuriya
Palitha Fernando
Suraj Bansajayah
Shantha Tirunawakarusu
Deepal Subasinghe
Ralph Nugera
Primal Rodrigo
Jayavi Fernando
Ananda Alwis
Priyath Munasinghe
Vikum Siriwardena
Dudley Weeraman
Nandana Udawatte
A.W.M.Ranawana
Wasantha Jayaweera
Daya Ratnayake
Nirmal Dharmaratne
Udaya Perera

Twelve members of the Special Forces and Commando Long Range Patrol Teams

Navy
Wasantha Karannagoda
Somatilleke Dissanayake
Jayantha Perera
R.C.Wijegunaratne
Piyal Silva
D.K.P.Dassanayake
Sujeewa Seneviratne
Udaya Bandara
Mahesh Goonesekera

Air Force
Roshan Gunatilleke
Harsha Abeywickrema
Kolitha Gunatilleke
Gagan Bulathsinhala
S.Fernando
Senaka Dharmawardhana
Mohan Balasooriya

Police/STF
Keerthi Gajanayake
Nimal Wakishta
Anura Senanayake
Ravi Seneviratne
Nimal Leuke
Varuna Jayasundara

Tamil Militants and Politicians
Varatharajah Perumal
Suresh Premachandran
Karuna Amman (Vinayagamurthy Muralitharan)
Kumaran Pathmanathan
Douglas Devananda
V.Anandasangaree
Dharmalingam Siddharthan

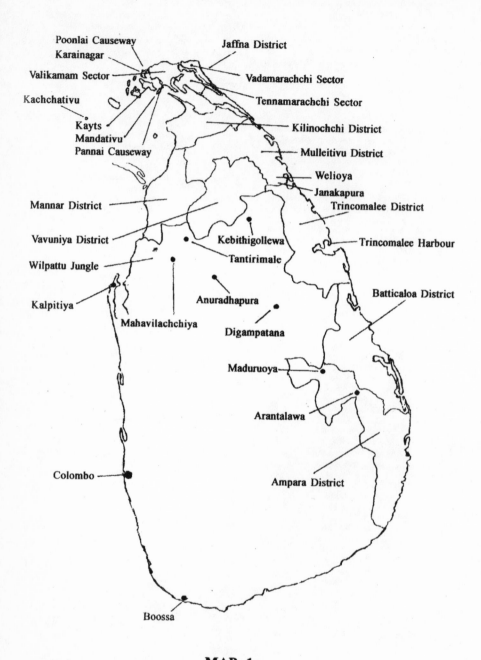

MAP 1

SRI LANKA

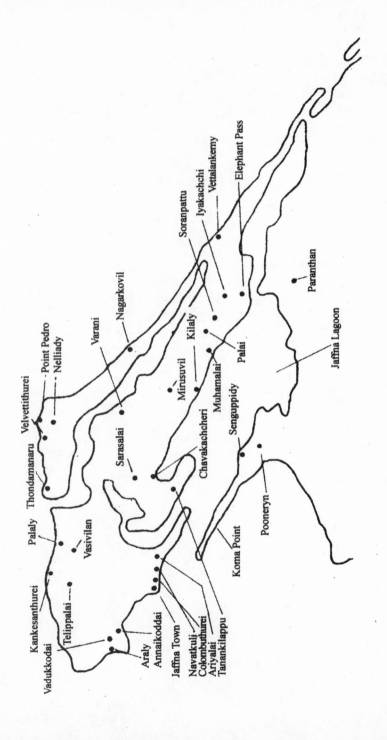

MAP 3
JAFFNA PENNINSULA

Point Pedro
Nelliady
Velvettithurei
Thondamanaru
Palaly
Vadukkodai
Kankesanthurei
Telippalai
Vasivilan
Araly
Annaikoddai
Jaffna Town
Navatkuli
Colombuthurei
Ariyalai
Tanankilappu
Koma Point
Pooneryn
Senguppidy
Muhamalai
Chavakachcheri
Mirusuvil
Sarasalai
Varani
Nagarkovil
Palai
Kilaly
Jaffna Lagoon
Paranthan
Soranpattu
Iyakachchi
Vettalankemy
Elephant Pass

MAP 3

VANNI

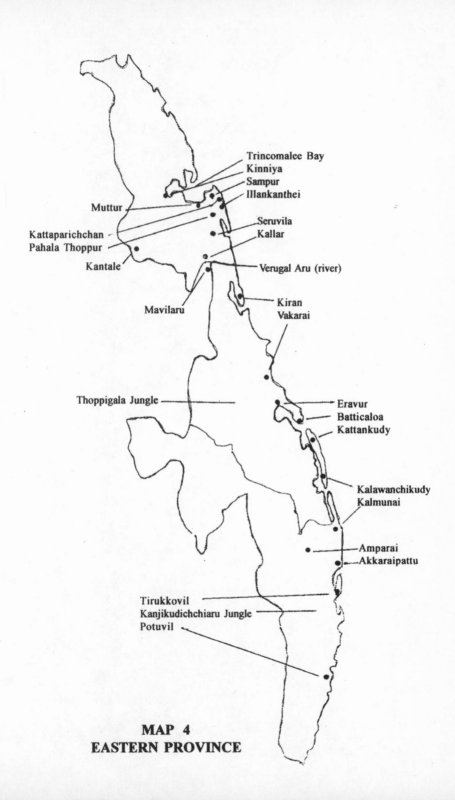

Trincomalee Bay
Kinniya
Sampur
Illankanthei

Muttur

Kattaparichchan
Pahala Thoppur

Seruvila
Kallar

Kantale

Verugal Aru (river)

Mavilaru

Kiran
Vakarai

Thoppigala Jungle

Eravur
Batticaloa
Kattankudy

Kalawanchikudy
Kalmunai

Amparai
Akkaraipattu

Tirukkovil
Kanjikudichchiaru Jungle
Potuvil

MAP 4
EASTERN PROVINCE

*Sinha Regiment days: Standing 6th from left Gōta , 7th Sarath Fonseka, 9th Susantha Mendis (KIA),
10th Neomal Palipana (KIA), 12th H.R.Stephen (KIA), 13th Malik Deen (KIA)*

Gôta (second from left)during an operation (early 1990s)

Janaka Perera (far left, seated), Gôta standing (left) Sarath Fonseka seated (far right)
(early 1990s)

Prabhakaran (third from left) liked to catch them young

*Terrorist's perspective: The hole through which an LTTE sniper shot
Foreign Minister Lakshman Kadirgarmar*

Prabhakaran in India

Mahattaya, Balasingham and Prabhakaran with Dixit

Inspecting trainee terrorists in India (Mid-1980s)

Kittu at target practice while Prabhakaran looks on

Tamil Nadu politicians trying out LTTE weaponry

Pottu Amman: The quintessential terrorist

Cooking was Prabhakaran's second hobby

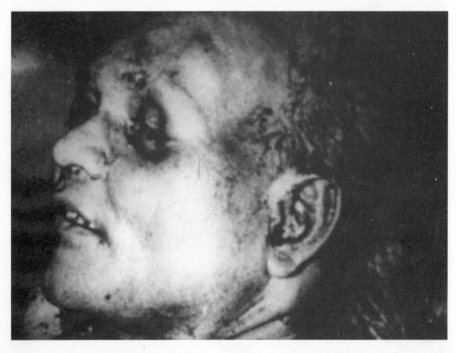

A. Amirthalingam, a victim of Tamil terrorism